Game Creation a  *:*

Insider Secrets from
Industry Experts

Contents at a Glance

Game Creation and Careers:
Insider Secrets from Industry Experts

Marc Saltzman

New Riders

201 West 103rd Street, Indianapolis, Indiana 46290
An Imprint of Pearson Education
Boston • Indianapolis • London • Munich • New York • San Francisco

Game Creation and Careers: Insider Secrets from Industry Experts

International Standard Book Number: 0-7357-1367-7

Library of Congress Catalog Card Number: 20033105822

Printed in the United States of America

First edition: July 2003

07 06 05 04   7 6 5 4 3 2

Interpretation of the printing code: The rightmost double-digit number is the year of the book's printing; the rightmost single-digit number is the number of the book's printing. For example, the printing code 04-1 shows that the first printing of the book occurred in 2004.

Trademarks

Warning and Disclaimer

Associate Publisher
Stephanie Wall

Production Manager
Gina Kanouse

Acquisitions Editor
Chris Zahn

Development Editor
Chris Zahn

Senior Project Editor
Lori Lyons

Copy Editor
Nancy Sixsmith

Senior Indexer
Cheryl Lenser

Composition
Gloria Schurick

Manufacturing Coordinator
Dan Urhig

Interior Designers
Will Cruz
Kim Scott

Cover Designer
Aren Howell

Media Developer
Jay Payne

Marketing
Scott Cowlin
Tammy Detrich
Hannah Onstad Latham

Publicity
Susan Nixon

This book is dedicated to my beautiful wife and soul mate, Kellie,
and to the new additions to the family—our twins, Jacob and Maya.

✾

Table of Contents

About the Author

 **Marc Saltzman** has reported on the bourgeoning consumer technology industry for the past seven years as a freelance journalist, author, lecturer, consultant, and radio and TV personality. His specialties lie in video gaming, computer software and hardware, Internet trends, gadgets, and consumer electronics.

Along with his weekly syndicated columns with Gannett News Service, USAToday.com, and CNN.com, Marc contributes to more than three dozen prominent publications, including *USA Today*, *LA Times*, *Newsweek*, *Modern Maturity*, *Playboy*, Playboy.com, *Golf Digest*, *National Post*, GlobeTechnology.com, *Access* magazine, and *Tribute* magazine.

Gannett News Service is the USA's largest newspaper group in terms of circulation. The company's 99 daily newspapers throughout the U.S. have a combined daily paid circulation of 7.8 million.

Marc Saltzman was one of the first journalists in the world to break open the MP3 phenomenon in late 1997 on CNN Interactive (CNN.com). He correctly predicted this controversial audio file format would revolutionize the recording industry.

His 10 books with Pearson Education and McGraw-Hill/Osborne are: *Internet Games Directory* (1996), *Gamer's Web Directory: Sites, Cheats and Secrets* (1997), *Quake II Strategy Master* (1998), *Game Design: Secrets of the Sages* (1999), *Game Design: Secrets of the Sages*, Second Edition (2000), *Game Design: Secrets of the Sages*, Third Edition (2001), *Marc Saltzman's 250 Best Palm Games* (2001, on CD), *Marc Saltzman's Top 300 Games for the PocketPC* (2002, on CD), *Game Design: Secrets of the Sages*, Fourth Edition (2002), and *DVD Confidential: Hundreds of Hidden Easter Eggs Revealed* (2002).

Marc also contributed to *Supercade*, Van Burnham's book chronicling the visual history of the video game industry (MIT press). Marc has also written popular in-game manuals for *Quake II* (id Software/Activision) and *Sin* (Ritual Entertainment/Activision).

Beginning in May of 2001, Marc became a technology expert at CNN, the Cable News Network. Marc is often a guest to talk about an array of high-tech issues, be it video games, the Internet, computers, or consumer electronics. He can be seen on the television show, *Next @ CNN*, which airs Saturdays at 3 p.m. (EST) and 4 p.m. (EST) each Sunday. The show won first place in the News Magazine category of the National Headliner Awards, announced Friday, March 16, 2001, by the Press Club of Atlantic City.

Marc also makes regular appearances as a high-tech expert on the *CBS Early Show*, *CNN Headline News*, *Breakfast Television (BT!)* in Toronto, and *TechTV Canada*.

Beginning in April 2003, Marc began hosting his own TV show, dubbed *TKO*. Considered "*Entertainment Tonight* meets consumer technology," *TKO* appears on four national networks in Canada: Global, Prime, CH, and MenTV. More information on the show can be found at www.pyramidproductions.tv.

Speaking of Global, Marc is also the host of "TechWise," a twice-a-week feature on the national *MoneyWise* program in Canada, hosted by Peter Kent and Dierdre McMurdy. The popular show airs coast-to-coast on CanWest Global and the Prime Network.

Marc also writes for and hosts two radio shows. The first is "Tech Talk with Marc Saltzman" on Canada's largest talk station, CFRB (1010AM in Toronto). The hour-long call-in program airs live on Sunday evenings. CFRB's parent company is Standard Radio. The second radio program is heard exclusively on Canada's largest new rock/alternative station, Edge 102 (102.1 FM in Toronto). Now in its seventh year, the pre-recorded segment airs twice a day, entitled "Cyber Escapes with Marc Saltzman." Edge 102's parent company is Corus Entertainment.

Marc enjoys delivering seminars on the ever-changing world of high-tech (as far as Hong Kong!) on how to best break into the interactive entertainment industry. Marc also moderates a panel each year at the annual Electronic Entertainment Expo (E3) on this very same topic. Marc has also been an official "Best of E3" judge for the past five years, nominating the best computer and console games and most promising hardware for the annual trade show.

Marc is also a judge for the annual "Codie Awards" established by the SIIA (Software and Information Industry Association) to recognize innovative software and information products.

Marc is a paid member of the International Game Developers Association (IGDA), contributing to the violence committee.

In August, 1997, Marc was decorated by the University of Toronto's Alumni Association as an "outstanding graduate" for his success across many mediums: print (books, newspapers, magazines), the Internet, television, and radio.

About the Contributors

The following game and level designers, programmers, musicians, producers, sound engineers—and many other titles and job functions could be added here—provided the core of this book: their insights into and experiences with the fascinating world of game design. (For biographical information on many of the contributors, see the appendix at the end of this book.)

Craig Alexander

Éric Allard

Michel Ancel

Kevin Bachus

Clint Bajakian

Bill Bales

Pat Bigley

Mary Bihr

Cliff Bleszinksi

Don Bluth

George Broussard

Jeff Brunner

Nolan Bushnell

Tim Cain

Melanie Cambron

Stevie Case

Jeff Castaneda

Louis Castle

Steven Chiang

Jason Chu

Doug Church

Kevin Cloud

Chris Cross

Shane Dabiri

Dave Davis

Ed Del Castillo

Jason Della Rocca

Mark Dickenson

David Dienstbier

Peter Dille

Alex Dunne

Denis Dyack

Jason Enos

Richard Evans

Noah Falstein

Mathieu Ferland

Mike Fischer

Chris Foster

Toby Gard

Alex Garden

Richard "Lord British" Garriott

Mark Gibbons

Ron Gilbert

Rick Goodman

Harry Gottlieb

Richard "Levelord" Gray

Daniel Greenberg

Rodney Greenblat

Jack Grillo

Peter Hirschmann

Don Hopkins

Matt Householder

Todd Howard

Steve Hunt

Tsunekazu Ishihara

David Jaffe

Paul Jaquays

Joel Jewett

Matthew Lee Johnston

Kenji Kanno

Chris Kantrowitz

Bartosz Kijanka

Jeff Kliment

Hideo Kojima

Erik Kraber

Richard Kriegler

Jeff Lane

Lorne Lanning

Alan Lawrance

Minh Le

Mark Linn

Ian Lloyd

Doug Lombardi

Ed Magnin

Fred Markus

Ed Martin

Michael McCartie

Ernest McCay

Mike McCoy

American McGee

Brendan McNamara

Brad McQuaid

Sid Meier

Marc Mencher

Dan Michelson

Shinji Mikami

John Miles

Jay Miller

Scott Miller

Shigeru Miyamoto

Peter Molyneux

Steve Moraff

Ray Muzyka

Toshihiro Nagoshi

Yuji Naka

Gabe Newell

Tetsuya Nomura

Marty O'Donnell

Chris Olmstead

Mike Olsen

Alexey Pajitnov

Rob Pardo

David Perry

Lee Petty

Michael Raymond-July

Steve Rechtschaffner

Brian Reynolds

Bob Riley

Pierre Rivest

Erin Roberts

John Romero

Bill Roper

Catherine Roy

Jason Rubin

Michael Rubinelli

Hironobu Sakaguchi

George "The Fat Man" Sanger

Tom Sarris

Takiyoshi Sato

Phil Saunders

Chris Sawyer

Tammy Schachter

Tim Schafer

James Schmalz

Reid Schneider

John Scott

Shawnee Sequeira

Bruce C. Shelley

John Slagel

Harvey Smith

Randy Smith

Warren Spector

Phil Steinmeyer

Jeremy Strauser

Greg Street

Rick Stringfellow

Yu Suzuki

Tim Sweeney

Max Szlagor

Tommy Tallarico

Chris Taylor

Chance Thomas

Greg Thomas

Denny Thorley

Howard Tomlinson

Ragnar Tørnquist

Eric Tremblay

Emmanuel Valdez

Michael Waite

Ian Wall

Gordon Walton

Thomas Warfield

Stephen White

Kevin Wilkinson

Bruce Williams

Tim Willits

Jeane Wong

Will Wright

David Wu

Greg Zeschuk

Acknowledgments

A very special thank you goes out to all of the members of the electronic gaming industry who have taken the time and effort to contribute to this book.

Thanks to Stephanie Wall, Associate Publisher for New Riders, who was inspired by the original *Game Design: Secrets of the Sages* book series and wanted to take it to the next level. Thank you to development editor Chris Zahn and senior project editor Lori Lyons for their incredible professionalism and commitment to create an invaluable resource for those who want to make or market video games for a living! A big thank you also goes out to Nancy Sixsmith (copy editor), Cheryl Lenser (senior indexer), and Gloria Schurick (compositor) for their tireless work on this exciting project. Lastly, thank you to those talented folks who worked on the original *Game Design: Secrets of the Sages* series—namely, editor extraordinaire Robin Drake, and of course, to Steve Schafer, Paul Reese, and Leigh Davis.

Tell Us What You Think

As the reader of this book, you are the most important critic and commentator. We value your opinion and want to know what we're doing right, what we could do better, what areas you'd like to see us publish in, and any other words of wisdom you're willing to pass our way.

As the senior acquisitions editor for New Riders Publishing, I welcome your comments. You can fax, email, or write me directly to let me know what you did or didn't like about this book—as well as what we can do to make our books stronger. When you write, please be sure to include this book's title, ISBN, and author, as well as your name and phone or fax number. I will carefully review your comments and share them with the author and editors who worked on the book.

Please note that I cannot help you with technical problems related to the topic of this book, and that due to the high volume of email I receive, I might not be able to reply to every message.

Fax: 317-581-4663

Email: `linda.bump@newriders.com`

Mail: Linda Anne Bump
         Senior Acquisitions Editor
         New Riders Publishing
         201 West 103rd Street
         Indianapolis, IN 46290 USA

Foreword

A book that combines my two loves—games and entrepreneurship—is special to me. What better way to spend your life than to build a business devoted to creating fun for millions of people?

There are those who think of the '70s as the golden era—but to me, the best is yet to come. The software tools now available allow even simple games to have great graphics and super play value. People love to compete, and simple games allow the casual player—one who doesn't want to learn complex rules or elaborate storylines—to challenge and interact with people in the same room or across the world.

Many games have become more complex, and storylines are more dramatic and deep. That allows game designers to inject more tension into their games, tempting the player to react and interact—to move, explore, build, shoot, or create. That evolution can be good for games and for the gaming industry's diversity of gameplay, providing something for everyone. People play more and play longer, driving the games to be even more interesting and the developers to be more creative and skillful.

To succeed in the industry today, you need to be somewhat of a polymorph—or to have a good idea and know how to find experts in a host of areas from video production to character development to computer programming to graphic design. It also helps to be a visionary. The most important development since the introduction of the home console is the capability to connect it to the Internet—think about the ramifications of a global network of interconnected gamers. What kind of game will you plug into that network to help it evolve?

It's truly exciting to create for a medium that allows people to interact with each other…so different from other creative outlets, in which there is a wall between art and appreciator. In games, the art is different every time and can serve as a direct conduit for people appreciating it on opposite sides of the world.

We all know that games are big business. In 1983, people spent $22 billion in arcades on video games made by my company, Atari, and our competitors. The U.S. Secretary of the Treasury called me to ask me to empty the coin boxes more often because the country was running out of quarters.

People still spend billions of dollars one quarter at a time, but the home market is the focus of most game designers. The connected world is a world that allows the gaming world to expand; to create new experiences for new media, whether Palm, WAP, 3G, home consoles, or cable set-top boxes. Any one of those devices can be a gateway to a whole new world.

Of course, things are different now from the way they were 30 years ago. There's a lot of talent out there, and there are several first steps you can take as a budding game designer besides striking out on your own. This book discusses the many ways to break into the business, such as joining up with a development studio or publisher. It would be a stretch to say I wish this book had been around when I was starting because I had a lot of fun finding success on my own terms. But now that there is more competition and there are more established rules, it can be helpful to hear from people who have made it to the top of today's gaming world—and then proceeded to rewrite the rules after they got there.

My advice: Think out of the box, think connected, and jump into the game world. The water's fine.

—**Nolan Bushnell**
CEO and Founder of uWink, Inc.
Founder of Atari
Launcher of Pong

Introduction: So, You Wanna Make Games for a Living, Huh?

What a treat and honor it is to have Nolan Bushnell—the father of the video game industry, who founded Atari and launched *Pong*—write the forward to this book, *Game Creation and Careers: Insider Secrets from Industry Experts*. And how fitting. Although the video game industry has certainly changed quite a bit over the past quarter-century, Bushnell's accomplishments embody the spirit of this book, which looks to the future.

The premise of this book is a simple one: Making video games for a living may sound like the ultimate "dream job," but it's an attainable (and often lucrative) reality.

Quite simply, there has never been a better time to break into the industry or to advance up the ranks and become a lead designer on a project. The tools have never been better and easier to use; the industry has never been more ripe; and the Internet, as a distribution medium and gaming platform, is one of the most incredible technologies for gamers and game developers alike. And there have never been as many gaming platforms available simultaneously in the history of the industry: the Sony PlayStation/PSone, Sony PlayStation 2, Nintendo GameCube, Microsoft Xbox, Nintendo Game Boy Advance SP, PC, Macintosh, the Web, arcades, Pocket PC, Palm, and cell phones. Whew!

And lest we forget—all three consoles are now online, which expands the possibilities of game design and development even further.

Therefore, it's no wonder why the video game industry has broken the $10 billion dollar-a-year mark in the U.S. alone, which is significantly more than the revenues generated from movie box office receipts. Wowza.

Here are some other impressive stats:

➤ According to a 2003 survey from Zanthus, a market research company in Portland, Oregon, a whopping 92% of American teenagers own and play video games.

➤ Forrester Research forecasts that video game consoles will be in nearly 70 million American households by 2005.

➤ According to a survey conducted by the Interactive Digital Software Association (IDSA), an incredible 60% of all Americans age 6 and older—or about 145 million people—play computer and video games.

➤ The same report concludes that about 43% of game players are women. And the average age of a gamer is 28 years old. (Thought it was younger, didn't you?)

➤ In 2002, more than 221 million computer and video games were sold, or almost 2 games for every U.S. household.

So, the question begs—what do you want to be doing in the 21st century?

Game Creation and Careers: Insider Secrets from Industry Experts is an extension of the popular book series, *Game Design: Secrets of the Sages*. A bit of history: The first *Game Design: Secrets of the Sages* was released in the spring of 1999, and I'm pleased to report that it garnered quite a bit of critical praise and worldwide commercial success. In fact, it's been translated into several other languages, and I've had the distinct pleasure of traveling the world to speak to budding game designers and developers based on this book (even as far as Hong Kong!). The second edition, released a year later, added more than three dozen new interviews to the already-spectacular lineup of gaming celebrities. The third edition, released in 2001, added even more content, this time on massively multiplayer game design, writing design documents, specific programming tips and techniques, and an updated look at key gaming schools and courses. For the fourth edition in 2002, we worked on ways to make this book even better—and more comprehensive—by squeezing in more than 50 new interviews with the best minds of the gaming industry.

Game Creation and Careers: Insider Secrets from Industry Experts has all of that and more.

But let's talk for a minute about what this book *isn't*. This book doesn't require budding game programmers to be familiar with advanced concepts such as data structures, algorithm analysis, or anything like that. For the most part, the entire book is in easy-to-comprehend language; if acronyms, technical jargon, or industry slang are used, the words are followed with a brief definition or clarification. In addition, although the book was originally called *Game Design: Secrets of the Sages*, it covers much more than just game design. Sure, it explains how to write a solid design document and how to decide what kind of game to create, but it also caters to all the members of a development team: programmers, artists and animators, sound engineers, and musicians. And more than one-third of this book is devoted to the business side of gaming. This discussion includes how to properly market your game, how to work with the press, the best ways to test your product, the do's and don'ts of technical support and customer service, and much, much more. Last, but certainly not least, a good chunk of this book is devoted to breaking into the exciting gaming industry—whether you want to be a solo shareware game designer, you want to start your own full-blown development company and need to pitch your idea to a publisher, or perhaps you prefer to squeeze in at an existing development studio or publishing company.

Because this book covers so much ground, you may or may not want to read it all the way through. Feel free to jump back and forth from chapter to chapter, as dictated by your personal tastes.

Also, be sure to keep in mind that each chapter could really be expanded into a book itself—or even a series of books, for that matter. Therefore, in case further reading is desired, most chapters contain a handful of great web site addresses and Usenet newsgroups to surf to or books to pick up. Plus, there's a chapter toward the end of the book reserved for the best game design resources out there.

Finally, we listened to the feedback collected from those who read the first four editions of *Game Design: Secrets of the Sages*, and have polished this edition considerably. You wanted more console game design? You got it—we talked to Nintendo's Shigeru Miyamoto, Capcom's Shinji Mikami, Square's Hironobu Sakaguchi, and Naughty Dog's Jason Rubin, to name a few. You asked for more PC game designers? We tracked down the likes of Will Wright, Warren Spector, Greg Zeschuk, Ray Muzyka, Chris Taylor, Sid Meier, and Tim Sweeney to add to the existing stellar lineup. You wished for massively multiplayer online RPG design advice? How about Brad McQuaid of *EverQuest* fame and Ultima's Richard "Lord British" Garriott? Finally, for this edition, we added a bunch of "extras," such as Chris Taylor's master design document template, Tommy Tallarico's standard audio agreement, and much more—including rare, behind-the-scenes images provided for the purposes of this book.

Whether you're into action games or strategy, sims or sports, adventure games or role-playing games or puzzles, we've got more than 150 of the gaming industry's most savvy developers ready and anxious to pour out advice on a myriad of topics, pooled from their many years of experience in the limelight.

Consider this book the world's largest roundtable of game designers and developers discussing their tips, tricks, and techniques for creating the perfect game; and offering their do's and don'ts of breaking into the industry.

So go ahead, dive right in and get in the game. With help from our sages over the next few hundred pages, the only thing between you and your hit game is your imagination and ambition.

Part I

Pre-Production

Chapter 1

Game Genres and Playing Perspectives

KEY TOPICS

- Game Genres
- Playing Perspectives

Before diving into this book, let's first cover a few of the basics. The first section of this chapter clarifies the differences between the various gaming genres or styles of play. This way, we'll all be on the same wavelength. Plus, before you sit down to design your game, you will ultimately need to choose a genre or a combination of genres to help solidify your vision.

There will also be a number of terms thrown around over the next few hundred pages to explain how the game is played and/or the view the player has of the action. Words such as top-down, first-person perspective, and isometric will be explained and illustrated with an example.

Everybody in? Let's begin!

Game Genres

Game genres are simply the main categories into which various types of games fall. They include action, strategy, adventure, role-playing, sports, simulations, and puzzle or "classic" games.

Action

Quite simply, action games rely more on hand/eye coordination than on story or strategy. They're generally fast-paced and reflex-oriented. The most popular type of action game for the PC is the first-person perspective 3D shooter (more on this later). id Software's *DOOM* or *Quake* series, Epic Games' *Unreal* series, THQ's *Red Faction* games, and Microsoft's *Halo* are all good examples.

Fighting games such as Tecmo's *Dead or Alive 3* or Namco's *Tekken 4* fall into this "action" category, as do the classic 2D side-scroller games (such as the old *Sonic* and *Mario* platform games or *Rayman Advance* for the Game Boy Advance). "Over-the-shoulder" perspective games (described later in the chapter) such as the *Tomb Raider* series from Eidos Interactive, Activision's *Tony Hawk's Pro Skater* series, or Rockstar Games' *Grand Theft Auto* titles also fall into this category.

Action games are still the most popular genre for both console and PC systems. But of course there are many different flavors of action games. *Max Payne*, for example, is a dark and gritty shooter that fused "The Matrix"–style moves with a film noir storyline.
(Used with permission by 3D Realms.)

Strategy

Strategy games emphasize logical thinking and planning. They often stress resource and time management, which usually take precedence over fast action and character involvement. Tactical organization and execution are necessary, and the game creators usually place the decision-making skills and delivery of commands in the player's hands.

As opposed to turn-based games such as Firaxis' *Civilization III* or 3DO's *Heroes of Might and Magic* series, real-time strategy (RTS) games add an active element and force the player to consider multiple events occurring at the same time. Examples of such games include Blizzard's *Warcraft III: Reign of Chaos*, Microsoft's *Age of Mythology*, and Westwood's *Command & Conquer* series.

A Farseer calls down a storm on a squad of Skeletons in Blizzard's Warcraft III: Reign of Chaos, a shining example
of a real-time strategy game. The Warcraft series is one of the most beloved franchises on the PC.
(Used with permission by Blizzard Entertainment, Inc.)

Adventure

Adventure games involve the player in a journey of exploration and puzzle-solving. These
games usually have a linear storyline in which you, the protagonist, set out to accomplish a
main goal through character interaction and inventory manipulation. Some traces of the action
genre may be found in these games. Good examples of adventure games include The Adventure
Company's *Syberia*, Konami's *Shadow of Destiny*, Ubi Soft's *Myst* series, and Funcom's *The
Longest Journey*.

Role-Playing Games (RPGs)

Role-playing games (RPGs) are similar to adventure games, but rely more on character growth
and development (usually involving player statistics), conversation, and strategic combat than
on puzzle-solving. Huge epic quests and fantasy worlds with non-player characters (NPCs) are
common, and storylines are not always linear as in traditional adventure games. Side quests are
also not uncommon to the genre. Computer role-playing games are often referred to as CRPGs.

Action may play a significant role in an RPG, as in Microsoft's *Dungeon Siege*, Blizzard's *Diablo*
series, and Squaresoft's *Final Fantasy* series. Older RPGs, referred to as MUDs (short for multiuser domains or multiuser dungeons), are exclusive to the Internet and are text-only. The
majority of them are played via Telnet instead of over the World Wide Web. Most gamers,
however, have shifted interest over to the more graphical and online RPGs, such as Sony Online
Entertainment mega-popular *EverQuest*.

More than 450,000 gamers pay $13 a month to play the massively multiplayer game *EverQuest*. Seen here is a screen grab from one of the many *EverQuest* expansion CDs: *Shadows of Luclin*.
(Used with permission by Sony Online Entertainment, Inc.)

Sports

Sports titles simulate a single-player or team game from an instructional or a player perspective. Realism is important, as are fast action and tactical strategy. Examples of popular sports games include the Madden football series from Electronic Arts; Sega Sports' "2K" football, basketball, and hockey series; THQ's many wrestling games; and Midway's *NHL Hitz*. (Though *Hitz* is more over-the-top than realistic!)

Simulations or Sims

Sims realistically simulate a given animate or inanimate object or process. Sims often place the gamer in a 3D first-person perspective and re-create machinery such as planes, tanks, helicopters, and submarines. Examples include Microsoft's *Flight Simulator* or *Combat Flight Simulator* series, Ubi Soft's *IL-2 Sturmovik* series, and iEntertainment's *WarBirds III*.

Moreover, a simulation can create machinery that doesn't even exist, such as spaceships—LucasArts' *Rogue Leader: Rogue Squadron II* for the Nintendo GameCube is a perfect example.

Finally, "God-game" sims require the (often megalomaniac!) gamer to build and manage cities, communities, and other resources on a grander scale; Electronic Arts' *The Sims* and *SimCity 4* are good examples, as is Atari's *RollerCoaster Tycoon* series.

NOTE

So where exactly do racing/driving games fit into the picture? Well, if you think about it, these games can fit into their own category of game genre or fall into the action/arcade genre (such as Incognito Studios' *Twisted Metal: Black*), the simulation genre (Codemasters' *Colin McRae Rally* series), or the sports genre (EA Sports' *NASCAR Thunder* series).

The best-selling PC game of all time is Electronic Arts' *The Sims*, a simulation game in which your goal is to create and maintain a household of virtual residents, successfully work your way up the career ladder, and take care of business at home. A massively-multiplayer version—*The Sims Online*—debuted in early 2003.

(Used with permission by Electronic Arts, Inc.)

Arguably the most popular racing game series on the planet is the *Gran Turismo* series, created in Japan by Polyphony and published by Sony for its PSOne and PlayStation 2 platforms. One lap around the track and you're hooked for months on end.

(Used with permission by Sony Computer Entertainment America, Inc.)

Puzzle or "Classic" Games

The puzzle or "classic" games include older and more historic games of leisure such as cards; tile games; and trivia, word, or board games. Chess, checkers, backgammon, Mah Jongg, and Solitaire are perfect examples. Recently, "classic" games have also included simpler and smaller-scale computer games, such as older arcade favorites and games that may lack a deep story or player commitment. (*Tetris*, *Bust-A-Move*, *Bejeweled*, *Bounce Out*, *Snood*, and *Minesweeper* are great examples.) Keep in mind that some of these games borrow elements from multiple genres (as illustrated in the RPG examples) or toy with different playing perspectives.

> **NOTE**
> A "new" genre of games has evolved over the past couple of years, both in arcades and on the home front, known as the music genre. Games such as Komani's *Dance Dance Revolution*, Sony's *Frequency* and *PaRappa the Rappa* series, and Sega's *Space Channel 5* focus on music, singing, and dancing. This is an exciting new trend that's sure to continue well into the future.

Playing Perspectives

Playing perspectives define the role or point of view that the player has on the game. These perspectives include first-person, third-person, top-down, isometric, flat, side-view, and text-based.

First-Person Perspective

As touched on earlier in this chapter, first-person perspective is a popular choice among action game designers. In 3D shooters, the view of the gaming environment is as if the player is seeing it through the character's eyes, such as in Electronic Arts' *Medal of Honor: Allied Assault*, Fox Interactive's *No One Lives Forever* series, or id Software's *DOOM III*.

Genres other than action games take advantage of this popular perspective, too, including most simulations (such as Microsoft's *Flight Simulator* series), adventure games (Ubi Soft's *Myst* series), strategy games (Simon & Schuster's *Star Trek: Dominion Wars*), and role-playing games (Bethesda Softworks' *The Elder Scrolls III: Morrowind*).

A first-person perspective view is often preferred because it adds to the believability of the world and overall immersion factor. Pictured here is Activision's eagerly anticipated *DOOM III*.
(Images from DOOM III™ © 2002 Id Software, Inc. All rights reserved. Used under license. DOOM®, DOOM III™, and the id Software™ name are either registered trademarks or trademarks of Id Software, Inc. in the United States and/or other countries. Used with permission by Activision, Inc.)

Third-Person Perspective

Also known as the "over-the-shoulder" view, the third-person perspective is another popular choice among game designers these days, especially because most games are in 3D. A third-person perspective is when the player can see the character he or she is playing onscreen. This perspective has its advantages, too, because more of the environment can be seen while playing, plus you can see the moves your character can make—which is impossible in a first-person perspective view.

Many console and PC games use this view, including *Grand Theft Auto III* and *Grand Theft Auto: Vice City*, the *Tomb Raider* series, the *Spider-Man* series, the *Tony Hawk's Pro Skater* series, the *Metal Gear Solid* series, and the *Resident Evil* series.

Eidos Interactive's *Tomb Raider* was one of the first big hits to use a third-person perspective with an "intelligent" camera that followed heroine Lara Croft around. This is a screen shot from the latest game in the series, *Lara Croft Tomb Raider: The Angel of Darkness*.
(Used with permission by Eidos Interactive, Inc.)

This perspective is not limited to just action/arcade games; sports games (almost all of them) honor this view, as well as RPGs (*Final Fantasy* series) and adventure games (LucasArts' *Escape from Monkey Island*).

Some games—such as Microsoft's *Halo*, shown here—switch between the first-person and third-person perspective. While on foot, the game is played from a first-person perspective. Inside one of the many vehicles, it swaps to a third-person view so players can see more of the environment.
(Used with permission by Microsoft, Inc.)

Top-Down Perspective

Top-down perspective is exactly as it sounds. The game is viewed looking down, as if the "camera" were hovering over the game itself. The genre that uses this perspective the most is the strategy game genre—both turn-based and real-time versions. This is because of all the minute micro-management details and tactical placement of troops on a landscape for battle. The player must be able to access the units and survey the situation with one glance. Good examples of top-down games are the various *Pokémon* games for the Game Boy and Monkeystone's *Hyperspace Delivery Boy!* for the PC and PocketPC platforms.

Non-strategy games that use this perspective include older *Ultima* and *Zelda* games, and many classic 2D games of yesteryear, including the arcade hits *Centipede* and *Frogger*.

Nintendo's *Pokémon Crystal* for the Game Boy platform utilizes a top-down perspective.
(Used with permission by Nintendo of America, Inc.)

Isometric

Often confused with top-down is the isometric point of view. This is a slightly tilted "three-quarter" view that hovers up and off to the side of the gameplay and gives the impression of 3D. Good examples of this kind of perspective are Blizzard's *Diablo* series, Interplay's *Neverwinter Nights*, and Electronic Arts' *The Sims*.

Blizzard's *Diablo II* is an isometric action/RPG. Many game developers prefer this view because the characters and the environments can be seen by the player at the same time. In this shot, the Sorceress unleashes her Flame Jet against a group of Corrupt Rogues.
(Used with permission by Blizzard Entertainment, Inc.)

Flat, Side-View

The flat, side-view is the traditional two-dimensional "side view" of the action, a perspective that has become less and less popular over the years as 3D became the norm. This view was popularized with the once-common "side-scroller" or "platform" games in the late 1980s and early 1990s, such as a few *Mario Brothers* and *Sonic the Hedgehog* games.

Some current games still use this perspective, and it may prove to be a refreshing change from all the first-person and third-person perspective games these days. Examples include Titus' *Worms* series, ARUSH Entertainment's *Duke Nukem: Manhattan Project*, and the first two *Oddworld* titles from Oddworld Inhabitants.

Text-Based Games

There are very few text-based games that don't use graphics at all or very sparingly. Aside from the classic text adventures from the early 1980s, such as the famous *Zork* series from Infocom, Douglas Adams' *Hitchhiker's Guide to the Galaxy*, and today's *Outsmart* online game (Microsoft) are good examples of this type of game.

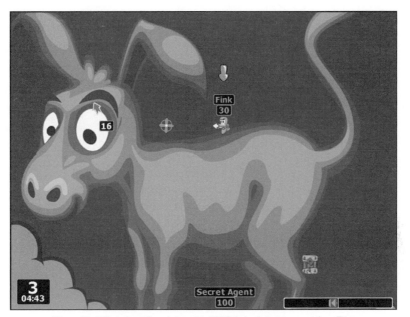

Worms World Party is a silly yet charming 2D "flat view" strategy game from Titus.
(Used with permission by the Titus Software Corporation.)

Chapter 2

General Game Design: Action/Arcade Games

Considering that good game design is more of an art form than a science, it can often be difficult to ask someone to "teach" it to you. As an analogy, it's like asking McCartney how he co-wrote a song like "Yesterday" or how Salvador Dali conceived a painting such as *Persistence of Memory*. In fact, it's often more difficult to analyze and tutor on game design because it incorporates more senses than any other art form, not to mention that it's often a group effort and an interactive medium, to boot.

Having said that, we're very fortunate to have some talented game designers who can put their avenues of inspiration into words and their game design processes onto paper. Naturally, there are as many ideas about approaching game design as there are developers, but we have some inspiring and enlightening advice from some of our young and bustling industry's finest over the next few chapters.

Before diving into these words of wisdom, remember one thing: All the glitz and glitter poured into games these days—expensive art, animation, real actors, the best musicians—can't cover up for poor gameplay.

This chapter features designers from the action/arcade category. Chapter 3, "General Game Design: Strategy Games," delves into the strategy game genre.

Here we go!

Jason Rubin, Naughty Dog

As a wholly owned subsidiary of Sony Computer Entertainment, Inc., Naughty Dog has won worldwide acclaim for its *Crash Bandicoot* games (1996 to 1999) and *Jak & Daxter: The Precursor Legacy*, a "sleeper" hit in 2001. "Jak II" is in the works.

We chatted with Jason Rubin, cofounder and lead designer at Naughty Dog, about game design theory and practice, and he has this to share with those who may be just starting out or pondering it seriously:

> ➤ The first choice to make when designing a game is "art" or "sales." The art world has government funding for "passion projects"; games don't. To be successful, you can't necessarily set out to make the game you want to make; you have to set out to make the game that gamers will want to play. At Naughty Dog, we always put the needs and desires of the gamer above our own likes and dislikes. Then, once we know what game we should be making, we do the best job designing the product that we can under those constraints. I'd like to believe that in the end, we do produce art...but art that leaves the shelf!

> ➤ I've realized from watching the video game industry for the last 16 years that if any of the "camps" of development are given more weight than the others in the development process, the game is destined for trouble. When artists rule, you end up with a beautiful...well, it's not a game. When programmers run the show, you end up with a tech demo that falls flat in the visuals and gameplay department. And when game designers rule, the programmers are sent off on impossible tasks just to please a whim of design, when something more practical could be substituted without damaging fun value. Artists are frustrated by design that doesn't take visuals into account, and game design isn't improved on-the-fly because the designers don't allow their work to be questioned. I remember a massive failure from a large publisher that came out late, was over budget, and didn't play well because the game designer forced the team to stick with his pre-production design document—the Bible—regardless of the results. The three-party system works; keep that in mind as a game designer, and you'll end up with a better product.

> ➤ There's only one opinion that matters in balancing, tuning, and refining a game: the voice of many focus testers in unison. I can't tell you how many times Naughty Dog has brought a feature or character to the gamer—sure either that it had to go or that it was the best thing ever created—only to walk away knowing that we were wrong. Against our instincts, we'll always change in the face of a well-set-up public opinion poll to the contrary. One way to test whether game designers are worth their weight is if they're as comfortable with being wrong as they are with being right.

Asked how you create a game that stands out from the crowd but isn't too "out there"—that is, how you combine ingenuity with familiarity—Rubin responds:

Lately, it seems that detail, detail, detail is the name of the day—not necessarily ingenuity. The trend is the same in the movies. Better effects and characters, average stories—even remakes in some cases. Games are competing with each other to see which can be the most dense—but as a result they end quickly. Can you shoot every bottle? Can you read the magazines on the stand? Are the players wearing the correct shoes? Every hour spent supporting "realistic jersey wear" in a hockey game is an hour lost on the AI [artificial intelligence—see Chapter 12, "Artificial Intelligence (AI)"]. Every extra detail in a level, from rain that realistically pools and flows to mirrors on the wall, is an additional level that never gets done or an enemy that could have been more complex. The gamers realize that this is a direct result of the additional details that they have come to expect. Our goal in *Jak & Daxter: The Precursor Legacy* was to spend the time and energy to add the detail and keep the length and value. The cost of this is directly felt in the budget. More people, more time, more effort.

See more of Jason Rubin's advice in Chapter 6, "Creating Characters, Storyboarding, and Design Documents."

> **NOTE**
>
> *Jak & Daxter: The Precursor Legacy* was arguably the first PS2 game with no load times whatsoever. How was this achieved? Chapter 11, "Programming Theory," dishes out advice by Stephen White, Naughty Dog's clever programming director.

Shinji Mikami, Capcom

Shinji Mikami, general manager of production at Studio 4 for Capcom in Japan, has worked on various Super Nintendo Entertainment System (SNES) games such as *Aladdin* and *Goof Troop*, but is best-known for creating many of today's most beloved "survival horror" titles, such as the *Resident Evil, Dino Crisis*, and *Devil May Cry* series. *Resident Evil* is enjoying somewhat of a renaissance. A feature film based on the franchise was released in 2001 (the official site is http://residentevil.station.sony.com/), and the video games have been re-released on the Nintendo GameCube platform, in stunning detail.

Concerning general game design, Mikami lists the most important considerations for game designers to keep in mind:

➤ Make it crystal-clear what you want to achieve with your game.

➤ Think in advance of the most effective way to shape up the initial game specs so the game fits within various limitations/restrictions (development time, hardware specs, and so on).

➤ Never give up. Trust yourself. Patience is the key.

➤ Always listen to people's opinions.

➤ Whatever methods or means you take, creating a game is always a painful job. Because of this nature, it's very important for you to try having fun with your work whenever you can.

A new generation of video gamers can experience the chills, thrills, and spills from the *Resident Evil* series as it has been reborn on the Nintendo GameCube platform. Pictured here are shots from the chilling re-release of the original *Resident Evil*.
(Used with permission by Capcom Entertainment, Inc.)

Mikami believes that much of the success and strong word-of-mouth of the *Resident Evil* series is due to the fact that he followed the preceding rules strictly:

> It was easy for a person to convey the horror factor in *Resident Evil* to his or her friends, to explain what [he or she loved] about *Resident Evil*. I made it my goal to represent the fear/horror factor in a video game and never stopped until the end.

How do you make a game scary?

> I make it the first priority to keep a scary atmosphere throughout the game; also, it's very important to time various events so they work most effectively in conjunction with what the player is doing at that moment.

Mikami believes that the market must also be ripe for a game to be a huge hit.

> Few games keep a good balance between "video games as an art" and "video games as a business commodity." That's the biggest problem, in my opinion, with many of today's games. I wish players would pay more attention to original/fresh concepts of games. It seems to me we're always expected to develop a sequel to the already established series.

Chapter 17, "Proper Game Testing," discusses various ways to test games in development to ensure a bug-free and balanced experience. How does Mikami test games such as the *Resident Evil* series and *Dino Crisis*?

> I usually test my game for a month before release. I first list all of the points in the game where a bug can be expected. Then I assign several different groups to each different "suspicious" part of the game and have them test it systematically.

Mikami is proud of the results of the re-release of the *Resident Evil* games on the GameCube. "In terms of visual quality, it exceeds the level of any of the past *Resident Evil* series by a couple of notches, to say the least!" New features were also introduced to the game, such as new puzzles and cinematics, more weapons and combat options, tougher enemies, and extra areas to explore.

Brendan McNamara, Sony Computer Entertainment Europe/Team Soho

As director of development at SCEE (Sony Computer Entertainment Europe) in Soho, UK, McNamara has worked on many console games over the past years, including *Kingsley*, the *This Is Football* series, and (most recently) *The Getaway*.

The Getaway, which debuted in early 2003, is an ambitious project that looks and plays more like an interactive movie than a video game: Actors were motion-captured for realistic animation and interaction. More than 40 square kilometers of downtown London were realistically re-created (down to each bus stop and restaurant). The game is based on a 100-page script, yielding more than an hour of dialogue.

In the game, players first assume the role of an ex-con who is framed for the murder of his wife. To make matters worse, his son is kidnapped and held captive by a deranged crime boss. Later in the game, the adventure is played all over again as an ex-"copper."

McNamara provides some advice to anyone working on his or her first game:

> ➤ **Keep things simple.** There's a huge temptation by everyone in a technology company to overcomplicate things, and less is often more in most areas of life. I often ask a designer or a programmer to do something quite simple, and I'll come back a couple of hours later and they have completely gone off [creating something elaborate].

➤ **Working within constraints is good.** The best designs in any walk of life are made by making the constraints the strengths. Find out what all of those constraints are before you design anything.

➤ **Make the controls simple.** The designer's job first and foremost is to put the fun in. It's a pretty intangible process, but the designer has to make what the player is seeing onscreen feel good in the player's hands. Test your control mechanics on as many people as you can, especially people who don't play as many games as you.

What lessons did McNamara learn in creating *The Getaway*?

Communicating in a huge team is difficult. The best move we ever made was to have one large open-plan floor and mix up all of the disciplines. We have game designers sitting next to programmers who sit next to artists. The worst move we ever made was not to insist that everyone who was on the team or joined the team thoroughly read the design document. [See Chapter 6 and Chapter 7, "Master Design Document Template," on how to create a design document.]

Anything else he'd do differently if he had a chance to go back to the early days of *The Getaway*?

I would try to get a lot of the technology issues out of the way before we actually started to produce the game. It would be similar to a pre-production phase in a feature film. *The Getaway* has [taken] two years developing technology and one year implementing the game. That's the wrong ratio. Luckily, the sequel will have the benefit of all that development, so it should be a fun game to work on. However, when PS3 comes around, I imagine we'll have to rethink our development process. I'm not sure that it will be sustainable both mentally or financially to have a huge team on a project for three years. It's difficult for 55 people to stay focused for that long. It becomes an exercise in willpower. I think as games inevitably get bigger that we'll see more freelance art teams come in to do parts of the project and move on to the next project, as they do on features.

McNamara says that *The Getaway* was strongly influenced by films, especially British gangster pictures from the '70s, '80s, and '90s.

Get Carter; *The Long Good Friday*; *Mona Lisa*; *Lock, Stock and Two Smoking Barrels*; and *Face* were all important. Two Jake Arnott books, *The Long Firm* and *He Kills Coppers*, were influential, as well as a documentary called *100% White*.

Where should game designers look for inspiration?

Obviously, game designers should look to their favorite games, but I'd also firmly advise designers to look forward and not always back into the past. It's a funny thing, but the resistance you get to new ideas in game companies is very alarming, considering how young the industry is. I can't tell you how many times I've been pitched revamps of *Jetpack* and *Tron*. Games are about popular culture. Inspiration should come from all of the regular sources, although I'd say that reading is probably best because it makes you visualize possibilities—which is often necessary for game designers, especially when they're waiting for tools and technology that aren't ready yet.

In Chapter 21, "Breaking into the Industry," Brendan McNamara offers good advice on how to best break into the biz. What should go on your résumé and in your portfolio when you apply? Flip the pages to find out…

Three separate scenes from Sony's ambitious *The Getaway*, played exclusively on the PlayStation 2 system.
(Used with permission by Sony Computer Entertainment America, Inc.)

Yu Suzuki, Sega

The honorable Yu Suzuki is a representative director at Sega-AM2 Co. Ltd. in Japan. He has worked on a number of worldwide products over the past few years, including *Beach Spikers*, the *Virtua Fighter* series (1 through 4), the *Shenmue* series, the *Virtua Cop* series, *Hang On*, *Space Harrier*, *Afterburner*, *Virtua Racing*, and many others. Whew!

His dream is for Sega-AM2 to be a top studio by the world's standards. "We would like to be a company that, when someone talks about 'a game company,' they immediately mention Sega-AM2," says Suzuki. He provides several pieces of good advice for a new game designer:

> ➤ **Senior team members.** As game development is in most cases a group effort, the most important matter is communication. In order to learn techniques effectively, it's important to find "good seniors." I recommend you go out and play other than in a place of work, and have a good friendship with them. By having a good relationship with them, you'll be able to obtain

various kinds of information or advice. By combining obtained information/advice and your own ideas, you'll be able to work toward the goal without vain efforts.

➤ **On-the-job training.** Some companies provide educational programs for a certain period after entering the company. There are general or special programs, but the most effective one is "on-the-job training."

If they want to practice processing words, planners should not only type words, but try writing the imaginary planning document of a game. Programmers should try programming according to the plan their company may carry out (fly something, move cars, etc.). For example, if you have information that you'll be developing a game featuring a Porsche, instead of giving a test for other cars, start with Porsche cars from the beginning.

The same can be said for designers. For example, if you have information that you'll develop a fantasy game, you can create fairies or creatures that suit fantasy, instead of flowers or glasses that have nothing to do with the game. I think that it's very important to always train yourself with images that you're likely to use in actual work.

➤ **Self-investment.** After you enter a company, you'll be salaried. Use your salary as much as possible for "self-investment" in order to add value to yourself. By raising your value in the company, their evaluation of you will rise.

➤ **Pursue your hobbies as much as possible.** For example, if you like watching movies, watch a lot of movies. Have at least one thing you're more familiar with than anyone else. Seen from other people's eyes, you might seem to waste your money. However, it will be your own experience and a great help to create good games in the future.

Yu Suzuki has helped create numerous Sega games for the home and arcade, including the *Virtua Fighter* series.
Virtua Fighter 4 is shown here.
(Used with permission by Sega of America, Inc.)

Suzuki says the most appealing part of the *Virtua Fighter* series is its multiplayer gameplay. He explains that it's not just simple "person versus CPU" gameplay: "For players, their opponent is a person through the medium of CPU. If a player changes, the gameplay itself will change, so it has a potential of limitless variation without running to pattern."

Asked to provide some do's and don'ts in game design, Suzuki says that it boils down to experiencing success or failure in a game:

> Players often have the opportunity to feel success or failure playing games. For instance, if it's a car-driving game, if you fail to turn curves for speeding too much, you'll feel you've failed. And if you succeed in turning curves, you'll feel you've achieved.

> "Don'ts" include situations in which you can't explain how a player has failed, and he or she can't realize the reason in a clear way. For example, if a player suddenly gets shot from outside the screen and the game is over, no one will play that game again.

Where does Suzuki look for inspiration?

> When watching movies, playing sports that have nothing to do with games, waking up in the morning, dreams, etc. I can't really specify occasions where inspiration comes. Generally, when I keep on thinking all the time, inspiration comes to me.

> It's important to bring your mind, in which you'll meet inspiration. Even if you don't have an answer, by continually thinking, it will enter into your deep mind and by some chance you'll meet inspiration. Continual thinking [improves] the probability for inspiration to come. Conversely, if you think nothing, no inspiration comes.

What separates a great game from a good game?

> ➤ Passion.

> ➤ Never give up.

> ➤ Create a game carefully, thinking about the people who will play it.

In Chapter 6, Yu Suzuki expounds on what makes for a great lead character in a game.

Hironobu Sakaguchi, Square, Ltd.

It's a great honor to welcome Hironobu Sakaguchi, executive producer on all *Final Fantasy* titles. Believe it or not, the *Final Fantasy* video games combined have sold more than 45 million units to date (as of March 2003). Sakaguchi also aided in the development of the official *Final Fantasy CGI* movie at the SQUARE USA Honolulu, Hawaii studios.

Sakaguchi says that the most important consideration for a game designer is "understanding and grasping the player's psychology. What will the player feel from the images, sounds, and movements?" He says it's necessary to take into account and predict how the player will react in response to those stimuli.

Consideration must be taken so that the player feels that he or she can freely move about the world. There will be constraints, of course, but the key is to create movements within the system and the game itself so that the constraints and limitations are not felt by the player.

Sakaguchi says that the most important factor in terms of storytelling and visuals is "a setting that allows the user to relate to the characters."

How do you create memorable characters in a video game such as *Cloud* or *Squall*? Sakaguchi responds briefly: "Uniqueness of the character, romance, a character that can become a master, and someone to protect." Indeed, this is all true for the protagonists for the *Final Fantasy* series. (Creating characters is covered in more detail in Chapter 6.)

What's missing or wrong in today's console or PC games? Lack of originality? Poor control? Not enough emotion?

Many factors are lacking in today's games. They range from the constraints of the hardware itself to problems stemming from the network or user interface. Of course, the story, characters, and world settings aren't being given much thought, either. But this is part of the evolutionary process of the industry in which we work. It gives us reason to evolve, to do better each time around. Actually, the process of evolving may be the best place to be because of the excitement associated with thinking about the future and how things will change.

The pre-rendered cinematics in *"Final Fantasy X"* are absolutely stunning, and serve as key turns in the ongoing saga. Will gameplay one day look this good? We're getting pretty close!

(© Square.)

Asked about user interface and control, Sakaguchi answers in light of the external and in-game limitations of today:

> In the household, we've been limited to the NTSC, a simple stereo environment, and the joystick. I believe that if the images were all 3D and we had a physical sensation system (with chairs that slant and shake), it would be much more fun, but I guess that's not realistic at present. But I believe that the interface within the screen, the GUI, is very important. Even if the story and game system are good, if the GUI is not created well, such as in the menu system, there are times when the game cannot be enjoyed and appreciated.

For more on graphical user interfaces, visit Chapter 14, "The All-Important User Interface (UI) and Game Control."

Chris Cross, Electronic Arts Los Angeles (EALA)

Christopher L. Cross is a lead designer at Electronic Arts' L.A. studios. Cross has worked as a tester for *Warcraft II* (localized versions), *Warcraft II: Expansion*, and *Warcraft II: Diablo*; and serves as a designer for EA on *Small Soldiers: Squad Commander*, *Trespasser*, *Medal of Honor*, and *Medal of Honor: Frontline*.

Pooling from his vast experience, Cross gives us the three most important things to keep in mind when designing games and how the spectacular *Medal of Honor* series fits into this advice.

"Keep it simple—don't overstep your experience or capabilities," begins Cross. "Make the design only as complex as it needs to be."

With the original *Medal of Honor*, Cross says they discussed having an inventory system that would allow you to pick up objects and keep them for later use, such as health, keys, ammo, and so forth. "But I quickly realized that this was going to overcomplicate things. Our main game mechanic is shooting; keeping that in mind, managing inventory distracts from the main goal of action."

The following is an excerpt from the original design doc that sums it up:

> Items in the inventory are used by pressing the action button when the player is in the proper location. If the player has the correct item for the place where he's standing, the item will automatically be used.
>
> When a new item is picked up, a text prompt will show what was acquired.
>
> When an object is used, the player is alerted by a text message.
>
> When an object is missing, the player will be alerted by a text message. (Say the player is at a locked door, but is missing the proper key.)
>
> When pressing the action button, a text message pops up and tells the player that he needs the blue key. Note: There are no blue keys—or keys of any other color—in *Medal of Honor*.

When you run over a key and pick it up, you're not really getting an object. Then, somewhere else in the level, a door can now be opened because it got a message saying that the player has the key to the door, so it should open when the action key is pressed in its vicinity. The inventory system is passive, so the player doesn't have to shuffle through his inventory to select the key and then activate it in the correct place. Instead, the player merely has to walk up to the door in question and press the action button. This could prompt a text message saying "KEY USED" if deemed necessary.

Cross' second piece of advice is this: "Consider the product as a whole—don't sacrifice having a better product for a favorite feature. Evaluate how much of the product is affected by any feature." A good example is the train level in *Medal of Honor: Frontline*.

As neat as that level is, it was only one out of 18, and was constantly at risk of getting cut. We couldn't afford the engineering man-hours to make the terrain move correctly, so one of our designers tackled the problem through script. He succeeded and it worked out kind of nicely, but we were all willing to cut the level in a heartbeat if we couldn't prove that it was going to work and be fun, no matter how cool we all thought the level was.

Cross believes that "Designing is not a dictatorship—being a designer doesn't mean standing around and handing out assignments. It's really about driving the vision of the whole team." He explains:

Keep an open ear—you might be surprised at the great ideas other people on your team may have. If the idea doesn't completely fit the vision of the game, take what does fit and incorporate it. Remember, there are never any bad ideas.

Can he offer specific examples for this last piece of advice? No, "mainly because I try to practice this every day."

I definitely try to influence decisions to my way of thinking, but I also keep my eye open for untapped or overlooked possibilities and incorporate them into the design. I always try to keep in mind that we are making a game, and input from as many people as possible is good as long as the final decisions on design are from me.

Why does Cross think the *Medal of Honor* series is so popular? He offers "WWII and accessibility."

World War II seems like ancient history to some, but it was "the war to end all wars." It was the last time that we had clear delineation between good and evil on a massive scale. The iconography of the Nazi war machine and the Third Reich is still a touchy subject and evokes powerful emotions for many around the world. Part of what we tried to achieve was to stay faithful with representing a historical view without losing the gameplay. Many of our game missions could have happened. The setting is also modern enough and the technology was advancing so fast at the time that we were never at a loss for some new interesting weapon or objective.

Gamespot magazine (`www.gamespot.com`) says this about *Medal of Honor: Frontline*: "[It'll] surprise PlayStation 2 owners by dazzling them with terrific gameplay, visual flair, and some of the best sound yet heard on Sony's console."
(Used with permission by Electronic Arts, Inc.)

On accessibility, which Cross also calls "simplicity of design," he says that designing a first-person shooter (FPS) for the console market involves making that kind of game work on a potentially awkward controller. "Keeping this in mind, you won't find many circle-strafing enemies or other unnecessary complexities in the game." He continues:

> It's hard enough for most players, who may not have ever played an FPS before, to navigate around the world. Enemies were also approached differently. In most FPS games preceding the first *Medal of Honor*, the blue enemy had this behavior and this weapon; the red enemy had another. We didn't have that luxury. All of our enemies were basically human, so we had to find ways to tie them into the backgrounds and make them seem like they really existed there. This also affected our approach to AI and animation. All our non-player characters have animations based on reality and can make complex decisions about self-preservation. In summation, I think all of our efforts were put into the idea of accessibility and recruiting new gamers into the FPS genre.

What drives Cross nuts when playing a game?

> I play games for fun first and then for research. I take a game apart and analyze it only when it stops being fun, something really impresses me, or I'm finished with it. My biggest beef is when games stop being fun. This usually involves a seemingly arbitrary decision on the level designer's part to force me to play or think a certain way. I especially don't appreciate cheap shots. It's very difficult to lay out an ambush successfully in most games without making the player feel cheated. The best way is to design some way for the player to learn that in some situations there is a chance for an ambush or surprise. This is something that has to be taught very carefully, to set up a grammar that the player understands and can recognize later in the game. Then the player has a chance to figure out when and where an ambush may happen and possibly find a smart or clever way to deal with it. A good example from *Medal of Honor* where we learned that lesson: at some random time, spawning three Panzershrek soldiers behind the player that almost instantly do major damage to the player.

In Chapter 21, Chris Cross chats about how to break into the industry.

American McGee, Carbon6 Entertainment

American James McGee (yes, that's his real name) is the creative director of Carbon6 Entertainment, based in Los Angeles, CA. His past projects include some little games known as *DOOM*, *DOOM II*, *Quake*, *Quake II*, and multiple *DOOM* and *Quake*-related spinoffs. Most recently, he created *American McGee's Alice* for Electronic Arts (EA), and he is currently involved in a number of other projects at EA as well as working on the official *Alice* feature film with Dimension Films.

McGee discusses a number of game design tips, with personal examples to support his suggestions:

> ➤ **Keep things simple.** When things start getting out of hand, you always have your basic ideas to fall back on. Make sure that you know what your core ideas are. What makes your concept stick together? Music, art, characters—know what those are and stay true to them.
>
> This was applied to everything: from story, to characters we decided on using, to the environments that we built. I tore the original story apart, extracted only those characters and environments that were needed to tell our story, and then crafted as simple yet compelling a story as possible to drive the action. Basically, we did what we knew we could do, and tried to do it as well as possible. Some risks were taken, but they were balanced against the complexity they would bring to the production of the game.
>
> ➤ **Know what you're trying to create.** Our team spent two months in pre-production. We sketched out most of our main characters, locations, and weapons long before we ever turned on a computer. This gave the guys responsible for creating the content a really solid base to build on once production started.
>
> ➤ **Create as if you were building a toy.** Things like interface, character interaction, weapon design and implementation, and game mechanics were all built to be as simple and usable as possible. One thing I really hate is games that force you to learn a new way of interfacing with the controls just to get up and running.
>
> A good example of the "toy" philosophy can be found in the jump reticle that we implemented. Jumping is a necessary evil created by the complex world geometry that we use to communicate our vision of Wonderland. It's not a lot of fun, and I've found that many people give up in frustration while playing a third/first-person game because of jumping. So we took the pain out of it and made it so even a novice could understand and enjoy moving around the world.
>
> And finally, remember that what you're creating is about fun. People want a game play experience, not painful lessons in interface, game mechanics, and control mechanisms.

Asked whether it's more difficult or much easier to work with a familiar universe such as Alice in Wonderland, McGee responds:

I think it was a mix of both. Easier because in a way a lot of the world and characters were already laid out for us. More difficult because we felt a strong desire to create an experience worthy of the Wonderland mythos. In the end, I really enjoyed working on something that had a place in the collective subconscious because it meant that a lot of work had already been done for us in terms of establishing our characters and environments. That left us free to explore new twists to those elements, which I think really paid off well.

If he could change something with today's computer/video games, what would it be?

I think that today's games suffer from the accelerated advance of the technology that they rely on to communicate their content. Basically, I feel that if computer technology would stop moving forward for a few years, we would spend more time creating content for a stationary target. The content would improve since we'd no longer be racing against time to get the game out before our platform slid out from under us.

In Chapter 21, American McGee gives some compelling advice on how to break into the interactive entertainment industry.

Asked to donate some never-before-seen images for this book, renowned designer American
McGee submitted this rare early sketch of the Mad Hatter from *American McGee's Alice*. Jump to Chapter 6
to read some text McGee wrote when trying to flesh out the intro to the game. Enjoy!
(Used with permission by Electronic Arts, Inc.)

Cliff Bleszinski, Epic Games

Cliff Bleszinski, or "Cliffy B" as many in the biz call him, is a lead designer and producer at Epic Games. He served as lead level designer/co-designer on both *Unreal* and *Unreal Tournament*, a producer and level designer on *Unreal Tournament 2003*, producer on *Unreal 2: The Awakening*, and lead designer on *Unreal Warfare*.

After a decade in the business, what are the three best pieces of advice Cliff can give to up-and-coming game designers looking to make their mark?

➤ **Be a benevolent dictator.** You may have your own vision and ideas about the game that you're going to create, but so does the team that you're working with day in and day out.

➤ **Be a hands-on designer.** Make sure that you're working on one element of the game—programming, art, or level design. Otherwise, you'll be an out-of-touch designer who finds himself wondering why his team harbors resentment.

➤ **Value "real life" experience.** Remember, you're working in an industry that, above and beyond everything else, is about fun. So, make sure you leave the office every so often to experience that thing we call "real life."

With *Unreal* and *Unreal Tournament* as examples, Bleszinski supports his advice:

A team-driven design is something that's always been in place at Epic. We simply find that it works. If an artist makes a gun, a programmer puts it in, and then the gun causes balancing issues, it's discussed in an open forum.

Throughout *Unreal* and *Unreal Tournament*, I made my own levels for the game. This allowed me to remain in the loop with how far along the title was, how fun the weapons were, and what state the toolset was in.

Whenever I can make time, I try to experience new things. I've gone skydiving, scuba diving, horseback riding, fishing, etc. ...and all of these things have made me a better designer!

Cliffy B applies his advice to his work on *Unreal Tournament* 2003:

Keep in mind that both *Unreal Tournament 2003* and *Unreal 2* are projects that have been developed externally.

Although Epic Games owns the *Unreal* franchise, we frequently work with outside teams to develop games within the intellectual property. Most recently, I've been working with Digital Extremes, who co-developed *Unreal* and *Unreal Tournament* with Epic in the past. Digital Extremes was the primary developer of the title, so we have had to walk a tricky line between collaboration and direction.

In this situation, Epic had a pretty good idea of what we wanted to see in the title. Occasionally, there would be creative differences on the project between the two companies. In these instances, we opted for "choosing our battles." As far as I was concerned, any time Epic said, "We want the game to do it this way—because we said so," it would be a failure of communication and would result in de-motivating the talented team that we were working with. We could have nitpicked with the developers to the point of driving them crazy, but we chose instead to trust their judgment in many areas and only "require" changes whenever we felt it was an absolute must.

This would be an example of being a "benevolent dictator." Yes, we own the franchise, but it is not in anyone's best interest to babysit and nitpick.

With regard to being a "hands-on designer": I was the primary designer of two levels in *Unreal Tournament 2003* and secondary on two other levels. Traditional corporate mentality seems to dictate that the higher you go in a company, the further you get from actually getting your hands dirty. At a small company like Epic, this paradigm doesn't hold true. My title may be Lead Designer, but I make it a point to make my own content on a regular basis. This allows me to be in touch with the team, tools, and development pipeline. It also helps prevent the "out-of-touch manager" syndrome that seems to plague many corporations.

How important is creating an "innovative title"? Isn't it possible to simply improve on a proven, existing formula?

I welcome innovative titles! Anyone in this business should recognize that the only way we'll move forward is by having new and innovative products that push the envelope in many different directions.

That said, I think there's plenty of room for titles that are evolutionary rather than revolutionary. I've heard cries from various industry folks: "We shouldn't make any more first-person shooters!" Well, if that was the case, we never would have had such great titles as *Half-Life* and *Medal of Honor*. Sometimes, it's okay to simply build the better mousetrap.

Bleszinski says *Unreal Tournament 2003* is what everyone expected—a better *Unreal Tournament*.

Polished, beautiful, fun, and packed with variety. The game has improved on the elements that made the first so successful, without messing with the formula too much. Remember, *Unreal Tournament* was the first "you-versus-bots" game of its kind, and it continues to lead that genre.

As you can see by this photo, Cliff Bleszinski is all about fun and games. Shown here: *Unreal Tournament 2003*.
(Used with permission by Epic Games, Inc. and Infogrames, Inc. Epic™,
Epic Games™, and Unreal™ are registered trademarks of Epic Games, Inc.)

Any personal beefs with the current crop of action games on the market? Cliffy B believes that single-player games are too long and too expensive: "I'd rather have a game that took 5–10 hours to complete, cost 10–20 dollars to purchase, and cost less to produce—I think there's a big market for low-priced quality titles."

Bleszinski chats about the differences in creating a console game versus a computer game.

> I've come to believe that the best console games are the ones where you and a few friends are sitting in the living room playing a game on the big screen together. Either your friends are playing the game with you—competitively or cooperating—or the game is visually interesting enough to want to watch. The environment that a console is played in is crucial to keep in mind when designing the title.

He cites *Soul Calibur*, the *Madden* series, and *Halo* as good examples. Here's why:

> *Soul Calibur* hits well on several fronts—it's fun to watch, because the characters are gorgeous and animate so well. Their attacks are exquisite. And, of course, since it's a fighting game, players love to jump in and bash each other.

> The *Madden* games look amazing—many folks have commented that the titles are near-broadcast quality. So they're fun to watch. Plus, they're multiplayer, so they work well in the living room environment.

> *Halo* had great cooperative play through the single-player experience alongside a solid competitive multiplayer selection. And, of course, it looked great.

With regard to the PC, Bleszinski believes that the titles that are most successful on this platform are the titles that take advantage of the platform's strengths. He explains:

> The genres that sell the most tend to be first-person shooters, real-time strategy and RPG titles (online and offline). Titles that do well on the PC tend to do some of the following:
>
> ➤ Play best with keyboard and mouse.
>
> ➤ Run best in higher resolutions (with a user who is a few feet from the screen).
>
> ➤ Take advantage of hard drive and Internet use (such as having the ability to download modifications, as well as playing with other players).
>
> ➤ Use the open-ended nature of the PC hardware to produce titles that are bleeding-edge graphically.

Bleszinski has many more good points to share. See Chapter 8, "Level Design," for some level design tips and techniques and Chapter 21 to read what Epic Games seeks in new developers.

NOTE

Epic Games' Cliff Bleszinski believes that creating a good user interface should be easy. His advice? "Keep it simple, stupid. Don't reinvent the wheel. The interface doesn't have to be a remarkable work of art—it has to WORK." For more on creating user interfaces, see Chapter 14.

David Jaffe, Sony Computer Entertainment America

As game director and lead designer at Sony Computer Entertainment America (Santa Monica Studios), David Jaffe has created a handful of memorable products for the Sony PlayStation 1 and 2—but is probably most widely known as the creator of the *Twisted Metal* franchise. Jaffe provides to-the-point advice for anyone looking for tips on game design:

➤ **Clearly define the interactivity of the game.** Cool themes, settings, and characters are great, but that's only part of the process. The main thing is to understand what you want the player to do. And you must understand this on a nuts-and-bolts level. Not only must you know the high concept of the interactivity (for example, a game where the player must navigate complex 3D environments while getting skilled at hard-to-pull-off d-pad fighting moves), but you must get down to brass tacks, really understanding what makes the gameplay you've selected tick, why it's fun, and how to improve it. This is obvious, but you'd be surprised by how many people come to me with "designs" that are simply scenarios and settings. ("I wanna do a game that feels like an action movie shootout!") They have no clue what they want the player to do over the course of 10–80 hours. This is one of the number one causes why games get canceled or delayed. The team gears up, they build an engine, they make some art, and about 6–12 months in they start to wonder what the hell the game is. Then they scramble and things go bad.

➤ **Break new ground in subject matter.** I'm making assumptions here, but most people in this business (myself included) seem to draw from the same well of inspiration. It's a well filled with comic books, summer movies, and Hong Kong action films. Oh, and *Blade Runner*. If we continue down this road, we will not only limit games to a small minority of the population, but eventually push away the players we currently have (who'll get bored and move on). There's a whole world out there, and the subjects of today's games seem to deal with only a very small portion of it.

At the same time, I'd advise taking small/medium steps down the road to making games with new themes. As much as I'd love to see *American Beauty: The Game* on store shelves, we need to get to that place gradually. With game budgets being around six million bucks these days, we have a responsibility to appeal to the current fan base (who do seem to really like the sci-fi, fantasy, and action genres). But at the same time, we must slowly expand the borders of what games can be about. Look at the incredibly original but highly esoteric lineup for the Sega Dreamcast (*Seaman*, *Jet Grind Radio*, *Space Channel 5*) and realize—assuming you want to sell your games and not just get critical acclaim—that innovation is a baby step process. The "talking to the virtual pet" mechanic of Seaman was one of the freshest in games in the last five years. And someone will use that mechanic soon in a context the buying public will care about (shouting out orders to Navy Seals in the middle of a harrowing mission, for example). But asking the public (the American public, anyway) to buy into the idea of shouting orders to a fish with a human head was just a bit too odd for most people. And sadly, the context kept many people from experiencing a wonderful game!

➤ **Break new ground in interactivity.** When's the last time you were given a game where what you needed to do (that is, the play) felt really fresh? About 1–2 new games each year truly introduce something new to the interactive canon. The rest of the games are—on a purely interactive level—remakes of something that has come before. Try to figure out totally new things (while still being fun) to ask a player to do…

Can Jaffe support his words of wisdom with the *Twisted Metal* franchise?

The first step in designing *Twisted Metal* (1, 2, and *Twisted Metal: Black*) was defining the interactivity. We had to figure out what the player was doing in the game. And what it came down to was this: *Twisted Metal* calls upon the player to quickly and precisely maneuver through complex 3D environments (the driving part) while also using a variety of weapons that call upon the player to master different play mechanics (the fighting part), while also asking the player to manage his resources of weapons and health, while also struggling to learn the strengths and weaknesses of the enemy vehicles. It's a long, run-on sentence, but with this, we had the map. We knew what the player would be doing on every level of the game.

From this high-level description, we tried to figure out how to make each of these elements more fun (this is where we tried to break new ground in interactivity). For example: Asking the player to quickly and precisely maneuver through complex 3D environments was something we had done in *Twisted Metal* 1 and 2. How could we make it new and better for T*wisted Metal: Black*? We introduced topography (which added strategic value in that players could now duck behind hills and use the rolling topography to avoid incoming missiles).

Asking the player to use weapons with different play mechanics is something every *Twisted Metal* game has. In *Twisted Metal: Black*, we tried to create weapon mechanics that players had not seen before, but that would still be fun. For example, we made up an attack where the longer the player can keep a laser site on the enemy, the more powerful the attack would be. We also introduced weapons that rewarded the player with more damage based on the player's skill at using that weapon (something we hadn't seen in a car combat game before) and introduced the idea of moving pickups that the player had to chase down.

As for new subject matter, while *Twisted Metal: Black* did exist in the horror genre (a well-represented genre on the console), we tried to create characters that were psychological monsters, not bogeymen. Basically, we wanted a game that felt like [the films] *Seven* or *Silence of the Lambs*, not *Friday the 13th* (which is what a lot of the console horror games tend to feel like).

David Jaffe supplies some rare preliminary sketches from 2001's best-selling *Twisted Metal: Black*. For more images and info about the game, visit www.scea.com/games/categories/shooter/tmb.

(Used with permission by Sony Computer Entertainment America, Inc.)

There have been many car combat games over the past few years; why has the *Twisted Metal* franchise risen to the top? In Jaffe's opinion, it's the personality of the characters and presentation of the game world:

> We spent a lot of time on the characters and mood of the game (from music to movies to game shell presentation). We really wanted players to feel like they were living in the *Twisted Metal* universe, not just playing a game. And I think we did a good job of giving players that experience. So—in that realm—no other console car combat game has come close to us. ([Activision's] *Interstate '76* on the PC did a good job of it, however.)

The other element is play tuning and balancing, adds Jaffe:

> You'd be surprised how many teams don't really tune their games…they get so comfortable playing the game over the course of 12–18 months that they start to go blind to its problems. But on *Twisted*, we were always aware of the players, worried about them having fun. I think this is key to our success. A well-tuned game is such a rare thing in the business that when one comes along, the public responds.

> **NOTE**
>
> *Twisted Metal: Black Online* is one of Sony's first PlayStation 2 games that has made the leap online via the PS2 network adapter. What other franchises can we expect Sony to resurrect for the Net?

Although Jaffe has beefs with some of today's games, he admits to being guilty of some of these mistakes himself:

➤ **Too many hardcore gamer cooks in the kitchen.** Many games are made by hardcore gamers, and this is a problem if that's all you have on your development team. While it's great to have team members who live, drink, and sleep games, you also need people who are going to push for unique ideas that come from other areas of life, other mediums than just video/computer games. These same "non-hardcore" folks tend to have a less cynical view about trying new things that (often) make the game even better.

➤ **No play balancing.** As touched on earlier, people just don't make the time for it. They don't take the game and show it to everyone they can; they don't do focus tests. This is what keeps two-star games from being three- and four-star games.

➤ **Lack of passion.** I'm lucky to work at a company where they allow me to choose (for the most part) what game I'll be working on next. Because of this, I make sure that I only work on things that I'm passionate about. Several other companies are this way, but many aren't. The thing is, there needs to be at least one person on the team who is so in love with the product that they're willing to really put their soul into the game. Players notice this and respond to it. But most games feel like they come out of some mass-production factory. It's a real shame; I hope as the industry matures, more and more people will begin to look at games as a real opportunity for expression; a real outlet for their passions. With this, games will get better and better. But for now, only a small percentage of game makers look at games this way. The rest, to be honest, seem to lack the vision to see that making games can be something more than a job—it can be a truly artistic experience.

➤ **Open E3 to the public.** Okay, so it doesn't hurt the actual play experience of the games themselves, but man that would be cool—open it for just one day and let gamers come play. What's the harm? It would be a madhouse!

For more from David Jaffe, check out Chapter 17 on proper game testing and Chapter 21 on the best ways to break into the industry.

Hideo Kojima, Konami

One of Konami's brightest stars is Hideo Kojima, creator of the *Metal Gear Solid* franchise, among many other video games for the Sega Saturn and Sony PlayStation platforms. Easily one of the most successful titles of 2001 was *Metal Gear Solid 2: Sons of Liberty* for PlayStation 2. *Metal Gear Solid 2: Substance* for the Xbox and PS2 platforms came out in 2002 and 2003, respectively. At last check, Kojima was working on—you guessed it—*Metal Gear Solid 3: Snake Eater*, slated for a 2004 release.

When asked the secret of the *Metal Gear Solid* (*MGS*) franchise's worldwide success, Kojima humbly admits that he doesn't understand the craze:

> Honestly, I don't know why MGS was so successful. However, one of the reasons, I think, is that it's an action game. Action transcends language barriers. The MGS world was very "Hollywood," cinematic, and that made it easier for the game to be accepted in the international market. Japanese traits (virtues) such as excessive service and detailed support mix well with the game medium. This is why Japanese games are well-received internationally—suppressing one's ego and trying to be nice and helpful to others works well with the interactive medium of games.

> [Because I] grew up with international film, music, and culture, the story, characters, and world of MGS that came from [me] probably ended up being somewhat distorted. This turned out to be a fresh experience for all.

For those who are just starting out, what can he share from his experience while working on the *Metal Gear Solid* games?

> Games are entertainment. Only after the player uses it and enjoys it does a game transform from a product to a work of art. It's not a work of art from the very beginning. There's always someone who is going to use (play) it. This is why game development is a service industry for the heart. It's a counselor as well. It involves pleasing people. You need the talent and perseverance to understand people's feelings and lead them. Therefore, you must be able to understand people. You have to read people's thoughts. Developing games is understanding and studying people. Valuing human relations is more important than the technological aspect. Game development is human research.

According to Kojima, the biggest problem with games today is that they don't "go beyond the realm of toys."

> Although games are an interactive medium, games can do their own message delivery. Movies and novels inspire and impress people and also do their own "preaching" that influences people's lives. They make a difference in people's lives. They're not simply a means to kill time; they offer more. Being fun is not enough; [by itself it won't] lead to a higher level. I don't know which comes first—players demanding such games or developers supplying them.

Lorne Lanning, Oddworld Inhabitants

As president and creative director at Oddworld Inhabitants, Lorne Lanning has overseen the development of all the popular Oddworld games, such as *Oddworld: Abe's Oddysee* (PSX, PC), *Oddworld: Abe's Exoddus* (PSX, PC), and most recently, *Oddworld: Munch's Oddysee* (for the Microsoft Xbox). One of his ambitions is to "continually evolve the Oddworld universe into one of the premier entertainment properties for the 21st century."

Lanning offers these important tips for those just starting out in the business:

> ➤ **Play hard.** Most importantly, you must play games—many games. Study them and analyze the technical constraints that the designers have had to deal with. It doesn't matter if you can "beat the end boss" (though it helps to be a good game player); what matters is whether you can understand what's making the games fun and also what's not working. Recognize the patterns of successful gameplay and also the patterns of the unsuccessful. There are lessons to be learned from the good and the bad.

> ➤ **Plan hard.** You need to do a lot of research to fuel your creative ideas, while also finding practical feasibility within the technological limitations of the hardware. Good games are all about limitations and constraints. Great games trick you into thinking that they're much more. Study the issues that the people who build games need to deal with. The artists, the programmers, the designers, the producers, the music and sound people—they all have different problems to solve and real limiting issues to confront. A good game designer must consider the issues of the various disciplines and incorporate this knowledge into the thinking, creative, and communication process to the rest of the team. You must be able to weave creative ideas into practical solutions and nurture the planning process all the way through. Then you must be completely flexible when nothing is working out as you planned!

> ➤ **Work hard.** If you don't believe in working hard, then you don't stand a chance at making it as a game designer. Working 9 to 5 is not an option for the aspiring or even the successful game designer. Building good games takes a lot of long and hard hours. You must love games; you must live, eat, sleep, and dream games if you're going to grow in the industry. If you don't have the discipline and commitment to do whatever it takes to get a good job done, then your career will be very short-lived, or mediocre at best. You also need to be proficient at the tools of the trade (today it's virtually all 3D). No one wants to listen to someone who doesn't understand the tools or the constraints of the systems, regardless of how brilliant or wonderful the ideas are. You must understand and respect the team, with its various disciplines. You must take pride in your work, and you must be passionate in achieving your goals.

Does Lanning heed his own advice when it comes to the Oddworld games? He replies, exhaustively:

> Our games have always been story-driven as well as gameplay-driven. This creates additional consistency challenges that must be foreseen, as aspects of movie sequence production need to be happening at the same time that gameplay production is happening. This means that by the time both are done, they need to fit seamlessly together, and yet they are two completely different disciplines. In order to

achieve this, we must have a final script of the story and gameplay treatments before we begin the production. The story script is based on how many minutes the computer graphics team will be capable of producing within the time allotted. We always want to create more than we actually can, so we need to be careful and make sure that our story can actually be completed with the team that we have. Otherwise, you could wind up with only a percentage of your footage done at the end of the schedule, and then you're in big trouble.

The first stage of the gameplay treatment is a rough 10–15 page document (see Chapters 6 and 7), explaining what we would like to make happen. The second stage identifies, in granular detail, exactly how the tools, game mechanics, characters, etc. will work in the game and how the designers should be able to control them. This is usually over 100 pages. This is heavily supported by feedback from the programming team to keep you in check from being overly ambitious. Just like the movies, you don't want to be only partially done by the time you're supposed to be finished. Be very careful in assessing the abilities of your teams and their feedback. If you miscalculate, the results could be disastrous to your project and the company.

Throughout the production process, you're adjusting gameplay and story based on things you couldn't have predicted earlier. Each time things change, you need to make sure that the consistency of how the game ramps and works itself into the movies…maintains compatibility. The typical course for production usually encounters many unhappy surprises. You need to keep faith in the project, stay focused, and work harder to make sure that in the end you haven't compromised the game to a degree that the audience begins to notice.

Lanning comments on what went right with *Munch's Oddysee* for the Xbox (from a game design standpoint):

> In the big picture, I think that more things went wrong with the design than went right. The original design was greatly hindered and completely compromised by the engine technology that failed to hit the original target. This meant the worst case for game design, which is what I call "reactionary design." It's what happens when the technology that you're planning for, and that you're being told will be delivered, never comes through. You get promising signs along the way, but ultimately it's quite easy to be fooled by supposed progress. By the time you figure out that it's not happening, you're too deep into the project to turn around, yet you must figure out how to still deliver. As the technology fails, you scramble. Much of what you've constructed has been planned for a different application than you now have accessible. Yet, what's left is all you have to work with and you must deliver. In hindsight, I guess what went right was that we were able to "reactionary design" ourselves out of a terrible code mess and still deliver a unique, quality title.

Was this "engine technology" timing failure an error on Microsoft's part? That is, were the Xbox development tools not readily available at that time?

> The engine technology issues had nothing to do with Microsoft. It was entirely an in-house issue on the programming side, compounded by various constraints embedded in the middleware we were using. However, if you run a company (as [my business partner] Sherry McKenna is always quick to point out), then you're ultimately responsible for all of its mistakes. There are always plenty of good excuses, but in the end it's the boss' fault when something goes wrong.

Microsoft helped us bring the project home [by finding] capable talent who could do the job we needed. They supplied us with some of their in-house people who came down to Oddworld and worked as part of our team, helping us to bring it all in on time. Sherry McKenna was honest with Microsoft about all of our issues as soon as we discovered them, which was at a very early stage in the relationship. It kind of surprised Microsoft because developers typically try to hide their problems and rarely, if ever, reveal their issues as quickly and as early in a project as Sherry had done. Microsoft responded as a true partner, and together we were able to bring the project home in time for the release of the Xbox.

Lanning says that Microsoft, despite its enormous size, proved to be an understanding partner throughout these development problems.

In light of these various difficulties, it became clear that Microsoft was the strongest partner we've ever had. Although they're a huge company that has its share of the typical issues that come from being so large, they're still incredibly capable. It was proven to us, especially in a difficult situation, that people like Ed Fries [vice president of Microsoft Game Studios] really care about the games they're funding. He wants great material and he's willing to pay for it and support it if he thinks the team can actually deliver it. He tries to surround himself with other individuals, like Scott Bayless, who also really want to see the genres of video games evolve in more interesting and entertaining ways.

On another note, Lanning says he's most proud of the evolution of Oddworld's beloved characters:

In terms of practical design successes, I think that our characters continued a line of mechanical thinking that makes Oddworld's characters unique. The characters' abilities are directly tied to who the characters are and what their plot is. Their strengths and weaknesses are part of them, their story, and their plight. Abe and Munch's abilities are not just traditional game functionalities that are tacked onto the characters as a need for general play value. The abilities of our heroes are actually highly designed and conceived aspects of the characters in a larger context. They offer new types of play abilities and balancing of powers and play strategy, yet they still function as solid game mechanics.

If he could turn back the hands of time to create this game again, Lanning says he would "make absolutely sure that the team is composed of passionate and capable people—ones who are dedicated to creating great work and willing to do what it takes."

> **NOTE**
>
> In Chapter 6, Lanning discusses how to create a successful lead character, as well as the importance of a concise design document. In Chapter 9, "Puzzle Design," he outlines what makes for a good puzzle in a game and how to create challenging and entertaining puzzles for your games. He talks about creating a good user interface and the importance of control in Chapter 14. And finally, in Chapter 21, he offers his best advice on breaking into "da biz." Whew!

Gabe Newell, Valve Software

Talk about catching a break—*Half-Life* was Valve Software's debut product, and not only has it sold hundreds of thousands of copies worldwide, but it racked up a number of "best of" awards—including winning the #1 spot on *PC Gamer* magazine's "50 Best Games of All Time" in both 1999 and 2001, the only two times this list has been compiled by the editors. (And heck, if you've ever played *Half-Life*, you know why it has received such critical acclaim and commercial success.) *Half-Life 2*, published by Vivendi Universal Games, should be out by the time you read this. Gabe Newell, managing director at Valve, shares some tips on creating successful games:

> ➤ **Be part of a good team.** The auteur approach may work for movies, but it doesn't apply to game design. A successful design is the result of iteration and collaboration, where the people around you are critical.

> ➤ **Keep it simple.** Another way of saying this is "know exactly what you're doing, what you're trying to achieve, and why." Throw everything else away—not because it's guaranteed not to be cool, but because it will make it really hard to make good decisions overall.

> ➤ **Get your hands dirty.** Write code. Build models. Paint textures. The more you understand the details of how your design will be realized, the more you'll be able to connect the abstractions you have in your head with the realities of the player's experience. For example, writing some AI code—even if it never ships—is a great way of formalizing your thinking about creature behavior.

Newell supports these three pieces of advice with examples from his work on *Half-Life*:

> ➤ The primary goal of building Valve was to create a company of highly skilled and experienced developers who had [or could have had] game companies of their own. It makes everything infinitely easier.

> ➤ I can give an example of where I didn't pay attention to [keeping it simple], and it really hurt us. I had a bunch of monster designs for *Half-Life* that involved creature-to-creature interactions (like the tail swipe the bullsquid will use on headcrabs). Even though we had been very careful in thinking about making the world as responsive to the player as possible, I had these ill-formed ideas about a monster ecology and having monsters do interesting things if you could watch them, which interacted with some other really ill-formed ideas about visibility. This ended up being a huge waste of time and a distraction from what really mattered—how the world reacted to the player.

> ➤ This is what actually rescued me from [the mistake mentioned in the preceding bullet item]. Trying to actually implement these goofy ideas made me realize how brain-damaged it was.

What's the best way to break into the industry? Newell recommends being part of one of the MOD teams that have sprung up around the world. "More and more games give players the abilities to extend or modify the content and code of the game. Some of these have been hugely successful, such as *Day of Defeat* and *Counter-Strike* (see the later interview with Minh Le). We absolutely pay attention to the people who are part of those teams and evaluate them as potential hires." 'Nuff said.

Gabe Newell talks about storyboarding and creating characters in Chapter 6.

George Broussard, 3D Realms

George Broussard is the president of 3D Realms and has overseen many successful properties for the PC, including *Rise of the Triad*, *Duke Nukem 3D*, *Shadow Warrior*, and *Max Payne*. (*Duke Nukem Forever* seems to be taking, er, forever to be released. Hopefully, it'll see the light of day by the end of 2003!) Future aspirations? "To continue to push character-driven action games."

Given Broussard's vast experience in this area, what is some of his best advice for those who want to create the next big 3D shooter? He first cautions game designers by reminding them that it's a very crowded market, so you need a better mousetrap or some other way to improve the genre:

> Make sure your gameplay is more interesting and involved than your predecessors'. And this doesn't mean things like blowing off more limbs, higher resolution textures, or other purely visual things. It means solid play mechanics that actually affect gameplay and what you "do" to progress as you play the game. Don't create marketing bullet points. Be innovative here. Be different. Create gameplay. If you do your job correctly, you create bullet points in the process.

Next, Broussard says to try to do at least one key thing that nobody has done before:

> This is important. Everyone will ask why your game is different. If you've done your job, that answer will be obvious. A good example is *Max Payne's Bullet Time* slow-motion gameplay. *Deus Ex* also did a good job by adding RPG elements into an FPS [first-person shooter] game (like *System Shock 2*, before it). In the end, just try to create some new spin on the action FPS genre that will keep it fresh and moving forward.

Finally, his advice is to learn about movie screenplays and story structure:

> Study how movies are designed into three major acts: setup, confrontation, and resolution. This will help you construct a properly developed story that will keep players interested as they play through your game. There are dozens of books on the subject, but I recommend *The Screenwriter's Workbook* by Syd Field [DTP, 1988] as a starting point. "Why do I need story in my FPS action game?" you ask. Because, after nearly 10 years of major FPS games, people have been there and done that. Story and presentation are the difference between *Half-Life* and *Serious Sam*.

What irks George Broussard about the 3D shooters available today?

> Probably lack of gameplay and innovation. Most of them don't do enough to differentiate from games that have come in the past and end up being straight shooters with little to do except shoot guys. They don't try to raise the bar, and in most cases barely meet it. They're like Hollywood formula movies. Pick a random TV/movie/book license (or generic theme), take 15–20 levels, 10 weapons, 15 bad guys, mix

it up, and presto, new game! This is also why we've seen dozens of FPS games in the past few years and yet there are maybe six or seven games that really did something new and different and weren't just more of the same. I realize that people don't always have the freedom they want when creating a game and have time pressure to ship, but sometimes it seems as if people aren't even trying.

George Broussard gives us a sneak peek at the eagerly anticipated *Duke Nukem Forever*. No, this is not pre-rendered—
this is a screenshot from the actual gameplay.
(Used with permission by 3D Realms.)

In Chapter 6, George Broussard teaches how to create a successful lead character (such as the macho Duke Nukem); in Chapter 9, he covers how to write good puzzles in a 3D shooter; and in Chapter 14, he discusses how to create a user-friendly interface.

Scott Miller, 3D Realms

Along with George Broussard, Scott Miller has been involved with all the games at 3D Realms (and at sister company Apogee before that). Managing the company includes setting goals and a company mission, dealing with publishers and other partners, making agreements/deals with these partners, and providing their developers with whatever is needed to help them do their jobs better.

Miller was asked to share his most precious rules of game design and to provide examples of his own games that support his advice. Notice how closely his comments resemble George Broussard's advice. Now that's focus!

➤ All successful games have one thing in common: They all do something unique. They cut a new path. They take a big risk. Always look for ways to differentiate your game in a significantly unique way, and try your best to position it as the first game in a subcategory. By positioning your game as doing something first, you automatically make it the leader and king of a new category, and this makes it newsworthy. One day, some other developer will figure out how 3D Realms' games get all the great (and free) buzz we do—with amazingly little advertising and hype. For example, the following are the "firsts" for some of 3D Realms' games:

   ➤ *Duke Nukem 3D* was the first 3D action game with a real character. [Technically the game isn't in 3D, but is played from a first-person perspective.]

   ➤ *Max Payne* was the first game with slow-motion gameplay.

   ➤ *Prey* was the first game with "portal" technology.

   ➤ *Tomb Raider* was the first 3D action game with a female hero.

   ➤ *Deer Hunter* was the first game in the 3D hunting category.

   ➤ *Unreal Tournament* was the first game in the play-against-lifelike-bots category (and therefore outsold id Software's *Quake III: Arena*, even though id is world-renowned for being the leader in 3D action games).

   ➤ *Half-Life* was the first 3D action game with a solid story.

   ➤ *Total Annihilation* was the first 3D RTS [real-time strategy game].

➤ Only develop games that in some way introduce a new facet to gameplay that's never been done before, or raise the bar significantly on an existing type of gameplay. But don't confuse the word *gameplay* with the word *feature*. Gameplay is the underlying rules that govern how the player interacts with the game. A feature can be a specific rule of gameplay or a feature can have nothing to do with gameplay, such as a technology feature. New gameplay excites players with the possibility of doing something new.

➤ [*Max Payne*] introduced slow-motion gameplay, something we'd never seen before, which adds a lot of newness and excitement to the play experience. In *Duke Nukem 3D*, we significantly raised the bar on level interactivity. In fact, few if any 3D action games have matched this game in this department, years after its release.

➤ The title of your game is one of the most important marketing decisions you can make. A bad name can incorrectly position a game, hurting its sales potential badly, and a good name is worth a million dollars of free advertising. Try to pick a name that has franchise value and doesn't pigeonhole your game. For example, bad names include *Descent*, which forces every sequel to take place in mines or tunnels (otherwise, the name doesn't make sense); and *Unreal*, a name with an entirely vague meaning that fails to say anything of value about the game itself—in fact, *Unreal* has come to mean "game engine" more than it means "fun game."

As another bad example, Miller cites *Tomb Raider*:

> Will all sequels be forced to include tombs to raid? Had Eidos understood proper positioning principles, they'd have named the game Lara Croft, which would have given all sequels the freedom to explore any location without making the name seem out of place. Also, by naming the game *Tomb Raider*, Eidos effectively created two brands they had to promote and spend marketing dollars on, when they should have just focused all their efforts on the one name that really matters: Lara Croft. The *Tomb Raider* name is costly dead weight to that franchise.

Bottom line with game names: Think long-term, think big, and think about your game's positioning and branding value. Character-based games, quite simply, should always be named the character's name. Otherwise, naming failure has been achieved.

> **NOTE**
>
> Eidos is calling the new series *Lara Croft Tomb Raider*, so apparently they're keeping the older *Tomb Raider* as part of the title, too—even though Croft is finished with raiding tombs! Good or bad idea? Tell 'em what you think at www.eidos.com.

After you have that first big hit, what are the do's and don'ts for building on that franchise?

> The best way to create a franchise is proper positioning and proper differentiation. A game needs to be the first and best game in its particular category, so it needs to be positioned in this way. This positioning starts with the game's title and with its original concept—it really needs to be one of the foremost thoughts for the designers, and this is where I think most game designs fail—because they don't take into account the ideas of positioning and being unique in one or more pivotal ways.

Miller advises seeking inspiration from the bestsellers that took a chance, such as *Black & White*, *RollerCoaster Tycoon*, and *The Sims*: "It's really true that you have to take a big risk to go for the big reward. Playing it safe is what everyone else is already doing, and you're not going to get far following in their footsteps. Cut a new path."

For any developer or publisher, he suggests reading these books:

➤ *Positioning: The Battle for Your Mind* (20th Anniversary Edition), by Al Ries and Jack Trout (McGraw-Hill, 2000)

➤ *Differentiate or Die: Survival in Our Era of Killer Competition*, by Jack Trout and Steve Rivkin (Wiley, 2000)

➤ *Focus: The Future of Your Company Depends on It*, by Al Ries (Harperbusiness, 1997)

In Chapter 6, along with his 3D Realms colleague George Broussard, Scott Miller discusses how to create a hit character in a computer game.

Pierre Rivest, Ubi Soft Entertainment, and Reid Schneider, BAM! Entertainment

For this segment, lead designer Pierre Rivest and producer Reid Schneider discuss working on action games. Their last project together was the gorgeous *Batman: Vengeance*, which was created in Montreal, Canada, and based on the dark animated series. Schneider left Ubi Soft in 2002 to work for BAM! Entertainment in the U.S.

From a production standpoint, Schneider says the most important things for him to keep in mind while working on *Batman: Vengeance* were to overcome the bad rap that previous Batman games had, to be true to the license, and to prove that a licensed game could be done right:

> First, we had a lot to overcome when we began to develop *Batman: Vengeance*—the previous games had not done justice to the license and the public had its doubts that the Batman license could yield a fun game. Next, we had to be true to the license from a visual style. We also had to adapt the 2D world of the series to 3D, yet retain the look and feel that made the show so popular. Our artists did an incredible job of capturing that stylized look while creating their own version of that world in 3D. Finally, we had to create a game that would appeal to gamers, since this was the primary demographic of the PS2/Xbox. When hearing about licensed products, gamers tend to be skeptical of these games. It was our job to convince them otherwise.

Rivest agrees with Schneider:

> The most important consideration was to remain true to the license—the need for actions, opponents, and environments of the game to reflect the feel of the Batman animated series. Also, to provide Batman with interesting actions and gadgets that will have to be mastered by the player to succeed in completing the game. Working hand-in-hand with this is intensive level design and situations derived from the story that will push the Batman actions to the limit.

Despite the pressure to handle the license with kid gloves, are there advantages to working with a name like *Batman*?

> As a positive, Batman is one of the world's best-known characters. We also had the benefit that almost everyone knew his past, and we didn't have to create it for him. Another positive was that the villains in the series had already been strongly developed, so we didn't have to create those from scratch either. As anyone in the industry will tell you, developing a character from scratch can be an extremely risky and costly venture, and there is always a chance that your character will not grab people's attention or be adopted by gamers. We had a character that was a staple of U.S. pop culture.

From a game design standpoint, Rivest admits it was pretty easy to work with the Batman license: "There are so many resources available about the Batman universe—during the conception phase of the game, we used comic books, novels, videos, and more to help us create the game."

Rivest discusses an obstacle he and his team faced when designing *Batman: Vengeance* and how it was overcome:

Batman is equipped with a grappling hook. This created some problems. Most of the levels where the grapple is used are outdoors. At first, we wanted to allow grappling on any surface and location. The outdoor locations more often than not are composed of a multitude of typical Gotham City skyscrapers. If we would have allowed the player to grapple anywhere, the player would have fallen to his death one too many times, which would have proven to be quite frustrating. This was our main problem with the grapple.

We decided to place grappling points throughout the levels and help the player find them by creating a unique aiming system. All grappling is done using the Bat-grapple in a first-person view mode. When the player navigates the maps in standard third-person perspective and a grapple is nearby, a small grappling icon appears onscreen, informing the player of nearby grappling points. To help the player find the grappling point, we added a small arrow around the crosshair. The arrow moves around the Bat-grapple crosshair and always points toward the closest grappling point. The crosshair itself changes color when the player has successfully targeted a grappling point. The player can then proceed to use the grapple and venture forward.

In Chapter 13, "Game Art and Animation," Schneider and Rivest talk about the animation used in *Batman: Vengeance*; in Chapter 14, Rivest talks about the importance of control and a smooth user interface. And for more on *Batman: Vengeance*, visit the official web site at www.ubisoft.com/batmanvengeance.

David Perry, Shiny Entertainment

David Perry is one of the most widely known and respected game designers of our time. He is president of Shiny Entertainment and has been in the business for more than 20 years, creating such memorable console games as the *Earthworm Jim* series, *MDK*, *Messiah*, *Sacrifice*, and the first game based on the movie *The Matrix*. In Perry's opinion, these are the most important pieces of advice to offer someone just starting out in the business:

> ➤ Play games, and not just for fun. Have a notepad handy and write down what they did right in that game and what they did wrong. This list will grow quickly; then it will slowly seem to start repeating itself. You'll be amazed how few components make up just about all the games out there. This list will then be a source of reference for you, and also a source of "Let's see if I can find a fresh new way to accomplish this" in the future.

> ➤ When you come up with a cool idea, write it down. Even if you have to get out of bed and go and find a pen.

> ➤ You need a hook to grab people's interest in your designs. That hook can be many different things, but without one, it's gonna be tough to sell. Good hooks are things like a.) a great license from a hit movie or a previous hit game; b.) a new amazing graphics technology that drops jaws; c.) better still, a new amazing graphics technology that actually improves gameplay, like being able to have an army of 1,000 characters instead of the usual four; d.) a new play mechanic, like when sniper mode first came along; e.) a great character that's really fun to play.

Can Perry support his advice with examples from his own past?

> ➤ I'm a "list-a-holic," but I do it for movies and video games.

> ➤ I keep thinking that I'll remember the idea, and when I wake up the next day, it's gone. I used to argue that if you forget an idea, it was probably not worth remembering in the first place. I changed my mind on that and now have pieces of paper on my bedside table with lots of crazy ideas jotted down. This way, you always have more ideas than you can even work on.

> ➤ The hook is crucial. A good hook means that you can describe your game in one sentence. For *MDK*: "He has a weapon so accurate, you can shoot your enemy in the eye from a mile away"—sniper mode was born. For our *Matrix* video game that we're making now, we should have plenty of hooks (if I get my way).

Also, there's good ambiance. Take the gamer off into a world that he can explore and have fun in. It can be the real world, but if so, he must be able to do things that he doesn't personally have the skill to perform. If it's a fantasy world, make sure that everything makes sense and has consistency. And keep the gameplay challenging, but don't let players get lost or blame the game for their problems. A good game designer always knows what players are thinking and is looking over their shoulders every step of the way.

I think design is all about vision—seeing the game in your mind—being able to see when something is wrong at a glance. When someone asks you what would happen in a complex situation, you have the answer. When you play other games, you question why things are done the way they are. And the most important thing—you have solutions! Many "designers" complain and moan, but rarely have a solution. I have met gamers who are true visionaries and they don't even know it. Just listen to their comments as they play; you slap yourself on the head and think, "Damn, why didn't I think of that? It's obvious!"

Having created games for both PC and console platforms, what are the primary differences from a game design point of view? What are the challenges for each, and how do they differ?

Designing games for the PC is fantastic because you have lots more RAM. So you have lots more storage space for graphics, sound effects, speech, world topography, etc. These are all really good things to have in a designer's toolbox, if they can provide freedom. The dark side of the PC world is the fact that there's such a spread of hardware prowess around the world. We have to design our game for some guy in Greece playing on a Pentium 166 so that his old machine gives him a great experience, yet the latest Intel 2GHz machine also needs to get a great experience.

How do you design a game for both? The answer is scalable engines. That means that the game internally says to itself, "This machine kinda sucks; let's just have 50 particles in the explosions instead of 500." Or "Instead of 8,000 polygons on this character, let's just use 1,000." The latest engines do this in real time. Another great benefit is that now you can add lots of characters onscreen. As the machine begins to choke, it just removes polygons to keep the game speed constant. It's a fantastic tool for a designer's toolbox because it means you don't have to always design for situations with a maximum of just five or six guys. If you want 75 guys to get in a giant fight, that's just fine. You can also use this technology on console. It doesn't help you with the different processor speeds because, for example, the Sony PlayStation 2s all share the same heart. But it will give you the ability to have maybe 100 characters with you at one time—great for Braveheart scenes!

Another great benefit of PCs is the hard disk. Xbox brings that to the console world. This gives you the ability to load quickly, stream movies/audio/textures into the game world, and modify the game permanently. So if you dig a hole, it's there forever.

Are any recent technological advancements making the gaming experience richer?

Storage space has greatly increased with CD, then DVD, and now hard drive space—we really cannot complain any more. Processors are insane also. The excuses are over. 3D hardware is jaw-dropping. I think every part has moved forward so much that it's up to us to take the leaps forward in pushing ourselves. To stop accepting things because "that's the way it's always been done." The two things that still need attention are control devices and voice recognition.

If Perry could change something with today's computer or console games, what would it be? That is, what's wrong with many of today's games?

I wish that stores would focus gamers on the good games in the store instead of just letting them walk out with terrible titles. I want gamers to buy games, have great experiences, then buy more games. Not buy games, think they suck, buy more, think they suck also, then start renting or take up some other hobby. There are many great games on the shelves; I just wish the big chain stores (that sell most of the games) would help gamers out. There is a great web site that I love, www.gamerankings.com. It's bullsh*t-proof. It averages all the reviews that each game gets, so it's not biased. It's just the information you need to buy only great games. Try it out and see if you disagree with the highest-ranked games in each genre.

How do you create a game that stands out from the crowd but isn't too "out there?" In other words, how do you straddle ingenuity with familiarity?

Generally, this is difficult. The more "out there" you get, the more the general public becomes concerned about risking hard-earned money. Imagine you're hungry. In front of you are McDonald's, Burger King, and Flambé Eel Burger Company. Which do you risk your money on? The general public plays it safe—they go with what they know. So I think the trick is to give them what they know, but add some secret sauce!

Perry's *Sacrifice* (2000) still sets the bar for one of the most graphically intensive PC strategy games to date.
(Used with permission by Sacrifice © Shiny Entertainment, Inc.)

Development cycles seem to be getting longer and longer. What's a "reasonable" development cycle for a console game?

> Today, it's about 18–24 months. The problem we run into is that we keep starting from scratch with a new engine and all-new technology. If you need to cut back development time, go with what you know and what you already have that works well. Westwood has done this really well with its *Command & Conquer* franchise. It's a smart way to run a business.

Be sure to read Perry's advice on creating a hit character in Chapter 6 and comments on breaking into the video games industry in Chapter 21.

Minh Le, Valve Software

Minh Le was hired by Valve after he created one of the most notorious *Half-Life (HL)* mods (modifications), dubbed *Counter-Strike* (www.counter-strike.net), and before that, *Navy SEALs* for *Quake* and *Action* for *Quake II*. His duties at Valve include coding, modeling, animating, and texturing.

To start, Le explains how he came up with the concept and carried through with the execution of *Counter-Strike (CS)*.

> I basically started working on CS by myself as soon as *Half-Life* was released (actually a little earlier). When the HL SDK [software development kit] was released (about 4–5 months after HL was released in stores), I was then able to code the initial version of CS. From then on, I kept releasing version after

version every couple of months. Initially we just mass-emailed every web site out there to get some word-of-mouth going for BETA1. We did the same thing as the versions progressed, and eventually more and more people came on.

But why *Counter-Strike*? What was your inspiration?

Well, I find terrorism intriguing, and I just wanted to do a game based on it. The whole teamplay aspect was just a logical extension to the theme, because you never see deathmatch terrorism in real life. My decision to not allow re-spawning was influenced by my work with a previous game. I felt it added a whole new level of tension to the experience. The key is to not make dying too tedious, so I decided to put a time limit on the rounds and offer up a snazzy spectator cam when you're dead.

Le says that thanks to the tools offered today with many PC games, creating your own title shouldn't be too expensive a proposition:

I was able to produce CS on a shoestring budget, but I had to sacrifice a lot of time. I believe I spent about 30 hours a week on the initial versions of CS. The maps were not produced by me, as I was able to "persuade" the public to do them for me—that really offset a lot of work for me. If you plan on making a game and don't really have a strict deadline to adhere to, you can do it as long as you're motivated and have a fair amount of time on your hands. It's also a lot easier to make a multiplayer game than to make a single-player game.

Le shares some advice on action game design:

➤ Have a clearly defined idea for what your game will be, and try not to incorporate too many unproven features.

➤ Always play test your game as early as you can and often as you can, as this helps give you an idea of how much fun your game is.

➤ When producing artwork for your game, it's a good idea to produce at the highest quality you can and down-sample (if necessary) to the minimum specs your game engine will allow. For example, when making a texture map for a model, make it in very high resolution and then down-sample so it doesn't eat up as much memory. What this allows you to do is to reuse your old artwork as your game engine becomes more efficient.

Mathieu Ferland, Ubi Soft

As senior producer at Ubi Soft's Montreal studios, Mathieu Ferland has worked on many console and PC games, including *Monaco Grand Prix Racing Championship* (1998), *F1 Racing Championship* (1999), *Donald Duck Goin' Quackers* (2000), *Tom Clancy's Rainbow Six: Rogue Spear—Black Thorn* (2001), *Tom Clancy's Rainbow Six: Raven Shield* (2002) and *Tom Clancy's Splinter Cell* (2002). Ferland offers his top pointers first, and then explains them in great detail:

➤ Create specific first; then think global. If you don't, you may leave behind very interesting concepts.

➤ Consider and integrate technical and graphical features in the game design.

➤ You're not the one who will play the game after release. Don't create it for you.

Ferland elaborates on the first point:

Before you define the rules or the general mechanisms of the game, make sure that these will end up with interesting specific gameplay elements that will serve each level of the game. The best way of doing it is to do the contrary; that is, create all specific gameplay elements to end up with the general rules and mechanisms.

In the very beginning of the conception phase, brainstorm on what specific gameplay elements it would be cool to have in the game. What do you want the players to see? What do you want them to feel? Many ideas will come out of this exercise. Try to follow the basic guidelines of the game concept, but also experiment so you don't kill a good idea much too soon in the process.

After a few sessions, you should have a huge bank of specific game design or level design ideas [that you could use to] build three or four games! You should have tons of possible (or impossible) movement and controls for the characters, many ideas of super powers or gadget uses, ideas of cool sections of your levels, surprises in the story, etc.

Starting from all these specific and archaic concepts, you should then "think global" and create rules that will fit with the best ideas proposed. In other words, you must begin to design the game having these ideas in your mind. Global mechanics will cover character movement and controls, special power use or gadget use, environment interaction system, inventory system, rewards, and so forth. Of course, you'll have to discard many ideas during the process.

After a few days or months, once you believe that the global system serves the best specific ideas, you must brainstorm again, considering these game design restrictions and finding more interesting specific gameplay ideas to serve the game even better.

Many game designers are focusing on the global systems first and then on specific actions, which I think is a mistake because it limits the creativity and the diversity of what you want the players to feel when playing the game.

Ferland goes into even more depth with his second piece of advice:

All development teams have strengths and weaknesses. During pre-production and development, it will turn out that some features (technical, graphic, or others) of the game will be more impressive than others. A good game designer should consider this aspect and adapt its design in order to promote and use the best features developed. This aspect is often very hard to deal with because changes in game design usually affect schedule, budget, and motivation of the team(s). However, if this is properly done and communicated, the added value of the game may be quite surprising. Exploit the team's strengths and avoid its weaknesses.

Ferland discusses why the game should not only appeal to you:

> After months or years of time and effort spent on a single game, it becomes quite natural to take criticisms personally. But a game is not a piece of art for you to use as a means of expressing your personal artistic skills. We're in the entertainment industry, and the first goal is to make people enjoy the time they'll spend on your game, and make their $50 a good investment.
>
> Is it hard to find this balance? Not really. Trust your thoughts and communicate to the team the reasons why you think the game you're building will be awesome. But remember that an idea isn't final until it's validated by play testing. Never underestimate the necessity of play tests; they're a window to the future, a good way to tell whether the game will be successful.
>
> Try to conduct play tests as soon as possible during the development cycle. Focus on one feature at a time and slowly validate or refuse each element of the game. Start these tests with general mechanics observations, then level design consistencies, and finish with the game calibration.

The award-winning *Tom Clancy's Splinter Cell* is the first of this popular series to appear on the Xbox platform. The game was developed by Ubi Soft's Montreal, Canada, studios under the direction of Mathieu Ferland.
(© 2002 Ubi Soft Entertainment Inc. Ubi Soft Entertainment is a registered trademark of Ubi Soft Entertainment and Splinter Cell is a trademark of Ubi Soft Entertainment Inc. All rights reserved.)

For *Splinter Cell*, Ubi Soft did a lot of research about the NSA, U.S. military weapons, and SWAT gadgets:

> We also got a lot of inspirations [from films] for the character's movements. With these inspirations, we established what would be interesting to do, to see, and to communicate in the game. We had a brainstorming session following this basic game concept guideline: "Create a third-person action/adventure game using Tom Clancy's highly realistic environment, geopolitical context, and high-tech military material." We started to talk about these concepts and to gather all the specific ideas, such as escaping from a building that was on fire, using enemies as a body shield, surprising the player while the roof is falling apart, using a sticky camera to provide critical information, etc. When we had more gameplay ideas than

needed, we started to think about how to make it work. This is where game designers need to perform; the challenge is to provide unlimited possibilities of gameplay ideas/elements with a highly limited general system. With *Splinter Cell*, the system works quite well considering all the stuff that Sam Fisher [the main character] can do and use. I believe that we've reached the objectives.

On the integration of graphical and technical elements of the game, Ferland recalls:

During *Splinter Cell* development, if we would have "fixed" the game design too soon, we would have missed many opportunities. For example, when we developed our dynamic lighting system, we had clear objectives and gameplay ideas. When we've developed the physics on soft bodies, we also had clear expectations. However, when we mixed the soft bodies and the dynamic lighting, we discovered that we could see an enemy through the soft bodies. This was a new feature for the game that could have stayed at a research stage if the game design would not have been flexible enough to consider it. It turned out that it became one of the most impressive features of the game.

Unfortunately, Ferland says they learned that their game was too difficult to play:

Splinter Cell was much too hard a game to play before it was play tested. We discovered that the mapping of the controller wasn't intuitive enough. Many elements of the game, including the inventory system, have been reviewed. The game was submitted to play testers for a two-month period, providing a new build every two days, starting with the alpha build. Without play tests, the general level of quality for *Splinter Cell* would have been much lower.

How does *Splinter Cell* differ from other stealth-based tactical action games?

When you're creating a game, it's very hard to not be inspired by existing or previous games. Most developers reuse what worked before, improving and adapting it to their own unique games. With *Splinter Cell*, we spent a lot of effort on providing a strong variety of actions for the main character. He can do different basic moves (walk, run, jump, crouch, etc.), but he can also do athletic action moves like wall jump, split jump, zip line, climb on pipes, etc. So, the amount of movements that Sam Fisher can do is quite innovative. Moreover, the gadgets Sam can use—optic cable camera, shocker, night and thermal goggles, etc.—create many possibilities for the player and a great freedom of action. Players must think and pick one of the best combinations to succeed. The story, and the way it's communicated to the player, is quite original.

Is it easier or more difficult to work with an existing franchise? Ferland says it's a bit of both:

Tom Clancy knows what he wants. The world he has defined through the years is quite impressive and is a great source of inspiration. The main strength of Tom Clancy's stories is that they feel realistic, and details are justified to make it even more realistic. People are interested in Clancy stories because they occur in a very close future and the politics are close to the existing geopolitical situations in the world. For a team to create a game, it's so nice to get inspired from the actual world and to slightly modify it to make it just a bit ahead. For example, night vision and thermal visions are gadgets that exist, but not on the same goggle set. We've been inspired by an existing prototype and have projected what it could become in the near future, in a realistic and credible way.

The cons of working on this franchise are to justify every detail. This means that we needed to spend a lot of effort in researching and sticking to the franchise. The approval process is also quite complex. This is not the case with other sci-fi environments, where any creation has a better chance to fit with the original concept.

Any beefs when playing console games? "I think that games are generally too long," begins Ferland. "Even if a game is interesting, I personally have completed only very few games."

We must keep in mind that this is entertainment and only entertainment. People like diversity. They enjoy trying different kinds of games, and they'll switch to another game if it's too long. It's important to enjoy the time you're playing a game, but if you're ready to pay $10 to see a two-hour movie, why would you be upset after playing a 15-hour game for $50? It's not worth it to develop games that may never be finished.

Ferland offers some final advice on successful game design:

➤ Try to work on the kind of game you like to play and know a lot about. This is the only way to progress quickly.

➤ Don't underestimate the importance of research of any kind. Playing games or watching movies is a good start, but research that will allow you to get into even greater detail will provide you innovative concepts, and is even more important.

➤ Do more than your best, and communicate your knowledge and tricks to your teammates so they can also improve their skills. You'll also gain respect and credibility.

Mike McCoy, Ubi Soft

Continuing our discussion of the Tom Clancy computer/console game phenomenon, we're joined by Mike McCoy, lead designer on *Rainbow Six III: Raven Shield*. McCoy is also based out of Montreal's Ubi Soft offices. Interestingly, McCoy's advice varies somewhat from that of his colleague, Mathieu Ferland:

Always make time to listen to your team and anyone else who has an idea. If the idea is good, use it. If it's bad, explain why and ask them to continue to bring their ideas in the future. As a game designer, you're not the only person who has great ideas. Lots of times I get incredible ideas from the least likely of places. Consider your job to be that of collecting all the good ideas and rejecting all the bad ideas.

When possible, use implied complexity instead of explicit complexity. What I mean by this is use as many complex ideas and rules as you need to create a fun and realistic game, but always present them to players in easy-to-understand terms. People play games to escape reality and to do things they could never do in real life. If you're making a modern flight simulator and use advanced equations to simulate flight, don't throw them at the player. Don't force players to go to the Air Force Academy in order to play your game. What they need to understand is how to fly their aircraft in the simplest of terms.

Finally, your design document [see Chapter 6] represents the ideas, feelings, and images you want players to experience in your game. Let's say you write an incredibly detailed document describing how terrorist artificial intelligence works. When programmers get their hands on it, expect a lot of questions. What is clear and concise to you is not necessarily that way to others. After the programmers gain an understanding of your document, don't be surprised if they come up with other ways to get the same thing done. If it has the same or better final effect and is easier to implement for them, great! Your job is to create a great game, not to micromanage how the programmers implement one of the features of the game. Also, expect the team to come up with lots of questions for which you don't have answers. There's no way you can anticipate all the implementation problems, but you can fix them as they arise.

McCoy uses *Raven Shield* to support these three pieces of advice. For "always listen," McCoy says throughout the development of *Raven Shield*, level designers and AI programmers have come to the design team with suggestions on how to make the terrorist AI better. "Just because I designed it, that didn't mean that I made it perfectly," admits McCoy. He continues:

They were laying out and using terrorist AI every day and came up with quite a few improvements. The level designers were especially good at finding ways to have the terrorists know about their surroundings and use them appropriately, such as using a car for cover while firing.

For "implied complexity over explicit complexity," McCoy offers the following:

To create all the variables that we use for weapons in *Raven Shield*, we use real data and complex equations. This data includes muzzle energy, bullet diameter, barrel length, weapon weight, weapon length, and fire rate, along with many other items. Most players aren't really interested in this stuff, and if we forced it on them they might even shy away from the game. So when we present weapons to players, we give them five bar graphs to explain a weapon: Range, Damage, Accuracy, Recoil/Jump, and Recovery. These bars allow them to compare weapons in simple terms and decide which one they want to use. If you know about guns and understand how they work, you can pick your weapons based on your knowledge, and because we used realistic physical data, weapons work as you expect. If you don't [have any experience], you simply use the bars and make your choice. The complexity is in the weapon mechanics, but we present it to players in simpler terms. Everyone enjoys the results, both expert and novice alike.

And on design documents:

When I originally wrote the Rainbow AI document for *Raven Shield*, I tried to think of every possible situation a Rainbow could get into. However, a programmer quickly analyzed it and found many missing pieces. We sat down and began to talk through all the problems. After about an hour, she said that my method didn't work in every situation. Then she proposed a different method that worked much better than mine.

"What makes *Rainbow Six* such a unique and successful franchise is its uncompromising realism," says McCoy.

When Red Storm first developed the idea of "one shot, one kill" lethality, everyone said it wouldn't work. Until then, the reigning hypothesis on games was that players wanted them to be forgiving and allow them to make mistakes. Since *Rainbow Six* hit the shelves, almost every successful first-person shooter has had a "one shot, one kill" mod [user-made modification].

The real fun in *Rainbow Six* is the suspense before combat, expecting to see a tango behind every corner and door. After you start shooting, it's an emotional release as either you or the tango get taken out. I can't tell you how many times I've peeked around a corner, taken a bullet in the forehead, and jumped out of my seat! "Where the hell was that guy? Next time, I'll find him first."

The main thing I think a new game designer can get from this franchise is "Don't always conform to what everyone else is doing." Try unconventional things and see if they're fun. Be willing to take risks with your ideas in order to innovate and stay ahead of the crowd.

On the pros and cons of working on a Tom Clancy game, McCoy breaks it down into the following:

Pros:

➤ **Incredible Clancy universe.** The Tom Clancy universe is a rich and seemingly endless realm based on our reality. Nothing in it seems farfetched or futuristic, but everything is cutting-edge.

➤ **Constrained reality.** Because the Tom Clancy universe is based on our reality, it's really easy to shoot down fantastic (fantasy-based) and futuristic ideas that don't fit. It really helped us stay focused and heading in the right direction. If we couldn't confirm its existence or the possibility of its existence with our technical advisor, it wasn't considered for the game.

➤ **Established gameplay, look, and feel.** Because the *Rainbow Six* franchise is so well-established, people know when something feels like *Rainbow* and when it doesn't. Therefore, our first goal with *Raven Shield* was to make it look, smell, sound, and taste like *Rainbow*. After that, we went about enhancing and improving on the previous *Rainbow* titles.

➤ **Huge existing customer base.** When developing *Raven Shield*, we always had in the back of our minds how successful the previous two titles were. This puts a lot of pressure on you and the team, but I believe this was a positive thing that helped us to excel and make an even better game.

Cons:

➤ **Constrained reality.** Having a reality based on the real world limits your imagination and creativity. Not that we wanted to, but we couldn't add laser rifles to the game.

➤ **Huge existing customer base.** Having an existing customer base limits the number and size of the gameplay changes that you can implement at one time. If you implement too many too fast, people don't feel that your game belongs to the franchise. Also, if you innovate or change features that are near and dear to fans, you run the risk of alienating them and losing them as customers. And after all, what's a franchise without its fans?

Finally, McCoy chats about what he dislikes when playing computer games. "I can't stand to play games that are inconsistent and/or too hard."

> If in the user interface you teach the player that to go to the next screen you press a button on the lower right, never move the next screen button. I've played a game where loading my last saved game required me to click in the lower-right corner twice, but then in the lower-left corner the last time:
>
> 1. Game—lower right
>
> 2. Select Campaign—lower right
>
> 3. Load Level—lower left
>
> Guess what button was in the lower right on the third screen, exactly where the Load Level button should have been: Delete Saved Level! Can you believe it?

McCoy says his second gripe is about games that are too hard to play:

> Inexperienced designers increase the difficulty of all the difficulty levels instead of just adding a fourth or fifth even-harder level. They believe what challenges them, challenges all. In reality, they've been playing the game so long that they're experts, and what's easy to them is moderate to hard for others. When I worked on *Shadow Company*, we added a "Sinister" difficulty level that was nearly impossible to beat. But we didn't change the difficulty of the first three levels.
>
> The first time I play a game I usually play on easy mode, to experience the game. If I like it, then I play through on a harder mode, to challenge myself. If the game forces me to struggle to experience it, I usually put it away.

Mike McCoy also offers some inspiration on breaking into the industry; see Chapter 21.

David Dienstbier

David Dienstbier began working at Acclaim as a game designer who worked on such projects as the *Turok: Dinosaur Hunter* series for the Nintendo 64, the *All-Star Baseball* series, the *NFL Quarterback Club* football series, and many others.

In 2002, David Dienstbier left his post as creative director at Acclaim Studios Austin to pursue other interests.

When asked for the most important things for a new game designer to keep in mind when creating his/her first "masterpiece," Dienstbier first cautions by saying that any truly creative person probably never creates their masterpiece:

> It's a term that's frequently used by consumers and the press when expressing their appreciation for a game, but one that seldom has the same meaning to a creative individual. The very nature of our business means that we can always improve, always innovate, and always create better product. We can't afford to rely on past successes if we are to continue moving forward.

Dienstbier says it's also key to remember that we're in the business of making games:

> While there's certainly an art to making any game, we're part of the entertainment industry. The realities that we face every day have to do with deadlines, scheduling, marketing, funding, practicality, and recognizing the fact that while there's no limit to what we can accomplish [artistically], there are definite limits to what can be accomplished by a set number of people within a set amount of time. It's often difficult for people to accept the fact that every endeavor, every creative urge, and every risk we choose to take are dependent on the success of a product. If our games make money, we earn money to fund our next project. [Otherwise,] where will that money come from? It's naïve to think that merely throwing more time or money at any project will ensure its success. Becoming comfortable with the business of making games creates a more functional relationship with everyone involved and creates a unified understanding of not only how the business works, but why certain decisions are made by developers and publishers.

Not to deter an inexperienced game designer/developer, but Dienstbier says that certain aspects of the business are often very frustrating and run counter to the designer's creative impulses: "And I'll be the first to admit that I'm often at odds with these exact problems. I've found that the more I learn about the business of games, the better I'm able to cope with my own frustrations."

The third bit of advice Dienstbier gives is that the success of any game cannot be attributed to a single person, or a single discipline:

> It's common to hear people debating or even arguing about the significance or insignificance of technology, design, or art in the development process. Such arguments, in my opinion, serve no purpose but to create division and resentment. They're a trap. As members of a team, every single person should value and respect the challenges and effort that are necessary for anyone to excel in their field and appreciate the dedication that's required by all of them to help deliver a great game.

Dienstbier says that inspiration can come from multiple places:

> When I was studying art in college, I often found myself looking to nature for inspiration, and I still do today. I have a fascination with bones, fossils, animals, and evolution, and it influenced a lot of my art. In looking for inspiration for a game concept, I draw from a diverse pool of creative sources—books, comics, film, photography, poetry, music, and history are all invaluable to me as I set out to take on a new challenge. Other games are always a source for inspiration, of course.

Where did the concept for *Turok* originate?

> The game came about as a result of a number of things that were going on with Acclaim when I was hired. The company had acquired a comic book company called Valiant Comics, with the intention of developing some of its key properties into game franchises. The decision to base the first game on the Turok comic was made at the corporate level. At the time, Acclaim wanted its first effort to be based on

one of the stronger properties they owned. Turok was not its best-selling comic, but it was a solid performer and a property that many people thought was strong. It was my job to try to decide how to translate the comic property into a video game. At the time, the first-person shooter was the hottest "new" genre in gaming. The problem was that it was pretty much confined to the PC in terms of really pushing the technology. This was all taking place while the wave of powerful new game consoles were preparing to launch, and machines like the Sega Saturn, PSX, and N64 were all designed to take console games from two dimensions to three. The decision to make Turok a first-person shooter was what I felt was natural. We had the opportunity to bring a world to life on a console, and do it in a way that not only took advantage of the huge popularity of FPS games, but that also created a world that was very different visually. While most FPS games took place in corridors, we built jungles. While most games were devoid of life except for the enemies, our world was full of birds and deer and fish and monkeys. It was a desire to do something that stood out, more than anything.

With today's crop of video games, Dienstbier admits to one main pet peeve: an over-reliance on sequels:

Sequels are an important part of our business. They give fans of hugely popular games more of what they want, and one cannot really argue the numbers. My problem has nothing to do with the fact that the industry produces sequels; it has to do with the fact that often companies become so sequel-centric that they're less willing to approve new properties or take risks with new ideas. Publishers often would rather invest in a sequel to a modest seller than take the chance to invest in new properties. The same patterns exist in all aspects of the entertainment industry, from film to television to books and music. From a business standpoint, it's totally logical. However, it's frustrating when these patterns actually work against the creation of exciting new experiences.

What are the fundamental differences between developing a game for a PC versus a console? Dienstbier's first answer looks at the technical challenges for both:

Hardware specifications for PC games are in a constant state of flux. New standards in processing speed, graphics cards, controllers, etc. create a constantly changing series of variables to consider. The fact that developers must support devices made by any number of different companies is also an issue. The majority of these are not issues with console development because the hardware tends to stay fixed. There are still some exceptions, of course. For *Turok 2*, we added a high-resolution mode that could be activated only if the player purchased a RAM expansion pack for their machine. The PS2 will soon have a hard drive, and developers will have to decide whether they're going to support these devices and how they'll make use of them. So the problem does exist, but it's quite insignificant when compared to the PC. They don't change what the hardware is capable of, but they do provide developers with options for new features and present new possibilities.

Dienstbier discusses some differences in the audiences for PC games and console games:

A hit RPG for the PC doesn't ensure a hit if the game is ported to a console, and vice versa. There are different types of games and different experiences that have historically had homes on either the PC or consoles. Some of that is changing as new consoles become more powerful, but at the same time, players often crave different experiences when buying a game for a console versus a PC. There is a huge rift in the core age group between the average PC gamer and the average console gamer, but this too has been changing. Being aware of these differences is crucial because the potential audience for a console game can be very different from [the audience for] a PC title.

We revisit Acclaim's Dienstbier in Chapters 17 and 21, in which he offers up some advice on proper game testing and how to break into the industry, respectively.

Randy Smith, Ion Storm Austin

Before joining Ion Storm, Randy Smith, project director and lead designer of *Thief 3*, worked at Looking Glass Studios as a designer on the groundbreaking *Thief* and *Thief 2*. In fact, it may not be fair to place *Thief* under the category of action because it's considered a "3D sneaker" rather than a "3D shooter." For the uninitiated, the *Thief* series places a much stronger emphasis on silent and cunning maneuverability.

What does Randy Smith think are the three most important things for game designers to keep in mind when working on their first "masterpiece"?

Game designers need to be in a learning frame of mind, open to new ideas, and ready to assimilate information about what the game design process is all about. Don't work on your "masterpiece" first. You probably aren't ready to design any game by yourself, much less the one game you really hope comes out brilliantly. Start by working on someone else's project, and do your best to contribute effectively.

Also, learn from the people around you! Work closely with designers and other developers whose work you admire. Ask them what goes into their decision-making process, how they evaluate design ideas, and what general principles they use when designing. Collaborate with everybody on your team and be open-minded to any input you get. Learning by making mistakes is very effective, as long as you're able to recognize and fix them before the game ships. To do so, you first need to admit to yourself that you sometimes make mistakes, so get ready for it.

Finally, a common misconception is that game design is all about thinking up creative new ideas. That's part of it, certainly, but not nearly as much as you might think. Most teams are creative enough to provide far more cool ideas than you could (or should) implement in your game. Being a good designer is as much about picking and choosing intelligently between the possibilities as it is about thinking up the ideas in the first place. To evaluate ideas effectively, you need foresight to predict potential problems and [you need] abstract design tools and thought models to iron out those issues. Then you need to assess how much effort will go into implementing the idea and make a budgeting decision about which ideas you should pursue given your finite project resources (such as time). A lot of this stuff takes time and experience to get good at, so that's why you should start your career ready to learn.

Thief had a distinctive look and style. Where should a game designer look for inspiration? And how can inspiration be successfully and uniquely implemented into a game? Smith says inspiration for game fiction can come from many sources. In the next few segments, he discusses how this can affect a game as it relates to mission design (be sure to read his excellent advice in Chapter 10, "Mission Design") and general gameplay mechanics:

Media such as books, movies, and games are obviously useful, but real-world references such as history, science, and architecture have always proved invaluable to me. I do a ton of research before I begin planning a mission, and I believe that having a thorough mental image of the space, the characters, and the history of both helps to keep the mission consistent and believable and helps to flesh out important details. Personal experience in the real world is not to be overlooked. If you want to build a cathedral, go visit a cathedral. Use your imagination as you observe the space, and think of fun things you could do if you were the character in your game.

It's even more important to have inspiration for gameplay design. You need to know how to construct fun experiences and evaluate and tune your designs when they're implemented. To do so, collect a library of abstract design tools, principles, and mental models that you can apply to any design problem. Treat game design like a formal science, not like an inexplicable art form. Inspiration can come from existing video games and your fellow developers. Working with a group of designers, identify game mechanics and game experiences—in your game or other games—that you think work really well, and reverse-engineer them. Deconstruct them to figure out which design principles motivate them and make them work. Then attempt to use those same design tools and principles to achieve results in your game. Evaluate your attempts for success and modify your mental models based on the evaluation. This is a hard process, but getting good at it will help you become a rigorous and effective designer.

Randy Smith explains how he and his team properly test games such as the *Thief* series, and how you can do the same to ensure proper balancing and bug fixing. Turn to Chapter 17 for this advice on testing during the game's development.

Erin Roberts, Digital Anvil

Erin Roberts serves as a producer at Digital Anvil's studios in Austin, Texas, part of the Microsoft Game Group. His credits include designer on the classic *Wing Commander* game (alongside brother Chris Roberts); associate producer on *Strike Commander*, *Privateer*, and *Shadowcaster*; and producer on *Privateer 2*, *Starlancer*, and most recently *Brute Force* for the Xbox platform. Pooled from his more than a decade of experience, Roberts offers some helpful advice on game design.

1. **Understand your design.** And realize you're part of a team! This, for me, is one of the most important areas that designers often overlook, and will always come back to bite you in the ass. To be able to design a mission or a level in a game, every member of the design team must really understand the whole design of the game, from story to characters to the gameplay mechanic. If you don't understand your game, you're not going to be able to make your part merge seamlessly into the rest of the design. So before you do anything or run off in a random direction, make sure you know what your cog in the machine is meant to do. This may sound pretty obvious, but I see this happen all the time.

2. **Does it make sense?** When designing anything, from the original concept down to the level of separate missions, pull yourself back from the design and ask yourself if it makes sense. The most important part of this is your overall plot and story. You can get very involved in wanting

something to happen because it would make a really cool mission rather than that it works in the story. Adversely, you can have something in your story that you feel is really cool, but will never work in a mission. Ask these questions first, and it will save you a lot of pain later. Are you contradicting your story? Does each area of the game/mission support the overall plot and storyline? In actual missions, are you doing stuff that really make sense? Would the enemy be surprised if you land in a drop ship 100 meters from them? My guess is that they would be well-prepared by the time you step off your ship.

3. **Understand your limitations.** But don't be afraid to push the boundaries! This is really key to making and completing a game in a reasonable amount of time. It's pointless creating an all-encompassing game design if the best programming team in the world either says it's impossible or needs to spend two to three years creating technology and tools to support your needs. When creating your design, include the rest of the team who will make it happen. Get feedback from both your technology and art counterparts. Understand what the limitation of your platform of choice is now, or what it will be when you plan to ship your game. Having said that, once you know what you can get away with, push as hard as possible to make sure you use every ounce of what you have.

Using his latest project, *Brute Force*, as an example, Roberts supports his advice. "I've seen every mistake I talked about above happen in *Brute Force* to some degree, which is why I feel very strongly about exposing these issues."

There have been circumstances in Brute Force where missions have been created that don't work inside the storyline of the game. Sometimes that was because the original design was asking for [something that was] too difficult to implement, or in some cases because the designer didn't really understand the importance of making sure that his work meshed with the rest of the design. Other issues include making sure you understand the gameplay mechanic before creating a level/mission. In *Brute Force*, we have four very different squad members who have their own very different strengths and weaknesses. To support these characters and make missions interesting, maps have to be created that take into account each of their abilities. For example, it's pointless having a sniper in the group if you don't create a number of high areas that the player can snipe from. You'd be surprised at how often a map is created by a designer who has an idea of what he wants to see, without taking into account how it will be used by the characters.

Roberts thinks everyone finds inspiration in many different places:

You can play games and work out what you like and don't like. You can read a great novel or you can come up with something completely new inspired by something else. I always find that actually coming up with a concept is never the hardest thing; taking that concept, building a real design, and making it become reality is where the real work is involved. As for *Brute Force*, I had always wanted to work on a ground-based combat game—all my other projects had been (space) flight action adventure games— and I wanted to work on something new. Having a squad of kickass commandos to control and getting to beat up on lots of bad guys was where I wanted to go.

Any complaints about today's action games?

> My biggest problem is that we seem to be stuck in a rut of getting more of the same. When one game type is successful, it seems that a whole bunch of people go out and make a similar game, hoping to grab the coattails of the original game's success. One of the main pressures for this comes from the publishers, who see the amount of money the first game made and, hoping they'll see that type of cash, they greenlight only those types of projects. It's very hard to get the money to do something original unless you have a proven track record and someone is prepared to take a risk on you. I think you have to be brave enough to offer something new and be prepared to get knocked back a lot. Also it's important to remember that as a game designer, it's not just about having a concept or design for a game; you also have to have the means to get the game done. A concept without a team rarely goes anywhere.

In Chapter 21, Roberts offers some tidbits on breaking into the biz.

Denny Thorley, Day 1 Studios

Denny Thorley is an executive producer at Day 1 Studios, the developer responsible for the popular *MechAssault* game for Microsoft's Xbox platform. Prior to that, Thorley had a hand in previous FASA Mech games: *MechCommander* (for PC) and *BattleTech* (for Sega Genesis). Future aspirations? "Revolutionary multiplayer products on console platforms."

Creating action games isn't as easy as it may seem, says Thorley:

> ➤ **Focus!** Decide what's going to be fun about your game and concentrate your design on reinforcing that "fun." Don't give in to the temptation of adding features because they might be cool. Every feature in your game must be scrutinized to make sure it contributes to the core gameplay experience. Every game has budget and timeframe constraints, and a tightly focused design will allow you more time to tune and polish your game.

> ➤ **Research.** There's so much to learn from existing products. Designers can benefit from studying competitive products to evaluate the game mechanics that are effective and those that fail—without spending expensive programming time. There's something to learn from even the worst games. Scrutinizing existing games can't necessarily tell you what to do, but this process can bring to light potential problems with your design.

> ➤ **Clear, concise communication.** Many inexperienced designers end up writing like a frustrated novelist: so wordy they lose their audience. This is not the most effective communication for the programming team charged with the task of implementing the design. The design document must clearly lay out the details of the game and how all the components will harmonize to make a compelling product. It doesn't need to sell the programmers on how wonderful the game is going to be.

With *MechAssault* as an example, how does Thorley take to his own advice?

> *MechAssault* design is focused on huge, devastatingly powerful 'Mechs that stomp around the battlefield wreaking havoc wherever they choose. It was designed as a faster-paced game than traditional

'Mech simulations, giving the player more action and less 'Mech systems management. We also created robust destruction sequences for the buildings and environmental objects to reinforce the intoxicating power of the 'Mechs. The design's last major focus was ensuring that the *MechAssault* experience could be shared cooperatively and competitively around the world in an online format. Many features were considered, and if they didn't directly contribute to reinforcing the player being this "Tactical Godzilla" in a destructive and immersive world, then those features were dismissed.

Research played a large role in determining what design direction to pursue with *MechAssault*. Games in the 'Mech genre are plentiful, but few have enjoyed the commercial success we were striving for. With in-depth play evaluation, it was apparent that these games were difficult to just pick up and play. They also contained layers of complexity that hurt the "fun" factor and prevented the player from accessing the "fun" quickly. Our research helped to convince us to pursue an action-oriented *MechAssault* and persuaded us to abandon several control schemes we were considering prior to the competitive evaluation.

Unfortunately, we didn't achieve clear and concise communication with *MechAssault* for the entire project. We started strong and were lauded for our documentation process, but as deadlines approached, the importance of these documents staying current diminished. I think this shifting of priorities is typical in the industry, but negatively impacts the development process. In the future, we'll make our designs even less wordy and rely more heavily on visualization and prototyping.

What does Thorley consider to be the biggest problem with most console games today? "The biggest problem with console games, in my opinion, is the similarity between many of the titles."

Many developers are being directed by their publishers to skate to where the puck is now (to use a hockey term)—not to where it's going. The hits of this year will spawn a bunch of "me, too" products two years from now. Few of them will be successful. Designers can avoid this by not falling in love with their own product and finding inspiration outside of interactive games. To keep a realistic perspective, the designer should evaluate, on a periodic basis, how his or her product is going to fit into the marketplace, and how the game will differentiate itself in the market. Is the design and execution still unique enough to get above the noise at retail?

Speaking of "design and execution," what are the key differences in working on a console game versus a PC game?

The play experience on the PC is typically one player viewing the screen from two feet away. The screen resolution allows for more complex information to be presented to the player. Input devices on the PC also allow the handling of more complex tasks easily and efficiently. Evaluating successful games on the PC leads us to believe that PC players are more willing to read manuals and enjoy in-depth, more cerebral game designs.

We're starting to see the convergence of PC game design and console game design as the first-person shooters are gaining popularity on the console platforms. This design convergence is largely due to the impressive graphics and sophisticated controllers shipping with the new consoles.

Consoles, on the other hand, are often placed in more "social" rooms in the house, says Thorley:

> And they're generally located near the family's primary television. The location lends itself to more people participating simultaneously on console games. Additionally, console games are played from four to six feet away from the TV, further enhancing the multiplayer/single system experience. Game designs that maximize cooperative play and/or competitive play on the consoles have been rewarded with strong sales. Designers should consider this unique social aspect of the console experience when designing for these platforms.

For more information and media on *MechAssault*, visit www.xbox.com/mechassault. For job postings at Day 1 Studios, visit www.day1studios.com/jobs.htm.

In Chapter 21, Thorley offers some advice on breaking into the industry.

MechAssault is a sci-fi action/shooter game based on the highly successful *BattleTech* franchise. Players must battle foes and take out enemy structures while maneuvering the huge BattleMech, or "Mech," through a variety of environments.
(Used with permission by Microsoft Corp.)

Chapter 3

General Game Design: Strategy Games

THE EXPERTS

- Sid Meier, Firaxis
- Bill Roper, Blizzard North
- Brian Reynolds, Big Huge Games
- Bruce C. Shelley, Ensemble Studios
- Peter Molyneux, Lionhead Studios
- Alex Garden, Relic Entertainment
- Louis Castle, Electronic Arts/ Westwood Studios
- Chris Sawyer, Freelance
- Rick Goodman, Stainless Steel Studios
- Phil Steinmeyer, PopTop Software
- Ed Del Castillo, Liquid Entertainment

Do you like to use some brains along with (or instead of) brawn when gaming? This chapter is for you—how to create breathtaking strategy games. And do we have a roundtable of celebrities for you!

Sid Meier, Firaxis

There's a very good reason why Sid Meier is one of the most accomplished and respected game designers in the business. He pioneered the industry with a number of unprecedented instant classics, such as the very first combat flight simulator, *F-15 Strike Eagle*; then *Pirates*, *Railroad Tycoon*, and of course, a game often voted the number one game of all time, *Civilization*. Meier has contributed to a number of chapters in this book, but here he offers a few words on game inspiration.

"Find something you as a designer are excited about," begins Meier. "If not, it will likely show through your work." Meier also reminds designers that this is a project that they'll be working on for about two years, and designers have to ask themselves whether this is something they want to work on every day for that length of time. From a practical point of view, Meier says, "You probably don't want to get into a genre that's overly exhausted."

> For me, working on *SimGolf* is a fine example, and *Gettysburg* is another—something I've been fascinated with all my life, and it wasn't mainstream, but was a lot of fun to write—a fun game to put together.

To Meier, it all boils back down to passion:

> What do you get excited about, and what are you good at? Do an RPG, not an action shooter just because it's in style. Find something new and fresh—publishers want to be leading-edge, too, so they're usually receptive to new ideas. But remember, for every 20 guys who walk into the door, maybe two ideas are worth considering.

There's a temptation to create "the ultimate game of all time," so keep your focus on a couple of cool features, make sure those are great, and leave some room for a second game.

Be sure to read Meier's advice on programming, artificial intelligence, proper game testing, breaking into the industry, and more in later chapters.

Bill Roper, Blizzard North

Blizzard North VP Bill Roper is an industry veteran with countless triple-A titles under his belt, including *WarCraft II: Tides of Darkness* (producer), *Diablo* (producer), *StarCraft* (producer), *Diablo II* (senior producer), and *StarCraft: Brood War* (executive producer). Most recently, he has participated on the oversight team for *WarCraft III: Reign of Chaos*, in which he was instrumental in shaping the direction of the game.

We chat in depth with Roper in Chapter 5, "General Game Design: Role-Playing Games (RPGs) and Persistent Online Worlds," on role-playing game development, but here we have his inspiring and enlightening words on strategy game design, and how *WarCraft III: Reign of Chaos* could serve as a benchmark to others. Roper was first asked to discuss what he personally learned from working on such epic projects as *WarCraft III*. Following is his thorough response.

Persistence of Vision

The main goal of *WarCraft III* was to create a real-time strategy game that was heavily influenced by role-playing sensibilities. Although we went through innumerable changes, both grand and minute, we strove to keep the concept of the game in the forefront of discussions. This often proved challenging when we would have to try to balance the needs of a strategy game with the mechanics of a role-playing game. One of the key features of the game is the "Legendary Hero" units, and to emphasize their importance, we originally used an over-the-shoulder camera angle and required that regular units be "attached" to the Hero. This gave the game a very distinct look and feel while immediately driving home the point that role-playing elements were going to play a big part in the experience. Unfortunately, we discovered that this design prevented us from doing many things that we felt were necessary to create a strategy game. While the camera angle needed to be changed, we also didn't want to lose the immersion we had attained, so we also made sure that the environment had a much more organic feel as we pulled back the camera, making it easier to strategically control multiple units while at the same time eliminating the "game board" feel from which many strategy games suffer. Keeping our eye on the overall vision for the project allowed us to make major changes to even key elements of the game, with the knowledge that we would end up with a cohesive and fun game design.

Letting Go

During the creative process of designing a game, you come up with thousands of great ideas and not-so-great ideas. Sometimes you come up with ideas that seem like amazing groundbreaking concepts. Occasionally, these ideas just don't work. Whether for technical reasons, world continuity and design considerations, or simply because they're just not fun to play, these ideas need to be changed—or set aside. Sometimes, this can be a simple matter when you try something out and realize that it isn't fun or simply doesn't look right. Other times, this can be an extremely difficult decision because you can see how it might work and are willing to try and find ways to keep the idea alive. For example, we had a major shift in the look and the associated design elements of *WarCraft III* after a year or so of development, when we moved away from the over-the-shoulder angle associated with Hero units. The interesting aspect of this decision was that although it probably caused some concern and confusion to our players, the development team actually found that they could now make the game they envisioned; the rest of our design concepts related to melding role-playing elements into a strategy game were basically unaffected.

Dumping an idea that you have conceived, fostered, and perhaps even implemented is a painful but necessary process. Not everything works out as planned, and it's difficult to admit when that gameplay mechanic you thought would revolutionize the industry turns out to be an adventure into tedium. When you're faced with the need to pull the plug on something in the game—no matter what the cause—you have to do so as quickly and painlessly as possible. Don't be afraid to scrap ideas because many times you'll replace them with something far better or simply find that [you don't need] anything there at all.

Bill Roper says that *WarCraft III* is "one of our greatest accomplishments to date. We started out hoping to create a fitting sequel to *WarCraft II*, and we ended up crafting a world of epic proportions. *WarCraft III* offers players an incredibly fun and dynamic experience."

(Used with permission by Blizzard Entertainment, Inc.)

Taking Time for Tools

The design and implementation of the "World Editor" for *WarCraft III* was key to the successful realization of the role-playing game aspects found in the single-player campaign. The level designers worked hand-in-hand with the editor programmer to create a tool that was not only powerful but also easy enough for them to use day in and day out. While it's not uncommon to see tools created without much thought given to the end user, the growth of the World Editor was a cooperative venture between the people making it and the people using it. This was essential, not just because we intended to ship it as a part of the game, but also because we knew that we wanted to free up our game programmers as much as possible from having to do special-case programming for the campaign. By putting a heavy focus on designing a robust tool that the level designers could use to modify their work and then immediately review it in the game, we streamlined our development process [and gained] many more chances to iterate on those designs while reducing our required quality assurance testing time [see Chapter 17, "Proper Game Testing"]. It's said that a craftsman is only as good as his tools, so giving your craftsmen the best possible tools will help them create the best product they can.

Is there anything that Roper would've done differently? "We should have spent more time in designing the game before we put as many programmers and artists on the project as we did," he admits. Roper explains:

By nature, game design is a very organic and iterative process, but in our excitement to start making the game, we honestly put too many people on the project at too early a stage. It's difficult to gauge the proper numbers to assign to a project in the first weeks and months, but the biggest lesson we learned was to put as many designers into the mix as possible. Also, keeping multiple high-end designers in addition to the level designers on the project until the end was something we didn't address until later in the development process. Fortunately, we caught this issue before it was critical, but it certainly set back our balance and campaign designs to some extent.

In addition to the *Legendary Heroes* and the role-playing game flavor, what else makes *WarCraft III* stand out from other real-time strategy games? "While there are many elements that go into any successful game, I honestly feel the character and emotional bond gamers get while playing *WarCraft III* makes it far different from any strategy game we have ever created."

Movies have come a long way in the past 20 to 30 years in terms of what can be technologically created and brought to life onscreen. Games have leaped forward in the past 5 to 10 years in terms of what can be accomplished and represented with much of that same type of technology. Games provide potential immersion mainly because they're interactive, placing the player in control of the situation—something that movies simply can't do. But movies have traditionally provided something that games don't—an emotional connection between the entertained and the entertainment. This is an area where we as game developers can grow, and it was a major focus of the unit and level designers as well as the writers, cinematic artists, sound designers, and musicians on *WarCraft III*.

In terms of gameplay, the units in *WarCraft III* play an even more important and unique role within the composition of an army than in any of our previous games. Even the most basic unit has some special twist that makes him different and a viable choice throughout the course of a game. The top-end units—

the Legendary Heroes—are the epic leaders of those armies and can greatly influence the outcome of any battle in which they're employed. These special units really show how we used the sensibilities of role-playing games within a real-time strategy game as the units grow in experience, gain levels, and find and purchase items that they carry in an inventory. They even have their own names, making them a very personal element in the scope of any game. When one of these Heroes dies in battle, a message is sent throughout the game announcing his or her defeat, and the death animation is far more grand and dramatic than those of his less-epic compatriots. Although *WarCraft III* is first and foremost a real-time strategy game, these elements provide an interesting and unique gaming experience.

Roper says that in terms of making an emotional connection with the player, they spent a huge amount of time crafting a rich storyline that's expressed through the single-player campaign:

The use of pre-rendered and in-game cinematic sequences, professional voice acting, and missions that are centered around a story (and not the other way around) create a compelling game that involves not only the skills of the players, but also their feelings. As the story unfolds, both the world and the characters within undergo changes. Reaching someone on a deeper level only makes for a more satisfying experience, and this is something that other forms of entertainment do extremely well. With *WarCraft III*, we wanted to involve the player on many levels while still tapping into the adrenal responses that have served games so well for so many years. If we can succeed in this endeavor, we can reach a wider variety of people than just the traditional core gamer.

Anything and everything that touches your life is potential fodder for the creation of a game. Did you ever get stuck on the expressway and wish you could just jump the center divider, blast through oncoming traffic, and cinematically sail into the local 7-Eleven parking lot so you could grab a Slurpee while waiting for traffic to break? *Grand Theft Auto 3*. Have you ever sat through a long boring dinner, lazily arranging and rearranging the vegetables on your plate into new and interesting patterns—eating only the ones that line up three-in-a-row? *Bejeweled*. Have you ever listened to "Ride of the Valkyries" by Wagner while staring into a clear blue summer sky? The Wyvern Riders in *WarCraft III*.

What about the origins of *WarCraft III*?

WarCraft III came from (a) wanting to expand the world we had already created and grown; and (b) not wanting to waste an exceptionally strong storyline that had been created for a canceled game. When we looked at where to go with the WarCraft universe after destroying the Dark Portal in the expansion set to *WarCraft II*, our creative director, Chris Metzen, set to crafting a story that would focus on what happened to the orcs who were trapped in Azeroth. Elements of the story and the background of where the orcs came from as a people were inspired by the culture and plight of the American Indians. The internment camps of World War II also played a part in shaping the background of how the orcs were marshaled and corralled after the war in Azeroth. The gladiatorial rings of ancient Rome and the way their combatants were both revered and feared as they lived out violent lives as valuable property also played a major part in shaping the character of Thrall, the main character of the orc campaign.

Music, literature, television, animation, art, sports, music, food, love of debate, social interaction—these are all things that can spark ideas for a game designer. Also, playing other games is key—especially with other people on your team. The best solos in jazz are a fusion of the mind and skill of the soloist with a responsive and iterative rhythm section. They listen to what the soloist is doing and then play with it and off of it. In turn, the soloist responds with his own intuitive iterations or departures. When a second soloist joins the fray, his performance is augmented by what he has just heard only if he can build on and learn from that experience. As game developers, we shouldn't be afraid to play other companies' games and learn from what they did. We also need to play our games and learn from our own mistakes and failures. The rest of the equation is to listen to the people who buy our games and see what they want out of a play experience. All these things can inspire new chains of thought and can lead to new ideas in the design of game mechanics, world concept, and story.

In Chapter 21, "Breaking into the Industry," Bill Roper offers some advice on breaking into the industry.

Brian Reynolds, Big Huge Games

Throughout his illustrious career as a programmer and game designer, Brian Reynolds, now president of Big Huge Games, worked alongside Sid Meier at Microprose and Firaxis on such remarkable strategy games as *Colonization*, *Civilization II*, and *Alpha Centauri*. His latest project is *Rise of Nations*. Read more about this game, published by Microsoft Game Studios, at www.bighugegames.com. It seemed a simple task for Reynolds to list his best advice for strategy game designers and support these words with an example from past or current projects:

1. Get something running in the first month that you can actually play. (It doesn't matter if graphics aren't so great.) With Civilization II, we had the game to where you could play it all the way through over a year before it shipped (even though it was all-new code from the original Civilization). We knew that we needed to play and try out all the new things we wanted to add and that we'd need that much time to get the balance and AI tuned. For our current game at Big Huge, we had something playable by our first milestone, even though all we were actually required to "deliver" was a design document.

    Strategy games are extremely complex to design—although the individual components look deceptively simple, having a lot of "simple" moving parts makes for a very complex overall balancing task. It's easy to look at a strategy game and say, "I could make this better; I'd add this and this and this," but very hard to actually integrate lots of new parts into a game system without breaking the things that were already fun. To balance all the moving parts correctly, there's no substitute for actually playing your own game—the combinatorial explosion from all the moving parts makes it impossible to truly anticipate or tune results "on paper" in a design document. The sooner you get your game running, the sooner you can actually get to work on making the game fun and making it balanced. Both fun and balance tend to be taken for granted by novice designers. They think, "If I make a game about topic X and it has features A, B, and C and technology J, then it will be fun," but as it turns out, fun and balance both take a lot of hard work.

2. Each strategy should have both a unique strength to make it cool and a unique weakness to keep it from being too powerful. "Rock, paper, scissors" is the best model for game balance. Our current real-time game is based around a "rock, paper, scissors" model for game balance. That is, unit A is really strong against unit B, but weak against unit C; whereas B is weak against A and strong against C, etc. That way, no unit is so powerful that it's "unbalanced." Also, all units are strong against something, so they're cool to build in the correct context.

3. Play your game regularly. If you have multiplayer [capability], get that running early so that you can balance it. By the time our new game ships, we'll have had our multiplayer running for at least 18 months. We've built a special "multiplayer lab" with eight workstations side by side (it's modeled on the lab we saw at Ensemble Studios), and we run at least one multiplayer game a day there—often several. We have "novice days," "pro days," "intermediate days," "free-for-all days," and so forth—everyone in the company signs up and plays. Everybody in the company gets to see their own work interacting with the rest of the game, gets to see the "big picture," and has a chance to contribute to the design and balance. The progress on design and game balance was dramatic once we got the lab in, and we have plenty of time left.

Most of Brian Reynold's advice in this book is found in the chapters on programming (see Chapter 11, "Programming Theory") and artificial intelligence (Chapter 12, "Artificial Intelligence [AI]"), as well as on how best to break into the industry (Chapter 21).

Bruce C. Shelley, Ensemble Studios

Bruce Shelley is a lead game designer and spokesman for Ensemble Studios, the development studio that has created award-winning and critically acclaimed real-time strategy games for Microsoft. In the past, Shelley has worked on computer games such as *Civilization* (Microprose), *Railroad Tycoon* (Microprose), and others. His latest project was the million-unit-seller, *Age of Mythology*. Shelley offers some key tips for those starting out in the industry:

Be familiar with lots of games, but especially those most like the game you most want to design. Consider which parts of a game are working and which are not.

Providing a player with interesting decisions is the rocket science of game design. If you agree, then consider whether a game you're playing or designing is providing interesting decisions. When you attempt to add a new piece to a game, ask yourself whether it will add interesting decisions for the player to deal with.

When considering a new game, look at the competition first and make lists of features they do well, poorly, or not at all. The features they do well are the minimum requirements for your game. The features they do poorly or not at all are a list of opportunities where you can differentiate your game and offer innovation. Always seek to differentiate and innovate—don't clone around.

On providing direct examples, Shelley says this:

> When we set out to make the original *Age of Empires (AOE)*, we made our lists of features that were done well, poorly, or not at all in games like *Civilization*, *WarCraft*, and *Command & Conquer*. From these, we built our list of must-have features for *AOE*, such as hidden maps, economic buildup phase, empire building, town conquest, great multiplayer, scenario editor, and differentiated civilizations. Then we built the list of features that would differentiate *Age of Empires* because other games were not doing them well, such as historical theme, random maps, non-cheating AI, levels of difficulty, realistic graphics (not cartoonish), and multiple victory conditions. By meeting the competition where they were strong and providing clear differentiation and innovation in *AOE*, we created a game that was able to be quite successful in a very competitive genre (50+ RTS games in development in 1997). Competing games that fell by the side came up short mainly because they didn't sufficiently differentiate and innovate from the best games in the genre already available.

Check out this screen grab from Shelley's latest, *Age of Mythology*, published by Microsoft Game Studios in 2002.
Talk about gorgeous graphics!
(Used with permission by Microsoft Corp. and Ensemble Studios, Inc.)

Shelley says it's critical for a game designer to keep these three pointers in mind when starting out:

1. Design for a broad global audience, not a narrowly focused, especially hardcore audience. The majority of game buyers are casual gamers, and too many games are beyond their skill or tastes.

2. Within a specific genre, make your game different in terms of topic, look, and feel. At the gameplay level, innovate new features and gameplay. Don't imitate successful games only to the point of being at least as good as they are on their strong points. Create a new experience with your game. Nobody buys imitations.

3. After you have a basic design document, prototype the game quickly and thereafter design by playing. Play every day, make adjustments, get opinions, recode for tomorrow, and play again. If you have enough good gamers giving comments and your instincts as a designer are good, you'll design a fun game.

Shelley supports this advice in light of his latest project, *Age of Mythology*:

1. Included within *Age of Mythology* are multiplayer games, a single-player campaign, random map Solitaire games, and a variety of game types such as death match. We believe that gamers of all skill levels and from all global PC markets will find a satisfying way to enjoy our game. We think this is reaching out to a broad global market, as all of our past games have done.

2. Adding the mythological elements and moving to 3D technology will make our game different from other RTS games, including the *Age of Empires* games. At the gameplay level, we think we've innovated with myth creatures, god powers, and more subtle changes. Overall, we've made *Age of Mythology* both different and innovative to provide a new experience. No one will consider it a clone of something else.

3. *Age of Mythology* has been playable since early 2001. Since then, we continued to design the game by playing every day, making changes, and recoding through thousands of iterations.

Shelley is also known for this piece of advice: "A game has to have a great first 15 minutes!"

The concept of a great first 15 minutes was Sid Meier's. He mentioned to me that one of the reasons he thought *AOE* did well was because it had a great first 15 minutes. The point is that a game has to engage a new player within 15 minutes of that person sitting down to play. If not, the player is likely to give up and never try the game again. So the start of the game has to be engaging—get the player absorbed by presenting a lot of interesting decisions that pile on top of one another. Another one of Sid's phrases was the "inverted pyramid of decision-making." You want the player to deal with only a few decisions at first, which multiply quickly, fully absorbing the player. Games that do this pull the new player in.

In the original *AOE* game, for example, the map is almost entirely hidden at the start. The new player has a few villagers to put to work and use to explore. Once he or she has built more villagers and begun exploring, there are more decisions to be made: what tasks to assign to newcomers, where to place gathering buildings, which new directions to explore, what strategic choke points to watch, etc.

It's been said that a game designer need not reinvent the wheel—that it's perfectly acceptable to improve on an existing formula. Does Shelley agree or disagree?

The most valuable resource any game designer has is all the games that already exist from which we can get ideas. The risk is that we may do too much copying and not enough creating. Gamers want a new experience. It can be familiar or similar to other games they've played, but it must also be different and innovative to be successful. *Age of Mythology* is a big RTS similar to many others, including our own *Age of Empires* games. We've played and considered everything in the games that have been published. But we've also tried to create something that's different and innovative.

On creating an innovative yet accessible game, Shelley adds the following:

Basically, cloning a successful game is a recipe for disaster. We believe a new game must be clearly different from existing products or people will ignore it. For the *Age of Empires* games, the big differentiation was choosing historic themes when the competition was doing mostly sci-fi and fantasy. As a bonus, it turned out that there was a huge interest in the casual market for a historical RTS, which no one else was trying to fill. Innovation is important also, perhaps mainly with the hardcore gamers. They want a new experience. If a new game doesn't add much that's new and fun, they won't bother to put in the time to learn it. Graphic look and feel can be an important differentiation. Tony Goodman, our CEO and early art director, championed a fairly realistic graphic look and bright colors. The competition at the time was going with a more cartoonish look and often very dark and gloomy colors. We think now that our look was an important differentiator and another important key to attracting casual gamers. We think too many developers largely ignore the casual market, to their loss. Most game sales reside in the casual market, yet developers often try to outdo themselves focusing on what only the hardcores seem to want. Make commercial art, not fine art. When someone says they're making the game they've always wanted to make, the question is, how many of them does that person intend to buy? It makes much more business sense to say that you're going to make the game that you think millions of average casual gamers are going to want to own. That's the kind of thinking that publishers want to hear.

Finally, Shelley was asked to be frank about what it's like working with a powerful publisher such as Microsoft—something many game designers are likely curious about! Shelley says the pros are that "big publishers get shelf space; have marketing muscle; have PR departments; and are usually well organized for testing, localization, and manual creation. They do virtually everything better than the alternatives (small publisher, self-publishing)." But he discusses some of the cons as well: "They usually control the purse strings and can dictate schedule dates and budgets. Your game is just one in their portfolio. They may use it for strategic purposes good for their company, but not necessarily for yours (loss leader, bundling deals)."

Bruce Shelley offers advice on many other topics in this book, including writing design documents (Chapter 6, "Creating Characters, Storyboarding, and Design Documents), coding realistic AI (Chapter 12), creating a good user interface (Chapter 14, "The All-Important User Interface [UI] and Game Control), and breaking into the industry (Chapter 21).

Peter Molyneux, Lionhead Studios

One of the computer game industry's most revered game designers is Peter Molyneux, the brilliant (and soft-spoken) managing director at Lionhead Studios. And talk about a track record! Molyneux is responsible for some of the most beloved PC games, including *Populous*, *Magic Carpet*, *Theme Park*, *Dungeon Keeper*, and the *Black & White* series. Molyneux is currently overseeing a number of new projects, including *Project Ego*, *Black & White 2*, *Black and White: Next Generation*, and *The Movies*.

Molyneux shares some advice he wishes he was told before he got involved in this industry:

1. Come up with a concept that's easy to explain in a sentence or so. This was highlighted to me by Bing Gordon at Electronic Arts back in 1993. I was heading up to a meeting to try to sell the concept of *Magic Carpet*. [As we rode up together in the elevator] I said that I was looking forward to making the presentation, and Bing replied that if I couldn't explain the concept on the way up then it probably wasn't a good concept. We were on the first floor, and the meeting was on the second floor.

   Games that are easy to explain and that deal with subjects people can easily understand are always going to be more successful than more abstract ideas.

2. The most brilliant concept is useless unless you can think of the way that people will play the game. In the end, game design comes down to interface design—the key to making games playable is how you'll get people to interact with your concept and how simple the interface is.

3. Don't be frightened to be original and innovative. Remember that the greatest game concepts and interfaces are yet to be designed; just because everyone else has done things a certain way previously doesn't necessarily make it the right and only way to do something.

Put to the test—to support his advice with real-world examples—Molyneux passes brilliantly:

The idea of "designing and building your own theme park" was very accessible and clear—in one sentence, you know all about the game and what you need to do to play it. Although this is the most perfect example, I can think of others. You "play God" in *Populous*, you play the bad guy in *Dungeon Keeper*, and you find out who you are in *Black & White*—all are examples of games that explain themselves.

In *Black & White*, we wanted people to be able to do anything they wanted in the game world, so using the hand meant we didn't have to use a lot of explanations in the interface (although for this reason I think the tutorial should have been longer).

Molyneux once said in an interview that he would prefer to make games with a shorter development period. He clarifies this point:

The length of time a project takes is becoming a real issue. More power means bigger teams, having to take care of more than just graphics and programming—AI, physics, interfaces, gameplay—and all of these elements need coding to be built from scratch. It makes the task of developing a game quite overwhelming. For a game to have the best graphics, sounds, and animation means that developing a game is becoming a Herculean effort. I hope that with better internal organization of our team, it will be possible to compress 3–4 years into 2–3 years.

Molyneux talks briefly about programming in Chapter 11 and breaking into the industry in Chapter 21.

Peter Molyneux says, "The greatest game concepts and interfaces are yet to be designed." Pictured here are a couple of sneak peeks at the upcoming *Black & White 2*.
(Used with permission by Lionhead Studios.)

Alex Garden, Relic Entertainment

Alex Garden's most recent venture, Relic Entertainment, is one of North America's premiere game-development studios. Relic's first title, *Homeworld*, has won more than 50 awards, including the prestigious "Game of the Year" award from CNN.com, MSNBC, and the world's largest computer game magazine, *PC Gamer*. Garden's latest game is *Impossible Creatures*, released in early 2003. This game allows players to make war-hungry creatures by combining animal traits.

Garden was cornered to surrender some of his best-kept game design theories. Interestingly, his answers are similar to Sid Meier's advice:

1. Design around themes that you're passionate about. Life is short, and making games is supposed to be fun. Make sure you're having fun making games, and chances are that people will have fun playing them.

2. When you're coming up with concepts, focus more on what makes your game fundamentally fun to play, not what the story is. Understand that as a game player you rarely consider the underlying mechanics of the experience you're having. More often, you focus on the story that you're playing through. When you read a book, you rarely think about the fundamental appeal of the book; you think about the setting, characters, etc. As a game designer, the paramount rule you must obey is to make sure that the core experience is appealing before you worry about the story. If story is your only concern, write a book.

3. When making decisions about your game, ask yourself two questions: "What do I think is the right thing to do?" and "What does the paying public think is the right thing to do?" A totally uncompromising commitment to your own personal vision creates art. But art alone doesn't sell. You must make fun art.

As examples, Garden provides the following:

Homeworld had a totally freeform 3D camera. Some people loved it, but most people found it too hard to use. With *Impossible Creatures*, we've included the option to play with a totally freeform 3D camera, but by default the game is played from a fixed viewpoint, which dramatically simplifies the learning curve, thereby making *Impossible Creatures* accessible to a wider audience.

How can you create a new concept yet still include enough familiar concepts so the game isn't too obscure to the gamer?

Our design rule at Relic is "One revolutionary step, multiple evolutionary steps." Basically, we try to do one fundamental thing that will set us apart from everyone else, then we try to do everything standard better than everyone else. In *Impossible Creatures*, the revolutionary leap we took was to add a totally user-created army-building system with real-world animals. The evolutionary steps are all based on the lessons we learned through our experience with *Homeworld* and *Homeworld: Cataclysm*.

Does anything about today's games irk Garden?

I think that most games (and indeed, most game designers) today are afraid to take risks. When you take risks, bad things can happen (*Daikatana*), but truly magical, wonderful things can happen, too (*The Sims*).

Later in the book, Alex Garden talks about design documents and storyboards (Chapter 6) and breaking into the industry (Chapter 21). Read more about Relic Studios, Alex Garden, and *Impossible Creatures* at www.relic.com.

Louis Castle, Electronic Arts/Westwood Studios

Louis Castle is the general manager and co-founder of Westwood Studios, one of the most successful game development houses in the world. Westwood is best known for its *Command & Conquer* franchise, as well as *Blade Runner*, *Monopoly*, *The Lion King*, *Earth and Beyond*, and others. In early 2003, Westwood Studios become integrated with its parent company and publisher, Electronic Arts.

Castle provides some advice on creating successful computer games:

1. **Know your audience.** Spend the time to figure out who is likely to buy your product and research competitive or similar products. If none exist, spend time playing the best-selling and respected titles on your platform of choice. Be your best and worst customer.

2. **Make design a deliberate process.** Abstract the activities, emotional beats, and just about everything you can think of. Use the abstractions as filters and compare them to your favorite products. Design in any form is a deliberate action that requires planning, execution, and ongoing analysis.

3. **Listen to others.** The more exposure you can get and the sooner you can get it, the better your chances are to realize design flaws before you're committed to them. Be able to give up your best idea if it doesn't work in the context of your vision. Don't "make it fit."

Asked to comment on the key differences when creating a game for a console versus a PC, Castle has these comments:

The main difference between consoles and a PC is that a console game is one in which you're "playing" the interface device. You need to treat the controller as the actual game and let the audiovisual systems be subordinate to the device. The console player builds skill in a game through manipulating the interface device. The PC player builds skill from understanding the game and environment. The interface needs to be transparent, and the best PC games don't require "skill" in manipulating the keyboard and mouse—but rather, knowledge of what to do and when. Of course, both of these points are important on both platforms, but the emphasis is different. Console games are about instant satisfaction and long-term skill development. PC games are about quick entertainment and accomplishment followed by in-depth understanding and mastery.

How can you acquire a "dev kit" to work on a console game?

Console development kits are acquired through well-known publishers who support the platform. Developers can get systems directly through the manufacturer, but it usually requires a track record and volume of titles to be of interest. The very early systems typically cost tens of thousands of dollars and are in very limited supply. (They're considerably less now, although developers are not allowed to reveal exact prices. Formerly of THQ, Mike Rubinelli talks more in depth about dev kits in Chapter 21.)

Chapter 21 thoroughly discusses the various ways to break into the industry, but Castle offers some sound advice here:

> Take a low-paying job in any discipline you can. This minimizes the exposure for a company and gives you an opportunity to prove yourself. Learn to follow and execute; then worry about leading. Put your ego on hold and let your professionalism win you the creative jobs. I've always found the best way to get a job is to prove you can do it first, with the blessing of your boss and peers.

Chris Sawyer, Freelance

Although Chris Sawyer may not be a household name, this game developer, designer, and programmer created some of the most popular computer strategy/simulation games in the industry, including *Transport Tycoon*, *Transport Tycoon Deluxe*, the *RollerCoaster Tycoon* series, and its add-on packs *Corkscrew Follies* and *Loopy Landscapes*. Sawyer has also been in charge of many PC conversions of Amiga games, including *Frontier Elite 2*, *Xenomorph*, *Conqueror*, *Campaign*, *Virus*, *Goal*, and *Birds of Prey*.

Sawyer's contribution to the sage advice in this chapter:

1. Create something original and unique. Your game should look and play differently from other products to stand out.

2. Don't be put off if publishers initially discard your ideas and designs. When *RollerCoaster Tycoon* was in early development, I was told by everyone that it wouldn't succeed. The best way to convince people of a game's potential is to get the game to a playable state and actually let them play it.

3. Never forget that the ultimate aim of any computer game is to be fun. It's all very well coming up with a novel gameplay idea or an ever-more-immersive 3D world, but if it's not actually fun to play then it's worthless.

What was the most challenging aspect of creating *RollerCoaster Tycoon*?

> Perhaps the biggest challenge was to create a business model that was reasonably realistic but primarily "fun." I did this in *RollerCoaster Tycoon* by ignoring many of the financial and managerial aspects of running a theme park and concentrating more on the design and construction side.

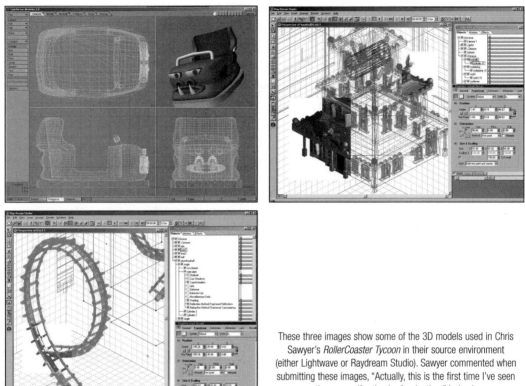

These three images show some of the 3D models used in Chris Sawyer's *RollerCoaster Tycoon* in their source environment (either Lightwave or Raydream Studio). Sawyer commented when submitting these images, "Actually, this is the first time I've seen these myself—they're fascinating." Indeed.
(Used with permission by Chris Sawyer.)

If Sawyer could go back and create the original *RollerCoaster Tycoon* all over again, would anything be done differently?

> Very little would change if I were re-creating the game to work with today's PCs. However, given more processing power, I'd reduce some of the compromises in the game, improve the graphical detail, and improve some of the AI.

Any pet peeves with today's computer games?

> Too many violent games, and not enough that focus on the more "positive" things we all enjoy, like building things and "nurturing" things.

Chris Sawyer returns in Chapter 12 to discuss artificial intelligence.

Rick Goodman, Stainless Steel Studios

While at Ensemble Studios, a company formed in 1995 with his brother Tony, Rick Goodman was the lead designer on the tremendously popular *Age of Empires* for Microsoft. He left Ensemble to form Stainless Steel Studios, where Goodman created the epic real-time strategy

(RTS) game *Empire Earth*, published by Sierra Studios in 2001. The game won "Best Strategy Game of 2001" by the readers at IGN (http://pc.ign.com). Goodman's latest game was *Empires: Dawn of the Modern World*, published by Activision.

Goodman offers us his "Ten Commandments of RTS Game Design," here in its entirety. Thou shalt pay attention:

1. The healthiest plants have the strongest roots. Goodman says to know your roots, whether comic books, sci-fi, board games, puzzles, toy soldiers, chess, *Dungeons & Dragons*, or anything else.

2. Paper never refuses ink. The key here is how to separate your good ideas from bad, otherwise known as "Hey, I have this great idea for a strategy game." Goodman says anyone can write a good design document, but there are four keys to success:

   ➤ Play the game through in your head.

   ➤ Model everything in a spreadsheet.

   ➤ Prototype user interfaces.

   ➤ Compose your "strike team" of play testers.

   In fact, Goodman used the Internet to recruit 12 savvy *Age of Empires* players and uses them all the time for guidance on *Empire Earth*, and to flush out bad ideas. Goodman reminds designers to welcome advice from others, with the adage "It's hard to see the picture when you're inside the frame."

3. A person who walks in another's tracks leaves no footprints. To innovate or to clone? Goodman reminds designers that we tend to criticize clones and then religiously follow up with new ones. He cites a phrase coined by Sid Meier, "innovative continuity," who came up with this term to not preclude him from doing anything he wanted. "Balance is key—add some innovative new things but make players comfortable in the game's surroundings so that they understand the rules and won't have to read the manual."

   Goodman says to "enhance the positive, eliminate the negative, and don't fiddle with the middle."

4. If I really wanted reality, would I have booted up the computer? Reinforce the fun factor over reality. Goodman refers to *Computer Gaming World* magazine polls that suggest that fantasy strategy games are often more popular than historical or reality-based ones. Even though *Age of Empires* is a historical strategy game, not everything is realistic: priest conversions, moving catapults, naval units attacking land units, and so forth.

5. If I had been present at creation, I would have given some useful hints. Goodman advises knowing your limits. Recognize your strengths and passions, and take advantage of them. For example, Goodman knew his knowledge of board games was very strong when he approached *Age of Empires*.

6. By the mile it's a trial, by the inch it's a cinch. Creating a game usually follows a top-down methodology, with game vision on top of the pyramid, game ideas and features in the middle, and low-level game mechanics on the bottom. Goodman explains, "There is a method to this process. The top is where the vision is generated ('How about a game where you're on a desert island?'); the middle is the game's features ('And this is what we'll do on this island'); and the bottom, the most crucial of the three, is how to implement these ideas in the game.

   According to Goodman, many game designers concentrate too much on the top two levels and not enough on how the play mechanics will work in the game. "The bottom level is the hardest; the implementation of the details is key," says Goodman. He also says most design docs seem to rely on the first two levels, when the emphasis should be on the implementation of the ideas into the computer and not just the ideas themselves.

7. Take note of the future; you're going to spend the rest of your life there. For the RTS genre to move forward, Goodman says, there has to be more to the game, and not just more of the same. He cites 3D action shooters as a genre that has evolved graphically, but not in gameplay (barring a few recent exceptions). With RTS games, try to foresee what will come down the pike and work toward bettering the genre.

8. Trees that are slow to grow bear the best fruit. "Time is your friend," says Goodman. "Use your project schedule well. *Age of Empires* was a 1,000-day project; 500 of those were spent internally at Ensemble Studios, the other half play-testing by Microsoft."

   "Beware—the only thing that can kill a good game is a great game. Be realistic at the beginning of your project and keep in mind that many of the great RTS games, such as *StarCraft* and *Age of Empires*, took longer than average to complete, but look at the outcome!"

9. Communicate your vision. One of the most important considerations while developing a game is communication. This is not only between a designer and his team, but between designer and publisher, the public, marketing, game critics, and testers.

10. Never put a glazed donut on a mouse pad. "…And other lessons learned the hard way," says Goodman. Some of his other lessons:

    ➤ Schedules are not more important than quality.

> ➤ "Let's not tell them and maybe they won't find out" always backfires; it's no different than when you were a kid.

For more information on *Empire Earth* and the design team at Stainless Steel Studios, visit `www.stainlesssteelstudios.com`.

Phil Steinmeyer, PopTop Software

For the past few editions of this book, PopTop Software's president and lead programmer, Phil Steinmeyer, has shared savvy strategy design tips. Steinmeyer has a number of games under his belt, including *Railroad Tycoon 2* and the *Tropico* series.

When it comes to general game design, Steinmeyer says to focus on a small niche somewhere within the gaming universe for your first project:

> If you can, create something with a built-in audience that will find your product with little marketing or distribution clout on your end, and with no big-budget competition. Some excellent niches to start in are war games, detailed 4X space games, games about semi-obscure sports or hobbies, gambling games, and so forth.

> Too many beginning game developers overshoot on their first game and never get it done. First, games are rarely brilliant—better to get something completely done and published and shoot for the moon on your second game.

Where does *Tropico* fit in?

> *Tropico* was my fifth major game; I had a much bigger budget and a more experienced team than anybody would typically have starting out. My first game (released in 1994) was a low-budget war game called *Iron Cross*. I did all the programming, most of the art and sound, and it was my first game—a true garage effort. There was a built-in audience (World War II enthusiasts), and little big-budget competition. It didn't sell nearly as many copies as my later games like *Railroad Tycoon 2* and *Tropico*, but it did all right given its budget—I made a decent amount for my time invested, and more important, I got my start in the industry and moved on to bigger and better things.

But is it possible to make a game easy to get into and understand while trying something new at the same time?

> It's hard to define it—this is sort of a "gut feeling" thing. I think *Tropico* was pretty good with this. The concept was quite novel (playing a Caribbean dictator, à la Fidel Castro). There had been few if any games set in the Caribbean or Latin America before, and our humorous Latin/Caribbean feel was very fresh, I think. At the same time, we grounded our gameplay in previous successful titles, particularly the *SimCity* series, although that was only a rough gameplay guide. But we thought the millions of buyers of *SimCity* and *RollerCoaster Tycoon* would immediately be able to "get" *Tropico* just by looking at the screenshots or seeing a little snippet of gameplay.

For more from Steinmeyer, flip to Chapters 6 and 21.

Ed Del Castillo, Liquid Entertainment

As president and co-founder of Liquid Entertainment, Ed Del Castillo juggles his management responsibilities with active participation in all aspects of product development: especially design and art direction. Liquid's first release was the eagerly anticipated *Battle Realms*. Before co-founding Liquid, Ed Del Castillo was probably best known as producer in charge of Westwood Studios' *Command & Conquer* franchise, including *Red Alert* and its expansion packs, various ports to other platforms, and foreign language versions.

Del Castillo was asked to provide three pieces of advice to a new strategy game designer looking to be successful in this industry. He responds as follows:

➤ Go to film school to learn how to tell a story, develop characters, light a scene, set a mood, and evoke an emotion.

➤ Never stop reading, watching, and playing everything.

➤ Consider another line of work if having a family is one of your goals!

According to Del Castillo, the most challenging obstacle when creating a real-time strategy (RTS) game is getting people to innovate:

The RTS genre has been in stagnation for so long with only micro-improvements that it's hard for people to create stuff that's truly better and not just different. Overcoming it is a matter of vision. You have to have a clear picture of what you're trying to achieve.

If Del Castillo could create *Command & Conquer (C&C)* all over again, would he do anything differently?

That's tough because *C&C* taught me so much. I think that I would change two things:

➤ A less-limiting universe. *C&C* is very limited, which is why you see things like *Red Alert* and *Emperor*. They're both attempts to use the *C&C* model in other worlds.

➤ More controlled presentations prior to ship. A few people, who shall be nameless, went on to great success due to their good memories and timely use of video cameras during our presentations prior to our release.

It had its place and time, and I'm having a hard time messing with that. The original *C&C* is my third favorite RTS after [Blizzard's] *StarCraft* and [Bungie Studios'] *Myth*.

Any pet peeves with today's strategy games?

Yes, too much iteration, not enough innovation. We need fewer people just trying to squeeze all they can out of an engine and more people crafting emotional experiences.

As a programmer, Del Castillo offers these words for others:

Think before you act. The days of the hacker are over. Think modular, flexible, expandable, well-organized, and well-documented code. Truly grasping these tenets will make you incredibly wanted by everyone.

On artificial intelligence (AI):

I think the biggest mistake you can make, and not just in AI, is to believe your own marketing. There's no such thing as a "learning" AI yet. Everything is still incrementing and decrementing weighting variables on algorithms based on specific and predefined data. AI is hard because most games aren't in the oven long enough to bake up a proper one. I think the best AIs are written for people who understand how little time they have and work to distill the decision-making tree of a human down to the essentials for that given game. I'm afraid that the only tip I have is to study the player. Most of his decisions can be simple to understand and emulate.

Del Castillo gives some examples of his past or present work that reinforce what he's suggesting here on innovation and on adding an emotional layer to a game:

➤ Innovation. When we conceived this game, it came from our ideas. We all came together and designed an RTS with no restrictions, no legacy, no need to be in the same universe as a predecessor. We were unbound by the past, and that allowed us to more fully reach for an ideal. It's the way it should be done. Too many people are held back by what they've already created and the desire to get more money out of it in the form of an incrementally improved sequel.

Battle Realms (BR) endeavored to innovate in two major ways. The first is combat. First-generation RTSs did a great job of showing the potential of this genre, but inadvertently they were very production-oriented. Building was more important than fighting. In *BR*, terrain matters. Height makes a difference to combat effectiveness. Real line of sight makes reconnaissance, sneaking, and ambushing a real element in the game. The unit dynamics focus on the combat dynamic and "incentivize" spending more of your attention commanding the battles rather than landlording the village.

The second major thing is to create more of a living world. There are a number of prongs to this, but it basically revolves around distilling more elements of reality and turning them into fun elements for the game. We incorporated a Living Resource System, which allows the player much more freedom. Horses are gathered and harnessed as pack animals or war steeds; water is used to put out fires, grow rice, and quench the thirst of peasants. We've tried to connect everything in some way, like the real world.

➤ Inspiration. It's about what I love, not what makes money this week. The inspiration comes from my childhood. Way too much *D&D* and the like mixed with way too many Kung Fu movies. I've been a game master for paper RPGs since I was 14, so the world-creation part is definitely something I love.

➤ Living world and the Living Resource System. This affects things in three ways:

  ➤ It makes things easier to understand. It feels right when the men run at each other, when the fire burns down a building or catches another building on fire or is put out by your peasants. Players of RTSs have learned a "vocabulary" of what they can and can't do and what things mean. We're allowing them to do more, and that means changing how things work a bit.

  ➤ It connects everything. Water, as an example, can be used for many things—put out fires, domesticate horses, quench the thirst of peasants toiling to build a building or soldiers training, even make the rice grow faster. Connecting things in this way not only feels more "natural" or "right," but also allows the player to easily shift his strategy and adapt to the enemy.

  ➤ It brings the world to life. We have units with more animations than ever before. Combats look alive as the units do different types of attacks. Birds fly from the trees when men move through the forest. Vultures gather on the battlefield. Soldiers juggle or clean their weapons when left alone too long, and it affects their abilities!

➤ Removal of artificial genre boundaries with the introduction of what other people would call "RPG elements," but what I call "character-investment elements." Genres are a thing of the past. Bringing in some of the growth and motivations from RPGs is very natural and allows for new cool possibilities in the game, to feel natural, and leave you asking, "Why couldn't I do this before?" It's all part of bringing the battlefield more to life. Allowing you to customize the characters is the first step to giving them individual characters and allowing you to fall in love with them. If you fall in love with them, you won't want them to die—thus creating the battlefield drama.

Ed Del Castillo offers some helpful advice on breaking into the industry in Chapter 21.

Chapter 4

General Game Design: Sports, Simulations, Adventure Games, and Puzzles

This large chapter covers a handful of game genres—sports, simulations, adventure games, and puzzles—each divided into specific sections for your convenience.

Let's start off with sports games—so grab a soda, put your feet up, and flip through the next few pages to read advice on creating football, baseball, basketball, and golf games (and even a couple of "extreme sports" entries, as well). Enjoy!

> **NOTE**
>
> As touched on in Chapter 1, "Game Genres and Playing Perspectives," racing games can be considered action/arcade games, simulations (if mimicking reality is the goal), or sports games (after all, NASCAR and F1 racing are sports). So you'll find racing games in this chapter (split between the sports and simulations sections). But if you're looking for advice from folks behind EA's *Motor City Online*, you'll have to flip to Chapter 5, "General Game Design: Role-Playing Games (RPGs) and Persistent Online Worlds," because it's a massively multiplayer game—therefore it fits that chapter best. Confusing, huh?

THE EXPERTS

- Kevin Wilkinson, EA Sports
- Mark Dickenson, The 3DO Company
- Jeremy Strauser, EA Sports
- Steven Chiang, EA Sports
- Mike Olsen, EA Sports
- Steven Rechtschaffner, Electronic Arts Canada
- Dave Davis, Electronic Arts
- Kenji Kanno, Hitmaker Studios/Sega
- Will Wright, Maxis Software
- Bruce Williams, Microsoft
- Steve Hunt
- Fred Markus, Rockstar San Diego
- Ed Martin, Electronic Arts
- Tim Schafer, Double Fine Productions
- Denis Dyack, Silicon Knights
- Phil Saunders, Presto Studios
- Ragnar Tørnquist, Funcom
- Ron Gilbert, Hulabee Entertainment
- Harry Gottlieb, Jellyvision
- Alexey Pajitnov, Microsoft
- Toshihiro Nagoshi, Amusement Vision/Sega

Sports Games

It should come as no surprise that most of the people interviewed here work for EA. But there are a few who don't, and they offer you valuable insights as well.

Kevin Wilkinson, EA Sports

Based in beautiful Burnaby, British Columbia, Kevin Wilkinson is a senior producer at Electronic Arts Canada, and has worked on many of the beloved hockey and basketball games that EA Sports is known for. Wilkinson's last project was the sneaker-squeaking hit *NBA Live 2003*.

Wilkinson was asked to reveal his secrets on successful game design for the purposes of this book.

> All of your game ideas (or call them "features") must include the following components for a user to appreciate them over time. These are the minimum requirements: 1. They must have a cool audio/visual component. 2. They must have a strategic risk/reward component. 3. They must have a learned skill component.

Wilkinson expands on the "risk/reward component:"

> Users want a competitive challenge, especially from the CPU team. Users want to know that there will be a payoff (reward) for attempting something strategic in a game. On the other hand, they don't want it to come for free. They actually want to work for it. They want to learn under what game circumstances and with which players they are more likely to be successful. If there are negative (or risk) consequences to their actions—now you've got their competitive juices flowing! Without the risk component, the feature dies a quick death.

> Once users have learned the strategic risk/reward to the feature, they still want more. Very similar to how athletes practice and perfect moves on the court, ice, and field; users want to master their gaming skills. "How'd you do that?" is the sweetest compliment you could give any "gamer"...your feature has now moved them beyond competitive challenge—it's now a pride thing!

Wilkinson says newbie designers often neglect one or more of these three components, resulting in a feature set that wears thin very quickly.

> Blow your features out. The best games in the industry provide a fourth component—individual expression—so when users feel they can express themselves as individuals by playing the game, they will feel a powerful bond with your game.

With *NBA Live 2003* as an example, Wilkinson points out a cool "feature:"

> We introduced a new patent-pending feature using the Right Analog stick. In all basketball games to date, crossover dribble moves are triggered by hitting a "crossover" button. The end result is a random selection in the code that chooses a "between-the-legs" or "around-the-back" crossover, etc.

The idea of using the Right Analog is that it acts as your arms—something you desperately need control of when playing hoops. So…move the stick to the left, and the players' arm and ball move left; move it right, and the ball switches (crosses over) to the right. Move the stick down and around (like drawing the letter J), and the ball goes behind your back to the left. There are 10 base moves that all string together in any order you choose, so you can imagine how many permutations of moves you have at your fingertips. The beauty of this feature is that a) you can control which crossover you want to perform; b) you can control the timing of when you want to cross the ball over; c) you can string a number of crossovers together to "school" your defender however you choose.

How does this "feature" apply to the first three pieces of advice?

Audio/Visual

Shoe squeaks are triggered to the ball carrier's foot plants; a quick cut results in a louder squeak. Commentary gets triggered on exceptional crossover moves. The visual is the fluidity of the motion.

Strategic Risk/Reward

Performing difficult crossover moves with your center results in him dribbling the ball off his foot or a higher likelihood of a steal or strip (that is, a risk). Performing the crossover with an exceptional ball handler results in beating your defender off the dribble, causing a double team and one of your teammates being wide open (that is, a reward). There is far more strategy here (probably 10 pages in all); this is the simplest example I could think of!

Learned Skill Factor

It takes time to learn which button movements trigger specific crossovers. The acquired skill is learning the timing involved in stringing the moves together.

Individual Expression

Users have complete control over how they use this feature. Over time, individual users will develop a customized set of moves that they can call their own. The permutations of moves are so deep, it is guaranteed that users will "bring their own game" when playing *NBA Live 2003*.

Let's face it: The competition is getting pretty steep in the basketball video games category, with products published by the likes of Sony, Sega Sports, Microsoft, Midway, Nintendo, and Konami. Does this newfound competition hurt or help the EA Sports team?

We love what we do and are competitive by nature. Our primary motivation comes from within rather than industry competition. We are motivated by other great EA Sports games. There is a healthy competition between *NHL*, *Live*, *Madden*, *MVP Baseball* [formerly the *Triple Play* series], and *FIFA*.

Are there any pet peeves while playing other basketball video games?

It's no fun playing defense. Most games concentrate on the offensive game and forget that 50 percent of the experience is feeling in control on the defensive side of the ball. *NBA Live 2003* changed that forever.

EA Sports' senior producer Kevin Wilkinson offers four "must-have" features a designer must implement into a successful sports game, and explains how *NBA Live 2003* meets these minimum requirements.
(Used with permission by Electronic Arts, Inc.)

How will the game offer more control to the player?

> In *NBA Live 2003*, players finally have control over your arms using the Right Analog stick. You are in control of which arm you want to steal the ball with. You are also provided with a "Take Charge" option on defense. By learning when and how to use the "Take Charge" button, you now have your opponent second-guessing as to when and how aggressively to drive into open lanes. It has provided a layer of defensive strategy missing in previous basketball games.

Although Chapter 21, "Breaking into the Industry," is focused on breaking into the business, Wilkinson offers his thoughts on the matter here. His advice?

> First, approach every day with a willingness and expectation to learn. You're not really "as good as your last game;" you are as good as what you learned yesterday. Second, use the strengths of the people around you. Making great games today involves strong communication and collaborative teamwork.

> Finally, make sure every idea gets a chance to grow. Don't rush to the "how-are-we-going-to-implement-this?" discussion. Too many great ideas get shut down too early by co-workers before they get to breathe life.

> Ideas need a little sunshine and rain sprinkled on them. Once they are fully developed, you can figure out how to implement them.

Mark Dickenson, The 3DO Company

The talented Mark Dickenson, senior director at the 3DO Company, has worked on a number of PC and console titles such as *High Heat Baseball* (arguably one of the best baseball video games on the planet), *Army Men: Sarge's War, Alien Legacy, The Shadow of Yserbius, Spellcraft,* and *Hard Nova.*

But we're only interested in sports games here—and, in particular, whatever discerning advice Mark can offer to those who are interested in creating sports games, baseball or otherwise. Right off the…er…bat, Dickenson offers the following:

1. **Know the sport; know it very well!** The nuances of the sport that come from this knowledge can lead to a great game.

2. **Do some research!** Your competitors in the sports game industry are going to do some things very well. However, along the way, they're probably going to miss some key attributes that are integral to the sport you're portraying. Find out what these things are and exploit them. Honestly, though, if you haven't already played the games and know what these weaknesses are, you might want to think of developing a different kind of game. For me, the frustration I had with other baseball games directly led to my passion for developing one.

3. **Develop a clear understanding of what's going to be special about the game.** Hammer on this in the development process. You can make compromises with other aspects of the game, but don't compromise in the key areas you've targeted.

How did this advice apply to his work with *High Heat Baseball*?

With *High Heat*, it's very easy. In the development of the first *High Heat Baseball*, we had very simple goals: great batter/pitcher interface, combined with a fast pace. We compromised many, many other features to be able to succeed at these two things. There were even people who laughed at us because we had so few features and sprite-based players, but along the way, we also brought baseball back to baseball video games. We wanted to bring some key features to video baseball games that had been missing—legitimate walks, triples, and deeper counts—and we did.

Dickenson dispels the myth that realism has to be sacrificed to make sports games accessible to players and to keep game pacing fast: "It may require a little more work and creative thinking, but pace, accessibility, and realism can be achieved in a single sports title." So, where can a game designer look for inspiration?

I think the inspiration really comes from playing other sports games and knowing they can be better. That simple desire to add the experiences that you feel are missing from the game. I really disliked the fact that in most baseball games before *High Heat*, you couldn't draw a walk. The idea of working the count to get the pitch you want to hit had disappeared in video baseball games. I wanted to fix that. Voilà, inspiration!

Finally, Dickenson discusses some challenges in working on a sports title compared to other genres:

I think one of the disadvantages, if you want to call it that, is that your end user is aware of what should be occurring on the screen. In fantasy genres, that's not the case. The end user might not even know that the game is not behaving properly. However, in sports games, the players are painfully aware of each error. One of the other key challenges in sports games is what I call "organic behavior." In baseball, you'll see single after single, but each one is different. You don't want users to feel that they're seeing the same thing over and over, so you have to make sure there's a certain amount of "fuzziness." In the end, though, it all has to look and feel real.

Unless your goal is to develop an over-the-top arcade game, don't give up on the small touches of realism. Don't believe the people who tell you that a particular thing can't be achieved. Patience is key. Play the game, review the results, work with the team to address issues, repeat as necessary, and then repeat again. Get the basic system working well before adding features, and even then be sure to stay focused on the integral gameplay required for the sport.

In Chapter 14, "The All-Important User Interface (UI) and Game Control," Dickenson delivers wise advice on creating a successful user interface for your sports games, so check it out when you're ready.

Jeremy Strauser, EA Sports

As producer at the Florida-based Tiburon Studios, Jeremy Strauser is in charge of one of the best-selling franchises on American soil—the *Madden NFL* series for EA Sports. To be specific, Strauser has produced *Madden NFL 96, 97, 2001, 2002, 2003,* and *NCAA Football 98, 99, 2000,* and *2001* editions.

Asked to discuss the three major areas of focus in a sports game, Strauser presents the following list:

> ➤ **Detail.** Can be graphics, sounds, general refinement, or any combination.

> ➤ **Gameplay.** The game has to be fun to play; without that, there isn't a game.

> ➤ **Depth.** The game needs to give the user a reason to play again and again, either in the game engine or as an external feature.

How does this advice fit Strauser's own products?

A good example of depth is the Dynasty Mode (NCAA) and Franchise Mode (Madden) features. These features basically are external to the game—but allow users to progress through multiple seasons and grow "their" teams over many years. These features have given people the ability to evolve their games beyond quick one-off games or even just one season.

Strauser admits that one of the most difficult tasks in a game is creating an effective and intuitive user interface (see Chapter 14), but he can offer some pointers when working on a sports video game:

The best advice here is thorough planning and design. Everything must be designed out first with an interface, including possible evolution of the feature set. Trying to shoehorn features into an existing interface, which is unfortunately done too often, is the biggest culprit of poor interfaces.

To take advantage of new hardware, EA Sports releases the *Madden NFL* franchise for most console platforms,
including the Sony PlayStation and PlayStation 2, the PC, the Nintendo GameCube,
and the Microsoft Xbox. Now that's market dominance! Pictured here is *Madden NFL 2002*.
(Used with permission by Electronic Arts, Inc.)

And on the issue of smooth control, Strauser adds:

> I think this is the whole fun of sports games. I'm not an athlete, I can't break three tackles en route to the end zone or make a diving catch for a first down, so I think the fun part comes in when I do that in a video game. A great game lets users feel like they "did" that.

> I think that sense of control is lacking in a lot of games, often at the expense of fancy graphics or canned animation sequences. That and frustrations with bad AI are my biggest issues.

This brings up a good point—along with control, what are some of the challenges in working on a sports title compared to other genres, and how does Strauser overcome them?

> The biggest thing is it can be somewhat limiting. At the end of the day, we're emulating the physical world and a real-life sport with real-life players. We're bound to that above all things. Also, working on the same type of game year after year can sometimes be difficult creatively, although we seem to come up with new ideas each year. Finally, we put a lot of pressure on ourselves to be timely—no one wants to buy a football game after football season, so we have very little room for lateness.

Finally, he offers a couple of do's and don'ts to keep in mind when creating sports video games. Do: Spend the time (and money) needed to make the game that is designed! Don't: Compromise the overall game design just to put a game out in a certain time.

Steven Chiang, EA Sports

Also at EA Sports' Tiburon studios in Florida is Steven Chiang—a co-founder and studio general manager—and someone who has had a hand in almost every Madden NFL game since *Madden NFL 97*. Chiang also worked on the last couple *NASCAR Thunder* racing games.

From a game design standpoint (not a financial one), what are the most important things to keep in mind for a newbie game designer who is working on his or her first sports video game?

> Make it a fun one-player game, design new ways to do the same thing, give it depth, and pay attention to the details.

With *Madden NFL 2003* under the microscope, Chiang was asked to support his advice. He responds as follows:

> *Madden NFL 2003* has a new mode called "Mini-Camp," in which the user participates in fun addictive drills that teach the user how to play the game. For instance, we have a precision passing drill, in which you pass the ball through rings to a receiver in order to learn the timing on a route. We also have added a new game control called the "defensive strafe," in which the user can press a button and stay facing forward. This helps the defensive game by making it easier to contain the offense.

> And our franchise mode has a full off-season with retiring players, free agency, a draft, and rookie scouting. *Madden NFL 2003* is a very deep game.

So, is this why each Madden game is the hottest football seller each year, despite increasing competition?

> The folks at Tiburon feel that *Madden NFL 2003* is critically acclaimed and commercially successful for several reasons:

> 1. Designed for the hardcore and mass-market consumer. The franchise mode satisfies our hardcore users, and Madden Cards and Mini-Camp appeal to the mass-market consumers.

> 2. Strong focus on realistic gameplay. Real plays, new defensive schemes, players that act like their counterparts in real life. We also revamp our gameplay and improve it every year

> 3. Value and consistency. *Madden NFL 2003* is a very deep and wide game, and every year users can count on a feature-rich Madden title.

Chiang also says that it's very important for sports game designers to be aware of slow frame rates in their games. "Sports games need to move fluidly—a game running at 12 frames a second isn't really playable."

Chapter 21 offers a deeper discussion on how to best break into the industry, but Chiang offers a few tidbits here:

> ➤ Be prepared for your interview. Know what company you are applying to and learn all about their products, their competition, their sales, etc.

➤ Do what it takes to get the job done. Work hard; work long hours. At the end of the day, get your work done and done well.

➤ Set the bar high; push for and expect the best-quality work. This is what sets the good games apart.

> **NOTE**
>
> Are you a fan of Sega Sports games? If so, you're certainly not alone. Be sure to check out Chapter 11, "Programming Theory," and Chapter 13, "Game Art and Animation," for advice from Greg Thomas, who's responsible for such Sega Sports games as the bone-crushing NFL2K3.

Mike Olsen, EA Sports

Lead designer Mike Olsen has been with Electronic Arts for seven years now, and is currently responsible for the *Tiger Woods PGA TOUR* golf console franchise. Prior to this series, Olsen worked on other sports titles, including *Knockout Kings*, *NCAA Football*, *NCAA March Madness*, and *NHL*. As a future aspiration, Olsen says he'd someday like to be the creative director of an original character action title. On developing sports video games, Olsen says game designers should heed the following advice:

Know Your Audience

It is very important to design a game for your audience. If you are targeting a younger audience, you may want to find out what's cool now. Your research may show that younger audiences tend to enjoy an arcade experience more then a simulation experience. In that case, you would want to be careful not to go too strongly down a hardcore simulation route.

Know Your Competitors

What are other publishers doing? What are the successful games doing? A lot of your ideas may actually be generated from other games' successes. If your competition is getting rave reviews on a feature that you don't have in your product, you may try to implement something similar, but in a way that makes it feel unique to your game. This includes play-testing many other products and staying current with the latest titles.

Determine and Evaluate Originality (Define Your Feature Set)

I believe it is critical to be innovative in your genre. I qualify innovative within the genre, meaning that even though a feature may not be innovative to the industry, it could still be new to your style of game. You can also innovate by simply reshaping older ideas in new ways. As a designer, you need to be able to take risks and try new things. It is important to allow yourself time to research and develop new content and technologies.

But can Olsen "drive home" his advice in light of the latest Tiger Woods golf game?

When it comes to "knowing the audience," Olsen says that *Tiger Woods PGA TOUR* took a slightly different path, hoping to broaden the appeal to reach a newer and younger audience. He explains:

> With this, we had to make careful choices to ensure that we created both a "gamer's game" and a game that would not offend our traditional golf fans who have supported the franchise over the years. When you try to be all things to all consumers, you can try to do too much for both and end up satisfying none of them. I feel that what we ended up with was a very effective hybrid that exceeded the expectations of BOTH types of players.

As for innovation, Olsen says the "True Precision Swing Mechanic" in the last couple of *Tiger Woods PGA TOUR* titles revolutionized the way gamers swing a golf club in the cyber world:

> We felt that the swing meters of traditional golf video games detached the player from his character. The user ends up playing the meter instead of playing his golfer. With an analog back-and-forth swing that provided immediate visual feedback on the golfer himself, we feel we've captured the essence of how a real golf swing would feel.

> In addition, we also implemented a new feature we called "Speed Golf." This mode consisted of hitting shots, running after your ball to find it, then hitting it again. You can play a full round of golf in less than five minutes in this mode—not your typical stodgy golf game!

Olsen discusses a few other features found in the *Tiger Woods* series that separate this golf game from the competition:

> A few more things that made Tiger Woods different/unique were the new feature set that we put into the game, as well as our prestigious licenses. We hold exclusive licenses to many different golfers/courses/tournaments, etc. We are the most "true-to-life simulation" golf game currently in the market; and also feature tons of original content between our many "challenge" courses and newly created characters.

Does having a huge sports celebrity such as Tiger Woods as a spokesperson (on the cover of the box and inside the game) make it easier or more difficult to create compelling content?

"Obviously, having Tiger on the cover of your game doesn't hurt you!" laughs Olsen. "He is arguably the most recognizable athlete in the world."

> With someone like Tiger, you also are able to gain access to other licenses that you may have not otherwise been able to pursue…you find people wanting to associate themselves with him.

> But any time you get involved with a licensing partner, your creativity with the design can be limited somewhat on occasion. Tiger approves each and every aspect of the game, so some things that you may think would be great features, he may not feel the same way. But as with any business relationship, there's give-and-take, and we never feel that we have to make any significant compromises that could hurt the product.

Finally, Olsen offers some advice to those starting out:

Thrive On Inspiration

Great games are made by passionate people. A group of talented people who feel passion for an idea is a powerful tool that can create amazing things. A group that "goes through the motions" on an idea that isn't fully supported by everyone will only produce mediocrity.

Think Your Thoughts Through and Log Your Ideas

Jotting down my ideas as I get them is very important. I have pieces of paper with design notes everywhere; you never know when an idea will hit your brain. I often keep a "would be cool..." document open on my desktop year round, and throw any new ideas in there as they happen. When it comes time to write my next design, I'll reference this document for new ideas.

NOTE

Game designer Dave Perry also admits to being a "list-o-holic" with a notepad always on his bedside night table. Flip back to Chapter 2, "General Game Design: Action/Arcade Games," to read why it's critical to jot down ideas as they come!

Steven Rechtschaffner, Electronic Arts Canada

If you've ever played the award-winning and best-selling *SSX* franchise games from EA Sports BIG, you've gotten a taste of Steven Rechtschaffner's magic touch. As studio vice president and executive producer at Electronic Arts Canada (EAC), Steve has a hit franchise under his belt and is here to share some of his knowledge with us.

Rechtschaffner says the first key is to decide who you're building the game for:

Is it for a diehard, need-every-detail simulation? Or for someone who likes sports and is looking for a fun experience? You need to pick your targeted user because you just can't make everybody happy. We're not always loved [by critics] for how we made baseball into a more fun experience with *Triple Play* [Note: the franchise is now referred to as *MVP Baseball*], although sales results always put us at the top of the baseball charts by a long margin. At EA, we work day-to-day on an art form with many scientific processes and technologies. However, at the end of the day, it's up to us to make the game that has the greatest potential to sell the most copies. We owe that to our stockholders.

Once you know who you're building your game for, adds Rechtschaffner, you need to identify what's going to give the greatest emotional impact for that type of user. "Then you can start to think about how you're going to bring your game to life and where you will focus your team's efforts. There's never enough time to do it all, so prioritizing the key impact areas of your design is paramount."

How did this strategy affect the design of *SSX* and *SSX Tricky*?

For *SSX Tricky*, we decided that tricks were going to be a key area where we would focus our efforts. We decided this because so many users of *SSX* were playing in Showoff (trick) mode and more into doing tricks than racing. With that objective [in mind], we started designing in a number of areas, new ways to create more emotional responses to playing in Showoff mode. These included a new level and more difficult, over-the-top tricks called "Uber Tricks." We also went back to each course and made a special version of it for Showoff mode only. It would now include additional rails, jumps, "grindable" objects, and shortcut paths that would show up only in Showoff mode. We also created a new system for scoring trick points, as well as combined trick points.

SSX Tricky executive producer Steve Rechtschaffner admits, "I'm much more about stimulation than simulation." He believes that the best way to break into the gaming industry is to work your way up the ranks. "There's so much learning to do along the way, before you can be the person driving a project with a 30- to 40-person team—so we've had great luck bringing people into our Quality Assurance system and using that as a launching pad for a production and design career."
(Used with permission by Electronic Arts, Inc.)

Does Rechtschaffner have any beefs about today's sports video games? Why is it so hard to get it right?

I'm much more about stimulation than simulation. I tend to be more interested in sports games with more immediate gratification and more consistent emotional payoffs, along the lines of an *NBA Street* or *SSX*. Having been involved with *Triple Play* for so long, I think taking what's great about baseball and translating it into a well-paced game is a big challenge. That said, the team here at EAC that's now working on *Triple Play* have created some pretty innovative ideas looking forward...so maybe they'll get there in the next year or two.

I play or have played all the games in the EA Sports line, and have had some good times. I like the fact that there's a level of familiarity across most of the games. It's less interesting to me to pick up another brand of sports game that feels like an EA Sports clone. I wish other people trying to break into this arena would take more risks and try to break through in new and innovative ways. We like competition.

Deciding who your customer is seems to be a problem for many sports games. They try to do it all, not going deep enough in any one direction. I think it's great that we now have both an *NBA Live* and an *NBA Street* game. I play them both, depending on what kind of experience I'm looking for (like channel surfing on the TV).

Read more from Steve Rechtschaffner in Chapter 14 and Chapter 17, "Proper Game Testing," on creating a slick user interface and proper game testing, respectively.

Dave Davis, Electronic Arts

While on the trend of "extreme sports" (see also Chapter 21 to read some words by Neversoft's Joel Jewett and the *Tony Hawk's Pro Skater* franchise), let's chat with EA Sports BIG's executive producer of *Freekstyle*. Naturally, we're referring to Dave Davis.

In addition to being the visionary behind *Freekstyle*, Dave is the executive producer for *Knockout Kings* and was the instigator of the massive reworking of the franchise. In the past, Davis produced the highly successful *MotoRacer* series as well as the EA Sports *Supercross* series.

When it comes to designing video games, Davis says there are three rules everyone should adhere to:

> ➤ Start with an original idea—and be true to it.

> ➤ Always remember that you are not building a game just for you and your friends—make it accessible.

> ➤ Create a compelling risk and reward structure—get the player invested.

Davis applies these words of wisdom (pooled from his 17+ years in the business) with his latest project, *Freekstyle*, as the shining example:

Have an Original Idea and Be True to It

With *Freekstyle*, we knew that we wanted to build a freestyle motocross game that was unlike any before. In the past, motocross games had been dry and boring and fell more into the simulation category. *Freekstyle* needed to capture the attitude and style that make up freestyle motocross. Everything in the game was verified against this goal. Based on all the feedback that has been written by people who have played the game, we were successful.

Build for Your Audience, Not Yourself

Far too often, we lose sight of who we are making our games for, and we make poor design decisions because of it. Remember that a game is not successful if only you and your friends buy it and want to play it. Understand that to be a top-selling game, it needs to appeal to 1.5 to 2 million gamers. That is precisely the reason we moved *Freekstyle* away from being a true motocross sim. I wanted *Freekstyle* to appeal to the casual video game player as well as to the hardcore moto-head.

Get the Player Invested

For a game to be successful, you need to engage the players as quickly as possible and provide them with a path that is rewarding enough for them to continue playing. In *Freekstyle*, players could identify with the characters and would select one that best represented their self-image. As they played through the game, they built up skill points and also unlocked new bikes, tracks, and gear. These mechanisms served to entice the player to continue playing and investing in his character.

Now, Davis referred to other motocross sims as sometimes "dry and boring." Are there any beefs he has about the industry that may help a budding game designer who is just starting out?

My main problem is more global: There are still way too many bad games being released into the market.

As we mature as an industry, we need to be more careful about dumping junk product on the consumers. If we don't exercise some self-restraint and kill the bad products, we run the risk of alienating our customers.

From a game design standpoint, I am very tired of playing games that are chock-full of great features (track builders, slow-mo replay that you can edit, franchise, etc.) but then quickly realizing that the developer or publisher failed to make a good game core.

If I can give any advice here, I would say: Please, please, please build a fun, compelling core first before you build out the entire game.

But let's face it: A smaller development studio (or even one sole gamemaker) will not have the money or resources like Electronic Arts does. So, how can a budding developer who is on his own compete in this space?

It's quickly becoming impossible for individuals or small groups to compete with the size and magnitude of the products that companies like EA are releasing. I think that the best way to be successful is to not try to compete with *Medal of Honor* or *SSX* because you will probably fall short unless you have the same amount of time, money, and resources available to you. Focus on building a small, tight, compelling experience with an original twist.

Dave Davis offers some advice in Chapter 21 on how to break into the industry. What works, what doesn't, and what has changed over the past couple of years? Check in to find out...

Get your freak on with EA Sports BIG's *Freekstyle* for the PlayStation 2 and GameCube. Executive producer Dave Davis chats about what budding game designers can learn from the gameplay mechanics in this extreme sports game.

(Used with permission by Electronic Arts, Inc.)

Kenji Kanno, Hitmaker Studios/Sega

Kenji Kanno, general manager of Sega's Hitmaker studio, also served as a producer on the coveted *Crazy Taxi* franchise. He joins us here to chat about game theory, design, and inspiration. He starts off by saying that human behavior is at the core of game design.

> This is because it can be applied to everything that concerns entertainment—it is significant to consider what sentiments gamers have and then use game design to control these emotions. Therefore, it is important to make it a rule to observe human behavior every day and then utilize this knowledge.

Another key to success is to study the trends of the time. Says Kanno:

> You first have to acquire the knowledge of what is in fashion today in the world. This "trend" does not just mean something in game development, but in everything (movies, music, or fashion). Then, you should remember the words, "To know new things, learn by studying the old." It may sound like I am giving myself airs, but it is important to polish your sensibilities. Humans have feelings that cannot be

described in words, which are so-called "sensibilities." Although it is not something to learn but to feel, it is meaningful to keep on giving yourself stimuli in order to always maintain these sensibilities.

If I were to add another point, it would be logic. Games are, after all, made with a combination of 0s and 1s—game design is to put pieces together using logic based on the aforementioned points.

Kanno was asked to use *Crazy Taxi* as an example in support of his advice.

What I wanted to express most with *Crazy Taxi* was for users to feel the dynamism of car action scenes that you often see in the Hollywood movies.

In order to convey this, I decided to express in a more effective way the feelings that many people have (for example, "thrills you will feel when your car drives down the opposite lane and when you drive through coming and going traffic"). One example of tricks is shown when you will get chips with sound after you and ordinary cars pass each other. This is a way to evoke joyful feelings as an award after tension. I judged that players would have positive feelings, with both their sight and auditory senses, when this process is repeated again and again.

As for the sensibility side, the team in one united body wanted players to feel that "this is cool!" I suppose there are a few people who have a "blue-collar" impression toward the taxi element. However, we utilized the image to make the game look cool. This part cannot be described in words, but I think it was successful, anyway.

When Kanno was asked to explain why he thinks *Crazy Taxi* was such an international hit, he responds: "Actually, it is US who want to ask YOU the reason why!"

We creators release works into the world thinking, "This definitely is fun!" Therefore, if it turns out to be a success, it will be just like "we have been right." Analysis of a success is a kind of nonsense to developers because we analyze various things and develop a title to win a great success.

But Kanno does talk about what he doesn't like in a video game:

After seeing this year's E3, I feel strongly that there are too many similar products. Certainly, everyone likes to play their favorite type of games; however, it is quite obvious that they will get bored in a couple of years as a feeling of repeating the same old things grows. So I think that it is important to always attempt new things. To betray users' expectations in a good sense is one means that can lead the game industry to improvement.

Finally, Kanno was asked about the inspiration behind *Crazy Taxi*:

I am not sure if this can be called the origin, but it was while I was driving my car and caught in a traffic jam that I decided to write up the project's plan. The opposite lane was totally empty, while our lane was not moving at all. I was thinking at that time: "I would feel great if I jumped my car out to the opposite lane and drove there at the fastest speed to my heart's content…I wonder how many people are here with the same sentiment as mine in this (traffic jam line)." When I went to the office the next day, I started to write the project plan.

As for others who are looking for inspiration, Kanno leaves us with the following: "There is no telling when you hit upon a game plan; therefore, it is essential to always closely observe things and people."

For more information on Hitmaker Studios, visit `www.hitmaker.co.jp`.

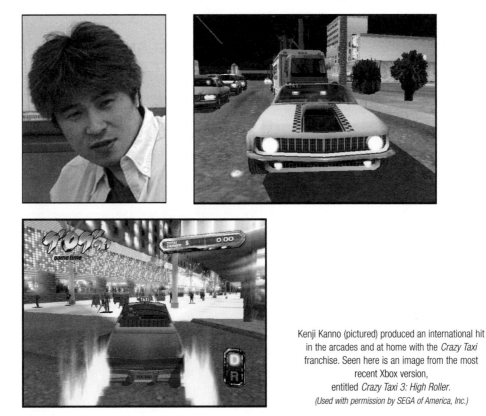

Kenji Kanno (pictured) produced an international hit in the arcades and at home with the *Crazy Taxi* franchise. Seen here is an image from the most recent Xbox version, entitled *Crazy Taxi 3: High Roller*.
(Used with permission by SEGA of America, Inc.)

Simulations

Of course, you can't discuss simulations without talking to the creator of the various incarnations of *The Sims*.

Will Wright, Maxis Software

One of the legendary superstars we're thrilled to have in this book is Will Wright, creator of such beloved computer games such as *SimCity*, *SimEarth*, *SimAnt*, *SimCity2000*, *SimCopter*, *The Sims*, and *The Sims Online*. His future aspiration? "[To] simulate the entire universe."

Despite his arduous schedule, Wright takes time to chat about game design, innovation, and the possible reasons behind the immense popularity of his games.

What are some key game design rules?

1. Games are about players having fun, not about programmers solving problems.

2. Be open to inspiration from unusual sources.

3. Know as much about every aspect of game production as you possibly can (especially programming).

Wright supports this advice with examples from his work at Maxis:

SimEarth was a great example of why rule #1 is important. In this game, we created a really cool simulation that we (the programmers) were very proud of. Unfortunately, this cool simulation we made was not very fun to play with.

From rule #2: *The Sims* was originally inspired by a rather academic book on architecture (*A Pattern Language* [Oxford University Press, 1977]). The final game bears very little resemblance to the book, but owes a lot to it.

As for rule #3, you need to understand the nature of your materials (code, art, sound) before you can become a good artist. Imagine trying to be a master painter while not knowing how to mix colors or stretch a canvas. As you begin to understand both the limits and the possibilities of your materials, the full range of creative possibilities becomes much more visible to you as a designer.

The Sims may have been influenced by a book on architecture, but where else can you find inspiration?

I mostly get my inspiration from books, both fiction and nonfiction. I really enjoy learning new subjects. When I find a new subject especially intriguing, I try to design a game that will help spread my fascination with that subject to the game players. Sometimes the game that emerges from this process seems very removed from the original subject, but that's okay, too.

As examples of inspiration, Wright says *SimCity* was inspired by train sets and a book by Stanislaw Lem, *The Cyberiad* (Harvest Books, 1985); *SimEarth* was inspired by many science fiction books, evolution, and climate; while *SimAnt* was inspired by Wright's backyard!

Is there a tangible reason why Wright's games are so sought-after? The designer responds:

I think one reason these games are so popular is because they allow the players to be creative in their gameplay. Many games are structured with a more linear or branching topology. This means that the problems that are encountered in the game have a very small number of possible solutions and are solved mostly the same way by different players. In contrast, a more open-ended game like *SimCity* or *The Sims* allows each player to find creative solutions to the problems that maybe no one else has found.

The upside of all this is that the creativity helps to promote empathy in the game. I care more about my City or my Family because no one else has one just like it. Not only that, but I remember all the good things and bad things that happened to it and how I managed to deal with those issues. It seems more "real" to me.

In 2003's *The Sims Online*, Will Wright (pictured here holding one of his sims) helps
you take your sims to an online world where you get to be yourself—
or whoever you want to be, for that matter. In this multiplayer world, players have their
own piece of land to do with as they please: Create a house,
coffee bar, dance club, museum, or whatever you can imagine.
(Used with permission by Electronic Arts, Inc.)

Wright was asked to explain what he has learned the most from working on *The Sims*.

> The most interesting lessons I've learned from *The Sims* are centered around the player community that
> has formed around the game. The interlocking dynamics of this community share many features of an
> ecosystem. What we need to learn going forward is how to nurture, grow, and protect these communities.

So, would there be anything he would change in creating this game if he could do it all over
again?

> No. I think so many things came together just right for *The Sims* that anything I changed would proba-
> bly have decreased the success.

On the other side of the coin, what's missing with many of today's computer games?

> I think in the future, games will be more about the story that the player is constructing through the play
> process and less about the story that the game designer is trying to tell through the design process. *The
> Sims* was an early attempt at just that: to make the players become the scriptwriters. I believe this will
> push empathy even further in the player's mind as we draw them into these complex little microworlds.

> **NOTE**
>
> Don't be discouraged if you're unable to sell your game to a publisher right away. Would you believe that Will Wright received rejection letters when he shopped *SimCity* back in the 1980s? He comments, "I showed to it to several publishers (Spectrum Holobyte, Broderbund, and so on). Nobody wanted to publish it, so the Commodore 64 version sat on the shelf for several years until I met Jeff Braun and we started Maxis together."

Be sure to read Will Wright's advice on creating online-only games in Chapter 5 and on programming artificial intelligence in Chapter 12, "Artificial Intelligence (AI)".

Bruce Williams, Microsoft

Talk about a veteran—Bruce Williams has worked at Microsoft for 15 years and has been with the *Flight Simulator* team since Flight Simulator for Windows 95. Williams, now a product planner for the *Flight Simulator* team, has also been a pilot since the early 1970s, so the connection with the *Flight Simulator* franchise is a natural one.

Asked to provide some advice for game designers looking to create simulations, Williams responds with the following:

> Game design isn't like writing novels or movie scripts. It's a collaborative effort involving the designer (author), artists, developers, program managers, business and marketing experts, etc. Although you must have a strong, clear vision when you set out to create a game, you must also be flexible and able to separate your ego from the product and process.

While the *Flight Simulator* series isn't a game per se, Williams pools from his own experience to help support his aforementioned words on collaboration and developing a clear vision for your product.

> [*Flight Simulator*] is a re-creation of the real world of aviation. In that sense, we don't make up a world, characters, and situation. Everything is modeled on what happens in the real world of flying. That said, we have to make tough decisions about how much emphasis to place on particular aspects of the simulation to balance the goals of appealing to a broad audience, matching the simulation to the horsepower available in the marketplace, schedules, international considerations, and so forth. It's a complex matrix. I can think of many examples, ranging from selecting aircraft (we all have our favorites), to deciding which cities to render in high detail, to how creative we get in developing scenarios for users to fly. Each decision involves many players, and if you adopt an "over my dead body" mentality, well, you just might get run over.

What are the advantages and disadvantages of creating a simulation rather than a game?

> On the one hand, creating a simulation is fairly straightforward. You look at the thing you're simulating and set out to emulate it in as much detail as possible. You don't have to create an entire world from a blank screen. On the other hand, you have to make a series of decisions about how to convert the experience in the real world to a computer screen, figure out how to re-create such details as cockpit controls, weather, etc. in a compelling way. I suppose the process is much like making a movie that involves depicting an historic event, period, or characters. You have to be realistic, but you also have to make

adjustments that deliver a compelling experience. And, of course, you have to do it all on budget and on time. It's not an infinite sandbox.

Creating a game that's really a fantasy is different in some ways. For example, you have more freedom to create a world and situations that don't correspond to anything that anyone has ever seen or experienced on Earth. But you still have many of the same technical and practical constraints. It's rather like the difference between filming a documentary and making a drama.

What would Williams like to see more of with today's simulations on the PC?

I'd love to have more advanced technology available at a reasonable price so that users could have a wider field of view, more realistic controls, and a better sense of motion. Whether you're flying, driving, or zooming through space, the limitations of today's computer displays, joysticks, etc. take something away from the experience.

Exactly how important is a good user interface (UI) in a game such as *Flight Simulator 2002*?

A good UI is always important. Experienced users figure things out on their own, but when you're trying to bring new users into the fold, it's critical to make everything inviting and easy to use. It's also very important to make sure that people can find all the cool stuff to do, especially when creating a simulation that's as complex and detailed as *Flight Simulator*. The UI takes the place of the instructor in the real world of flying, where you have someone who points things out and helps you understand how everything works. Creating a useful, compelling UI is one of the hardest tasks we face.

For Williams' advice on how flight simulations are properly tested before they fly off the shelves, turn to Chapter 17.

As real as it gets? Take a gander at this screen shot from the latest Microsoft *Flight Simulator* product for the PC. Bruce Williams says creating a compelling user interface is one of the team's biggest challenges. To read up on how to create a good UI, jump over to Chapter 14.
(Used with permission by Microsoft Corp.)

Steve Hunt

So far, we've explored people sims and civilian aircraft sims, so now let's jump into aerial combat sims. Before Rage Software shut its doors in January of 2003, Steve Hunt wore many hats at the U.K. company, including project manager, lead designer, and programmer. Past products include a handful of games for the Atari in the 1980s (such as *River Rally* and *Planet Attack*). Then it was all combat flight simulations in the 1990s and 2000s: *EF2000*, *Super EF2000*, *F-22 ADF*, *Total Air War,* and *Eurofighter Typhoon*.

Although most of Hunt's advice in this book falls into the programming chapters, he says that to be a successful game designer, you need to find the right balance between creating a fun product and creating a fun product that will sell:

> I think a good design has to take into account and mix two main things. The product is supposed to be entertaining to the player, and secondly to be successful from a business point of view. This might sound obvious, but I've seen many designs that are just showing off some technology rather than entertaining the player—it's very easy to fall into this one. From the business point of view, the game needs to make money; there's no point in designing a game that may sell well but is so expensive to develop that it never makes a profit.

> I think game designing is both an art and a science, and therefore you need to appreciate both sides to come up with a good design.

Hunt offers three pieces of advice for game designers:

1. Have a good core idea that's there to entertain the player. Don't fall into the trap of designing a big technology demo or a mishmash of games ideas in one.

2. Think of the business side. How much is this likely to cost, will it easily port to other platforms (this one is very important), how long will the product take to make, what are the big risks?

3. Believe in the game you design and know it inside out. Play it in your head so you can feel what your game will be like. Be able to answer any questions about it.

Skip up to Chapter 11 to read Steve Hunt's advice on programming aerial combat simulations.

Fred Markus, Rockstar San Diego

As director of game design at Rockstar San Diego (formerly Angel Studios), Fred Markus has overseen, programmed for, and designed a number of action sim products, including the *Midtown Madness* games for Microsoft and the popular *Smuggler's Run* titles for Take-Two Publishing. Markus chats about fleshing out the vision of the game:

> You don't know if an idea is going to be fun until you play it. Games are not made on paper, but with a joystick in your hands, looking at a screen. A good game design document [see Chapter 6, "Creating Characters, Storyboarding, and Design Documents," and Chapter 7, "Master Design Document

Template"] should be a list of questions, a list of experiments you want to try. Once you've collected enough really fun game experiments for the kind of title you want to work on, then and only then should you write a big fat document with storyline and character descriptions. It then becomes a production document. The world is full of good ideas. Only a few of them end up being really fun, though.

Although it's not an easy realization, Markus says it's also key to know when something isn't working out.

Be cold-blooded enough to give up your great ideas if they end up not working, and iterate on new ones as soon as possible. You have to be able to lose your ego-driven preconceptions. Only then can you progress and start working on new things. The faster you're able to recognize the fact that something is not as fun as you expected it to be, the more new experiments you'll be able to work on. You'll have more chances to find great and fun gameplay if you experiment a lot.

"Game designer" is a really bad way to define the person who needs to carry the vision of the game during the entire development but also lead his team. The game designer needs to make his team members do things they didn't know they could do. He needs to make them all participate in the creative process. A game designer is not a know-it-all. He'll get tremendous input from his teammates to discover new ideas and new perspectives, and he'll filter them.

Markus supports his advice with some examples from Rockstar San Diego:

Without any input from me, the team created some of the best races in *Midtown Madness*: the 18-wheeler, the bus. The "cops-and-robbers mode" was also a common effort in *Midtown Madness*. And it lead to *Smuggler's Run*. We thought that the most interesting thing in *Midtown Madness* would be racing, but in the end people love just to be able to drive around the cities freely!

How were some of the other Rockstar San Diego games conceived?

Some of the original seeds for these game ideas came from publisher needs or from observation. *GTI Club* from Konami inspired Microsoft, and we designed *Midtown Madness*. *Sky Pirates* is based on a great piece of hardware designed by Steven Spielberg. It needed a game that would fully use it and make people play a ride. The game was designed to accomplish just that. It seems that good games all play with feelings we all have deep in us. Maybe that's where we should get inspired.

> **NOTE**
>
> In Chapter 10, "Mission Design," Markus discusses what it takes to create fun and challenging missions in a game, details a couple of his personal favorites, and offers an opinion as to why so many games fail in this category.

On the key differences between creating games for a console versus a PC, Markus says it boils down to the target audience:

Good PC games sell worldwide, just like good console games. The games that don't are designed for a very specific audience. Consoles are mass-market, so if you want your game to be played, design it for everyone to play and not just hardcore gamers. Also, mouse and keyboard controls are really different from a joypad. You won't have access to hundreds of keys, which is a really good example of really bad game design, anyway!

Chapter 17 focuses on how to properly—and thoroughly—test your game prior to its release. Markus divulges how Rockstar San Diego approaches testing:

Focus groups are important. Get your audience to play your game and see how they react. It's really useful if you have enough experience to filter the good feedback from the bad! Bad feedback? "You know, you should really have a bunch of naked girls at the end of this level—that would be so cooool!"

Markus says knowing a lot of games won't necessarily make you a good game designer or director:

If you really want to make games, then you already know about all the authoring tools that are available out there and/or you've already started to make little game experiments. Showing us that you've already started to work on experiments would be the best way to get a job with us! Other than that, be open to suggestions and get ready to be a team leader: Making games is teamwork!

Ed Martin, Electronic Arts

We can't have a simulation section without chatting about America's fastest growing sport: NASCAR. Ed Martin happens to be the director of *NASCAR Thunder* production at Electronic Arts.

Needless to say, there are many budding game designers who'd love to create car sims or arcade-based driving games for a living. In this section, Martin opens up the floodgates and gives his opinion on what to do to maximize your success.

Realize that you are not the only audience for the game; the customers are the audience, and you need to do your best to balance your subjective opinions and desires from the objective of "what people are going to like."

Face it, not a single person you'll work with is actually going to have to buy a copy of the game you're working on. If you're interested in people buying and enjoying what you're creating, create it for the audience.

Now that's not to say that the designer/producer doesn't have a tremendously valuable perspective; in the end, we have to make all the calls, and we are in these positions because we know what the heck we're doing. But there's a fine line that constantly needs to be balanced. And it's incredibly tempting to head toward "the dark side." It's incredibly difficult to know where your own personal line is. There's vision and there's passion—those are the things that make the magic. But in all aspects of our lives, we all know that passion can get the best of you, and it can go too far. It's always a balance.

With *NASCAR Thunder 2002* as the shining example, Martin was asked to support his advice.

I've always said that I'd be the worst person in the world to create a Star Trek game. I'm a Trekker. I'd have a horrible time fighting to create the game I want versus the game the buyers want. I'd get totally caught up in the "Oh, my God! I'm on the set of Star Trek, and I get to sit in the captain's chair…this is SO cool!" (Yeah, I'm a geek.)

Don't get me wrong; I'm a big NASCAR fan. But to be honest, I didn't know a lot about the sport eight years ago when I first got involved in the video game side of it. But as soon as I got involved, I got it. It's a great sport filled with great people.

But I attribute a lot of my success to the fact that I'm not too much of a fan. I don't get star-struck around the celebrities in the sport, and I don't take advantage of the incredible access I get to all of it as part of my job. In the end, I'm there to do a job, just like the drivers are there to do a job.

What this gives me is a balanced perspective of what I think is cool and fun, but also the balanced insight of what the fans think is cool.

My favorite place at the track, believe it or not, is souvenir row: the row of trucks where all the teams sell their stuff. It's an incredible sight. Dozens and dozens of trucks lined up, and hundreds—thousands—of fans lining up to buy that latest Jeff Gordon die-cast; Dale Earnhardt, Jr. T-shirt; Tony Stewart hat; or Bobby Labonte jacket. Why are they all there? Why are they tripping over each other with credit cards to buy these things? That (understanding why), to me is the key to making a great game. Why? Well, in the end, all we're creating with the *NASCAR Thunder* franchise is an interactive, electronic "souvenir." We are giving the fans a really cool way to be more a part of the sport and perhaps closer to their favorite driver(s). Is that really all that different from buying that Richard Petty belt buckle? All the fans are there because the events that happen on the track are phenomenal entertainment; the drivers are cool role models and heroes. The rest of it is just a wide variety of ways to extend that enjoyment.

So, when I make my calls throughout *NASCAR Thunder*, I always keep "souvenir row" in mind. Not because we sell a lot of our products there (in fact, we don't—through the complexities of distribution, we're restricted at most at-track venues), but because those people are the fans who are looking to go beyond the on-track events and "take a piece of it home." We're creating one of those pieces that the fans can take home (of course, I think it's the coolest "piece"). Bet you never thought you'd see video games compared to Richard Petty's belt buckle, huh?

Martin was asked if he had any beefs when playing other NASCAR video games, and his response was a tad surprising, to say the least.

"It's funny, but I typically enjoy playing other NASCAR games more than I like playing my own," says Martin. He explains:

The fact of the matter is that by the time we're done with it, it's been in front of me orders of magnitude longer than any gamer typically spends with any game. I'm proud of it, I love it, but I've played it to death. Okay, yes, part of my enjoyment in playing other games is the feeling that "yeah, we did that better." But I'm always playing them to look for the things maybe they did better.

As a global answer, though, I'd have to say that the thing I typically like the least is when others just try to just copy what someone else has done without pushing the envelope to make something new, better, and different.

The world really doesn't need another NASCAR game where all you get to do is to pick a car, pick a track, drive fast, and turn left. I've been involved in making games that did that since 1994. Let those creative juices flow! Come up with new, cool, innovative ways to enjoy whatever you're presenting. There are unlimited things that we can do in the video game world that can't happen in the real world and/or things that we can do better in the video game world. Tap into those things; be creative; push the envelope; do something new and different. That's my challenge for every game. It makes it fun for me and it sure makes it fun for the gamers out there.

"All we're creating with the *NASCAR Thunder* franchise is an interactive electronic 'souvenir,'" says EA Sports' Martin. "We are giving the fans a really cool way to be more a part of the sport and perhaps closer to their favorite driver(s)."
Pictured here is *NASCAR Thunder 2003* for the Xbox platform.
(Used with permission by Electronic Arts, Inc.)

But a small designer/developer obviously won't get a NASCAR license, nor will they have a team of 50 people. What advice can Martin give for those who want to create a stock car racing game with only a couple of people? Perhaps a shareware release? Or a PDA game?

Well, back in 1994, there was a little 30-ish person company in Somerville, Massachusetts. They had some pretty cool 3D technology and a founder who had an incredible passion for racing. They didn't have a lot of money, nor did they have a huge team. I joined that place as employee #34. It was Papyrus (now part of Sierra/Vivendi). They got that NASCAR license, and the rest is history.

To me, the moral of that story is that timing and an idea are everything. You're right—it's highly unlikely that a small group is going to be able to get a NASCAR license today and take on the likes of EA, Sierra, and Infogrames. But why the hell would you want to? There's a lot more out there that we don't know and a lot more out there that we haven't done than there is that we do, and have.

"The world is full of knock-offs. Do something different. Take a different spin on things," encourages Martin.

> I think an amazing example of this is Will Wright. He created the *SimCity* franchise years ago. It got knocked-off to death, both within the franchise and by competitors. But then he took what was great, went in an amazing new direction, and created *The Sims*. That's now the best-selling PC game of all time."

Martin has an important caveat for new developers:

> Oh, and by the way, be very careful not to step on licensed properties. When you're dealing with things like Star Wars, the NFL, NASCAR, etc., you're talking about properties that are worth millions, maybe billions of dollars. You're dealing with properties that companies like EA pay an awful lot of money to license. The people or organizations that own those properties are very protective, and with good reason. So, you might be able to do a, let's say, shareware Star Trek game and stay under the radar for awhile. But if it takes off, you will get noticed and you will get some very unpleasant calls and letters— or worse. Be careful.

In Chapter 21, EA's Ed Martin offers more advice on the do's and don'ts of breaking into the biz.

Adventure Games

We can't forget this popular genre.

Tim Schafer, Double Fine Productions

One of the more eagerly anticipated console games for the fall of 2003 is *Psychonauts*, the latest project by game design veteran Tim Schafer.

Before leaving to start his own development company, Double Fine Productions, Tim Schafer spent the previous decade at LucasArts as a programmer and assistant designer on the first two *Secret of Monkey Island* games, co-designer and co-project leader on *Day of the Tentacle*, and designer/project leader on *Full Throttle* and *Grim Fandango*. Needless to say, Schafer has become somewhat of a legend to adventure game enthusiasts. Here, Schafer offers some advice on adventure game design and then chats about his latest game, what it's like to work on a console (rather than PC game development), and whether or not someone should start their own game company.

But first, Schafer spent some time discussing adventure game design for those looking to get into "interactive storytelling." Three golden rules for adventure game design, as advised by the master himself:

1. **Never stop playing games.** You have to have input. A lot of people in the games industry work too hard—all night and all day, sometimes for months on end. After a long day (and night) of making a game, the last thing you want to do when you get home is play one. But that's a

bad habit to get into. You have to keep playing. Playing games is what inspires you and what stimulates new ideas in your head, and it's easy to forget that.

2. **Diversify your sources.** Don't only play games. Watch movies, read books, see shows. And not just science fiction and fantasy. One of the biggest problems with games is that the people who make them seem to be limited in their interests. There are a lot of other cool things going on in the world besides science fiction and fantasy, and very few of them are being properly plundered for game ideas.

3. **No ice levels.** Come on. That's so played out.

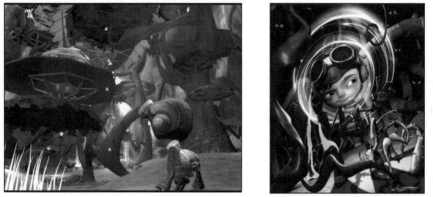

Veteran game designer Tim Schafer has this to say about his latest action/adventure, *Psychonauts*: "The adults will get all the jokes, and the kids will just laugh at the crazy animation; and if you don't like either, then you can have fun blasting enemies."
For more on the Xbox game, visit `www.xbox.com/psychonauts`.
(Used with permission by Microsoft Corp.)

Schafer supports these words with examples from his personal and professional experiences:

1. Have you ever finished *Skies of Arcadia*? You think that was easy?

2. *Grim Fandango* was inspired by the folklore of Mexico. Folklore is just one area of culture that's not raided enough for games. And Mexican folklore is just one area within that realm. There are a million folk tales outside of Arthurian legend that are worth telling.

3. The only ice I've ever put in a game was that frozen hamster in *Day of the Tentacle*. And I'm very, very sorry about it.

What are Schafer's pet peeves with today's crop of adventure games?

As far as classic adventure games on the PC, well, I really haven't even played one in awhile. Are there any? They just haven't kept up with the times. Ever since *Tomb Raider*, *Final Fantasy IV*, and even *Super Mario 64*, it's been apparent that you can explore fantastic worlds and experience a story without putting up with clunky interfaces; lethargic pacing; and obscure, self-indulgent, impossible puzzles.

Everyone paying attention?

Could this be the reason why adventure games aren't as hot in North America as they once were? Says Schafer:

> I really think the adventure game market hasn't shrunk. It just hasn't grown as much as the rest of the games industry. There are probably just as many people wanting them as always. But unfortunately, there were only 100,000 of those people max, ever. Hmmm…of course, there is that damn *Myst* example, which always throws off any adventure game discussion. I think if someone makes a really great adventure game now and it has adequate commercial hooks in it, people will show up and buy it.

At the heart of a good adventure game is a lovable main character and some challenging and entertaining puzzles. In Chapter 6 and Chapter 9, "Puzzle Design," Tim Schafer offers some tips, tricks, and techniques on storyboarding, creating a successful protagonist, and infusing puzzles into your adventure game.

Okay, now let's get down to business about Schafer's latest project: *Psychonauts*. What can a budding designer learn from this game?

> I think *Psychonauts* shows that video games let you take your strangest, most surreal ideas and present them in a way that is incredibly accessible to a wide audience.

> The adults will get all the jokes, and the kids will just laugh at the crazy animation; and if you don't like either, then you can have fun blasting enemies. I also hope to show that you can take the simple mechanics of games—puzzles, combat, power-ups, collecting, etc.—and use them to explore psychological themes more meaningfully than we've been led to expect from games. ("Okay, the theme here is BANANAS. This game is all about how much everybody wants bananas.")

Schafer explains why *Psychonauts* won "Best Original Game" at E3 2002 (www.e3awards.com). What makes it unique, and is unique good?

> I think we won "Best Original Game" at E3 2002 because people responded to the uniqueness of our idea.

> The press will almost always react to a unique game because they have to look at so many games a week that they all start to look the same. When one comes along that looks different, everybody gets excited. But you have to watch out—the public doesn't always share their enthusiasm. You can get the press' attention by being different, but when it comes time to ship, being different isn't enough. You have to have the gameplay to match.

Schafer started out creating content for computer gamers, and now *Psychonauts* is an exclusive Microsoft Xbox game. He was asked about the obvious and perhaps not-so-obvious differences between creating a console game and a PC game (in light of both technical differences and game design).

> I think console game design is more rigorous. Your designs have to be tighter, technically and creatively. This demand comes from the limitations of the hardware, but also from the expectations of the audience. For instance, the amount of available memory on consoles has always been less than on the PC, so you have to plan your memory usage more carefully. This is a pain, but it leads to a more efficient

engine in the end, so it's a good thing. Likewise, when designing gameplay, you have to remember that PC players are a more patient group than console players. PC users are used to installing software and troubleshooting compatibility issues. They don't like bugs and blue-screen crashes, but they are used to them, and I think they take that attitude into their gameplay experience. When things are weird or confusing or have lags or pauses in a PC game, the player is more likely to work around the problem or wait for things to pick up than a console player. A console player wants progress and action at all times. No lags. No downtime. No waiting. So you have to cut all the fat out of your gameplay experience. Take out the waiting and the long expository cut scenes, and as far as expecting them to read a manual? Forget about it. And if a console game crashed on a console player, I think his head would explode. This tightening of design and code leads to better games, I believe.

In Chapter 21, Schafer reveals all his secrets—no, not his personal ones—about how to get a job in the video game industry!

Denis Dyack, Silicon Knights

Denis Dyack is the founder of the Canadian-based Silicon Knights, a second-party developer for Nintendo. Dyack served as director for its latest game, *Eternal Darkness: Sanity's Requiem*. Some of his previous works include *Blood Omen: Legacy of Kain*, *Dark Legions*, *Fantasy Empires*, and *Cyber Empires*. Silicon Knights recently announced it will be bringing *Metal Gear Solid: The Twin Snakes* to the Nintendo GameCube system.

Dyack has been creating games for more than 11 years, and he has this to say to those who are just starting out:

> ➤ Always design something you like and are passionate about.
>
> ➤ Have a clear vision of the game.
>
> ➤ Understand that the content is the key.

Having a passion and a love for your work is very important. The game design should always try to incorporate something new. When doing this, there is no formula for creating something you know everyone will like; so by doing something you like, you will at least be sure to please one person. Passion and a love for the work are the keys to creating something successful. Remember that technology is secondary to the content that you provide to the gamer. Despite what many people believe, the gaming industry is an entertainment industry and not a technological industry; therefore, you should focus on the content.

So, does Dyack have any beefs with today's games?

Many developers place too much emphasis on technology and not enough focus on quality, substance, and content. Most games today are built like cars with a nice exterior but nothing under the hood. They may look good at first glance, but once you drive them, the flaws are obvious and apparent. To avoid these pitfalls, always strive to create something meaningful in your work. Remember that there needs to be a message in your work.

In terms of inspiration, Dyack says the roots of *Eternal Darkness* were the "classics." He explains:

> In order to create something new, we believe we have to look to the past and incorporate our knowledge of the arts into the modern nonlinear genre of video games. The structure of Shakespearean plays was a great inspiration, as well as other classical writers. When Shakespeare would write a play, he would write it to reach as many people as possible. He would write dirty jokes for everyone who was inebriated in the front rows of the theater, and he would also write cerebral metaphors for the aristocracy in the balconies. All this was done to please as many people as possible. We believe that if video games are truly to become the dominant form of entertainment in the next century, we also should have this goal.

Dyack says these three simple rules should ensure your success in this industry:

- ➤ Stay true to yourself.

- ➤ Stay true to others.

- ➤ Never forget that the secret to any success is 1% inspiration and 99% perspiration.

Eternal Darkness: Sanity's Requiem begins in the year 2000, as the young Alexandra Roivas is called to her grandfather's estate following his brutal murder. She decides to stay in his Rhode Island mansion to find out what led up to his tragic death and unknowingly stumbles upon a detailed family history that spans 20 centuries.
(Used with permission by Nintendo of America, Inc.)

Phil Saunders, Presto Studios

Phil Saunders is the creative director at Presto Studios, the game development house responsible for such beloved adventure games as *The Journeyman Project (1, 2, and 3)* and most recently, *Myst III: Exile* (2001) for the PC and a quirky action game called *Whacked!* (2002) for the Xbox.

Challenged to explain why adventure games are so hard to get right, Saunders shares some helpful tips on creating a successful adventure game:

1. Always role-play the user. As the designer of an adventure game, you already know everything. You know how the puzzles are solved, how the environments are laid out, and how the story will progress. Essentially, you know the secrets of the game. It's too easy for a designer to make assumptions for what players are going to know and what their experiences and backgrounds are. You can't take for granted that the average player is going to understand the principle of a fulcrum in a lever, for instance, or the relationship of one area of a level to another… Clear your mind of all the foreknowledge that you have and truly try to experience the game from the inside, from the player's point of view.

   The end result of this should be that you know when you need to make the path more clear, and when you need to educate players in order to properly equip them with the intellectual tools and background experience to solve the puzzle set in front of them.

2. Design your story, gameplay, and environments organically. In the real world, obstacles to a goal come out of environment and circumstance. Environment is also the product of the people who created it, while circumstances emerge from the interaction of people with each other and with their environment. All of these elements are interconnected. To create a seamless and immersive gameplay experience, you need to develop each of these major elements—story, gameplay, and environment design—simultaneously, so that the ideas of each one can inform and develop the other.

   When you first start out, explore story ideas, gameplay structure, and aesthetic direction at the same time. Don't let anything restrict your imagination for what your environments could be. In parallel to that, write different story directions as well. Sometimes the writing and the design will feed off of each other and you'll get these really interesting ideas. Sometimes they'll be completely separate and isolated from any dramatic context, but just suggest some really intriguing possibilities. If the story is written, then your gameplay and aesthetic design have already been constrained. Your creative freedom has been inhibited. While you're designing, the writer will feed off of these visuals and perhaps find inspiration from your designs to continue the story in a certain direction. At the same time, story ideas become a launching point for potential visuals; and throughout this gameplay structure, ideas and puzzle ideas can lead to both intriguing plot lines and compelling settings. When everything comes together at the end of the process, what you've created is a world where the obstacles that create the gameplay emerge naturally from a story that fits the world in which it's being told.

3. A game is a series of meaningful choices in order to reach a clear goal. To create an immersive experience, it's important to make sure that players feel invested in what they're doing. Even games such as *Myst*, which relies on freedom of exploration and discovery, need to make you feel that this wandering has a purpose. Otherwise, the player can take or leave the experience at leisure and may never return to complete the game. As soon as possible in the experience, you should make sure that the player knows what he or she is there for. What the purpose is. The choices made and the puzzles solved also need to have meaning. Each element should tie to the larger goal and feel like a significant decision that has consequences to the success or failure of the journey.

Using *Myst III: Exile* as an example, Saunders puts this advice into perspective:

> The really early decision that we made in the design of *Myst III: Exile* was to try to create a story context that would offer us the opportunity to create a lot of deliberate puzzles. It's very, very difficult to create challenges that are integral to a story without them feeling out of place. So the Lesson Age concept of J'nanin gave us a great foundation of these worlds that were created in order to teach someone something. And in teaching them, you've essentially got a basis for a puzzle.

Is anything wrong with today's adventure games?

> I think a lot of adventure games lose focus on creating an immersive experience that tells a story. In the wake of the success of the original *Myst*, a lot of game designers felt that simply creating a cinematic experience, occasionally interrupted by a deliberate puzzle or two, was a surefire recipe for success. What they missed was the nature of the game, in that it's an interactive experience. One that, at its best, makes you feel like you're an integral part of the unfolding of the story, not just a casual observer. In recent years, adventure games have blended in action elements in real time to create a much more visceral experience, but often at the expense of depth of storytelling. I believe we're still trying to find the balance between the two, but when we finally succeed, the result will be a tremendously fulfilling game.

Speaking of puzzles—a key component of most adventure games—Phil Saunders discusses, at great length, what makes for a good adventure game puzzle and cites some examples from Presto Studios' work. Head on over to Chapter 9 to read this enlightening excerpt from the interview.

Saunders also chats about creating a design document and the importance of storyboarding in Chapter 6, developing a good user interface in Chapter 14, and ways to break into the industry in Chapter 21.

Ragnar Tørnquist, Funcom

Ragnar Tørnquist may not yet be a household name in the adventure game industry. At Funcom, he is a creative director and lead designer, with a number of titles under his belt—including one of the deepest and most gratifying computer games to debut in a long, long while: *The Longest Journey*. Along with creating *The Longest Journey* (and its upcoming sequel, *The Longest Journey 2*), Tørnquist has recently worked on the story for *Anarchy Online* and another online multiplayer game, *Midgard*.

It seems that Ragnar Tørnquist has quite a lot to say on the subject of adventure game design—and if you've ever played *The Longest Journey*, you'll know what a lot of text is! Without further ado, he first discusses some key rules of good adventure game design. To Tørnquist, it's a focus on interaction, immersion, and storytelling, in that order:

> Engage the player with constant interaction. In other words, never let the player wander about with no idea of what to do or where to go. Make the interaction between the player and the game the driving force behind the story, not the other way around. Successful adventures are great games first, great stories second. The interaction should never feel arbitrary or unnecessarily complicated; while players enjoy a challenge, they won't tolerate artificial barriers constructed to slow down process and extend playing time.

"Interaction also means variety; ideally, you want to challenge the player mentally, physically, and emotionally," advises Ragnar Tørnquist, creator of *The Longest Journey*, a game that touches players on all of these levels. Read more about the game at `www.longestjourney.com`.
(Used with permission by Funcom, Inc.)

Immersion means that you have to create an entire living world for your adventure game, a place that feels as real as the real world. It doesn't matter if you're dealing with fantasy, science fiction, historical, or contemporary settings. No matter how fundamentally "unreal" the setting is, players need to feel like they're inhabiting a real place, with an internally consistent logic. The *Monkey Island* series had a thoroughly defined setting, and you never questioned the existence of any of the eccentric characters Guybrush met, the hysterical situations he got into, or the absurd problems he was faced with. *Shenmue Dreamcast* also had an extraordinary sense of reality to it, and every action Ryo had to perform—locate a specific person in town, beat up some gangsters, or work for a week hauling cargo—stayed true to the setting. While the former was an entirely imaginary place and the latter was firmly based on 1980s Japan but with mythological and mystical overtones, they both made sense; playing either game, you felt as though you were in a real place.

Last but not least: The story is what gives an adventure a real sense of purpose. It's not about getting the highest score or killing the most aliens; it's about finding out what happens next [WHN]. WHN is an incredibly strong tool to have and something that makes adventure games potentially the most intriguing game genre, especially for the casual gamer who won't naturally gravitate toward games; he or she could choose to go to the movies or watch TV instead, and it's all about what provides the most entertainment, where to find the most intriguing story. Stories are, of course, an important part of our culture, and if you manage to hook people early on, to get them to wonder about the next scene, what's behind that door, where the story and the characters will lead you—in effect, WHN—that's the strongest drug of all.

He tacks on one last thought on the matter:

It's quite telling that, in recent years, most (if not all) genres—[even] bar sports games and simulators—have introduced the story as one of their main features. I like to think that the adventure invented the story in games, as well as the puzzle, and that other genres have been slowly but surely gravitating toward the kind of experience adventure games have given players for decades.

Tørnquist says that every puzzle in *The Longest Journey* was devised to be an integral part of the storyline, but admits that he didn't always follow his own advice:

Part of the fun in playing *The Longest Journey* is just to wander around exploring the diverse environments, meeting strange new characters, picking up bits and pieces of the background story, and learning about April Ryan's destiny—immersion, story, and interaction. But, of course, puzzles are at the core of the traditional adventure, and there was a definite focus on giving players a variety of challenges, from conversational puzzles to logical challenges.

While Tørnquist talks more about puzzle design in Chapter 9, the following anecdote explains why he believes *The Longest Journey* to be a well-designed puzzle:

In one particular scene, April—in other words, the player—had to figure out how to get inside a cinema. The reason April (and the player) wanted to get inside that cinema was, essentially, WHN—what happens next. The player knew there was someone inside the cinema who could explain a lot of the strange events that had been happening to April, and this provided a strong incentive for solving a somewhat convoluted series of puzzles, including an undercover detective, a dimwitted theatre employee, some candy, a fuse box, a trashcan, and a lighter. The interaction with the environment and the characters had to be interesting in and of itself; it had to provide a challenge that made sense. But the motivation for taking up the challenge was in the story, and the fun and excitement was in the immersion: the dingy street and alley, the surly detective, and the dangerously stupid employee.

Any beefs with today's adventure games? "Most current adventure games look to the past rather than the future," says Tørnquist. He expands:

While it's good to see the odd traditional adventure from time to time (*The Longest Journey*, for example, was purposely designed to be "old school"), I think the market at large is looking for something more revolutionary in terms of immersion, storytelling, characterization, and (most importantly) interaction. I'm not talking about games that require the latest hardware; often, adventure games will appeal to the more casual gamer who may not care to invest in expensive technology just to play the odd game or two. I'm talking about games that push the barriers in other ways, like *System Shock 2*, *Deus Ex*, and (on the consoles), *Shenmue*, *Metal Gear Solid*, *Silent Hill*, and the *Final Fantasy* series. In my opinion, these games are (to a greater or lesser degree) adventure games. They may contain role-playing or action elements, but the focus of these games is on storytelling, immersing the player in a world, creating believable environments and characters. These games introduce obstacles for the player that don't necessarily require violence to get past, but [do need] a great deal of lateral thinking. All of these games have inventories that the player can manipulate. Most of them have extensive cut scenes and lots of dialogue. In other words, they fulfill all the requirements of the "traditional adventure," except that in a lot of ways they take the genre to the next level by introducing fresh play mechanics, injecting the adventure with a much-needed shot of adrenaline and a healthy dose of invention.

Tørnquist believes that the future of the adventure game isn't just offline, or on the consoles—it's also online:

Huge environments where thousands of people can interact with each other; with NPCs [non-player characters]; and with a constantly evolving, and constantly surprising, environment…done right, this will definitely give adventures a whole new lease on life.

I really do think that, consciously or not, gamers will always gravitate toward the kind of immersive experience an adventure game provides—though they may not be aware of it because the games won't be marketed as such. Instead, games will increasingly be recognized as hybrid genres, mixing role-playing, action, strategy, puzzles, and plain old adventures to provide the most intriguing gaming worlds possible.

Chapters such as 5 and 8, "Level Design," include more words of wisdom from Ragnar Tørnquist. Be sure to read his thoughts on creating a successful character and writing good adventure game puzzles, respectively.

Ron Gilbert, Hulabee Entertainment

Veteran Ron Gilbert is personally responsible for many of our best-loved computer games, such as *Maniac Mansion*, the *Monkey Island* series, and a handful of children's adventure games for Humongous Entertainment. He left Humongous in 2000 to start a new company: Hulabee Entertainment.

Here he talks about the root of it all—inspiration.

Sometimes it comes from playing someone else's game. It may come from watching a movie or reading a book—just something will give you a spark. Adventure games are built on stories, and you must approach the game design from that angle, as if you were writing a script or a book.

Be aware of who the audience is; if you're making a game just to please yourself, you may not be too successful unless you're really in sync with the market. But, at the same time, it has to come from your heart and not your head. If you do market research, it may come out too much from the head.

Are there any examples Gilbert can give, based on his past works? How did the *Monkey Island* idea come about? According to Gilbert, it was a bit of market watching (there were no pirate games of this kind), but it was primarily a personal preference:

> I wanted to make a fantasy game since *Maniac Mansion* was set in a contemporary world, and I liked pirates. It took me a couple of years for *Monkey Island*, actually. I wrote five stories before I settled on one. But on the other hand, *Monkey Island II* was done in less than a year.

We hear from Gilbert again in Chapter 6 about creating a hit character, so stay "tooned!"

Puzzle Games

Many gamers still like these more traditional types of games.

Harry Gottlieb, Jellyvision

If you've enjoyed even a round of the irreverent *You Don't Know Jack* trivia games (and if you haven't, shame on you), you can thank Jellyvision founder and chief designer Harry Gottlieb. Along with the many, many incarnations of *You Don't Know Jack* (*YDKJ*), Gottlieb and his savvy team of developers also created questions for the *Who Wants to Be a Millionaire* games, *Smush*, and most recently, MSN Zone's *OutSmart!* (www.outsmart.com)

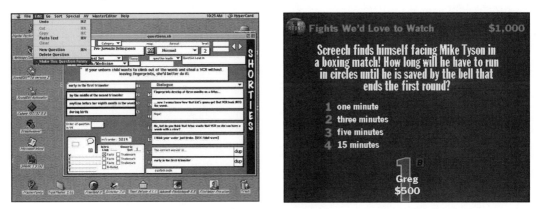

Want a peek behind the scenes of the *You Don't Know Jack* series? You got it. Here's an image of a program Jellyvision uses, called "FunkMaster," which allows them to quickly write, edit, and record all Jack questions. On the Edit menu, a menu item called Make This Question Funny adds words to the end of the question, such as "...with a banana." Also shown, a screen grab from *You Don't Know Jack: Sports.*
(Used with permission by Jellyvision, Inc.)

When asked to provide advice for those looking to make interactive trivia games, Gottlieb says to remember that "the game's the thing." That is, expensive graphics mean nothing if you don't have a game that's fun to play in black-and-white with rudimentary graphics. He adds, "Don't start coding until the game works with your friends sitting around a table with paper, pencils, a whiteboard, and squeezy toys."

What's the most challenging component of creating a trivia game such as *YDKJ*, and how did Gottlieb & Co. overcome it? Is it making it fast and flashy? Writing the questions? Hiring a good voice actor? Eliminating repetition among the questions?

Frankly, doing almost everything on the first volume of *You Don't Know Jack* was hard. But the hardest part for others to replicate is the writing. When companies create programs that involve language and communication (whether it's a TV show or an interactive game), usually lots of money is spent on high-end production, and people forget about the pivotal role of writing. I say pivotal because with any form of mass communication, the foundation is almost always writing. The best technology and creative talent in the world can't make a great program with a bad script.

Make games that you want to play yourself. The original creative team for YDKJ didn't particularly like trivia games, so we asked ourselves, "How can we make a trivia game that we would like?" The answer: Make it funny.

Alexey Pajitnov, Microsoft

Alexey Pajitnov is the famous designer responsible for *Tetris*, one of the most addictive video games of all time. Pajitnov moved from Russia to work for the Microsoft Games group in Redmond, Washington to create all-new puzzle games.

Pajitnov divulges his top three game design secrets and states that he adheres to them when creating puzzle games:

> ➤ **Nothing is too simple.** Pajitnov mentions this first because "When you get too close to your work and you're involved with it for so long, things tend to look simple to you." With the puzzle games Pajitnov has worked on in the past, everything looked to be trivial after a while, but he later realized that someone who hasn't seen the game yet would likely find it challenging.

> ➤ **Don't neglect the hard puzzles, either.** "No matter how difficult the task, there will be the player who figures it out," says Pajitnov. He admits that this seems to contradict his first point, but they're both correct. "Don't neglect the hard puzzles because you don't think someone will figure them out; there will always be a smarter gamer than you."

> ➤ **Is the game fun?** Pajitnov believes that if you don't get fun from your game, nobody will. "I tell all three of these things to my team all the time."

What about inspiration? Is there a way to find it? Pajitnov says, "Inspiration cannot be rationalized. It usually comes during the work; I'm never waiting for it." He continues:

Ideas are everywhere. Usually, I get them from other board game puzzles. I have a huge collection of puzzles in my office. I like Rubik's Cube, 3D rotational puzzles, putting pieces together, or jigsaw puzzles. The idea doesn't come by itself; you need to keep working. That's my motto—work all the time. If you don't have very good inspiration, try to improve what you can. If you sit, it won't come.

How was *Tetris* conceived? Pajitnov laughs:

> It was in 1984; it was a boring period for me. I didn't have good ideas. But I was always playing this game, it's a well-known puzzle where I lived, called Pentomino. It's a set of 12 shapes or pieces you can make out of 5 squares, and the puzzle is to put all the pieces in a box of 10 × 6, if I recall. And this looks like a strange kind of jigsaw puzzle. I love this puzzle. It takes about 40 minutes to finish it—for experienced people, maybe 10 minutes. I decided this was very good and tried to make a two-player game. I started programming all of this (but 5 squares was too much, so I cut it to 4 pieces). I realized that it looked funny. And then I made it a real-time game. So that's it. It was finished for the PC in 1985. It was called *Tetris* from the very beginning.

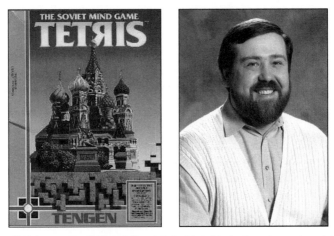

Ever wanted to know how *Tetris* was conceived? Alexey Pajitnov tells the tale in this chapter, so be sure to read about the origins of one of the greatest—and most recognizable—video games of all time. One of the original boxes of the game from the 1980s.
(Used with permission by Microsoft Corp.)

Pajitnov discusses the hardest part about bringing an idea into reality:

> [When] you start the professional game design, you've got to make a long list of decisions. That's the most torturing part of the process. You then need to decide to do something you don't like. Intuitively, you know you can't put in a complicated score system or can't make people play too long without any success, so there are intuitive rules and you need to follow them. Sometimes you need to give up cool small ideas, and that's probably the most painful and difficult part about the process.

Assuming that you've got the idea fleshed out on paper, and you've made some cuts for the sake of gameplay, what's next? Pajitnov says to get some code up and running. "And then you'll know if you're satisfied with the way the game mechanic works." He expands:

> Work out the main purpose of the game. Then you can add more parts as they come, but you need to develop the game, put in the small features such as power-ups, and so forth. It's quite boring!

Do puzzle games need to be in 3D these days? How about multiplayer games? Does a single-player game stand a chance in the 21st century? Pajitnov's reply:

> 2D games still have great chances. The technology has been changing dramatically for the last 10 years, but not the human brain. And there are lots of people enjoying the Solitaire games, but multiplayer mode is such a great advantage that it's a crime to skip it.

Finally, a few notes on user interfaces. Pajitnov says, "This is not a technical problem; it's a psychological one. There is nothing too simple; nothing too primitive. The designer who works on the game for weeks or months becomes so involved in it, it may seem elementary to you." He cautions game designers at this stage to take a step back and make sure that the game is easily accessible for all:

> Some designers make it good for the people who make the game and not the gamers. I call this "professional adoration"—you have an illusion that the interface is simple and it's hard to get rid of it, so you need to put the prototype out into a play testing environment. This cures it immediately. You'll know what to do. And it's usually not too hard to fix it. Take yourself away from it and see how [users] play and what kind of trouble they have with the game. You'll immediately have a clear picture.

Toshihiro Nagoshi, Amusement Vision/Sega

Super Monkey Ball was one of the first (and one of the most critically acclaimed) games for the Nintendo GameCube platform. Formerly known as AM4, Amusement Vision is the development team at Sega responsible for this "party" puzzle game—and its sequel, *Super Monkey Ball 2*—under the advisement of President Toshihiro Nagoshi.

For the purposes of this book, Nagoshi shares with us his top pieces of advice for those looking to be a success in the video game industry.

> Discover how to establish your vision, keeping in line with one goal. This can be said mainly about game design, but also about programming. At the beginning of a project, it is common to have a lack of clear goals, even if you know how to create something in a technical sense. You need a stance in which you always are working toward a common goal, and make sure all the content supports that goal.

Nagoshi says to "keep professional awareness toward deadlines," although he admits this is tough to be aware of at first:

> When you are starting out, even if you can understand the concept of deadlines, you may not know that it is not enough for you to just complete your work on time in an ordinary sense. Once you become a professional and you are surrounded by other strong competitive companies, you realize that it is important for you to aim at further efficiency, while at the same time you handle your work at hand.

Nagoshi says to "think about relationships between vision and the professional awareness":

> These two skills can be considered the minimum requirements for becoming a game developer, but are not things learned in school. The notion of time limits and establishment of vision always go together. If your vision is weak, it takes a lot of time, and content will be thin. But when you have a clear vision, that problem can be solved. In the end, it is most important to understand the significance of this relationship.

Where does *Super Monkey Ball* fit into this equation?

> First, as a basic vision for the game, we took the concept that people purely and simply enjoy rolling a ball. Then, we made it clear that we would adopt ideas required in this basic concept, but deny everything that would hinder it. We made the whole game—from project planning to design to programming—follow this style. Even though this is a simple awareness, it is nonetheless the most effective instruction in group work.

So, have you ever considered creating a deep and immersive role-playing game (RPG)? What about a massively multiplayer online world such as *EverQuest* or Star *Wars Galaxies: An Empire Divided*? Read the next chapter for RPG Game Design 101.

Chapter 5

General Game Design: Role-Playing Games (RPGs) and Persistent Online Worlds

Without a doubt, the genre of role-playing games (RPGs) is one of the most popular on the planet. And for good reason: RPGs appeal to gamers of all ages and both genders, they're enjoyed by both console players and PC gamers, the stories usually have universal appeal, and RPGs combine a deep story and character growth with combat and puzzle-solving. What more can you ask?

This chapter discusses RPG game development at great length, plus the latter portion looks at persistent online worlds for multiplayer fanatics. These include RPGs such as the smash hit *EverQuest*, as well as other genres entering the fray.

Go forth, brave knight.

Role-Playing Games

Creating a fun and challenging RPG is not going to be a walk in the park. So take heed of the following advice offered by some of the world's wisest gaming sages.

Bill Roper, Blizzard Entertainment

As Vice President of Blizzard North in San Mateo, California, Bill Roper oversees and manages all external projects, coordinates internal development teams, and heads Blizzard's project oversight teams. Most recently, he was instrumental in shaping the direction of *WarCraft III: Reign of Chaos*. Oh, and you may have heard of some of these *little* projects that Roper has worked on in the past: *Diablo* (producer), *Diablo II* (senior producer), *Starcraft* (producer), *Starcraft: Brood War* (executive producer), and *WarCraft II: Beyond the Dark Portal* (executive producer).

THE EXPERTS

- Bill Roper, Blizzard Entertainment
- Matt Householder, Blizzard North
- Tim Cain, Troika Games
- Chris Taylor, Gas Powered Games
- Todd Howard, Bethesda Softworks
- Warren Spector, Ion Storm Austin
- Ray Muzyka and Greg Zeschuk, BioWare
- Harvey Smith, Ion Storm Austin
- Brad McQuaid, Sigil Games Online
- Richard "Lord British" Garriott, NCsoft
- Michael Waite, Electronic Arts
- Will Wright, Maxis Software
- Gordon Walton, Maxis Software
- Craig Alexander, Electronic Arts/Westwood Studios
- Shane Dabiri, Blizzard Entertainment

Needless to say, Roper has picked up on a number of tricks and techniques over the years and was kind enough to share them with us here in detail. First on the agenda is to discuss some important pieces of advice when it comes to working on your first game. The following are Roper's top three:

➤ **Simple interface.** The way that players interact with the game should be as easy to understand and use as possible. This means that whenever possible there should be no hidden elements to the way a player makes something happen. If you need to open an inventory screen for your character in an RPG, make sure there's an easy and understandable way to do so with the mouse, in a logical place in your interface. Although having keyboard shortcuts for advanced users is acceptable and encouraged, you shouldn't require someone to memorize a cryptic keystroke combination to access features in the game. Keeping the interface simple and clean in design is key to making the game accessible to any player. A complex interface can be daunting for novice gamers, even if it's well-laid-out. Manipulating the game, whether commanding massive armies or a single character, should be as intuitive and easy as possible.

➤ **Easy learning curve.** A gradual and integrated learning curve will get players into your game quickly and help them master the intricacies of more advanced strategies as they play. Make the first goals of the game easy to accomplish while not making them trivial. Next, give the player an early reward for his success as a means of positive reinforcement and, if possible, as a way to teach him even more about the game. Then, slowly add more complex situations and commands into the player's palette through the building of the story and basic gameplay mechanic. The goal is to let players build their skills through practical application that moves the entire game forward. And before they know it, they'll be able to utilize more intricate tactics than they first thought possible.

➤ **Fun factor.** While this would seem to be a natural requirement of a game, it's important to make sure that it's fun to play. Don't get caught up in the technology you're creating or the feature set that you've spent weeks designing. If you play the game and it isn't fun, you have to have the courage to change it. Many ideas seem great until they're put into practice and then they fall flat. It's vital to be able to stay fluid and alter your implementation of every element of the game to ensure that it's a fun and entertaining experience. If a game has stunning 3D graphics, fully destructible terrain, intuitive AI, an exhaustive technology tree, full surround sound, and an orchestral score recorded with the London Symphony Orchestra, but it's not fun to play, it will sit on store shelves and—worse yet—player's shelves.

On the topic of good game design, Bill Roper instructs readers not to get caught up in the technology—the gameplay is much more important: "By definition, a game is an activity engaged in for amusement. It's as simple as that." Seen here is a shot from *Diablo II*.
(Used with permission by Blizzard Entertainment, Inc.)

Can Roper pass the test by applying his top three pieces of game design advice to his work at Blizzard Entertainment?

> ➤ Simple interface: *Diablo*. The *Diablo* series is a good example of an intuitive interface that's easy to use. If you want to walk somewhere, just select the target with your mouse and click. If you want to fight a monster, just select the target with your mouse and click. If you want to open a chest or a door, just select the target with your mouse and click. Opening your character's inventory or statistic sheet is as easy as clicking a button onscreen. Using potions is also done through a simple mouse click. Although there are keyboard shortcuts for the vast majority of these actions, one of our goals was to ensure that you could play and win the game using only the mouse.

> ➤ Easy learning curve: *WarCraft II and Starcraft*. With *WarCraft II* and *Starcraft*, we worked hard to provide a gradual learning curve that showed players how to use our interface while introducing them to the basics of our resource model, technology tree, building construction, and unit production before they ever have to engage in combat. Once the basics of building and running a base of operations is under the player's belt, we slowly bring in the elements of scouting and basic combat. This then naturally leads into more complex tactics, such as cloaking and detection, multiple attack fronts, and "spells." Next, we mix in the concept of using

more advanced units and units of different sides (or races), and over the course of numerous missions we have given the player a wide variety of skills and knowledge from which to draw upon. Finally, we allow players to test and hone their proficiency with the game against other players from around the world over Battle.net, making for a never-ending learning experience. We strive to make our games easy to learn and difficult to master, hoping that gamers will enjoy the challenge of getting better and better, especially against others.

➤ Fun factor: All games. We have thrown out more artwork, code, and design ideas than I could have ever imagined possible in the pursuit of making our games as fun as possible. We have even canceled projects that we felt were not living up to the standards both we and the fans of our games expected. Sometimes these are relatively minor things, like the maximum number of players in a game of *WarCraft II*. Other times, it's deceptively complex, as in how much damage a Terran Marine does against flying units. There are even times when we have to make massive changes, like when we changed the original *Diablo* from turn-based to real-time. In every case, the decision was made to make the game fun, and this is why we take so much time and place so much effort into the final balance and polish of our games.

> **NOTE**
> In Chapter 3, "General Game Design: Strategy Games," Blizzard's Bill Roper chats in-depth about real-time strategy game design and the ups and downs of developing an epic game such as *WarCraft III: Reign of Chaos*.

Are RPGs more difficult to create than other kinds of computer games? "The massive amount of content creation required for an RPG is difficult to describe or, in many cases, to prepare a team to undertake," begins Roper. He continues:

Diablo II had more animations, sounds, voiceover, items, spells, backgrounds, and network support than anything we had done to date. The really frightening thing is that there are RPGs that do much more in many regards. Look at the massive amount of logic and writing involved in the quests found in *Baldur's Gate II*, for example—it's staggering! In *Diablo II*, we created separate art teams for backgrounds, monsters and characters, and items. The programmers had to integrate this massive amount of resources into the game while also constructing the quests, integrating the NPCs [non-player characters] and making it all work over Battle.net. It was a huge, coordinated effort to not only get all of these elements into the game and then balance them, but also to test them as thoroughly as possible with our Quality Assurance department. It's one thing to have hundreds of thousands of randomly generated items in the game. It's a whole other thing to make sure they all work.

Bill Roper offers much more sage advice in other chapters in this book, including a discussion on the importance of a game design document and storyboarding, how to properly test single-player and multiplayer role-playing games, and some words of wisdom on how to break into the business. Flip to Chapter 17, "Proper Game Testing," and Chapter 21, "Breaking into the Industry."

Matt Householder, Blizzard North

Before joining Blizzard North to produce *Diablo II* (and to help recruit game developers for the project), Matt Householder worked on many computer, console, and arcade games dating back to 1981, when he began working on his first coin-op game, *Krull*, an action/RPG published two years later. Be sure to read the bio appendix at the back of this book to peruse his impressive list of game credits.

For this book, Householder presents the following "Axioms of Interactive Game Design:"

1. Play a wide variety of computer and console games, but especially the big sellers. You can learn a lot by studying the hits. Take note of what the hits did right and what they did wrong.

2. Bide your time while you learn the craft of game design and production at an entry-level job in the industry. You need to pay the rent somehow.

3. Once you're ready to take the big leap—either creatively or economically (by starting your own game development shop)—design the game you want to play, not just what others tell you will sell. A well-grounded self-confidence is essential to any risky, creative endeavor. However, don't let your confidence develop into a blinding arrogance.

Householder says Blizzard games are always designed to be the games that the development team wants to play—but it's not without a cost:

It takes longer to arrive at a completed game by developing this way and we can't make a game be "all things to all players," but we feel this is the only way to be true to both our loyal fans and ourselves. To keep our pride in check, we pay plenty of attention to the vocal fans and critics who point out our shortcomings on the major pro and amateur web sites.

Taking note of what the hits did right and what they did wrong, as Householder suggested earlier, how did *Diablo's* success affect *Diablo II*?

After the original *Diablo* shipped in January 1997, everyone at Blizzard North took a well-deserved break before buckling down again to work on our next game, *Diablo II*. Our first order of business was to determine what people liked and disliked about *Diablo* to help us focus on making *Diablo II* even better and more fun to play.

We compiled huge lists of complaints (and praise) from customer service emails, Battle.net forums, Usenet newsgroups, online fan sites, game reviewers, and (of course) our own QA [quality assurance] and development staff. We boiled these lists down to just a few pages and used them as the seed for our *Diablo II* design/development process. Following are some of the issues that we addressed early on.

In order to improve on the RPG aspects of *Diablo*, we increased the number of player character classes to five and added skill trees to the character leveling/spell system. We also added a much larger, more integrated story in the improved *Diablo II* Quest system.

Diablo was often criticized as a "clickfest." Clearly, the gameplay in *Diablo II* had to remain action-oriented, but we reduced the need for repeated mouse-clicking by adding the "click and hold" feature to repeat-attack the same monster.

The wide variety of items in *Diablo* when combined with the suffix/prefix Magic naming system made for a mind-boggling range of cool stuff for players to find and use. We amplified this in *Diablo II* by creating the new classes of Rare and Socketed items. We also redesigned the graphics system in *Diablo II* to display "components" to allow players to see a much greater variety of the armor-and-weapon combinations on the characters while in the game and in the Battle.net chat rooms. This made owning and showing off cool items a lot easier and more fun. The component system also allowed us to populate the world with a larger variety of monsters outfitted with different-looking items.

We eliminated level load screens by streaming data constantly off the hard drive and CD. This also made it possible to create large open outdoor areas to complement the original's interior dungeons.

The most ambitious and fundamental improvement in *Diablo II* was to create the Battle.net Realms, a true client/server system that would minimize the sorts of hacks that interfered with the original *Diablo* online play experience. In making the decision to go with a client/server system, we studied (that is, played) *Ultima Online* and *EverQuest* for many months (actually years, in the case of *UO*) and learned from their experiences. The Realm system has prevented the simple editing of "god-like" characters and "town kill" hacks. Still, *Diablo II* has been the subject of various hacks and bug exploits by some members of our fan base.

Householder offers this parting thought on creating a solid user interface:

Don't frustrate the player's desire for perfect control within the game world. Any sense by the player of lack of control (however brief) can be fatal. The user interface must be intuitive and consistent. This makes it easy for new players to learn and encourages experienced players to become experts.

Matt Householder contributed to many other sections in this book; be sure to see his comments on creating storyboards and design documents (Chapter 6), proper game testing (Chapter 17), and breaking into the industry (Chapter 21).

Tim Cain, Troika Games

The ingenious Tim Cain created several games at Interplay, including the award-winning RPG *Fallout*, and juggled the roles of programmer, designer, and producer. In 1998, Tim co-founded his own company, Troika Games, whose first game was *Arcanum*, a deep computer-based RPG released in the fall of 2001. The studios' next project is another PC RPG, *The Temple of Elemental Evil*. As if he weren't busy enough, Tim has also taught undergraduate courses in computer game design at UCI.

Cain offers some important advice on becoming a success in this industry:

1. **Work hard.** There are a lot of people who would like your job. Make sure you're better than they are. Yes, you should enjoy yourself too, but always keep your personal standards high.

2. **Get the right people.** This not only means hiring people who know their stuff; it means hiring people who are easy to work with. An antisocial genius is just as frustrating to have on your team as a friendly moron.

3. **Be original.** Try to do something new and different in each game you make. While it's instructive to mimic an existing game just to see how they did something, you don't want to build a career out of making wannabe games that are compared (usually unfavorably) to more popular games. Try to have a fresh perspective when making your game, and you'll have more fun making it, too.

How does Cain's advice apply to *Arcanum*?

The game is huge, and was made with only 10 people in the development group. So we obviously worked very hard. And we obviously hired good people who knew their stuff, or we wouldn't have been able to make such a large complex game with only a fraction of the number of people that other development houses use. And I don't think there is any argument that our game is original. *Arcanum's* setting and skill system is unique, and both are tied into the magic/technology dichotomy inherent in the world of *Arcanum*. It's a very different game, and we had a blast making it.

Chapter 6, "Creating Characters, Storyboarding, and Design Documents," looks at design documents and storyboarding a game—a few of the tools needed to help flesh out a unified, focused vision between all members of a development team. Cain comments here on the importance of these tools:

Design docs and storyboards are very important. *Arcanum* had a 150-page design doc before any code or art was done. By the time it shipped, there were more than 1,000 pages of documentation, including tool docs and process docs. Anyone who tries to make a game these days without using such docs is probably setting up for a big disappointment when the game fails to come together at the important milestones, like alpha or beta. Instead, they'll find themselves with lots of pieces of a game, instead of a whole game.

Is anything missing with today's RPGs? Answers Cain:

I think most games have too much flash and too little substance. There are a lot of games out there that talk about their frame-rate or poly count, but that isn't important after five minutes of playing. People want to be entertained, and the eye candy loses its appeal very quickly. There needs to be something more: a good story, interesting characters to talk to, and quests that lead to new places and give fun and useful rewards.

Of course, like many developers, I feel pressured to put in the eye candy. Most reviewers tell you it attracts the masses, and they won't put a game on their magazine covers unless it's pretty. And a game with a lot of features is often said to be "too complex" or have "a high learning curve," at least compared to the twitch-based shooters. So a developer has to balance these issues when making the game.

Tim Cain makes a point about games having too much flash and not enough substance—because in the end it'll be the gameplay (and not high production values) that you'll remember. "I think 10 years from now, people will remember that epic battle with the Overlord that lasted 30 minutes and used every charge on their Supreme Weapon, but they won't be talking about the awesome graphics of an older game. If pretty art is all your game has, then I don't think anyone will be remembering it a few years from now."
(Used with permission by Sierra Studios, Inc.)

Finally, Cain chats about some of the challenges when working on an RPG, compared to other genres, and how to overcome them.

RPGs are very complex games, perhaps the most complex of any game genre. You also need to look good, of course, which means a good graphics engine and good artists. You also need a good combat system that's balanced for all the different characters that the player can have, and that alone demands a great design team. But then add the hundreds or thousands of quests—with the associated NPCs, dialogues, items, and new areas to explore—and you need a dedicated team that can handle the wide variety of tasks that confront them. They may need to lay out a nice-looking dungeon, decide on a good balance of items and monsters inside it, hook in quests to NPCs and items that are located inside or are related to the dungeon, and then write witty dialogue to tie everything together. It's a tough job.

Chris Taylor, Gas Powered Games

As president, project leader, and chief designer at Gas Powered Games, the gregarious (and busy!) Chris Taylor has made quite the name for himself in the computer game industry. While at Electronic Arts and Cavedog Entertainment, his past games included *Hardball 2*, *4D Sports Boxing*, *Triple Play Baseball*, *Total Annihilation*, and *Total Annihilation: The Core Contingency*. His latest project was the popular *Dungeon Siege* for Microsoft Games, released in the spring of 2002. *Dungeon Siege II* was announced in May of 2003, slated for a 2004 release.

Although Taylor's words of wisdom can be found in many chapters in this book, here he chats about finding inspiration as a budding game designer. What key pieces of advice can he share?

1. There has to be an overall vision of the game that you're about to design. It's really hard to design something if you just have the mandate to make a great game.

2. Implementation is very important, and you have to find the right team of people to build the game.

3. You must understand a long list of principles when designing—principles such as not designing it all up front, working with the team, experimentation, paying attention to the market, breaking some rules, not being afraid of copying what the competition has proven to be fun, and not being afraid of throwing stuff away if it sucks!

"For any game, you also need to keep these three things in mind: your audience, the technology, and the gameplay mechanics," reiterates Taylor.

In addition to these areas of focus, the designer needs a good understanding of the genre (including all the established design paradigms), the game interface, and the style or artistic direction of the game—the order in which these are prioritized is up to the designer.

With *Dungeon Siege* as the example, Taylor supports his advice:

When we started the development process for *Dungeon Siege*, we started by creating a list of all the things we thought players were looking for in an action RPG. We then thought about what new forms of technology we would introduce to the game experience: our continuous world, for example. Next, we talked about how we would innovate in terms of actual gameplay. Then, we integrated these goals into what was already established in the genre. We then established goals for "ease of use" with the game's interface and finally began to craft the actual world, which includes the way it looks and the style we wanted to present to the player.

Taylor was asked what he thought—strictly from a game design standpoint—was the single most impressive element to *Dungeon Siege*.

On the design side, I believe it was the ease at which players learned how to play (shallow learning curve) and the simple yet powerful interface. We achieved this by starting the player off with a rich and interesting environment, but not one that demanded some level of understanding of the world to create a fun experience. We don't overload the players with the complex exploration of a starting town, or have them interacting with a bunch of characters; we simply let them get straight to work on the core experience in the game (combat, exploration, and looting). It was important that the first hour of gameplay was not too difficult because nobody likes getting killed while they are learning the gameplay mechanics, camera control, and interface. As the game progresses, we introduce "pop-up" gameplay tips to give the player information at about the time this information may actually be useful to them. By slowly feeding them this information, as they become "invested" into the game, they can absorb it slowly and not feel overwhelmed...hence, the shallow learning curve.

Taylor was asked the same question about what made *Dungeon Siege* special and/or unique compared to the action/RPGs—but this time from a technical standpoint.

> Easily the most impressive technical accomplishment was the "continuous world" technology that eliminated load screens (once the game has been loaded initially). The engineers really had their work cut out for them and did an awesome job on this. This technological advancement impacted almost every aspect of how the game was engineered and thus how the game was experienced.

> **NOTE**
>
> If you want to learn more about eliminating load times as in *Dungeon Siege*, flip to Chapter 11, "Programming Theory," in which Gas Powered Games' engineer Bartosz Kijanka explains how this was achieved. A similar conversation for consoles can be found in the same chapter with Naughty Dog's Stephen White, who achieved a similar feat in *Jak & Daxter: The Precursor Legacy!*

Taylor was asked if there was anything he would change if he could go back a couple of years to begin work on *Dungeon Siege* all over again.

> That's a tricky question. If I knew then what I knew now, I would spend more time in preproduction and design. I would spend more time creating tools to help almost every aspect of the development process and work on improving communication between team members. These are all things we are doing moving forward on future versions of *Dungeon Siege*.

Now, let's shift our direction to game inspiration—something needed before the first line of code is written! Taylor says that inspiration often comes from the gamer inside yourself:

> What do you like? What makes you nuts? How could you change something to make it better? I play games and always ask myself those basic questions. I also try to learn from movies, books, and music. These are areas where artists struggle to create new ideas, tell new stories, or evoke emotions that have never been felt before.

The genesis of *Total Annihilation* provides an example:

> After playing *Command & Conquer*, I wanted to do an RTS game, but in 3D. I didn't know how much of the game would run in 3D at the time, but I knew that if I could get the units to render at any angle, things like being able to shoot while retreating would be possible. I also knew that if the units were 3D, I could have many more of them in memory than if they were all pre-rendered bitmaps.

> When I told Ron [Gilbert] about the idea, he immediately liked it and supported the project by having me join Humongous [Entertainment, Cavedog's sister company] and start working on it.

Being market-sensitive is often an important determinant of a game's success, believes Taylor, and he explains how to achieve this without having to compromise the designer's original vision:

> Well, first of all, let's define "market-sensitive." I see this as meaning "paying attention to what people are buying, what people are ignoring, and an extrasensory perception of what people might want if it were there to buy." I think if you have a strong vision of the product you want to build, nothing will get in the way. Even a market with a constantly shifting focus.
>
> I don't think it will ever pay to jump off the deep end and deliver a new experience that's so alien that [players] can't relate. Creating a means of allowing the gamer to relate to the game is one of the most important things that a designer should keep in mind. People need to feel comfortable with what they're seeing and interacting with.

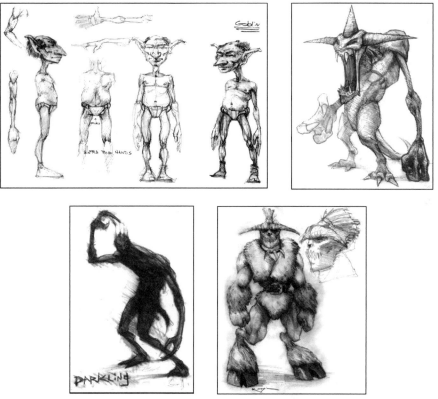

Kirkland, Washington's Gas Powered Games was founded in May 1998 by Chris Taylor, creator of the award-winning *Total Annihilation*.
Its first release was a fantasy RPG epic, dubbed *Dungeon Siege*, published by Microsoft in 2002.
Enjoy this collage of rare, behind-the-scenes sketches from the development of the game.
(Used with permission by Microsoft Corp.)

How can someone begin building his/her development team on a shoestring budget?

Well, if you have no money, then everyone involved should have another job to pay the rent and a lot of spare time afterward to devote to the project. If you have that, then you have a chance.

Someone on the team should have the vision, someone else should be an ace at code, and someone else should kick some huge butt in the art department. Sound is important but that can come later, and be damn sure they know what they're doing because nothing can make a game come alive like sound and music.

> **NOTE**
>
> The honorable Chris Taylor was kind enough to share with us his "master design document" template, so that budding game designers can use it as a handy guide for their own game design and implementation. You'll find it in Chapter 7, "Master Design Document Template."

When you're working on something on-the-sly, you'll need to have something special, something that's brilliant and that makes the difference in a way that high production values won't. Think of an art film that captures the imagination of the audience for $100 grand, not $100 million. Even when you're in the business, you need to come up with tricks to cut corners and make a thousand dollars look like something that cost ten times that. Heck, I think that's where the magic can come from. A limited budget can help to focus you on the game experience and not all the expensive fluff that so many games have.

Asked to comment on straddling innovation with familiarity—that is, how to create a game that stands out from the crowd but isn't too "out there"—Taylor responds as follows:

A good game can't be so unique that you need to explain it to people so they know what it is you're making. There's an industry term for a game that has a concept that's very easy to understand; it's called a "high concept." A high concept game is immediately recognizable. This [kind of game] includes all sports games, flight sims, game-show games that 50 million people watch, licenses from movies, and anything that will immediately communicate to the gamer who walks into the store looking to make a purchase. After you settle on your high concept, then you need to bring something new to the experience that will excite and amaze. This can be done with a cleaner, more intuitive design, a more accessible interface, a sexier graphics engine that uses the latest and greatest 3D technology. Whatever that is, it will be immediately more accessible because everyone will know what it is you're making, and easily make the leap to how your game is going to be better than what's currently on the market.

Though not confirmed by the company at the time of this writing, *Dungeon Siege 2* is currently in the works at Gas Powered Games.

For more from the vocal Chris Taylor, jump to Chapters 6, 17, and 21. Whew!

Todd Howard, Bethesda Softworks

Todd Howard has been a computer game designer and producer for Bethesda Softworks since 1994 and was the project leader for *Morrowind*, the third chapter in *The Elder Scrolls* RPG series, released earlier in 2002 for the PC and Xbox platforms. His major credits include design on *Daggerfall* (designated 1996 Role Playing Game of the Year by *Computer Gaming World* and *PC Gamer*); producer and designer of *The Terminator: Future Shock* and *SkyNET* (1996 *PC Gamer* Editor's Choice, 5 Stars Next Generation); and project leader and designer of *Redguard* (1998 Adventure Game of the Year and Finalist, *Computer Gaming World* and *PC Gamer*).

Howard first offers his top three pieces of advice for those looking to create computer games for a living:

1. **Great games are played, not made.** You can write the biggest, most thorough design document ever, and half of it will change when you see it in the game. Try to prototype as fast as possible. Play your own game and be prepared to change your ideas. You may have to change your favorite feature to make your game better.

2. **Keep it simple.** Doing something really well and making it polished takes time—more time than you probably have. Try to keep your ideas simple and make them work as well as possible.

3. **Define the experience.** Don't define your game as a list of features. Try to write what the experience will be. This will help you weed out and/or change features and keep the heart of your game intact.

How does this advice apply to such deep and involved games as *The Elder Scrolls: Morrowind*?

Even with super-complicated games like *The Elder Scrolls*, I try to design systems that by themselves are very simple. And design simple world rules, like how you put an object down. When you get many simple systems working together, you actually can get very complex actions and behaviors. In addition, we've built our game tools to allow us to modify things very easily. We realize that when we play the game, we'll want to change everything from monster stats to skills balance with a simple click.

Howard chats about what a user interface consists of, its importance, and how to create a solid UI for the player:

Interface is everything. It's the player's way of using the game. From the controls to the aesthetics of the menus, it all plays a huge part. And never expect the players to read the manual. That's too much effort. They want to put the game in and just play. The other thing, especially when doing a console game, is to really pay attention to what buttons you use. Play your game for a while and see if your hand starts to cramp up. If so, try another combination. Spend time tweaking the turning speeds on your character and see how the stick feels. This can make a big difference in how much fun your game is.

> **NOTE**
> Chapter 14, "The All-Important User Interface (UI) and Game Control," focuses on how to create the all-important interface and how it relates to (and works with) character control.

Pictured here is the PC and Xbox RPG, *The Elder Scrolls III: Morrowind*, which has also spawned two expansion packs: *Tribunal* and *Bloodmoon* (PC only). You can read more from Bethesda's Todd Howard in other chapters; he discusses art techniques, how to properly test an RPG, and breaking into the industry.
(Used with permission by Bethesda Softworks, Inc.)

Warren Spector, Ion Storm Austin

Talk about being a seasoned veteran—Warren Spector was project director and in-house producer for Ion Storm's *Deus Ex* (for Eidos Interactive). At Origin, he co-produced *Ultima VI* and *Wing Commander*, produced *Bad Blood, Martian Dreams, Shadowcaster* (uncredited), *Ultima VII Part 2: Serpent Isle, Ultima Underworld, Ultima Underworld II, Wings of Glory, System Shock, Crusader: No Remorse, Cybermage*, and more. He currently is the studio director at Ion Storm Austin.

Before Spector reveals some of his sought-after rules of game design, he cautions that rules are made to be broken, and these pieces of advice reflect a lifetime of prejudices and a host of genre-specific assumptions. "That having been said, here are some rules that might be of interest."

1. Don't think of yourself as being more important than the player. Game design should never be about how clever you are; it should be about how clever the player is.

2. Bound player experience only when not doing so would result in player confusion and frustration. Give players as much freedom as possible and then provide them with gameplay tools and game worlds that maximize the possibilities for self-expression. Exception #1 to rule #2: Give beginners a break—limiting options and bounding player experience in early missions or levels or tracks or whatever isn't the worst idea in the world. Ease players into your game; don't overwhelm them with options right at the outset.

3. Give players clear goals and a variety of ways to achieve those goals. Wondering what you're supposed to do isn't fun—what is fun is figuring out how to do something you know you're supposed to do. Guessing what the designer had in mind also isn't fun—single-solution puzzles are a nice way to pass the time, but they're kind of second-rate game design, if you ask me. If you've followed the advice in [steps] #1 and #2, players will find their own solutions to the problems you've put in their paths—that's where the real magic of gaming happens.

4. If you give players choices, make sure there are consequences associated with those choices. Pulling a virtual trigger or setting off an alarm or offending someone in conversation (or conversely, being extra-friendly to them) should all mean something. Building one kind of base should burn resources that could have been spent to build something else. Choosing to move a square block to the lower-left corner of the screen should have some impact on where you can put the squiggly z-shaped piece that shows up next. Choice without consequence is meaningless in life, it's meaningless in literature, and it's meaningless in games (where it's also horrifyingly common). Meaningless is a bad thing if we really believe that interactivity is what makes games work.

With *Deus Ex* as an example, can Spector support his "rules" with direct examples from the critically acclaimed game?

Deus Ex is all about player expression. You can create a unique alter ego by selecting specific skills, augmentations, and equipment. And those choices make it easier to interact with the game world in specific ways. In other words, a character who picks silent, non-lethal-ranged weapon skills (and carries around weapons of that sort) and then upgrades his or her character with augmentations that allow silent movement and invisibility is inevitably going to have a different experience than a player who chooses heavy weapons skills, targeting augmentations, and so on. And that player is going to have a different experience than one who builds a character who can pick locks with ease, hack computers to access keycodes and passwords, and so on. Making the choice to be one kind of character essentially closes the door to being another kind of character.

Of course, all of that means nothing if the game world doesn't offer something more sophisticated than single-solution puzzles. We tried to make sure that every single problem in *Deus Ex* could be solved in a variety of ways, that there was always more than one path to reach a given location, and that every character choice and problem solution was equally rewarded. You tell me whether we achieved our goals or not! Assuming we did, the character choices I mentioned earlier are significant because they make it more difficult (if not impossible) to solve problems in some ways, even as they make it possible to solve problems in other ways.

Spector believes there were some ways in which they failed to live up to their goals, however—where they lost sight of the rules mentioned earlier:

> There were a couple of points in the game (which I can't really mention specifically without a spoiler alert) where we forced players to fail—at those moments, the needs of the story (and our need for creative expression) were more important to us than the needs of the player. Similarly, there were characters we had to keep alive early in the game, so they'd be around to play vital roles later in the game. Given our overall adherence to "the rules," these mistakes stood out glaringly in the context of a game about player choice.

In Chapter 6, Warren Spector discusses storyboarding and writing design documents. Watch for more from Spector on ways of programming realistic artificial intelligence (Chapter 12, "Artificial Intelligence [AI]"), properly testing a game (Chapter 17), and the do's and don'ts of breaking into the industry (Chapter 21).

Ray Muzyka and Greg Zeschuk, BioWare

Founded in 1995, Canada's BioWare has become one of the more renowned computer role-playing game development studios on the planet. The *Baldur's Gate* and *Neverwinter Nights* series have both garnered critical acclaim and enjoyed commercial success worldwide, and for good reason—they're extremely polished, well-written, and incredibly fun RPGs. BioWare's latest—and arguably most ambitious project—was the first *Star Wars* RPG, *Knights of the Old Republic*, for the Xbox and PC.

Interestingly, co-founders and joint CEOs Greg Zeschuk and Ray Muzyka left their posts as family physicians to launch BioWare. We've got them both here to wax lyrical about creating RPGs for the new millennium.

What do Zeschuk and Muzyka offer as the three most important pieces of advice for new game makers? First, let's hear from Greg Zeschuk:

1. **Make it fun.** RPGs are the most joyous type of game when made correctly. Making them correctly involves the player spending a lot of time on the fun activities (combat, collecting treasure, experiencing the story) and as little time as possible on the mundane (scrounging for food and water; running from empty area to empty area; reading endless dialogue).

2. **Focus the player's experience.** RPGs are not fun if you don't know what you're supposed to be doing. Aimless wandering and pointless dialogue become old very quickly. Remember that there are hundreds of other games to play; yours must grip the player as quickly as possible!

3. **See the game through the player's eyes.** When you're making a game, it's very hard not to become so involved in your creation that you can't objectively look at the monstrosity you're building. As a game designer, you need to be able to step back and see your game for what it is. Play-test it yourself and try to imitate the first-time player—don't use shortcuts or cheats and see if it's still what you think it is.

Ray Muzyka chimes in with a few more:

1. **Characterization, story, and pacing.** The player needs to feel that the characters in the game are rich and well-developed. They should have plausible lives—adding in friends, romances, jobs, hobbies, and other elements of back story will help create characters that are more likable heroes, more despicable villains, and more believable townsfolk. Also, take time to develop a storyline that's engaging and immersive. This isn't easy, and we haven't succeeded completely in achieving this in all of our games yet, but we're working on making each storyline better than the last. Part of a rich storyline is a well-developed world—consider things like geography, ecology, economy, and an array of other back story items. Further, as Greg noted, focus is very important in role-playing games, and this brings in another issue: pacing. A well-paced game provides regular rewards, and these can take many different forms: new items, leveling up, cut scenes, new areas to explore, and new subquests or additional parts to the main storyline.

2. **Scope.** RPGs are big. This means that they can be complex to create. Expect to see loads of data and art, intricate underlying rules systems that are complex to program, a large dev team, long development schedules, and potentially more testing time at the end to allow your play testers to work their way through the title over and over again in all its permutations.

3. **Interface.** The essence of a good interface is one that's transparent to the user, provides a learning curve for the more advanced users, and is simultaneously easy to use yet powerful from the start. Many games fail, not because the story isn't good or the basic gameplay design isn't fun, but rather because people can't figure out how to play them because the interface isn't good enough!

Zeschuk and Muzyka support their advice with examples from games they've worked on. Zeschuk starts us off:

Early in the development of the *Baldur's Gate* series, we made a decision to "streamline" the *Dungeons & Dragons* experience by allowing the user to set the level of detail of the game system. By modifying a few game options, hardcore players of the *Baldur's Gate* series can see every dice roll along with the multitudes of modifiers during combat; casual players are treated to a more simple default setting, showing only combat highlights. By having optional detail levels, we catered to the varied tastes of the players—the results made both hardcore and casual players happy. We also decided to remove mundane elements such as hunger and thirst from the game system in Baldur's Gate so the player could concentrate on fun activities like vanquishing monsters and gathering treasure.

And now Muzyka:

The folks at BioWare also make a great effort to test our games ourselves—Greg and I have a rule that we finish all of them ourselves, sometimes multiple times, and work hard to find bugs and spot areas that just don't have the right pacing or that don't make sense to the user. We do analyses of other games in the market to try to find good features to emulate and bad features to avoid. We study interfaces and try to design our game interfaces to reflect both the comfort of a familiar interface (of a popular game already released) while we add some new design improvements to that interface. We've also gotten better at designing storylines, creating design documents, and planning milestone schedules in our role-playing games over the years as our teams gain experience; as a result, we think that games like *Neverwinter Nights* and *Star Wars: Knights of the Old Republic* are our best games yet.

Speaking of *Neverwinter Nights*, what have you learned the most from working on the game?

Ray: I think we learned a lot about a number of different things during the course of developing *Neverwinter Nights*. One thing we learned was about how to develop and design a very large game. *Neverwinter Nights* is a huge game—the single-player/multiplayer campaign alone takes over 100 hours to play through; the team size on *Neverwinter Nights* was over 75 near the end of development, and we worked on the game for nearly five years, all told. To allow for people to play through the game in manageable chunks of gameplay, we had originally planned for there to be nearly 30 modules in the official campaign, but we rapidly realized that for there to be meaningful, designed consequences to the player's actions—people reacting to what you did while playing through the game, for example—the modules needed to be a bit larger. What we ended up doing was merging modules together, so we ended up with seven final modules: four main chapters, a tutorial, and two smaller subchapters. This final design choice was a blended approach midway between the smaller modules we had initially planned and the larger chapters of a game like *Baldur's Gate*, for example. We also learned about how to make a game simultaneously multiplayer and single-player, and also how to provide tools to our fans that would allow them to both create new content and serve as virtual *Dungeon Masters* in the modules they were running.

Can you give us an example?

Ray: To enable the official campaign in both the single-player and multiplayer modes, we had to ensure that the player was always the center of the action. Unlike the storyline in some of our past RPGs, where there was one character who was special in some way, the characters in a multiplayer game of *Neverwinter* had to all be important, much as the characters in any session of *Dungeons & Dragons* are. In terms of the tools, we had to design systems in the game that were flexible enough to allow people to create new content with the tools, while also allowing us to create the official campaign storyline at a quality level exceeding all of our past games.

Greg: In developing *Neverwinter Nights*, BioWare learned a lot about creating customer-ready tools that function apart from the main game. *Neverwinter Nights* is our first foray into creating editing tools for use by the community (as well as our internal designers), and we learned a few good lessons in their development. The biggest lesson we learned was to try and lock the tools down as quickly as possible to first let designers do their work in developing the game content, and second to make sure that the tools can reach their final iteration as early as possible. Our extremely dedicated tools programmers worked extremely hard in improving and optimizing the tools—the result is evident in the tools' functionality and ease of use. Starting the completion process even earlier would have made the tools even better by the end of the project.

Muzyka and Zeschuk were also asked what they'd do again and not do again during the development of *Neverwinter Nights* if they had the chance to go back in time.

Ray: Though it would be easy to look retrospectively and say "if only…" or "I wish we had…" I don't think we have any such regrets with *Neverwinter*, at least in terms of design. The original vision of *Neverwinter* involved four key pillars: the single-player game, the multiplayer game, the dungeon master tools, and the content creation tools (aka the BioWare Aurora *Neverwinter* toolset). Trent (the producer here at BioWare), Greg, I, and the rest of the team all really felt strongly about achieving these four design goals simultaneously. Accordingly, we didn't make many, if any, compromises on the original design that Trent, Greg, and I began mapping out in 1997/1998, and we're all really happy with the end result that is *Neverwinter*! Probably the only thing we could have done better was to fully understand the scope of the game. *Neverwinter Nights* really is huge, so it took much longer to finish than we had originally anticipated it would back in 1997…but then again, we've learned a lot since then!

Greg: I have to echo Ray on this—even though *Neverwinter Nights* was a huge game that took a Herculean effort to complete, we're really happy with how it turned out. Looking back at those design documents from 1997 is an uncanny experience because practically all the features we planned for the game made it into the final release. Not a lot of games have that kind of focused vision—we've been very fortunate in being able to follow *Neverwinter Nights* through to its proper completion.

What are some of the challenges in working on an RPG compared to other genres, and how do you overcome them?

Ray: RPGs are very complicated and difficult to make, with large storylines, a lot of underlying rules, and a lot of assets such as art and design—they also require huge resource commitments in time and personnel.

Greg: Yes, and current standards dictate that RPGs should feature graphics as pretty as any action game, stories and characters as compelling as the best novels, and gameplay in a fully interactive world that responds to the player's actions.

So how do you overcome this seemingly endless demand for more depth and options? Greg Zeschuk responds:

The best way to overcome these impossible hurdles is to pick a few things to do well, and do them better than any other game. Meanwhile, make sure that everything else is still quite good!

We chat in-depth about the importance of a good user interface (UI) in Chapter 14. Meanwhile, harking back to Ray's earlier comment about game failure due to poor interface, he and Greg offer some quick advice on how to build a successful graphical user interface (GUI):

Ray: Some other tips we've learned over the years:

1. Provide at least 50% extra space on all buttons to allow for localization—German, French, Spanish, and other languages can take a lot more space for phrases than English does.

2. Choose your font carefully. If your players can't read the text in the game, it doesn't matter if the font looks cool—legibility is at least as important as appearance!

As a treat for computer role-playing game fanatics, two rare sketches from the making of *Baldur's Gate II* and early concept character art for *Neverwinter Nights*.
(Used with permission by Interplay Productions, Inc., BioWare Corp., and Infogrames, Inc.)

3. Concept and prototype your interfaces and try to make an editor that will allow you to create new interfaces quickly. Programming interfaces is a time-consuming affair, and we have been surprised many times (hopefully not any more) by the number of interfaces required for a game like *Baldur's Gate* once you start to include all buttons, floating panels, multiplayer GUIs, and the myriad of other unexpected GUI screens.

4. If you're planning a multi-platform release like *MDK2*, make sure that your user interface is capable of handling different inputs—this is particularly important for PC games with console SKUs. PC games use the mouse and keyboard and console games use controllers—which often require completely different interface design. This can be one of the slowest parts of getting a game to another platform if you haven't planned ahead for it in your early interface design and programming.

Greg: We've got a couple of easy interface tips—for a PC game, count the number of times you need to click through the menus to get to common destinations. If more than a few are required to reach a menu destination, your menus are too complex. On a console, a newbie (but an experienced console player) should be able to pick up a controller and immediately figure how to do all common actions in your game. If someone needs to look at the instructions to figure out the controls in a console game, you're really sunk!

Do these gaming experts have any beefs with today's RPGs?

Greg: My biggest pet peeve is experiencing a game in which the designers became self-indulgent and made the game not for the player, but for themselves. As a game designer, the enjoyment and experiences of the player must always be first and foremost in your mind. Games featuring excessive "inside jokes" or over-reliance on a moderately cool feature make me very angry. It's almost as though the designers' egos caused them to forget they're making the game for the player—it really bothers me to see such disregard for the experience of the player.

Ray: Those questions on interface design made me think how some games I played could have been fun with a better interface or control scheme—grr!

What technical or theoretical advice can Zeschuk and Muzyka offer a newbie game programmer?

Greg: Fortunately, the programming experience I do have is all bad, so it will be quite easy to explain where I went wrong! My answer is very straightforward—if a piece of code is broken, and no matter how hard you try you are unable to debug it, then rewrite it! It will probably be better the second time around than it ever could have been the first time. I didn't do this, and some very bad things happened, so heed my advice!

Ray: The last time I did any programming was more than seven years ago, and that wasn't very good programming, either (horrible would be a better description!). Nowadays, Greg and I are lucky that BioWare has some programmers who, like the rest of our staff, are smart, creative, and know how to program far better than we ever could! However, it is very helpful to have done some programming in the past, even if you are a producer, an artist, an animator, or a designer rather than a programmer—having this experience will allow you to understand the basic logic behind the way a programmer thinks. The worst error that neophyte programmers probably make is not planning enough in advance—creating a detailed design document is very important to know what you need to program, and not having a detailed enough design doc (as we've found out, painfully, several times in the past) will always result in having to throw away work and redo it.

What about creating console games versus PC games?

Ray: From a game design standpoint, there are distinct differences between developing for console and PC. Perhaps they are related in part to the inputs for both types of games (keyboard and mouse for PC versus controller for console), but even games in the same genre (for example, RPGs) are quite distinct on PC versus console. Developing the same game for both PC and console is challenging, but it can be done to great effect. We co-developed *MDK2* for Dreamcast PC and later ported it to PS2, for example, and all of these were reviewed very favorably by the press and by fans. Certainly in terms of hardware differences, the big ones relate to the variety of configurations available on PC (versus on console, where each console system is locked in its configuration), the lack of a hard drive on most console systems (with the notable exception of the Xbox), and the memory limitations on console. (Again, the Xbox has the greatest amount of available memory, which helps when designing a game—it allows you to make textures and graphic effects larger and more impressive than on lower memory systems).

Greg: Console players have a completely different mindset compared to PC players when they sit down to try a game. Console games succeed by being easily accessible and providing quick rewards right out of the box, while PC games employ a more gradual reward scheme and more gameplay depth than the average console game. When designing a game for either platform, you need to account for differences in the players as well as the hardware. One really great feature of consoles is they require no compatibility testing because their hardware configurations are static (as Ray mentions). Until you make a PC game, it's really hard to fully comprehend the impact that as many as five different operating systems (Windows 95, 98, Millennium, 2000, and XP), billions of possible hardware configurations, and user-controlled driver updates can have on your game's stability. Games that are completely stable on one PC often will not work on another one—it's somewhat of an art to make a game that functions on all PC systems.

What about working on a *Star Wars* game such as *Knights of the Old Republic*? What was it like?

Ray: Working with LucasArts on the *Star Wars: Knights of the Old Republic* game was very positive. Naturally, there are certain approvals that need to occur, as with any licensed property, but they are generally quite reasonable at LucasArts, and as well because *Knights of the Old Republic* is set 4000 years before the movies. This allowed us a bit more creative latitude in designing the storyline and game events than if we were making the game set in the same time period as *Episode II* or *III*, for example.

Greg: Many of the people at BioWare are huge *Star Wars* fans (including us), so you can probably imagine the excitement in the office when we first announced the title. One of the most impressive things about doing a *Star Wars* game is that everyone is just as excited today as they were when the game was first announced nearly two years ago. It's just that much fun to work on, and the team is really pumped about the game.

Any do's, don'ts, tips, tricks, or techniques on how to become a successful game designer?

Ray: First off, never forget to dream big. Because Greg and I originally trained as medical doctors, not in business or computer science (though I did get my M.B.A. a couple of years ago, and Greg is also planning to get one in the future), many people we encountered in the first few years of BioWare didn't think we could pull it off. But we were fortunate to be able to attract and retain some very smart, creative people here at BioWare who have helped us to build a great company and great games. Hence, my second piece of advice is to work hard to attract and retain great people to work with and always strive to build a great environment for those people to work in. We have two core values at BioWare, and one of them relates to the quality of our workplace. We try to ensure that BioWare is the kind of place where we would want to work ourselves, and where our employees are very comfortable. The third piece of advice relates to our second core value: maintaining the highest possible quality in our products.

At BioWare, we work hard to ensure that we never compromise the quality of our games, and we always strive to be the market leader in our games, setting the standard of quality for our competitors.

Greg: Another good quality to have is patience. We've been in the industry now for more than eight years, and we're just getting to the point where we feel we've got a solid vision of our future and the ability to attain our goals. We've been very fortunate with the projects we've had over the years, but it has taken a very long time to get to the point where we feel we are controlling our destiny. If you're not patient, you're not going to last. Developing games is somewhat like a marathon—you have to be prepared for the long haul, but you also have to pace yourself to reach the end of the race.

> **NOTE**
>
> If you're short on cash, but want to see if you have what it takes to create a role-playing game on your PC, visit www.rpgtoolkit.com to obtain a free RPG toolkit development system. Upload your game to the same site when you're done creating your masterpiece.

Harvey Smith, Ion Storm Austin

Harvey Smith was the lead designer on the groundbreaking RPG *Deus Ex* and is currently the project director on *Deus Ex 2* at Ion Storm Austin. Prior to Ion Storm Austin, Smith was the lead designer on *FireTeam* (an underrated Internet squad-level action game that allowed players to cooperate using real-time speech) and also worked at Origin Systems in Texas with Warren Spector's development group.

Drawing from his past (and vast!) experience, Smith offers some game design advice for newbies:

> At a high level, I'd say that three key (non-technical) elements that aid in creating a game are passion for the project, understanding of the holistic vision, and good communication/team interaction. But specifically in regard to people working on their "dream" games, I'd warn against losing objectivity. At some level, the dream game is counter to the best game-creation process: One of the critical aspects of game development is, I believe, the ability to let the design unfold organically. I learned the hard way how important it is to escape the Tyranny of the Idea. That is, initially, you can have a powerfully defined idea for how something should work, but you eventually learn to let the idea morph (or go away completely) as the needs of the game dictate. The important part is adhering to some high-level vision of the game, while letting the low-level features change as needed. That's harder to do when you're working on your dream game.

Where should a game designer look for inspiration?

> Nature is my favorite resource for creatures and ecologies. Learning about the symbiotic relations in the flora/fauna world has often given me good ideas for the relations between game units, the player, and the environment. But fiction, film, and architecture are also useful inspirations for creating man-made environments and dramatic situations. Overall, it helps to play games, but it also helps to get away from games—to look into atypical areas for inspiration. This might sound obvious, but going out and doing

something in the real world is often a great source of inspiration—anything from a pub-crawl to a camping trip will often give you a half dozen interesting ideas.

In Chapter 17, Harvey Smith provides some helpful tips on proper game testing. In Chapter 10, "Mission Design," he shares some secrets on how to create challenging missions, such as those found in *Deus Ex*.

Massively Multiplayer Games

This portion of the role-playing game chapter is devoted to massively multiplayer games played over the Internet, also known as persistent online worlds or persistent state worlds (PSWs) because the game continues even if the player logs off. Although the majority of the games discussed here are role-playing games, we also hear from the folks who revved up *Motor City Online*, the world's first massively multiplayer car racing game with an economic component.

Brad McQuaid, Sigil Games Online

Before leaving in January 2002 to start up Sigil Games Online (www.sigilgames.com), Brad McQuaid served as Vice President of Sony Online Entertainment, the developers of the smash hit massively multiplayer online role-playing game (MMORPG) *EverQuest*. McQuaid was the producer on *EverQuest* and for the first official expansion pack, *The Ruins of Kunark*.

From a game design standpoint, McQuaid offers some important pieces of advice for those looking to create a massively multiplayer game:

1. Play the MMORPGs that exist now, study their strengths and weaknesses with objectivity, and think about what could be done to improve them. Don't limit yourself to one perspective or angle in your analysis. Include some of the better free-text MUDs/MUSHes/MOOs that are out there—in many ways, some are actually more advanced and further involved than commercial, graphical MMORPGs.

2. Make an effort to understand basic human nature and what's necessary to make a virtual society viable (economy, player interdependence, and so on). Make provisions in your design that support these elements as they relate to dynamic online worlds. Don't lose sight of the fact that these elements must be designed to support and enhance the structure of an enjoyable game.

3. Don't try to achieve or accomplish too much in your design. Focus on either depth or breadth of gameplay, but don't bite off more than you can chew. It's better to create a more limited but fun game in terms of scope than to attempt to make huge new strides in the evolution of online gaming, but end up creating something incomplete and/or un-fun.

McQuaid thinks part of *EverQuest's* success is that "we did a decent job of following all three elements of advice!" He expands:

> First, we played a lot of MUDs and learned a great deal from them. The great experiment with *EverQuest* was to see if that which compelled a niche group of college kids to spend ungodly amounts of hours virtually addicted to text MUDs would be viable commercially, when coupled with graphics and professional support and distribution. And it turned out that what was true for the goose was true for the gander— the core game mechanics that worked in popular text MUDs also create a compelling and immersive experience in commercial massively multiplayer games.

> Also, we really attempted to focus on adventuring. We set out to make a virtual world and a game, but when the two were at odds, we chose the game. *EverQuest* has been labeled, and sometimes negatively, a combat-only game, or too "hack-'n-slash." Well, that's what we set out to make: a game focused on adventure with a lot of depth and detail associated with that adventure. And that, I'm proud to say, is not only what we ended up with, but something 400,000 people enjoy almost daily [and for $10 a month!].

Getting enough content into the game is the most important challenge of designing a massively multiplayer game, says McQuaid. Another big challenge is to create and maintain a balanced game.

> It takes an author perhaps six months to write a novel, but the reader a week to read it. Players consume content at a rapid pace, and the game designer must create a system and environment in which content is self-generating but not repetitive.

> MMORPGs change and evolve, both due to new content being added and also because the game's player base is constantly changing and advancing. This means constant tweaks must be made both before and after commercial launch.

The elements of persistence and nonlinearity must be at the core of the game design, says McQuaid.

> Unlike a traditional single-player game, there is no "end"—there is no all-encompassing storyline that the player follows from introduction to conclusion. And, of course, MMORPGs must keep players playing for periods orders of magnitude longer than single-player games, which means the focus needs to be on character development, in-game ownership, and building relationships with other players."

McQuaid was lead programmer on *EverQuest* for a brief period of time. To programmers, he offers the following comments:

> Go to school, but also study on your own. Unfortunately, many colleges and universities are still behind in terms of what they teach. Learn C++. Study mathematics. Try to determine what aspects of math will help you with 3D programming and focus on them. And, most importantly, start programming something. A mini-game, a demo, something that shows off both your talent and that you have the fortitude to complete a project. There are too many programmers in this industry who may be talented and intelligent, but can't seem to finish what they start.

In a previous edition of *Game Design: Secrets of the Sages*, the book series that led to what you're holding in your hands now, McQuaid stressed the importance of a good user interface (UI). The following discussion explains why this is and why McQuaid believes that *EverQuest* (*EQ*) excels in this department:

Sony Online Entertainment's critically acclaimed *EverQuest* is a true 3D massively multiplayer fantasy role-playing game. More than 450,000 gamers are paying $13 a month to "live" in this virtual community each month. Pictured here is the *EverQuest* expansion pack *Scars of Velious*.
(Used with permission by Sony Computer Entertainment America, Inc.)

A good user interface is very important, both short- and long-term, as it relates to a player's experience and use of the game. Short-term, a good interface doesn't overwhelm a new player with too much information or with operations and functions that aren't intuitive. Long-term, a good interface is very user-customizable, allowing the player to configure the interface as it relates to his or her style of gameplay and what functions and commands he or she uses most often.

I think *EverQuest* did a decent job with our user interface, but there is much room for improvement in both areas. One aspect of *EQ*'s interface I am most proud of are what we call "hot buttons," which is functionality that allows the player to set up a series of buttons representing commands and/or functionality that he or she uses most often. It's quite similar to customizable icon bars in popular spreadsheets and word processors. Credit goes out to Bill Trost, *EQ*'s lead game designer, for the idea and implementation.

Study everything on the market with an objective eye and learn to recognize what interface elements add to "immersiveness" and ease of use. Understand what interface properties detract from immersion and distract from gameplay. Think about how existing interfaces could be improved.

With so many MMORPGs popping up, something must irk McQuaid about them:

Probably the "trend" that annoys me the most is the move toward random content. Creating content, of course, is the most challenging aspect of making MMORPGs. Like I said earlier, it takes perhaps six months on average to write a novel, but maybe a week to read one. The same applies with these games, and they need to be designed to entertain thousands of people for years at a time.

So coming up with all that content is indeed challenging, but I see elements in our industry trying to solve that problem by creating content randomly. Whether it's random quest generators or dynamically creating dungeons and other adventure areas, and so on—to me, it's taking the easy way out. Hand-crafting content (worlds, quests, adventures, items, NPCs, and so on) will always be, in my opinion, harder to do—but superior. I guess I'm just not for taking the easy road; and large, crazy, ambitious projects are more my cup of tea.

McQuaid discusses some challenges in working on an MMORPG compared to other genres.

1. **Development time.** These games take a long time to create and a lot of people. Three years minimum, and probably teams of more than 20 people, are what's really needed. Some people just don't want to be on projects that long—I guess they either lack the fortitude or get bored easily.

2. **Budgets.** This, of course, relates to point #1. If a project has 20+ people on it and runs three or more years, you're probably talking budgets in the neighborhood of $12+ million dollars. It's not easy to get that sort of funding, that's for sure.

3. **Designing for a group of people and creating a functional world.** As opposed to the traditional linear story-based game where the player is the protagonist and center of the universe, it simply takes a very different approach—creating a virtual world and keeping everyone happy (and subscribing) for month after month, year after year.

4. **Player expectations.** Typically, a game player will purchase a game, decide whether he likes it or not, and if he does, play it for a few weeks. If he doesn't like it, no harm, no foul—he either throws it on the shelf or returns it. Massively multiplayer games, however, are designed to keep people around for a long time by focusing on gameplay elements such as community and character development. Over time, players begin to belong to the world they're playing in, and they become very attached to their characters and relationships with other players. And so when they finally do get burned-out on the game (and this can vary greatly in time because there is no "end game"), they're often very upset at the game and its creators. Managing the expectations of your player base can help minimize these long-term feelings players often develop.

5. **Non-development-related infrastructure.** Keep in mind that when developing a massively multiplayer game, there's much more than simply writing the game. These products require large groups of operations and customer service people, as well as a huge infrastructure in terms of servers, routers, switches, tons of bandwidth, and so on. How your client and server relate to and support all of this is very important to consider and plan early on.

Be sure to read McQuaid's thoughts on how to test a massively multiplayer online role-playing game in Chapter 17.

> **NOTE**
>
> *EverQuest* made its way over to the PS2 in early 2003, known as *EverQuest Online Adventures*. If you're interested in console-based massively multiplayer role-playing games, in the next chapter, we hear from Yuji Naka, creator of the beloved *Phantasy Star Online*.

Richard "Lord British" Garriott, NCsoft

"Lord British" is one of the pioneers of the computer gaming industry, best known for his mega-successful *Ultima* role-playing game series. To date, there have been over a dozen sequels, plus countless other products—including children's cartoons, comic books, novels, and songs. In 2000, Garriott left Origin, a company he founded, to start Destination Games, which then became part of NCsoft, a Korean-based company that currently operates the largest subscription-based online game in the world: *Lineage: The Blood Pledge*.

Garriott takes time out of his busy schedule to chat about game design theory and implementation, with an emphasis on massively multiplayer persistent online games (MMP):

1. Hire experienced personnel. The pitfalls of developing and shipping an MMP are vast! Only experience will help you avoid these.

2. Coding standards are the key to a stable expandable game.

3. Back-end support costs are the most important financial metric. If a game does well, the up-front costs are a small piece of the issue.

In light of his sage advice, Garriott gives examples from his own current and past projects to hit the points home. The following numbers correspond to Garriott's previous answers:

1. The team that's creating *Tabula Rasa*, my current project, is built exclusively on experienced top-notch MMP developers. Examples: Starr Long, co-creator and director of *Ultima Online 1*; Jake Song, creator of *Lineage*; and myself, a principal creator of computer RPGs and MMPs. Plus most all of the best staff from *Ultima IX* and *Ultima Online*, both from the original creation standpoint and the live support side. With great skilled folks from Turbine, Sierra, and so on.

2. *Ultima Online 1* was started by a group of hackers. They were the visionary early adopters that we could cram into our skunk works. As we learned the importance of coding standards, we slowly shifted to well-written code that's stable and expandable.

3. *Ultima Online 1* started out earning only 25 cents on the dollar. Over time, with code and process improvements, it has improved to 50 cents, which makes a huge difference in the profit numbers. On a relative scale, the original product development spending is hardly noticed.

Garriott also offers some guidance for those looking to create a single-player RPG:

1. Keep it simple. Most RPG creators create games for themselves, not for the market. Thus, most RPGs become too complex and hard to understand for customers.

2. Stay the course. RPG creation is the most prone to "creeping featurism" of any game style. I think this is due to simulating a "real world," which is quite open-ended. Containing the problem is key!

3. Be prepared for periodic lacks of faith by publishers. RPGs are the hardest to understand by large-scale publishers who, for instance, might publish lots of sports games. Despite the release of the *Harry Potter* and *Lord of the Rings* movies, both of which are potential candidates for RPG computer games, many publishers see RPGs as long, expensive, and risky.

Now that Garriott has left Origin to start another company, what are a few things he has learned that he will apply to NCSoft?

Don't partner with a company that doesn't understand online games as its primary focus! And launch MMPs with a relatively small feature set and grow. Finally, quality people with MMP experience are rare but incredibly valuable—especially those with good future visions, not old-school hacks or paper game designers.

During an interview for a previous edition of this book, Garriott stressed the importance of a good user interface. Here he reiterates:

My best example is stolen from Starr Long. Starr proposes that instead of inventing a new interface for people to learn, you base your designs on what people must already know: Windows. Now that sounds obvious, but usually people invent some new way to interact with the sophisticated world they create. Instead, consider limiting your world interaction to one with a Windows-style paradigm.

> **NOTE**
> In Chapter 14, Lord British elaborates on how to create an effective user interface. Be sure to read this comprehensive piece.

Having started the graphical online role-playing game phenomenon with *Ultima Online*, Garriott comments on what's missing in today's MMORPGs:

"Role-playing" is not inventory management and purely combat-based advancement. Thus, games like *Diablo* and most other so-called role-playing games—where the general play style is advancement and inventory control—are not role-playing! In a role-playing game, you should succeed based on how well you play your role, which is a much harder but often more rewarding experience. Thus, in *Ultima*, if you didn't play the role of a true Avatar of Virtue, you didn't become the Avatar! In most RPGs, you pillage and plunder while becoming a "hero." Not very heroic in my book. I'd love to see more role-playing games!

Any do's and don'ts for getting a job in the computer gaming industry today? "Education," begins Garriott. He continues:

> Wow, has that come full circle! When I started, school had little to offer over real-world experience. Now there is a great deal to know that must be learned, and most businesses can't afford to train these basic ideas. Also, I'm very negative on designers who are not either incredibly well-proven programmers or artists. All too often, people who are not trained programmers or artists want into the games business and end up as designers because of this lack of programming or art skills. This is a mistake. Likewise, paper game designers believe they're good computer game designers. Usually, these types of people don't convert well to computer games. Technical education and/or skills are critical to writing computer games. This shouldn't really be a big surprise, but many people don't have the basic requirements.

Along with his words of wisdom in Chapter 14, Chapter 17 contains Garriott's advice on properly testing your MMORPG.

NOTE

Looking to build a massively multiplayer role-playing game? The world's very first MMORPG construction kit is available at `www.trinityofdarkness.com`. Users can create and host their very own online world.

Michael Waite, Electronic Arts

As a special treat for those itching to create massively multiplayer Internet-based games—but not role-playing games—we have Michael Waite, the producer and lead designer of EA's *Motor City Online*. His past projects include four EA Sports titles and several games for Sierra (now Vivendi)—including puzzle games (*The Incredible Machine*), shooters (*Tribes*, back when it was called *Fear*), and fighting games (*CyberGladiators*).

NOTE

If you'd rather be steering and veering than hacking and slashing, Electronic Arts' latest massively multiplayer online game may be for you. In *Motor City Online* (`www.motorcityonline.com`), players can climb behind the wheel of more than 60 classic American cars, such as a '49 Mercury Coupe, a '57 Chevy, or a '64 Ford Mustang. Racing and winning against other players rakes in more cash to buy better parts and additional cars. And talk about depth—choose from more than 2,000 authentic car parts to tweak your hot rod's performance—not to mention the limitless cosmetic modifications such as customized paint jobs and hubcaps and such. Cherry Coke and black leather jacket optional!

Waite says to keep the following tips in mind when creating a persistent state world (PSW):

> A PSW designer needs to plan for much greater game depth than a console or PC game designer. Design objectives need to account for different types of players: those looking for a predominantly social experience, those looking for a competitive experience, and those looking to immerse themselves in exploration of the game world.

You have to provide a balanced range of experiences and rewards for each type of player.

Think systems. Every feature you build into a PSW needs to be scalable, editable, and friendly to new content. If you can't patch in changes quickly and easily, you're screwed. Both the technology and game administrators need to be able to respond almost instantly to bugs, exploits, abuses, and server outages. The more powerful your toolset, the smoother things will run.

Design features that let users run the game for you once it's live. Design ways to let users communicate easily, form groups, mentor each other, host their own events, and, if possible, create actual game content. This will do a number of things for your game. The users will feel a greater sense of ownership, so they'll want to stick around and they'll have a stake in keeping peace and fairness in the world. And every activity or piece of content generated by users is one fewer task for your "live team." Ultimately, you'll want things to run so that a small number of community staff are working as managers, editors, and content gatherers, dealing with all the input coming from the players.

With *Motor City Online (MCO)* to support his aforementioned advice, Waite says features for the competitive player style are racing (street, drag, circuit, and time trials), level advancement, salary and race rewards, pink slip challenges, and turf wars. For the social player style, features include club activities, chatting, trading, community stories, and "friendly" racing (no purse or wager). Finally, features for the player who likes to explore are workshops with more than 100,000 car modification variations possible, 20+ tracks to race, 59+ cars to drive or own, and the test drive.

"Every piece of technology in *MCO* is a system, from the front-end graphics engine to the true-physics car construction engine," says Waite. "We can add new screens, car parts, persona models (and so on) at any time via autopatch at login." He continues:

Motor City Online players own and operate the community. Club leaders invite members whom they train, help with resources, and lead into "turf wars" against rival clubs. We've got a car-painting tool that we'll be releasing to the public after it's tuned—this will allow users to create paint jobs that can be entered in contests; the winning "skins" are sold in the game, and the painters are rewarded with *MCO* cash. The Community Center contains a series of HTML pages where player stories, interviews, and screenshots can be published to the game community.

What does Waite think of other massively multiplayer online games available today?

The major PSWs that have stayed afloat—*Ultima Online, Asheron's Call, EverQuest*—are all awesome. If you've never worked on a PSW, you can't appreciate what an amazing achievement these games are—the play-balancing nightmare, the massive scale and clunky coordination of multiple dev and support teams, the re-re-reconfiguration of server technology. *Ultima Online* is the best in terms of gameplay depth, but the look is starting to feel outdated. I like *EverQuest's* graphic world the best, but my first two hours in the game were a yawn. (I got killed by a guard within the first five minutes—not a great new user experience.)

On the subject of his pet peeves with today's PSWs, Waite targets the inherent learning curve in these games, "…and I'm not sure I see a way around it if you're going to keep the game depth."

> There is no immediate sense of objective in any of the leading PSWs—you don't know where to start, what you're trying to achieve, or even what it means to be a Magical Dwarf with Archery Skills. But even as I bitch about this in the other PSWs, I'm hearing the same complaints from some *MCO* users. The cool thing is, it's a live game, so we can patch in improvements as quickly as we develop them.

This brings up a good point about PSWs. Waite discusses some of the key challenges or obstacles when creating a "living" game such as *Motor City Online*.

> We joke a lot about the absurd enormity of *MCO*: The core game mechanic is the most complex racing sim ever built; there's an Outlook-style instant messaging and contacts system; the game runs on a dedicated network play system (with shards of 24+ boxes); it employs an eBay-like auction system; the front end has its own in-game HTML parser (the only one in existence, to my knowledge); there's a car modification workshop that runs 49 true-physics diagnostics on every change you make to your car; there's an in-game publishing system, persistent in-game chat, a Club creation and competition system, and tons and tons of content. The biggest challenge is finding people talented enough (and insane enough) to sign on for this complicated project. The second biggest challenge is trying to keep everything straight in your head.

Scenes from EA's *Motor City Online*.
(Used with permission by Electronic Arts, Inc.)

An interesting note about competition versus cooperation:

> One challenge specific to *MCO* as a PSW lies primarily with the fact that racing games are inherently competitive in game mechanic, whereas online gaming is foremost a social platform.

> We knew if we wanted to win in the online market, we'd have to find a way to make racing a positive social experience, and we'd have to find a way to get players to form groups. Our key solution was clubs, which work similarly to team sports. You join a club where you train, strategize, and share resources; then you team up out on the racetrack against other clubs to see who can claim victory in a "turf war."

Finally, Waite gives some advice to engineers who want to work on PSWs:

> Before you start coding a feature, make sure you've done a thorough review of the design document [see the next chapter] with the designers, an art lead, and any other programmers who will touch the feature. You will always find flaws in the design. You can head off a lot of unnecessary (and frustrating) recoding by forcing some redesign work ahead of the fact.

See Chapter 14 for Waite's suggestions on creating a good user interface in PSWs.

Will Wright, Maxis Software

In Chapter 4, "General Game Design: Sports, Simulations, Adventure Games, and Puzzles," game designer extraordinaire Will Wright chats about creating games such as *The Sims*. Here, he offers some advice on creating massively multiplayer games such as *The Sims Online*.

Wright submits these three important online gaming factors for those who want to create a massively multiplayer computer or console game:

Player Motivation

In some sense, the primary components the designer is working with in an online game are the players rather than software mechanisms. Understanding the subtle, often chaotic details that drive this motivation is crucial to building a successful online game, I'm beginning to learn.

Diversity

In a world full of real people, there isn't a one-size-fits-all solution. Online worlds need to appeal to a broad range of player interests and abilities. The tricky part is getting these different player types to interact and depend on each other.

Social Landscape

The social landscape of online games is the real topography that the players are moving through. Just like a real landscape, the social topography needs to be interesting, navigable, and motivating.

Gordon Walton, Maxis Software

This talented V.P. and Executive Producer of *The Sims Online* has been authoring games and managing game development since 1977, believe it or not! He has personally developed more than two dozen games, and managed the development of hundreds of other games.

When asked what is the single most important thing to remember when creating a massively multiplayer game, Walton says, "community, community, and community." He explains:

> We were focused on community from the very beginning of *The Sims Online*. Will Wright started the project as a way to explore what he calls "social landscapes," made up of the connections between people. Most of our new features revolve around connecting people in interesting ways, while allowing them to control and direct their experiences in the world of *The Sims Online*. Roommates, messaging, overhead

chat, letters, bookmarks, and friendship all come to mind as community features. Basically, we wanted familiar web and chat tools to be integral to *The Sims Online* experience.

Walton continues to discuss the importance of "community" in any massively multiplayer game:

Massively multiplayer online games are, at their core, about community. The people in the game and their relationships are what make it continually interesting. Being able to communicate with other people who share a common interest in a safe anonymous setting can be extremely compelling, and leads to real relationships (the game itself is a good starting point for a common interest). Being able to meet people without being judged for your looks, social standing, geography, or any of the other real-world filters that separate us as human beings allows something magical to happen in human socialization. You can be yourself in the world or experiment by role-playing someone you always wanted to be. A game designer should focus on mechanics that bring like-minded people together as quickly as possible and that allow them to stay connected within the game world.

Walton says the social element cannot be lost during the gameplay:

You have to build in support for your community members, like easy ways to chat, ways to remember and track their friends, ways to group with other people, and to find groups of people among others. Let the players expose their game status, both inside the game and out on the web, and if at all possible let them have the potential to have a permanent effect on the world. All of these things encourage the players to build their own micro-groups within the game environment based on these so-called "virtual" relationships.

Interestingly, all the emotions you experience in these relationships are as real as those you experience in real-world relationships. The full game community is the aggregate of all the game members and the micro-groups they have formed. If these micro-groups are strong, the overall community will be so, too. I recommend taking the time to study the communities of the massively multiplayer games currently in existence to see what they have done well and where the communities have filled the gaps that these games left in their community support tools.

In discussing the various challenges in creating these kinds of games, Walton says the biggest problem isn't the games themselves:

The biggest problem is communicating how compelling this medium is to the average person. It sounds a little strange to people who have not experienced a persistent world game, but in fact, the emotions you feel and friends you make in these online worlds are as genuine as your so-called "real-life" experiences. I believe this medium has the ability to touch an audience in a way no other can, so the sooner we get better at communicating this value, the better!

When it comes to game design, Walton authored a piece titled "Seven Deadly Sins" in *Game Developer* magazine. He explains the premise:

> Well, that article was a bit of a rant on the state of game development, and the seven sins just seemed like a convenient structure for it. The core message was really that our flaws as people and game developers show up in our games, greatly limiting the potential audience. Simple things like making games that work only on the latest hardware, making games that appeal only to the most hardcore of gamers, and/or putting games out unpolished and incomplete really hold our industry back from its potential. Not collaborating with our players, lacking trust in their innate intelligence and creativity by giving them the ability to customize their gaming experience is also detrimental. Finally, not taking responsibility for our key role in the process of making games and not being willing to stand up to our management when decisions are made that will harm our game and consuming public. To have our work and industry taken seriously, we need to raise the level of professionalism to match our level of creativity. These two elements, professionalism and creativity, are more powerful together than when practiced separately. I think we will be much more effective and appreciated as an industry when these elements are in better balance.

On breaking into the industry, Walton offers the following words:

> ➤ Get a solid education in your area of choice. If nothing else, it shows you are committed and can complete what you start.

> ➤ Learn everything you can about games, but also about mainstream entertainment. You are competing for time people spend on all other entertainment forms, after all.

> ➤ Get ready to suffer for your art. In all seriousness, game development is something you should do only if you love it and are willing to commit yourself far beyond the level of a "day job." I personally wouldn't do anything else, even with the sacrifices involved, but it simply isn't for everyone.

NOTE
For more on breaking into the industry, sink your teeth into the meaty Chapter 21!

Craig Alexander, Electronic Arts/Westwood Studios

What discussion on massively multiplayer games would be complete without Westwood Studios' ambitious *Earth & Beyond*?

In the game, players climb into a ship and set out across a vast universe populated by tens of thousands of other players simultaneously over Electronic Arts' EA.com.

And who better to be the Executive Producer on the project than Craig Alexander; prior to getting into the gaming industry, Craig began his career at TRW in the project control office, scheduling large NASA spacecraft programs! (Be sure to read Craig's bio in the appendix of this book.)

OK, let's get down to business. What are the three most important considerations when creating a massively multiplayer online game?

"There are so many things for developers to keep in mind," cautions Alexander, but here are his highlights:

> The first—and most important—thing to remember is that you are creating a service. Stand-alone games are often linear with a short time span. Forty to 50 hours, and the game experience is over. An MMORPG, on the other hand, must continue to entertain the player for thousands of hours. It's similar to any subscription-based entertainment service, such as a magazine, premium TV channel, or cable/satellite network—they must be working correctly and providing enjoyment all the time.

> Another way to think of MMORPGs is like an episodic television show. Developers must always have things going on in-game; not just now, but 5 to 10 years down the line. You have to be much more forward-looking in the development planning process.

> The last thing to keep in mind is the sheer scale of an MMORPG. This type of game is enormous compared to a traditional stand-alone game. In addition, it requires skills you don't normally attribute to game design. Knowledge, practice in setting up, and managing back-end infrastructures and networks is absolutely essential. Also, managerial skills are important. MMORPG development teams are typically three times the size of a traditional team, so implementing managerial processes will have a huge impact in streamlining development.

Alexander refers to his years of experience while working on *Earth & Beyond*:

> Early on, we hired a community management team and a customer service team. We did this about two years earlier than we would for any other project, and they've proven to be invaluable...especially when we started the public test a year later. We already had the community and customer support systems in place to handle a large influx of people.

> We also hired a large team of writers to flesh out the story structure...and this started 4 years ago! Much like episodic television, we currently have 12 to 18 months of concrete story ideas planned out, along with a vague idea of what we'll be doing 5 years from now.

> As for the large skill set, we've staffed our team with more than 100 people with a large variety of skills. For example, we have 3 dedicated Oracle database programmers, several network programmers, 6 audio designers, and 20 game designers. Many of our team members have technical degrees from schools such as Cal Tech and MIT. In addition, our leadership team is larger than the entire development team of many early projects. *Earth & Beyond* has 2 development directors, 2 producers, 1 associate producer, and an executive producer. Not to mention the art, design, programming, and audio team leads.

Whew! Alexander says from a player standpoint, the biggest problem with MMORPGs is that they are becoming very repetitive:

> The "leveling treadmill" that was novel in the early days of the genre is quickly becoming tired. Players now want an active involving story and more diverse gameplay.

From a developer standpoint, the biggest challenge is managing the complexity of an MMORPG, says Alexander:

> This is because it has so many dynamic systems that interact with each other. Managing takes hyper levels of programming, planning, and processes. These were always nice to have in a standard PC game, but they are absolutely essential on an MMORPG.

Are there were any misconceptions about working on a massively multiplayer persistent world?

> The biggest misconception about working on an MMORPG is that it can be developed in the same time-frame, and for the same price, as a single-player PC game.

> But in truth, if you don't have an established architecture, development will take a minimum of three years, and the costs are substantially more. If you're not a well-funded developer or publisher, beware.

Left, a Jenquai Explorer surveys the landscape of an alien world. Right, a Progen Fighter comes to the aid of a Jenquai explorer who has taken on more than he can handle. Two scenes from Westwood Studios' *Earth & Beyond*. For more on the game, visit www.earthandbeyond.ea.com.
(Used with permission by Electronic Arts, Inc.)

If the roots of *Earth & Beyond* started more than four years ago—and it's only in its beta stage at the time of writing this—are there any regrets?

> Well, I've been on the project for less than a year, but I will say that I wouldn't have underestimated the staffing requirements for the game, nor how long it would take to complete it. As a general rule, estimate how much staff, how much money, and how long you'll need to finish the title…then double it.

In Chapter 21, Craig Alexander offers some insight on breaking into the biz. After all, he does have 17 years of experience under his belt!

Shane Dabiri, Blizzard Entertainment

Earlier in this chapter, we heard from Blizzard's Bill Roper and Matt Householder on working on RPGs such as the coveted *Diablo* series.

Now, we're joined by Blizzard's Shane Dabiri, who currently sits as Producer on the upcoming *World of WarCraft*, an eagerly anticipated massively multiplayer online role-playing game (MMORPG). In the past, Dabiri has worked on *WarCraft II*, *Starcraft*, *Starcraft Expansion: Brood War*, and *Diablo*. When it comes to designing an MMORPG, Dabiri says willing game designers or developers must keep these pointers in mind:

World of WarCraft is a persistent online world that allows players to visit familiar landmarks and explore uncharted lands, experience a dynamic world with constantly changing events and situations, trade with thousands of other players simultaneously, and, of course, engage in fast-paced combat against multiple opponents.

(Used with permission by Blizzard Entertainment, Inc.)

Be Prepared to Be Surprised

Players will figure out things that you never expected them to. Be prepared to be flexible with the design to adapt the gameplay style to what the customers adopt. If you say, "Players will never do that," more than likely they'll figure out a way. Doesn't mean you need to try and fill all the holes, just acknowledge that an MMORPG grows as the players do.

Content Is King

If players run out of cool places to go, items to find, monsters to beat, quests to complete, they will eventually become bored and start to leave your world. You need to continually challenge players.

A Few Minutes to Learn, a Lifetime to Master

That is the goal of many games. Much like chess, one can learn in but a few minutes how to play, but it would take a lifetime to be the best at the game. An MMORPG needs to evolve in the same fashion and let players jump right in, play, and have fun; but the true strategies and nuances will take you a long time to develop.

So, where does *World of WarCraft* fit in here?

World of WarCraft wasn't designed by an economist, social theorist, or military scientist. The game was developed by avid gamers. One can easily get sidetracked with 100 different avenues of research that might be "cool" to make in a game world, but in the end it needs to be easy to learn, fun to play, and a game you'll always want to come back to. All the "technology" in the world will never make a good game if you don't have the basics. Blizzard products adhere to this common idea.

Dabiri was asked whether he had any beefs with today's persistent online worlds. In fact, he has two of them:

First, poor customer support after the product goes live. Consumers expect quality service, especially if they're going to be paying per month for it. Make sure you have the customer support staff to support your population.

Second, poor launch strategies—meaning unstable servers or buggy code at launch. Many players could leave the game in the first several weeks because of poor performance or server stability. These players rarely come back...and bad impressions spread. Players don't pay monthly to become part of a beta product. They do expect there to be an ever-evolving world (and that changes will be made in that sense), but they do not expect or will not tolerate server downtime, slow game performance, or other bugs.

Finally, Dabiri offers his advice to those who want to create games for a living:

Play games. Play every game under the sun. Then play even more games.

Okay, so we get the point!

Flip the page to Chapter 6—it's a thorough discussion about how to create storyboards, write design documents, and create a hit video game character.

Chapter 6

Creating Characters, Storyboarding, and Design Documents

Mario. Pikachu. Donkey Kong. Lara Croft. Solid Snake. Sonic. Pac-Man. Crash Bandicoot. Duke Nukem. Earthworm Jim.

THE EXPERTS

- Shigeru Miyamoto
- Lorne Lanning
- Tsunekazu Ishihara
- Toshihiro Nagoshi
- David Perry
- George Broussard
- Scott Miller
- Jason Rubin
- Toby Gard
- Yuji Naka
- Yu Suzuki
- Hideo Kojima
- Michel Ancel
- Tim Schafer
- Gabe Newell
- Alex Garden
- Bruce C. Shelley
- Noah Falstein
- Phil Steinmeyer
- Phil Saunders
- Ragnar Tørnquist
- Ron Gilbert
- Daniel Greenberg
- Bill Roper
- Matt Householder
- Chris Taylor
- Warren Spector
- American McGee

What do these words have in common? The answer is simple—all of them are household names, but they're not famous actors from a Hollywood movie or some hit TV show. They're not Saturday morning cartoon characters (okay, some of them went on to that), and they're not the latest toy craze for kids. These are the video game heroes—the stars of the interactive screen whose marketing potential has kept them in the limelight for many years and lined the pockets of their creators with green.

Many developers and publishers have tried desperately to create the next billion-dollar game icon, but a catchy name or cute look often isn't enough. So what's the secret? This chapter contains words of wisdom from many of those aforementioned creators. But that's not all we're going to explore here.

If there were a common theme running through this chapter, it would be "how to get your ideas down on paper." Some game designers prefer to sketch out rough characters or backgrounds on paper (or work with artists to do so). Others draw sequential storyboards to help shape the vision and flow of the game or a cinematic cut-scene sequence. In other cases, designers write fiction or game screenplays (usually for adventure games or RPGs in which there's a lot of dialogue).

Design documents are often lengthy paper reports used to communicate the entire blueprint of the game, covering all its features, story elements, characters, locations, dialogue, puzzles, artwork, sound effects, music, and much more. These documents are usually designed in a modular fashion, so they can be updated and modified if the design of the game takes a new form.

This chapter highlights how some of the more famous characters in the gaming industry were born. Plus, we talk with game designers and artists about storyboarding, script writing, design documents, and other ways to flesh out your hit game before you type your first line of code.

As a special addition to this lengthy chapter, veteran freelance game designer Daniel Greenberg (www.danielgreenberg.com) has written an educational and enlightening essay on interactive script writing. But wait—there's more—designer American McGee has provided us with the complete narrative to the beginning of *American McGee's Alice*.

> **NOTE**
>
> See Chapter 13, "Game Art and Animation," for a discussion from legendary Hollywood animator Don Bluth (www.donbluth.com) on how to create a successful game character such as "Dirk the Daring" from the *Dragon's Lair* series.

Shigeru Miyamoto, Nintendo

A man who needs little introduction, the humble Mr. Miyamoto is a living legend in the interactive entertainment industry. He has conceived some of our most beloved electronic characters, such as Mario, Luigi, Donkey Kong, and Link from the *Legend of Zelda* series.

When asked how to create such internationally recognizable and deeply loved characters, Miyamoto said it all boils down to the fun factor:

> Making games "fun" is our only objective, and we're always making an effort to accomplish this goal. I believe that the creation of game characters is simply one of the processes to achieve this goal. If *Mario* games hadn't been fun to play, the character wouldn't be popular at all.

Exactly what makes a character fun? Is it solely appearance? A cute voice? Ease of control? Why do many game developers fail when trying to create the next Mario?

> I'm not sure why some fail to create a memorable character. A player can emotionally relate to the video game character as his/her other self, which is the decisive difference from the characters in other media. Mario, for instance, can be a character with completely different meaning when he's driving a car and when he's jumping. The other design elements will affect the look and feel of the character.

Miyamoto recognizes that his characters are quite cute and family-friendly and therefore won't appeal to all kinds of gamers: "I think a number of game players feel, 'If Miyamoto's characters had cooler appearances, I could love them.' All I can say to them is, "I am sorry."

Of course, you know these famous characters: Samus Aran returned in *Metroid Prime*, Link is from *The Legend of Zelda: The Wind Waker*, and Mario starred last in *Super Mario Sunshine*.
(Used with permission by Nintendo of America, Inc.)

Where does Miyamoto find inspiration for his beloved games and characters? How exactly did Mario come to life?

> The inspirations come from all over: my childhood adventures; the stories I heard growing up; the legends in Japan. After all, we can get inspiration from the ordinary things that everyone is experiencing in our daily lives by looking at them from a different angle. In the case of Mario, back in or around 1980, when we couldn't reproduce sophisticated designs on TV game machines due to the technological limitations, I had to make his nose bigger and put on a mustache so that players could notice he had the nose. I had to let him wear overalls so that his arm movements became noticeable. Mario was the result of these rational ideas plus the Italian design touch that I loved.

One last note: Miyamoto warns that designers may not be able to objectively comprehend how players will feel when playing the game for the first time because the designer is so close to the project.

Lorne Lanning, Oddworld Inhabitants

In Chapter 2, "General Game Design: Action/Arcade Games," Lorne Lanning, who is responsible in part for the memorable characters found in the various *Oddworld* games, talks about game design theory and production. Here, he discusses the "secret" of creating protagonists such as Abe or Munch.

> First, you have to know what you're after when designing lead characters. Is it a heroic character? An outlaw? A spy? What are they all about, and what do they represent? You have to know exactly how you want them to communicate to the viewer. You need to know as much about them as you can conjure

up: What they like and dislike, what their dilemmas are, what makes them tick. These are the things that give characters depth. The depth of the character is something that you should understand before you even start to design how it looks visually.

What's the first step, then? Lanning references *Oddworld's* lovable aliens:

Before we hit the drawing table, our focus was to create hero characters who were true underdogs. They're unlikely heroes who couldn't believe what had happened to them, their species, their cultures, and so on. These characters would be considered the garbage of society. They come from the native aboriginal class, the working class, or from the wild. They're looked upon as pure commodity in their world, but not as living sensitive beings. They're not the muscle-bound superheroes that you wish you could be; they're the poor schmucks that we already are. We wanted characters that embrace the notion of finding their inner strength and purpose.

You then have to be willing to go through a ton of design iterations. When Farzad Varahramyan [a production designer on the *Oddworld* games] started to design Munch, we went through literally hundreds of designs. We already knew that Munch was an amphibious creature who hopped on one leg like a bird on land, yet swam like a dolphin in the water. We knew he had only one leg, two little arms, a big mouth, and a big head. We knew he had a remote zap port implanted in his skull. We knew that he was young and the last of his kind. We knew that he was in denial regarding the condition of his species. We knew that he was lonely and searching out others of his kind. He was uneducated. He was really just a child in the scheme of things. We knew all of these things when Farzad began to create many, many cool designs…but still we weren't hitting the emotional mark of our goal.

Next, Lanning says they passed different iterations past Sherry McKenna, Executive Producer/CEO of Oddworld Inhabitants.

Her read is predictably non-biased—as she puts it, "completely pedestrian." She looks at things and just registers how it makes her feel. She's a great litmus test for us in this respect. We wanted to make sure that Munch held a place in the hearts of males and females. It was a very difficult character to design, and we spent a lot of time finalizing him. Farzad stuck to it and didn't get discouraged. In the end, he came through and we were able to create a new hero who hooked those who saw him. He had to look like he came from *Oddworld*; he had to look as though he could have evolved there, and he had to capture our hearts.

Interestingly, Lanning says their various publishers were skeptical at first that this critter could win people's hearts.

However, we believed we had hit the mark on our final iteration, and after much debate, the final Munch design prevailed. Since then, it has gone over extremely well with all the audiences who have seen him. Had the publishing forces had their way, Munch could have been watered down into something less strange-looking, and thus less edgy. You need to believe when you have something that communicates to an audience, and you need to be prepared to defend and substantiate what you believe works and why it works. You also need to listen to feedback, in case you're wrong. It's one thing to believe you have a solid design; it's another to be able to convince others.

Lorne Lanning says his team went through many iterations of *Oddworld's* beloved characters,
Munch and Abe. Here are a couple of publicity shots of Abe, used to help promote its last game.
(© 2001 Oddworld Inhabitants, Inc. All rights reserved. Used with permission by Microsoft Corp.)

When you're on the creative front, the people who are paying for the product want assurances that the "creative" will work for the target audience. Of course, to have assurances usually means that it's proven historically. Unfortunately, history doesn't reveal what will creatively work for today's and tomorrow's audience. So the dance of selling something new and different is almost as important as the ability to create it.

NOTE

Many gamers want to know why Oddworld Inhabitants made the switch from developing for Sony to developing for Xbox. Type this address into your web browser to read an interview with Lorne Lanning and Sherry McKenna, co-founders of Oddworld Inhabitants:

`www.oddworld.com/oddworld/company/ow_inhabitants4_bio.html`

This chapter also discusses the importance of design documents and storyboarding. Lanning contributes his thoughts on these topics:

Design documents are critical. They are the equivalent of a movie script or a business plan; without one, you don't have a roadmap that will keep you on course throughout the storm that is production—let alone getting you financing in the first place.

In addition, today games take large teams of people and have multimillion-dollar budgets. This means that everyone needs to have clear communication, or else a lot of money can be wasted very quickly. The team, the publisher, the management—everyone needs to know what you're getting into if you're to pull it off and have production go smoothly. It also becomes the basis of your schedule at the beginning of the project.

Lanning offers some advice on how to approach drafting a design document:

> I would first point toward Gamasutra [www.gamasutra.com] as a place for aspiring designers to look at game design reference materials. This is a great site, where many working designers have taken the time to share their experiences and post formats they use or find helpful. Overall, I see game design as largely an exercise in creative structured thinking. One must be able to organize and systematize ideas if one is able to conceive something as large and complicated as a contemporary game. This means understanding the core of your game and being able to clearly identify and isolate each of its key components and critical functionalities. These aspects will need to be communicated to the people who will be funding, managing, and building the game. So, the designer should really master being able to intelligently communicate the vision of a game and also communicate why it will work for the gaming audience.
>
> The designer also needs to fully understand what the game will be and how it will be built—and most importantly *if* it can be built. It is often that you'll hear concepts that sound great, but they will never see the light of day because they are too ambitious, not grounded in repeatable core mechanics that scale well, or are ultimately non-produceable due to lack of time, money, and talent.

Lanning says storyboarding is critical to the team at Oddworld Inhabitants—primarily in the video sequences:

> We used to do storyboards for gameplay, but this became more of a burden than an asset. Then we started doing actual visualizations, which helped to communicate ideas much more clearly. For these, we used 3D data to illustrate the moves, lighting, effects, animations, etc. that the game engine would eventually run. There's nothing like seeing something do exactly what you want it to do—before it has been coded—to help communicate new ideas to a team of people.

Be sure to visit Chapter 9, "Puzzle Design," which contains some stellar advice from Lorne Lanning on how to create good puzzles in your games.

Tsunekazu Ishihara, Pokémon Co.

It's hard to argue that *Pokémon* has become one of the world's biggest phenomena over the past few years. It first started out as a Game Boy title in Japan and then became a popular kid's TV show, collectible card game, successful toy line, movie franchise, and more.

Here to speak about creating successful video game characters is Tsunekazu Ishihara, the producer on all *Pokémon* and *Pokémon*-related products for Nintendo.

Naturally, the first question is whether there's a formula, secret, or technique to creating characters such as Pikachu and other mega-popular *Pokémon* icons. Ishihara responds:

> When talking about Pokémon games, its success is because the characters are described in thorough detail, I believe. More specifically, for each Pokémon, there's weight, height, effective offense/defense, and other attributes. These details help make Pokémon video games very well balanced; on the other hand, they help make such imaginary Pokémon characters as Pikachu have more of a realistic existence.

With this information, children form their images of each Pokémon in their minds, empathizing with each of the characters and feeling as if they were actually traveling with Pokémon. Such well-detailed characteristics may be the secret of why Pokémon characters such as Pikachu are well-received by children around the world.

On its international success, Ishihara says, "It was not something we had originally intended." Instead, Pokémon was designed originally for the Japanese people, says Ishihara. Honestly, he later admits, it was designed for his nephews and nieces!

After the success in Japan, when we were to bring them to the U.S., our U.S. people demanded a variety of modifications in order to Americanize them. For example, they said that Pokémons are too cute and that they wanted to add muscular nature and such themes as fighting against evil. In the end, however, we haven't complied with their requests. If we were to do so, Pokémon would not be Pokémon. As a result, children around the world fell in love with Pokémon.

One final funny note. "It has turned out that my nephew and niece are happy they sort of brought Pokémon to the rest of the children in the world!" jokes Ishihara.

Believe it or not, Tsunekazu Ishihara says he created Pokémon to please his niece and nephew and never dreamed it would become an unprecedented international success. Nintendo estimates worldwide Pokémon franchise revenue in 2002 alone at $1 billion. Wowza. In the spring of 2003, the phenomenon returned to America with Pokémon *Ruby* and Pokémon *Sapphire* for the Game Boy Advance.

(Used with permission by Nintendo of America, Inc.)

Toshihiro Nagoshi, Amusement Vision/Sega

How can anyone not fall in love with the cute little monkey in Sega's *Super Monkey Ball*? Well, in Chapter 4, "General Game Design: Sports, Simulations, Adventure Games, and Puzzles," Amusement Vision president Toshihito Nagoshi chats about game design theory, and here he shares his insight on creating a successful video game character.

How did Nagoshi come up with the monkey from *Super Monkey Ball*? Interestingly, this character came from a game design problem. Explains Nagoshi:

> At one point in the process of creating *Super Monkey Ball*, we ran into two problems supporting the basic concept of rolling a ball through various environments. The first was that it was not very easy to intuitively tell which direction the ball was rolling; the second was that on a flat surface, gameplay was monotonous. To correct this, at first we painted patterns and characters on the surface. Later, we had an inspiration that we could make the ball itself transparent and enclose the characters inside it. The character turned out to be a monkey, but there was no special reason. We took care to make it look catchy and cute. If I am forced to mention one reason for choosing a monkey, I would say we wanted the game to be called "XXXX Ball" and ended up liking the title "Monkey Ball" best.

Just how and why did Nagoshi and the folks at Sega's Amusement Vision studio come up with the monkey from the popular *Super Monkey Ball* series? It's probably not what you think! Pictured here is Toshihiro Nagoshi, our lovable monkey, and a screen shot from 2002's *Super Monkey Ball 2* for the Nintendo GameCube platform.
(Used with permission by SEGA of America, Inc.)

Great story! So, how can others learn from this? What are the most important things to keep in mind when creating a successful video game character?

> I have one thing that I always place a lot of value in. That is to make players feel that there is a style to the game that demonstrates the developer's VISION. This can happen when a character's looks and actions match each other or when there is a surprise element to the game. This is most important.

> In *Super Monkey Ball*, the characters were functional. They were there to lead movement of the ball through their actions and to improve the game interface through the nature of their interactions.

> Thus, we succeed in communicating to players the condition of the ball in the game through actions of the characters. For example, the ball rolls at a slow speed when the character walks slowly. The speed of the ball increases when the character runs, the ball rolls at a greater speed when the character dashes, and the ball bounds when the character jumps. I think this is truly an innovative idea.

Finally, Nagoshi adds:

> In the end, if a game has only nice graphics or only operability, it is incomplete. It is impossible to have an excellent character if those two things are not working together.

David Perry, Shiny Entertainment

President of Shiny Entertainment and game designer extraordinaire David Perry has brought to life a number of hit characters over the years. These characters include protagonists from the *Earthworm Jim* games, *MDK*, *Wild 9*, *Messiah*, *Sacrifice*, and a little ol' movie franchise known as *The Matrix*.

Perry was asked to provide three (in)valuable pieces of advice on creating a successful game character, and all three of his answers are thought-provoking:

> 1. Humor is a very important part of entertainment. So if you can make it amusing, that's the easiest way to go. Unique abilities are also good. Earthworm Jim's suit would use him to achieve its goals. Funny stuff like that adds spice to the characters you're creating.

> 2. Somebody once said that a great character has a unique silhouette—if you can identify a character just by its outline, you know you've made something that will stand out in a crowd.

> 3. New and interesting weapons are also important. Nothing is worse than playing a game with a leaky peashooter. So great firepower is a good way to pat a gamer on the head.

Perry says he hates to advertise this, but…

> I have to say that the best way to learn how to make a great character is to take this class: www.beyondstructure.com. I highly recommend it. If you're new to the business, you're not going to get away with *Pac-Man* any more; you have to make real, intelligent, interesting characters. This seminar will tell you exactly how to do just that.

Many times throughout this book, you may see conflicting advice on certain topics. Case in point: Asked about the importance of design documents, Perry directly contradicts Lorne Lanning and others:

I used to think they were a waste of time. I still do, to be honest. I prefer different documents that matter to certain people that they will bother to read:

➤ **The game walkthrough script**. We write in a program called Final Draft (`www.finaldraft.com`), and we write the experience we would love to see from the beginning to the end of the game. It's written kinda like a movie, but describes the ambiance, who's there, what you see, what you don't see, the action, what they say, etc.

➤ **The lists**. These are done in Microsoft Excel and are tracked. These are lists of everything: objects, weapons, characters, balance statistics, etc.

Game designer extraordinaire David Perry says humor can spice up your characters quite a bit. Seen here are characters from *Earthworm Jim, MDK, Messiah,* and *Sacrifice.*
(© Shiny.)

Does Perry storyboard his games?

> Over the years, I've worked with all sorts of business people. Some "get it," but some are completely flatline when it comes to any ability to think creatively. I found that the saying is indeed true, "A picture paints a thousand words." We extensively draw storyboards now, so that anyone who needs to understand the vision can just look at the pictures like a comic book. It saves a lot of discussion.

> I've found that taking 3D sculptures of your characters to meetings is great because it's an instant conversation piece, and the people you're pitching become mesmerized by the sculpture as you describe the design. How do you get a good sculpture? There are several ways, but these are the best two I know:

> ➤ Use a great sculptor who works with action/pitch characters. Just ask for photos of previous work.

> ➤ Use a technology called rapid prototyping (search on the Net). Companies like Gentle Giant will take your game's 3D model data and then sculpt it using lasers so you get an exact replica of your character. We have some quite amazing sculptures from these guys that took zero effort at our end.

Perry's words of wisdom can be found in other places throughout this book—be sure to read his thoughts on general game design theory and implementation (Chapter 2) and on breaking into the industry (Chapter 21, "Breaking Into the Industry").

George Broussard, 3D Realms

Ever since the third game in 3D Realms' popular *Duke Nukem* series came out in 1996, countless others have tried to create a successful lead character by mimicking its overly macho, mouthy, bad-ass hero, Duke Nukem. (Heck, his name says it alone!)

3D Realms president George Broussard offers some advice to those looking to create character-driven action games:

> First off, your game has to be great. Without that, nothing you do with a character matters. We try to create catchy character names—like Duke Nukem or Max Payne—that instantly get a reaction from people or create an image in someone's mind. That's the "hook." Once you have a hook that people find interesting, you just flesh out the character with personality traits, mannerisms, and catchphrases.

Broussard explains why Max Payne is more than just a cool name:

> Remedy Entertainment did a great job with Max Payne. His name has a unique hook, and people usually get the pun—that he delivers "maximum pain." Then you give Max a compelling reason to act and be motivated. He's an undercover cop with his back against the wall, out for revenge after the death of his wife and daughter. Finally, you give Max his "personality" through the way he speaks. Max narrates his journey metaphorically, in the style of detective films of the 1940s and 1950s. What you end up with

is an interesting character who's fairly unique to games, and hopefully people respond to that. Our gaming audience is getting more sophisticated every day and won't settle for less.

Broussard adds that this advice really depends on the types of characters you want to make. He explains:

We typically create over-the-top characters that lean more toward what you might find in comic books or high-action movies. Characters that are larger than life—and for those types of characters, there's a pretty basic starting point.

To reiterate and summarize his points made previously, Broussard says you can break down any character into the following characteristics:

➤ **Personality traits**. These define the character's personality and how he or she reacts to situations.

➤ **Appearance**. There should be a distinctive look to your character, so people will learn to recognize the character from appearance alone. Examples: Lara Croft; Superman (almost any superhero); Darth Vader.

➤ **Motivation**. Why do your characters do what they do? What drives them? Once this is established, your characters will get stronger from doing things the way people expect them to.

➤ **Catchphrase**. The best characters become famous and well-known for a simple catchphrase that sticks in people's minds, and usually becomes part of pop culture. (Remember the "Where's the Beef?" commercials for Wendy's?) Examples: "What's up, doc?" (Bugs Bunny); "Up, up, and away!" (Superman); "Holy hand grenades, Batman!" (Robin); "I'll be back!" (The Terminator); "Go ahead, make my day." (Dirty Harry).

➤ **Name**. A character's name should be "catchy" and unique in some way, so people hear the name and get an instant image in their minds. Rhyming and alliteration are good tools to come up with a catchy character name. Examples: Duke Nukem, Sonic the Hedgehog, Earthworm Jim.

To further illustrate his point on the "parts" of a distinguishable character, Broussard provides these examples:

See if you can guess the character before the name is given, simply from the basic elements.

Personality trait: Egotistical

Appearance: Sunglasses, red muscle shirt, bandoliers, blond flattop

Motivation: Kick alien ass/score with babes

Catchphrase: "Come get some"

Name: Duke Nukem

Personality traits: Determined, inquisitive, loner

Appearance: Black suit, white shirt, tie, cell phone

Motivation: FBI agent/uncover conspiracies

Catchphrase: "The Truth Is Out There"

Name: Fox Mulder, from *The X-Files*

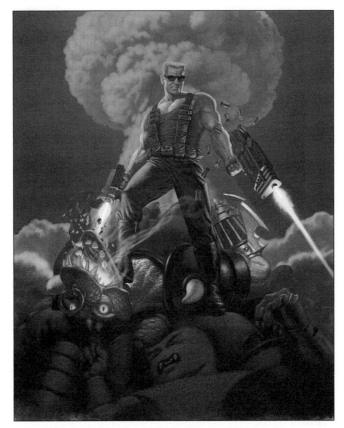

Broussard suggests hiring a writer: "We're at the point today where all games need a real writer who can breathe real personalities, dialogue, and life into characters." Here's a shot of the Duke in all his glory, which eventually made the box front for the bad boy, *Duke Nukem 3D*.
(Used with permission by 3D Realms, Inc.)

Says Broussard, "The preceding is merely a starting point for developing your own characters, and you can make them more or less complex, depending on your needs. But in the end, these characteristics are needed for a really memorable character."

How do you translate sketches to real characters in the game? Is it necessary for a series such as *Duke Nukem*?

As video games have gotten more and more complex, we've started to adopt the ways that movies do things. A lot of games today have scripts much like a movie, where all the action, cut scenes, and dialogue are carefully laid out in every detail. Another thing that has been adopted is the idea of concept sketches. These sketches serve to solidify the look and feel of elements in the game, such as characters, locations, and action sequences.

But what about design documents? Are they necessary for all types of games?

Let me tell you about design docs. *Duke Nukem 3D* didn't even have one. We did stuff as we went, adding bits that were cool and discarding ideas that didn't work. Look how the game turned out. All we had was a vague notion that the game would be based in a future seedy L.A. The rest came from a dynamic development process.

Duke Nukem Forever has substantially more on paper from the start because it's a much more cohesive and large game. But people who write 300-page design docs beforehand are wasting their time. The game design process (for most) is an evolutionary process. You refine and redesign as you go, learning and making things better. It's insane to write a 300-page doc; then just make the game. There's no way you can think of every cool idea before you make the game, and you have to be flexible enough to roll with the punches and add and refine ideas as you go, all according to the timeline.

Speaking from our experience, design docs are merely a general guideline that gets more and more polished as you go. You just try to stay three to four months ahead of things as you go. The design doc isn't done until the game is.

Also bear in mind that 3D action games are not that complex. They have bad guys, guns, items, and level locations. Not exactly rocket science or something needing 300 pages.

Be sure to read all about the exciting *Duke Nukem* happenings at 3D Realms' official web site (www.3drealms.com).

Scott Miller, 3D Realms

We just heard from George Broussard, president of 3D Realms, about creating such hit characters as Duke Nukem—but we'll also turn to 3D Realms' CEO Scott Miller to reveal the "secret" to creating successful characters while so many others have failed.

Positioning and differentiation. Duke is the first white male action hero. No other character will ever have a chance knocking Duke off his particular pedestal because it's better to be first than it is to be better (a key concept of positioning). Likewise, Max Payne is the first character of his type—a true antihero vigilante cop—and no other developer will ever have a chance making a better character with this description. Thanks to the well-known psychology of the human mind, better doesn't win; being first is what really matters.

George [Broussard] and I have studied and discussed characters for almost a decade, and finally in the last 6–7 years we think we've put together the key pieces of the puzzle better than anyone else in this industry. A bold statement, maybe, but consider that we planned Max to be the next great male action character and franchise from day one of the games design, and guided Remedy (the developers) in the key ways to make it happen. And we're going to do it again with two more coming game characters: Bombshell (appearing first in *Duke Nukem Forever* before starring in her own games) and another game I can't announce yet.

Miller acknowledges that this is a tough topic to cover in brief because, as he puts it, "It's worthy of its own book."

But there are specific guidelines to naming a character properly so that the name is better remembered and has a catchy hook. A character-based game should be named with the character's name (much like most comic books do—which was our inspiration for this particular idea years ago). One commonality of catchy, memorable names is that one of the names is only one syllable long. For example: Johnny Quest, James Bond, Darth Vadar, Luke Skywalker, Duke Nukem, Commander Keen, Indiana Jones, Max Payne, Han Solo, Lara Croft, on and on. There are several important rules like this that should be followed to create a great character name.

Another piece of advice, something that was also touched on by Broussard, is that a character's name should reflect something about the character. Explains Miller:

Duke Nukem and Max Payne do this very well. Other game character names like Lara Croft, Kate Archer, John Mullins, John Blade are just generic, valueless names that say nothing about the personality of the character they represent.

In other areas of this book, Miller shares a lot of great advice on general game design, on building a franchise (Chapter 2), and on breaking into the industry (Chapter 21).

Jason Rubin, Naughty Dog

As a wholly owned subsidiary of Sony Computer Entertainment, Inc., Naughty Dog won worldwide acclaim for its *Crash Bandicoot* games (1996 to 1999). Jason Rubin is the co-founder of the company and also served as lead designer on its latest title, *Jak & Daxter: The Precursor Legacy*, a 3D platformer for the PlayStation 2. *Jak II* is scheduled for a fall 2003 launch.

Is there a formula for creating a successful game character?

Ah, the impossible question to answer. Certainly, there are many things that contribute. Good design, which means making sure that the right people are involved and the right opinions are sought. Good integration, which involves making sure that the character fits the game and the game is worth playing. Good marketing, to make sure that the character is positioned correctly and the public wants to know more about it. And good follow-through, including derivative products like toys and shirts to reinforce the connection; as well as properly timed sequels and continued placement of the character in the public eye. Certainly, no successful character that I can think of has failed in any of these categories. The best, like Pokémon and Mario, have not only done well in each, but have always excelled.

So, how important is a cute/cool character in a video game today, such as *Crash Bandicoot* or *Jak & Daxter*?

The further into the broader marketplace gaming goes, the more important "characters" become. That might mean a lead character, or a license like *Tony Hawk*, or the official NBA teams and logos. The reason that video games are interesting to more people today than they were in the '80s is that people who couldn't identify with a *Pong* paddle or *Pac-Man* are interested in playing *Lara Croft*. As the gap between reality or fantasy and the visuals in games narrows, more people are drawn to the medium. And as story and plot become more involving in games, even the non-competitive have a reason to play. A look across recent bestsellers yields (besides the venerable *Tetris*) a list of games that focus on characters broadly defined, and the trend should continue.

It's not always easy whipping up a hit character—Naughty Dog's Jason Rubin admits that *Jak & Daxter* took about four months to flesh out, which is twice as long as it took to get *Crash Bandicoot* right.
(Used with permission by Sony Computer Entertainment America, Inc. and Naughty Dog, Inc.)

Without a doubt, many readers of this chapter would be interested in how Rubin and company came up with the Crash Bandicoot character. He answers with the following anecdote:

> Crash was designed by multiple Naughty Dogs and two Hollywood cartoon designers named Charles Zembillas and Joe Pearson. We did dozens of paper sketches and then we bred them together, picking the best features from each and adding new mutations along the way. After dozens of generations, we had a 2D Crash. Then we modeled him in a 3D package and further refined his attributes to work with the added dimension. Finally, we put him on the PlayStation and refined him yet again to make sure that features stood out and that he worked at the resolution and with the number of polygons that we were using. The whole process took about four months.

Speaking of Crash, if Rubin had to summarize it into a paragraph, what would he say is the key to Crash's success? He ponders the question, and then answers:

> Crash Bandicoot, the character, appeals to the broadest variety of people: young and old; male and female; Japanese, North American, or European. Most first-time *Crash* purchasers, regardless of nationality, are buying from advertising, promotional material, or the box cover. If the character fails, then the game fails. *Crash* excelled in this department, thanks to both a good original design and Sony Computer Entertainment's amazing worldwide marketing campaign.

With this in mind, was Jak & Daxter any easier, more difficult, or about the same?

> Jak & Daxter's design process was similar to Crash's, but it took twice as long. We asked more opinions and had more experience as a group. We also designed Jak & Daxter in conjunction with our producers and marketing teams from Sony America, Sony Europe, and Sony Japan. We set out from the beginning to make a character that appealed to the whole world. Crash was designed in a less global manner, and I think that only luck and a great marketing effort by Sony facilitated his international appeal. Overall, I'm more excited about Jak & Daxter than I was with Crash. I love the way they look, and I think that they have more possibilities for growth as characters.

Want to catch Rubin's advice on game design? Fling yourself back to Chapter 2.

Toby Gard, Confounding Factor

You may not be too familiar with this designer's name, but chances are that you're aware of his most beloved creation: Lara Croft. Toby Gard left Core Design as lead graphic artist and game designer on the revolutionary title *Tomb Raider* to launch his own development studio, Confounding Factor (www.confounding-factor.com), alongside fellow Core Design lead programmer Paul Douglas. Their first game, *Galleon*, will be an epic action/adventure for multiple platforms.

In a minute, we'll get into creating successful characters. (And *Tomb Raider*'s Lara Croft is as successful as it gets—complete with her own live action movie series starring Angelina Jolie!) First, a few words from Gard on general game design.

Your objectives should be contingent upon your resources. If you're forced into using a type of technology, such as a certain engine, or are limited in any other way by your platform or programming, then you have to come at your design from that direction first. For instance, at its most severe, if you're making a Game Boy game, then you already know you're limited to it being 2D and having pretty serious speed and memory restrictions. No *Quake 12* for you.

Assuming that you'll be making a game for the PC or one of the newer 3D consoles, however, as is more often the case these days, your restrictions are pretty loose. I prefer working from this direction because you can take a pure idea and you know that in some form you'll be able to make it happen—however hard that route is. So then you need an idea, right? Well, I think we all have about a million of them each—it's whatever gets you excited, like wanting to be in *Star Wars* or showing people how much fun snowboarding is. Then all you need to do is go down to the pub and talk endlessly with your mates (or preferably with whoever you're going to make the game with) about what would be cool about it.

During that time, you need to be constantly solving the "How the hell can we do that?" technical questions. Even if you're just saying stuff like, "Well, we need shadows. *Quake* does shadows, so how are they doing that, and can we use a similar technique?" During this period, you should be thinking an awful lot about how your control system will work. I'm a believer in compressing your control system down to the minimum number of buttons to achieve your aims; that way, you tend to get an elegant rather than a cumbersome control system. You're basically aiming to be in the position where you have such a clear idea of what the game will be like that you can actually play it in your head. When you can do that, if you're visualizing it hard enough, you'll be able to see and address loads of the flaws in the idea before you've implemented a damn thing!

Therefore, the three most important things for me are a) visualize the control system, including game mechanics; b) have technology ideas for how to implement all of the above; and c) write it all down!

When creating a lead character for a video game, Gard says to be sure you really *like* what you've designed; then other people have a good chance of liking it, too. He expands on this notion:

If you aren't sure about your character, dump it. If you experiment all the time, drawing without any particular purpose and exploring avenues that look good in a fairly freeform sort of way, at some point you'll get something that you just instinctively know works. Then, you see, you'll start to love the character, and that will shine through in your work because the character starts to take on its own personality through your drawings. I think that's probably it—you need to design and redesign again and again until you can't any more. Then just draw that character about a hundred times (having fun with it), and you'll be there. Well, that's the method I use.

Can Gard offer any specific do's or don'ts for creating a hit character like Lara Croft?

➤ Make a character simple and clear; look at comics to see why. Your art should be an iconic piece of graphic art, as well as a nicely rendered piece of art. Example: gray, black, and yellow = Batman. Bold sections of color and a simple overall design. Whatever style you draw him in, Batman is always Batman because he's so iconic he's almost a logo in his own right.

➤ Do something radical. Almost everything can work equally well turned on its head. Most people are sick of seeing the same sorts of characters, so break the rules.

➤ If you want people to take to your character, then you should have respect for it. It should have admirable qualities; it should be something you kind of wouldn't mind spending a few hours stepping into the shoes of.

After all, that's the whole point, right?

Tomb Raider's Lara Croft is Gard's claim to fame. Also, a shot from Gard's latest project, an action/adventure epic for the PC, PlayStation 2, GameCube and Xbox, dubbed *Galleon*. *(Lara Croft's image is used with permission by Eidos Interactive, Inc.; Galleon image used with permission by Confounding Factor, Inc.)*

Yuji Naka, Sega

As president of Sonic Team Corporation, Yuji Naka has worked on a number of beloved Sega games, including *Nights*, *Samba de Amigo*, *Phantasy Star Online*, *Sonic Adventure*, and others.

Through an interpreter, we chatted with Mr. Naka about game design and creating successful lead characters.

Asked to give some advice for those interested in making games for a living, Naka's answer was to try and create a game with its own unique identity (regardless of what others are doing) and to add as much feeling and character into the game as possible.

Speaking of characters, Sonic the Hedgehog is one of the world's most recognizable video game mascots. How can someone create the next Sonic?

> Characters produced from the games are naturally born of the fun elements of the games. Because it's much different in that respect from animated cartoons and movies, think about the game itself and then create characters.

> The game's movement and flow are the necessary reason why Sonic was born. There originally was Super Mario, and although much different from Nintendo's character, we designed—not as his rival—but as a game that we can be proud of on the same level…and Sonic was born.

On finding inspiration for games, Naka says he tries to direct his attention to various kinds of things in his everyday life—like everyday entertainment, for example.

What's the best advice Naka can give for creating massively multiplayer console games such as *Phantasy Star Online*? "Carefully create the means of communication." That is, one of the most important points is the communication among the game players. So when you create a game such as *Phantasy Star Online*, you should think about what communication means to the game-play.

Does Naka believe that multiplayer games are the future for consoles? He responds, "I guess it is in a way, but I don't think it's the only way. I would say that 30% of players will become multiplayers and the rest won't."

Naka emphasizes that the user interface (see Chapter 14, "The All-Important User Interface [UI] and Game Control") is one of the most important considerations for the game designer: "Games that don't take the interface and controls into account have not been successful in the past—they're the most important points in the game itself."

Yu Suzuki, Sega

Also at Sega is the one and only Yu Suzuki, who is responsible for such fantastic games as the character-driven *Shenmue* series, the *Virtua Fighter* series, the *Virtua Cop* series, *Hang On*, *Space Harrier*, and others.

Although Chapter 2 houses Suzuki's answers on creating fun and challenging video games, here we just asked him one question: How does he create such great characters as Ryo in *Shenmue*? Suzuki says:

> What's most important is originality. Also, by tightly creating invisible parts like background stories or personalities of the characters, later development opportunity will be broadened. And lastly, a note on self-promotion: It's necessary to make an active effort to gain more recognition, like exposure or advertisement to media such as magazines or home pages.

Hideo Kojima, Konami

The celebrated game designer responsible for the *Metal Gear Solid* games was asked to discuss the importance of a lead character, such as Solid Snake, and how to create a successful one.

> This is a tough question. The lead character of a story is the most important element. If you can't associate yourself with the lead character of a movie or novel, you won't enjoy the storyline, no matter how great the storyline is. This holds true for games. What's different is that in games you control the main character. This is why it's necessary to take into consideration the character's "compatibility" to the viewpoints and psychology of all the people who would potentially play the game. Maintaining this balance is very difficult. The basic character description/setting, along with the character itself, is one thing. When the player actually moves the character, the character becomes complete. The player is the one who adds to the character what's missing.

Be sure to turn back to Chapter 2 to read Kojima's advice on general video game design.

Hideo Kojima, creator of the insanely popular *Metal Gear Solid* games, believes that the success of a video game character is directly related to how well the player can control him or her.
(Used with permission by Konami of America, Inc.)

> **NOTE**
>
> If you've ever seen the wacky and wonderful paper-thin characters such as those found in PaRappa the Rapper or Um Jammer Lammy, then you've gotten a taste of the imagination of Rodney Greenblat. Check out Chapter 13 on art and animation to read how he came up with these characters and his trademark artistic style.

Michel Ancel, Ubi Soft Entertainment

As project director at Ubi Soft in Paris, France, Michel Ancel is the designer who created the character Rayman, a huge international hit. He stars in all the versions of the *Rayman* games (available on multiple platforms), including the latest, *Rayman 3: Hoodlum Havoc*. To date, the *Rayman* games have sold more than 11 million units worldwide.

Before we dive into Rayman as a character, Ancel offers some game design tips. "Be creative, be logical, and understand the player's point of view," he begins. Using *Rayman* as an example, Ancel continues:

> The creativity aspect of *Rayman* comes from its graphic style. We also tried to imagine some unique game sequences, like being chased by a pirate spaceship or cooperating with a powerful but fearful friend. The logic part is about the rules, the gameplay techniques that you have to follow precisely, like the evolutions of *Rayman*, the level of skills, the puzzles. And to understand the player's view, the game must be playable for maybe millions of people. It means that we must consider how people will react when playing. The typical questions are about the controls, the story, the challenge, the rewards, and so on. Are they good enough? Easy to understand? And so on. These questions must be answered early in the game's creation.

How is Rayman visually original? Well, for one thing, he's got no arms or legs—the hands and feet just magically appear where they should!
(Used with permission by Ubi Soft Entertainment, Inc.)

Is there a special technique for creating world-renowned characters such as Rayman?

When I created Rayman, I didn't really analyze it. I just made it like this because it was fun for me and my friends. I also wanted an easy-to-animate character. Your character must not look like [other characters], but at the same time he must appear familiar to people. That's a challenge between originality and an easy-to-understand character.

Rayman is visually original, but in some aspects he's close to what young people are wanting from a hero. The visual aspect is important for the first impact. After this first feeling, the next one is about animation. A lot of the personality is revealed by the animations—the way your character moves in common actions. The next and most important step—especially for games—comes from his powers, his specific actions. What can he do that will surprise the player? This is an important question. The next and deepest aspect will come from his feelings, his personality, the way he reacts in particular situations: danger, love, surprises, victory, and so on. You must consider all these steps of perceptions and be sure that you're not completely copying another hero!

"Rayman is 50% action and 50% humor. That's what most young people care about," says Ancel.

Finally, he discusses the issue of control (discussed in depth in Chapter 14). Ancel agrees that one of the biggest challenges when making a game is to make the control intuitive and comfortable. The *Rayman* series is a good example of it done right. Ancel explains why:

You must look at the player's reflexes. To avoid frustration, you must think about what's natural for people. Test your new control with your friends, wife, children—everyone who will give you feedback. A single delay on the buttons, the acceleration curve of the camera—all these parameters are important to tune if you want good control. You must have more than 100 of these kinds of parameters in your game and must be able to change them easily, depending on the player's feedback.

Tim Schafer, Double Fine Productions

Some of the computer game industry's most beloved characters were created by the affable Tim Schafer, who recently left an eight-year stint at LucasArts to start Double Fine Productions (www.doublefine.com). His first project at DFP will be *Psychonauts* for the Xbox. Schafer has brought such memorable, time-withstanding characters to life as Manuel "Manny" Calavera and Hector Lemans from *Grim Fandango* and Ben and Malcolm Corley from *Full Throttle*.

According to Schafer, wish-fulfillment is the main secret to character (and game) design. He explains:

Never forget that you're providing players with the chance to do something they can't do in their daily lives. It should be something that they really want to do, if just for a little while. With *Full Throttle*, we were banking on the secret desire to be a biker: big, tough, cool. Riding a huge hog around. Without a helmet. Ask yourself, what's the wish-fulfillment that I'm providing with my game? What secret desire am I satisfying? This is more important in adventure games than in a game like, say, *Sonic the Hedgehog* because adventure games are always about fantasy.

Schafer comments on the importance of storyboarding and design documents for creating adventure games:

> We storyboarded every single shot that appears in *Grim Fandango*, and it was invaluable. It helps the artists know what to build, what angles it has to look good from. It tells the people who are placing the characters in the scenes where everybody should be standing. People have been doing it in movies for years, and games are just figuring it out now.

> A design document is the game designer's bible for the development of the game. It shouldn't just be a burst of ideas you scribble down in the beginning of the process and then forget about as you enter the heat of production. It should be a living document that you revise after every brainstorming session to keep fresh and up-to-date. It's for the team to reference when they (or you) forget what the plan was.

Take heed to this veteran's advice: "If you don't have one, you'll drift off-target, I promise."

Read more from Schafer on general game design tips and techniques (Chapter 4) and how to create good puzzles in an adventure game (Chapter 9).

Gabe Newell, Valve Software

In Chapter 2, Gabe Newell, founder and managing director of Kirkland, Washington's Valve Software, talks about creating successful action games such as *Half-Life*. He briefly comments here on creating lead characters and writing design documents.

"Actually, I'm not sure that a lead character is necessary or even beneficial in first-person games," admits Newell. He continues:

> We made Gordon [Freeman, the protagonist in *Half-Life*] as transparent to the player as possible. The only time you ever hear yourself is when you're breathing during the disaster sequence. We had a bunch of third-person scenes, and we slowly realized that they were hurting the experience, not helping.

However, Newell does admit to using design documents:

> We couldn't work without design documents. We have too many people who need to think through all of the implications of the design in all of the millions of details that go into a next-generation game. Each hour spent on the design probably saves us 10 hours of implementation.

Alex Garden, Relic Entertainment

The young game designer responsible for *Homeworld* and *Impossible Creatures* talks about the importance of a design document and how to best tackle one:

> A design document is a road map for a team tasked with creating your wacky idea. Members of your team should be able to reference your design document when they have questions. Practically speaking, game design is a somewhat organic process, though, so the design document has to be somewhat organic as well to keep people informed correctly. At Relic, we have one mega central design document that's used as the basis of the game; then we supplement it with "Design Updates" that are much shorter and easier to update.

How important is storyboarding a game today?

Considering the cost and complexity of cinematic and animatic sequences, it's critically important to do as much pre-production as you can (which is relatively cheap) before you start working on full product (which is very, very expensive). Planning may look like a waste of time, but it is in fact the single easiest and cheapest way to make your game good in the end.

> **TIP**
>
> Garden brings up a great point here: Understandably, money is a very big issue, so the more gameplay mechanics that a designer/developer can work out before the clock starts ticking (when a publisher begins funding the project), the better!

Bruce C. Shelley, Ensemble Studios

Ensemble Studios designer Bruce Shelley—whose *Age of Empires* and *Age of Mythology* computer games have become one of the most successful real-time strategy series on the planet—offers his advice on using design documents:

The design document (DD) is the blueprint of the game design. It begins with a short paragraph or a long vision statement that sums up what the game is about. This is followed by a longer two- or three-page vision document, which provides more detail on the look and feel of the game. This grows into a full-blown DD that may reach several hundred pages for one of our games. All major systems have separate chapters that explain in detail how each system will work. For example, in the *Age of Empires* games, the DDs had a chapter on buildings. Here, we listed all the buildings, their functions, their costs, their prerequisites, when they could be built, their attributes (hit points, armor), and so on. Everyone on the project could go to that part of the DD to see how a particular building was supposed to work. From this document, the programming team would create its technical design document, which would list all the programming tasks, who was assigned to them, and estimates of creation time. The art team builds a list of art components from the DD. The test team builds its list of systems to be tested. The publisher compares the DD to the build it receives. The DD is the backbone of the development process. It's a living document, updated regularly. We keep it on our intranet so it's easily available to all. We also create a "DD Lite" that someone can read more easily for a quick overview of the product.

Read more on Ensemble Studios at www.ensemblestudios.com.

Noah Falstein, The Inspiracy

Believe it or not, Noah Falstein programmed his first computer game in 1976 and has been employed in the games industry since 1980. Now, that's an industry veteran! Falstein is the President of The Inspiracy, a design consulting company with clients such as Disney Interactive, Dreamworks Interactive, Shell Oil, I-Imagine Entertainment, Electronic Arts, and Intel. Be sure to read his lengthy bio at the back of this book.

Simply, The Inspiracy provides game design and production expertise for entertainment, education, and corporate training. In Falstein's own words:

> The Inspiracy is my freelance design/production business. It's mostly me, with some help from some very experienced friends when I find it is helpful to bring them in. There's more info in my bio [at the back of the book], so briefly I find that my clients are split between two main groups. There are the established game companies that need an expert designer to review and polish their own designs, or help them through a rough spot when they don't have the in-house resources. And there are startups or people from outside the games industry who can use my help in putting together business plans, meeting with publishers, or designing games based on their initial concepts. I love variety and have worked on everything from corporate training games to kid's edutainment titles, to full-scale PS2 and Xbox and PC games. Recently, I've found work through the new interest in massively multiplayer games and games played on cell phones.

Before we discuss fleshing out ideas onto paper, Falstein offers some important tips to those just starting out in the business. According to Falstein, budding game designers should pay attention to these three pointers:

Be collaborative

Often, there's a sense of having to prove yourself on your first game, and sometimes people interpret that as requiring them to make it on their own. But even small games are complicated things to design, and large games today take huge teams, even on the design side. Also, if you develop the ability to work well with other people and incorporate their ideas into a unified whole, you'll benefit both from the synergy of collaboration and the politically savvy move of gaining their support through shared ownership of the project.

Study the competition

One mistake some developers who are new to the games industry can make is to assume that if they play a lot of other games, their designs will become compromised and derivative. I sometimes hear the complaint, "There's nothing out there that I like." And "I don't play games because they're all bad [usually a stronger phrase is substituted here]—but my idea has never been done before, and it will be much more fun than anything out there!" Of course, the paradox is that if they don't play games, how can they know it's never been done? Invariably, it turns out their idea HAS been done before, often more than once, and they miss out on learning from other people's mistakes. Some of the best designers I know (people like Sid Meier, Will Wright, or Ron Gilbert) freely borrow ideas from other people, but then apply their own personal style and expertise to make them their own.

Be confident, not arrogant

Good game designers need a lot of confidence; there are invariably times when they have ideas that no one else understands or can visualize, and it's important to have the assurance to sell your vision. On the other hand, confidence can turn into overconfidence or even arrogance. Good game designers have the will to carry on when they know they're right. Great game designers have the humility to be honest about realizing they will sometimes be wrong.

Now onto the topic of a design document: Is drafting one before and/or during the game's development all that necessary?

This should be a simple question, and yet it's actually hard to answer. That's because every design document is different. Not just different in content, like two movie scripts, but potentially different in format, size, detail, and style. I've seen games made based on design documents that were two pages long and 800 pages long. Some are filled with beautiful drawings, others have lots of bare-bones diagrams, and some are all text—but most employ some combination of those three things, as well as lists, maps, and reference material. In my experience, there is no one right format for a design document (which is why they vary so much), and ideally each project will have a design that is hand-crafted to the needs of the idea, the company, and particularly the team that makes it.

A design document does have to convey the vision for a game effectively to the team that has to make it. Really short documents work fine when the team is small; experienced; working in close proximity; in agreement about how the game should look, feel, and play; and when the scope of the game is small. Really long documents work best when the team is large, may have newbies involved, is distributed among different locations, and when the scope of the game is large. I didn't mention agreement there because a large team always has a variety of ideas about what the game could be like, and it's the job of the designer to provide a unifying vision, with the design document as the best tool to accomplish that.

In his advice on making it as a game designer, Falstein says to "be collaborative." Pictured here is the educational title *Hungry Red Planet*, which was built by an all-freelance team spread out in six locations across the U.S.

(Used with permission by Noah Falstein)

So, should someone outsource their design document writing to The Inspiracy?

They shouldn't. One of the first points I advise any potential client about is that it is usually preferable to have a full-time internal designer instead of using one from the outside.

But the key word is "usually." If they can't find someone with the proper experience, or if they have someone they like who may be tackling a larger project than they've ever done, or if they're trying something really new, it can help to bring in an experienced, collaborative, knowledgeable freelance designer—like me.

I also have found that people appreciate the fact that I have a technical background as well as an extensive background as a producer, so my designs are practical to build and take the strengths and weaknesses of the team, the concept or license, and the market niche into account. It's hard to accumulate the knowledge and expertise to do this sort of thing, so I'm appreciated by those who see the wisdom in that kind of multifaceted approach.

What's the most annoying problem with video game pre-production today?

Overoptimism. It's easy to fall into the trap of thinking that you can pull something off that is really too hard or too ambitious to do, given the resources you have. Then the project crashes and burns later on, when reality sets in. One of the clearest differences I see between experienced and raw teams is in the scope of their plans. A novice group will design everything into their game, on the "more is better" principle, and throw in lots of hyperbolic statements like "kick-ass graphics that are ten times better than *Quake 3*" (statements that belong in ads after the game is done, not in design documents). I'm not suggesting that people shouldn't aim high—that's a prerequisite to AAA status—but it's even more important to know the strengths and limitations of the individuals, the whole team, and even the company that's making the game. Only when everything can be smoothly and effectively integrated do you end up with a smash hit, and even then it takes a lot of hard work.

Finally, although Chapter 21 focuses on the topic of breaking into the industry in great depth, Falstein offers some advice on the matter here:

I'm tempted to paraphrase the old real estate saw of "Location, location, location" with the game developer equivalent: "Persistence, persistence, persistence." I've seen persistent wannabes with very little talent, and talented wannabes with very little persistence; the former individuals almost always make it, while the latter seldom do. Not giving up is the single most important way to get a start.

"But just one piece of advice here is a bit of a cop-out," says Falstein:

I'd also say that being willing, even eager to do something besides your final aim is very helpful. If you want to be a designer, great. But if you're not willing to start by doing anything less than being a lead designer, you're not going to make it. Test yourself with the idea of spending a year or two in QA; then perhaps being a level designer on a project before having a chance to lead a small design. If that sounds exciting, great. If it sounds like a lot of boring stuff until you get to be in control, you're probably not cut out for the industry—and this applies to the other disciplines of art, programming, and project management.

Finally, he advises to "learn to network."

This is an industry that has tremendous volatility, with people moving around all the time. That can be a big advantage—get to know people at one company, and in a few years, you'll have contacts in several; in 10 years, you'll have contact in dozens. Even if you intend to find a place and stick with it, it pays to be social and get to know other people who are in the industry. The GDC is the primary place to do this sort of networking [see Chapter 25, "Key Conventions, Organizations, and Awards"], but company parties, IGDA local chapters, and other industry conferences are also good for this.

Phil Steinmeyer, PopTop Software

The creator of *Railroad Tycoon*, the *Tropico* series, and others says there are all kinds of design documents, so it's important to clarify the differences between them:

[They can] range from publisher summaries, which can be 1–10 pages, to general game design documents, running 15–50 pages, to detailed technical architecture documents listing every bit of code and art asset that will be needed by the game (sometimes running 1,000 pages and more).

Steinmeyer says he typically writes and follows two design documents. The first is a short summary for his publisher that highlights projected marketing, budget, sales, and competing games. The second is a longer document for internal use.

For *Tropico*, it was about 40 pages of text, plus lots of spreadsheets. My team has complained that the *Tropico* design document wasn't detailed enough, and it wasn't kept up-to-date, so I'm going to try for more detail and keeping it up better on our next game.

Phil Saunders, Presto Studios

Earlier in this chapter, we heard from Tim Schafer, best known for his games when employed by LucasArts. Now we have Phil Saunders from Presto Studios to chat further about design docs and storyboarding in adventure games.

"In our process, storyboarding is really only used for cinematic sequences where we're in complete control of the player's viewpoint," begins Saunders. He continues:

In environments that are fully realized and navigable, the important part of pre-production is prototyping. We create simple models early on in the process to define the path and to show what will and won't be visible to the player in any given location. At this stage, we're able to discover what players will and won't learn and when, what we can hide from them, as well as what's revealed. As an additional benefit, prototyping allows us to have a good grasp of the size and scope of our production. We can tell what level of detail must be put into what part of the environment, based on its distance and accessibility to the player.

Why this amount of effort?

> We've learned the hard way that preliminary planning pays off in the end. It's sad to see someone's designs being cut from the game because you've run out of time, or technically it just won't work. For *Myst III: Exile*, we spent about a year developing the gameplay, story, and early visual ideas. At the end of about 11 months, we had a design document 160 pages long. The design document saves you from overdesigning and eventually cutting out work that took someone months to prepare. Months that could have been better spent fine-tuning other areas.

Is a design document necessary? "In my opinion," concludes Saunders, "it's the most important part of production."

For more about the creation of *Myst III: Exile* and what can be learned from it, hop back to Chapter 4.

Ragnar Tørnquist, Funcom

The brilliant and articulate Ragnar Tørnquist—creator of *The Longest Journey*, arguably one of the most critically acclaimed adventure games of late—talks in this chapter about creating a successful protagonist and the importance of design docs and storyboard sequences.

"Creating strong characters in a game is not as hard as people think," begins Tørnquist, when asked to reveal the "secret" to creating a successful lead character such as April Ryan in *The Longest Journey*.

> Most of it has to do with depth: depth of personality, depth of background, depth of characterization. It's important to avoid clichés and stereotypes, and one way to go about it (at least initially) is to use real people as models for your characters. Think about what it is that makes a person unique: Is it the way he or she talks, walks, laughs? Observe his or her expressions—facial, verbal, body language—and dig deep into that person's full history. The more complex the background, the more thorough your preparation and the easier it is to develop a strong character. Even if it isn't mentioned in the game, take the time to write down personal details such as family history, likes and dislikes, favorite pets—anything and everything that's suitable for the kind of character you want to create.

> In other words, if your character is a butt-kicking Marine with a grudge, you probably don't need to think about his favorite color, but you'll need to find out why this guy became a soldier in the first place, what makes him tick, and what he wants to accomplish.

Okay, so what about the creation of April Ryan?

> With April Ryan in *The Longest Journey (TLJ)*, there was actually a ton of background material that's only briefly hinted at in the game, but that gave her depth and character. There's a reason for everything she says and does, and I think that's quite apparent. Long before I started writing her dialogue, I knew everything that had happened to her from the day she was born to the day the game started. I knew what made her tick. I knew how she spoke, how she would react in any given situation. At that point, it's a lot easier to develop the character and to have him or her become a natural part of the story and the setting.

I said earlier to avoid clichés and stereotypes, but sometimes clichés and stereotypes are great ways to establish a character immediately, without a lot of dialogue—especially in the case of supporting characters who may not get a lot of screen time. Don't knock stereotyping; there's a good reason why some people do conform to stereotypes. With *TLJ*, we had The Surly Detective, The Funny Sidekick, The Mysterious Stranger, The Mad Wizard, and so on. These types of characters, done right, appeal to us on a very basic level: We understand them. We've seen them before. We know where they fit in. While you don't want your lead character(s) to fit into an easy mold, clichés and stereotypes are tools that can be used to fill out your character gallery. After awhile, you'll probably want to play with these clichés and stereotypes, twisting them ever so slightly to keep the players on their toes throughout.

The Longest Journey creator Ragnar Tørnquist says he creates thorough background dossiers for most of the important characters in the game. Of April, Tørnquist says, "There's a reason for everything she says and does, and I think that's quite apparent. Long before I started writing her dialogue, I knew everything that had happened to her from the day she was born to the day the game started."
(Used with permission by Funcom, Inc.)

And on the development of these characters, and using the story—or, more precisely, the plot—Tørnquist says to keep in mind that good characterization (at least in games) comes from placing ordinary people in extraordinary situations.

This is usually a lot more interesting than extraordinary people in extraordinary situations: By virtue of the changes in the game world and the way your characters react to these changes, you'll find that your protagonist(s) often start to evolve and grow on you, regardless of your original intent. Let the player experience the world through the eyes of the protagonist; if the protagonist's eyes are jaded or all-knowing, it's not particularly interesting. But if, as with April, the extraordinary things that happen on her journey are as surprising to her as to the player, there's an instant link between the person playing and the character he or she is controlling. And that's a good thing.

On design docs for an adventure game, Tørnquist mirrors many of the sentiments found in this chapter:

A design document is a blueprint for the programmers, artists, and level designers. It describes in detail the concept and ideas, the systems and functions, and the suggested implementation of all game features—both the obvious ones (visual interface, for example) and the not-so-obvious ones (AI, scripts, saving and loading, and so on).

Tørnquist expands on this comment and also touches on storyboarding:

> The designer's job is to think of every eventuality that might occur, every action the player may want to perform, every problem that could pop up; as well as create an interesting world, a strong story, intriguing characters, and fun gameplay. It's impossible to cover every eventuality—to second-guess all possibilities—but the point is to be as well-prepared as possible. Design will happen, whether you want it to or not, throughout the production until the day the game ships (or, in the case of online games, even after the game has shipped and for years to come). A design document is therefore an evolving document, constantly updated by the designers, providing a living record of intent as well as result.
>
> A storyboard is a visual representation of what occurs onscreen, which is only the tip of the iceberg in terms of the actual design. A storyboard visualizes what the player will see and do, and so it's an interesting way to "play the game" long before the game is up and running, but it doesn't replace the design document. For *The Longest Journey*, we storyboarded a few important in-game sequences, but not all of them—not even most of them. However, we did make detailed concept drawings of all locations and every single character in the game—this is called the *visual* or *graphic* design. By doing that, we were able to plan out what animations, sound effects, dialogue, and code we needed. Of course, all of the game's cut scenes were fully storyboarded, much like with an animated movie.

And lest we forget about a script—arguably the most important part of creating an adventure game—Tørnquist has a few words to say on that topic:

> Last but not least, an adventure game needs a script; this is the document that "tells the story," in dialogue, scripted events, every possible response to every possible action—much like a movie script, but much, much bigger. Combine the three—the design (technical, systems, interface), the storyboard, and the script—and you're ready to start production, at which point you'll realize that making adventure games is even more fun than playing them!

Ragnar Tørnquist offers sage advice on creating adventure games in Chapter 3, "General Game Design: Strategy Games."

Ron Gilbert, Hulabee Entertainment

The gaming genius behind many of our most lovable characters, such as *Monkey Island's* Guybrush Threepwood, *Maniac Mansion's* Bernard, and Pajama Sam, believes that "there has to be something about the character that's visually recognizable, and simply understood." He explains:

> We don't have the bandwidth yet for complex characters like in film, so we simplify and often rely on stereotypes and then we build them up through storytelling. In action or real-time strategy games, we rely on these stereotypes for you to instantly understand who the character is. The story is secondary, more of an afterthought, but not for adventure games, of course.

Many of Gilbert's latest and greatest characters can be seen at his past companies' web sites, such as www.lucasarts.com and www.humongous.com, and (soon) his new company's site, www.hulabee.com.

Daniel Greenberg, Freelance

The talented Daniel Greenberg is an award-winning freelance game designer with almost two decades of experience making critically acclaimed and commercially successful games. Some of these include *Star Trek: Starfleet Academy*, *Vampire: The Masquerade—Redemption*, *Star Control III*, *Tenchu II: Birth of the Stealth Assassins*, *Independence War II: The Edge of Chaos*, *Sea Dogs*, *Advanced Dungeons and Dragons: Al Qadim/The Genie's Curse*, and *X-Men: The Mutant Wars*. He is also a consultant for a number of well-known computer and console publishers.

Greenberg was first asked to provide some important pieces of advice to share with newbie game designers on becoming a success in the industry. His answers are quite thorough, so dig in and get comfortable.

1. **Apprenticeship: Learn the rules**. Stay in school. There's a lot more to game design than being really into deathmatching. The best way to learn it is to absorb the distilled essence of what mankind has learned over the last few thousand years. There's a shocking amount of good stuff in college and even high school—if you keep your ears open. Learn the basics—at least enough English to write crackling dialogue and avoid passive voice; at least enough dramatic theory to understand why Aristotelian theory is still essential 2,000 years later; at least enough programming to create flowcharts that are efficient and meaningful; at least enough art theory to be able to speak intelligently to artists about color, form, motion, and asset management; and at least enough business and marketing and corporate culture to talk coherently to people who will turn your games into cash. None of this stuff is dull to an active mind that is restlessly churning everything it digests into fodder for games. Once you're firmly grounded in a multidisciplinary approach, get inside the business any way you can: quality assurance, administrative assistant, etc. Once you're inside, it's easy to learn the ropes and even find mentors. Knowing the rules will help you avoid the pitfalls that tripped up so many designers before you.

2. **Professionalism: Follow the rules**. It doesn't matter if you're 16 or 60; there's no excuse for unprofessional conduct. Handle the basic stuff. When you give your word, can your boss and co-workers and employees count on you? Make sure they can—every time. Underpromise and overdeliver. The temptation to do just the opposite is often overwhelming. Resist it.

   The rules are there for a reason: they work. The rules can help you isolate bad ideas and eliminate the pressures that result in crappy games.

3. **Revolution: Break the rules**. Game design is full of devotion to stupid conventions that are slavishly copied in hopes of duplicating success. Innovation requires a leap of faith into the void. And that's the easy part. Once you've created a brilliant, unconventional, defiant design, harness your creative powers to create imaginative ways to sell your innovations to marketing. If you learned how risk-averse corporate culture is during step 1 (apprenticeship), you should have an edge in this process. Following the rules makes good games. To make *great* games, you have to know which rules to break.

With the nearly 20 years of experience Greenberg has under his belt, he can easily support his previous advice with real-world personal/professional examples.

I'm still pillaging classes I took years ago for good ideas. My psychological studies into reaching autistic children became the basis for the secret final mission in *Starfleet Academy* ("A World of Their Own"), in which the only way to survive a confrontation with a planet-killing vessel is to not try to get them to understand you, but to understand them by getting into their dissociative world.

In my *Advanced Dungeons and Dragons* computer game, *The Genie's Curse*, I drew on notions of honor and sacrifice from a Philosophy of the Middle Ages course in order to let players make meaningful choices about expediency versus the difficult but honorable path. (The *Computer Shopper* magazine reviewer said "…it is refreshing to see a game where honor and courtesy are an integral part and portrayed in a way that isn't trite.")

Much of this chapter looks at storyboarding, the various theories on why storyboards are important, and how to approach them. Greenberg looks at the importance of the story itself and offers the following paragraphs:

Aristotelian dramatic structure has not been repealed in the digital age, but it needs some adaptation to account for user input. Story structure needs to follow the basic pattern of rising and falling action, but the player needs some ability to alter the pacing, or the story will feel forced and labored. But just as Arthur Miller had to seriously rework Aristotle to reach a modern audience with "Death of a Salesman," good games need to rethink dramatic structure for the new medium.

Many games have paper-thin characters because our art form is still in its infancy. For all their rapidly accelerating power, PCs are actually still a very crude canvas. They're bursting at the seams to contain an art form as potentially explosive as interactive storytelling. Unlike mature art forms like books or films, our medium is in its infancy, and our ultimate structure is utterly unknown to us—though many of us suspect it will make the Holodeck look like a child's toy. (Wait. The Holodeck *is* a child's toy.)

The people in our audience who "get" interactive entertainment are still a small subset of the general population (though this subset is growing and evolving faster than the keepers of our culture understand or imagine). So we can be excused for catering more to the more primal interactivity needs of our audience than the more subtle forms of characterization and intricate plot construction. It only makes sense that we (and our audience) are more enthralled by the gimcrackery of the exponentially increasing technology than exploring the depths of the human psyche via video games (though that, too, is happening). So the simple conclusion is that Lara Croft is about as developed as she needs to be for the style of game she appears in. That style of gameplay is evolving, however, as we find what's really meaningful in storytelling.

Great stories resonate in us because somewhere the story relates to journeys we have taken, struggles we have endured, and burdens we have borne. Even the most fantastic story can connect with us on a symbolic level. This has tremendous power, even if most people are not fully conscious of the effects of story on their emotions, actions, and lives. Games can illuminate our own inner landscape just as books and movies can, showing us a little bit about ourselves as we play. Good games let us take charge of that process and let us explore that inner landscape. One secret to illuminate that path is the tool of multiple good outcomes.

Any secrets Greenberg can share on storytelling in an interactive medium? Indeed there are. Greenberg provides the following, and supports his comprehensive words of wisdom with examples from games such as Activision's *Vampire: The Masquerade—Redemption* and Interplay's *Star Trek: Starfleet Academy*.

Multiple "good" outcomes: A big secret of superior interactive storytelling is the concept of multiple good outcomes, with varying degrees of "good."

When I first began designing, most games had a very linear storyline. Interactive choices offered were largely illusory because any deviation from the storyline was punishable by death (or at least game over). This became too obvious, so some games decided not to kill characters immediately after the player chose the death path. This made the game livelier, but led to terrible frustration when players realized they were "dead without knowing it." It was often quite difficult for players to locate the killer choice point and start over from there. Eventually, interactive story design evolved to the point where games could offer a third, more ambiguous choice to spice up the mix of a fairly obvious survival choice and a fairly obvious insta-death choice. These good, bad, and ugly choices improved the mix, but were still very limited.

My favorite solution was to make the insta-death choice very rare (You chose door number two? You're dead!) and focus on a wide range of variables to track choices within the main story. Players don't have cut-and-dried choices that point in obvious directions, but more subtle choices that could each turn out well. Each choice has real consequences and real rewards far beyond issues of death and survival. They take the player along differing paths through the main story and result in a range of consequences and endings, depending on the preponderance of choices made throughout the game. This lets the player feel more in charge of his destiny.

This "multiple good options" approach has another beneficial effect. Players can personalize their character to a greater extent and therefore feel a closer connection to their avatar. For example, if the player needs to question a non-player character, consider providing a range of dialogue approaches. Choosing between dialogue options like browbeating and sweet-talking lets players sculpt their characters' emerging personalities. Players not only control their destinies, but shape the kind of ride they have on the way to that destiny.

Technical note: If you're going to offer the player these kinds of choices throughout the game, it's important to reveal this experientially early on by setting up a simple low-impact choice and result early in the game. The player needs to feel the consequences of his choice very quickly to know that the game is indeed responding qualitatively to his decisions.

The trick is tracking all the variables set in play and making sure they're all paid off. It's also important that the player has a sense of why he gets the outcome he did. He doesn't need to understand the direct consequences of each choice, but should have some idea. (If he wants to know the direct consequences of each choice, he's free to replay from a myriad of saved games, and believe me, a lot of players will. And then they'll post the consequences in great detail on gaming sites.)

One of the best ways to offer multiple good options is to use the approach of short-term pain for long-term gain versus short-term gain for long-term pain. Tempt the player with expedient choices, but hint that there's a price to pay later. And offer a price to be paid now for hope of a return later. This is a diabolical bind, and makes for very textured choices for the player—neither of which is obviously objectively bad. When players are wracked with nervous apprehension while making choices, you have done your job.

Examples (and reviews to show how the goal was accomplished):

Vampire: The Masquerade—Redemption offers the player multiple endings based on ethical conduct during the game. While ethical vampires might sound confusingly contradictory, in practice it works well. We implemented the Humanity system that we had used quite successfully in the paper game version. Vampires are unliving creatures who either cling to the tattered shreds of their former humanity or yield to the beast within and become ravening monsters. So if the player made difficult but ethical choices in his dealings with others, he could forestall the slide to oblivion and even find a kind of redemption. If he acts like the monster he's becoming, he hastens his slide into oblivion. However, even this "bad" ending can give him power to defeat the boss villain, but at the cost of his soul. In the end, the game's basic choices became a meditation on what we sacrifice for power, on defeat in victory, and on victory in defeat.

Adrenaline Vault said: "The well-constructed storyline and character development system give *VTM: Redemption* an overpoweringly immersive quality, possessed in very few offerings today."

Star Trek: Starfleet Academy requires that the player manage a crew of raw cadets and mold them into a team. Besides having to make career path decisions, resolve inter-crew squabbling, and deal with opportunities to cheat (just like James T. Kirk), the player has the option to neglect his studies to help solve a serious problem he and his science officer have stumbled upon. From the very beginning of the game, it appears that the top victory condition is graduating first in the class. Therefore, all the academic choices seem far more important than more-fun distractions. And for the most part, they are. But the player gets an inkling that the fringe research project he has embarked upon could have tremendous, far-reaching consequences, saving more than a few lives. The player will have to sacrifice what appears to be the whole point of the game—winning command of his own ship by graduating first in his class. The research plan that will let him crack the problem is presented as yet another tempting distraction from his limited study time. But clues interspersed throughout the game, including interactions with Academy Special Instructor Kirk, hint that it could be far more than that. If you actually dare to ask Kirk audacious questions about his notorious defiance of the Prime Directive, you learn all about how and when to break rules. Many players figure out the special ending the first time through the game, but not all. Which is as it should be.

c|Net GameCenter's review said that *Starfleet Academy*'s "…clever writing and an understanding of the *Trek* mythos (and its implications) surpasses most of the current TV shows and movies. In fact, the question of what we are to learn from Kirk himself and his 'Cowboy Diplomacy' (based on the original series and first set of movies) is one of the major themes of this story."

For more on Greenberg's work, visit his web site at www.danielgreenberg.com.

Bill Roper, Blizzard Entertainment

Do design docs and storyboarding play an important role in RPGs? To enlighten us, Blizzard Entertainment's Bill Roper and Blizzard North's Matt Householder (see the next section) speak on these issues. First, let's hear from Bill Roper:

> The different teams within Blizzard approach design documents from different angles. The *Diablo II* team kept most of the design within the game. If a change was made to the way monsters worked, those changes were made directly in the spreadsheets and were recorded that way as well. The *Warcraft III* team had integrated its design documents into a web-based format to make it easier for non-programmers to follow the changes to the game. Both ways have their strengths and weaknesses, and in the end, it's up to each team to find the method that best suits their particular needs and group of developers.
>
> The common ground that our teams share in regard to design documents is in defining and following the vision of the project. In the case of *Warcraft III*, this is to create a real-time strategy game that infuses elements of role-playing into the design. We created the term *role-playing strategy (RPS)* to help focus the decisions made by the team. From this basic idea came the concepts of focusing on fewer and more powerful units, simplifying the resource model, making exploration a key component of the game, creating more organic campaigns, and making the game even more immersive than *Starcraft*. Finding the core essence of the game and then building upon that concept is how we grow our games, and the documentation involved is recording decisions and ideas that are made along the way.

With Blizzard's stunning cinematic sequences, you can bet these start out as storyboards before the computer graphic (CG) artists begin animating these short films. Roper explains how the process works at Blizzard:

> Storyboarding is essential in regard to campaign creation and cinematic sequences. The cinematic department at Blizzard has walls filled with storyboards scripting out each sequence they're going to create for each game. They work closely with the development teams to ensure that the look and spirit of the game are translated into the cinematic sequences and to make sure that [they've created] the proper continuity. Models are shared when appropriate, and artists from both the cinematic and development teams get together to brainstorm and eventually create the storyboards. The writers utilize these storyboards to shape the dialogue, and this can result in a change in the visuals as well as the acting performances or sound and music design.
>
> Of course, this all has to tie into the game's campaign storyline, and so the level designers get involved in the process as well. They also create storyboards, although these tend to be with both words and level outlines. With the ability to create in-game cinematic sequences using the game engine, we've found it necessary to find key elements in the campaign maps in which to integrate story elements or give players rewards for completing portions of the campaign. All in all, it's a very collaborative process involving several different groups within the company.

Matt Householder, Blizzard North

Another key member of the *Diablo II* group is Matt Householder, who also shares some comments in Chapter 5, "General Game Design: Role-Playing Games (RPGs) and Persistent Online Worlds." He adds to Roper's discussion on the importance of a design documents and storyboarding of these mega-popular RPGs:

> The purpose of a design document is to present the look and feel of the game to the production team (and publisher's management) in an efficient and maintainable way. Begin with a one- or two-page overview, briefly describing the player's viewpoint, gameplay, and controls.
>
> Explain why it will be fun to play. Be sure to cover all the basic issues in brief: single-player, multiplayer, console versus PC, player characters, opponent/enemy characters, animation style, background settings, sound/music, story, and so on; and then elaborate on them in later sections devoted to one major topic at a time. Drawings—sketches, character designs, screen mockups—are very helpful to visualize the game. For a large game, the document could grow to hundreds of pages!
>
> A design document is a lot like a recipe for the building of a game, but the best cooks often experiment and modify recipes as they go. Likewise, Blizzard North uses a design document more as a general guideline rather than as a "bible," and encourages creative expression by all the production team members—even exploring major design changes during the development process.

And on storyboarding:

> It's essential for cinematic production, but not strictly necessary for the production of game code and artwork. One place where storyboarding can help a great deal in game production, however, is in flowcharting the user interactions of making choices to start up a game, navigating through game menu screens, and the like.

Both Householder and Roper discuss the art and science that is RPG game design in Chapter 5.

Chris Taylor, Gas Powered Games

The creator of such beloved games as *Total Annihilation* (when at Cavedog Entertainment) and *Dungeon Siege* (at Gas Powered Games) has provided this book with a design document template (see Chapter 7) that you can use as a basis for your own custom document, plugging in the necessary game details to suit your project.

Here, Taylor explains that creating a design document can be approached in many different ways:

> Design documents can vary from highly theoretical to very technical and detailed. Over the years I've settled on a system in which I create an overview document and then a series of appendices that add the details. From this, I then produce specification documents that break down everything for the person who will implement the specifics. It's great to have a template to work from because then you can just go through and fill in each section. You begin with the high concept; then the feature set. Then you must answer the 10 most jaded and difficult questions that you think someone might ask you about your

design. If you can't answer them right from the beginning, you may need to go back and think about why you want to make a game like that in the first place.

Taylor says the importance of storyboarding depends on the type of game:

When there are a huge number of art assets involved, you absolutely must do concept sketches, storyboards, and anything else you can to reduce risk and any chance of doing stuff over and over again. Poor planning will frustrate people and demotivate them, so storyboarding is a great way to communicate the overall plan, look and feel, style, and scope of the game.

Warren Spector, Ion Storm Austin

In Chapter 5, Warren Spector—best known for games such as the *Ultima Underworld* series, *System Shock* and *Deus Ex*—chats at great length about creating award-winning role-playing games. His suggestions can also be found in Chapter 12, "Artificial Intelligence (AI)," Chapter 17, "Proper Game Testing," and Chapter 21.

Here he discusses the importance of a design doc:

A design doc is absolutely vital to me. I know some other hugely successful developers (who will remain nameless) who insist they never bother trying to document their games. I can't imagine that!

For me, a design doc is many things: It's a roadmap—an abstract, iconic version of your proposed game. If you keep it updated during pre-production and even during production, it's a snapshot—a picture of where your project stands today, right now. If done "right," it includes materials, assets, and information that marketing can use to generate early press coverage of your game (without bugging the development team too much!). Toward the end of the project, a design doc that has been updated appropriately can be a vital tool for manual and cluebook writers, as well as for QA teams looking to generate playthrough and feature checklists. Most important, though, a design doc is a vital communications tool, both internally (ensuring that everyone on the dev team is on the same page) and externally (for publisher, marketing, and even press). I just wouldn't know how to make or manage a game without one.

So, how does Spector—or any game designer, for that matter—write a design document?

Unfortunately, no two projects are the same, no two teams are the same, no two genres have the same requirements, and therefore no two design docs are going to be the same. You just have to find the elements necessary to describe *your* game to your team and to your publisher. Figure out what you need to provide to ensure that your team has enough information to implement the vision of a game. Allow each person on the team to contribute to the extent of their capabilities and/or interests, but give one person "ownership" of the doc. (In other words, one person should say yes or no to any idea before it's incorporated into the final doc.) Plan on revising throughout development to ensure that the doc reflects the changing reality of your game's development. Recognize that a time will come when reality overtakes your doc and continued updating may (*may*) be unnecessary. And then read the book I obviously have to write on this subject! I'm completely overwhelmed by how much there is to say, so I'd better stop. Sorry...

Spector admits that storyboarding has never been a big part of his development process:

It's vital, obviously, when planning cinematics, but that's about it. You always want concept art for characters and locations/maps/levels before you spend a lot of money modeling and creating them, but that isn't really storyboarding, per se. I remember reading a fine little book, called *Behind the Scenes at Sega*, about the making of a platform game that said every aspect of the game should be storyboarded. That idea just isn't applicable to the kinds of games my studio produces (and illustrates the fact that development processes have to be appropriate to the game you're making—there's no single Right Way to make a game...). Storyboarding is probably vital to games in which you know exactly what path players will take every step of their journey and where you pre-plan every puzzle and its one solution.

Storyboards were certainly an important part of the *Wing Commander* games, with their emphasis on cinematics, and I bet the LucasArts adventure games use them heavily. But if you're making something more open-ended than that, storyboards just don't seem all that useful. We're not (or shouldn't be) making movies here...

American McGee, Carbon6 Entertainment

American McGee, creative director at Carbon6 Entertainment, has worked on such renowned PC titles as *DOOM*, *DOOM III*, *Quake*, *Quake II*, and most recently, *American McGee's Alice* for Electronic Arts.

For this chapter on storyboarding, McGee gives us his vision for the cinematic intro to Alice. Read on, and enjoy. If you've ever played the game (and you should!), you'll get a lot more out of this having experienced the breathtaking intro sequence.

American McGee's Alice intro, written by American McGee:

Alice Story

Intro:

EXT HOUSE

Snow flurries dot the night sky. Storm has passed.

Camera glides through leaded glass French doors into the library of a comfortable Victorian manor.

[Full] moon's glow, intensified by snow, lights the room. Shelves overflow with books and papers.

Camera moves toward a large fireplace.

A napping cat stands, arches his back, and uses the leg of a nearby desk to sharpen his claws.

Retreating, he catches a claw on a damask cloth, which is decoratively draped over part of the desk.

An oil lamp sits on the cloth.

Trying to get free, the cat pulls the cloth. The lamp is drawn to and over the edge. Smashes on floor.

Oil covers the cat and flows towards the glowing embers in the fireplace.

Flame explodes out of the cinders and engulfs the cat and paper-filled desk.

Fire spreads through the library at an alarming pace.

Smoke slithers the door and up the stairs—along the hallway—and slips under Alice's door.

Camera moves to sleeping Alice.

A tendril of smoke wisps up her nostril.

Camera follows.

WONDERLAND—GNOME GARDEN—TEA PARTY

Alice and a small assortment of Wonderland characters—Mad Hatter, Gryphon, March Hare, Dormouse, White Rabbit—having tea around a huge table. Mood is light and playful.

Mad Hatter, pouring tea for Alice, drops the pot, which shatters with the sounds of breaking glass. Suddenly, the ground around the table splits open and fire comes through the fissures.

Smoke billows around everyone. The shadow of the Jabberwock passes overhead. Screams.

Fade back to Alice's moonlit, smoke-filled room.

INT HOUSE

Alice awakens from her interrupted dream.

The [muffled] screams are coming from inside the house.

Alice leaps out of bed, clutching her beloved white rabbit, and runs to the door.

Hallway is filled with smoke and licks of fire.

She bolts toward her parents' room, and trying the doorknob, burns her hand severely.

She pushes the door in a little—flames come billowing out.

Alice, driven back by heat, distraught, screaming in agony and frustration, retreats.

Camera follows as she runs wildly down hall.

EXT HOUSE

Camera watches as Alice exits house through the front door and stumbles down the steps.

Screaming, coughing, covered with soot, she collapses on the front yard in a large snow drift.

House is completely engulfed in flames; a section of roof/wall dramatically collapses.

She curls up in fetal position, eyes locked on the burning house.

Camera flies into the fire burning in Alice's right eye.

Alice faints.

FADE

Cut to asylum...LET MUSIC MAKE THE TRANSITION

INT CHILDRENS HOSPITAL/ASYLUM

Rain is falling outside.

Camera slowly pulls away from Alice's vacant eye. She's curled on a bed in a private room.

Sterile, impersonal except for framed facing photos of her mum and dad on bedside table. Shares space with a bowl of food and a large spoon. A chair is the only other piece of furniture.

No longer the pretty little girl of earlier sequences, Alice is a drawn young woman; has not seen the sun in ages.

She clutches a dirty and threadbare stuffed rabbit, whose only eye stares off into space.

We see numerous scars on Alice's wrists. Some fresh. One wrist is bandaged.

The night, visible through a barred window, is boiling with bad weather.

A nurse in the foreground turns and walks slowly to the door shaking her head, speaking to herself.

NURSE

Glad I saved that moth-eaten relic [the rabbit] from the dustbin.

(Turns and says, in full voice)

Please try to eat something, dear. Good night, Alice.

(The nurse will resemble the Duchess in game.)

Nurse locks the door behind her as the darkened sky outside unleashes a burst of lightning.

Alice flinches and grasps the rabbit tight.

Camera pulls in again on Alice.

Every time there is a lightning flash, she flinches slightly; she exhibits no other signs of activity.

Another flash offers the opportunity to cut to a close-up of her head and torso, where the rabbit in her hand slowly turns its head to look at Alice.

It whispers in a raspy voice, sounding like the worn-out toy it is.

RABBIT

Alice, pull yourself together, girl. You must help us!

Another flash pulls the camera back out; Alice slowly turns her head to look downward at the rabbit.

Another flash and the rabbit is gone from her hand, but something else is in the room with Alice.

Camera pans as if to look out of Alice's eye and finds a large white rabbit dressed in undertakers' garb standing before her.

RABBIT

You must help us, Alice. You really must. Follow me—we haven't much time.

Walking toward to the door, the rabbit pulls a key from its waistcoat and unlocks the door. Pushing it open, the rabbit steps through into darkness and begins to run away, again exclaiming:

RABBIT

Hurry, Alice; we're very late already!

Alice slowly rises from the bed; she takes the spoon (this will become her knife) and shambles slowly to the door. Grasping the frame, she propels herself through the door and into the darkness beyond.

WONDERLAND—INT RABBIT HOLE

Alice is falling.

Alice cries out as she falls. She is once again tossed down the rabbit hole and through the entrance to Wonderland. But this feels different.

She falls for quite some time, with the images of her parents, her childhood lifestyle, and her years at the asylum blending together. Images twist and warp, and several of the twisted Wonderland creatures are briefly introduced here.

The shadow of the Jabberwock flies across Alice. The Mad Hatter rides a Victorian bicycle across her path; only his coattails and top hat visible. Furniture twists and changes; the walls are pure darkness.

(End Intro)

Chapter 7

Master Design Document Template

As discussed in Chapter 6, "Creating Characters, Storyboarding, and Design Documents," a design document is the master blueprint to your game—before the clock starts ticking and the money begins to burn, it's the key to thoroughly fleshing out the game in depth, on paper, or in a word processing document to cover all the key components.

Throughout the game's development, various members of the team will refer to this document, and in most cases modify it. But where on earth do you start?

To help us along, celebrated game designer Chris Taylor—responsible for such games as Microsoft's *Dungeon Siege* series and Cavedog's *Total Annihilation*—has provided a master design document template to help solidify and organize your vision. Taylor stresses that this is merely a guideline to the way a master design document could be written, and will vary greatly between game designers and development studios. That is, there's no official "right" way to write one of these.

After the game starts development, additional technical data is stuffed into appendices inside the master design (this keeps total document count down to a minimum). When more is known about the game, Taylor adds, technical specifications are created.

> Often, they follow my appendix model, but now I believe they should be their own doc. In other words, on *Dungeon Siege*, I have something called the Interface Appendix that grew out of the master design doc. However, 20/20 hindsight has me believing that this should just be called the Dungeon Siege Interface Specification v1.0 or whatever version the doc is.

So, in the end, the original doc grows appendices, which each grow to become stand-alone specifications. Then, all the implementors on the team—artists, designers (level designers, typically), engineering, UE (user education, or what most would call the manual writer), testing/QA (quality assurance), the localization teams, the "Setup.exe" people, strategy guide writers—will use these specification documents because there is a very accurate one-to-one correlation between what appears in the game and what's written in the specification docs. The original design doc is simply a lofty goal that the lead designer shoots for and more often than not, many of the features don't make it.

So, without further ado, consider the following your very own template for creating a master design document in which you can plug in all the specific variables for your game. Chris Taylor provides loads of notes on the kinds of information to include in each section. (You can find the Word document template on the New Riders web site at www.newriders.com.)

Title Page

The title page should include the following information:

➤ *Your company name or logo*

➤ **Design Document for:** *Name of game*

➤ **One line description, such as** *The Ultimate Racing Game*

➤ *"Something funny here!"*™

➤ All work Copyright ©(*DATE*) by *Your Company Name*

➤ Written by *Your Name*

➤ Version #

➤ Current Date

Table of Contents

The table of contents should include a list of all the major and minor sections in the design document and the correct page number for each. (Among the advantages of using a word processing program to create the design document is the fact that the software can provide the page numbers!) The following is a typical table of contents for a design document. (Each of these items is explained briefly in the following pages.)

Name of Game

Design History

Version 1.10

Version 2.00

Version 2.10

Game Overview

Philosophy

Philosophical point #1

Philosophical point #2

Philosophical point #3

Common Questions

What is the game?

Why create this game?

Where does the game take place?

What do I control?

How many characters do I control?

What is the main focus?

What's different?

Feature Set

General Features

Multiplayer Features

Editor

Game Play

The Game World

Overview

World Feature #1

World Feature #2

The Physical World

Overview

Key Locations

Travel

Scale

Objects

Weather

Day and Night

Time

Rendering System

Overview

2D/3D Rendering

Camera

Overview

Camera Detail #1

Camera Detail #2

Game Engine

Overview

Game Engine Detail #1

Water

Collision Detection

Lighting Models

Overview

Lighting Model Detail #1

Lighting Model Detail #2

The World Layout

Overview

World Layout Detail #1

World Layout Detail #2

Game Characters

Overview

Creating a Character

Enemies and Monsters

User Interface

Overview

User Interface Detail #1

User Interface Detail #2

Weapons

Overview

Weapons Detail #1

Weapons Detail #2

Musical Scores and Sound Effects

Overview

Red Book Audio

3D Sound

Sound Design

Single-Player Game

Overview

Single-Player Game Detail #1

Single-Player Game Detail #2

Story

Hours of Gameplay

Victory Conditions

Multiplayer Game

Overview

Max Players

Servers

Customization

Internet

Gaming Sites

Persistence

Saving and Loading

Character Rendering

Overview

Character Rendering Detail #1

Character Rendering Detail #2

World Editing

Overview

World Editing Detail #1

World Editing Detail #2

Extra Miscellaneous Stuff

Overview

Junk I am working on…

XYZ Appendix

Objects Appendix

User Interface Appendix

Networking Appendix

Character Rendering and Animation Appendix

Story Appendix

Design History

This is a brief (one-paragraph) explanation of the history of this document. In this paragraph, describe to the reader what you're trying to achieve with the design history. It's possible that they don't know what this is for, so you need to explain it to them.

Version 1.10

Version 1.10 includes some tuning and tweaking that I did after making my initial pass at the design. Here is what I changed:

1. I rewrote the section about what systems the game runs on.

2. I incorporated feedback from the team into all parts of the design; however, no major changes were made.

3. Just keep listing your changes like this.

Version 2.00

Version 2.00 is the first version of the design in which a major revision has been made now that much more is known about the game. After many hours of design, many decisions have been made. Most of these large design decisions are now reflected in this document.

Included in the changes are the following:

1. Paring down of the design scope (scope, not design).

2. More detailed descriptions in many areas, specifically A, B, and C.

3. Story details.

4. World layout and design.

Version 2.10

Version 2.10 has several small changes over version 2.00. The key areas are in many of the appendixes.

Included in the changes are the following:

1. Minor revisions throughout entire document.

2. Added "User Interface Appendix."

3. Added "Game Object Properties Appendix."

4. Added concept sketch for world.

Game Overview

Philosophy

Philosophical point #1

This game is trying to do this and that. Fundamentally, I am trying to achieve something that has never been achieved before. Or: This game will not try and change the world. We are ripping off the competition so exactly that I can't believe it. The world will be shocked at how we are using an existing engine with new art.

Philosophical point #2

Our game runs only on Compaq computers. The reason for this is such and such. We believe the world is coming to an end anyhow, so what difference does it make?

Philosophical point #3

When you create some of these overarching philosophical points about your design, say whatever you want. Also, feel free to change it to "My game design goals" or whatever you want to call it.

Common Questions

What is the game?

Describe the game in a paragraph. This is the answer to the most common question that you will be asked: What are you working on?

Why create this game?

Why are you creating this game? Do you love 3D shooters? Do you think there is a hole in the market for Jell-O tossing midgets?

Where does the game take place?

Describe the world that your game takes place in. Simple as that. Help frame it in the reader's mind by spending a few sentences on it here. You can go into lengthy detail later in a section solely dedicated to describing the world. Remember that we want to keep this part of the design light and readable.

What do I control?

Describe what the player will control. You will be in charge of a band of rabid, mutant fiddle players. If you want, you can switch on the AI and turn it into a fishbowl simulation.

How many characters do I control?

If this applies, talk a little more about the control choices. Remember to add answers to questions that you think the reader will ask. This is totally dependent on your design.

What is the main focus?

Now that we know where the game takes place and what the player controls, what are they supposed to achieve in this world? Angry fiddle players take over the U.N. building. Be careful not to add a bunch of salesmanship here. Your design wants to stay light and informative.

What's different?

Tell them what's different from the games that are attempting this in the market right now. This question comes up a lot.

Feature Set

General Features

Huge world

Mutant fiddle players

3D graphics

32-bit color

Multiplayer Features

Up to 10 million players

Easy to find a game

Easy to find your pal in huge world

Can chat over voice link

Editor

Comes with world editor

Get levels from Internet

Editor is super-easy to use

Gameplay

List stuff here that is key to the gameplay experience

List a lot of stuff here

Hey, if you got nothing here, is this game worth doing?

The Game World

Overview

Provide an overview to the game world.

World Feature #1

This section is not supposed to be called *World Feature #1* but is supposed to be titled with some major thing about the world. This is where you break down what is so great about the game world into component pieces and describe each one.

World Feature #2

Same thing here. Don't sell too hard. These features should be awesome and be selling the game on its own.

The Physical World

Overview

Describe an overview of the physical world. Then start talking about the components of the physical world in each following paragraph.

The following describes the key components of the physical world.

Key Locations

Describe the key locations in the world here.

Travel

Describe how the player moves characters around in the world.

Scale

Describe the scale that you will use to represent the world. Scale is important!

Objects

Describe the different objects that can be found in the world.

See the "Objects Appendix" for a list of all the objects found in the world.

Weather

Describe what sort of weather will be found in the world, if any. Otherwise, omit this section. Add sections that apply to your game design.

Day and Night

Does your game have a day and night mode? If so, describe it here.

Time

Describe the way time will work in your game or whatever will be used.

Rendering System

Overview

Give an overview of how your game will be rendered and then go into detail in the following paragraphs.

2D/3D Rendering

Describe what sort of 2D/3D rendering engine will be used.

Camera

Overview

Describe the way the camera will work and then go into details in subsections if the camera is very complicated.

Camera Detail #1

The camera will move around like this and that.

Camera Detail #2

The camera will sometimes move like this in this special circumstance.

Game Engine

Overview

Describe an overview of the game engine.

Game Engine Detail #1

The game engine will keep track of everything in the world like such and such.

Water

There will be water in the world that looks awesome and our game engine will handle it beautifully.

Collision Detection

Our game engine handles collision detection really well. It uses the such and such technique and will be quite excellent. Can you see I am having a hard time making up stupid placeholder text here?

Lighting Models

Overview

Describe the lighting model you are going to use and then go into the different aspects of it below.

Lighting Model Detail #1

We are using the xyz technique to light our world.

Lighting Model Detail #2

We won't be lighting the eggplants in the game because they are purple.

The World Layout

Overview

Provide an overview here.

World Layout Detail #1

World Layout Detail #2

Game Characters

Overview

Overview of what your characters are like.

Creating a Character

How you create or personalize your character.

Enemies and Monsters

Describe enemies or monsters in the world or whomever the player is trying to defeat. Naturally, this depends heavily on your game idea, but generally games are trying to kill something.

User Interface

Overview

Provide some sort of an overview to your interface and as in all the previous sections, break down the components of the following UI.

User Interface Detail #1

User Interface Detail #2

Weapons

Overview

Overview of weapons used in game.

Weapons Details #1

Weapons Details #2

Musical Scores and Sound Effects

Overview

This should probably be broken down into two sections but I think you get the point.

Red Book Audio

If you're using Red Book, describe what your plan is here. If not, what are you using?

3D Sound

Talk about what sort of sound APIs you're going to use or not use, as the case may be.

Sound Design

Take a shot at what you're going to do for sound design at this early stage. Hey, good to let your reader know what you're thinking.

Single-Player Game

Overview

Describe the single-player game experience in a few sentences.

Here's a breakdown of the key components of the single-player game.

Single Player Game Detail #1

Single Player Game Detail #2

Story

Describe your story idea here and then refer to an appendix or separate document that provides all the details on the story if it's really big.

Hours of Gameplay

Talk about how long the single-player game experience is supposed to last or what your thoughts are at this point.

Victory Conditions

How does the player win the single-player game?

Multiplayer Game

Overview

Describe how the multiplayer game will work in a few sentences and then go into details following.

Max Players

Describe how many players can play at once or whatever.

Servers

Is your game client/server, peer-to-peer, or whatever.

Customization

Describe how the players can customize the multiplayer experience.

Internet

Describe how your game will work over the Internet.

Gaming Sites

Describe what gaming sites you want to support and what technology you intend to use to achieve this. Perhaps Dplay or TCP/IP or whatever. It's probably a good idea to break the tech stuff out into a separate area; you decide.

Persistence

Describe whether your world is persistent or not.

Saving and Loading

Explain how you can save a multiplayer game and then reload it if you can, or explain why this is not possible.

Character Rendering

Overview

Provide an overview as to how your characters will be rendered. You may have decided to include this elsewhere or break it out to provide more detail to a specific reader.

Character Rendering Detail #1

Character Rendering Detail #2

World Editing

Overview

Provide an overview about the world editor.

World Editing Detail #1

World Editing Detail #2

Extra Miscellaneous Stuff

Overview

Drop anything you're working on and don't have a good home for here.

Junk I am working on...

Crazy idea #1

Crazy idea #2

XYZ Appendix

Provide a brief description of what this appendix is for, and then get down to business and provide data to the reader.

Here are a few examples of some of the appendices in my latest design...

➤ Objects Appendix

➤ User Interface Appendix

➤ Networking Appendix

➤ Character Rendering and Animation Appendix

➤ Story Appendix

Okay, that's it. I wanted to spend more time on this and really make it a great roadmap for putting a game design together. Unfortunately, it would take a ton of time, and that's something that we don't have enough of in this business. I think you get the idea, anyhow. Also, don't get the impression that I think a design should provide the information in any particular order; this just happened to be the way it fell out of my head when I sat down. Change this template any way you want and if you feel you have improved on it, send it back to me and I can pass it out as an alternative to anyone who asks me in the future.

Good luck and all that!

Chris Taylor, www.gaspoweredgames.com

Chapter 8

Level Design

The worldwide PC gaming community hasn't been the same since id Software's *Wolfenstein 3D* was unleashed in the spring of 1992. More than a quarter-million people scrambled to download this racy, 700KB shareware game from their local bulletin board system (BBS) and thus, the first-person perspective 3D shooter was born.

The next decade yielded many memorable "shooters"—*DOOM, Dark Forces, Duke Nukem 3D, Quake,* the *Jedi Knight* series, *GoldenEye 007, Unreal, Half-Life, Soldier of Fortune,* the *Medal of Honor* series, *No One Lives Forever, Halo, Red Faction, Return to Castle Wolfenstein*—and in so doing, launched a specialized and necessary art form known as level design.

Loosely speaking, *level design* pertains to creating the architecture of maps in the game, plus dealing with object placement, with the mission or goal of the map, and often with mini-missions within the level.

So, what makes for a well-laid-out and challenging level to complete? What are some of the more common mistakes found in amateur level design? Is there a science to it? You bet. This chapter features the world's top-level designers and their invaluable opinions on what makes or breaks level architecture in 3D shooters. Keep in mind that many of these pointers can also apply to other 3D games, including third-person perspective action games (such as *Max Payne*) and action/adventure hybrids (such as *Tomb Raider*).

Paul Jaquays, Ensemble Studios

We are once again honored to have Paul Jaquays, content designer at Ensemble Studios, to discuss level design. And a sage he is: While at id Software, Paul created some of the most memorable levels for *Quake II, Quake III Arena, Quake III: Team Arena,* and (currently in development) the all-new *DOOM*. At Ensemble, he's working on an undisclosed product.

When designing levels in a game, Jaquays says that there are three very important considerations to keep in mind:

1. **Stay focused on the goal**. Design a game level to fulfill the purpose required of it. The initial design should include only those elements, design, structural or play content that are needed to set up what must be accomplished in the level. If you're building a deathmatch map, don't try to make it play or feel like a single-player map.

> **NOTE**
>
> *Deathmatch (DM)* refers to non-team-based multiplayer maps, typically played over the Internet or on a LAN with other human players. It's a "kill-or-be-killed" scenario, in which the goal is to stay alive and rack up as many frags (points) as possible. Kill a player, get a frag; die yourself, lose one—hence the name *deathmatch*.

2. **Include a focal point for the map—something that becomes the definition of the map**. This piece of architecture, or model, or clever play gimmick, or even a unique bit of gameplay interaction that occurs, will be how players remember your map. If the players remember nothing else about the map, the focal point stays with them.

3. **"The play's the thing."** Pardon my poor Shakespeare, but when all else is said and done, if the map didn't play well, all the graphics, all the special effects, and all the clever gimmicks will have gone to waste.

Does Jaquays sketch out his ideas on paper?

Originally, I would have an image in my head and work toward that. But now, I must say that I'm starting to see the light about putting as much down on paper first as you can. Scratching out a layout on paper allows you to see important relationships between encounter sites. For a single-player game, it allows you to set up a walkthrough of events and see how they relate to each other. It allows you to lay out, design, and redesign spaces without spending a lot of time creating 3D architecture. And most importantly, it allows other members of your design team to see what you're doing, and when you try to explain (or defend) your intentions, it can reveal design flaws before they're implemented.

Jaquays offers some specific advice:

Big thoughts:

➤ Imagine grandiosely; block in sparingly; finish the design somewhere in the middle.

➤ Imagine grand vistas and dream mighty dreams, but know how to implement something that works.

➤ Don't always choose the easiest or the safest solutions to a development problem. Even if the schedule is tight, take risks.

➤ Frame-rate is not god. Make games that look good and have an acceptable frame-rate.

➤ Be known as a designer who can finish things. If you can finish them on schedule, all the better.

Practical thoughts:

➤ Your initial block-in of a game map should use less than 33% to 50% of your allowed resources. The less, the better. Making it look good will use up all the rest and most of what the software team finds in optimizations.

➤ Regularly try to look at your game development as if you were seeing it for the first time.

➤ The game designer, like the artist, needs to be an observer of the world at large.

Although the focus of gameplay in *Quake III: Arena* was deathmatch and the individual player, the focus of *Quake III: Team Arena* was—you guessed it—team play. How does this affect level design? Read the excerpts from id Software's Paul Jaquays and Tim Willits. Check out the official web site at `www.idsoftware.com/games/quake/quake3-teamarena`.
(Images from *Quake III Team Arena 2003* Id Software, Inc. All rights reserved. Used under license. *Quake* and *Quake III Team Arena* are either registered trademarks or trademarks of Id Software, Inc. in the United States and/or other countries.
(Used with permission by Activision, Inc.)

Paul Jaquays' 26 Level Design Tips

To summarize some of the aforementioned points, and to add a whole whack more, Jaquays offers 26 points to keep in mind if you want to become a successful level designer. Take heed, young Jedi, and read on:

1. Know what you want to do with a level before you start. Don't expect a map that you start as a single-player map to be easily changed into a multiplayer map. The reverse holds true for trying to make a deathmatch map into a single-player challenge.

2. Sketch out a diagram of the map to use as an initial guide.

3. Don't start with grandiose projects. Try making something fun with a few rooms.

4. If possible, build your level with a "gimmick" in mind—some tricky gamism bit that players will remember. Popular gimmicks that have been used in the past include wind tunnels, numerous portals, lava maps, trap maps, water-filled maps, maps with large slow-moving hazards, and low-gravity maps.

5. Try to be fresh and original with every new design. Do something that you haven't seen done before.

6. Test gimmicks of gameplay, tricks, and traps in test levels before building them into your game level.

7. Do architecture and texture studies ahead of time to establish an architectural style. Stick to that style.

8. Block out your level with large pieces of geometry. Think of the architecture you'll use, but concentrate more on how gameplay will flow through the level. At this stage, I try to keep my map grid at the largest possible setting (in *Quake II* or *Quake III*, that's the "64" grid). Avoid fussy details at this point and go for massiveness. At this stage of development, try to keep your frame-rate speeds well below the amount allowed by the game (for *Quake II*, we aimed to be below a maximum count of 500 triangles of architecture in any view). A good rule might be to try for no more than one-third of your total possible polygon count in the worst views in and near your larger rooms.

9. After the flow is established, you can start adding architectural detail and refining hall and room shapes.

10. Build in a modular manner. Make prefabricated pieces that can fit together easily to make your level. Build tricky pieces of detailed architecture (such as doorframes, complicated cornices, or furniture) once and set them outside the boundaries of your map. Clone them as needed for placement in the map.

11. When designing architectural elements, study the real world. Try to duplicate the look and feel of impressive works, but with less complicated geometry. Set yourself challenges in this regard.

12. Strike a balance between the use of real geometry and textures that imply three-dimensional depth when building architectural details. Textures that appear to be 3D should be used with caution. When viewed from a distance, they can fool the eye into believing that the architectural geometry is significantly more complex than it actually is. But the same texture viewed up close and at eye-level completely destroys the illusion of depth.

13. Compile the map often. Don't wait until everything is placed to see what things look like (or if you have leaks in the map hull).

14. Complete your map geometry before adding monsters and items.

15. When building single-player game maps, don't put every game feature in the level. Having every monster possible in the game in a single game level is a glaring sign of amateur work. Generally speaking, the only place you will see all the monsters at once is in the AI programmer's test level.

16. The same goes for tricks, traps, items, weapons, and power-ups. Unless your map is as massive as the 64-player DM maps created for *Quake II*, restrict the number of different items you put in the map. Use a few things cleverly, rather than [using] many poorly.

17. Small maps can be relatively similar throughout. Large maps should have distinctive, memorable locations that the player can use to orient himself in the map. "City64," a large DM map for *Quake II*, featured a huge canyon area, a massive alien temple, underwater caverns, a vast deep tank with water in the bottom, and numerous stretches of twisty corridors. The corridors were often similar, but they ended in distinctive large play areas.

18. For DM maps, give the player frequent opportunities to avoid pursuit and dodge for cover. Long hallways with no exits are bad. Avoid forcing players to make long trips to dead-end rooms—even to get good power-ups.

19. Place lights to achieve drama. If you have a choice between underlighting an area and overlighting it, err on the side of darkness. Just don't go overboard. Dark levels may look nifty, but stumbling around in the dark while playing gets old fast.

20. Light as you go—even if you're placing only temporary lights.

21. Don't forget the audio elements of a map. Sounds can provide important game clues.

22. If possible, allow multiple solutions for puzzles. You can still reserve the greatest rewards for players who solve them in what the designer has decided is the "best way."

23. Give the player a variety of game experiences and challenges in each map. All combat or all puzzles can get old quickly.

24. Be kind to your players; don't overchallenge them unnecessarily. Well-placed environmental hazards add to the tension of gameplay, but falling into lava or slime every third step or being crushed to death by falling weights every time you turn around quickly becomes frustrating.

25. Study maps you like, and make an effort to duplicate or even improve situations and settings.

26. Finish what you begin.

Many other programmers, artists, animators, musicians, and level designers chime in with Paul Jaquays on this point: Finishing a project instead of starting 10 new ones is essential, and not easy for beginners.

Paul's Advice on Game Design

Through a long career in the gaming industry, Jaquays has accumulated quite a bit of knowledge on the art of game design. Although he covered many individual points in the preceding section on map creation, the following details serve as more broad advice on game design, drawing from Paul's own experiences.

➤ **Stop imitating yourself**. I started in the game business as a designer of game adventures for a new (at the time) game called *Dungeons & Dragons* and later for *Runequest*. There was a time when I was considered one of the best adventure writers in the field. One of the reasons that I quit designing pencil-and-paper–type role-playing games was because I found that I had started to imitate myself, rehashing the same storyline over and over. I was no longer fresh. Thankfully, I had other career options within the game business that I could pursue. But the problem still remains—how to keep your ideas alive and new.

Innovation is the process of developing and improving upon what has gone before. *Invention* is the process of creating things that are significantly different from what has been previously created. Innovation and invention both have their places in game design and development. Innovation works best at improving on systems and procedures, such as control interfaces in a first-person shooter, which have become almost standardized over the years. Yet, for high-level aspects of game design, invention is best. The truly memorable games over the years have been those that broke the mold and created game concepts—and in some cases entire game genres—that didn't exist in computer game form.

➤ **Choose the unconventional solution**. There's a tendency in game design to use familiar or tried-and-true solutions to design. In the latter part of the Golden Age of Video Games (the classic 8-bit years), the solution for nearly every game based on a character or movie license was to create a side-scrolling game. During my tenure at Coleco, we were given very few opportunities to create new games. Most of our work was to analyze and translate arcade titles. The *WarGames* movie license gave us the opportunity to create a game that broke the mold. The conventional solution would have been to make a side-scrolling "solve the puzzles, find the hidden goodies, and avoid the bad guys" game, until at last you confronted the computer in the last scene. At that point, the game would start you back at the beginning and ratchet up the level of difficulty a notch. After seeing a special preview screening of the movie *WarGames*, I was inspired by the sequence near the end of the movie, in which the computer runs simulated scenario after scenario in which the outcome was always the same: nuclear war and complete world devastation. I was taken by the graphics that plotted the arcs of missiles as they approached their targets. If I could convince the powers-that-be, that short sequence of the movie would be our game. The actual gameplay derived from several unrelated concepts. The goal of the player would be to stop bombers, subs, and missiles (which were drawn on-the-fly as lines—no simple trick in the 8-bit pattern tile game systems of the day) from reaching their targets on a map of the United States.

In a way, it had similarities to the popular arcade game *Missile Command*, in which the player fires antiballistic missiles at incoming missiles dropping down from the top of the screen. Unlike the arcade, the play took place on six separate maps simultaneously. Like the juggler who keeps numerous plates spinning at once atop thin sticks, the player had to rapidly switch his attention between a radar map showing the whole U.S. and six sub-maps that contained closer views of target cities and military installations. The player had to rapidly commit resources (missiles, interceptor planes, and attack subs) to deal with enemy attacks; then shift to the next map and do the same. If the player had the right stuff, he or she could defeat the game.

➤ **Blend flavors**. Some of the most popular foods are those that blend unlike or even opposite flavors together in one tasty package. Sweet-and-sour Chinese dishes and Chicago-style hot dogs are just two examples. What does this have to do with game design? One of the products of which I'm most proud is a book series called *Central Casting*. The purpose of the products was to create vivid back-stories or histories for characters in role-playing games. I created separate books that covered three distinct genre groups of games: fantasy, science fiction (or futuristic), and 20th century games. Players rolled dice and compared the results against a series of tables and lists. Roll by roll, they selected events and personality traits that they could use to define their game characters. Quite often, the results of dice rolls would seem unlikely to be combined, but with a little creative thought, the widely disparate events would blend together, like the myriad of flavors in a Chicago-style hot dog, into a uniquely original result.

➤ **Make it real**. Even if you plan on making your game setting wildly fantastic—that is, nothing you would ever see in the real world—take care to make it seem real. This is something I learned as a fantasy illustrator, painting covers for games and books. The way to make the fantastic elements of a painting believable is to realistically paint the mundane things in the picture. This establishes a setting that appears as if it could actually exist somewhere. You then paint the fantastic elements in the painting with an equal amount of care so that they partake of the reality of the rest of the painting. The same holds true when making 3D game levels. Give the player one or more familiar elements that he can relate to. By comparison with the real elements, the unreal things in the game should seem more real, or perhaps a better term is that they seem more plausible. And by contrast with the mundane, they'll seem that much more fantastic.

To keep up-to-date on Paul's work, visit `www.idsoftware.com` or one of the many news sites, such as Blue's News (`www.bluesnews.com`).

Tim Willits, id Software

As level designer on *Ultimate DOOM* and *Quake*; lead level designer on the legendary *Quake II*, *Quake III: Arena*, and *Quake III: Team Arena*; and senior designer and project director on *DOOM III*, Tim Willits has gathered quite a bit of knowledge on how to create a successful map for 3D shooters. He shares his take on this exciting facet of 3D game development:

When designing any level, the most important thing for a level designer to keep in mind is this: "What's the purpose of this map and what do you want to achieve?" [This basic concept is] often forgotten when planning the map. Some designers just start building without knowing exactly what they want to build or what purpose the map has in the greater scheme of the game. Later, after it's built, when pieces of the map require rework or deleting, it adds precious time onto the project—time [that might have been] saved if only the designer had a clear idea of the map before he or she started. When maps are built without purpose and then later fitted into a game, they always seem forced or contrived—they stand out as examples of poor planning.

Before Willits sits down to create a map, he asks himself whether it will be a single-player map or a deathmatch map:

Before you can do anything, you need to figure out what kind of level you want. It's a lot easier if you stick to either deathmatch (DM) or single player (SP). Though it can be done, making a map great for both DM and SP is a very difficult task. Usually, if it's great for DM, it'll be too circular for SP; and if it's a fun SP map, it's usually too straight for DM.

Although many of the same principles can be applied to creating both SP and DM maps, Willits breaks up his advice into separate groups for SP and DM.

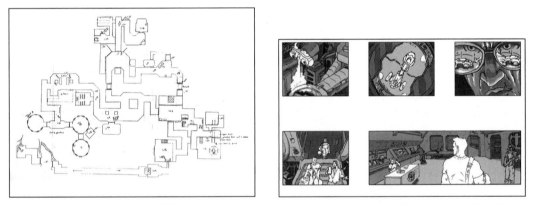

Tim Willits' hand-drawn sketches of a *DOOM III* storyline and overhead map for the game. He comments, "I create a simple 2D sketch of a map before I start work in the editor." (Images from *DOOM III* © 2002 Id Software, Inc. All rights reserved. Used under license. *DOOM*, *DOOM III*, and the Id Software name are either registered trademarks or trademarks of Id Software, Inc. in the United States and/or other countries.)

(Used with permission by Activision, Inc.)

Single-Player Levels

According to Willits, there are a number of rules to adhere to when devising successful single-player levels. The following are the most significant rules to keep in mind.

Focus and Continuity

Of the utmost importance, in Willits' opinion, are focus and continuity of the task. And, as he explains, it can be easy to lose both during a game's cycle:

Every game has one overall mission or goal. The game then is made up of many single levels. Every level in turn must also have one overall mission. And every map must have a reason why it exists. It's important that the designer doesn't forget this—it happens a lot. A designer will be working on a level with a goal in mind. And then something happens—sometimes a technology is introduced into the game or a technical problem arises, and the focus of the map shifts. Sometimes designers don't even realize that they've lost focus on their original goals of the level, but they have. When this happens, the designer must step back, look at where things are going, and focus more attention on the overall design and goals of the level, sometimes reworking areas or changing the goals to accommodate the map's mission. Basically, it's crucial that designers stay focused on their ultimate goals in designing a level.

As a side note, Willits reminds level designers that there must be one person who focuses on the entire design process, to ensure that levels don't stray too far from their original goal. A fresh set of eyes from someone not too close to the level is ideal for all games.

Architecture Design and Gameplay Elements

According to Willits, SP maps require a pretty linear flow, and they need to guide the player through the level with both architecture design and gameplay elements. To clarify, *architecture design* is basically how the areas are constructed. There should be natural breaks in levels that separate the major components of that level, as well as the level's mini-missions (we'll get to this in a moment). *Gameplay elements*, on the other hand, follow the events orchestrated by the story of the level within the game. Willits cites an example:

> If the player's mission on the power station level is to destroy the nuclear reactor; then the level may be broken down into areas such as the control center, waste pumping station, core reactor, and coolant subsystems. Each one of these areas must look like it's supposed to look as well as perform some function in the overall level. The player may need to enter the security codes in the control center to gain access to the coolant subsystems. Once in the coolant subsystems, the player could drain the core reactor's coolant, causing an unstable heat exchange within the core. Finally, the player could reverse the waste in the waste pumping station, creating a chain reaction that would destroy the entire nuclear reactor.

Risks and Rewards

Risks and rewards must be peppered throughout SP maps to challenge the gamer while plowing toward the end of a game. Willits believes it's essential that each new area contain these kinds of obstacles. Here's an example:

> The player enters a new area of a map, and there's a slime pool that's too far to jump across. On the other side of the slime pool is a button that extends the bridge, but it's guarded by a monster. The player's mini-mission is to extend the bridge. The obstacles to accomplishing that mission are the monster and the fact that the button is on the other side of the slime pool—too far away to push. To accomplish this mini-mission, all the player needs to do is shoot the button from his side and then avoid the monster while crossing the bridge; that's it. Simple. It may not seem like a mission, but it is. It's a challenge that the player must face and overcome in order to continue with the game. A single-player level is a collection of these mini-missions, tied closely around unique areas in some cohesive manner.

Willits describes an example of not rewarding the player enough:

> I once played a game in which there was a tower in the middle of a courtyard with some monsters in it. It looked important, and it was a centerpiece of that courtyard. I killed the two guys in the upper portion and navigated to the top. I was pretty disappointed when I finally reached the top and there was nothing there. Every time you have an area in the map that looks important and there's a fight to reach it, you need to reward the player with "goodies."

Environmental Feel, Teasers, and Flow

An important consideration of an SP map, according to Willits, is the overall environmental feel. Aside from looking good and playing well, what does he mean by this?

> A designer must make the level look the way the player expects it to. If the designer calls a map a *warehouse*, there had better be some crates lying around because players will be looking for them. Also, a designer must try to make the level seem as if it fits into the rest of the world. Don't mix time periods if you're not traveling in time; don't mix construction materials along similar time periods. For example, don't build your first map out of sheets of metal and have the follow-up map made mostly of brick and stucco. Players want consistency; they're comfortable with it because it surrounds their everyday lives.

Another nice touch in creating a good environmental feel is to build the map with the hint that there's more out there. "Create fake facades that can be viewed through windows but are unreachable on foot. Have boxes come out of walls and vanish through other walls on the other side of the room. Create architecture that sweeps out past the playing area," says Willits. If these items are placed in the levels by the designer, players will feel like they're involved in something "bigger."

Along with these "teasers," a few outstanding visual scenes or landmarks will also help capture the environment that the designer wants to create, says Willits.

> Spend some time developing a spectacular view. Maybe a grand entrance, a detailed outer building, or even a super-advanced control center. Make players turn a corner for the first time and say to themselves, "Wow." It stays with the players, and they remember the level long after they completed it if they were impressed by something cool-looking. This isn't so important in DM maps, mainly because once you run past it no one cares what it looks like time after time. Don't spend too much time on something visually stunning in DM; spend more time on flow.

In terms of flow, the levels need to start out pretty easy and then advance in difficulty, maintains Willits. As a rule, he builds the first level as a training level.

> If you want to build some cool objects that move or some sort of complex geometry to showcase the engine, put it out of the path of the player. For example, air vents with spinning blades look just as good horizontal behind grates. Or moving pumps alongside walls is another good use of moving things that are non-threatening. I know you want to add a lot of interesting things in the first couple of levels, but just keep them as non-intrusive as possible.

Perhaps you're interested in creating only top-notch multiplayer maps? If that's the case, pull up a chair to Willits' DM 101 and get a few pointers on *capture the flag*-style games as well.

Deathmatch Levels

There are basically five popular styles of deathmatch levels: arena, circular, linear, location-based, and theme-centered. Many of these styles can be included in one map, and some have crossover traits, according to Willits.

Arena

In a nutshell, *arena* levels usually have one central area in which most of the combat takes place. Most of the hallways and passages either lead from this central area or to it. Says Willits:

> The map has very few other large rooms or areas of significance. The arena style of DM is very focused, very refined; the maps are quickly learned and easy to master. Players will always know where they are, and should never get lost navigating the hallways around the arena area. Players will find these maps fast-paced with high frag limits, which will be reached quickly. An example level is MAP07 from *DOOM II*.

And a word of caution to designers:

> Try not to make the arena areas too architecturally complex. This is the area in which all the fighting occurs, so it has to run fast. Complex architecture may look good, but it only slows down the game. Try to build this area as simply as possible.

Circular

As the name suggests, these *circular* maps are circular in design, or, as Willits says, "built in such a fashion that the player would never need to stop and turn around along its main path." He expands:

> Build with as few dead ends as possible—they're best built with none. Use numerous entrances and exits around its central core, which would allow free-flowing movement without hitches. The map also needs good weapon distribution—in which neither side has an advantage—and as little holding ground as possible. (*Holding ground* is a place in which a player can stock up on health and ammo in a room and camp.) An example level here is DM6 from *Quake*.

Linear

Linear maps are built with only a few alternate paths. Willits amplifies:

> The architecture becomes a roadmap in which people instantly know which side of the map they're on. Include nice open areas or wide hallways in which players can enjoy jousting-type combat. Even weapon distribution to force players to move back and forth. Have the ammo for the weapons on the opposite side of the map, forcing players who want to stock to travel. An example level is E1M1 from *DOOM*.

Location-Based

Location-based DM allows players to always know where they are. You may not be able to figure out how to get somewhere else fast, but you immediately know your location. These maps are not free-flowing as in circular or linear maps, but instead are made up of many unique identifiable areas. Each area should have some distinct combat areas or mini-themes included in it. For example, in DM3 from *Quake* is a water area for swimming, a thin staircase for vertical fighting, and a computer room made for close fighting. Each area has a special weapon or power-up that fits the environment. These maps are great for team games.

Theme-Centered

And last on the list for DM maps are *theme-based* maps. As Willits puts it, a theme-based map uses something unique to combat and overexaggerates it all over the map. Perhaps this is better explained by an example:

An example of this is E1M4 from *Quake*, a.k.a. The Sewage System. This map is covered with water; most of the fighting is in or around water. Everywhere the player looks, he sees water or something related to water. In almost every area, the player can enter or exit the water. The water is the "theme" or the special combat characterization throughout the map. Theme maps are great for players who enjoy something totally unique. Theme-based maps are also more difficult to navigate through and should be used only for medium or advanced play. Themes need to enhance gameplay, not detract from it.

Good id Software examples of theme-based maps include wind tunnels (*Quake*, E3M5); low gravity (*Quake*, E1M8); low light, such as the mine levels in *Quake II*; hazardous materials such as lava, slime, or pits of death (*Quake*, DM4); torturous devices such as spike shooters or security lasers (*Quake II*); wide and open areas (*Quake II*); and teleport craziness (*Quake*, DM1).

"Capture the Flag" Games

"Capture the flag" (CTF) is a popular team-based multiplayer game in which the object is to steal the other team's flag and bring it safely back to your own base. There are many variations of CTF games. In the following section, Willits offers advice on creating maps for CTF fanatics.

Symmetric Levels

With CTF games, it's important that levels be nearly mirrors of each other to make things even between the two teams. Willits maintains, "In theory, it's possible to have two bases look different, but even in practice this has rarely worked." He cites a bad example of a CTF map from *Quake II*:

Strike is a fairly big failure in that regard, due to BFG and teleporter placement (putting the red team at a large disadvantage). Also, there are more methods of entering the red base than the blue base, making the blue base easily defensible. This map also has uneven ammo and weapon placement; the blue base has far better resources within. All this is solved very easily by making both sides identical.

Asymmetrical Levels

Willits says that if the level is not symmetrical, there should be a balanced strategy that needs to be employed by each individual team. For example, if one side is largely covered by water, the team should be given rebreathers. Similarly, protective environment suits should be accessible on the slime side.

Random Tips for CTF Maps

Willits grants us an assorted medley of tips on creating CTF maps:

➤ There should be a good supply of weapons and ammo near a base, but don't overdo it. This makes the base too easy to defend and difficult to attack. If a designer is using power-ups, they should never start off within the base.

➤ While still making it defensible, there should be multiple entry points and exits to a base.

➤ Centralized placement of major power-ups is a good idea. The power-ups still need to be located far enough from each other to prevent players from using a single power-up and crushing everyone on the map.

➤ Create some good sniper locations; but if players are going to snipe, they should be vulnerable in some way, too.

➤ There should be obvious color-coding of areas, but don't rely on colored lighting because colored lighting tends to neutralize player colors, and you can't see what team they're on. Use colored textures instead.

➤ Focus on good weapon placement and think it through. Weapon placement may be more important in CTF than normal DM because it can greatly shift the balance of power from one side to the other.

Does Willits sketch out ideas on paper or boot up the PC right way?

Sketching ideas out on paper is something I do before every level I start. I like to separate myself from the computer, finding someplace comfortable where I can relax and think. I start by roughing things out, simple and quick; flushing the ideas as fast as I can draw them or write them. I use the drawings and text descriptions as a starting point for the map creation. I may not exactly create what I draw, but it does give me some direction and reminds me of the "purpose and focus" of the map. As I stated before, planning will save a designer lots of pain and suffering down the road.

Willits also offers some advice in Chapter 21, "Breaking into the Industry," on the best way to break into the industry.

Richard "Levelord" Gray, Ritual Entertainment

Richard Gray, known more familiarly in the industry as the "Levelord," began his career in game design by building amateur levels for *DOOM* (id Software) and *Blood* (Apogee/3D Realms). The Levelord created roughly half of the levels in the outstanding shooter *Duke Nukem 3D* in 1996, before co-founding Ritual Entertainment, at which he created levels for a *Quake* add-on pack, *Sin*, and *Heavy Metal*. At last check, he was putting the finishing touches on *Condition Zero: Counter Strike* and *Star Trek: Elite Forces II*.

The "fun factor" is one of the Levelord's main mandates when building a level. He explains:

> Nothing else is more important! The game must, of course, perform well on its target platform. Ultimately, though, the game must be fun to play. Many games are filled with flashy new technology and special effects. Many of these same games are also short, boring, and lack any serious attention to what makes the game fun.

> What makes a game fun is hard to describe in words. This quality changes from game genre to genre. It's really something that you put into a game as you develop it. Attention must be paid to the fun factor during the design process, but this phase usually yields only broad general concepts. The fun factor, more often than not, seeps in during the implementation phase.

> Game designers spend a lot of time chasing new engine features and cutting-edge paraphernalia. They also chase deadlines. For our genre of first-person action games, some of the important aspects to the fun factor are immersion, player interaction, the invocation of such emotions as fear and being threatened, as well as puzzle solving.

And on the all-important immersion factor, the Levelord comments:

> As a level designer, I must make environments in which players can truly feel as though they are "there." That is, the level must be believable. Often, this only requires realism, even in a sci-fi or fantasy setting, and enough details to portray that realism. Details can also hurt frame-rate, so this process is often a wrestling match between what I want to put in the level and what the platform will allow for performance.

> Player interaction is usually easy, but it frequently falls by the wayside because we spend so much time tackling new technology. Player interaction is adding things such as breakable objects at which to shoot, telephones that work, toilets that flush, and so on. These activities go far to promote extended gameplay time as well as player satisfaction when discovering them.

On emotion:

> Provoking emotions and puzzle-solving are typically implemented during the design phase. These aspects are usually intrinsic to the level's basic intentions. It's hard to truly scare players nowadays, and keeping them at the edge of their seat is harder as the spectrum of experienced players grows wider. Edge-of-your-seat design requires a fine-lined balance between too little ammo and health and too much. Providing fear can also too easily escalate into a level that's too hard.

A good example of the fun factor at its simplest in shooters is the game *Serious Sam*. The game is not outstanding technologically. The game's story and character development are comparatively absent by today's standards. However, it's nonstop action and edge-of-your-seat excitement. The game is immersive enough, and there's a lot of player interaction. The game is fun, and that's all that matters.

Does the Levelord sketch ideas on paper?

Sometimes I do; sometimes I don't—sometimes I'll draw an entire level before casting the actual geometry in my editor; other times, though, I'll fly by the seat of my pants and just start building. Both approaches are good, but as games get more complicated, with embedded storylines and character development and sheer complexity, we tend to design everything on paper before making the actual game. We always use concept sketches for levels now, but we still let implementation phase additions be added as the level is actually engineered.

The Levelord finds inspiration in many places:

I look at books and movies, I look at pictures on the Internet, and I even look at other levels. Many people are afraid to look at other sources for inspiration because they fear being caught as a thief. In the art world, looking to others for inspiration is called "appropriation." As long as you don't outright copy someone else's work, you're not a thief.

Because he finds inspiration everywhere—including his dreams—the Levelord does the same thing as David Perry (as revealed in Chapter 2, "General Game Design: Action/Arcade Games"):

I find inspiration in my own dreams and thoughts. I keep a pad of paper and pencil next to my bed to write ideas that seem to come to my mind on their own. Many of these ideas come during that semi-sleep state just before or just after falling into real sleep.

What are the differences when creating levels for a console game versus a PC game?

The biggest difference is that consoles are more restrictive. Although dedicated to games, they have higher demands on constraints such as frame-rate and memory. This is partially due to their higher performance requirements. A PC game can satisfactorily run at 30–40 frames per second, whereas a console game can never go below 60 frames per second.

Consoles are in many ways better than PCs, too. Because they're a game-specific platform, they're far more reliable. There aren't 12 different video cards to test for compatibility. There aren't five different sound cards. The operating system won't change halfway through the development cycle. There's one set of performance parameters to deal with, not a range of "minimum" to "recommended" systems. When we release a console game, we're very sure that we have released a well-verified and fully validated game.

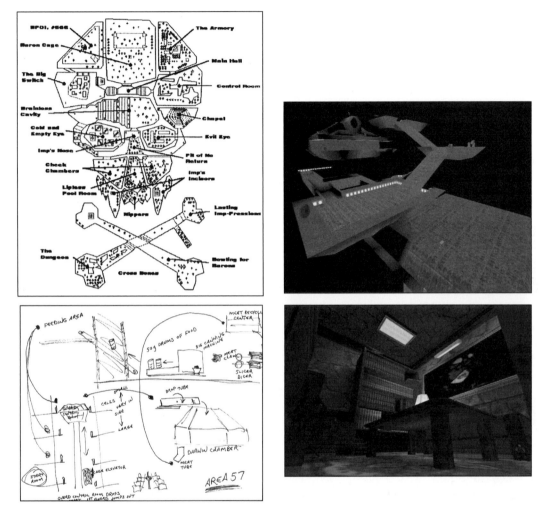

Check out this collection of behind-the-scenes images from the Levelord's work: hand-drawn sketches for a skull level in *DOOM* (back in 1994); a deathmatch level in *Quake: Scourge of Armagon*; plus a design sketch and snapshot from the game *Sin*. The image of the book-shelf is from a deathmatch level in *Sin* called "Spry," which places the player in a reading room as the size of a rat. "I believe this was the first professional micro-level, which is now semi-popular," adds Gray.

(Used with permission by Richard Gray.)

Chapter 21 focuses on the do's and don'ts of breaking into the interactive entertainment industry. Here, the Levelord offers some keen advice on the matter:

> There is only one "do" to get into this industry, and that's "do"! So many people ask me how I got in. It was simple for me; I had an unyielding passion to design levels. Even if I hadn't been hired, I would still be designing levels today. Most professional game developers are the same. They didn't ask how to get in; they just crafted their specialty and got noticed by a company. I believe id Software's hiring motto is "If you have to ask, we probably don't want you." [The staff we've hired are all] people that we found rather than them finding us.
>
> There really is no excuse not to get hired. The tools are free on the Internet, and anyone who really wants to get in only needs to do what they say they want to do. I've believed that I want to play the harmonica for years. Why don't I, though? The tool is cheap to acquire and fairly simple to learn. However, I never have gone beyond buying a harmonica and blowing into it a few dozen times. [Obviously,] I really don't want to play the harmonica, and will never get hired to do so.

> **NOTE**
> John Romero of id Software fame offers his advice on creating games for the bourgeoning PDA gaming market (see Chapter 20, "Doing It Yourself and the Shareware Revolution"). Romero is currently the CEO and chairman of Monkeystone Games (www.monkeystone.com).

Cliff Bleszinski, Epic Games

In Chapter 2, "Cliffy B" (as he's affectionately known in the industry), designer on the beloved *Unreal* series, gives some discerning advice on general game design. Here, he shares some level design tips for creating 3D shooters.

> It seems so obvious, but the golden rule of design is "Make the kind of experience you want to play." This ties into the overall concept of fun—balancing a good task-to-reward ratio. A *task* could be anything from solving a puzzle to destroying a villain to traversing a hazardous terrain. A *reward* might be discovering a new area, finding a new item, or uncovering a new piece of the story. If the player spends too much time in one area or finds himself lost, confused, or bored, you're not doing your job.

According to Bleszinski, the rules of design can vary from game to game, so it's best to understand what the evolving position of "level designer" involves.

> As we move forward with level design, we're no longer finding designers working in a vacuum. Artists and designers must work hand-in-hand to make sure that the game looks great, plays well, and runs at an acceptable frame-rate. Tight coordination and great communication are becoming crucial parts of making a great game experience.

A level designer is one-quarter architect, one-quarter game designer, one-quarter artist, and one-quarter play tester:

➤ **Architect**. The designer is building environments that must look believable to the most scrutinizing of gamers. Basic architectural knowledge is a must.

➤ **Game designer**. An intelligent lead designer will keep the project's design focused while allowing for creative elbow room by the level designers who are contributing to the game. Individual designers must have a level of control over the events that occur within their game space.

➤ **Artist**. In a perfect world, every single level designer would also be an artist capable of producing top-notch texture, geometry, and lighting work. But these people are few and far between. Most designers' strengths lie in game flow, game design, and balancing; artists are best at making things look good. That said, each designer must still possess some level of artistic knowledge. Even the initial simple blocking out of an environment must require a good level of composition.

➤ **Play tester**. A level designer will play the level he builds more than anyone else—he is responsible for making sure the level runs well, the AI handles the game space well, and the level is FUN!

To summarize, a level designer must understand the multiple hats that his position requires him to wear to excel at his job and make great games.

In a previous edition of this book, legendary game designer John Romero (one of the *DOOM* creators) said he felt that "fear" was a crucial element in level design—to always keep the gamers on their toes and edge of their seat! Bleszinski adds his own twist:

Pacing is also very important. If the player is constantly in fear, he'll become numb; if he's constantly surprised, it will wear off and not be effective. The key to scaring the player in a level is knowing when, where, and how often to spring a surprise. If there are, say, five minutes of idle time exploring and chatting with peaceful aliens, you can bet the player will be shaking in his boots when the door bursts in and a lava monster stomps in screaming bloody hell. This is why good horror movies don't spring surprise after surprise on the audience—because it loses its impact.

Good pacing is a skill that applies to every element of level design. Pace your flow of monsters, and have areas where the player feels like he is being engulfed by less-intelligent "cannon fodder" foes, as well as areas that have just a few devious baddies that are hard as nails to take out. Know how often to reward the player with goodies or health. Don't cover the level with items; rather, give him the prizes after monsters are killed, doors are opened, or a ledge is reached.

What's a "DemonMan"? Enjoy this early concept drawing of a soldier from *Unreal Warfare*, Cliff Bleszinski's next project.
(Used with permission by Epic Games, Inc.)

Bleszinski recognizes that there's a lot more to level design than the "fear factor" and "good pacing," so he also provides his own five-step crash course in good level design. Pencils in hand? Here we go…

1. **Geometry building and world texturing**. Naturally, you need to construct your environment first. Ideally, the texture artists should have a head start on the level designers so that the level designers have content with which to texture their areas while building. Then the level designers can tell the artists, "I need a 32 × 128 girder with three bolts on it and no directional rust, and please put it into the FACTORY texture set!"

2. **Lighting the environment**. The right kind of lighting can make or break a beautiful scene. Low lights tend to illuminate   monsters more dramatically, whereas bright rooms reduce fumbling around in the dark. A level designer needs to be creative with his lighting; if the player is going deeper into a volcano, the lighting should get "hotter" by getting brighter and more orange and red; or, if you're sending him through a swampy area, use drab, depressing colors, such as green and gray.

   Using the *Unreal* or *Quake* engine gives a level designer amazing control over realistic shadows. Building architecture that allows for shadows is essential; try putting support beams beneath a skylight to encourage sharp moody shadows on the floor or put a flame behind a polygonal grate to cast harsh shadows on the opposite wall.

3. **Tricks, traps, and puzzles**. Never force the player to learn by dying. Always give him a chance to figure out a puzzle without slapping his wrists. Remember: the person playing your game is playing it for fun, not for work. If you want to have slicing blades pop up from the floor of your Incan temple, make sure that you put some blood splotches and body parts around the exact spot that the blades spring forth, so that the attentive player won't be killed. Even if the player is killed, he'll think, "Oh, I should have seen those warnings, how stupid of me!" instead of "This game cheats! How was I supposed to know there was a trap there?"

4. **Monster, ammo, and health placement ("gameflow")**. During the course of *Unreal's* development, I harassed the level designers to always make their monsters patrol a local area, or to have them spring out of the dark, or even crash through glass at the player. If the player walks into a room and the monsters are just standing there waiting for him, he's not going to feel that this is a very believable world. However, if he walks into a room and his foe is just walking past him to go work on a computer terminal, he'll appreciate the extra effort that has been taken to further the believability.

   Ammunition is always tricky to get right in a level. Too much ammo, and the gamer breezes through the level without a sweat; not enough ammo, and your gamer is running around the level hacking at your foes with his default weapon while pondering looking for cheats online. Right when the player is thinking, "Boy, I'm going to be needing some ammunition soon," there should be a box of bullets waiting for him. The same rules apply for health.

5. **Drama**! In *Unreal*, we tried to create a sense of being in a hostile alien world. This believability is greatly helped by what I refer to as drama. Hearing a scene occur behind a locked door. Watching an evil alien punish a friendly alien who assists the player. Witnessing the murder of a comrade before your eyes. Real events that occur real time in the game, many of which the player can interfere with. Well-done drama will stick in the player's head for years to come.

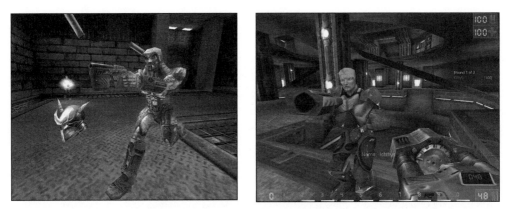

If the primary objective of your game is to kill and kill fast, don't slow the player down with boring, cumbersome puzzles. It's one thing to have three switches that need to be turned on in order to pass; it's another to have 12 switches that have a combination code three levels away that the player must physically write on a piece of paper to remember.

(Used with permission by Epic Games, Inc. and Atari/IESA.)

So how important is level design, anyway? Why is this such an integral part of the game design? "Level design is where the rubber hits the road," are the first words Jay Wilbur, former "biz guy" and CEO of id Software, told Cliff Bleszinski during their initial telephone conversation a couple of years ago. This has stuck with Cliff as an "absolute truth." He expands on the analogy:

> Game development can be compared to building a car. You have all these different parts that are created by talented people—programming, modeling, sound, and artwork—and at some point, everyone's hard work on a car comes together, and the tires hit the road. With a game, everyone's work is held together by the levels that use all of that, and they'd better be exceptional or the game falters.

With *Unreal Tournament 2003* as the shining example, Bleszinksi applies the aforementioned advice:

> In *Unreal Tournament 2003*, the majority of the levels are designed with a modular system of architecture. Environments are built as pieces, not unlike the toy Lego. From this angle, level design has changed significantly from *Unreal Tournament* to *Unreal Tournament 2003*. In the previous title, the designer was the one responsible for everything—he would touch every triangle in his environment and, other than texture maps, would seldom work with an artist on the level. Now, the designer is the one responsible for assembling prefabricated architecture in a way that yields an enjoyable game dynamic. The artists are the ones who are responsible for building said prefabs as well as assisting in level lighting and composition.

> These changes allow us to maintain the ability to quickly modify levels that are not enjoyable or those that have issues with balance or AI. This was something that we were able to use to leverage *Unreal Tournament* into a very enjoyable game; level design was a significant part of that. Build a level, play it, and then FIX what doesn't work and provide MORE of what does work. Much of this working and reworking has taken place in the new *Unreal Tournament* and has yielded excellent results—well-balanced levels that take place in a variety of settings.

More of Cliff Bleszinski's wisdom can be found in Chapters 2 and 21.

Peter Hirschmann, LucasArts

The *Medal of Honor* series (originally for the Sony PlayStation) is an authentic World War II-based action game that's played from a first-person perspective. Consider these games an interactive *Saving Private Ryan* (especially *Medal of Honor: Allied Assault* for the PC and the PS2)—complete with a breathtakingly real re-enactment of landing on Omaha Beach and other WWII scenarios. In this segment, lead designer Peter Hirschmann chats about general game design and level design.

In 2002, Hirschmann left Electronic Arts to work for LucasArts.

What are some personal or professional attributes you need to be a successful level designer?

> The most important thing is to have a passion not just for playing games, but making them. Consume all you can about the industry. Learn about the people who make the games you like and follow their careers. I make a point to always be up on what Sid Meier, Shigeru Miyamoto, Larry Holland, Will Wright, Brian Reynolds, Chris Taylor, Tim Schafer, Alex Garden, and Noah Falstein are up to. Pore through online designer diaries and read chat transcripts. Though they tend to be somewhat PC-centric, I always enjoy reading the postmortems in *Game Developer* magazine, also available at `www.gamasutra.com` [see Chapter 24, "Game Design Resources on the Internet"].

Is level design for a console any different from design for a PC game?

> From a production perspective, they can be quite different. It tends to be a lot easier to develop a robust design toolset when the game and the editor are running on the same platform (a PC). For a console title, the feedback loop tends to be longer from tweak to runtime, which can sometimes be quite frustrating. A positive aspect of console game design, obviously, is that you're designing for a closed system in which everyone in your target audience has, for the most part, the same equipment. But regardless of platform, the ultimate goal is always to make a fun, accessible game—and that can only come from having a deep understanding of what you want your game to be.

What key game/level design software tools does Hirschmann use? "Like a lot of development studios, we rely heavily on 3D Studio Max in our production pipeline, and it's probably safe to say that, moving forward, having a firm grasp of how three dimensions are manipulated on a two-dimensional screen is an essential skill."

> Making a game is certainly an art, but it's also a very demanding craft. Learn the nuts and bolts of how things work, from the underpinnings of the Windows OS to how a PlayStation 2 gets data off the CD. Electronic gaming is just that, so understand the technology and how it affects the way a game is designed. (To quote William Shatner from *Star Trek II*: "Learn why things work on a starship.") Always play around with the design tools that may come with a shrink-wrapped product—certainly more common on the PC side, but it's great to see console games like *Tony Hawk's Pro Skater 2* shipping with a basic map editor. But keep in mind that these polished end-user editors are often a far cry from the ugly and messy tools that you actually use in development.

How did the team at DreamWorks approach level design when creating the award-winning *Medal of Honor (MOH)*? Would this protocol be the same regardless of the game genre? As a special treat, Hirschmann chronicles the entire development approach to game design for *MOH*:

> Process is incredibly important, and the process really depends on the kind of game you're trying to make. Our goal with *Medal of Honor* was to create an environment that felt as authentic as possible, though not necessarily realistic. One of our rules during production was that when it was fun versus realism, fun won. There were several well-established gaming conventions that we embraced, like the fact that despite the caliber and country of origin, weapon types (pistols, rifles, submachine guns) all shared the same ammunition; you could carry over 100 pounds of gear and never get tired; and, most importantly, you could come back to life as many times as you wanted after you'd been hit in the head with a German Panzershrek bazooka.
>
> The process for building each *Medal of Honor* level was long, complex, and, ultimately, very rewarding for the team. During the first few months of production, we just immersed ourselves in the subject matter, reading all the reference material we could find (Stephen Ambrose's *Citizen Soldiers* being a team favorite and providing a lot of personal inspiration); building scale models of tanks, half-tracks, and field artillery; and, most importantly, working with (read: getting our butts kicked by) our consultant, Captain Dale Dye, USMC (Ret.). A quick tangent: I often get asked how many war movies we watched, and I think it would surprise people how few we actually viewed together as a team. Watching a movie about a subject that you're researching can sometimes have a detrimental effect, as it can irrevocably influence you on how something should look, as opposed to what your imagination might come up with on its own. The exception to this was obviously *Saving Private Ryan*, which we all saw for the first time about nine months into production. It was a moving experience, because it was head-and-shoulders above almost the entire canon of WWII cinema.
>
> We were continuously prototyping the engine code, creating concept art (both 2D and 3D), and testing character animation during this research phase, so after a few months we had a good idea of where we wanted to go with the game, both in terms of scope and design. The next step was formalizing the game flow, which was ultimately organized into seven missions, each composed of three thematic levels: infiltration, mission execution, and ex-filtration. This breakdown came directly from Capt. Dye, who early on pointed out to us that the hardest part of any mission is usually getting back home. This structure lent itself beautifully to gameplay, as it has a ramping naturally built into it. Infiltration levels tended to emphasize more stealthy gameplay as you're trying to sneak into wherever it is you need to get to (such as creeping through giant pipes into a heavy water plant). The mission execution levels were generally where you actually accomplish the primary goal of the mission (sabotaging the heavy water plant), made up of more intense combat and complex mission objectives. Finally, there was ex-filtration (escape from the heavy water plant through the snow), which were levels consisting of all-out combat from start to finish against the toughest of those particular enemies (arctic troopers armed with Panzershreks).

The process for building each *Medal of Honor: Allied Assault* level involved dedication: "We just immersed ourselves in the subject matter, reading all the reference material we could find; building scale models of tanks, half-tracks, and field artillery; and, most importantly, working with our consultant, Captain Dale Dye, USMC (Ret.)," says Peter Hirschmann.
(Used with permission by Electronic Arts, Inc.)

Once this structure was in place, the team went about filling in all the blanks. The player character of Lt. Jimmy Patterson and his story of a C-47 transport pilot-turned-reluctant-OSS-agent was fleshed out early on, and our wish list of missions was whittled down to the seven that ultimately appeared in the game. From there, each mission was broken down into its three levels (and sometimes a level was split into two parts to accommodate art needs), and the designers got to work.

Here are the three key things we learned, in ascending order, that went into making a successful single-player mission for *MOH*:

1. **Start with a good, well-developed idea**. Seems like common sense, but it's very easy to get excited about a cool-sounding idea that ultimately won't work within the parameters of your game. The list of rejected *MOH* levels ranges from a fight aboard a Zeppelin to being caught in a POW prison riot. Both have some nifty potential, but could never be pulled off in the original *MOH* game engine. One that did work successfully was the Scuttle U-4901

mission, in which Jimmy has to sink the prototype of a new giant class of German U-boat sub-marines. Laid out by co-lead designer Lynn Henson, this mission takes what everyone on the team agreed was a cool idea (doing something on a U-boat) and fleshes it out into an epic *Medal of Honor* adventure. You start out in disguise mode on a ship taking you to the subma-rine facility in Germany where the U-boat is being built. After disabling the ship's engines, you have to disembark via a cargo crane; then sneak along the rooftops of the bustling port and into the U-boat production yard. Once inside, you have to secure plans to the sub you're about to sink; then get aboard as she departs on her maiden voyage—ultimately blowing the sub's dive controls to smithereens before escaping out the conning tower as she sinks to the ocean floor.

Thinking things through, before pen is put to paper and polygon is rendered onscreen, will inform the countless decisions you have to make in the course of bringing a mission alive. Here's a partial list of the U-boat mission objectives: find wrench, gain access to engineering, jam engine, exit ship through cargo hold, locate smuggled weapons, secure deployment timetable, blow up truck with demo charges, find hatchway to production facility, find engine specs, procure hull blueprints, destroy sea door control, locate and board U-4901, radio coor-dinates to Allied intelligence, lock fins to dive setting, destroy fin controls, blow ballast to sur-face boat, find exit hatch. All in a day's work, eh?

2. **Design with an emphasis on ramping**. Not just ramping difficulty, but new objectives, new enemies, new mechanics, and new terrain—both indoor and outdoor. Tell a story through the level design. As you work your way through the sub pen in level 3.3, "The Hunter's Den" built by lead artist Dmitri Ellingson, you initially see only welding tanks and scattered industrial equip-ment. As you move further, though, you begin to come across drive shafts and propellers, tor-pedoes and fuel—even a pair of half-finished submarine hulls. Travel even deeper, and you dis-cover a complete U-boat in dry dock, along with its well-armed crew on deck. This is not your final destination, however. If you survive and make it to the end of the level, you discover the gargantuan U-4901 prototype ready for launch.

3. **Enemies are everything**. For *Medal of Honor*, this was the key. You can have the prettiest graphics in the world, the slickest level layout, the coolest mechanics—but if you don't have smart enemies, you don't have anything. *MOH* was about the tactical relationship between the player and the enemy Germans he or she encountered, so the animation and AI systems were where we always poured the bulk of engineering resources. The amazing enemy behavior states created by animation director Sunil Thankamushy, combined with incredibly robust message handler scripting done by co-lead designer Chris Cross, led to the polygonal army that populated the *MOH* universe. Things like getting enemies to pick up grenades and throw them back to you took a lot of time, but without that effort, our virtual European Theater 1944 would not have been worth the trip.

As one last piece of advice, Hirschmann offers the following:

> Always keep your quality bar raised as high as Mount Everest. The nuts and bolts of game production are incredibly diverse and complex, but there's no secret to making a game other than it's hard and it takes a long time. However, if you have a passion for seeing it through, getting up and going to work every day will feel like a privilege.

In Chapter 10, "Mission Design," Hirschmann discusses some of the mission structure in the *Medal of Honor* games; and in Chapter 21, he outlines how he broke into the industry and offers advice for others looking to do the same.

Chris Foster, Raven Software

Chris Foster started work at Madison, Wisconsin's Raven Software in the spring of 1995 and has worked on nearly all the titles begun by the company since that time, including *Heretic II*. In addition to his work at Raven, Chris is creating his own role-playing game. He's also a published poet and prose writer, as well as the assistant editor for a small, independently run local magazine, *The Writer's Block*. Chris was lead designer on *Star Trek: Voyager—Elite Force* and *Jedi Knight II: Jedi Outcast*.

Although Foster chats more in the chapters on programming, he offers these tips for budding level designers:

1. **Have a plan in place**. I can't tell you how much it helps to plan out what you're going to work on. It not only saves you time in the long run, but you'll have a concrete vision to refer to if you ever need or are forced to put aside your level for any significant amount of time. Freeform design works for multiplayer maps, but due to the complexity of today's games, having a design goal in mind for single-player is essential.

2. **Start simple**. I generally build my maps with one or two neutral textures to begin with. I spend time blocking in the shapes of all major features and then run around in it. If I feel they're too small, I expand the simple shapes; if they're too big, I rein them in. When you deal with a map in this way, you can experiment a lot before you make the final calls. If you fall in love with a specific feature...refer to step 3!

3. **Cut!** Your worst enemy in level design is usually your own complacency. If I feel that a feature in a map I'm building is really, really cool, but may be in the way of solidifying the design, I cut it out and save it in my prefab folder. I can always try and use it later or even on another map. Never be afraid to totally tear into your own map and really shore it up. It may look horrible while you're remodeling, but in the end you'll have a stronger level.

Be sure to click www.ravensoft.com.

Michael Raymond-July

Before leaving Raven Software in 2002, Michael Raymond-July served as a game designer for nine years on *Shadowcaster*, *Heretic* (including *Shadow of the Serpent Riders*), *Hexen* (as well as *DeathKings of the Dark Citadel*), *Necrodome*, *Take No Prisoners*, *Heretic II*, *Star Trek: Voyager—Elite Force* and *Star Wars: Jedi Knight 2—Jedi Outcast*.

Asked how to create such enjoyable and challenging game levels, Raymond-July responds with some key pieces of advice:

1. Know what you want to do in advance, and stick to it. A complete plan ensures not only time-ly delivery and ease of building; it also ensures that the level fits properly into the "big picture" of the game. In the days of *DOOM*, when there was no real "big picture," this was not an issue; but in today's games, it's vital.

2. "Real" and "fun" are not always compatible. I try for "real-ish," which is to say that I try to evoke the atmosphere and sense that the player is in a "real" place, without being so concerned with details that making the map takes forever or ends up being no fun to play.

3. Someone else will tell you to change something you love, and you will have to do it. Even when you're the boss, sometimes you make things that you think are cool, but for one reason or another don't fit what the game needs. Learning to accept this fact gracefully not only allows you to move on to the next thing (and hopefully still meet the deadline); it also ensures that you'll still have a job when the project is done.

Game designer Michael Raymond-July, who last worked on *Star Wars: Jedi Knight 2—Jedi Outcast*, says "real" and "fun" are not always compatible when creating levels for a game.

(© 2002 LucasArts Entertainment Company LLC and its licensors. LucasArts and the LucasArts logo are registered trademarks of Lucasfilm Ltd. All rights reserved.)

Be sure to read Raymond-July's suggestions on creating a good puzzle in a game (see Chapter 9, "Puzzle Design") and programming (see Chapter 11, "Programming Theory").

Jeff Lane, Valve Software

After more than 12 years as a graphic designer, Jeff Lane jumped right into computer games and hasn't looked back. Lane spent five years at Sierra Studios, in which he worked as an art director on *Phantasmagoria 2* and as a level designer for *SWAT 3*, before coming to Valve. At Valve, Jeff has worked on *Team Fortress Classic* and *Team Fortress 2* as a level designer.

Lane divulges his level design secret: "The bottom line for me is that you want to create an immersive and fun environment for the player."

Just how do you go about this?

> There are a ton of things that you need to inject and balance to make that happen, but that's the end result that should be the goal of all you create. For example, even something like a good constant frame-rate is part of the goal of making it immersive. If people are distracted by a sideshow-level frame-rate, you've lost them.

> Some of the other elements to consider in a single-player level: visual consistency, interactivity, proper audio cues, appropriate difficulty level, a continuing narrative, a sense of momentum, and an opportunity for exploration. All of these things must be combined to keep the player engrossed in the level and the game as a whole.

Lane says the issues for multiplayer levels are different, but the basic ideas and principles of balancing all the elements are the same:

> I'm sure you can think of multiplayer levels where, for example, they looked great but had incredibly unbalanced gameplay toward one of the teams. If you ignore any of these issues, you do it at your own risk—the environment is unlikely to have a level of interest and excitement that will pull the player into the game world. The best level designers understand and recognize these elements and know how to apply them properly when they create environments.

How does this process work? Lane usually begins by brainstorming on paper, with words, to get basic ideas about the kind of themes and some overall design goals:

> I find that it's really important to decide what we want to accomplish with the design, and what interesting gameplay aspects I'm striving for. I usually look for some visual references (sometimes a lot) next, but that depends on the level. Then I draw out some basic layouts on paper. Sometimes I create fairly elaborate paper layouts, but often I have a good idea of what I want and just start to "sketch" some shapes in 3D after only a simple paper sketch. As it probably sounds, I never stick to an exact formula other than the brainstorm at the start. Flexibility is important to me.

Lane's sources of inspiration echo those mentioned by most of the game designers interviewed for this book:

A level designer looks for inspiration anywhere and everywhere. Books, movies, photos, other games, outside your window, in a foreign country, or an ancient civilization. A good designer should always come up with new and interesting ideas, but should also know the true power of cliché and familiar references. Inspiration can come from any number of sources, and you should be open to them. It all comes back to immersion and believability. If you take design elements that are familiar and put a new spin on them, you'll have the players hooked. The familiar elements give them a solid frame of reference, and the spin you add provides the excitement and keeps the player interested. For example, take Darth Vader. He's big and dressed all in black. The second you saw him, you knew he was the ultimate bad guy. That's the power of clichés. I'm not saying all bad guys should be dressed in black, but injecting some components of familiarity into your designs will go a long way toward making players feel like they're really present in the environment you created. It's up to the designers to let themselves be inspired and create the spin on the familiar elements that will make that level a truly memorable one.

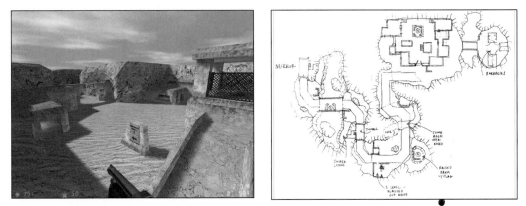

To support his advice, Lane provides a level design sketch and screen grab from *Team Fortress Classic*. In the "Warpath" level, the goal was to have a interesting visual theme while creating balanced and exciting team-oriented gameplay, says Lane.
(Used with permission by Sierra Studios, Inc.)

Stevie Case, Monkeystone Games

Last but certainly not least is a rising celebrity of the computer game world: Stevie Case. Before leaving Ion Storm to become vice president and production coordinator of Monkeystone Games, Case worked on titles such as *Daikatana* and *Anachronox* as a level designer. Monkeystone Games' first title was *Hyperspace Delivery Boy!*, which was released for the PC and Pocket PC platforms in 2002.

When designing levels in a game, Case says these are the three most important things for a level designer to keep in mind:

1. **Speed, speed, speed**. A slow-running map can turn a fun experience into total frustration. Speed is my best friend and my worst enemy! One thing that can set a level designer apart from a pure modeler is the ability to make beautiful and exciting environments that appear complex but run fast on the required hardware. During my time working on *Anachronox*, I spent many an hour tweaking some gorgeous maps that were just too slow. Maps like Tensil look phenomenal, but it took some tricks and major effort to get it running in the *Quake II* engine at a reasonable speed. Know your engine inside and out, and master all the tricks that can be used to speed up a level. Talk to your coders and get their input on how to make things go fast.

2. **Fun**. If it's not fun, what's the point? It's fantastic to design maps that are everything to everyone: great gameplay, stunning aesthetics, and fast as lightning. However, people play games to have fun. Rewarding gameplay should take priority above aesthetic concerns. Fill your map with unique interactions, nooks and crannies, secrets, and anything else that fits the style. Be sure that your map is easy to navigate and that irritating or repetitive obstacles don't get in the way of the player. If it's not fun, take it out of the map. Mastering the fun factor often requires outside input and lots of testing. It's easy to get jaded about your own work. Let your friends and co-workers play your stuff. They'll help you discover what's fun and what's got to go.

3. **Surprise**. The element of surprise adds depth and excitement to a virtual world. Pure architecture can get quite monotonous without some twists and turns to get the player scared and thinking. It's always nice to avoid placing items and enemies in predictable locations. Unique and surprising events will keep the player on his toes and his mind on the game! One of the best examples of the element of surprise is Cliffy B's Skaarj encounter in the very first map of *Unreal*. The player is suddenly trapped, the lights go out, and a growling Skaarj enters the room. That's some terrifying, wonderful stuff!

Case says she sometimes sketches ideas on paper before hitting the PC, but it depends on the requirements of the level that she's working on:

I almost always work from a sketch for single-player maps. I find that spending the time to think through the intricacies of a design before beginning is extremely useful. When a map isn't preplanned, it can quickly become too rambling or unfocused. On the other hand, I generally avoid sketches for my deathmatch maps. DM maps are smaller and much easier to see mentally, though I'll occasionally draft an overhead layout on paper to consider all of the possible area connections.

Any tips for newbies?

Know your game's engine inside and out. A deep understanding of the technical elements of the game will aid you in designing a map that fits within the bounds of the code. If you're working with licensed technology, consult any and all mapping tutorials and design sites that you can find on the Net. They're a fantastic resource. Talk to your coders, and don't be afraid to ask questions! Get to know anyone else you can find who's working on maps within the same engine. Always get outside feedback on your work, and be prepared to take constructive criticism. Listen to what less-hardcore gamers have to say about your game—their perspective will differ from yours. Most of all, do the job only if you love it. Being creative under a deadline is tough, but if you push through the tough times, map creation will get more and more comfortable.

NOTE

Case admits that level design is always on her mind. "Level designers often see the world around them in wireframe and assess whether it's too complex or might run slow in the engine. It's an obsession, I tell you!" She has even gathered many ideas from dreams she's had about architecture after long nights of mapping. "Observe everything in minute detail. Inspiration is everywhere!"

Be sure to stop by Chapter 21 to read Stevie Case's advice on breaking into the industry, regardless of what position you're after.

Stevie "Killcreek" Case provides some visual examples to support her advice on creating detailed and immersive levels. As an example of speed, *Anachronox's* "Tensil" level was beautiful, but needed to be optimized to run more smoothly, says Case. For fun, *Daikatana's* "Acropolis" area contained many unique and memorable gameplay moments. And for surprise, she cites *Unreal's* frightening first Skaarj sighting.

(Used with permission by Eidos Interactive Inc. and Infogrames Inc.)

Chapter 9

Puzzle Design

THE EXPERTS

- Lorne Lanning, Oddworld Inhabitants

- George Broussard, 3D Realms

- Tim Schafer, Double Fine Productions

- Phil Saunders, Presto Studios

- Ragnar Tørnquist, Funcom

- Gabe Newell, Valve Software

- Michael Raymond-July

- Chris Foster, Raven Software

You look through the keyhole into the next room, and there it is—the book of spells you've been yearning to find throughout this treacherous journey. With this precious collection of magic potions and chants, you will surely be able to get past the grunts guarding the castle up ahead. Alas, the door is locked, but a second glimpse into the keyhole reveals something sticking out of the other side. It's the key! You hastily look around the room to find a scrap piece of paper lying on the table. And then it hits like a bolt of lightning. You slide the paper halfway under the locked door and bang your fists on it until the key falls out of the keyhole and onto the paper. Slowly sliding the paper back toward you exposes the key, and into the room you go to snag the book.

This hypothetical example is meant to illustrate puzzle design—the game designer's sneaky way of inserting a challenging obstacle the player must solve with brains and not brawn (usually) to continue playing the game. These kinds of puzzles are found in adventure, role-playing, and some action games. There are usually various kinds of puzzles littered throughout such games:

➤ Environmental puzzles can be solved by analyzing and often altering your surroundings in the game. For example, in Nintendo's *Legend of Zelda: Ocarina of Time*, the player must light torches on each side of a door to enter a new area of the cave.

➤ In inventory puzzles, objects in your possession may solve the puzzle. It's fair to say that environmental and inventory puzzles work together quite a bit, such as in the preceding example or in a game such as LucasArts' *Day of the Tentacle*, in which you must place your bottle of wine in a time machine and pick it up in the future if you need vinegar!

➤ Conversation-based puzzles are usually solved by saying the right piece of dialogue when conversing with a character or perhaps recalling an earlier exchange between characters in the game that may be used in the present situation. An example of this is Microïd's stellar *Syberia*, in which the heroine Kate Walker must talk to various characters to unlock a family mystery.

➤ Finally, many adventure games, especially those that came out in the mid 1990s, used puzzles that had no relevance whatsoever to the task at hand. For instance, in DreamWorks Interactive's *The Neverhood Chronicles*, the player had to solve a sliding tile puzzle in one instance and play a game of *Concentration* in another, although it had nothing to do with the game.

Lorne Lanning, Oddworld Inhabitants

Lorne Lanning, creator of the beloved *Oddworld* series, explains how to create a good puzzle in a game, with an example of a well-conceived and well-executed puzzle from one of his games:

> You must first create a fun chemistry of basic moves and mechanics. A *mechanic* is what we call anything that can be done in the game. There are basic moves (a character can run, jump, sneak, punch, talk, and so on), and then there are mechanics (a character can pull a lever, possess other characters, ride vehicles, use weapons, operate cranes, and so on).

Lorne Lanning says many of the puzzles in *Oddworld: Munch's Oddysee* were designed to take advantage of the fact that Abe and Munch had different physical attributes and skills, requiring cooperation between them.
(© 2001 Oddworld Inhabitants, Inc. All rights reserved.
Used with permission by Microsoft Corp.)

> The combination of these had better be fun. Once you have a fun chemistry, then it's all in how you lay out a level or environment. You build upon the mechanics so that they ramp fairly to the user. Then you get more clever as the user has a chance to get familiar with the mechanics of the game. Once players

understand the basics, then you start to throw more at them. Done well, and you have an experience that doesn't overwhelm them, yet teaches them just enough along the way that they have a feeling of being challenged as well as a feeling of being successful.

A simple example would be our first hero's (Abe's) basic move: a sneak. The idea was simple. If he sneaked around, other characters (enemies) wouldn't hear him, but they could see him. This would often be used with another mechanic, which we called *hide zones*. Hide zones allowed Abe to stand in a dark area and not be seen. But he could still be heard in a dark hide zone, so he needed to stay quiet when using them. When used successfully, the two mechanics could be used to build tension and progress gameplay. A weaponless Abe could hide in a shadow area as an armed enemy walked right past him. Abe could then sneak out of the hide zone and slowly sneak behind the enemy as it walked away. It's a classic image that we all understand. Its play value was solid and it not only pulled off a challenge, but offered some humor value. The one basic move, sneak, offered being seen but not heard. The other mechanic, hide, offered being heard but not seen. Together, these polarities could be combined to create something unusual yet understandable.

George Broussard, 3D Realms

This industry veteran, responsible in part for the *Duke Nukem* games among many others, has chatted about many topics in this book. Here, Broussard shares some advice on creating good puzzles in a game:

Good puzzles are, first and foremost, fair. They won't have giant leaps of logic to solve, and there may be multiple solutions. A good puzzle isn't arbitrary and makes sense in the game world and supports it. Good puzzles allow the player a little leeway in experimentation and don't force you to die to discover how to solve them.

As an example, Broussard refers to a puzzle from Fox Interactive's *No One Lives Forever*:

There's a security vault you have to get through. The first area is guarded by static laser trip mines that you jump around and navigate easily. The second area introduces moving laser beams, which makes things slightly more difficult. Finally, in the last area, you face a room with about 50 rapidly moving laser trip mines and a door 30 feet away. I looked at the room and thought the level designer must be crazy to expect that of me. But I tried anyway, and died. I tried again and again, getting a little closer each time. Finally, I took a break from the puzzle and came back later. After failing a couple more times, I was really frustrated and looked around. At my feet, on the floor, was a simple access grate I had missed. I opened it and went under the floor, bypassing the impossible laser room.

What makes it a good puzzle is that the solution was placed literally at my feet. I was so focused on the red herring puzzle in front of my face that I missed the obvious. It was my fault. I know several players who found the grate in 30 seconds, and I know others who took 30 minutes—due to their determination to try and do the impossible.

Scenes from Fox Interactive's *No One Lives Forever*. Tom Goodman, a cocky American operative, surprises Agent Archer in her hotel room. H.A.R.M. has co-opted a forgotten alpine fortress to serve as their base of operations in the area. Archer must be careful to avoid search-lights as she sneaks through the area.

(© 2000 Twentieth Century Fox Film Corporation. LithTech© game engine © 1998–1999 LithTech, Inc. All Rights Reserved. Fox, Fox Interactive, Inc.)

Tim Schafer, Double Fine Productions

Tim Schafer, the mastermind behind such beloved adventure games as *Grim Fandango* and *Day of the Tentacle*, and soon, *Psychonauts*, offers these words of wisdom on creating successful puzzles on a game:

> Don't have backwards puzzles, in which the player finds the key and then the door. Players should find the problem and *then* the solution, so that they have time to enjoy the puzzled feeling, the scratching of the head when they can't figure out how to cross the ravine, and then that great sense of relief when they find the key. (Wait, how do you cross a ravine with a key? Oh, wait. I know. You tie a string to it and then lure a hawk down to pick it up…) This rule sounds obvious, but you'd be surprised how easy it is to let players find the key first and then open the door before they even realize there's a puzzle there.
>
> Always ask yourself, "How does the player know to do this?" If you have a puzzle about getting onto the roof, ask yourself how the player even knows he *wants* to get on the roof. Don't leave the player wondering what's supposed to be going on. He should know where the action is at all times, so he can push toward it.

Schafer says the old adage is true—less is more:

> Don't write too much. We found when play testing *The Secret of Monkey Island* that people start tapping their fingers after three consecutive lines of non-interactive dialogue. It's okay for big scenes that herald new game chapters, but not all over the game. Learn to edit yourself ruthlessly.

Phil Saunders, Presto Studios

If you've ever played *Myst III: Exile* or any of the *Journeyman Project* titles, then you've had a taste of well-written, challenging, and entertaining puzzles to solve. Presto Studios' creative director Phil Saunders offers the following for those looking to create good puzzles in a game:

> Educate the player. One of the things that we really felt was important with the puzzle creations of *Myst III: Exile* was educating players and preparing them for the challenges ahead. We didn't want to cheap out just because this was the mass market—and create puzzles that weren't challenging, puzzles that were easy. What we did feel the need to do was to make these puzzles intuitive. A lot of the Ages [in the game] are filled with things that you've never seen before, and we can't expect players to be able to look at them and, just through their design, be able to figure out what they do. So we decided that we had to educate players early by putting interactive elements in the very early Ages of the game that they could play with. Things that they didn't necessarily realize would be related to something later on. When they approached a puzzle later on in the game, we wanted them to have something in the back of their minds, something that they had seen before that they would intuitively relate to the challenge that was placed in front of them.

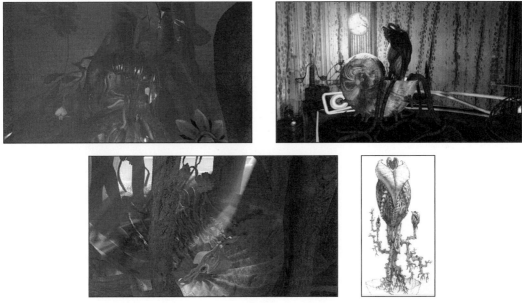

In the darkened hollows of the 700-foot inverted tree environment of Edanna, the Venus Flytrap plays an important role in the solution to this particular Age. Placing a Venus Flytrap in the villain's lair, which players encounter early in the game, arms them with the knowledge of what it will take to make this plant open later in the game. This is the designer's clever way of educating the player, without seeming like a lesson. The Electra Ray patrols the flower basin. Note how the fish electrifies the plant roots it feeds on—another subtle clue to aid in the completion of tasks/goals. As a special treat, Presto Studios' Phil Saunders provides a sketch of the Venus Flytrap from *Myst III: Exile*.

(Used with permission by Ubi Soft Entertainment, Inc. and Presto Studios, Inc.)

It served a story purpose in showing the development that Saavedro had put into these traps that he had laid for Atrus, but at the same time, it gave us a way of foreshadowing the puzzle that was to come. It gave players something they could see and understand in a non-threatening environment, where they could just play around with it. Later on, when they came to the actual puzzle of freeing the bird in the Age of Edanna, they would be informed as to how that would work.

Ragnar Tørnquist, Funcom

The inventive mind behind *The Longest Journey*, Funcom's Ragnar Tørnquist, chats about what makes for a good puzzle:

> The perfect puzzle is one that can be solved in several ways, depending on the player's mindset. It's one that doesn't feel arbitrary or obscure. The player won't have to figure out how the designer thinks; instead, the puzzle feels perfectly integrated with the world, the setting, the internal logic of the game, and the storyline.

Tørnquist adds that the perfect puzzle is hard to find, but a good puzzle adheres to at least a couple of the preceding criteria. He offers the following as examples:

> A great example is my favorite adventure game of all time, LucasArts' brilliant *Day of the Tentacle*. In this game, all the puzzles were interlinked. Because the past affected the present, which again affected the future—the game took place in three time periods simultaneously—the puzzles were both surprising and perfectly logical, and so amazingly well-scripted that you never thought, "Huh, wait a second…" Like painting a tree to look like a cherry tree so that George Washington would cut it down in the past, thus allowing a character to get down from the (now nonexistent) tree in the future. Just brilliant. Although *Day of the Tentacle* didn't have multiple solutions for any of its puzzles, they were perfectly integrated with the story and setting.
>
> Another good example is from *Deus Ex* (call it what you want—at heart, it was a highly original adventure game). Most barriers (puzzles) in that game could be handled in at least two different ways: stealth or brute force. Using stealth, finding passcodes, using lockpicks, disabling security cameras and sentry robots, stabbing guards in the back, you could pretty much move unharmed through most levels. Or you could go in, guns blazing, and hope for the best. This level of interaction and immersion—the number of choices the player can make that directly affect his or her progress in the game—is not only a clear indication of how the adventure genre (in an evolved form) is moving in the right direction, but also a good example of how to design great puzzles.

Gabe Newell, Valve Software

Valve's founder and managing director, Gabe Newell, has an interesting take on the importance of puzzles:

> I'm not sure I believe in puzzles so much as experiences. Creating "puzzles" puts too small a box around what designers should be thinking about. Separating cognition out of the other aspects of the player's experience seems to be trivializing what we need to be achieving. A simple puzzle under a lot of real stress is a lot more interesting than a clever puzzle. One of my favorite "puzzles" in *Half-Life* was the

elevator shortly after the disaster sequence. There's an elevator button with the notice "In Case of Emergency, Do Not Use." If you press the button, the elevator falls with a bunch of screaming people in it. Most people figure it out after a couple of seconds and usually laugh, "Oh, so that's what would happen."

Michael Raymond-July

We hear from Michael in Chapter 8, "Level Design," and in Chapter 11, "Programming Theory." In this chapter, the assistant lead designer on Raven's *Star Wars: Jedi Knight 2—Jedi Outcast* talks about creating thought-provoking and fresh puzzles in its games.

I think one of the most important things to realize is that for most games (RPGs and true story-driven games like *Myst* aside), every puzzle is ultimately still a key-and-lock puzzle. The trick is to make a believable and fun "disguise" for that puzzle—either the "lock" is something unusual (perhaps a ship without air pressure that you have to get into), or it's the key that's unique (finding a spacesuit or pumping atmosphere from one craft to another). It helps if you can have "big-picture" puzzles that are broken into smaller bits—maybe getting atmosphere requires you to complete several tasks, each of which has a subtask to perform. Variety is also important. Solving the same type of puzzle over and over, even if the details are not the same, is boring. Shake people up, surprise them, and they'll be happier. Finally, make the puzzle make sense in the context of the game.

Raymond-July cites *Star Trek: Voyager—Elite Force* as a good example:

We tried keeping to the "accepted norms" of the *Star Trek* universe—thinking was as important as fighting, certain alien races acted in expected ways, and technology conformed with the "canon" set out in the shows. This made the puzzles and world more real to the people who were familiar with it, and ensured a consistent set of guidelines for planning them. Failing to follow those norms would have immediately thrown players out of that "world" and ruined the puzzle.

Basically, it boils down to hiding the fact that it's still a key and lock—the better you are at hiding it, the more fun the player will have.

Chris Foster, Raven Software

As lead designer on the aforementioned *Star Trek: Voyager—Elite Force* and *Jedi Knight II: Jedi Outcast*, Chris Foster knows a thing or two about designing puzzles for a game and offers some trade secrets.

In my opinion, you have to remember that everything you do in a game, puzzle-wise, can be broken down into a few simple elements. We recognize that getting the key card for the door and getting the detonator for the nuclear bomb are essentially the same goal. You get A to interact with B, and you get result C. We try to make sure that the journey to the end result is varying and interesting. Once the journey to the item/object/person is completed, you still face the fact that you only have so many mechanics at your disposal in a game world. How do you get around this? Well, you don't. What you do is make the interaction of the items/people interesting or challenging in a unique way. The reward the player gets from figuring out the new way in which you need to interact with the world to get a result is most often what pushes a puzzle into the realm of "cool."

Having more than one way to solve a puzzle or mission is exceedingly cool, but difficult to do very often. We do it in many places, but the problem is that players often end up not seeing half of the work! Also, changing the rules of how a player must accomplish a goal in your level is fine as long as you clue them in as to the nature of your new way of doing things. Killing a player over and over in a level because he doesn't crouch-jump as well as you do is pretty lame. Remember: Demonstrate. Present. Reward.

> **NOTE**
>
> In case you breezed through Chapter 6, "Creating Characters, Storyboarding, and Design Documents," or perhaps skipped it altogether (we won't tell), be sure to at least read Daniel Greenberg's marvelous document on writing for an interactive medium.

Chapter 10

Mission Design

Chapter 8, "Level Design," dealt with *level design*—that is, how a map is laid out architecturally, and objects placed within it. *Mission* or *scenario design* refers to the specific objective(s) the player must carry out during the game. Mission design is an integral part of many kinds of games: strategy, simulations, RPGs, adventure, and some action titles, too. Missions can be historical in nature—such as in WWII combat flight sims or turn-based strategy war games—or can be purely fictional, as found in fantasy role-playing games or action games. In some cases, each mission may have a number of smaller goals to complete, or missions are tightly integrated into a grander story.

For an example of a mission, let's use Rockstar's *Grand Theft Auto III*, the best-selling (and controversial) action game for the PlayStation 2 and PC. In one of the early missions, the player is hired to find a mob boss eating lunch at a restaurant in Liberty City. The goal is to carjack his vehicle, take it to a secret garage to have a bomb planted underneath, return it to the same parking spot, and wait for him to get in. (And BOOM!) To make this mission even more difficult, this task must be completed within a certain amount of time, and if the car is damaged while driving to and from the garage, the player has to spend money to repair it before returning the car to the restaurant.

The term *campaign* in a game refers to a string of single-level scenarios or missions, often in a sequential order to complete an overall goal. For example, Blizzard's mega-successful sci-fi strategy game *Starcraft* contains three campaigns for the different races—the Zerg, Protoss, and Terrans—each containing 10 scenarios, for a total of 30.

THE EXPERTS

- Greg Street, Ensemble Studios

- Rob Pardo, Blizzard Entertainment

- James Schmalz, Digital Extremes

- Louis Castle, Electronic Arts/Westwood Studios

- Fred Markus, Angel Studios

- Harvey Smith, Ion Storm Austin

- Randy Smith, Ion Storm Austin

- Peter Hirschmann, LucasArts

In *dynamic campaigns*, the success or failure of missions is factored into the campaign and should affect the future of the campaign as a result. For example, if a country's radar bases are destroyed, it may be harder for them to detect rival forces approaching in future missions. Naturally, this breathes some life and additional satisfaction into the game experience, instead of the player feeling as if he or she is part of a canned script.

Hundreds of games each year fall short in the mission-writing department, and the player often stops playing because of lackluster missions, repetitive ones, confusing situations, or missions that can be too easily completed or are painstakingly difficult.

This chapter contains advice from hand-picked professionals on what can turn an average game into a veritable mission masterpiece.

Grand Theft Auto III has 100 or so of these missions, 60 of which are mandatory. Let's hope game designers begin to think of original missions like these instead of the canned ones we've seen copied over and over.
(Used with permission by Take Two Interactive, Inc.)

Greg Street, Ensemble Studios

Anyone who has stayed up until the wee hours playing any of the *Age of Empires* or *Age of Mythology* games should thank (or blame!) Greg Street, a game designer at Ensemble Studios (now part of the Microsoft collective), who wrote campaigns for *Age of Empires Expansion: The Rise of Rome* and *Age of Empires II: Age of Kings*. Street also headed the *Conquerors* expansion pack and finally the million unit-selling *Age of Mythology*.

Street discusses what goes into making such rich and detailed missions as those found in the *Age of Empires* series, offering his top three pieces of advice:

1. **The scenario must offer interesting decisions**. At Ensemble Studios, we believe this is the heart of a strategy game, if not all games. Remember, there are two key words to this statement. To be a decision, there must be choices; running a gauntlet is rarely a choice. This is not to say that a scenario must have a plot that branches. Choosing how to spend resources is a decision at the heart of all RTS [real-time strategy] games. Choosing to train a quantity of mediocre troops over a few quality troops can be a strategic decision. However, the decision

must also be interesting. Being given the choice to attack enemy 1 or enemy 2 first is pretty meaningless without some context. Taking the left or right fork is an arbitrary decision unless the player can see how the choice relates to the overall goal of the mission.

2. **The player needs some information in order to make an informed decision**. Bad designers love to have forks in the road where one way leads to riches and the other to certain death. So what is a player going to do? Save the game, take both routes, and then restore again. Is that fun? Designers need to remember that players never have as much information as the designers do. Making a player choose between a longer, easier route and a shorter, more dangerous route can be interesting if a player knows which is which.

3. **The player should theoretically be able to complete a scenario on the first try**. As game designers, we tend to side with the AI and root for the computer player to win after we've spent so much time crafting out its goals. This is generally a bad paradigm. Instead, we should be thinking from the player's point of view. Ultimately, a scenario needs to be fun first and challenging second. If players are punished for the consequences of making a decision in a vacuum, then they're just going to reload the game anyway. This is not to say that every scenario has to be won on the first try, but at least players should all have all the info and resources needed to win on a single try if they're lucky and use their resources wisely. Remember, many more games are abandoned from being too difficult than from being too easy. Most of us aren't working on arcade games any more, in which the object is to part the player from as many quarters as possible.

The following anecdote from Street serves as an example:

In the first Attila the Hun scenarios in the *Conquerors* expansion, the player knows he has to dispose of Attila's brother, Bleda, in order to gain control of the Hun horde. This can be done by just outright attacking Bleda, or by allowing a monstrous wild boar to kill him and refusing to lend aid. The player can also just run away and try to start his own rival nation of Huns. The rest of the scenario plays out the same way (the player must overcome the Roman fort nearby), but players feel like they have some control over how the scenario plays out.

When trying to provide players with some indication of which branch of a forked path to take, the simplest approach is to have some lieutenant or advisor say that one route might require a lot of fighting, and the other might require subterfuge. In the Manzikert scenario in *Conquerors*, the player leads an army of Turks trying to capture weapons from various Byzantine themes (towns). The player can choose to go for the nearest enemy theme, which will provide reinforcements right away; or hold out to attack the one that will provide siege weapons, which will then make subsequent invasions that much easier.

Ensemble Studios always provides a "Hints" panel as part of the mission objectives user interface. Street explains:

These were designed to help out more casual gamers who get stuck trying to solve the scenario. While working on *Age of Kings*, we found that more hardcore players also want a little bit of information on what strategies the enemy forces are using. [This] seemed natural, since any historical commander probably would have recon information on the enemy. As a result, we added a "Scouts Report" interface that suggests what kind of troops enemy forces are likely to use and whether they might be susceptible to an early attack or are heavily defended, which will require a later siege using long-distance weapons.

In the fifth Genghis Khan scenario from *Age of Kings*, the player needs to construct three castles to defend himself from the massive Bohemian army. The player knows that the Bohemians won't attack until the castles are done, so the player doesn't feel like he's fighting an invisible clock. We could have provided a countdown instead, but those seem better suited for modern or sci-fi genres and don't scale for difficulty very well.

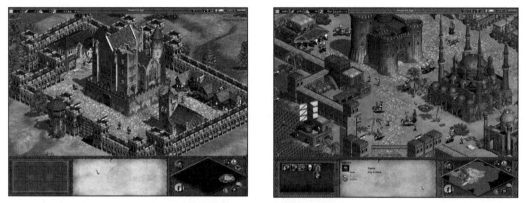

On why mission/scenario design falls short more often than not, Ensemble Studios' Greg Street says there are a few reasons, one of which is that scenario designers often don't put themselves into the player's perspective enough: "They forget that players are often dealing with an unexplored map, and don't know where they must go to find resources." Pictured here are two shots from *Age of Empires II: Age of Kings*.
(Used with permission by Microsoft Corp.)

Why do so many game designers seem to fall short when it comes to writing challenging/unique missions?

> ➤ Scenario design can't really begin in earnest until much of the rest of code and design work is stable. Plus, scenario designers are always dealing with changing data. I added sea walls to one of the Attila scenarios before we ended up taking them out of the game. In *Age of Mythology*, the scenario designers had to deal with incomplete AI and tech trees that kept changing as balance testing continues. This is the reason why expansion packs nearly always have better campaigns—the scenario designers are comfortable and familiar with the tools by then.

> ➤ Scenario designers often don't put themselves into the player's perspective enough. They forget that players are often dealing with an unexplored map, and don't know where they must go to find different resources. A player who fails to find a critical resource will have a much harder time playing the scenario. To mitigate this problem at ES, we play test the heck out of our scenarios and make the designers watch these play tests.

➤ Scenario designers play the game so much that they have a tendency to think their missions are easier than they really are. In addition (as mentioned previously), designers are usually rooting for the bad guys, which leads to making scenarios overly challenging.

➤ For RTS games, far too many designers require players to slog through heavily defended enemy bases. This is fun once or twice, but tedious when the computer opponent always starts with a well-defended town negating any early attack. These defenses are often added to make up for poor computer player AI.

➤ RTS game designers seem to be overly enamored of puzzle scenarios. Although puzzles can be a part of the challenges of any game, requiring players to figure out the single often illogical solution to get over a particular hurdle in an RTS can be as frustrating as a poorly written adventure game. Often, these puzzles involve using special abilities of units or complex triggers. Again, I think this is a function of professional designers being a little jaded. Ironically, it also seems to be the case with a lot of prolific amateur scenario designers, who may feel the pressure to produce something no one has ever seen before [in order] to stand out from the crowd. I don't think all puzzles are inherently bad, but I always remind our scenario designers that the game itself is fun—training units, gathering resources, and/or attacking the enemy should be the focus of most scenarios.

Street chats about his latest game, *Age of Mythology (AOM)*, and how the mission/scenario design differed from his work on *Age of Empires (AOE)* and *Age of Kings (AOK)*:

For one thing, *AOM* was the first time we've ever done a single, giant campaign. *AOE* and *AOK* had multiple smaller campaigns so that we could showcase different cultures. However, we were eager to try an epic story of our own creation that's long enough to have plot twists, recurring characters, and a dramatic climax. A single campaign also allows us to introduce concepts slowly, rather than having to assume that everyone played the learning campaign.

The story is of our own creation, as are many of the characters, although players will be sure to encounter plenty of the familiar names, places, and events from mythology. We also have detailed cinematics using the in-game engine that let us do closeups, [do] flyovers, and change camera angles to a greater extent than we've seen in any game so far.

As far as the scenarios themselves, we've worked to ensure that every scenario has a "hook" or something unique about it that makes the scenario interesting, even independent of the ambitious story. Scenarios in the *Age* series have to compete without the random map feature, so they need to put players in situations that they couldn't normally encounter in random map play. We've used a ton of scenario-specific art and programming this time around, and actually had three full-time content designers to work on the scenarios (compared to just me for nearly all of the two previous games).

For more information on *Age of Mythology*, visit www.ensemblestudios.com or www.microsoft.com/games.

Rob Pardo, Blizzard Entertainment

Rob Pardo is a senior game designer at the award-winning Blizzard Entertainment. He was the lead designer on *Warcraft III: Reign of Chaos* and *Starcraft: Brood War*, and was producer on several titles at Interplay Productions.

When designing specific campaigns and missions in a game such as *Starcraft* or *Warcraft*, what does Pardo suggest are the most important things to keep in mind?

> ➤ **Make it easy.** When you think you have the level so any child can play it, make it easier still. It's inevitable in most mission design to make the level too hard. The designer knows the level inside and out, and he or she will find many puzzles obvious that may stump a real player.

> ➤ **Explain the objectives properly.** I can't tell you the numbers of missions where I'm not sure what it is I'm supposed to accomplish. You must spoon-feed the level objectives to the player and reinforce those objectives over the course of the level.

> ➤ **Don't let the story overwhelm the game.** Ideally, all of your story will be told while the player is actually playing the level. Although it's sometimes necessary to do a non-interactive cinematic to explain a complicated story node, don't get carried away with this tool. If the player starts feeling like he's watching a movie, you're not doing your job.

Why do so many computer and console games fall short in this department?

I think the primary reason is that designers make games for themselves first, and almost all designers are gamers. It's very difficult to make a level that is fun for the gamer audience and still very approachable from the broad market perspective. Console games like *Zelda* and *Mario* are fantastic examples of level design, where the game is easy for the casual gamer and has enough depth to keep the interest of the hardcore gamer.

What works best in mission design: linearity (that is, a straight linear path to an end goal) or full freedom? "Somewhere in the middle," says Pardo. He continues:

There is no true "best" way, in my opinion. I've seen great levels that are completely linear and great missions that were open-ended. I personally like to make levels that have a clear linear path, but with other areas for the player to explore. The nonlinear areas typically add more to the story, but can be skipped by the player who just wants to finish the level.

In *Warcraft III*, we tried to design missions that combine the open feeling of an RTS mission with story elements of an RPG. Missions will give the player his objectives at the beginning of each mission, but as the player advances, more objectives may be added through staged events and in-game cinematics.

Where does a mission designer look for inspiration? "Everywhere, really," says Blizzard's Rob Pardo. "I get ideas from movies, books, and other games. Many times, I'll see an interesting scene in a movie and think, 'Hey, imagine if I took some of that dynamic and applied it to a level…'"

(Used with permission by Blizzard Entertainment, Inc.)

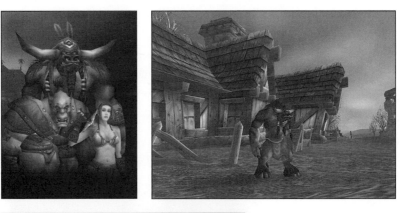

Blizzard Entertainment is busy readying its first massively multiplayer game based on the *Warcraft* universe, dubbed *World of Warcraft*. Read all about this exciting project at `www.blizzard.com/wow`.

(Used with permission by Blizzard Entertainment, Inc.)

James Schmalz, Digital Extremes

The groundbreaking and beautiful 3D shooter *Unreal* is a good example of infusing clever missions into a game. Co-developer James Schmalz offers some tips on creating unique missions:

> ➤ **Keep the player doing something as much as possible**. You don't want players wandering around aimlessly with nothing exciting happening around them.

> ➤ **Give the player interesting and new experiences**. You need to be creative and come up with events and actions that are fresh and exciting—not just the same old gameplay mechanisms that have been done to death.

> ➤ **Challenge the player with tasks that are not too difficult, not too easy, and not frustrating**. A very difficult balance.

With *Unreal Championship (UC)* as the shining example, Schmalz supports his aforementioned advice:

> *Unreal Championship* is an easy match up to that philosophy. In *UC*, you are constantly in combat against your opponents. Either you're attacking them or running to find new weapons and power-ups. Certainly never a boring moment because the moment you do rest, you're dead.

> Interesting and new experiences work well with *UC* because there are so many ways to play the game. Multiple game types, tons of maps. There's so much to experience that it will take a long time to get bored; and when you do start getting bored, there are online and new downloadable maps.

> Finally, on keeping the player challenged, it's fairly easy to do in the single-player game by allowing the player to select the difficulty of the 'bots; plus, we put a huge amount of time into making sure that the difficulty settings are accurate for newbies all the way up to the most advanced professional players.

So why do so many shooters have the same old "get the key, turn on a machine, kill the boss character," and so forth?

> They do this because it's an easy thing to fall back on. If you're pressured for time or resources, it's something that's simple to do and requires less effort than creating something original. It's always a mistake to fall back on this gameplay mechanism because it bores players quickly. They have done this in too many other games to be entertained for long.

Louis Castle, Electronic Arts/Westwood Studios

Westwood Studios' general manager Louis Castle refers to its best-selling *Command & Conquer* strategy series to offer this piece of advice on creating missions:

> Start with a good "story" that has the right pacing of activities for the particular point in the design. Make sure you pay attention to emotional and physical beats. Keep the activities limited to what the player is likely to know without extensive trial-and-error. A good design introduces concepts first, later rewards competence, and then requires mastery.

During the game's development, I played the beta mission of defending Parliament for Yuri's revenge in the *Command & Conquer: Red Alert* series of games. I felt it was a very sound design because it introduced new units in the Master Minds and Flying Disks, but also required competence with existing units and mastery of base defense when bridges are involved. The mission also puts you in the role of a defender, launching well-thought-out attacks with combinations of units that are a challenge to defend against if you're not thoughtful. When the mission is nearly complete, more of the map is opened—and now you must switch to the offensive, which strikes a great resource challenge. An excellent mission overall.

Fred Markus, Angel Studios

Fred Markus, one of the talented developers partially responsible for *Smuggler's Run* and *Midtown Madness* at Angel Studios, shares the following on creating good missions and why some designers create bad ones:

Unfortunately, making games is a real business. So there can be multiple reasons why missions will be bad in a game: bad level designers, a bad game director…but it can also come from a lack of time to finish the product properly. If you don't have enough time to go through your experiments cycle, and you have to ship the product at a specific date for marketing reasons, your game will have flawed missions, even if everyone in the team is super-competent.

To create fun missions, you need to first have enough to play with in your game. The experiments cycle will help you build your game vocabulary. If you have only a few words, then you won't be very interesting to talk to after awhile! It's the same for a game. If you stretch your only fun gameplay element for an entire game, your levels will become boring very quickly. Make sure you have enough to "say" before you start to build your missions. And make sure that what you have to say is consistent with what you want to express. You should be able to define your game in one sentence, and all the vocabulary you build belongs to the same theme. Don't mix too many things or styles of gameplay—none of them will be good. Make the player feel good and have fun.

How about some good mission examples from an Angel Studios game?

In *Midtown Madness 2*, we used a lot of examples of what could be done with cars in the new stunt mode. The intermediate exams combine three of the skills you need to master. The one I like the most happens in London, where you have to get out of an alley by doing a reverse 180, then lose the paparazzi chasing you, and finally cross the Thames by jumping from barge to barge!

In *Smuggler's Run*, the last mission happens mainly on ice, with a lot of diversity and action. You have to reach a frozen lake [and] do a 180 on it to reach a waterfall, where you take huge air, race on the frozen river, cross the village, and climb around a mountain without falling from the ledge. And you have to do all this with a bunch of crazy guys chasing you. Really frantic and fun!

Smuggler's Run 2 was released in the summer of 2002.

> **NOTE**
>
> Raven Software programmer John Scott offers these few words on clever mission design: "Preplanning is everything. Work out an overall story in brief and have a definite goal in mind for the player to complete the game. Then work out sub-missions on a level-by-level basis; this is when the whole team brainstorming works well. When you've decided on a plot, stick to it! Tweaking, cutting, and removing plot holes are all fine, but keep the overall feeling of the game intact. There's nothing more depressing for developers than to change the game midstream."

Harvey Smith, Ion Storm Austin

As project director of *Deus Ex 2* and lead designer of the original *Deus Ex*, Ion Storm's Harvey Smith was asked to discuss his talent for writing clever missions for these games:

> More than "writing" missions, we try to come up with interesting parameters (for the player and his tools). With regard to making the settings, characters, and situations as interesting and flexible as possible, I think you have to allow your work to undergo constant critical evaluation. Nothing is written in stone, and everything can be improved. (Escape the Tyranny of the Idea.) From a mission-fiction standpoint, one of the hardest things to avoid is repetition of the contextual clichés for your game environments. For the missions in *Deus Ex*, we had to constantly guard against repeating another "infiltrate the secret high-tech lab" mission. At one point in early story development, we realized (with a shock) that we had three missions in a row that told the player to "find an underground Illuminatus."

Any other examples?

> While working on *Deus Ex*, one of the things that helped us with mission design was using a different RPG-style mission designer for each location. For instance, designer Steve Powers worked out most of the Hong Kong fiction, working with lead writer Sheldon Pacotti. I worked on a lot of NYC and Paris, also working with Sheldon. The designers brought individual ideas, and Sheldon connected everything fictionally. We all reviewed each other's work constantly and aggressively throughout the project. We pushed each other, and all tried to do something different, yet something that fit within the overall vision of the project. For instance, I wanted to feature an abandoned house that could invoke a feeling of suspense and (adventuresome) intrigue without resorting to violence—a first-person "shooter" space with no combat. Sheldon and I worked out all the details, so that a character (Nicolette DuClare) followed the player around, commenting on her abandoned home and her mother's recent death. It was fairly unique to the game, yet it fit into the overall story.

Harvey Smith of *Deus Ex* and *Deus Ex 2* gives an example in this segment about a clever mission involving the character Nicolette DuClare (pictured here). Read how it fit well into the overall story and why it was a unique mission for the genre. *(Used with permission by Eidos Interactive, Inc.)*

Smith ponders why so many game designers fall short on writing challenging/unique missions:

I think part of this problem is related to the overall options granted to the player. If the player's only expression tools are guns, the range of what can be accomplished within the mission is limited. The game environments should be built around the player's toolset, and that toolset should be powerful enough to allow the player to express himself in interesting ways.

For instance, *Deus Ex* features an aquatic biotech lab, the (partially flooded) site of a disaster. (Designers Monte Martinez and Ricardo Bare worked on that map, along with me, and it was our homage to *System Shock*.) *DX* allows the player to choose Swimming as a skill and Aqualung as a nanotech augmentation. Some of the weapons are made to function underwater, and some of the "monsters" can swim in addition to moving on land. As a result of the interaction of these player tools and game units, we were able to create an interesting mission that stood out from the rest of the game (and from other games) in many ways. Control of air supply became a mini-dynamic, and the ammo for the water-based weapons became more important—the player was suddenly in an area that was novel in some ways, but otherwise consistent with the rest of the game. We allowed the player some atypical options that made the mission richer. Providing a broader range of player-expression tools makes it easier to create rich missions. [Of course,] communicating to the player the set of tools he has and how he can use them is then *another* problem that has to be solved.

Randy Smith, Ion Storm Austin

Also with Ion Storm Austin (but not related to Harvey Smith) is Randy Smith, project director and lead designer of *Thief 3*.

On why so many designers fail at writing interesting missions, Randy continues where colleague Harvey Smith left off:

> Good missions aren't written; they're *designed*. *Written* implies that you're trying to figure out what will happen to the player during the mission. The important agent in something that's written (such as a novel) is the author. The important agent in a video game is the player. The game is not about you, the designer; the game is about the player! Don't write a script that describes what will happen to the player every step of the way. Don't write a story where the only input the player has is pushing buttons to make the story click forward. Instead, design a mission in which the player can make his or her own meaningful choices—ones that you, the designer, couldn't predict. We call this "putting the player on stage," because the game systems and mission designs enable players to express themselves and solve problems creatively. The trick to accomplishing this is imposing very little of your own will upon players (just enough to give them direction and goals), and otherwise providing them with open-ended tools that can be used arbitrarily in a rich environment full of objects and agents that react predictably.

For an example, Randy refers to the wonderful *Thief*, developed by Looking Glass Studios and published by Eidos Interactive:

> In *Thief*, we split up the narrative in the following way. First, there's the *embedded narrative*—the parts of the story that the player has no control over and no input into. In *Thief*, this is all the story stuff that happens between missions: Garrett [the lead character in the game] gets a job offer from a mysterious contact; someone betrays Garrett; someone gets thrown in jail; and so on. Truly interactive fiction is poorly understood at best, and because we don't know how to give the player meaningful, arbitrary input into the story on such a high level, we don't even pretend to try. Instead, we impose it on the player; here's the situation Garrett has gotten himself into now, and therefore here are the goals for your next mission.

> Second, there's the *emergent narrative*. This is basically what happens on a low-level, minute-to-minute basis while Garrett is in a mission trying to accomplish his mission objectives. It's not as grandiose a story as the high-level one, but it's generally much more exciting; and because it's told through gameplay with the player at the controls, the player really does have meaningful input into it. For example, when Garrett is trying to open a door with a lockpick, he hears a guard coming down the hallway toward him, so he ducks back into a shadowy alcove, but in the process accidentally takes a loud misstep onto a metal grate. The guard yells, "Who's there?" and starts searching the area, and Garrett fires a noisemaker arrow off in another direction to distract the guard and draw him away. That's an emergent narrative. The player "wrote" it—not the designer. The designer's contribution was to provide the player with a goal (get past the locked door), the player's tools (lockpicks, noisemaker arrows, the ability to hide in shadows), and challenges in the environment (guards, loud metal plates). Players "write" the emergent narrative using their tools against challenges in the process of trying to achieve their goals.

Smith complains that he often finds missions too challenging—to the point of being frustrating:

> Often, this isn't because the player isn't good at playing the game; rather it's because the player doesn't know what the designer expects him to do. This comes up most often in puzzle-solving portions of games. Never assume that players think like you do. Just because something is obvious to you, the designer, doesn't mean it's obvious to the players. The players aren't stupid; they just have a completely different perception of the mission than you. To address this, keep in mind that the player is very often in the mindset of wondering what's expected of him, so [you need to] clearly explain the problem. Give as many liberal hints as necessary. Providing multiple solutions can also help players who have a different approach to problem-solving. If your game isn't a puzzle-based game, you might want to come right out and explicitly tell the player what to do.

> With respect to "unique" missions, I sometimes get frustrated at the lack of new ideas. Video games are a very young form of media, and there are plenty of new things that can be accomplished with them. Sadly, it's very common for the content of video games to be a thinly veiled celebration of some popular movie or book, with the gameplay locked into rehashing that one plot. Why set out to make a derivative product? At most, use those stories as reference, providing similar experiences and settings, but empower players to tell their own stories.

Peter Hirschmann, LucasArts

We first heard from the articulate Peter Hirschmann in Chapter 7, "Master Design Document Template," in which he discussed game design techniques as well as more specific advice on creating good levels in a game. In the following segment, Hirschmann explains why *Medal of Honor: Allied Assault (MOHAA)* was given to a new developer. He also explains the mission structure for the game and how it ties in tightly with the overall story, which was based on real World War II scenarios.

> **NOTE**
> Hirschmann left Electronic Arts to work for LucasArts in 2002, shortly after *Allied Assault* shipped to retailers.

Medal of Honor: Allied Assault is a milestone for the franchise because not only is it the first time the series has gone onto the PC, but it's the first *Medal of Honor (MOH)* title we've created externally with an outside developer.

2015 Inc., based in Tulsa, Oklahoma, designed and developed the game for our EALA studio (known in olden days as DreamWorks Interactive). The PlayStation and PlayStation2 games in the series are developed internally, but after we decided to take the franchise to the PC platform and create a brand new game, we went looking for a group of people outside the studio who could do the *MOH* series proud. The 2015 team has some of the best programmers, designers, artists, and animators that we've ever had the pleasure of working with, and their efforts on the game have been nothing short of stunning.

It's important that each game in the *Medal of Honor* series tell a good story. For *Allied Assault*, we're introducing a new character, Lt. Mike Powell, who is a professional soldier and already involved with fighting the ground war when the game starts. Lt. Powell joins the ranks of Lt. Jimmy Patterson (star of the original *Medal of Honor* game as well as *Medal of Honor: Frontline*), resistance fighter Manon Batiste (heroine of *Medal of Honor: Underground*), and USMC aviator Capt. Sam Hargrove (the player character in *Medal of Honor: Fighter Command*). Powell is a member of the elite U.S. Army Rangers, who were often at the front lines of each of the major battles in the European theater of operations—including D-Day on Omaha Beach. Fans of the previous games know that the Office of Strategic Services (the precursor to the CIA) has always played an important part in the series, and *MOHAA* is no different, but we added a few new twists this time.

Ever since the first game, the continuity of the *MOH* universe has been a priority for us, and all the missions in Allied Assault are intertwined with the established timeline. The design team at 2015 has done a lot of fun things that tie the game in with the rest of the series (including the other *MOH* games in production that will come out after *MOHAA*). There are a lot of little elements that careful observers should notice—if you remember back to the first game, a plane was shot down behind enemy lines, carrying a G3 operations officer that Jimmy has to rescue. The player's briefing comes via some intelligence gathered by the plane's pilot, who was rescued the night before in a daring search-and-rescue mission. Who rescued the pilot? Well, Lt. Mike Powell did, of course! We wanted to keep most of the other crossovers a secret, but Manon makes an appearance, and Jimmy helps Lt. Powell with some enemy intelligence regarding a certain rather infamous location in the *MOH* universe. *Allied Assault* not only expands on some of the established history of the earlier titles, but it also takes the series in new and exciting directions that will have repercussions on all the games that follow.

Most importantly, *MOHAA* builds on the gameplay established in previous games—fun missions filled with incredibly intelligent enemies. The biggest addition to gameplay is the "Allied" in *Allied Assault*—you now have AI troops fighting with you, not just against you. One of my favorite levels, designed by 2015's Mackey McCandlish, is called "Sniper Town," where the player hooks up with a demoralized and frightened squad of American soldiers who have been separated from their unit. The player can simply choose to ignore them and go about fulfilling his original orders, or join up with the guys and shepherd them through this incredibly dangerous environment filled with German troops and armor—and a few elite Nazi marksmen hidden in some very choice spots. If you choose to help the squad, the results (from a gameplay perspective) are quite amazing—you'll find yourself thrown into some of the most intense moments of squad-versus-squad urban combat that you can imagine. Because of this, the game world feels much more alive than it ever has before.

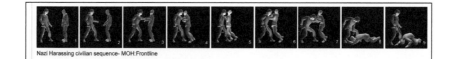

Nazi Harassing civilian sequence- MOH:Frontline

Peter Hirschmann offers these rare, behind-the-scenes images from the making of *Medal of Honor: Allied Assault*. To read more on this breathtakingly realistic action war game, visit `http://moh.ea.com/`.
(Used with permission by Electronic Arts, Inc.)

Part II

Production

Chapter 11

Programming Theory

In this chapter, we get down to the meat-and-potatoes of game design—programming.

Programming, of course, refers to designing and writing a computer program—in our case, a game or game engine. It's the programmer's job to decide what the game needs to do, develop the logic of how to do it, and write instructions for the computer in a language that the computer can translate into its own language and execute (such as Microsoft Visual C++).

Another definition of programming is "the most fun you can have with your clothes on, although clothes are not mandatory." (Okay, that's debatable, but it is a real tertiary definition at the *Online Computing Dictionary* web site at `www.instantweb.com/D/dictionary/contents.html!`)

Call 'em what you want—code-crunchers, number-munchers, algorithm analysts—programmers are the talented folks who create the backbone of the game. As an analogy, think of the game as a building under construction. Programming represents the girders or the skeleton that forms the shape of the structure. All the beautiful art on the walls or incredible music pumping through the PA system does not substitute for poor engineering. A game, like a building, must be built on a solid and secure foundation.

There's a lot more to programming than graduating with a degree in computer science and hacking around with some code on your PC. Game programming takes cunning, patience, and an intangible savoir faire developed after years of practice, discipline, and a passion for the trade.

Over the following pages, we'll hear from savvy programmers who want to share with us the knowledge gained from their years of experience with programming games and how to overcome the tribulations inherent in this growing profession.

THE EXPERTS

- Alan Lawrance, Volition
- John Slagel, Volition
- Tim Sweeney, Epic Games
- Sid Meier, Firaxis Games
- Shigeru Miyamoto, Nintendo
- Don Hopkins, Freelance
- Bartosz Kijanka, Gas Powered Games
- Stephen White, Naughty Dog
- Catherine Roy and Éric Allard, Ubi Soft Entertainment
- Brian Reynolds, Big Huge Games
- David Wu, Pseudo Interactive
- Peter Molyneux, Lionhead Studios
- Louis Castle, Electronic Arts/ Westwood Studios
- Greg Thomas, Sega of America/Visual Concepts
- Steve Hunt
- James Schmalz, Digital Extremes
- Doug Church, Freelance
- John Scott, Raven Software
- Michael Raymond-July
- Ed Magnin, Magnin & Associates

Alan Lawrance, Volition

Alan Lawrance is a senior programmer at Volition and was lead designer on the incredible *Red Faction* and *Red Faction 2*, published by THQ. Before that, he was a programmer on *FreeSpace*, a popular space combat simulation for Interplay Productions.

Lawrance has quite a bit to say on the topic of game programming, beginning with some general advice for those looking to become a success in the industry:

> The most important thing to keep in mind for a beginner is to choose a project that stands a chance at getting finished. If you're too ambitious with your first project, you'll likely get frustrated and give up. You have to start small and work your way up to more ambitious projects.

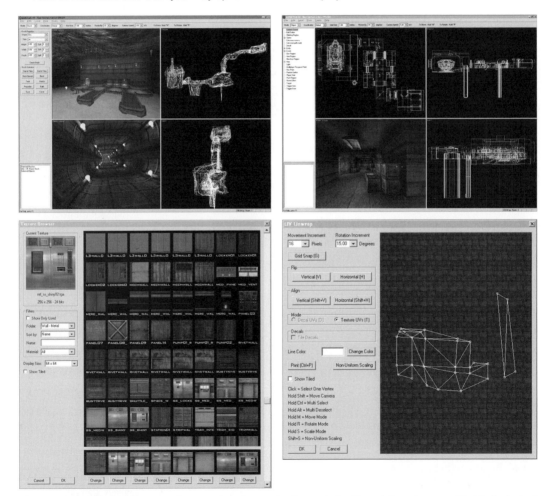

"One of the biggest obstacles in programming a game today is managing the complexity of the code," says Lawrance. "*Red Faction* is about 300,000 lines of C code, which is more code than any single programmer can manage well." Pictured here are a handful of never-before-seen *Red Faction* shots taken during the game's development. *(Used with permission by THQ, Inc.)*

Second, Lawrance advises writing code that's modular from a technical perspective: "You should try to write systems that are self-contained and don't have dependencies on other sections of the code." But how is this achieved?

The first step of writing modular code is not to write any code at all! Before jumping into coding, it's important to spend time designing the code on paper and discussing your design with another programmer if possible. You're much more likely to write modular code if you spend the time really thinking through the design of the system.

Modular code has its guts hidden from the rest of the program. The only entry point into modular code is through an interface. As long as the interface doesn't change, you can modify your modular code without worrying about breaking the rest of the game. This minimizes the dependencies between your modular code and the rest of the code in the game. When you're working on game code with 300,000+ lines, it's very important to have modular systems that are safe to modify. Managing the complexity of your game code by writing modular systems is critical with today's games.

The final piece of general advice from Lawrance is to strive for simplicity: "I would avoid trying to use a fancy object-oriented design, and instead focus on writing simple straight C code." He waxes more on the subject:

This is a philosophy of writing code that's easy to read and modify, rather than writing fancy code. It's tempting to write code that saves a few cycles by doing something tricky or writing dense code to save a few lines. [But] in a professional game company, it's likely that other programmers will have to read and modify your code, too. The K.I.S.S. principle (keep it simple, stupid) definitely applies to software development.

Red Faction was quite a technical achievement on the PlayStation 2. Surely, there were challenges to programming this game. Lawrance answers:

One of the biggest obstacles in programming a game today is managing the complexity of the code. *Red Faction* is about 300,000 lines of C code, which is more code than any single programmer can manage well. Each programmer on the team needs to be a specialist in one or more areas, and the programmers have to work well together so all the different systems can fit together.

Red Faction is also available for the PC. Were there similar challenges?

There are tradeoffs between PC and console development. The great thing about console development is that you're working on fixed hardware. You know exactly what your target machine will be, and if the game runs well on one console, it will run exactly the same on all consoles. When you program on a PC, you have to be concerned with being compatible with all the different system configurations your customers may have. This means your game has to be scalable on the PC, to run well on low-end systems and still have all the cool graphical features available for those with fast systems and the latest video cards.

Lawrance also mirrors the other tradeoffs mentioned in this chapter:

With PC programming, you generally don't have to be worried about your program running out of memory. If your game needs extra memory, there will almost always be virtual memory available. If your console game runs out of memory, though, it's going to crash. Console programmers tend to be very careful with memory in their games, and avoid dynamic allocation.

The tools for PC development are generally easier to use than tools for console development. For PC development, you're developing and testing your game on a PC, which is a flexible platform that everyone understands well. For console development, there is specialized hardware that you have to launch your game on, which is more cumbersome than working with an open PC system.

When asked whether it's better to license a 3D game engine or create your own, Lawrance says it really depends on the goals of the development team:

For *Red Faction*, we couldn't license a game engine because no available game engines had support for dynamic geometry modification. It would be extremely difficult to add support for geometry modification to an existing engine, so it was a clear choice for us to develop our own game engine.

NOTE

"Geomod" technology allows players to deform the environment in real-time, such as blasting through a wall and then climbing through it. Be sure to read our chat with Volition's senior programmer, John Slagel, on how this was achieved (see the next section).

Lawrance discusses the pros and cons of building your own game engine:

For some teams, it makes perfect sense to license an engine. It can reduce technical risk and cut many months (if not years) off the time to produce a game. There's still a lot of work to adapting an engine to your game, though, so it's not like you can just buy an engine and not expect to make changes to it.

What software should a game programmer know?

At a minimum, a programmer needs to know how to use a decent editor and a compiler. I would recommend using software that lets you edit/compile/debug within the same package, such as Microsoft Developer Studio or Metrowerks Codewarrior.

Pulling examples from his experience at Volition, Lawrance talks about the Geomod technology, a first for the gaming industry:

I'm very proud of the arbitrary geometry modification system in *Red Faction*. The ability to modify geometry in real-time is a groundbreaking feature for first-person action games. We spent well over a year of programmer time creating the core system, and it affected many other areas of the code. We had a vision at the start of the project to make it possible to destroy your environment, and we never gave up on that goal.

The glass-breaking system in *Red Faction* is very cool. When you fire a bullet through a window, the glass breaks apart from the impact point, and the entire pane of glass falls away in shards. The effect is spectacular and has to be seen to be appreciated. Like most systems in the game, they start in a basic form and progress as more features and polish get added. The glass-breaking system was like this. We started with the basic idea of having the glass break apart from the impact point, and built from there. After many iterations and feedback from the team, we had a polished glass-breaking system that's a very memorable part of *Red Faction*.

Finally, a few words on breaking into the industry (covered in depth in Chapter 21, "Breaking into the Industry"):

For a programmer, I would recommend getting a computer science or electrical/computer engineering degree first. While in school, you should work on programming projects in your spare time. If you can show you have a passion for programming outside of school, it goes a long way to proving you'll be able to make it as a game programmer. You should be ready to include a good game demo (with the source code) with your résumé when you apply to game companies. Besides proving you're a capable programmer, you should also prove that you love to play games. Become knowledgeable about games and the game industry in general, and be ready to talk about the games you like to play and why.

Be sure to jump to Chapter 12 to read Lawrance's advice on coding AI.

John Slagel, Volition

Also at Volition is senior programmer John Slagel, an engineer who has worked on games such as *Descent* (*I* and *II*), *Freespace*, and the *Red Faction* series. As touched on in the interview with Alan Lawrance, THQ's *Red Faction* garnered respect within the game programming community for its "Geomod" technology—the capability to destroy the environment in real-time.

We chatted with John Slagel about how this was achieved. But first, a few tidbits of general advice for game programmers.

Slagel's Three Pointers:

Unless you're writing a simple game, build on an existing engine. There is simply too much that goes into a game these days for one person to finish all the details, and nobody expects you to. But being able to take an existing library or engine and make it do something different and cool is good practice because when you get your job in the game industry, that is exactly what you will be doing. You'll probably be working with existing technology and engines for many years after starting. There is a lot of good source code out there; from us, there is *Descent I* and *II* and *Freespace II* source code. The *Freespace II* source code compiles with MSDEV right out of the box! Basically, if it works, use it and reuse it; don't rewrite it.

Keep it simple.

If you're writing code to solve a problem and it's getting very complex, take a step back and figure out how you can do something different and simpler. Simple is usually faster and more stable, two good qualities to have in game code. Find someone experienced who has published a game; someone you can talk to and ask questions.

If you ask someone who has done it before, they can usually tell you what works in the real world and what a good approach is. For example, in the *Descent I* days, Matt Toschlog wrote the 3D rendering pipeline, and I've never seen a better example of an overall good way to do the third pipeline in any book. We still follow his basic algorithms years later, in *Freespace*, *Summoner*, and *Red Faction*.

Slagel talks more in-depth about *Red Faction*:

> We built *Red Faction* off of the *Freespace* source code, which was built off of the *Descent* source code. We reused a lot. When we went to implement the Geomod code, we considered many different approaches, and picked the one that was simplest and fit the hardware the best. Even in the implementation of it, we kept things simple…the basic Geomod algorithm is very simple for what it does. We could have implemented different solutions using complex triangulation or bsp algorithms, but we just chose something we knew we could implement that would be simple and stable.

Now on to the beefy part of our discussion on Geomod technology. As Slagel explains, "Geomod technology basically lets you blast holes in the world." He expands:

> The obvious thing it does is to deform geometry, but there's more to it than that…you need to make some pieces of the world fall, you need to make the AI know about the holes so they can shoot through them, you need to let the rendering code know it now needs to render through that wall. You can't assume anything is static, like lighting or pathfinding or collision detection. Almost all data structures and algorithms in the game need to be more dynamic than their non-Geomodable counterparts.

On how it was achieved, Slagel submits the following document—which he wrote back in August 2001—that was going to be released to the public, but never made it. That is, until now! In this essay, Slagel explains the general process of Geomod code. Enjoy!

How *Red Faction 1* Geomod Technology Worked

A Geomod looks complex, but it's pretty simple. It's just a Boolean operation on the level geometry that happens in real-time during the game.

The Geomod itself is just a shape that is semi-spherical that one of the artists made once. We could use any shape, and we scale it up or down depending on the size of the Geomod that we want.

A *Red Faction* level is made up of a bunch of polygons organized into rooms, with portals connecting rooms. The rendering engine uses the portals to render *mostly* only what's visible. The rooms can be in any shape, which means that rooms within rooms may work, but aren't fully supported because we render rooms from back to front, so objects in a room inside another room may not render in the proper order. The rooms are watertight with invisible portal faces filling in gaps between rooms.

The polygons inside each room are just in a big list that is sorted by texture and alpha, and we let the z-buffer do the work.

Here's an example of how a simple Geomod works:

1. First, the faces from the Geomod are added to the world.

2. All the faces in the Geomod and in the level are split with all other faces that intersect them.

3. All the level faces inside of the Geomod are deleted.

4. Then, any of the Geomod faces inside of the level is deleted, the remaining Geomod faces are added to the room, and the Geomod is complete.

A more complex case occurs when the Geomod connects a room or two; in this example, the black sphere is a Geomod that is being done and touches three rooms.

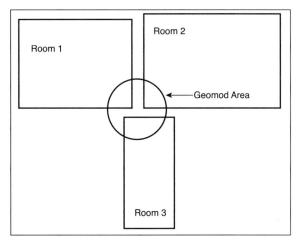

In the first step, all the faces are broken with all the other faces.

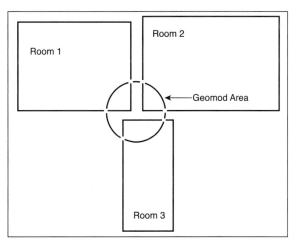

The code detects that room 1 is the room that is going to expand. (It picks the room with the lowest number.)

Then, the Geomod faces inside the world are thrown out, and the faces of the world inside the Geomod are thrown out—except for any faces from rooms other than room 1. They are kept and flagged as portals. So you see all other rooms will stay "watertight" because they always keep all of their faces and they start out watertight.

All faces that are kept from the Geomod sphere are then linked to room 1.

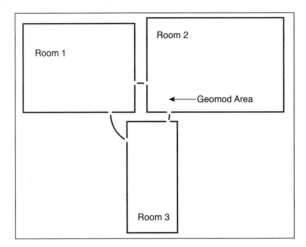

Then, all portal faces are copied and flipped, and those new faces are marked as portals and linked to room 1, thus making it a complete watertight solid.

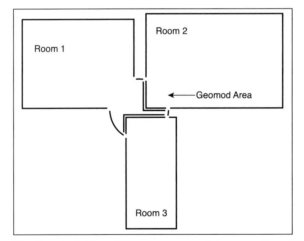

Ta da! It's done; everything is watertight, and there are new portals connecting all the rooms.

There are a few "trivial" details left, though:

➤ What is a face? A triangle? An *n*-sided polygon? Can it be concave?

➤ How to split any intersection faces quickly and accurately.

➤ How to classify a face as in or out.

➤ How to store and structure the data so that you can add/remove/split faces quickly.

➤ How to maintain proper polygon topology; no t-joints, sharing edges, or vertices.

➤ How to render this dynamically changing world with such odd-shaped rooms and possibly many portals.

➤ How to collide against this dynamically changing world.

➤ How to light/texture the new faces.

➤ How to make AI know it can go through the holes in walls, but avoid the holes in floors.

➤ How to determine that a piece of the world broke off.

➤ How to make that piece fall in a believable manner.

➤ How to make all of this happen at 24 fps.

Here are some good books and resources that I found useful:

➤ Martti Mantyla, An *Introduction to Solid Modeling*, 1988.

➤ Christoph M. Hoffman, *Geometric and Solid Modeling*, 1989.

➤ Philip M. Hubbard, *Constructive Solid Geometry for Triangulated Polyhedra*, 1990. (This paper can be found online; I highly recommend reading it.)

➤ Michael Muuss and Lee Butler, "Combinatorial Solid Geometry, B-Reps, and n-Manifold Geometry" from the book *State of the Art in Computer Graphics*, 1991.

Slagel was asked about the biggest problem(s) with most console or computer game programming today, and how a coder can avoid it/them. Quite simply, Slagel says the biggest problem is that "games are getting HUGE." He explains:

There is so much you need to do to "keep up with the Joneses." From engine details, such as supporting specular highlights and bumpmaps, to high-level features, such as multiplayer with a tracker server. There are platform details, such as an install program for the PC and memory card support on the console.

I don't think avoiding them is the solution; rather, planning for them. Pick a set of features you want to support that will make your game fun, and try to stick with it and not add every new thing that comes out just because it sounds cool or someone else is doing it.

Slagel says another problem is that sometimes programmers code with no limits or upper bounds, and the artists go nuts and make something that is too slow or uses too much RAM. He offers a better approach:

Design things with hard-and-fast limits, so you know where the time and memory is going, and let the content creators know the limits. Surprisingly, it makes their job easier because they know how far they can push things, and in all of our experience, it turns out better; you'd be amazed at some of the things artists can produce inside a fixed set of limits. Instead of being conservative, hoping it'll be small enough, they can do as much as possible because they know the limits. Everyone is happier.

Finally, Slagel offers some advice for a budding game programmer who wants to break into the video gaming industry:

> Write a demo or game or two on your own before you apply for a programming job, and send out the demo along with your résumé or at least a link to your demo. Make it easy to run and use.

> Go to college; get a B.S. in computer science. Not a Master's…usually, that doesn't pay off. The primary reason is that if things don't work out in the game industry for you, or if you someday decide you want a different job in a different field and maybe you need to move someplace where there isn't a game company around, you will need the B.S. to get a job. Plus, while you're in college, you should have plenty of time for #1: making your demo. Another benefit of college: You learn a lot of other stuff applicable to games programming…cinema classes, English/literature classes, AI classes, tight deadlines, all-nighters, how to order pizza.

> Research game companies. Pick the one or two you want to work for. Apply to them with all your heart, tell them why you want to work there specifically, and explain why you are a good hire. Don't go through a recruiter or spam all the game companies with a form cover letter and résumé.

Although Slagel says, "Don't go through a recruiter," the folks in Chapter 22, "Game Agents and Headhunters," may disagree!

Tim Sweeney, Epic Games

Tim Sweeney is the founder of Epic Games and the programmer behind the *Unreal* engine, which powers such games as *Unreal Tournament*, *Duke Nukem Forever*, and *Deus Ex*. A talented workaholic, it took quite a bit of arm-twisting to get Mr. Sweeney to take time for an interview, but he gave in at last!

When programming a 3D shooter, what are the most important things to keep in mind?

> First and foremost, realize that no matter how good a programmer you are, you won't find the best solution to every problem on your first try. So, always be prepared to go back to clean up, restructure, or even completely rewrite your old code as your project progresses. No development project ever failed because a programmer spent a few days cleaning up his code. However, many projects have failed because too much old, poorly structured code weighed the project down and hurt long-term productivity.

He offers the following somewhat technical anecdote as evidence:

> In the first year of writing the *Unreal* engine, in early 1996, I had written about 40,000 lines of engine code in C. The code was very object-oriented, which wasn't a very good match for C's syntax and limitations, and adding new features became error-prone: I had literally thousands of lines of code that were simply typecasts to get from superclasses to subclasses. Progress slowed to a halt. Frustrated, I spent a month ripping the code apart, rewriting and updating it to take full advantage of C++. The end result was a much simpler code base—25,000 lines of code instead of 40,000—and thereafter, I was much more productive.

Once the rendering engine was up and running, I rewrote the texture-mapping code no fewer than seven times, switching between three major approaches. At first, I was trying to render everything with a highly optimized texture mapper—one that Arjan Brussee (the Dutch programmer of *Jazz Jackrabbit*) and I had come up with over a few months of email exchanges, in a sort of competition to out-optimize each other. This was very speedy in theory, but it required a *Quake*-style texture-caching scheme to support light maps, and that was an insurmountable bottleneck in the kinds of large environments I was trying to render. Eventually, I just gave up and started rewriting the code.

The second approach was quite novel: I subdivided polygons into 16×16-pixel quads, and ran a fairly complex lighting algorithm and perspective correction for each quad vertex, combining static shadow maps with dynamic lighting calculations. Then lighting and texture coordinates were linearly interpolated internally. This was the breakthrough period of *Unreal* development, in which the engine's focus on dramatic lighting really started to take shape. This approach was very fast, but ran into major warping and aliasing problems as polygons rotated and experienced perspective skewing. As time went by, it became clear that my new lighting routine had to go.

The final approach was to precompute more information about lighting—full light maps, but no texture caching, and then subdivide polygons into 4×4 quads, sampling the light maps at each quad vertex and then linearly interpolating them. This was a complex routine, and it ended up being quite slow in its initial C++ implementation, but had great worst-case performance and great visible quality. Once I had the routine up and running, Erik de Neve (Epic optimization guru) did something you hardly ever see nowadays, and spent six months optimizing the renderer in assembly language, eventually getting the performance very acceptable (and approximately 2.5 times faster than the C++ implementation).

The point of all this is that if I had stayed with my first approach or second approach, *Unreal* would have never been practical; the game either wouldn't have been finished or would have been quite disappointing; its visual quality held back by code with major flaws. Yet, I never would have realized that my first several rendering approaches weren't suitable unless I had spent a few months trying them out. Every game seems to have a few key components like this, which have to be designed and redesigned several times to make them work.

Sweeney advises keeping an eye on the overall efficiency of your code and major algorithms:

Don't worry too much about optimizing code line by line; computers are so fast nowadays that unoptimized C++ is fast enough for shipping a game. Your algorithms make all the difference on performance. A merge sort written in Visual Basic can easily outperform a bubble sort written in hand-optimized assembly language!

One interesting war story is *Unreal's* file-loading code. During early development, it was taking several minutes to load our largest levels. For a long time, I just figured it was disk access speed. When I went in and actually timed the code, I found that I was bubble-sorting a large array of strings every time I loaded a file, and that was taking over two-thirds of the time. By rewriting a few lines of code, loading times fell into the 20-second range, in which they really were dominated by disk transfer rates.

Another example is *Unreal's* actor collision code, which checks for collision between game objects whenever one object moves. My original approach was to check for collision against every other object in the level, which seemed like a fine idea at the time—after all, it worked in my 2D side-scroller: *Jill of the Jungle*. Although that worked fine in the case of 50 to 100 objects in a level, we had levels with thousands of objects, and the collision code was terribly slow. So I spent a day restructuring it to keep a linked list of objects residing in every 256×256×256 cube of space in the level. Immediately, collision detection overhead went down from around 25% of CPU time to under 1%.

In *Unreal*, a 1998 game designed largely around a software renderer, there were several major routines that were worth assembly language-optimizing: the texture mapping inner and outer loops, the BSP transformation and projection routines, and the light map generation inner loop.

In our latest code, designed for hardware T&L, there is only one routine worth optimizing: the skeletal animation inner loop, which takes advantage of SSE instructions. When DirectX 9 comes out, even that won't be necessary.

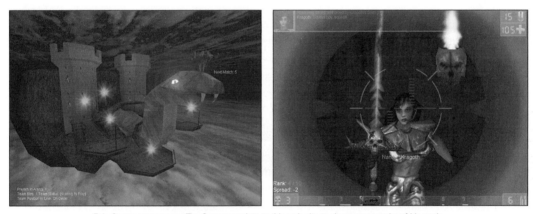

Epic Games programmer Tim Sweeney points to this web site to view screen grabs of his work:
`www.epicgames.com/_UnrealEngineNews.html`. He notes, "Keep in mind that everything here is a very collaborative effort between lots of artists and programmers; my work on the *Unreal* engine's core is just a little piece of it."
Now, that's a team player. Here, a couple of shots from *Unreal Tournament*.
(Used with permission by Epic Games, Inc. and Infogrames, Inc. Epic®, Epic Games®, and Unreal® are registered trademarks of Epic Games, Inc.)

Remember, you're writing a game, and programming is supposed to be fun, says Sweeney:

If you find yourself spending weeks doing tedious work you don't enjoy, ask yourself what you're doing wrong. Perhaps you're being held back by buggy old code, or perhaps you're working on a game that's not very fun. If you're unhappy with your work, figure out what you need to change in order to make it fun again. If you're not enjoying your work, you're probably not doing a very good job.

Is it feasible to purchase a game engine, or should you just start from scratch?

Whether to license an engine or build your own depends on your goals, skills, and budget. If you're making a game that will be similar in (at least) rendering paradigm to *Unreal* or *Quake*, licensing an off-the-shelf engine could save you a lot of time and enable you to focus most of your energy on gameplay innovations. Great examples of games built using licensed technology are Valve's *Half-Life* and Ion Storm's *Deus Ex*.

But if you're making a very different kind of game or are basing your entire game design on a new technical innovation that isn't practical in an existing engine, it makes more sense to build your own. One good example is *Red Faction*, the first 3D game to feature highly destructible environments—by building its own engine, the team was able to be the first with this new feature. Of course, building your own engine for a first-person action game entails a surprising amount of time and effort, so make your choices wisely.

But what if someone is just starting out as a game programmer?

If you're just starting out, and don't have a big budget—or don't have any budget at all—be realistic; you need to take on a relatively small project in order to have a chance at success. One possibility is to make a simple game; *Tetris* was a simple game developed by a single programmer with no budget. Don't expect to create the next phenomenal game such as *Tetris*, but it's certainly still possible for a single developer to make a simple game that wins critical acclaim and becomes popular with a dedicated following of users.

[Programmers can also] develop a mod for an existing game, such as *Half-Life*, *Quake*, or *Unreal*. By taking this route, you start with a great code base and an incredible amount of game content and documentation (whether official or created by other users); you can focus your efforts on creating a new variety of gameplay in one of these existing game universes. Many of the best game MODs—such as *CounterStrike* and *Team Fortress*—started out as small projects by a few developers with no budget.

Sid Meier, Firaxis Games

One of the gaming world's most admired game designers and programmers is Sid Meier, responsible for countless computer game classics over the past 17 years or so: *Civilization* and *Civilization II*, *F-15 Strike Eagle*, *Pirates*, *Railroad Tycoon*, and *Alpha Centauri*; and next, *SimGolf* and *Civilization III*.

Meier chats elsewhere about strategy game design (see Chapter 3, "General Game Design: Strategy Games"), but here he offers one key piece of game programming advice:

One thing I've learned over the years is to test your code often. I don't code for more than 10 or 15 minutes before checking it. If I code for an hour or two without testing my code, I get a much higher chance of horrendous results. I know it's unconventional, but it's fresh in my mind. Just test your code whenever you can. It's so easy to waste a whole day to track down a bug…but if you've programmed for a half-day, the bug can be 20 different bugs.

What tools must a programmer be familiar with? Firaxis Games uses Microsoft C++, which is pretty standard stuff. Meier comments, "We find it usable for 90% of everything we do. But we also use a little assembly, which is used a lot in video games."

For Sid Meier's words of wisdom on creating realistic AI, see Chapter 12, "Artificial Intelligence (AI)."

Shigeru Miyamoto, Nintendo

The beloved and respected Mr. Miyamoto comments elsewhere in this book on game design, creating successful characters, and the importance of a good user interface. Here, he discusses a bit of theory behind Nintendo's programming protocol:

> I believe a game designer must also be an engineer, to have the necessary technological knowledge as well as being a designer. Whenever a new designer joins Nintendo, we make it a point of letting him/her go through the technological lecture. By doing so, the designers learn what they can do and can't do in terms of the technology. Also, I'm always telling our designers and programmers that we shouldn't just make games, the most appealing point of which is the hardware technology. We should be proud of ourselves being the frontier of the unprecedented entertainment category called "interactive entertainment," and we must put our energies into the creation of this new entertainment that no one else can make.

Don Hopkins, Freelance

Since 1988, Don Hopkins has been developing "pie menus," a reliable and efficient gestural user-interface technique that has been implemented in many different products and platforms, including *The Sims* and Internet Explorer. Don worked with Will Wright at Maxis, developing the character animation system, user interface, programming, and content-creation tools for *The Sims*. And he also developed a free JavaScript implementation of pie menus, available at www.piemenu.com.

In the following segment, Hopkins covers quite a bit of ground—from general advice to budding game programmers, to the various kinds of programmers that a development studio typically hires, to explaining in-depth his proprietary pie menu interface.

First, Hopkins converses about the dozen specialties of game programming that a developer can pursue:

> Here's a breakdown of the various kinds of jobs and their usual responsibilities:
>
> ➤ **Simulation programmer**. This is someone who programs the inner workings of the game—designing and the implementing the model of the world.
>
> ➤ **Script programmer**. Many games have embedded scripting languages, so they can easily be programmed interactively, which is crucial for rapid development. Some scripting languages are special-purpose, such as SimAntics, which is a visual programming language for

controlling *The Sims'* behavior. It takes a lot of effort to develop and support programming and debugging tools for the script programmers to use. These days it's a lot more efficient to use an off-the-shelf plug-in scripting language, such as Python. That makes it possible to easily hire experienced script programmers and leverage the many existing programming tools and support services—programming higher-level behaviors, object customization, event handlers, non-player character AI, scenario scripting, user interface dialogs, and so on.

➤ **AI programmer**. The term *artificial intelligence* is often misused or trivialized in the game industry. It often refers to script programmers and simulation programmers who program non-player character behavior. But a hardcore artificial intelligence background is quite useful for game design these days, as computers become faster and games more complex.

➤ **Graphics programmer**. 2D graphics. 3D graphics. A very popular field, so there's not too much I can say that hasn't been covered. You should have a good practical understanding of math and enjoy reading conference proceedings. Learn how to simplify and apply academic research to solve practical problems. You can't just take a SIGGRAPH paper and implement it in a game. There are many compromises and tradeoffs that go into applying and optimizing academic research. Before deciding to implement the latest fad technology from SIGGRAPH, understand the goals and assumptions of other people's work and how they may or may not apply to the goals of your project.

➤ **User interface programmer**. Creates user interface toolkits and widgets. In graphics, programming skills are useful for user interface programmers, in games using immersive "direct manipulation" techniques, with user interface elements and feedback rendered in-game. These folks need to know about internationalization and accessibility.

➤ **Tool programmer**. Importers, exporters, content pipelines, scripts, databases. Implement tools to support the art department, so they can create and test out the content in the game. The content pipeline is the set of tools that move and process content from the artists into the game. These folks maintain and automate databases that keep track of all the content, source files, data files, dependencies, transformation processes, and so on.

➤ **Sound programmer**. Sound engine. Music. Effects. Speech. It's useful for sound programmers to know about music, drama, human perception, math, signal processing, and networking. They can be involved with the internationalization issues if a game uses speech. *The Sims* speak their own special language, which saved a lot of work by avoiding those issues.

➤ **Database programmer**. Keeping track of the game design, content, and bugs. Work with the designers to create models of the game and content in the database. Help the tool programmers and artists to develop and maintain the content pipeline.

➤ **Web programmer**. Interactive services, registration, updates, game lobby, support, and so on. Web server scripting. Working with databases.

➤ **BuildMeister (or BuildMeistress)**. Responsible for source code control; making sure the code builds every night on all platforms; badgering programmers who check in bugs. Might also take care of the content pipeline, making sure content exports as well as code builds, badgering artists who check in bogus content. Requires patience and attention to detail.

➤ **BugMeister (or BugMeistress)**. Keeps track of the bug database; prioritizing them; identifying and merging duplicates; discussing them with designers; assigning them to programmers; tracking their progress. Coordinates with QA, programmers, and designers to keep them working together and focused on shipping the game instead of murdering each other. Requires database experience and adept diplomatic skills.

➤ **Quality Assurance (QA)**. Test games, installers, manuals, web sites, assumptions. Diagnose and report bugs. Opportunities for advancement to game programming if you can prove yourself in QA. Analyzing bugs and understanding the behavior of a complex program is a steppingstone toward a more advanced programming career. Great way to learn the valuable skill of criticizing the work of touchy, overworked programmers without hurting their feelings. Could lead to a great career in politics. Some people get stuck in QA and never advance because they just like sitting around playing games all day and don't make any effort to expand their knowledge and stand out from the crowd. Playing games all day isn't such a bad life, but wouldn't you rather be playing games you helped write yourself?

NOTE

Forget the White House—Don Hopkins says summer internships can also be a great way to get into the industry. "Summer internships can be excellent opportunities if you're sufficiently motivated to jump in and learn," he says. Typically, summer interns are given interesting projects that are small enough to complete in the few months they're around. "It's a great ground-floor opportunity to learn from people working in the real world and to prove yourself, so don't waste it," says Hopkins. "It's the best way to learn about the real world, and makes it much easier to get a good full-time job in the future."

How about some advice to game programmers who are just starting out?

➤ Don't waste your time copying old worn-out designs that have been run into the ground, such as *Quake*. The world doesn't need another *Quake* clone, nor does it need another variation on *Space Invaders*.

➤ Don't try to implement general-purpose virtual reality systems or user interfaces as popularized in popular sci-fi books and TV. You can be sure that many other people have tried the same thing and failed. Even the most successful attempts aren't very fun.

➤ Don't make the mistake of trying to design a user interface look-and-feel based on what you saw on TV watching *Star Trek*. The *Star Trek* computer displays are purposefully designed to be illegible, so they look cool on the screen, but don't actually mean anything.

There are many other wonderful games and research projects to look to for inspiration. Play them, figure out why they're fun, and come up with original ideas for new games—don't just copy old ideas! Here's a master list: *Bill Budge's Pinball Construction Set*, *Little Computer People*, *Rockey's Boots*, *Robot Odyssey*, *M.U.L.E.*, *Zork*, *Habitat*, *SimCity*, *Ultima Online*, *Timothy Leary's Mind Mirror*, *Twisted Metal II*, *PaRappa the Rapper*, *Mario 64*, *Dungeon Keeper*, and *Black & White*.

Start interviewing for good jobs years in advance. Meet people you want to work with, and find out what they're working on and what skills it requires. Discover what you need to learn, and spend some time educating yourself. Continue your education after you graduate by working on projects that teach you skills needed to get better and better jobs. Don't get stuck doing the same thing. Learn from your experience; then move on to the next thing, building on top of what you've learned, in a pattern that fills in the gaps of your self-education. Don't get too attached to any particular piece of software or language, but seek out and learn good tools and techniques you can depend on for a long time.

This is all great advice that addresses how to approach game design, but what about specific programming tips and techniques? Hopkins answers with the following:

➤ Learn to read and assimilate other [programmers'] code, and write code that's easy for others to read and understand.

➤ Avoid the "Not Invented Here" syndrome. Stand on the shoulders of others, not their toes.

➤ Learn to appreciate not having to do everything yourself.

➤ Join the Open Source community, and share what you can.

➤ Write code for other people to read and understand, not just for the compiler to parse.

➤ Use lots of asserts in order to write down your mental assumptions, not just to catch errors at runtime. Asserts are better than comments because the compiler has no way to check the validity of comments.

Hopkins also provides advice for programmers and artists on working together:

➤ Artists and programmers have totally different ways of looking at the world, and use totally different languages, and solve problems with extremely different approaches. It's important for artists to at least understand the basics of programming (what can and can't be done).

➤ Artists who can program are wonderful; they can implement their own artistic designs with integrity, and bridge the gap between other artists and programmers.

➤ Programmers working with artists should sit down with the artists to see how they use the tools and learn how to use the tools themselves.

➤ Even if you don't have any artistic ability, you need to be familiar with the workflow and vocabulary, as well as the capabilities of the tools.

➤ Before you design an engine, learn what the tools and artists can do. Work with the artists to make some sample content first, instead of designing the ideal engine without thinking about how you're going to create content for it. If you have some sample content, you have a concrete goal to get that content into your engine and onto the screen, looking like it's supposed to. Keep in mind that the artists will have to produce hundreds or thousands of individual pieces of content, so keep track of it all in a database, and make sure that [info as well as] validating and exporting can be done automatically. All of the information required to export the content should be contained in the file or a database. The exporter should never prompt for any parameters, so there's no chance of human error; and so it's possible to batch validate and export all the content without human intervention.

What, you think it's easy programming a game like *The Sims*? Take a gander at Don Hopkins' list of 12 different kinds of game programmers in this section. Shown here: Two images from the expansion pack for *The Sims*, dubbed "Hot Date."
(Used with permission by Electronic Arts, Inc.)

And a personal anecdote:

At the time I started designing the character animation system for *The Sims*, we were using 3D Studio Max with an early version of Character Studio. We started out using biped skeletons, but not the Physique skin mesh deformer. The artists could use Physique to make deformable meshes, but at the time, there was no way for a plug-in to read that information back out of Physique; it was a black box. So at first, we had to attach rigid body parts to each of the bones instead of using a continuous deformable mesh like Physique supported. I could have written my own Physique-like plug-in to attach deformable meshes to skeleton, but it would have been a waste of time and a nightmare to support, as well as a moot point when Physique's new API became available. When a new version of Character Studio was released with an API for reading out the vertex-to-bone bindings, I upgraded the character animation system to support deformable meshes.

Don Hopkins offers more educational and enlightening advice on programming artificial intelligence (Chapter 12), animation (Chapter 13, "Game Art and Animation"), and creating a successful user interface (Chapter 14, "The All-Important User Interface[UI] and Game Control").

> **NOTE**
> If you're having trouble keeping up with all the technical lingo dropped in this chapter, head on over to the *Game Dictionary* at `www.gamedev.net/dict`. Their motto? "Defining the Game Industry, One Word at a Time."

Bartosz Kijanka, Gas Powered Games

Currently working as VP of technology at Gas Powered Games (and having held the position of tech lead on 2002's *Dungeon Siege*), Bartosz Kijanka is an admired programmer who in part solved the problem with constant load times while playing computer games.

In this discussion, Bartosz chats about general programming theory and divulges some information on how the streaming technology was achieved in *Dungeon Siege*. First, he starts with some general advice for game programmers:

> Assuming that programmers already have a foundation in the required knowledge of conventional data structures and algorithms, I would suggest they keep the practices of prototyping, refactoring, and data-driving close to heart. Prototyping will help them experiment with new ideas, and refactoring will help them turn the prototype into a solid engine. Lastly, if the engine is data-driven, it will enable them to prototype rapidly and will empower them during the main content-creation phase. If the engine is heavily data-driven, they will be able to make frequent changes without recompiling and restarting, which will lead to faster prototyping as well as regular development.

Bartosz was asked to support his advice on "prototyping, refactoring, and data-driving" with *Dungeon Siege* (*DS*) as the product in question:

Prototyping

Dungeon Siege had such lofty technical goals from the very onset that early in the development we faced a huge number of unknowns. To add to the challenges our own ambitions posed, we also faced a rapidly moving hardware platform. Hardware 3D acceleration was in the process of quickly becoming the norm, rather than the exception. RAM prices were plummeting, and CPUs were up to their usual growth overachievements. CPU growth was relatively predictable, but RAM prices and 3D hardware acceleration were not.

Making a prototype is very much like doing a feasibility study. The goals are to quantify risk and estimate cost. In other disciplines, you might be able to go about this with simple pen and paper, but not in games. History has shown that the most instructive thing we can do in this case is to try and build at least a shadow of what we're ultimately aiming to do. So, we made our best guesses as to the hardware platform and then proceeded to prototype just about everything we were thinking of doing. Repeatedly, these efforts led to findings that changed the course of the game's development. In fact, it could be said that the entire development of *DS* was based on the interactions of game design with the feasibility findings of prototypes. Frequently, we had to reconcile what we wanted to build with what we found was possible. Had we been less flexible and maintained certain goals in spite of what our prototypes showed, *DS* would be less of a game than it is today.

Refactoring

Although much has been said about refactoring (or "re-engineering") in recent history, it all boils down to this: If it's broken, fix it. It's a simple idea, but for a large piece of software, "broken" can mean a dozen subtler things in addition to the program simply crashing or producing incorrect results. Although *Dungeon Siege* was created with the particular goal of being "fun," it also had to meet numerous other more technical constraints. These constraints included such things as engine execution speed, working data size, disk data size, code maintenance, and ease of content creation. When any one of these criteria wasn't met, the engine was effectively "broken" and had to be "fixed." *Dungeon Siege* constitutes dozens of subsystems, and fixing *DS* each time it fell outside the constraints meant at the very minimum that one or several systems were heavily modified. Occasionally, a subsystem would have to be entirely rewritten, and in the course of nearly four years of development, I would estimate that every subsystem was rewritten an average of two times.

"In retrospect," Bartosz continues, "this was a very large amount of re-engineering work, but we were trying to build a new type of engine." He explains:

Because this engine was different from all the others we've worked on, sometimes we didn't realize it was operating outside the constraints until well into the content-creation phase. Many problems didn't become apparent until the content creators started to push the engine with ridiculous amounts of content. Given these circumstances, refactoring was simply a requirement, and a requirement that was present late into the game's development. Had we not fully embraced this practice, *DS* would take 3–10 times the RAM it does, and execute at anywhere from one-quarter to one-tenth of the speed.

Data-driving

Focusing on simply having all the features present in a game engine is not enough. Today's games continue to include ever-increasing quantities of content, and *DS* is no exception. Because all of this content is placed and tuned by people, the importance of the process of working with the content became paramount when we thought about the sheer amount of content we needed and our limited resources.

Bartosz says several requirements come to mind here:

> ➤ We have to start creating content right away.

> ➤ Content creation has to be easy so that it can proceed quickly.

> ➤ Content creation can't require engineering participation because we're already booked.

> ➤ Content creation will require a significant number of people.

> ➤ Content is qualitative; therefore, it will involve a lot of iteration.

I must point out that when I refer to creating content, I'm not referring to creating geometry, textures, or sound effects. Fortunately, as an industry, we now have standard tools that with some customization allow us to create these atomic pieces of content. What I am referring to is the schematic describing of how these atomic pieces connect and interact. The content I'm speaking of is the layout of the terrain, the environmental controls, the placement and tuning of all the active content such as monsters and treasures, the scripting of the AI, spells, and many other details that sum up to create gameplay.

"The first constraint really set the tone for the rest," says Bartosz. "Because we knew it would be some time before we had an editor, to meet this requirement we needed much of the game to exist in a human-readable form that can be viewed and edited with Notepad." He continues:

> We needed to define much of the game and its rules in these data files instead of coding the functionality into the core engine. Thus, our .gas files were born. Our .gas files can be described as hierarchical INI files that act as definition and configuration files for much of the content. They are plain text and relatively easy to work with.

> The size of the world we wanted to build was such that it would have been sadistic to expect level designers to build this entirely in Notepad. Even though data being edited lives in simple little text files, to be truly effective, we needed serious automation to produce the amount of content required, which came later in the form of the siege editor.

> The .gas files weren't the sole incarnation of the data-driving ideal. We also had a couple of scripting languages, in which things such as AI, animation controllers, and special effects were written. Like the .gas files, the scripts could be edited at game runtime and reloaded. One could create new content such as a new monster definition with new AI, casting a new spell, without being forced to recompile or restart the game engine. This allowed for rapid prototyping of new content because it made iteration and tweaking much faster.

Bartosz was asked to address *Dungeon Siege*'s lack of load times (aside from the initial one). How was this achieved?

> Publicly, we refer to this as the "Continuous World Technology." Internally, we refer to it as the "streamer," whereas at other times we may call it the "million-dollar feature." I think this is consistent with the fact that the streaming nature of the engine isn't as much a single feature as it is an overall architecture theme. This architectural theme affected just about every subsystem in *DS*.

> The principle behind the streamer is simple: The world is so large that you can't possibly hold all of the content in memory at once. Given this constraint, the only thing you can do is only partially load the content that is currently needed. To aid in this endeavor, all the content in the world has to break down to small atomic pieces. If you could picture *Dungeon Siege* as being built from Lego™ pieces, you'd get the idea. All of the terrain is built by snapping small pieces we call siege nodes together. About 54,000 of these pieces are snapped together to build the single-player world. Each piece in turn may have content placed on it. Content can be anything from a monster to a table, chair, door, or even "invisible" content such as controllers for triggering quest events or non-interactive sequences. There are about 67,000 pieces of such content in the single-player world.

So how did Bartosz manage to keep only a portion of this massive amount of content in memory?

> Imagine that every one of your heroes is surrounded by an invisible box. This box is very large in comparison with the hero. As the hero walks over the game world, everything you see as you play happens to be inside the box that the hero is carrying with him. Everything outside of the box simply doesn't exist. As the hero walks north, the Lego pieces of the world are thrown away at the southern extreme of the box as new content pieces are loaded at the northern extreme. The box is only large enough to conceal

the fact that beyond that hill you see in front of you, the road comes to an abrupt stop and basically leads to nowhere. So, this box is made large enough that as a player you have no idea that you're playing inside this box. To the player, the perceived environment feels vast and continuous.

So, why bother with this "million-dollar feature?"

It is specifically this feeling of continuity that we were aiming for. In an RPG game, the aesthetic and feeling of the world are very important.

As we looked at the games we were playing at the time, we identified that loading screens actually break this aesthetic and distract you from the experience. We all believe that the absence of loading screens in our game is a major contributor to how immersive the game feels.

Bartosz was asked to dig a bit deeper to explain exactly how this streamer technology worked.

Well, we didn't call the streamer the "million-dollar feature" without good cause. Although in the beginning we treated it much like just another feature, eventually it became apparent that it was much more than that. The ideas behind the streaming architecture were simple, but the implementation was not. So, in order to truly explain how the streamer works, I would have to detail most of the inner workings of the siege engine. Because I can't get into such detail here, what I can do is to briefly outline the approach and resulting constraints.

Due to memory and CPU constraints, the approach was to break the world into atomic pieces, and work only with a subset of the data at any one point. The natural place to start with this was the terrain, which is built out of atomic pieces we call siege nodes. The siege nodes can be of arbitrary shape and size, and can have an arbitrary number of connections with other nodes. For sanity's sake, the artists adopted some conventions, which allowed them to make many standard-sized and interchangeable pieces, but the flexibility was always there and occasionally used when the regular-sized pieces just didn't do the trick. The terrain is therefore a connected graph of meshes with arbitrary connections and orientations. This makes it possible to build a farmhouse and connect a basement to its bottom; then have the basement lead to a deep dungeon that can lead to other limitless twists, turns, and depths. Because the terrain-connected graph can literally extend in any direction to any distance, the working set must be determined before any simulation or rendering takes place. The working set consists of what we find to be inside the culling volumes, which happen to be centered at each human-controlled character.

Next, Bartosz explains the associated complications:

Getting the terrain graph traversal and culling alone was in itself a challenge. But the fun was far from over. The culling placed strict constraints on how the content could work. Culling content as you moved through the master set of data meant that at all times some content was getting thrown out while new content was being loaded in. Because many types of content may interact with each other, and because some content needs a segment of space instead of just a point, we were faced with having to address countless culling boundary conditions.

Bartosz offers an example to further explain the issue:

For example, you are walking toward a hut. Far behind the hut, a level designer placed two monsters that are supposed to fight. As you approach the hut, only one of the monsters is loaded. The second monster is farther down the path and won't load for another five seconds. Well, by the point you reach the hut, you can already see the first monster. The problem at this point is that it has explicit instructions to fight with the second monster. Unfortunately, at that moment the second monster is culled out, and for all practical purposes doesn't exist. What does it do? It can't just sit there, stuck and waiting for the day its fighting buddy materializes, so it has to improvise. To address such cases, we had to add logic to the AI scripts to allow the monsters to choose a sensible plan B.

"As always, the devil is in the details, so the challenge here was making the monster behave sensibly when it's improvising," explains Bartosz. He continues:

Another great example illustrating the discontinuity that culling of the world created is a simple trap that opens or closes a door far away. The trap will send an event when triggered, but the door itself may be culled out. If the door is not in the current active set of content, it simply doesn't exist. So, in these cases, we had to devise a system of queuing certain events while expiring others based on the context and an elaborate set of conventions.

There are many such examples of how the world culling added complexity to the engine. Where possible, we masked the discontinuity. But, in the majority of the cases, these problems had to be addressed by a combination of engine changes, level design, and special-case scripting work. So much work was done to address these issues that I'll have to leave most of the details to your imagination.

After having the mechanics of the streaming working, the engineers at Gas Powered Games still had to address performance issues, says Bartosz:

Because *DS* is loading constantly as you play, loading assets couldn't possibly be fast enough to not disturb the primary thread that was responsible for rendering. In order to minimize the frame rate irregularities, we were forced to move the content loading to a separate thread. We did this relatively late in development, so minimizing blocking between the main and the loader thread was a challenge. Fortunately, this change was ultimately successful and was the last piece of the streaming puzzle.

For more information about Gas Powered Games, visit www.gaspowered.com.

Stephen White, Naughty Dog

Stephen White is the programming director of Naughty Dog, Inc., and was instrumental in the development of Naughty Dog's extremely successful *Crash Bandicoot* games (more than 22 million copies sold!) for the PlayStation, as well as Naughty Dog's recent *Jak & Daxter* series for the PlayStation 2.

When it comes to programming a game, White says the three best pieces of advice he could give are as follows, but cautions that "this is a tricky question, depending on your situation and your final goal."

Game development is often quite expensive, so budget and development time play a major part in how you should go about programming your game. The budget and development cycle will strongly influence how long you can spend working on tools, the game's engine, and the various gameplay elements. For the sake of brevity, let's assume that your budget and project length seem reasonable for the type of game that you wish to create.

My first bit of advice relates to scheduling your programming tasks. Scheduling is one of the most difficult problems in creating a game, and in my opinion is rarely done effectively. Many people err on the side of making a programming schedule too detailed, trying to predict too far in advance what will need to be done and how long it will take to do it. A detailed schedule is rarely accurate for more than a month, can become quite time-consuming to maintain, and often is demoralizing due to inaccuracies. It can also stifle creativity and make it difficult to adapt to changing situations. Not following a schedule can be equally disastrous because programming tasks often take much longer to complete than expected, and you must be able to measure a game's development progress so that you can adapt as necessary to make certain that you meet your project deadlines.

White says he recommends figuring out the major milestones that you want to achieve and creating a rough schedule of when you expect to achieve those milestones:

Maintain a detailed schedule for tasks related to achieving the upcoming milestones. Use both the milestones and the short-term detailed schedule to monitor the progress of the game, and be prepared to adapt as you compare your scheduled estimates with the reality of actual development. You will often find that your end goals and milestones will change significantly after you've done some actual development and can better estimate the time required for future tasks.

White's next bit of advice is to answer the following questions: What type of game are you trying to make? How is it different from other similar games? Why will it be appealing to your target audience?

After you've initially answered those questions, you should focus on creating the tools and a game engine to demonstrate that what you're trying to achieve is indeed a good idea. Don't become bogged down in superfluous implementation details until you've prototyped several of the core elements of what defines your games. You may find that after you've mocked up something that it isn't as fun or as interesting as you'd hoped it would be, or you may find that the technology is much trickier to implement than you had originally predicted. You want to make those kinds of unpleasant discoveries as early as possible in the development process so that you can adapt accordingly.

White suggests planning to spend a significant amount of programming time tuning gameplay:

All too often, programmers spend practically all of the development cycle working on technology and don't leave enough time to properly tune the gameplay. Remember that you're trying to make a game that's fun to play, and although technology can greatly enhance the overall game experience, it's the actual gameplay that often determines the success of your game.

What are some of the biggest obstacles for game programmers?

Time. The biggest obstacle to a game programmer would have to be time. I don't believe that I've ever heard of a programmer saying he had too much time to make a game. There's always more that you want to accomplish than there is time to accomplish it, and it's always a race to try to get as much stuff into your game as you can. This is why effective time management is critical to successful game development.

Another big obstacle is technology, says White:

Back when I started programming, games were programmed by one or two programmers, and commonly had three-month development cycles. In those days, most of the technology was focused on writing optimized code for a relatively simple processor, and the math that was used rarely exceeded the complexity of simple physics computations. Today, games are commonly developed by large teams of programmers, have multiyear development cycles, and are written for complex multiprocessor platforms capable of doing complex mathematical computations. The skills required to make competitive games are becoming so extensive that the industry is rapidly switching to programmers specializing in certain areas of programming, similar to how doctors will specialize in various areas of medicine. In the near future, it will be rare to find a programmer who could be considered to be an expert in all aspects of what will be common game-programming practices.

And an all-too-common obstacle is poor external management, adds White.

The video game industry is maturing, but is still a relatively new industry; as such, it is filled with people in management roles who have poor managerial skills. A poor manager can be very disruptive with frequent meetings, status reports, and scheduling; can create havoc with design and vision changes; and can have an overall demoralizing effect on the team. Because of this, even a very talented team can be rendered ineffective by poor management. This is an unfortunate reality, and all too often, the lead programmer must develop skills for shielding the programmers on his team from negative aspects of external management.

Finally, as with Gas Powered Games' *Dungeon Siege* (discussed earlier in this chapter), Naughty Dog's *Jak & Daxter* had no load times whatsoever—an extraordinary feat considering that the PlayStation 2 has no hard drive to store data! How was this achieved?

There are several ways to achieve having no load times, but they all come down to proper planning in advance. The essential problem is how you can load things in advance so that everything is loaded for an area by the time the player reaches that area. In the case of *Jak & Daxter*, we carefully created our world out of levels that seamlessly joined each other. The designers made certain that the player wouldn't be able to see more than two detailed levels at any one time, and that there was sufficient time to load a level that was approached by the player before the player reached a point where he could see the loaded level. As an example, the villages in *Jak & Daxter* were used as central hubs. If the player was in the village and walked toward the jungle, at some threshold we started loading the jungle; if the player changed his mind and started walking toward the beach, we'd stop loading the jungle and instead load the beach. Conceptually, this is all very simple; however, it required careful planning of both load boundaries and visibility with regard to level layout.

Although Chapter 24, "Game Design Resources on the Internet," is devoted to key resources for game designers and developers, Stephen White offers a few of his own recommendations here:

> The resources available to programmers nowadays are quite staggering. We've come a long way from the days when the only resources were a few cryptic, poorly written technical manuals. Because there are far too many resources for me to list, I'll just mention a few of my favorites. I'm a big fan of technical books, and am especially fond of the *Graphics Gems* books (Academic Press) and the *Programming Gems* books (Charles River Media). Also, *Computer Graphics: Principles and Practice* (Addison-Wesley), known fondly as the "Foley and van Dam" book, is practically considered required reading despite how long the book has been around. The Knuth *Art of Computer Programming* (Addison-Wesley) books are a fantastic reference, and any book by Alan Watt is worth reading. For advanced C++ techniques, I highly recommend reading the books by Scott Meyers (Addison- Wesley) because these books are informative and extremely well-written. My favorite magazine is *Game Developer Magazine* (Miller Freeman, Inc.), which has many great articles concerning various aspects of video game development. The Internet is also a fantastic source for programmers; filled with many great web sites covering relevant technologies, such as `www.gamasutra.com`. Even a cursory search of the Internet will reveal many great web sites with many great technical articles.

Catherine Roy and Éric Allard, Ubi Soft Entertainment

As a producer for the past six years at Ubi Soft Entertainment, Catherine Roy has worked on a number of projects. Her last published game was Disney's *Tarzan Untamed* for the PlayStation 2 and Nintendo GameCube. Along with the *Tarzan Untamed* lead programmer, Éric Allard, Roy discusses programming advice, techniques, and the tricks employed when creating this action/adventure.

Allard starts off by acknowledging PlayStation 2 programming limitations:

> Keep in mind the PS2 constraints. The technical requirements checklist from Sony can be very tricky, the memory space is pretty limited, streaming problems can occur, and the filesystem structure is quite complex.

> You absolutely need to plan some time to learn how to work on the PS2. The learning curve is gradual; it really takes a lot of time before you master the console. If you're coming from PC development, you might set your deadline too short if you don't plan for this.

Allard focuses on setting goals:

> It's important to set your goals clearly, both in terms of design and performance. Your programming team is going to be much more efficient if they have a clear idea of what result is expected in the end. Also, their code will be more specific if they know that the design won't change all the time and they don't have to code for multiple possibilities. In terms of performance, it's important that the programming team can give some performance numbers early in the project, so that the modelers don't bust the memory with too many polygons, textures, or palettes.

Catherine Roy contributes some of the challenges in creating *Tarzan Untamed*:

> One of the biggest challenges in the production of *Tarzan* was the interrelationship between the modeling and the level design. At first, the level designers would mock up the topography of their level in 3D Studio Max and then the modeler would try to make it look good. We soon found out that this process was inefficient because each time the gameplay would change, the modeler would have to redo everything. Also, each branch had to be individually mapped and textured.

> We ended up creating branch modules that would allow the game designers to create all the paths they wanted by just changing the spline in the module in 3D Max. Because they were always using the same modules, the modelers had to map the modules only once. After the topography was done, all they had to do was to make sure the transitions looked good. Obviously, they still had a lot of work to do on the map, but it made it easier to work on the playable path. It saved us a lot of time and made the relations between graphic artists and game designers easier.

> Although this technique really helped us, I still consider that the relations between game designers and modelers could have been better—I'm still seeking the best way to coordinate those tasks that affect all the teams at once.

As *Tarzan Untamed* producer Catherine Roy explains, one of the challenges of the game was to coordinate efforts between the programmers, level designers, and artists. These images show the textures being added to the wireframe models and then implemented into the game. The programmer must create the invisible boundaries for where Tarzan is supposed to walk on the branch.
(Ubi Soft Entertainment S.A. All Rights Reserved. Under license by ©, Disney. All Rights Reserved.)

In a recent conference, Roy discussed some procedures used to combat memory/load issues with the PlayStation 2, so she was asked to go over this useful information again here.

> The memory space is always a constraint when you're trying to create a beautiful game. The more polygons you have, the rounder the shape can be, but the heavier it will be in memory. Having to create a jungle environment was a big challenge. We had to give the impression of depth and density while creating trees and vegetation that would look organic. It became really important to use wisely all the polygon count we were allowed to display or to load in memory.

We use the "instances" technique to reduce the space in memory that our maps take. We can use a rock, a tree, or any item, and duplicate it in the map. When we use the instances of the model, we count the polygons and textures of that object only once in memory, although we display it multiple times. We still have to manage the display limits, but we can get better results and still fit in the 32MB of memory on the PlayStation 2.

We also put a lot of energy into the creation of impressive skyboxes. They are big background textures, applied on a huge cylinder. On that cylinder is the horizon, the mountains far away, the sky, and so on. Only with this skybox, we immediately got the feeling of the map we wanted to create. Then when we put some 3D objects closer to the characters, it gave the sense of depth we were looking for.

Read more from Catherine Roy in Chapter 13 (on video game art and animation) and in Chapter 14 (on game control and creating a solid user interface).

Brian Reynolds, Big Huge Games

In Chapter 3, Brian Reynolds (who, at last check, was relishing in the critical success of his *Rise of Nations* game, published by Microsoft in May 2003) discusses some strategy game design techniques. This section outlines a few of his random programming tips as well as some do's and don'ts.

In a previous edition of this book, Reynolds advised programmers, "Get in there and make something you can play right away!" He elaborates here on that comment:

Strategy games are extremely complex to design—although the individual components look deceptively simple; having a *lot* of "simple" moving parts makes for a very complex overall balancing task. It's easy to look at a strategy game and say, "I could make this better—I'd add this and this and this," but very hard to actually integrate lots of new parts into a game system without breaking the things that were already fun. To balance all the moving parts correctly, there's no substitute for actually playing your own game—the combinatorial explosion from all the moving parts makes it impossible to truly anticipate or tune results "on paper" in a design document. The sooner you get your game running, the sooner you can actually get to work on making the game fun and making it balanced. Both fun and balance tend to be taken for granted by novice designers: They think, "If I make a game about topic X and it has features A, B, and C and technology J, it will be fun," but as it turns out, fun and balance both take a lot of hard work.

As far as do's and don'ts are concerned, Reynolds offers the following:

> ➤ Do play your own game at least once a week, preferably several times.

> ➤ Don't be afraid to write some code that you might have to throw away—when you think of a cool idea, whip up some code to try it. We end up throwing away a lot of ideas, but that's how we end up sifting out the good ideas. The same goes for art, by the way—don't be afraid to do some prototype art to try an idea that might not work.

➤ To designers and project leaders: Do learn how to program. Many people have great ideas for games, but only a few have the skills to actually bring their ideas to life. Even if you learn only the basics of C++, it can let you do some of your own balance tweaking and help you make informed decisions about whether it's really "too hard" to implement your cool idea.

➤ To programmers: Do learn how to balance, design, and write (English, that is). Immerse yourself in gameplay (both your own game and lots of other games—competitors' games, board games). Think about how games work. What are the specific things that you like in a game and the specific things that you dislike? Do you see themes and rules that seem to apply across many different situations and games? The better you understand the principles of game design and balance, the more effective your coding will be and the more cogent your contributions to the game itself.

Be sure to read Chapter 12 on programming artificial intelligence for some more words of wisdom from the one and only Brian Reynolds.

David Wu, Pseudo Interactive

Before becoming the president and a lead programmer at Canada's Pseudo Interactive, David Wu worked on games such as *Wing Commander: Prophecy* and *Ultima Ascension* at Origin Systems. His last project was *Cel Damage*, published for the Xbox and GameCube platforms in 2001 and 2002, respectively. In May 2003, Pseudo unveiled their latest project: *Vectorman* for the PlayStation 2, to be published by Sega of America, Inc. in 2004.

Wu dispenses some programming and game design advice. Let's start with general game design:

➤ **Distill your design**. Write a design doc that's more than 100 pages; then keep the best 16 pages. That's what you'll have time to accomplish. [See Chapter 6, "Creating Characters, Storyboarding, and Design Documents," on creating a design document; and Chapter 7, "Master Design Document Template," for the design document template provided by Chris Taylor.]

➤ **It's all about the experience**. Pay attention to people playing the game; pay attention to people listening to your pitch. Make sure they get it. What's in your mind may not be what game players experience when they sit down to play.

➤ **Keep the focus**. Make sure that your whole team is on the same page. You're the visionary of the game; make sure that everyone knows where they're going and why.

When programming a game, Wu says these are the most important considerations for a game programmer:

➤ **Get to "first playable" as soon as possible**. Get something up and running that demonstrates gameplay.

➤ **Work with the team**. Listen to your artists and designers and respect their ideas—even if they don't understand the finer points of numerical integration.

➤ **It's all about the experience**. Keep in mind the fact that you're creating a game, not a technical showpiece. The code serves to deliver the experience. Spend your time programming the features that make this possible.

David Wu offers three behind-the-scenes color drawings of
characters from *Cel Damage* and a never-before-seen sketch
of one of the levels in the game.
(Used with permission by Pseudo Interactive, Inc. and Electronic Arts, Inc.)

Wu says all that hard work programming your game won't pay off if no one cares about it—in fact, Wu recalls that *selling* the concept of *Cel Damage* was the most difficult obstacle to overcome.

The first and hardest hurdle that you face is creating a build that your producers, their marketing team, and your dev team understand and enjoy playing. If marketing gets it, your producer thinks that it will be profitable, and your team loves to play the game, you've got a winner. Until you reach this point, your game is in danger, like a frog playing in traffic.

People have written many papers on the art or science known as the "pitch." Some people think that you can sell a game on great ideas alone, or you can sell a game by learning exactly how to deliver the pitch. It's not that easy; I personally have been turned down more times than I can count. Imagine that you have a prototype and you've managed to earn the audience of a prospective producer who might fund your title. If you're as naïve as I was, you'll be rambling off design ideas, technical jargon, and plans for your title. Your prospective producer will be focusing his or her attention on the distillation of one facet of your game: the end user experience. Your prototype has to convince your producer beyond any reasonable doubt that the experience your game will deliver is worth $60. Your customers want a game that they can play; a game that they understand; a game that's fun. Far too many developers (myself included) focus on presenting a game that's technologically advanced; has breathtaking visuals; or has a deep, compelling, and complex design. Developers want to create a masterpiece; gamers want a fun game. Show your producer that you understand what gamers want—not a dream, but a down-to-earth, compelling, interactive experience.

Having created games for both PC and console platforms, Wu can speak knowledgeably about the differences between the two from a programming perspective:

[With a console], you have a fixed platform, which is nice. Unfortunately, your fixed platform doesn't have the resources of a PC, and your development environment may be primitive. Quality assurance is less forgiving: PC games crash; console games should not.

The most significant difference, however, is in the games that you create. The best console games are worlds apart from the best PC titles. If you have the luxury of choosing a platform, ask yourself, "Do I prefer console games or PC games?" The hardware differences are secondary to the overall design differences.

Can he support this advice with an example? Wu responds wryly, "It has taken me about six years to learn what I know. More than half of it is completely wrong—but *Cel Damage* is evidence that some of it has value, too."

Read more from Wu in Chapters 12 and 14, on programming AI and on creating a good user interface, respectively.

Peter Molyneux, Lionhead Studios

One of the computer gaming industry's most recognizable names and faces (and for good reason!) is Peter Molyneux, creator of many time-tested games such as *Populous*, *Magic Carpet*, *Dungeon Keeper*, and the *Black & White* series.

Molyneux speaks about general game design theory in Chapter 3; here, he shares some thoughts on game programming:

➤ Embrace C++ and the Standard Template Library fully, and don't be tempted to challenge people like Stroustrup.

➤ Don't expect to find all the answers to all your problems in papers and books—chances are that the solution doesn't exist, and this may mean that you'll be the person to invent it.

➤ Before starting a new project, get the foundation stones of library class design built.

Louis Castle, Electronic Arts/ Westwood Studios

"Programming is a vast discipline, but I'll try to be brief," begins Louis Castle, general manager and co-founder of Westwood Studios. Castle offers these do's and don'ts as programming tips:

➤ Plan your code to fulfill the design.

➤ Solve problems systemically.

➤ Allow for exceptions.

➤ Document your code design.

➤ Document your code.

➤ Read the ACM, books, and papers.

➤ Talk about your plan with other coders.

➤ Prototype ideas; plan systems.

➤ Don't code without a plan.

➤ Don't mix datatypes.

➤ Don't reinvent the wheel.

➤ Don't patch the patch.

➤ Don't plug in prototypes that don't fit the system design.

Greg Thomas, Sega of America/Visual Concepts

As president of visual concepts and vice president of product development at Sega of America, Greg Thomas brings more than a dozen years of experience to the table. As mentioned in his bio in Appendix A, "Biographies," Thomas is considered the mastermind behind the award-winning Sega Sports *NFL2K* series, along with more than 20 other games throughout his prolific career.

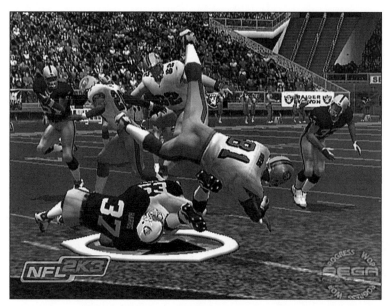

Greg Thomas says the biggest challenge of creating the coveted *NFL2K* football games is working out the collision system. Read here how Sega overcame this obstacle. This screen grab is from *NFL2K3* for the PlayStation 2 platform.
(Used with permission by Sega of America, Inc.)

When programming the *NFL2K* series, what were some of the biggest obstacles you faced, and how were they overcome?

> The biggest obstacle we faced with these games was our collision system. For our collisions to be accurate, we had to do true 3D collision. In the past, we had only done simpler cylinder collision, in which it's very easy to designate an object as a cylinder. But with *NFL2K*, this wasn't acceptable; we needed to collide with all parts of the body properly. We did this by putting collision spheres on our player model and moved them as the model animated. This was a bit tricky, but it ended up working well and making a large difference in the accuracy of our football game.

Any tips for newbie programmers who want to create the next big thing? Thomas responds by emphasizing that being a very structured programmer is extremely important. He expands on this notion:

> Games are getting to be huge projects. *NFL2K* had more than 500,000 lines of code in it! And the place where structured programmer is taught is college. So, even though I wouldn't have said this five years ago, today I believe going to programming classes in college is important in this regard.

Steve Hunt

Programming a simulation such as *Eurofighter Typhoon*? Who better to learn from than Steve Hunt, who served as lead designer and coder on the game at Rage in the UK. Unfortunately, Rage closed its doors in early 2003.

Hunt discusses some of the more crucial concerns to keep in mind when programming a simulation:

> ➤ **Focus your efforts in key areas**. Simulations are an approximation to real life. Don't try to simulate everything in the finest detail—you can't. The detail needs to go where the player will notice it. There's no point in modeling the crabs on the beach as you fly past at Mach 2 in your fighter aircraft. At the end of the day, simulation is illusion, and that's your job—you have to create the illusion that the player is in a battle with thousands of other units, without necessarily simulating all of it at a low level.

> ➤ **Debugging**. It's important to design and write your code in a way that will make it easy to debug. Simulations are complex anyway; don't make life harder by making the code harder to read, just so you can save a few bytes here and there. *Typhoon* has more than one million lines of code; when someone says, "The planes keep landing on the sea," you've got to be able to find and trace through the code that handles this. If you use overly complex or indirect coding styles, you'll be working a good few nights and weekends as a result.

> ➤ **Expect the unexpected. And believe what testers tell you**. The number of times I've had a bug report and thought, "There's no way my code will do that—the tester must be wrong," only to go and watch them play and suddenly think, "Oh, so you're doing *that*—well, that will make it go wrong"… If while you're writing your code, you find yourself thinking, "This could go wrong if *this* happens, but, hey, that doesn't matter—it's really unlikely," think again; it probably will happen. Either put in some safety code or make it more robust. You can almost guarantee that what you think of as unlikely will happen a hundred times *after* the game has gone out!

Were there any obstacles when creating *Eurofighter Typhoon*? Hunt responds:

One of the biggest problems with PC game development is the constantly changing hardware capabilities and the changing versions of DirectX that come with it. *Typhoon* took two years to develop, and in that time machine speed and features sets have gone wild. We started on DX6, went to DX7 halfway through development, and by the time *Typhoon* was released, DX8 was already available for public download. The big problem is that with PC games, "What you see is *not* what you get"—on one machine, the game will look great; on another, it will be slow and buggy. Just testing the product with the various graphics cards available is a total nightmare. Even worse, so-called obsolete cards that are no longer supported by the original manufacturer account for a large proportion of our potential customers—so we have to find a way to get these working, too. There's no real way around these problems on a PC; you just have to firefight your way through all the problems. It can be very stressful and frustrating; but on the other hand, it teaches you to be adaptive in your problem-solving abilities, which in turn helps you design and write better code.

I'm now developing on PS2, and it's such a great feeling to know that what I see on my dev box is what all the players will see when they play our game. Without all the distractions of constantly changing hardware and software—and not having to write for slow and fast PCs at the same time is a real release.

Among other tips, Steve Hunt says it's very important to write your code in a way that will make it easy to debug: "Simulations are complex anyway; don't make life harder by making the code harder to read just so you can save a few bytes here and there." Here are a couple of great shots from Hunt's latest game, *Eurofighter Typhoon*.
(Used with permission by Rage Games, Ltd. and Take Two Interactive, Inc.)

Hunt summarizes the difference in programming a PC versus a console game:

Console: What you see is what you get—you have to be very efficient in every aspect of the game.

PC: Loads of power can be relatively sloppy with code and art—but you'll never know what the end user is going to see or how well your game will run. You'll also spend a good six months testing and trying to keep up with hardware changes.

Although he's been heavily involved in PC flight simulations for the last six years, Hunt has now moved on to what he's always wanted to do—designing and producing an action game on a console.

Although I enjoyed my flight sim days, it's just so much more rewarding developing more mainstream games and working on a stable platform such as a console. I'm really excited about our current product, which I can't say anything about! As for the future, the technology will change and production methods probably will too (will we be writing code in 10 years' time?), but one thing I'm certain of is that you'll always need designers to come to you with ideas that will make a good game. This part of the process will never become obsolete. Designing and producing games is one of the most exciting and rewarding jobs I can think of. The industry is still young compared to that of film or music, and the technology is changing what we can do in games every six months (the most obvious is the emergence of console online gaming). I think there are going to be many interesting times ahead.

Be sure to flip to Chapter 12, where Hunt chats about coding realistic AI.

James Schmalz, Digital Extremes

James Schmalz of Digital Extremes co-developed *Unreal, Unreal Tournament,* and *Unreal Championship* along with Epic Games.

Asked whether it's best to license an existing game engine or design your own, Schmalz says it depends entirely on what your game design goals are, and should be evaluated on a game-by-game basis:

> If you're developing a game that requires a strong technology component and there's an engine that already does what you need, it's probably best to start with the licensed engine. A good example is if you're trying to create a new first-person shooter with a unique gameplay twist. It will definitely be best to start with an existing engine rather than trying to build one from scratch. Trying to build one from scratch for this type of game is an extremely difficult task. On the other hand, if you're trying to build a real-time strategy or adventure game, it probably doesn't make sense to license an engine.

What if you're just starting out in the business?

> If that's the case, it's much easier to prototype your game and get it up and running using an existing game engine. Usually, the supplier of the engine will let you develop a prototype or demo and let you attract a publisher before committing you to payment for use of the engine. So, in this sense, it's very practical to use an existing game engine. For that reason, it makes that much less sense to try to create your own engine if you have little or no money.

Although it may vary greatly, Schmalz says licensing a game engine—such as the *Unreal, Quake,* or LithTech engines—can cost a company anywhere from $100,000 with royalties to $750,000 without royalties. Ouch!

The obvious benefit of licensing an engine is time, says Schmalz:

> Without a doubt, it saves you a lot of time, as long as the engine does specifically what you want it to do. For example, if you are doing a new tactical FPS, you are probably much better off licensing an engine.

He believes the cons for licensing an engine are as follows:

> ➤ Working with an evolving technology, which is tricky whether you're doing it yourself or the engine licensing company is doing it.
>
> ➤ Coming up-to-speed on a huge amount of someone else's code is always difficult.
>
> ➤ If the technology is finished, it might start to become a little dated by the time you finish your game.

> The perfect engine-licensing situation is for a game that doesn't require bleeding-edge technology, in which the available engine has been built around a similar game.

Schmalz was asked to give some tips for those who want to program games. "If you want to code games for a living, you *must* do one of two things," says Schmalz:

> ➤ Make little games in your spare time. Make them better and better, and try to do some cool impressive stuff.

> ➤ Get into the MOD communities and work with a MOD team to make some awesome MODs.

There is nothing better to prepare yourself for a career in making games than to actually make games in your spare time. That is the absolute #1 piece of advice I could give a budding programmer who wants to code games for a living.

Regarding general game design, Schmalz says he can offer the following tips to those just starting out:

Make a "Fun" Game

Far, far too many people either don't understand how to make something fun or they lose focus on other things such as technology or visuals. Technology and visuals are great, but if the game is not fun, it's nothing. "Fun" is by far the overwhelmingly important factor in a good game, and it is often missed.

Schedule

Even the most advanced game developers still have problems with this. It takes a lot of experience just to understand all the things that will add up and eat away at your development time. If you make it too tight, you can be forced into releasing a crappy game because it's simply not finished.

Project Scope

It is certainly possible to make a really fun and successful small game on schedule that still makes a lot of money. Far too many new developers try to tackle the "be-all and end-all" game with no real idea of what it's going to take to finish it properly. That will no doubt result in disaster.

But can a game design create something compelling if it's not truly original? Where does *Unreal Championship* fit in?

You have to be really, really good to be able to come up with a completely new type of game. They are very few and far between. Most great games are either an evolution of a style of game or a combination of two or more styles, giving the player a fresh new experience. In addition, you don't want something too different in the game design that the users cannot relate to. They at least need the basic premise of the game to be somewhat familiar.

I applaud the designers who try things that are totally different and off the wall. Most of those types of games will fail, but the occasional gem comes out to define an entirely new type of game. I would point out *The Sims* as being a recent gem that defines a new style of game, but even that has its roots in the "God sim" games.

In addition, very few designers have the resources to try something completely different. Only the absolute premiere designers can say, "Trust me with your $10,000,000—really, even though it sounds crazy, the game will rock," and have someone with that kind of money believe them.

Having worked on both this year, Schmalz was asked to discuss the differences between working on a PC game and a console game.

> The biggest difference is memory. Nowadays, the consoles are far more limiting, even though the graphics horsepower is similar.

> Second is the controls—this is a huge issue. The PC is keyboard and mouse, and the consoles have their controller. Your game simply has to be designed to work best with the control system on the platform you are targeting.

> A third issue is the target audience. There are certainly different expectations for a console game than for a PC game.

As an example, Schmalz says the most obvious is fighting games—they simply don't sell on the PC, yet they're some of the largest sellers on the consoles.

Doug Church, Freelance

Doug Church has been involved in game design and programming for more than 12 years. His early projects included *Ultima Underworld* (with small teams of four to eight people) and *Ultima Underworld II*, whereas newer games include *System Shock*, *Flight Unlimited*, and *Thief*. Over the past two years, Church has been consulting as a game designer and programmer while working on a PlayStation 2 music game.

Church says there are many things to keep in mind if you want to program a successful game, and has provided a few suggestions here. He cautions that most of these comments focus on the design side of programming rather than "practical coding." Okay, here we go:

> ➤ Your first client is the player. If you're working on code that isn't going to positively impact the player experience, make sure there's a good reason for it. Being super clever isn't necessarily more fun. Writing the coolest-ever thing X isn't necessarily relevant. Sometimes, of course, it's exactly what should be done to maximize fun, but other times it's a programmer just wasting time.

> ➤ Your next clients are the designers. Coding to allow the designers to be more creative will result in a better game. It's always frustrating when you build a system and feel it's underutilized, but often the code or tools are to blame. Tightening the design loop is vital, so that a designer (whether that's someone else or you wearing your design hat) can make real changes to the game and see the effects instantly. If a change requires recompiles or re-releases of the code so that every tweak, change, or fix requires three days before you can see the results, it's very hard to really improve and squeeze every bit out of a system. To really improve quality, figure out what you can expose in the runtime environment to direct design input and then make sure it's easy to play with.

➤ Computer games require a synthesis of technology and design. However, it's the programmers' job to understand (and often create) that technology. So they have the responsibility for understanding the design goals and working with the designers to make sure that the gameplay takes full advantage of what the tech can do—and that the tech fits the goals of the design. As an example, simulation and emulation are vital but very different ways to have a game world respond to player input. Deciding which to use for various game systems will determine how the game feels. This is a fairly common decision to have to make, and one that's often made by default rather than by planning.

➤ Flexibility. This is related to the second item in this list. Good games rarely happen because a 200-page spec was slavishly followed. Changes, tuning, mistakes, opportunities—they all happen. The best games are ready to react, to find cool accidents and turn them into extra fun, and to abandon "cool ideas" that aren't working out. Much of this is a management/project vision/design problem. But without flexible code, which is understood by a tech team that's willing to make changes, there is little hope.

Any other real-world, real-game examples?

Of over-engineering/cool code that was irrelevant: In *Underworld*, our levels had chasms in them, which were deep and had to be jumped by the player. So, our AI non-player characters had to know how to deal with that and jump across them as well. To make it "fair," we wanted AIs to need running starts (well, to have enough velocity when they jumped). So our AIs, if they reached a chasm going too slowly following/chasing the player, would back up, start running, and jump the chasm. This was very cool, and using our detachable camera code in the editor we could make sure it worked and all that. That said, I'm sure no player of the game ever saw it happen because it pretty much only happened *behind* the player, by definition. Oh, well.

Of the importance of tools (and clients, really): In *Thief*, our initial AI scripting system was a simplified messaging wrapper, allowing designers to write OnXXXXXX() calls, which listened for a given event (OnNotify, OnAlert, and so on) and reacted to it. Then they could write fairly arbitrary code, check links, send messages, control the AI, and so on. This was very rarely used because it required some extra compilation tools and was essentially scary. Later in the project, Tom Leonard, our lead programmer and main AI guy, wrote a "pseudo-scripting" system, which was an in-world editor, menu-driven "script" system allowing designers to pick event triggers and have simple formulaic responses (OnAlertness 2, Go to Obj X, Go into combat mode, Run Away, or whatever). As soon as this went in, our designers started using them heavily, and the AI got about 10 times more interesting, even though the raw capabilities of pseudo-scripts were far *less* than the full scripting system. This is an obvious lesson that everyone knows (including us), but the mistake continues to be made and recovered from each time.

On the player experiencing "not cool" tech: In *Flight Unlimited*, for the longest time we had four separate programs, basically: a terrain renderer, a physics engine, a training/judging module, the FBO movement system. They all were fairly cool and interesting; however, they never got put together. Everyone assumed it would be easy to just take them and attach them with menus and UI and have a game. Needless to say, the "simple merge" took ages, was incredibly painful, and meant that when we were done we had a lot of mismatched systems and missed opportunities in which things could have really worked together, but didn't. Important to solve the problem of "what experience is the player getting, and how," not "how can we write neat stuff that we find cool."

On flexibility and feedback loop for designers: In *Ultima Underworld (UW)* and *System Shock*, our object systems were simple hierarchies of structures with the fields of their parents and themselves. This obviously was very easy to implement, and matches well the way C/C++ thinks about objects. However, it's really bad for games. When designers wanted to add a new object/behavior [or new] data, they had to fit it into a rigid hierarchy, explain it to a programmer, and wait for the next build. Adding behaviors to objects often required some bizarre new subclass (such as a talking door—in *UW*, we just had a hidden creature and wrote totally hacked special code to make this work).

In *Thief*, by contrast (and *System Shock 2*), we used a new object engine, which allowed designers to add properties to any object, create simple new properties, and so on. This made it much easier for them to experiment and iterate without getting blocked by programmers. Any fancy behavior would often require coding, of course, but the layout of the object tree and the assignment of behaviors was completely under designer control and far more flexible.

On the lessons front: a huge one that I've mentioned elsewhere ("Write a game, don't publish a paper"). In *Deus Ex*, the original design doc called for "realistic AI opponents." What this meant was that in early versions, you would round a corner and be shot dead by some guy on a catwalk with a rifle—you never saw or heard him because the alarm had sounded, he was on patrol, he was ready, he saw you, and he shot you. Perfectly reasonable, but totally un-fun. The real goal of the AI, of course, had nothing to do with being "realistic"; it had to do with being fun. By ship time, the DX guys had changed the AI behavior so they deliberately said things such as "My gosh, I see him," waited to fire while loading/reloading ammo, ran extra motions to indicate they were getting ready to fire, and so on. A paper (or research project) focused on "good" combat AI would not go this direction, but a game AI has to, or it will be no fun. Remember what your goal is—the player experience—not "the right thing" for some abstraction. Context is always vital.

Many new game developers wonder whether to spend the time, money, and effort to develop a custom game engine or scrape up the cash to purchase an existing engine and simply modify it. What's Church's take on this?

"It depends completely on what you want to do," Church answers. He elaborates:

The current engines are very cool and can be a big help, but they're still very young. Most engines are very good at doing games like their own and less flexible when it comes to changing the model. Games such as *Half-Life* and *Deus Ex* were licensed engines, but also had significant rewrite and cost just as much as an unlicensed game to make. So engines are not some silver bullet. If you're going to use one, the most important issue is probably to realize early on where your design is in conflict with the engine. Then either change the design or make sure you have time and resources to make changes to the engine.

I suppose anything is feasible. But the list of "good game engines" that have been made by a group just starting out is vanishingly small, and the list of engines that have produced really solid flexible tools without money is also short.

Titles such as *Thief* and the *Ultima Underworld* series were quite unique; how can you create something fun but different?

There are many ways people have done that, though I'm not sure how many of them were recognized as [unique] until the game came out and did well. Personally, I focus on the player and what I consider the cool thing about computers. I believe that our unique capability as a medium is to allow the player to be center stage, as opposed to the designer. Most other artistic media focus on the artist, who presents an authored work. Although we author our work as well, we can choose to focus on authoring procedures and systems. This allows for players to be the focus and explore themselves more directly than in other media. This isn't to say that all games should do this or that things that don't are somehow bad. But that's the part of creating computer games that I personally find most interesting. So I try to work out new ways to enable players to have control, and to express themselves and see what it's like. As someone who is into the player, I try to use simulation models for game state and so on as much as possible. Then I usually try to figure out a "more traditional" game like that and then try to mix the two.

I mostly have [my current projects] set up as almost Trojan horses, in which players start playing, assuming that they're playing a fairly straightforward RPG with some cool new stuff, and that's how the game starts. An hour or two in, when the player realizes how different it is, he hopefully is having so much fun that he just doesn't worry about it…

John Scott, Raven Software

As a technology programmer at Raven Software, John Scott has worked on many games, including *Heretic II*, *Star Trek: Voyager—Elite Force*, *Soldier of Fortune*, and *Soldier of Fortune 2*, published by Activision in 2002.

Scott helps budding game programmers by offering some advice on the trade.

The trick is to keep it simple; develop a system that does everything the designers ask it to do, code it so you can expand when the inevitable "Can you…?" questions come up, but don't do any more unless it's a native part of the system. If you're working with an existing system, work out what kind of data it can really chomp on and what drags it to a halt; experiment, find its limits and capabilities, and find what breaks it. Don't be too clever with tech; keep the code clean and easily maintainable. Also, put in plenty of code to be able to list what assets are resident, how much memory is being used, and what part of the system is having a hard time.

What if someone is creating game modifications (MODs)—extra levels, maps, or new game modes—to sharpen their skill? Scott comments:

From the perspective of a "modder," experiment with very simple ideas first, get them working, and then move on to concepts evolved from that. Don't try a really neat complex idea first because you'll most likely circumvent the correct way of doing things—leading to obscure bugs and performance problems later on.

What was the most challenging part about programming *Soldier of Fortune*?

> Random mission generator physics. This is because physics are extremely hard to code in a predicted networking environment. There's also very little in the way of audio or visual feedback. If you make an effect, you can see what you're doing; if you get stuck occasionally at arbitrary coordinates while crouching mid-jump, how do you know whether the problem is fixed? I just stuck at it, painfully getting exact reproducible cases until every little issue was fixed.

An example of networking woes:

> When the player moves forward, the client sends this message off to the server and moves the local player forward (this is the prediction bit). The server detects that someone has shot this player some fraction of a second ago, recalculates his coordinates, and sends that back down to the client. The client then sets the local player to the position the server says, resulting in a jump in positions. All well and good so far—in theory. However, in real life, the Internet suffers from packet loss and lag. What happens if the server never received the message from the client (due to packet loss), or if the client has a laggy connection, so the server message arrives well after the player has moved on?

Flip to Chapter 12 to read Scott's opinions on artificial intelligence.

Michael Raymond-July

Formerly a designer at Raven Software, Michael Raymond-July has worked on many games for the past 10 years. (We hear from him in Chapter 8, "Level Design," and Chapter 10, "Mission Design.") Here, he talks about programming *Star Wars: Jedi Knight 2—Jedi Outcast.*

First, some quick tips provided by Raymond-July:

> ➤ Fast and fun is better than pretty but slow. The reason it has taken so long to make games with near real-time lighting effects and nearly true curves isn't because the technical know-how wasn't there; it's because hardware couldn't make it fast enough. From past painful experience, I can say that pushing the envelope is good only to the point where players are impressed by appearance, but not distracted by slow or awkward gameplay.

> ➤ Do what has to be in the game before playing with what might be "cool," but isn't part of the core game. Elegant clean design that's fun to play beats a host of nice but irrelevant features every time.

> ➤ Have enough hands to carry the load. A single brilliant mind (okay, one exception here, maybe) can't make up for all the drudge work necessary to deliver a game on time and bug-free. "When it's done" makes a nice wall plaque, but it doesn't put product on the shelf in time to pay the bills—[that requires] having enough people to get all the work done.

Raymond-July discusses a hurdle he and his team faced on *Star Wars: Jedi Knight 2—Jedi Outcast*—the short timetable:

Ironically, we prevented this from being an impossible obstacle by not leaping right into building maps. We spent the first month or so (some people had longer than that) planning out all the missions in detail, including which enemies would be where and what resources you'd have to fight them, architecture and layout, concept sketches, everything. This meant that when designers started to actually build the map, they knew exactly what they had to do and what it should look like. This is so much faster than the traditional "build and then rebuild" method that it more than made up for the initial time investment.

And in case you wonder about leaving the designer feeling like a "brush monkey," the person assigned to build a given level was an important part of the team laying out that level and usually was responsible for coming up with a good part of the layout and content. There was no lack of "sense of ownership" at all.

"Have enough hands to carry the load," suggests Raymond-July, on programming a game. Pictured here is
Jedi Knight II—a popular PC action game released in the first half of 2002.
(© 2002 LucasArts Entertainment Company LLC and its Licensors. LucasArts and the LucasArts logo
are registered trademarks of Lucasfilm, Ltd. All rights reserved.)

Ed Magnin, Magnin & Associates

Ed Magnin has programmed many games for the Apple II/IIe, Super Nintendo (*NFL Football*), Game Boy (*Prince of Persia* and *Caesar's Palace*), and a handful for the Game Boy Color (*Extreme Sports with the Berenstain Bears, Arthur's Absolutely Fun Day!, Wings of Fury, Prince of*

Persia, *Moon Patrol*, and *Spy Hunter*). He also teaches video game programming at Palomar College in San Marcos, California (near San Diego). Several of his former students are now gainfully employed in the industry!

Magnin shares his vast game programming knowledge for those just starting out in the interactive entertainment industry. First, he reminds wannabe game programmers that it's hard work! "It's not all fun and games—there are long hours and lost summers." And Magnin says you often have to complete and submit a game earlier than you think:

> Computer games can be manufactured at the last minute, but with consoles (cartridge-based games), you have to send it off for Nintendo to approve it for a month…then wait in line to be manufactured, which takes another two to three months…then you wait in line to be tested…and so forth. Therefore, a development team has to finish a product in June or July for the holidays.

As an amusing anecdote on how much work this is, he recalls working on the *Three Stooges* game:

> I was working on the pie fight scene, and my daughter came in and [said] how fun it is, what I was working on—throwing pies at each other. Then she came in the next day and saw the same thing. And the next day after that. She finally asked, "How many times are you going to work on it?" My response was, "Oh, 300 to 400!"

So how long does an average Game Boy title take to develop? Magnin says seven to nine months.

When working on a game, Magnin comments, a programmer has to be a bit schizophrenic; while you're trying to enjoy it, you're also trying to destroy it at the same time in order to test it and find bugs and such. He suggests taking all the programming classes you can while you still have the time:

> Make sure that you have a good understanding of physics, trigonometry, probability, combinations and permutations, binary and hexadecimal numbers. Right now, if you're a student, you should take C and assembly language. Even though it may not be the same language you'll work on in the "real world," it'll be familiar and similar…it's kinda like learning French—you can learn Italian pretty easily after that.

Magnin's advice is to keep current:

> Read lots of books and articles. You have to keep learning new platforms, as new ones come out every two to three years. Because you won't have time later…you have to like learning, keeping current, buying books.

One thing Magnin teaches in his classes is the key difference between programming a game versus programming other software: Things need to run *fast*. In fact, this is a mandatory question on his midterm exams!

There's always some kind of main loop. (Did anyone hit me with a bullet? Was I running? Was I running and was hit by a bullet?) Many others are waiting for a keypress, not on a loop, redrawing the screen, seeing if anyone moved, seeing if a bullet has hit its target. Something is always happening. Unlike a word processing document, there's no safe place to stand in a game.

Another important note taught to Magnin's students is that projects cannot be late. To drive home the point, Magnin says if a project is late, he drops the student one letter grade; if it's late again, it drops yet again. This teaches them about the real world.

There are times when everyone is partying or playing volleyball at the beach, and you have to be disciplined—because it's going to happen. I had this student who was a genius, very talented, but he never finished anything. He won't make it in the industry—you have to finish something. GT Interactive [lost] 600 people because four games were late!

And here's another tip from Magnin he picked up from creating Game Boy titles: "If there's extra space on the cartridge, you'll need that space for multiple languages, so don't use it up!"

How can a game programmer get a job in the biz (covered in depth in Chapter 21)? Magnin says the first thing is to make a snazzy demo disk:

Companies want experienced programmers. Without experience, a good demo is your best chance to prove you can do the work. Spend the extra hours to make it as good as you can. Often, you get only one chance to try to impress someone.

Chapter 12

Artificial Intelligence (AI)

THE EXPERTS

- Brian Reynolds,
  Big Huge Games

- Sid Meier,
  Firaxis Games

- Bruce Shelley,
  Ensemble Studios

- Chris Sawyer,
  Freelance

- Will Wright,
  Maxis Software

- Warren Spector,
  Ion Storm Austin

- David Wu,
  Pseudo Interactive

- Steve Hunt

- Alan Lawrance,
  Volition

- Don Hopkins,
  Freelance

- John Scott,
  Raven Software

- Richard Evans,
  Lionhead Studios

You've seen the movie...now, read the chapter!

Artificial intelligence (AI) may best be described as an attempt to model aspects of human thought or behavior on computers. In computer or console gaming, it boils down to making players feel like they're playing against real, intelligent opponents. Unfortunately, this has been one of the most difficult challenges of game programming, so this chapter will be solely dedicated to AI, instead of being combined with the rest of the topics covered in the chapter on programming theory (see Chapter 11, "Programming Theory").

Another reason for giving AI its own chapter is that single-player gaming should not be neglected. With the growth of multiplayer gaming, many gamers fear that a developer's time, money, and effort will be spent on tweaking the multiplayer code rather than improving the AI. After all, if the AI is predictable or dumb, many gamers will flock online to play against real people instead. The key is to make a game that offers both a hearty multiplayer component and realistic AI for those who can't afford to go online or who prefer the solo gaming experience.

With a panel of AI specialists, each working in different genres, this chapter discusses different kinds of AI and how a game designer should approach this tricky matter.

Brian Reynolds, Big Huge Games

As one of Sid Meier's star pupils, Brian Reynolds went on to help create such PC strategy hits as *Colonization, Civilization II,* and *Alpha Centauri.* His latest project was *Rise of Nations,* published by Microsoft for the PC in 2003. Read more about the game at www.bighugegames.com.

"Contrary to popular belief, you don't need any black magic to write AI for computer games," says Reynolds. "You don't need any patented algorithms; you don't need the latest papers on neural nets. All you need is a little creativity and a lot of persistence." The following sections describe some of his favorite techniques.

The Iterative Design Process

First of all, with AI, as with game design, use the iterative design process. Start by just making a simple routine that moves the enemy pieces—even if your algorithm is nothing more complex than `switch(rnd(4))`. Then play the game against your AI and watch it make its moves. Watch until it does something dumb (it shouldn't take too long at first). Then think about a) what the computer did that was stupid—for example, moved its tanks slowly through the woods or built only artillery units and nothing else; b) what you would have done instead (moved your tanks along the road; built a healthy mix of infantry, artillery, armor, and air); and c) what piece of information led you to (or helped you to) make that decision (road squares cost less to enter; you already had an artillery unit, but no infantry). Then just go back and revise your algorithm to incorporate this data.

Now play your game again and watch the AI, wait until it does something else stupid, and repeat this process. Repeat it over and over and over again, and your AI will get better and better. It's the poor man's version of the proverbial "AI that learns from its mistakes." Through your playing and revising, the AI is essentially building up "experience" and getting better and better at the game.

To illustrate his point, Reynolds shares with us an anecdote from when he was a young programmer working on his first game as a designer (*Colonization*):

I was a little intimidated when it came time to start working on some AI. I mean, I had a game that you could play, move the pieces around; but the AI didn't know how to do any of that. Where was I to start? I can still remember Sid Meier's advice to me: Start by teaching it how to play one turn. Then teach it how to play two turns, and then worry about teaching it how to play 10 turns.

Start Simple

Start with simple building blocks. For instance, in a strategy game, a useful algorithm to have is a routine that tells a unit how to get from point A to point B, [which is] called a pathfinding or go-to algorithm. A go-to routine is a nice compartmentalized project to start out with—just teaching a unit how to get from here to there, and worrying later about how to decide where "there" ought to be. I'm not saying it's easy to write a great go-to routine, but it's easy to start with a simple adequate routine and work your way up to something more complex. Once you've got a go-to routine, you can have another routine that decides where on the map the pieces ought to move, and it doesn't need to worry about how they're going to go about getting there.

> **NOTE**
> Pathfinding refers to a unit or units moving from point A to point B, and what path is taken to get there. Ever notice how, in older real-time strategy games, units at times will get "stuck" in some places, while at other times they take a longer or illogical route to their destination?

Doubling or Splitting Your Values

Another excellent trick I learned from Sid Meier when I was getting started (and which, like almost all of our tricks, applies equally well to game design and AI) is this: If you have a value or an effect, and you think you need to adjust it, either double it or halve it. For example, if you think tanks are too cheap to build, double the cost. Spare yourself the frustration of increasing it from 10 to 11 and wondering whether you can tell the difference or not. Make it 20, even if that seems initially ridiculous, and try the game out that way. This will give you a clear-cut difference in effect and show you what the game is like with tanks that are definitely more expensive. If they feel too expensive, you can cut back to 15 to fine-tune. If you think your computer AI is making too many infantry units, halve the likelihood that they will build them. I can remember countless times when I've doubled or halved something, thinking it would be too drastic a change, but wound up doubling or halving again before I really achieved the effect I wanted. All of this once again depends on using the iterative process.

Reynolds leaves off with this simple piece of advice: "Try stuff out; see how it works; revise; repeat."

Sid Meier, Firaxis Games

The one and only Sid Meier (referred to by Brian Reynolds in the preceding entry!) also discusses the trick of splitting or doubling values, plus a few extra tips:

Put something dumb in there; play it again; fix its weaknesses instead of creating more. I let it evolve as I play against it. I teach it to counteract, and so on.

The other rule I have for AI is don't overestimate—you can't make your easiest level too easy or the hardest level too hard. You'd be surprised how slow people will be at the beginning...make it real easy. You'd be surprised how good at it [they'll get], so make [the hardest level] your hardest. Start off with a few elements.

The legendary Sid Meier takes a common-sense approach to testing the artificial intelligence in his games: "Put something dumb in there, play it again, fix its weaknesses instead of creating more." Pictured here are *Civilization III* and Sid Meier's *SimGolf*.
(Used with permission by Infogrames, Inc. Used with permission by Electronic Arts, Inc.)

As an example of the latter, Meier says that *Civilization* starts off easy and rewards the player, instead of dumping it all onto the player at once:

> Players then look forward to increases in complexity and new things; if it was all at the beginning, you'd be overwhelmed. With *Civilization*, you don't start off with other civilizations. Rather, the idea of the map is to start off with a small area; then, as the game goes on, the player explores mountain ranges, seas, and so forth, which adds yet another dimension, gradually increasing as the game goes on…

Be sure to read Chapter 3, "General Game Design: Strategy Games," in which Meier offers helpful advice on creating strategy games.

> **NOTE**
>
> Anyone who has ever played *Thief* likely remembers that this single-player game had some savvy AI. To read some tricks and techniques used by Doug Church and company, turn back to Chapter 10, "Mission Design," for general game programming advice.

Bruce Shelley, Ensemble Studios

The co-designer on the *Age of Empires* and *Age of Mythology* games speaks quite a bit in this book on game design. Here, he chats about the different kinds of artificial intelligence and some things to keep in mind when programming AI.

Shelley says there are three tiers of AI: pathing, unit behavior, and strategic AI. Following is a more thorough description of each:

> Pathing is just how units find their way around the map. Unit behavior is how a character in the game responds to things going on around it. These two AIs are basically logic puzzles. The really difficult part is the strategic AI—how the computer plays the game as a human equivalent. Our goal from the start has been that the computer AI would not cheat, but play with the same general handicaps that a human would. We also wanted to be able to scale back the skill of the AI so we could have levels of difficulty. A particular challenge for us was our implementation of randomly generated maps. It's much easier to build an AI when everything is fixed on known maps. It's more difficult to make an AI competent when the map can be different in every game.

Shelley says the key to Ensemble Studios' savvy AI is their scripting system:

> [The scripting systems allows us to] provide the AI player with something like recipes for exploring, economic expansion, army building, and battle fighting. The AI has a recipe to follow at the start of play but can switch to a new recipe, depending on what's encountered in the game. Say the AI is set up for hunting and berry gathering to acquire food, but encounters a seacoast. The AI may switch scripts and change to wood gathering and boat fishing. This is how our AI can adjust to what it finds on random maps. If the AI builds an army of archers and siege weapons, but you counter with cavalry, the AI may switch to building camels or pikemen. Here, the AI is reacting to game events. We can further tweak the scripts by setting the size of the AI army before it attacks, setting a level of aggression for the rapidity of attacks, or setting its priority for targets (economic or military).

And don't be frustrated if you can't get it right from the beginning. Says Shelley, "The AI in each of our games has built on our experience. We find that we can duplicate the AI in our previous game perhaps 25% of the time [required for the previous game]. That leaves a lot of time for making it better in the new version."

So how does the process work?

> Two teams create the AI. The programming team creates the functionality and the scripting tools. The scripting team actually uses the tools to write the scripts that set out how the AI will play. We're able to set up script battles, in which AI scripts fight against each other at very high speeds. Our designers can watch the script battles live onscreen and spot errors in the scripts. With each test and adjustment, the scripts get tougher and tougher.

Read more from Bruce Shelley on strategy game design in Chapter 3.

Bruce Shelley teaches that "pathing AI"—that is, how the units move around the level—is just one kind of artificial intelligence to be concerned with when programming a deep real-time strategy game like *Age of Empires* or, pictured here, *Age of Mythology*.
(Used with permission by Microsoft Corp.)

Chris Sawyer, Freelance

The mastermind behind MicroProse's highly polished and ultra-fun *RollerCoaster Tycoon* (and its expansion packs) offers some AI tips:

> AI is challenging to program because intelligence is so nonlinear, and trying to program a linear algorithm for it is impossibly difficult. You also have to make the algorithms fast and efficient in a game. It's no use creating highly intelligent people in RollerCoaster Tycoon if the game freezes for minutes or hours while each person decides which direction to walk next. The trick is to think laterally and design very efficient "trick" algorithms that create the illusion of intelligence most of the time.

Sawyer also offers a handful of do's and don'ts for general game programming:

1. **Dare to be different**. Many games programmers look at what other programmers are doing and try to do the same but better. Much better to try doing it differently. If you succeed, you have something unique that will stand out against all the clones out there, instead of just being "the same but a little bit better/faster/smoother, and so on."

2. **Don't get carried away with the technical aspects of the game engine or the graphical engine**. Always remember that the #1 priority is to make the game fun to play. Some games boast about numbers of polygons or types of shading used, but what good is that if the gameplay is an afterthought?

3. **Document everything**. Your code, notes, mistakes, changes, everything. You never know when you might need to refer to it, or when others need to understand your code.

Jump back to Chapter 3 to read more from Chris Sawyer on strategy game design.

Will Wright, Maxis Software

The creator of the *SimCity* series, *The Sims*, and *The Sims Online* admits that he doesn't do much programming any more ("though I rather miss it!" he confesses), but offers the following:

> Probably the best advice I can give is this: Make sure that you're solving the right problem. I've seen many programmer hours wasted building elaborate solutions that don't really address the real issues in a game (which are frequently better solved with design or content solutions).
>
> What I mean is this: Every problem can be seen from many levels (global view to down in the gutter). Frequently, picking the correct level to address a problem is the real art to problem solving. For instance, what you may be attacking as a user interface problem may in fact be a problem with the conceptual model you've given the player to work with (for example, it's a map, not a Lego set).
>
> AI is mostly about maintaining a strong chain of believability through a product. You usually want to keep looking at your system with fresh eyes (first-time play testers) and see which links in that chain are the weakest (routing, conversation, and so on). You then keep improving those weak links continually until the product ships. Sometimes the improvement is best accomplished through new technologies; other times, through better tuning.

Chapter 4, "General Game Design: Sports, Simulations, Adventure Games, and Puzzles," features words of wisdom from Will Wright on creating simulations.

Warren Spector, Ion Storm Austin

"Hmm…wish I could remember what excellent things I said!" teases Spector when reminded of a previous interview about artificial intelligence. The veteran developer—responsible for many instant classic PC games such as *Ultima Underworld*, *System Shock*, and *Deus Ex*—offers the following:

> I guess the best I can do is repeat something I learned during *Deus Ex* and something I was taught by the talented men and women of Looking Glass Studios. The lesson learned on *Deus Ex* was that re-creating human behavior, while an alluring goal, doesn't necessarily lead to good gameplay. Games and reality are (obviously) two very different things, and that's something we should bear in mind, especially as we make games that look more and more realistic. The lesson learned from the LG folks is that game AI shouldn't be about beating the player—game AI should be about challenging players and, in the case of games like *Thief* and *Deus Ex*, giving players information they can use to formulate reasonable plans of action. Too many AI programmers seem intent on crushing players. What fun! (Well, maybe for the programmer.) Refocusing on challenging and informing—providing an interesting foil for the player— sounds simple and even obvious, but it sure doesn't seem to be, if many of the games I've played recently are any indication. Frankly, it wasn't obvious to me until the Looking Glass folks beat it into my thick skull.

Hop back to Chapter 5, "General Game Design: Role-Playing Games (RPGs) and Persistent Online Worlds," to read more sage advice from Warren Spector.

David Wu, Pseudo Interactive

Cel Damage was one of the Xbox launch titles developed by Canada's Pseudo Interactive. Founder and lead designer David Wu offers a few techniques on coding AI in a video game.

His first piece of advice? Learn the basics, says Wu:

> Make sure that you understand the tools that you'll use to build your controllers, path planning, and decision logic. A lot of material out there is easy to learn and very effective from a practical standpoint. Take advantage of this.

> Then there's "personality." Unlike in academia, you're not finding the optimal solution; rather, you're finding the most entertaining solution.

Next, Wu says to iterate:

> AI will evolve throughout the game; it won't be perfect the first time you implement it. Get your system up and running early to provide a lot of time for iterations and tuning.

Finally, "Conduct field tests early and often," says Wu.

> Play against your AIs. Watch people playing against them. How do they perform in real-world tests? Are players exploiting their shortcomings? Are they frustrating? Do they appear stupid? Are they repeatedly head-butting a wall?

Wu waxes more about programming in Chapter 11.

Steve Hunt

When at the now-defunct Rage Software, Steve Hunt says his advice on coding realistic AI in a simulation like *Eurofighter Typhoon* would be the same as he'd recommend on general game design (see Chapter 4). Hunt elaborates:

> It's very easy to get carried away with AI and write a system that's totally overengineered for what it's going to be used for. You can fall into this trap because AI programming is really interesting, and it's very rewarding to get convincing behavior.

Hunt says his approach has always been to use a "state-based system." He explains:

> It's important to write down all the states that the entities you're modeling can be in and then work out what the fundamental behaviors are. From here, you can write a number of small modules that handle each state and a piece of higher-level code to decide when to change from one state to another. You may also find that you need a number of substates for one particular state. The main thing is to modularize each part and break down the problem into small, easy-to-manage chunks. As an example, a plane could be in cruising mode, in which it's just flying from point A to point B. This state is pretty

simple; you may just output a required speed, heading, and altitude. But say our plane enters a dogfight. This state is very complex, and in Typhoon we use a number of substates:

➤ **Evasive**. There is someone who is in a position where they can fire at us.

➤ **Turn on to**. The situation is neutral; try to get behind our target.

➤ **Attack**. We're behind our target, so maneuver into a firing position.

I've grossly oversimplified this example, but hopefully the general approach is clear.

With AI programming, things get really interesting when you're trying to get a number of entities to work as a group. This is the real sharp end, and it can be difficult to predict on paper what the emergent behavior of a number of interacting entities will be. In our dogfight example, we may have a two-on-two situation. If we want the planes to cooperate, we need to take this into account when we decide what states we're going to have. In Typhoon and in real life, a pair of planes will have a lead and a wingman. It's the wingman's job to cover the lead. The lead carries on as normal, but the wingman will hold back and engage only if the lead is directly threatened.

Hunt says there are a million and one ways to do this sort of thing, and he thinks it's the real problem with AI coding in games. It's not writing the code that's hard; it's defining and understanding what the different states are and how they will interact with each other. "So think about the design; but just as importantly, write the code so you'll be able to debug it," says Hunt.

Alan Lawrance, Volition

The developer responsible in part for the amazing *Red Faction* and *Red Faction 2* (for the PlayStation 2, Xbox, and PC) says one key to creating convincing AI is to make sure that your AI doesn't do anything obviously wrong.

If an enemy is stuck on a wall or doesn't react when you shoot someone standing beside him, you've just completely broken immersion for the player. If you can get rid of all the things that make your AI look stupid, you've gone a long way toward creating decent AI. What really makes AI convincing are the details that make your AI seem intelligent. If you can have enemies take cover, act cooperatively to flush the player out of hiding, throw grenades back, and so on, you'll create the illusion of intelligent enemies.

Read more from Lawrance in Chapter 11.

Volition's Alan Lawrance says what really makes AI convincing are the details that make the AI seem intelligent.
(Used with permission by THQ, Inc.)

Don Hopkins, Freelance

This freelance programmer speaks quite a bit about programming techniques in Chapter 11 but reserves his comments in this chapter to discuss some very interesting advice on AI and the psychology of creating savvy AI.

When asked what's the most important thing for a game programmer to keep in mind when coding AI, Hopkins says that not only should programmers have a model of the game, but also a model of the user and how he or she is expected to think about the game. He explains:

> There are two important but different models of a game: The designer's model, used to implement it; and the user's model, used to interact with it. These models are necessarily different. It's the job of the game designer to trick the users into imagining a much richer mental model than the computer is actually using to run the simulation. Implication is much more efficient than simulation. If you can imply a complex emotion instead of actually simulating it, you have saved many CPU cycles. Even if you could truly simulate emotions, you would still need a way to express them. But if you can express the appropriate emotions without actually simulating them very deeply, you've done your job. The user's imagination is much more powerful than the computer's number-crunching ability. Use that fact to your advantage instead of letting it be a liability.

On a slightly more technical note, Hopkins adds that interactive scripting languages are essential.

> *The Sims* has its own visual programming languages called "SimAntics." It's extremely costly and difficult to develop your own scripting languages because they're hard to get right and they require a lot of work to develop programming tools and debuggers, and to train and support script programmers. These days, it's much better to use a well-designed, off-the-shelf scripting language such as Python, which is well-known, documented, and supported, and has a rich set of libraries and programming and debugging tools.

John Scott, Raven Software

This programmer, who brought us *Soldier of Fortune* and other top-tier titles at Raven Software, says AI is a very nebulous concept and very difficult to make "look good." Scott clarifies:

> A computer can think, aim, and shoot 20 guys in a fraction of a second; the computer could make the NPCs [non-player characters] track you down and kill you in no time at all. Is this fun? Not even close. The difficulty is to make the enemies appear intelligent while not letting them get the better of the player. When your opponents are human, this is exceptionally difficult; everyone knows what a person would do in certain situations. If your opponents are zombies and demons, you can get away with very simple AI because no one can know what these creatures would do, so for them to act stupid would not look odd.

Scott says his personal approach is to make every parameter of the NPCs configurable:

> This includes their FOV [field of view], view distance, hearing distance, delay between shots, aiming ability, etc. This way, you can tweak these settings in-game until you find the "looking good" numbers. Design a good framework to enable easy modification of these values.

Finally, Scott reminds programmers that there's no right or wrong regarding AI; there are some things that computer-controlled characters shouldn't do, but the rest is purely up to personal opinion.

Richard Evans, Lionhead Studios

If you've ever marveled at the incredibly savvy AI found in *Black & White*, you can visit www.lionhead.co.uk and drop kudos and thanks to Richard Evans, the head of artificial intelligence at Lionhead Studios in the UK.

Evans starts off here with a brief "in-a-nutshell" description of game AI and then offers some general tidbits of game programming advice:

> AI is the black art of getting a computer to perform some task which, if performed by a human, would be deemed to require intelligence. AI is the Next Big Thing in games (along with realistic physics), now that the graphical issues are being solved. AI is extremely important in giving games longevity: The more realistic, plausible, and deep your characters are, the longer the player will be hooked.

> ➤ Keep in mind that getting your code right will take at least three times as long as you think it will.

> ➤ Regard testers as a useful resource, not as a hassle.

> ➤ Work all night and then get up early in the morning.

"There is no one unique 'trick' to coding very realistic AI," reveals Evans:

> The important thing is to take ideas from a wide variety of AI techniques. In *Black & White*, we used belief-desire-intention architectures, decision-tree learning, and perceptron training, among others. We also took inspiration from philosophical and psychological ideas.

Evans expands on belief-desire-intention architecture:

> Developing the creature AI has been a bit like looking after a newborn baby: sometimes painful, exhausting, and frustrating; and at other times deeply rewarding.
>
> The basic design was based on the belief-desires-intention (BDI) model, as pioneered by the philosopher Michael Bratman. The basic idea is that the agent has many different desires, but he also has an agenda that contains what he has decided to do. This agenda doesn't change unless something significantly more important comes along (which prevents *hysteriesis*, the phenomenon of an agent flitting between two equally important goals).
>
> With a basic BDI implemented, a number of significant new features were added:
>
> 1. **Learning using perceptron training**. Each desire that the creatures have is based on a number of different sources. For example, the creature might be angry because he has seen someone he hates, or he might be angry because he has been damaged, or he might be angry because he's frustrated. These are three different sources for the desire anger. The various weightings that decide when your creature gets angry are modified by perceptron training.
>
> 2. **Learning using decision trees**. Once a creature has learned to prefer to eat pigs to rocks, say, he represents this as a decision tree, which is modified at runtime to minimize the entropy in player feedback. (This was based on the work of Quinlan.)
>
> 3. **Building a mental model of the player**. The creature stores a mental model of his master so that he can empathize with him. The basic design approach is that empathy is essentially a reciprocal, two-way kind of thing. (The reason it's inappropriate/childish to try to empathize with a teddy is precisely because a teddy cannot empathize with you.) In order to encourage the player to feel some involvement with his creature, it was essential that the creature empathized, reciprocally, with [the player]. The creature keeps an elaborate model of his player to achieve this effect. He computes how much attention his master is giving him (and gets lonely if he's ignored.) More importantly, he tries to work out what the player is trying to do by observing his actions, and over time he builds up a picture of his master's goals. This isn't entirely trivial because one action may be used on different occasions to satisfy different goals. On occasion, the creature can misunderstand his master; for instance, if his master throws a rock at a town, trying to impress the villagers with his power, the creature may misinterpret this as the player trying to be aggressive.

NOTE

Richard Evans' detailed document on the AI in *Black & White* is available at `www.gameai.com/blackandwhite.html`.

Ever heard of "belief-desire-intention" architectures? If you're interested in programming artificial intelligence, be sure to peruse this segment featuring Richard Evans of Lionhead Studios fame. Shown here are creatures from *Black & White*.
(Used with permission by Electronic Arts, Inc.)

Chapter 13

Game Art and Animation

Computer and console game graphics are among the most important facets of game design: They eat up the biggest piece of the game budget pie; contribute more to a game's immersion factor; and from a marketing standpoint, are crucial selling points (think of all the prerelease screen shots in magazines or on the Internet, and on the outside of the box at retail).

Generally speaking, there are two kinds of art in gaming: concept and in-game. In most cases, concept artists work with the game designers to help flesh out the graphical vision of the product by sketching characters and backgrounds, and perhaps some 3D modeling as well. In-game artists may work on character art ("painting" textures on 2D sprites or 3D polygons, for example) and background art (game locations). There are also "art technicians," who work specifically on the programming side of placing the graphics in the game engine.

And working hand-in-hand with art is animation because objects rarely remain static throughout a game! Quite simply, the purpose of animation in games, movies, or television programs is to simulate life through frames of movement. Animation in games is particularly challenging because it must synchronize with the program's artificial intelligence to mimic life (or machinery) and must be easily controlled by the player at the same time.

There is also pre-rendered animation that is not interactive, such as the CG (computer graphics) intro movies and cut scenes that are popular in PC and console games today.

This chapter hosts a diverse collection of game artists and animators who want to share their advice and expertise with others on creating art for games, what tools to use, and the best ways to get into the industry as an artist. All genres are covered, but their order of appearance is purely random.

Let's get to it!

THE EXPERTS

- Ian Lloyd, Electronic Arts
- Rodney Alan Greenblat, Freelance
- John Miles, Electronic Arts UK
- Mark Gibbons, Sony Computer Entertainment Europe, Cambridge Studio
- Richard Kriegler, Electronic Arts/Westwood Studios
- Takiyoshi Sato, Konami
- Lee Petty, Circus Freak Studios
- Tetsuya Nomura, Square Enix
- Don Hopkins, Freelance
- Kevin Cloud, id Software
- Pierre Rivest, Ubi Soft Entertainment
- Reid Schneider, BAM! Entertainment
- Catherine Roy, Ubi Soft Entertainment
- Greg Thomas, Sega of America/Visual Concepts
- Todd Howard, Bethesda Softworks
- Emmanuel Valdez
- Rick Stringfellow
- Dan Michelson, Electronic Arts
- Don Bluth, Don Bluth Films

Ian Lloyd, Electronic Arts

Ian Lloyd was the character and animation lead on *SSX Tricky* at Electronic Arts Canada. Past products include three iterations of *Triple Play Baseball* for the PlayStation and the wildly successful *SSX* for the PlayStation 2.

Lloyd was first asked to give his top three most important pieces of advice for an artist or animator. The following are his responses:

➤ **Context**. As game hardware technology advances, it becomes increasingly critical to ensure that the gamer's experience is as contextual as possible. Everything should look and behave in specific rather than general ways, for discernible reasons. Characters are designed to achieve specific objectives and suggest specific associations with the audience; animations take into account a character's state of mind, motivations, conflicts, and so on; characters react to their environments and each other in very specific rather than generic ways. This also applies stylistically. It's no longer acceptable to create games that don't have strong visual languages and cohesive designs.

➤ **Quality**. Is the artwork—whether geometry, texture map, or animation—the very best it can be within the time constraints (see following point)? I try to stress fundamental understanding of anatomy and human kinetics with my teammates to ensure that nothing looks obviously wrong. From here, it's easy to go in and make something look special or super cool, but if you start with the super cool stuff on a fundamentally flawed base, it will never look right. We stress traditional sculpting principles for character modelers and classical animation theory for animators. An artist with this skill set can always learn new tools to communicate with, but an artist who doesn't even know what he or she is trying to communicate or can't figure out why something just doesn't look right is in for a much steeper learning curve.

Additionally, the artist needs to be intimately familiar with all the technical constraints and factors affecting how the art is displayed in-game. The interdependencies of the rendering code, lighting system, and the texture development is a key area for us. It's very difficult to predict what details need to be painted into a texture until the render engine and lighting system are complete. The better an artist understands what happens to the art once it leaves their hands and the more they interact with the programmers, the better the final artwork can become.

➤ **Speed/Efficiency**. High quality comes at a steep price, and there's always a fine balance between "good enough" and "This is taking too long/costing too much money." In this regard, it's critical to "pick your spots." It's impossible to do everything at the same level of quality and time investment, and it's unnecessary to do so in most cases. Just as filmmakers have been employing "false fronts" for years, video game artists need to understand where they can apply a few "false fronts" of their own. Being inherently lazy, I always try to prioritize the biggest-impact aspects of development and focus on making these areas shine. In the lower-impact areas, we try to take a modular and reusable approach wherever possible. Obviously, the more games move toward full interactivity and free-roaming models, the more important it is to ensure that all areas of the game appear to be of equal quality, resolution, and detail. One area in which we're trying to improve is in utilizing better pre-production processes to reduce the amount of reworking and revisions an artist needs on a given piece of art. We're getting better in this regard, but I'm sure the artists I work with would confirm that we still have a long way to go.

What software tools should a video game artist be familiar with?

Lloyd says they are currently using Alias' Maya (`www.aliaswavefront.com`) almost exclusively and "enjoying great success with it." But there are others, too:

In the past, we had divided various aspects of the game development between software packages and always experienced headaches trying to marry the assets from one package to another. For texturing, we're using Adobe Photoshop [`www.adobe.com`] and Deep Paint with Texture Weapons [both available at `www.us.righthemisphere.com`] in some applications. I also find Adobe Illustrator [`www.adobe.com`] useful for developing crisp, scalable graphics and logos for skin treatments. Although lately I find myself deeply immersed in Microsoft Word and Excel most of the time. I worry that the animator in me committed "hara kiri" a long, long time ago!

Talk about a rare find—Electronic Arts' Ian Lloyd has provided a handful of behind-the-scenes images for the game *SSX Tricky*. Seen here is a conceptual drawing and a detailed render of two new characters introduced in this popular game: Eddie Wachowski and Psymon Stark.

(Used with permission by Electronic Arts, Inc.)

And what about schooling? Necessary or not? Lloyd believes most artists would agree that the best artists never stop learning:

> I totally agree with this credo. It's never too early or too late to learn more about creating art. These days, one certainly needs to look into the legitimacy of any school or courses they plan to enroll in, as tuition fees in the CG education field have exploded and the number of fly-by-night institutions have kept pace. Even some of the better-known schools go through rough periods, so I highly recommend doing as much homework as possible to get an understanding of a particular school's current state of affairs. Talk to students, teachers, and graduates of the program. When was the last time they had a faculty strike? When did they last upgrade their equipment or facilities? How much has tuition risen over the last few years? Have the services improved to match this increase?

Lloyd says a lot of kids are jumping straight into the 3D software courses without fundamental art skills, "which I feel can often be a big mistake." He elaborates:

> Certainly a number of hugely talented artists have evolved from this path as they effectively utilize computer-based toolsets, but may not have embraced the messier or more time-consuming media such as painting or sculpting. But it's one thing to know how to use the software and quite another to understand what you're trying to communicate with it.

Lloyd also believes that animators should learn classic animation before jumping into the computer graphics software packages:

> I recommend that anyone who wants to become an animator take a classical animation course before moving into CG, or at least ensure that there is classical theory instruction at the school they attend. If not, I recommend taking acting and/or drama classes if they have the guts. I never did and regret it to this day. I was always terminally shy as a kid (the result, I'm sure to this day, of a traumatic kindergarten Christmas play incident) and have never been comfortable performing for an audience. But acting is the key to animation, and really getting into a character's head makes the difference between an animating CG character and a believable character, period. The animation team on *SSX Tricky* can testify to the hours logged performing sexy walks, dorky dance moves, and psychotic rages at their desks. Makes for a pretty entertaining day usually, not to mention the exercise benefits.

> Additionally and economically, there is a ton of material on the Internet relating to animation, notably the following sites: www.cg-char.com, www.anticz.com, www.3dark.com, www.anamie.com, www.animfound.com, and www.brianlemay.com. I'd also like to recommend a fantastic traditional sculpting book for all CG character modelers: *Modelling and Sculpting the Human Figure* by Edouard Lanteri [Dover Books, 1985, ISBN 0486250067].

It's hard to imagine that someone came up with the wild concepts behind *SSX* and *SSX Tricky*—character-driven border cross games that mesh high-speed racing on fantasy courses with impossible midair tricks and stunts—so Lloyd was asked where an artist can look for inspiration and how to apply it to his or her work.

In my opinion, an artist should try to be open to any potential source of inspiration at any time. Obviously, finding key inspiration during the brainstorming process is ideal, but often a light bulb simply can't turn on in many cases until one has traveled to a certain point in the creative process. It's amazing how often the pieces simply fall into place at a specific point in the process. It is true, however, that some designs ship with the final product for no reason other than that they were inoffensive, rather than being exceptional designs.

Sometimes, I find the need for a heavy dose of fresh inspiration when a design hits a creative roadblock. When this happens, I often find it useful to immerse myself in material that I personally find exciting or satisfying (cue the laugh track from people who know me well, but I'll try to keep a straight face here). This material can be almost anything: books, magazines, comics, film, music, theatre, dance, nature, and so on. I personally find music, comics, film, and nature to be some of my biggest sources of inspiration. I'm partial to the artwork of Masamune Shirow, Katushiro Otomo, John Byrne, Frank Miller, and Mike Mignola. These artists always surprise me with elegant and powerful storytelling solutions. These guys may not be the latest sensation, but their work has definitely helped shape my sensibilities. Lately, I've been watching some of Akira Kurosawa's film works and love what M. Night Shyamalan is doing with powerful comic book-derived storytelling in his films. It's nice to see such a derided medium growing up into such an influential and powerful storytelling tool. Games are great, but nothing beats a comic book's ability to give an audience a context to use their imagination effectively.

On *SSX*, Lloyd found that he responded strongly to character-specific speech and in-game music to better understand a character's attitude or envision how the character might move. "We had an incredible audio team on *SSX Tricky* and it's always exciting to hear their latest work. I find this cross-pollination to be incredibly invigorating, as they do when we provide them with equally inspiring animation to work with," says Lloyd.

Speaking of *SSX*, what was the most challenging aspect to the art in that game? Were there technical, creative, or time-related obstacles?

Some of the more obviously challenging aspects of creating art for *SSX* have been learning the strengths and limitations of new hardware (that is, the Sony's PlayStation 2 in 2000) as well as developing a solid language and methodology for providing direction to the team on a brand new original title. It's no secret that EA has a lock on effectively and efficiently producing iterative titles, but *SSX* was a very different creature. We experienced many false starts in trying to define what the game was going to be. As crazy as that sounds, particularly when one looks at the finished product (it just makes so much sense now), this proved to be the difference between getting a green light on the project and it getting canned. We eventually figured out what the game wanted to be and what we thought people wanted in a snowboarding game: an arcade-style snowboard racer. When we had this key vision, everything else solidified around it.

And on character design:

> One specifically challenging area of art development in *SSX* was (and still is) character design. We knew we wanted characters that balanced believability (not to be confused with realism) with a stylized representation. In this respect, the *Tekken* series has been a huge inspiration for the team in nearly all aspects of development, but the key aspect learned from *Tekken* was the beauty of a cast of equally balanced yet radically different-playing and -looking characters.

> When it came down to developing our characters, I struggled to champion the "cast of characters" approach rather than tackling them one at a time. We decided to create eight characters and tune each of them differently, so the user got a unique riding experience with each one. I wanted to make sure that physically we covered the obvious bases that varying gameplay required. The big, heavy, sturdy character in Jurgen versus the small, agile, tricky character in Kaori. This established our range, or scope, and it was a relatively simple task to fill in the remaining physical gaps.

One of Lloyd's most demanding challenges was selling the concept of a cool female character who wasn't necessarily a gorgeous supermodel with exaggerated proportions. He recalls:

> Yes, we had one of those in Elise, but I felt we could also afford a tough, punk-ass, super-cool character who also just happened to be a girl. Unfortunately, this is unsurprisingly an extremely tough sell in this industry. Zoe is about as close as we could get to this, and although I'm happy with how she turned out and how well she's been received, I still can't help feeling like she's a safer, watered-down version of a much more challenging character.

Lloyd discusses the move to *SSX Tricky*:

> On *SSX Tricky*, we had characters evolve from a few very different sources. A couple, such as Luther-Dwayne and Psymon, originated in early brainstorming sessions, whereas Eddie and Seeiah were developed in direct response to the voice talent who expressed interest in the project. Marisol fills the demographic desire to add a Spanish character, and Brodi gives the ladies something nice to play with. The trick is to try to address marketing and other desires while avoiding stereotypes and presenting new and interesting characters that fit logically within the *SSX* (and EA Sports BIG) universe. On the whole, our new characters have been very well-received.

There were animation challenges for these products, too:

> On the animation side of things, our biggest challenge was to get our three animators—Terry Sanderson, Yanick Lebel, and me—to learn enough about snowboarding to pull off convincing hand-animated motion in three different riding styles. I'm pretty pleased with the results. In a studio with such an incredible motion-capture team and studio, even getting a hand-animated project off the ground is a huge accomplishment. I'm extremely proud of the talents and efforts of the animation team on *SSX* and *SSX Tricky*.

Rodney Alan Greenblat, Freelance

Not only has this talented New York-based artist created paintings and sculpture exhibited in galleries and museums throughout the world, he's also an author and illustrator of children's books, director of the Center for Advanced Whimsy (an independent art, design, and music company), and the inventor of Sony's characters for the PlayStation hits *PaRappa the Rapper* (1997) and *Um Jammer Lammy* (1999), among others. His latest project was *PaRappa the Rapper 2*, published in early 2002 for the PS2 by Sony Computer Entertainment America.

Greenblat begins by discussing the different kinds of art in a game, focusing on PlayStation development.

> ➤ **Character designer (that's me)**. This artist basically supplies the personality of the game. Writers usually supply the character designer with the bare bones of what the characters are like. Sometimes it's the director. Sometimes the character designer gets to make things up.

> ➤ **Storyboard artist**. This artist takes what the director, writers, and character designer are saying and roughs out the action. This is a very powerful position. In a very complicated project, there is probably more than one storyboard artist.

> ➤ **Animators**. There is usually a chief animator who oversees the whole style of the project. Then there are many different animation specialists. I don't know what they all do. It depends on the style of the art, the complexity, and the budget of the project.

> ➤ **Special designers**. In a big 3D role-playing game, there might be special designers to do vehicles, spaceships, architectural interiors, backgrounds, costumes, and so on.

NOTE

How did Greenblat come up with the unique 2D, paper-thin-looking characters in the *PaRappa the Rapper* and *Um Jammer Lammy* games? "We felt like preserving as much of my original art style as possible. My work is primarily 2D cartoon style, and converting them into full low-res 3D just didn't seem natural. When we tested them as 3D 'cutouts,' it really worked," says Greenblat.

Greenblat shares some general art-related advice for those just starting out—suggesting that you ask yourself these questions when working on a project:

1. How is my game better than other games?

2. Why would anybody want to buy this game when it's finished?

3. If this game is a hit, will I make any money?

After some nudging, Greenblat provides some questions specifically for video game artists:

1. Does the style of the artwork and animation complement the story content?

2. Do the details add information to the storyline, or are they just filling space?

3. In the style you've chosen, can you get the project done on time?

4. Does the style of the animation match the technology of the delivery device?

> **NOTE**
>
> Rodney Greenblat, creator of the characters from the *PaRappa the Rapper* series and *Um Jammer Lammy*, says there are a few 2D software tools an artist and animator should be familiar with, but "today, many computer artists are working out ideas with Flash [`www.macromedia.com`]. It's very versatile because it can make illustrations that can be used for animation, web sites, and video. I've seen some pretty good storyboards done with Flash, too."

Chapter 6, "Creating Characters, Storyboarding, and Design Documents," focuses in part on creating a successful video game character. What are Greenblat's "secrets" to creating a hit character? Why do so many characters fail to attract an audience? He speculates:

In the case of PaRappa and Mario, I'd say simplicity and humor make the characters inviting. Both are characters that are instantly recognizable. Somehow they're both easy to relate to, also. Match this to the simple objectives of the games these characters star in, and you can see how it becomes catchy.

There are many reasons why characters fail. Even if they're lovable and ingenious, without a well-funded and experienced marketing machine behind them, they're probably doomed. It's sad to say. Things become popular when many people see them. That costs money.

Seen here is a shot of the entire "gang." Says Greenblat: "This is a group pose of all my main characters for the *PaRappa the Rapper* and *Um Jammer Lammy* games for Sony PlayStation. Despite the amazing amount of changes some of these characters have gone through, they manage to hold together stylistically, and each maintains his or her individuality. They are a funny wacky group, and I'm proud to say I designed them." Left to right: Mar-san, Yoko Teriaki, PJ Berri, Katy Kat, Cathy Pillar, Rammy, Instructor Mooselini, Lammy, PaRappa, Chop Chop Master Onion, Master Prince Fleaswallow, Sunny Funny, Cheap Cheap the Cooking Chicken, Captain Fussenpepper, Joe Chin, Paul Chuck, and Chief Puddle.
(Used with permission by Sony Computer Entertainment America, Inc.)

Where should a character design artist look for inspiration?

> TV and movies. No—I changed my mind. Books. No, comics and magazines. That's not right. Museums.
> Yes. Go to lots of museums. No wait, Grandma and Grandpa. They have a different perspective… but
> not as good as teachers at art school! Yes, teachers at art school are very inspiring. But sometimes they
> don't know what they're talking about! Forget it—follow your heart. That's it. But what if you're in a bad
> mood? Better stick with TV and movies.

But that vision could become confounded when there are huge teams making a game. Greenblat says this is the most challenging part about creating art for a video game: "So many *other people* are involved. What are they all doing? What do they want??? The hardest part is trying to please them all and feel that I am making something of my own at the same time."

Visit Greenblat's official web page at www.whimsyload.com.

John Miles, Electronic Arts UK

Talk about pressure—creating video game art based on one of the most beloved children's books in recent history is no easy task. But that's what John Miles, franchise art director at Electronic Arts UK, is responsible for.

Before working on the *Harry Potter* games, Miles had a hand in the creation of *Privateer 2: The Darkening*, *Populous 3*, *Dungeon Keeper 2*, *Theme Park World*, and others.

We spoke with Miles right after the first *Harry Potter* game shipped for multiple platforms.

When asked what his future aspirations were, Miles says in the short term "while we've spent the last two years bringing Harry Potter to the video game arena, the challenge now is to make him grow from a young boy, age 11, into an adult."

He admits: "This is something that hasn't been done before in games, and I'm looking forward to driving it. Harry is a complex individual, and making the player believe the subtleties of his nature is a real challenge."

Before we get into the *Harry Potter* games themselves, Miles had some advice for aspiring video game artists.

> Miles' Top Five Game Art Tips for Newbies
>
> ➤ **Look for inspiration outside of your own world**. Don't just look at other video games; look
> to all creative media—from film to theatre, graphic design to contemporary art installations.
>
> ➤ **Iterate quickly**. Cheap—Quick, not Expensive—Slow. Don't spend ages on each idea; create
> lots of ideas quickly; don't worry about them being finished, polished images. It's the ideas that
> count, not the execution in the early stages. After you clarify your direction, you can work more
> on the finer elements.

➤ **When making changes, double or half**. When changing the design of something, whether it's a character's proportions or the brightness of a light, make the changes big and not too subtle. This will help you get to all the possibilities quickly. Subtlety should come later in the polishing stage.

➤ **Be bold**. Don't be afraid to try something new. But also work with—not against—the team you're on. If people feel comfortable in approaching you and discussing your work, it's likely you'll be given more of the important work because directors will feel comfortable that they can work well with you on it.

➤ **Don't be afraid to kill your babies**. Don't become too attached to your ideas. That way, when one is chosen over another for reasons out of your control—such as budget, time, the director's preference, and so on—it won't be so emotional to let it go. This is one good reason to create a plethora of ideas; that way, there's a chance one will be suitable.

John Miles is responsible for the artwork in Electronic Arts' *Harry Potter* video game series, based on the hugely successful novels by J.K. Rowling.
(Used with permission by Electronic Arts, Inc.)

Okay, so let's now take a closer look at *Harry Potter*. Does the same advice apply here?

The design of Harry Potter, the character, took many months and involved much discussion. The challenge was that this famous character existed in the minds of millions of children and adults, but there wasn't one image that was truly representative of what he looked like.

There were the book covers; each one had a different look and style. There was also the forthcoming Warner Brothers film, with Daniel Radcliffe playing Harry.

The quandary was that some people thought we should take the look of Harry directly from the film: Cyberscan and motion-capture Daniel Radcliffe, re-creating him perfectly in 3D.

"Unfortunately, this never works as well as you might think," says Miles.

Why not?

"Frequently, a character will appear very wooden and often quite scary when created this way."
He explains:

> The closer we try to replicate reality in computer graphics, the more the subtleties of human mannerisms are important. It's far easier to stylize or produce a caricature.

Interestingly, another choice was to create a cartoon version of Harry, but author J.K. Rowling was clear that she didn't want this to happen.

So, Miles says the route they chose was to stylize a version of the WB film reference, and create their own version of Harry.

"This took a firm will because many senior people weren't convinced of this approach,"
admits Miles.

Miles outlines the advantages for going this route:

> We have a Harry and his world of Hogwarts that doesn't contradict the WB image, but we're also able to exaggerate Harry's features and movements, which suits the world of video games. Having larger facial features, hands, and feet gives us a better read when dealing with a third-person action adventure. In a game in which action is important, we don't want to be restricted to the limitations of real life. When Harry jumps or casts a spell, we want it to be dramatic and not look too feeble.

> People who haven't read the books have the misconception that *Harry Potter* is a kid's book, and consequently nothing bad ever really happens to him. The truth is, of course, that bad things do happen, and sometimes the consequences can be quite gruesome. This is probably partly why kids love it so much.

> We would never be able to get the malevolence of the world of Hogwarts across if we had a cartoon world. However, in our illustratory style world we can still carry this off.

I'm sure many video game artists (amateur or professional) want to know what it's like to work on such a celebrated franchise as *Harry Potter*. Miles discusses the pros and cons:

Pros

> When you work on a high-profile project such as *HP*, everyone knows what you're talking about when you're in the pub. Many times before *HP*, I would chat about games I was working on, and I could see people visibly switch off. *Potter's* a different matter, though. People just want to know more. The tie-in with the film also adds richness to my working day: dealing with the film producer and visiting the sets.

> I've worked long hours on many projects that barely glimpse the light of day or will only make it into the charts for a short period of time. That just doesn't happen with *Harry Potter*.

> *Harry Potter* is the biggest-selling game for EA. It will last for a number of years and will be seen by millions of people.

> Having a large budget also enables me to try things other projects wouldn't allow. We can dedicate people and resources to specific areas; experiment with new ideas and processes.

Cons

On the down side, the hugely popular nature of the license means that it's like developing in a goldfish bowl.

Everyone wants to know what you're doing and why you're doing it that way, and to make suggestions as to how they'd do it. It's possible to spend as much time discussing a point and trying to make people understand your perspective as you spend coming up with the ideas in the first place.

In addition, it's a film license, so you have boundaries to work within. There is a style and elements of background and character design already there. In contrast, it's nice to work on a completely new project with no preconceptions as to the visual style. However, this can in itself be daunting due to the option paralyses suffered when faced with a blank canvas.

Finally, to newbie artists looking to break into the industry, Miles offers the following words of wisdom:

> ➤ Collate a good, concise portfolio or show reel. Don't put everything in it. Put only your best work in it, and don't present just one type of medium.

> ➤ Many people have only computer graphic images—you should make an effort to include a selection of traditional art media, such as life drawing, sculpture, or painting. (Don't feel like you need to produce all of these, but make sure you have some non-computer graphics works.)

> ➤ Never underestimate the experience gained from observed study. Demonstrating that you can draw inspiration from a multitude of sources will make you look proactive and inspirational.

> ➤ Be enthusiastic. It's always offputting to interview an artist who comes across as blasé, arrogant, or just plain not interested. My personal theory on team building is to get good quality, sociable team members over and above talented prima donnas. In the long run, large egos on a team will only cause endless problems.

> ➤ Set your goal and remain focused. Decide what you want to do, get to know people in that industry, ask their advice, and ask to visit their studios or workplaces.

Mark Gibbons, Sony Computer Entertainment Europe, Cambridge Studio

Also out of the UK is Sony's Mark Gibbons, lead artist at SCEE's Cambridge studios. Gibbons' last project was the gorgeous *Primal*, which debuted on PlayStation 2 in March 2003.

Gibbons was asked to provide some inspiring words to video game artists just breaking into the business. What three things should they keep in mind when working on their first game?

Gibbons says it's "economy, time constraints, and the big picture." He elaborates:

Economy

Always be mindful of the delicate balance that exists between art and programming in video game development. Each additional polygon an artist adds to a character or scene shaves the tiniest fraction off the game's frame rate. The more detail onscreen, the slower the engine will run.

Let's look at *Primal* for an example. Late in the game, trapped in a vast ancient temple, enormous pillars tower up to a high vaulted ceiling 100 feet over the head of Jen, our beautifully detailed heroine. She leaps out of the way of exploding fireballs launched from the fists of a towering demonic statue brought to life by Iblis, Lord of the Djinn, who looks on, in true arch-villain tradition, laughing. Meanwhile, a dozen temple guards in shining armor charge at her across the brightly patterned mosaic floor, swinging flaming swords over their heads. Sounds great? Well, talk like that tends to give your programming team seizures.

Gibbons continues:

Now, of course, the programmers will do their utmost to deliver an engine that will allow even the most ambitious of art teams the scope to indulge their elaborate fantasies, but art and programming are joined in a fragile marriage of convenience that we as artists should do our best to make work.

"Spend the polygons, and place the elaborate textures where they'll be appreciated," offers Gibbons.

Gibbons gives a specific example of modeling economy:

If you're creating the environments for a first-person shoot-'em-up or a third-person action-adventure, move the camera through the scene you're modeling at your game character's head height. Make note of which environmental features you notice, and invest your efforts in those features. Returning to our ancient temple for a second, if Jen never reaches the tops of those 100-foot pillars, you'd be wasting your time creating elaborate detail around the area where they meet the ceiling. Focus your efforts at ground level. Spend those extra polygons on the gryphon statues hunched at the pillar's base; throw multitextures and bump maps on the metal surfaces on the floor.

Conversely, you don't want to be placing a flat texture of a beamed ceiling in a room if the player's character is likely to be climbing around in the rafters, says Gibbons. "That's going to require proper modeling to look convincing."

Time Constraints

The clock is always ticking. Although the time it takes and budget required to develop a cutting-edge video game has grown massively in recent years, anything the artist can do to increase the efficiency of his work is welcome. So adapt and revise. Get as much mileage out of a character model or piece of architecture as you can. In *Primal*, for example, we developed a swappable body part system, whereby an artist creates a single enemy character that can be split into several components (torso, legs, arms, and so on); and by producing different texture sets and additional pieces of geometry (weapons, shields, helmets, and so on), we're able to mix-and-match to generate an enormous variety of unique opponents for Jen to fight. It is far more efficient than modeling each and every character individually.

The Big Picture

Take pride in your work without being precious about it. Accept that the constantly shifting sands of video game development may mean that you find yourself adjusting, revising, and occasionally completely abandoning art that you may have spent a great deal of time on. You may also be required to incorporate other artist's efforts into your own or deliver your work into the hands of another. Video game artists need to be flexible, unselfish, resourceful, and sometimes prepared to compromise their artistic principles for the greater gaming good.

"Oh, and of course: Listen to every word your lead artist tells you!" laughs Gibbons.

He was asked to pool from his vast experience as a concept and in-game artist, and to offer a handful of do's and dont's for newbie artists:

You know that hoary old cliché that because you have two ears and only one mouth, you should listen twice as much as you speak? Well, it applies twice as much in video game development. Creating art for video games is a peculiar process and probably unlike any other discipline of computer graphics. You may be hugely experienced with the software you're being asked to use, but if you're new to the video game industry, seek out the sages in your studio. There will be at least one or two (and not necessarily the old dudes) with a razor-sharp understanding of what this craft is all about. Become a sponge...soak it up.

Gibbons also talks about the importance of a design document (see more in Chapter 6 on the subject):

Every game will have a design document: the developer's Bible that records the sacred text of all (game) creation. It's something every artist on the team should be intimately familiar with, and although rarely set in stone, it should read as the foundation on which the structure of the actual game art is constructed. The design document on *Primal* takes the form of an in-house web site that details every element of the game, from character sketches and written backgrounds to gameplay mechanics and lines of dialogue. It's updated frequently, and is ideally checked by everyone on the team on a regular basis.

Next, Gibbons tells artists to "become a librarian:"

Develop a body of reference for the work you do. Whether it's art books, photography books, or pictures you've taken yourself, strive to broaden your frames of reference by soaking up images from elsewhere. Maintain a texture library. Take photos. Take a lot of photos. Take a camera with you whenever you can. Photographs form the basis for a large number of the textures we create for *Primal*. The days of texturing an entire game with purely hand-drawn bitmaps are gone. As the geometry created for gaming environments and characters become increasingly sophisticated, there's an equal emphasis placed on producing textures that enhance and complement these additional polygons. They don't need to be truly photorealistic (in fact, I strongly advise against pursuing that crippling ideal), but they do need to have a convincing realism. Develop a library of base textures that you can then use to generate a wider variety of more specific stuff.

If you find yourself in the countryside, photograph tree bark, leaves, and grass. Photograph them straight on and, if possible, in flat lighting conditions—avoid strong directional sunlight. It doesn't matter that you may be currently working on a futuristic sci-fi game set aboard a giant spaceship with not a plant in sight. I guarantee you'll find yourself building a forest one day!

Gibbons also says to offer your work for review regularly: "Hopefully, you'll have senior staff around to offer guidance and advice as you go, but never be reluctant to show off your stuff."

"Game development is a genuine team effort, so embrace that spirit of sharing!" adds Gibbons. "And you should be prepared to take criticism on the chin…"

Gibbons wants to also add a few practical words on résumés and portfolios/show reels:

➤ Keep résumés short and snappy. Imagine that the recipient has already waded through a dozen applications that morning, so try to avoid any unnecessary padding or waffle. Whatever you do, don't make jokes, criticize software, or include irrelevant details of your private life. Ultimately, the résumé is inconsequential. The best you can hope for is that it will open the door to an interview. You will be hired on the strength of your portfolio or show reel.

➤ Tailor it to the job you're applying for. If you're looking for a position with a video game developer, include samples of your low polygon modeling and texturing skills. A beautiful render or two could be included to demonstrate your artistic flair, but that's no substitute for a fantastic 1,600-polygon game character.

➤ Don't worry about covering every aspect of game art creation in what you show. Most studios tend to have artists that specialize these days. Focus on your strengths. If architectural modeling is your forte, compose your show reel accordingly. If you're a great animator, show some walk and run cycles.

➤ Finally, if you have decent traditional art skills, always include a couple of sample sketches or illustrations. The ability to put a pencil to good use should be highly valued.

Gibbons was asked what he learned from creating the art for the game *Primal*. And what would he do differently if he could start all over again?

You can never devote too much time to careful planning in the early stages of a project's development. It's inevitable with a game such as *Primal*, which takes 30 staff members and three years to develop, that many changes are made along the way. Trying to do all you can in that initial preproduction phase to nail down content issues—be they creative or technical—will undoubtedly help to reduce the problems and convoluted design revisions made during full production.

On that note, Gibbons advises to "think simply:"

Sometimes, the best ideas for video games are the most straightforward—new technologies and the latest hardware can have an intoxicating effect on developers, tempting we artists and designers to indulge grand schemes for games that we imagine will change the face of the industry.

"You can never devote too much time to careful planning in the early stages of a project's development," says Cambridge Studio's Mark

Gibbons, lead artist on the gorgeous *Primal*. Pictured here are
some screen grabs and concept art from the *PS2* game.
(Used with permission by Sony Computer Entertainment
of America, Inc.)

I like the Hollywood expression "high concept," referring to a script or storyline that is easily reduced to a simple, appealing one-liner; a film in which a plot can easily be understood after hearing just a few words. Apply that expression to your video game or even just the level or mission you're working on. Think of gameplay [that] a person can easily understand after playing for just a few minutes. It may help you to remain focused on what's important.

Gibbons says, "What we've tried to do on *Primal* is to invest our time building interesting, dynamic characters with well-rounded personalities and then place them in a game environment in which a detailed story unfolds around them that gamers will want to experience." He continues:

"Interactive movie" used to be dirty words in this business, but we've all played games in which we grow to care about our onscreen characters in much the same way we (sometimes) care about the heroes and heroines in the blockbuster movies we watch.

About halfway though production, we found the need to regulate our art production better. All our art-work creation—whether character or environment modeling, cut scenes, or in-game animation—is now split into a two-part process we refer to imaginatively as Art1 and Art2.

With our animations, for example, the Art1 phase involves creating quick, functional moves that allow our programmers to implement them rapidly in-game. Designers can then begin play-testing immediately. We do the same thing with our environments. A modeler will block out a location with accurate but unpolished geometry and place basic textures on the surfaces. Only after it's been incorporated into the game engine and played through will the artist return to add the Art2 polish that includes proper lighting, detailed textures, and additional geometry refinements.

We do all this essentially to avoid our artists spending too much time on areas of the game that may need considerable adjustment and refining. Art1 allows us to make any necessary changes to charac-ters, environments, or animations early in the process; and thereby hopefully reduce the potential for tantrums.

Primal represented the Cambridge studio's first plunge into the deep and potentially dangerous waters of motion capture. Motion capture has brought our in-game characters a degree of realism and subtle-ty of movement that's damn hard (and time-consuming) to animate by hand. It's provided us with some beautifully realistic walk and run cycles. The interaction between characters in our cut scenes is won-derfully convincing, with gestures and movements that would have been painstaking to create by tradi-tional means. We also discovered quickly that what mo-cap can't do, unfortunately, is deliver the kind of extreme, explosive, comic book combat you need to see in a video game.

Originally, we recruited martial artists to capture a good deal of *Primal's* combat moves, but soon dis-covered that although amazing to watch in isolation, when implemented in-game, these moves felt very sluggish and distinctly underwhelming. We realized there's a dynamic, overblown quality to any decent combat game, and we struggled to create that sensation using motion-capture alone. The vast majori-ty of our fighting moves are now hand-animated, allowing our animators the freedom to produce exciting and energized encounters.

Gibbons was asked where a video game artist should look for inspiration:

Play lots of games. Have fun, but also try to understand what makes the good games worth playing and the bad ones worth avoiding. You're in game development now, and however much you may enjoy play-ing the latest console smash, you will find yourself looking at it through a developer's eyes. Pick out its strengths and weaknesses, noting everything from the resolution of its textures to the quality of its lip-syncing. You may see moments of graphical splendor and wonder how to incorporate something simi-lar into your work. You may encounter art so dreadful you wonder how that particular game ever got made. Try not to let any of that spoil your gaming enjoyment!

Furthermore, Gibbons says to watch lots of movies:

> Although even the most expensive video game is produced for a fraction of the cost of just an average Hollywood movie, games can now boast similar production values. On *Primal*, we hired professional scriptwriters and well-known American and British actors to voice our characters, and we're working with an L.A. rock band to provide music for the game. Look to the movies, particularly those with distinctive visual styles, for inspiration. Whether it's lighting, costume, set design, or special effects, remember that because the motion picture industry has been around since the end of the 19th century, they have a considerable head start on us.

"And, of course," concludes Gibbons, "do what every artist, in every discipline does…take a look around you!"

Richard Kriegler, Electronic Arts/Westwood Studios

One of the most eagerly anticipated computer games in 2002 was *Command & Conquer: Generals*.

Richard Kriegler was the lead artist on the game, and he was asked to give some tips to those artists just starting out in the gaming biz.

"The most important thing students need to remember when they begin their careers is to keep an open mind," begins Kriegler. "Most students come out of college with pretty similar portfolios, all filled with beginner work—nothing the game industry hasn't seen before. Students need to understand that they will essentially be beginning their education all over again. Knowledge will come at them at a rapid pace, and they need to be ready to absorb it all."

He continues:

> Also, many students come out of school with idealistic notions of exactly what they want to do. Although it's definitely important to have goals, students need to remember that they won't likely land their dream jobs right out of school. However, the industry is so diverse and ever-changing that they will eventually get a chance to work on the projects they want. Students should never overlook a good job just because it isn't exactly what they're looking for.

Kriegler was asked how important it is to be a trained as a 2D or 3D artist (that is, in school):

> Yes, it matters a great deal to be trained in both 2D and 3D art in school. Students need at least two years of 2D training—touching all the traditional art and 2D computer programs, such as Photoshop, Quark, Illustrator, and Life Drawing. Students also need two to three years to get all the 3D programs under their belt, such as Maya, 3D Studio Max, and Wave Front. To get the best jobs in games, you need to have experience with both of these disciplines. For example, I'm constantly drawing and sketching concepts before moving them to the computer to be rendered in 3D.

Kriegler was asked to discuss what he's most proud of in *Command & Conquer: Generals*:

> I think the thing I'm most proud of is the realistic look and feel we've captured in *Generals*. The level of detail in our buildings, units, and environments is really a step above our competition, and it adds to the overall believability of the world we've created. Most other RTS games on the market have storylines (and thus environments) that are rooted in fantasy. Although this allows the developers more freedom in their designs, it forces a disconnect between players and the world in which they're playing.

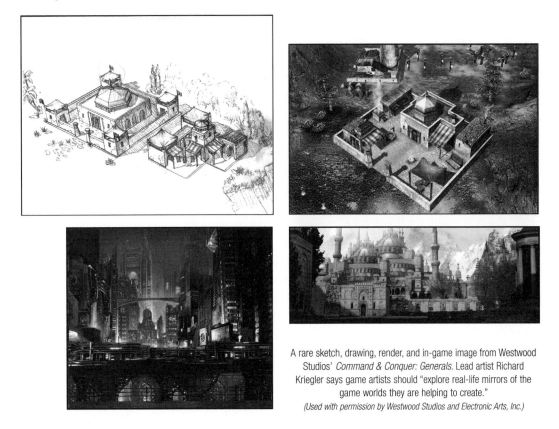

A rare sketch, drawing, render, and in-game image from Westwood Studios' *Command & Conquer: Generals*. Lead artist Richard Kriegler says game artists should "explore real-life mirrors of the game worlds they are helping to create."
(Used with permission by Westwood Studios and Electronic Arts, Inc.)

So, where should a video game artist look for inspiration? "All over the place! But a good place to begin is the video game industry itself; this industry produces a steady stream of original, high-quality material that can really inspire anyone. Similar outlets are movies, television, and comic books."

He continues:

> Beyond that, artists need to explore real-life mirrors of the game worlds they are helping to create. For example, in *Generals*, I've taken a great deal of inspiration from books and news accounts of the Middle East and China, so I can more accurately portray them in the modern warfare setting of our game.

"Of course, nature itself is the oldest and most ripe resource for gathering inspiration," adds Kriegler. "Plant and animal life, along with geological formations, have been inspiring artists since the beginning of mankind."

Takiyoshi Sato, Konami

After studying modern art and oil painting at Tama Art University in Tokyo, Takiyoshi Sato worked as a freelance artist before joining Konami. He is best known for his CG work for the creepy survival horror games *Silent Hill* and *Silent Hill 2* (for the Sony PlayStation and PlayStation 2/Xbox/PC, respectively).

First, some tips from Sato on creating art for video games:

➤ Observing and looking at other human beings is the best way to find something new and interesting around you.

➤ Putting ideas on paper is always better than doing it in your head. Always keep a notebook, explore different options, and write down your ideas about what you can do and what you should do.

➤ If you have a favorite thing or artist, be sure not to duplicate that work or artist. Be original!

How did Sato create the frightening scenes in the *Silent Hill* series?

I'm always thinking and making notes. I don't have any special technique other than that. When I was making *Silent Hill*, I watched a lot of horror movies and read all kinds of novels. I tried to visualize what was happening in the book or movie and then write it down—this is the best way to grow your imagination. When I'm planning a scene, I let ideas grow in my brain, create rough storyboards, and that's about it! I try to find what shocks people; I analyze everything; and then make an answer of my own.

To get the scenes from his mind into the game, Sato says they use Softimage [www.softimage.com] to generate models, animate, and render everything. Editing software such as After Effects and Photoshop [both at www.adobe.com] are important, too.

Believe it or not, Sato says the *Silent Hill 2* team is quite small. "Everybody does a bit of everything—modeling, texturing, animating, lighting, and rendering. In Japan, there's just the director, producer, programmers, and artists—that's it."

The most important part about the development of the *Silent Hill* games, according to Sato, is creating a believable fantasy world. "This requires strong skills to make images to realize that world; but making a balance between the gameplay and atmosphere—that's the most important part."

Finally, Sato's advice for young artists who want to make games for a living:

Games are just merchandise, so of course we have to sell them. But I always keep something in mind I call "religion." Always look at everything from a cultural point of view: Why do we need this work in this age; will this product affect people's notions; what kind of influence will this product have? I think that all creators have to think about these things. People should learn and study another aspect besides games. If you want to be a game artist, don't just focus on game production; you should study traditional subjects—for example, literature, architecture, and music.

Konami's Takiyoshi Sato says he finds inspiration everywhere, but mostly when traveling on his motorcycle! If you've seen the terrifying and gruesome images in *Silent Hill 2*, you might wonder what Sato was really seeing while driving.
(Used with permission by Konami of America, Inc.)

Lee Petty, Circus Freak Studios

Lee Petty is the co-founder and art director of Circus Freak Studios, whose last project was *Superman: The Man of Steel* for Infogrames. The same studio also provided character and cinematic work on a number of other projects, including *Test Drive*, *TransWorld Surf*, and *Test Drive: Offroad*.

Petty took a lot of time to discuss important game art tips and techniques, and how he adheres to the advice in his work on *Superman*.

First, the following are Petty's thoughts on what goes into successful video game artistry:

Preplan Your Work

It's critical that you take at least a few moments to think through any task you are assigned, and try to identify potential problems. These issues can be artistic or technical in nature. A lot of artists have the natural tendency just to "jump into" the work without planning the method or considering all of the consequences. Although this "spontaneous" way of working is often very valuable during an explorative phase of a project, it can cause a lot of problems during the production phase of a project, which is where most of the work is done. Even on a very short time schedule, a lot of problems can be avoided by spending a few moments thinking through the task.

Petty says he often starts with the game "function" of the object he is about to create. He explains:

It's often helpful to start by asking yourself questions about how the item will function in the game. Where will this object be seen? How close will the player get to the object? Does the object need multiple variations? Does the object need to break? In a well-organized project, a detailed design document or similar documentation will have already answered these questions. The reality is, though, that a lot of the tiny details of implementation always slip through the cracks, and it's everyone's job to make sure that what you're creating fits into the proper context.

After you establish the function of the object clearly in your head, says Petty, start to explore any artistic concerns you may have. He advises:

If a concept design has been provided for the object in question, re-evaluate the design in terms of the game context that you've just established. Does it still work? Does the design work artistically in all the contexts? Often, concept designs are little more than thumbnails due to the constant time pressures of game development, and further research may be required before that object can be fully realized in 3D. Find the time to create further sketches or additional detail refinements to the sketch provided, if needed. Research similar real-world objects on the Web or in books, and try to find a way to "meld" the concept design with the real-world details that will make it convincing to the player. Also, make sure that what you're about to create will "flow" with the rest of the art in the game and contribute to the vision as a whole, rather than stand out on its own as a testimony to your abilities.

"The last step you should consider before you begin is any technical limitations you may have," says Petty. He says that artists should ask themselves questions such as "How many polygons do I have for my creation?" or "What texture limitations do I have?" or "Does the object need to be set up for any in-game effects, or tagged in any way?"

Keep Your Work Scalable

In an ideal world, artists would have all the answers necessary at the start of the project to have to create their work only once. Unfortunately, I've never seen this happen. Throughout the course of production, many things change, get adjusted, or change focus. Even in extremely well-organized projects, this is part of the organic evolution that creative endeavors, such as video games, tend to follow.

"Because of this," continues Petty, "it's important that any work you create be kept as 'open' as possible, in terms of construction, to allow for changes." He continues:

Try to find ways of constructing your work to allow you to quickly change or enhance elements throughout the course of production. At Circus Freak Studios, we have many processes that help this.

In our texture work, we always keep a high-resolution, multilayered Photoshop original around. It's common practice by texture artists in this industry to work at higher resolutions than can be used in the game engine. This is usually done because it's quicker and easier to work larger, the process of image reduction tends to help hide any "rough" edges of the texture, and (most importantly from a scalable viewpoint), it allows you to use bigger textures whenever possible. This is most commonly seen in multi-sku game productions, in which one particular hardware platform has less texture memory than another. Without the high-resolution original, it would be a lot of work to "up-res" a texture from a smaller to a larger size. Also, by keeping as many elements on layers as possible, it allows the texture to be "massaged" after it's seen in its full game context; and tasks such as color changes, adding/removing detail from certain areas, and adding specific alpha to elements are quick and trivial to do.

Our character team also has evolved a process of working that allows the work to scale more easily. By making use of 3D Studio Max's external referencing system (or *x-ref'ing*, as it's known), we divide a character's production into two component parts. We have a character model file that contains the character model and texture. The character is modeled, UV'd, and textured in this file. This entire file is then referenced into an animation file, in which the skeleton is animated and the character is skinned. This allows for two people to do simultaneous production on the character. It also makes it simpler to account for changes because if UV work is needed on a character, the much-simpler model file can be used, with little risk of accidentally messing up the bones or rig. In addition to this simple division, the character team has made more extensive use of referencing external files for other elements, such as morph targeting. Even animations can be saved as discrete segments that can be loaded, blended, rearranged, and shared with other characters with similar skeletons.

Work in Passes (Iterations)

Working in passes is something most artists with a traditional background are used to. A final painting, for example, often goes through a series of quick studies, an initial under-painting, and a series of layers that are progressively built up until the final polished work is completed. This basic methodology is useful in creating art in the game industry for a number of reasons.

Because a lot of artists new to the industry have a tendency to try to work on something from start-to-finish in one pass and becoming bogged down in tiny details that may or may not ever be seen in the game, working in passes helps focus them. Working in passes also allows us to make sure that the art is always executed on time. At worst case, the work is in a rougher but functional state, and doesn't delay either the programming or design team from doing their work because we are adding extra detail too early on. Working in passes also allows us to keep our work scalable, as mentioned previously, and not lock down any detail too early in the game—before the proper context is up and running. Seeing your work in Max and seeing it rendered in the game engine with the game camera and AI behaviors functioning is completely different.

At Circus Freak Studios, we try to structure our work in multiple passes whenever possible, with clear definitions of a first, second, and final pass of a given type of asset. This helps keep everyone on track, and brings the game art up as a whole. It also allows the art team to spend the last phase of the project polishing the work and adding extra detail when more of the game context exists, instead of creating new levels and assets at the end of the project. All of this being said, there are times when we have to polish work earlier on than we'd like for things such as prototypes, magazine demos, or trying to demonstrate to a publisher or licensor what a polished section of the game will eventually look like.

Petty says he used the preceding techniques and concepts throughout the course of production on *Superman* (as much as possible). "*Superman: The Man of Steel* for the Xbox is an extremely challenging game to execute due to our relatively short development cycle, the huge scale of our environments, and our desire to take advantage of the power of the Xbox on our characters and environments," explains Petty.

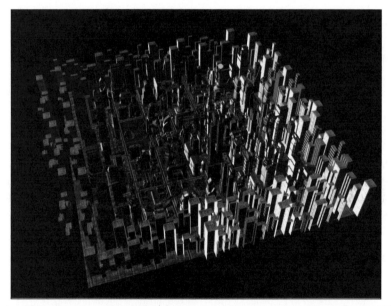

Petty illustrates how big the Superman world is in the game with this 3D model. Yup, those are buildings to fly around. Pretty cool, huh?
(Used with permission by Infogrames, Inc., SUPERMAN ™ & © DC Comics 2002.)

Petty says using their world as an example, he'll demonstrate how they applied the principles of preplanning, scalability, and working in passes to successfully execute the art on time and to a high quality standard:

From the moment we started *Superman*, we knew that we were going to focus on making sure the player was able to use all of his powers all the time. One of Superman's most often used powers is his ability to fly at high speeds throughout Metropolis. We wanted to give the player the freedom to fly and land on any arbitrary building in a big world without relying on fogging out the background or constraining Superman to be able to fly only a few hundred feet high.

To accomplish these goals, we had to plan our level construction to support the detail where it would be seen most: hundreds of feet up in the air. The world artists preplanned their work carefully by working with the game designers to define key areas in our environments where important encounters would take place. We married the key locations from the city of Metropolis, such as the *Daily Planet*, with key engagement areas that the designers had established. The world artists built quick first-pass "block worlds" built from simple shapes with no textures or lighting to establish the overall scale of the level. Key areas were defined by bright coloring. The designers were able to fly Superman through these levels, and they worked with the artists to adjust the placement of key areas and to help sculpt mission flow.

After this phase was complete, the artists began a second pass at their levels. This pass involved defining detailed building shapes, applying UVs and "proxy" textures (which mainly established color relationships and scale), and using simple lighting. At this point, the level artists were careful to keep their work scalable. This was accomplished in 3D Studio Max by keeping as many things as instanced as possible, so that the level artists would have fewer buildings to iterate than if every individual structure were a unique identity (we had a few thousand buildings per level in some cases). The thought was that if the level was too repetitive in appearance, the buildings could be collapsed into unique entities and modified during the very last phases of the project.

Next, Petty says that after this second pass had been completed, it was obvious they would need to make extensive use of the Xbox's multipass capabilities to deal with some of the texturing challenges that popped up:

In our game, more than any other, the player could fly right up to almost any object in the world, as well as get over one mile away and still see the very same object. If we textured our structures to look good when the player was close to them, they tended to look badly tiled when the player was far away. To combat this, we knew we would have to make extensive use of detail textures and other texture passes to break up the surface. At that stage of the project, however, we didn't have our multipass tools yet, so we had to keep our texture work very scalable so we could move detail from one texture to another pass.

The world scale issue also provided a similar problem with lighting. Because we had buildings that ranged from 20 feet to 2000 feet tall, combined with the sheer number of buildings in the world that were visible at once, we didn't have enough vertex resolution in all objects to create highly detailed vertex lighting. We knew that once multipass came online, we could leverage it to utilize additional lighting techniques such as per-pixel lighting. So, again, we kept our worlds scalable in this pass until later and avoided doing any detail lighting work or cutting any shadows into the meshes because they would just change later on.

Petty says that by the time the artists began their third pass on the levels, they had introduced multipass texturing, and better texturing and lighting schemes were available. He continues:

> Also, an LOD and streaming system were created to allow for such huge levels to exist while minimizing the memory footprint. Had the world artists polished their work too early in development and not kept their geometry, texturing, and lighting approaches scalable and in multiple passes, a lot of unnecessary rework would have occurred.

Is working with a franchise such as *Superman* a blessing, or is there too much pressure to deliver?

"Working with licensed productions presents both benefits and challenges to the game artist and development team as a whole," admits Petty. He elaborates:

> A license such as *Superman* offers a long history of interesting characters, cool environments, and story ideas. Being able to tap into that established wealth of information is a great boost to kicking off a game. Having this library of visual work makes it easier to focus the entire art team in the same visual direction without undergoing an extensive concept art phase. We were provided with a lot of very useful reference artwork for characters and environments.
>
> It's also nice with a license as big as *Superman* that the consumer is already familiar with Superman's character, motivations, and abilities. This really helps move an action game such as *Superman* along without having to go into unnecessary explanations; everyone expects that Superman can fly and use x-ray vision.

According to Petty, a licensed product can present many challenges, too, because of the many assumptions and restrictions that must be properly addressed to do the license justice.

Petty says that the biggest and most critical challenge for the artists is being able to "translate" the look of the original source media into that of the video game realm:

> In *Superman*, for example, the comic's look relies heavily on use of line weight, dynamic composition, and simple bold color schemes. As we created the artwork for *Superman: The Man of Steel*, we realized that we would have difficulty using those elements to communicate the look and feel. There really is no concept of comic-style "variable-weight line work" in video games (although for a very cartoon look, a lot of people use cell-shaded techniques to achieve this). With a free-roaming, third-person camera, the artists cannot create a dynamic "framed" composition. Also, simple bold color schemes were perceived as "too simple" and not convincing enough to "feel" like the future city of Metropolis. With all these variables in mind, it was our challenge to create something that upon detailed inspection is quite different from a comic book look, but still needed to embody the spirit and "feel" of Superman.

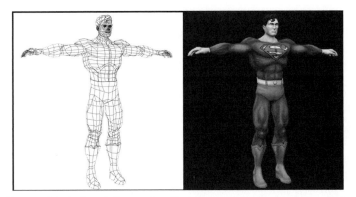

The man of steel gets ready for game time. Here's a shot of Superman as a wireframe (left)
and then with the textures painted on the 3D model (right).
(Used with permission by Infogrames, Inc., SUPERMAN ™ & © DC Comics 2002.)

Petty says there were a lot of challenges in creating Superman's powers, too:

> A hero that can fly, is invulnerable, and can see through any building in the world not only presented many game design challenges to our designers, but also meant that we had to plan very carefully where we put our art resources. With a licensed product, there is no "redesigning" the character to fit the gameplay. We couldn't decide to make Superman not fly because we wanted to focus more detail and gameplay on the ground. We couldn't use visibility-culling tricks on the world with the assumption that the player couldn't fly 1500 feet up in the air and use his telescopic vision to look across the entire level. We had to work with these constraints because not doing so wouldn't have made it a *Superman* game.

Petty was also asked to provide some artwork designed for the game (figures that follow) and discuss the techniques used to create it:

> Throughout the course of development on *Superman: The Man of Steel*, a large number of interactive objects have been created. I'll describe the basic process I used to create a simple object for the "Warworld" environment. This object was described by design as a large "rune stone" that Superman would have to use his super strength to move from one place to another in order to unlock a puzzle to provide clues to an object Superman needs to help him defeat his arch nemesis: Brainiac-13.

To go one step further, Petty applies the design and implantation of this rune stone in light of his preceding advice:

Preplanning

I started this process by asking the designers a number of questions. A number of conversations later, I had all the information I needed. There were to be three different rune stones, which the player must find and move next to one another in a certain sequence to reveal a clue. Superman will be able to read the runes after they are placed in a certain order to find his next objective. The runes were supposed to have some indication in their appearance of belonging next to other runes. I decided at this point that I would make one model with one "base" texture for most of the model and a second smaller texture that could be swapped out for variations. This second texture would contain the unique runes on the front of the rune block and would help guide the player on where to place the runes. Using this approach, I only needed one model, but could create all three rune blocks through texture variation, which would save me time as well as save memory: the most precious resource in game development.

In our chat, Circus Freak Studios' Lee Petty discusses the creation and implementation of these rune stones in the game *Superman: The Man of Steel*. Pictured here: rune block concept, its textures, and a render of it.
(Used with permission by Infogrames, Inc., SUPERMAN ™ & © DC Comics 2002.)

Petty says the runes were on an alien planet known as Warworld, in which the evil Mongul is in the process of building weapons and has scattered futuristic industrial structures all over the surface of this barren planet:

The runes were remnants of an ancient race that once inhabited the planet before Mongul devastated it. The world artists had already done a lot of work on the planet, and the look and feel of the environment was looking great. I did a small amount of research on the web and decided after looking at many rune patterns that I would go with something less European and more "cuneiform" in appearance because it was less familiar than the European runes and felt more ancient and alien to me.

Petty says that because this was essentially a one-day task, he quickly did a rough sketch to cement his ideas together and then proceeded to the modeling and texturing process.

Modeling

After a sketch was complete, I modeled the basic shape of the rune block, making sure it was the proper scale in the game, before I did any detail work on it. I set up the UVs inside of 3D Studio Max, and exported my texture coordinates to Photoshop using a plug-in for 3D Studio Max called "texporter."

Texturing

I created my textures directly in Photoshop. I used cement and stone patterns for the basic textures, keeping everything in layers. I wanted to have all of the edges of the object worn, to help give the illusion that more beveling existed on the object's edges. I wanted to keep the texture scalable enough to change how weathered the edges looked, in case it seemed out of place after it got into the game engine. To do this, I created a layer mask in Photoshop, and "erased" through the base texture to reveal the "worn" texture around the edges. By using the layer mask approach to most of my grunge and detail, I could tweak it later with minimal rework.

Petty says that after creating the base texture, he worked on three variants for the second texture, which would be used to differentiate the three different rune faces.

As if this Game Art 101 wasn't enough, Petty also took the time to give advice on breaking into the industry as an artist:

Strong demo reel

A good demo reel is necessary to get a good job. It's what prospective employers see first, and it leaves an impression.

The following are his tips for creating your demo reel:

➤ Don't use "pop techno" music as a backdrop to your piece; it's so commonly used that it causes most people to just turn down the volume.

➤ Don't make the reel more than four minutes in length. Make your reel short and sweet.

➤ Show only your best work in your strongest area. Too often, I see reels that have excellent models, but really horrible textures or material work. The most common error I see is bad animation. Unless you are a really good animator, don't show your animation. I see a lot of great models animated really badly. I think most people want to show their versatility, but odds are you won't be hired for your weak area anyway, and it only lowers the perceived quality of your whole reel. What you want to do is ride into a job on your strength and then expand your skill set internally, when you can be mentored.

➤ Along those same lines, if you're not a strong concept designer, don't model, texture, and animate only your own designs. If your initial design work isn't strong, the model will never be truly impressive. Use other sources to model, such as real-world references, or take inspiration from (don't copy) some of your favorite artists.

➤ Robots, spaceships, and heavily muscled guys with big guns are all fine and dandy, but if you really want your reel to stand out, try something more unique. Something more stylized. Right now, there's a lot of buzz in the industry about NPR (non-photorealistic rendering), yet I rarely see a demo reel that has any stylized rendering other than the straight "CG" look.

Strong traditional skills, but also technically competent

According to Petty, a lot of art directors say that they'd rather hire a talented artist who doesn't know the tools than a mediocre artist who knows the tools well: "They say that they can train a person to use the tools quickly, but to train someone to be a good artist takes years of time that they simply don't have," says Petty.

"In concept, I couldn't agree more," says Petty, but he points to an exception:

Knowing a specific tool isn't important, but knowing how tools fundamentally work and being able to understand their structures and to troubleshoot problems and arrive at creative but technical solutions is a critical skill to have. This skill is also not quick to impart to people who are not inclined in this way. Due to the horrible time restrictions in this industry, most production teams need someone who can produce quickly and problem-solve the myriad issues that arise during production. This usually means someone who knows the tools already. If you don't happen to know the tools, go out of your way to demonstrate that you are technically savvy enough to learn them quickly and troubleshoot problems on your own.

Petty believes that there are a lot of talented artists in this industry and a lot of talented artists trying to break into this industry. So, what does Petty look for when hiring?

Flexibility and working in a team

When I interview a person, I look for someone who is flexible enough to work on a project that has a certain amount of chaos built in. Throughout production, an artist will have to rework, re-export, and redo many pieces of work to get the best results. Someone who lacks the flexibility to do this and stay interested in the work will have trouble getting through a bigger project. I respect someone who voices his or her opinion, but doesn't whine at every change request.

Petty says this flexibility will go a long way to help that individual work within a team context:

In video game art production, there are a lot of very creative people having to work very closely under terrible deadlines. Knowing how to work, cooperate, and enhance others on your team, who may be very different people from yourself, is a key skill. If the team doesn't work well together, the work will never get past a certain point. People who are fundamentally interested in working with others to make something greater than they could do by themselves are people I want to hire. At Circus Freak Studios, all the great artwork that has been done on *Superman: The Man of Steel* is thanks to our art team.

It would be unfair of me to say this without thanking all of them: Mike Badillo, Norm Badillo, Judah Baron, Ken Brose, Jeremy Dale, David Gustlin, Mike Khoury, Randall Ng, Lee Rosenbaum, Seth Swanson, and Angus Wilson.

Tetsuya Nomura, Square Enix

As director and character designer on the celebrated *Final Fantasy* role-playing game series for the Sony PlayStation and PC, Tetsuya Nomura is internationally respected for his work on such memorable characters as Cloud and Aeris. Following the incredible success of *Final Fantasy VII*, Nomura went on to design characters for *Parasite Eve* and *Final Fantasy* games VIII through X, as well.

Once again, a *Final Fantasy* game pushes the boundaries for in-game and pre-rendered graphics. Pictured here are scenes from *Final Fantasy X* for the PlayStation 2.
(Used with permission by SQUARE USA, Inc.)

Asked to highlight three of the most important pieces of advice he could give to a game artist or animator just starting out, Nomura responds as follows:

> First, the most important aspect is the communication between the staff on the game development team. Game design involves character design, 3D models, textures, motion, and other details; so it's necessary to understand the overall flow of development and to be aware of progress.
>
> Second, it's also necessary to have interests other than games. In my case, I watch many movies. I tend to like action movies, but I watch movies in all genres. I also watch a lot of TV. I have an interest in images overall. I also am interested in fashion. I go through fashion magazines and I like to shop.
>
> The third point is not to mistake yourself for an "artist." We are not "artists," but "creators." Our goal is to create newer and more fun games. Art is not our goal. There are those who say that games are a form of art within digital entertainment, but I believe that games are toys that are to be enjoyed.

What tools are used by the artists at Square to create such breathtaking images in the *Final Fantasy* series?

> My work entails creating designs and storyboards that serve as blueprints in the process of creating images, so I use an HB mechanical pencil and size A4 copy paper. I use Photoshop for coloring and touching up the images. I have no special techniques; I draw and create images based on feeling and inspiration.

> **NOTE**
>
> David Perry, creator of hit characters from games such as *MDK*, *Earthworm Jim*, and *Messiah*, says he almost always employs model makers to create 3D representations of his characters to bring into business meetings when pitching a game. Read Chapter 6 for some ways to do this.

Don Hopkins, Freelance

This extremely bright and articulate freelance developer has worked on many games, including the best-selling and award-winning *The Sims* for Electronic Arts. In this book, he chats elsewhere about programming and AI (see Chapter 11, "Programming Theory"), and user interfaces (see Chapter 14, "The All-Important User Interface [UI] and Game Control").

Hopkins "talks tech" about how a character can be smoothly animated.

> The objects in *The Sims* are pre-rendered in 3D Studio Max [www.discreet.com], complete with z buffers of depth information, so they clip correctly in the 3D world. Object animations are accomplished by flipping between different sprites, which can be broken up into independently animated subcomponents (like the two doors, gas flame, and food on the grill). But the characters are rendered in real time as 3D texture-mapped polygons. The z buffers of the sprites allow the characters to closely interact with the objects, so they properly clip each other, like when the kids climb around inside the playground equipment.

The artists produce the character animation and objects in 3D Studio Max, loading them into the same file so they can get the registration correct. But they export the objects and animations separately because the sprite content pipeline is quite different from the character animation pipeline. Some artists specialize in making 3D objects, others specialize in character skin meshes and texture maps, and others specialize in character animation.

The Sims uses a character animation system inspired by Ken Perlin's work on *Improv*, according to Hopkins:

They have a skeleton, to which you can attach deformable meshes and animate. The skeletons, bodies, accessories, and animations are created in 3D Studio Max, using Character Studio's Biped for animating the skeleton and Physique for attaching the body to the skeleton. The artists use "note tracks" to mark up the skeletons, suits, skills, and events. A note track can be attached to any 3D object and contains text keys positioned in time. Note tracks are extremely useful and general purpose because they can identify a point in time and space and because they contain key/value pairs to control the exporter as well as the animation engine in the game. I implemented the character animation exporter as an extension to MaxScript scripting language in 3D Studio Max. The exporter looks for the note tracks that tell it what objects to export, including skeletons, suits, and skills.

Skeletons are the simplest. You put a tag on the root of the skeleton, giving it a name. The skeleton defines the names of a bunch of bones—their tree structure, translations, rotations, and degrees of freedom.

Suits are more complicated. A *suit* is a snapshot of one or more texture-mapped meshes attached to a skeleton at a particular point in time. There are two ways to attach meshes to the skeleton: by connecting a rigid mesh as a child of a single parent bone or by using the Physique modifier to attach a deformable mesh to any number of bones.

Rigid meshes—such as heads, hands, and accessories—are just exported as a special case of deformable mesh, attached to only one bone. Deformable meshes can have vertices that straddle two bones, whose position is blended between them, for smoothing the mesh along joints such as elbows and knees.

Animations are the most complicated. They have a begin time and an end time, marked by separate note track keys attached to the root bone of the skeleton. You can also make partial body animations by attaching tags lower down in the skeleton or explicitly listing bones to exclude or include in the note track key.

The playback engine in the game combines animations by blending and layering full and partial body animations together, kind of like Photoshop layers.

When switching between animations, the engine cross-fades from the end of the last animation to the beginning of the new animation, to smooth out small incompatibilities between poses in sequential animations. Partial body animations, such as one-arm carrying, are layered over full-body walking animations, so sims can carry objects around the house.

To learn more about Ken Perlin and creating dramatic character animation and computer graphics, visit www.kenperlin.com or http://mrl.nyu.edu/~perlin/.

Kevin Cloud, id Software

Kevin Cloud is an artist and part owner at id Software, who started way back during the development of the classic *Wolfenstein 3D*. Since then, he has worked on such hit series as *DOOM* and *Quake*. Cloud takes some time out of his busy schedule from working on the much-anticipated *DOOM III* to offer his expertise on creating art for games. He starts with the following:

> What's been most difficult for me is following good advice. Because everyone is different, with different talents and different circumstances, each individual must find his or her own way. But if you want to make sure you're going in the right direction, watch what other successful artists have done. So I guess my first bit of advice is to be a student of life. Always maintain your interest in the world around you and be open to understanding and learning from the successes and failures of other artists.

> The golden rule for being successful at anything is to do something you enjoy. I know it's a cliché, but that's because it's true. And this is a rule everyone tends to forget and relearn. Computer game artists need to like computer games, enjoy working with a team, and being part of a process. As a computer game artist, you'll be subject to creating things that other people design, making art that follows bizarre restrictions, and working under criticism from others. But if you love making worlds for people to play, you'll enjoy doing it all. Certainly, tons of game artists are ambivalent about games. But from my experience, these people are rarely happy doing their jobs. And trust me, you can't be successful unless you're happy. Happiness is a requirement for success.

The next stage may sound fairly obvious, says Cloud, but it tends to be overlooked quite a bit in today's gaming industry. Cloud admits even he has learned this way:

> Next, learn to be an artist, not just a computer artist. I graduated with a degree in political science. And although I took several art classes, I wish I would have taken more. I'm proud of my ability to learn new tools and take advantage of what's available to make the best art I can in the quickest possible time. But I've had to pick up on many fundamental skills as I've gone along. If I started out today with the skills I had in '85 when I started at my first job, I probably wouldn't be hired. The day of the hacker/computer artist is over. Either by reading books or going to school, learning the fundamentals of art is imperative. Color theory, animation, the human form, painting, drawing techniques, composition, and so on aren't skills you pick up on your own.

Imagine a realistic 3D shooter played from a first-person perspective fused with a disturbing horror theme, not unlike the *Resident Evil* games. The result is *DOOM III*, with graphics so good they looked like pre-rendered CG.
(Used with permission by id Software, Inc. and Activision, Inc.)

So what can someone do outside of school? What are the tools to learn first, and best?

Get set up at home with your own system. You can't learn to be a computer artist unless you spend time on the computer. Buy an old system and find public domain or used software on the Internet. Take the bus or bike to the university, but get a computer. You don't need the best software or system to get started, but you do need something. There are so many good programs out there, but you won't make a mistake by learning Photoshop [www.adobe.com] and 3D Studio [www.discreet.com]. If you can't find an old copy of one of those, then get any 32-bit art program and polygon modeling tool you can afford. Other alternatives to having a system at home are using a friend's system, using the school's system, or getting a job (any job) at a place that has computers. Some suggestions are a copy/fax place, a service bureau, or a small computer store. Although I applied for the position of artist at my first computer company, Softdisk, they said they didn't need an artist. Instead, I took the job of answering technical support calls. It took time to convince the people at Softdisk that they needed an artist, but in the meantime I got a chance to talk to their programmers and use their computers and software to learn.

> **NOTE**
> id Software's Kevin Cloud says Photoshop is still the best tool to use and is what most gaming companies are using. But "there is less of a consensus on 3D tools," says Cloud. "3D Studio, now generally called 3ds max or just max, has lost some ground to LightWave and Maya, but it is still probably the most common model and animation tool for games."

Cloud says that after you have some schooling and real-world experience behind you, the next step is to focus on being a better artist:

Avoid the millions of distractions that come your way. This is a lesson I have to learn over and over again. Although I never stop doing art, I often get sidetracked on other projects, and about a year later my head explodes. I have to learn once again that I'm an artist because that's what I like doing. Throughout your career, remain focused on being a better artist. Seek out more art resources—books, good web sites, art collections on disk. There are tons of biographies about artists, featuring their art and stories about their lives. Every artist should spend some time following the lives of favorite artists and emulating their styles. You'll learn so much just by trying to match the style of a great artist, and in the end you'll gain the flexibility to create your own style. Look for discussion groups on the web, and don't be afraid to ask questions. And ask for advice and comments from your coworkers. Surround yourself with positive people who are interested in becoming better artists. Focus on improving your art skills, and opportunities will be out there for you.

An extra piece of advice is this: Don't be afraid to move or take risks, and strive to be great. If possible, finish the project you're on—but if a better opportunity comes along, take it. Try to surround yourself with positive and talented people. Working with the best will always bring out the best in you. And keep in mind that your future is in your hands. Don't settle for being just one of the many. Do something different to set yourself apart. Develop a style or technique that is your own. Try to make a difference on any project you're on, so that people will know that your hands have been on that game.

Cloud was asked to discuss what he was most proud of—from an artistic standpoint—in the upcoming *DOOM III*, due out sometime in 2003.

First, let me say that unlike the original *DOOM*, in which Adrian [Carmack] and I were the only artists, the vast majority of the art for *DOOM III* is being created by the other artists here at id. id has been lucky enough to attract the best artistic talent in the industry, and the team we have here is creating things that I wouldn't have imagined possible back when we created the first *DOOM*.

That said, Cloud offers the following:

DOOM III is an evolutionary step in computer game graphics, offering the ability to create pre-rendered, cinematic-quality art in a real-time environment. If you've created a pre-rendered cinematic, you'll be familiar with the basic elements used to create art in *DOOM III*: things such as lighting, particle systems, material content, cameras, and so on. For an artist, working in *DOOM III* is better than creating traditional cinematics because the results of your work can be seen immediately. For example, change world geometry, a light, a texture, or a model, and immediately see the results inside the *DOOM* world.

Cloud says "heightmaps" are probably the coolest art element in *DOOM III*:

> *DOOM III* uses a heightmap to replicate the detail of a high-poly model. The artist creates a 3D model of, for example, a monster skin or a wall texture or whatever. Then this model is converted into a 24-bit, two-dimensional texture that works with the rendering and lighting systems to create the details of a surface (such as veins, hair, wrinkles, muscles, and so on).

From an artistic perspective, Cloud was asked to discuss the differences between creating art for a computer game versus a console game. "The differences vary, depending on the game and the console," answers Cloud. "However, in general, a console artist has more constraints and will have to do more with less total texture memory—this may mean making textures smaller or using fewer textures than he would for a PC game." He continues:

> Also, a television and a PC monitor's output are a little different. On a television, saturated colors of red, blue, or green tend to blur and are more intense than on a PC monitor. So, artists need to adjust for this when creating the textures or continue to check their textures on a television output.

Cloud says that at id, the technology constantly changes to make the best use of the latest PC hardware. Therefore, the development environment and toolsets are changing as well:

> We rarely have the time to create the perfect internal toolsets. However, the console is a stable platform in which the artist and programmers can work to evolve the techniques and toolsets over the lifetime of the console.

Cloud says another advantage a console artist has above a PC artist is that the console cannot be heavily modified:

> When creating art for a console, you don't have to worry about how the game will look on all the different hardware configurations. On the PC, a spectacular environment can look somewhat less impressive with lightmaps, shade layers, interpolation, mipmaps, and resolution—either reduced or turned off.

Finally, Cloud was asked whether the art of creating art for computer/video games has changed at all over the past couple of years. And if so, how has it changed?

> Creating art changes every year. Rather than creating a surface from one image, we now use several images or layers. How those layers are combined is based on a text file script called a *material defini-tion*. If you're familiar with creating art for pre-rendered scenes, you'll have a general understanding of how it's done. Each surface has surface detail generated from a bumpmap or heightmap layer; then another layer identifies the specular content or the shininess of the texture, and another layer identifies the color of the surface, and so on. The heightmap is created using a 3D modeling tool rather than Photoshop. The model is used to generate a texture in which each color channel of a pixel represents the amount of light hitting the surface from a consistent direction. The advantage of all of this, especially in a world that's lit in real-time, is that the surface can now respond to the color, amount, and angle of the light—similar to the way it would in the real world.

Pierre Rivest, Ubi Soft Entertainment and Reid Schneider, BAM! Entertainment

In other areas of this book, *Batman: Vengeance* producer Reid Schneider chats about creating the game's dark look and feel (and staying true to the Warner Bros. animated TV series). Here, he and artist Pierre Rivest talk about some of the art/animation techniques used to create the game. Schneider has since left Ubi Soft to work for BAM! Entertainment.

Schneider:

Our animators made it a point to create ultra-fluid movement for all the characters in the game, and they did an incredible job. One of the hardest parts of game animation is that you have to make sure that every move can link together seamlessly, or the illusion is broken. The gamer of today is extremely demanding (this is a good thing) and expects ultra-high quality. However, high-quality animation is only one side of the equation. The code that uses the animation must be extremely well-done and properly linked to the animation, or the result will be subpar.

This is true for the cape as well. The cape is a result of animators and programmers working together for one goal. It's a great example of collaboration between two very different fields for one result.

Rivest:

All animations within the game were hand-created. No motion-capture was used. We felt that by hand-animating, we'd have better control of the results and it would be easier to make Batman perform the superhero actions that players expect. Most of the character animations within the *Batman: Vengeance* game use a technique called blending. This technique allows us to blend two animations together quite easily. For example, Batman could be performing his running animation, and a nearby thug holding a shotgun fires and hits Batman. With the animation blending, it's very easy for us to blend both the running and getting-hit-by-shotgun animations together. This has the effect of Batman continuing to run but reacting to the shotgun impact.

The bat-cape is actually separate from Batman. It's a dynamic actor that follows and reacts dynamically to every movement Batman performs.

Catherine Roy, Ubi Soft Entertainment

We heard some interesting comments from this talented producer on the *Tarzan Untamed* and *Jungle Book* games earlier in this book. Here, Roy discusses how the animation in the game looks so fluid. How did they animate Tarzan's hair?

First, Roy says to animate the characters in Tarzan, their main tools were 3D Studio Max and Character Studio (both at www.discreet.com). And the two biggest challenges were the cinematic bosses and Tarzan's animations. She explains:

The gameplay related with the boss implicated that our animations would be playable forward and reverse to give the wrestle feeling. Each boss took more than two artists per month to animate. The three animators worked closely with the programmers in the beginning to make sure that our animation player would interpolate the frame correctly forward and backward.

For Tarzan, the challenge came from the quantity of animation we needed to do. Added to this, each animation needed to be retouched to animate Tarzan's hair. It made the animator's job very long and pretty boring. This is why we developed a hair mechanic in the engine that animates the hair on its own. It puts some wind and gravity on the hair dreads. Then the animator had to put collision zones on Tarzan's shoulder and neck so the hair wouldn't go through the body, and that was it. The time we saved not having to animate the hair was put on the important animations to make them as fluid as possible and allowed us to create a wider variety of trick moves.

Catherine Roy says real-world experiences can help to animate a not-so-real-world character, as seen here in *Tarzan Untamed*: "One of our animators was a skater since the age of 10. He was really excited to work on Tarzan's trick moves and he put all his energy and creativity to create the best moves he could for each sport. We looked at plenty of videos found on the Net for barefoot skiing, wakeboarding, snowboarding, skateboarding… and we came up with a selection of moves that would be cool in the sport we have in the game."
(Ubi Soft Entertainment S.A. All Rights Reserved. Under license by © Disney. All Rights Reserved.)

Greg Thomas, Sega of America/Visual Concepts

This veteran console game designer offers a number of programming tips for beginners. In the following passage, he outlines three excellent "rules" for game artists to adhere to.

> ➤ Leave your ego at the door. There are many creative people on a team. What I mean by this is that an artist needs to be able to take criticism well. Often there are many "redos."

> ➤ Remember that we're creating an interactive experience, not a movie. So gameplay comes before visuals. This may mean cutting frames of animation or slightly degrading elements of artwork, and so on. This is very important, though, and artists often don't fully understand this. If an artist wants to solely focus on visuals, the game industry is not the place for him or her.

➤ An artist needs to be somewhat technical in understanding what the machine is capable of doing. I've seen some awesome artists end up with more average work than an artist who has lesser base art skills, but understands technically what's going on. For example, an artist might be able to make a football player model that looks perfectly real, but the hardware can't use it. It's better to make the model simpler at first and then continue to add details until the limits are reached.

Sega's Greg Thomas says the tools used to create such stunning games as Sega Sports' *NBA2K3* (pictured here) and *NFL2K3* were Alias Power Animator/Power Modeling, Adobe Photoshop, some motion-capture work, and a few custom in-house tools.

(Used with permission by Sega of America, Inc.)

Todd Howard, Bethesda Softworks

We heard from Howard in Chapter 5, "General Game Design: Role-Playing Games (RPGs) and Persistent Online Worlds" on role-playing game (RPG) design. Here, he was asked to explain the different kinds of artists needed for the creation of a 3D RPG such as *Elder Scrolls: Morrowind*. What should be the most important consideration for an artist/animator before starting the project?

Everything now is 3D. Even most interfaces are 3D in some respect. You must learn 3D Studio Max [www.discreet.com], Maya [www.aliaswavefront.com], or something of the sort. But the art department will usually break into modeling, texturing, and animation. It's best to be good at all three. Modeling and texturing go together well, but animation really takes your full time if you do that.

Bethesda's Todd Howard has donated two never-before-seen images from the game *Morrowind*. Seen here is Vivec, one of the Dark Elven gods, in 3D Studio Max, plus a sketch of him fighting Ruddy Man.
(Used with permission by Bethesda Softworks, Inc.)

The first thing to know before you start doing art is how many polygons you can spend. Make a budget for your whole scene. How many for characters? How many for the environment and how many for special effects? You don't want to make a 10,000-polygon character and then find out that your game can only support 200. But aim high. There are two reasons for this: It's easier to scale down than up later on, and your game will most likely get further optimized by the time you're done, so you'll wish you had done more with the art.

Emmanuel Valdez

If you've ever laughed at the over-the-top animated faces of the fighters in Midway's *Ready 2 Rumble Boxing*, you've enjoyed the work of the very talented Emmanuel Valdez. Before leaving Midway in 2002 to pursue other interests, Valdez was the lead artist at Midway Home Entertainment, Inc, who created cyber-celebs such as Afro Thunder. Before that, he worked on *ESPN Extreme Games* and *Bio F.r.e.a.k.s.* His future aspirations include being in the industry long enough to work on games that "blur the line between the virtual world and the real world."

Valdez outlines three key rules for game artists to keep in mind.

Communication

"Game art and graphics are one of the first things most consumers relate to when they purchase a video game," says Valdez.

It's the goal of a computer graphics artist to clearly communicate the overall look and feel of the game in every aspect of the graphics, including the interface, the animations, and the gameplay graphics.

The interface of *Ready 2 Rumble Boxing* revolved around the use of a plain white background and "bouncing" cartoony fonts. Instead of cluttering the screen with cool and trendy graphics, we opted to concentrate on clearly defining your options while providing a fun and playful feeling because the game focuses on a comical approach to boxing and less simulation.

Attention to Detail

According to Valdez, every game artist should set goals in establishing the look of the game. He explains:

Go the extra mile and apply as much visual stimulation as you can to the art in the elements such as color, design, texture, and animation. The work applied to the computer graphics that scream to be looked at because of the extra put into them will draw praise from consumers and fellow game developers alike. The added details reflect the artist's and game developer's devotion to creating depth and show effort in making a game.

With *Ready 2 Rumble Boxing 2*, the advent of Sony PlayStation 2 and the Microsoft Xbox provided the opportunity to create highly detailed, cinema-quality computer graphics. We created characters that were more defined and had larger animation move sets and an abundance of texture memory, allowing texture-map artists to create details that were once deemed a luxury to pursue. Soon the video game industry will converge with the movie industry and create the next level in entertainment.

Know When to Say When

To balance out the level of detail, Valdez warns that it's important to know when to stop fiddling and fighting with the art.

An artist is usually never happy with the results and often spends a lot of time trying to experiment and rework the game graphics. Time to develop video games is getting shorter and shorter and is the single-most defining factor in game art compromises.

What tools were used to achieve the look and feel of the *Ready 2 Rumble Boxing* series?

Every art director or lead artist should always lay down the groundwork for the overall look that they want to base the graphics on. It may be just one idea on a character's costume or an elaborate level with complex lighting and geometry that dictates the flow and coherent quality of the entire game—a sort of "graphics bible." Any divergence from "the look" that is totally unrelated in quality or style, unless deliberately done, is game art that usually doesn't work. A good way to get started is to gather visual information on subjects that will relate to the game or visuals that inspire and motivate the computer artist. Often, you can draw from an assortment of influences that spark interesting and visually stimulating impressions, which can help the artist convey a message that reflects the overall vision for a game.

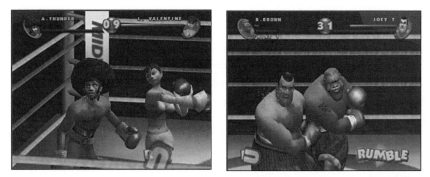

"The animation in *Ready 2 Rumble Boxing: Round 2* reflects the attention to detail that goes into creating a video game character,"
says Valdez. Pictured here is the funkadelic Afro Thunder, among other characters. Can you dig it?
(Used with permission by Midway Games, Inc.)

On the various positions to fill at a game development studio, Valdez says computer game artists usually come in three different flavors: texture-map artist, model builder, and animator. Here's a brief breakdown of each:

➤ A *texture-map artist* creates 2D materials and textures, such as clothing, hair, and skin, and applies that data onto 3D models.

➤ A *model builder* creates the 3D geometry that the texture mappers use as the base for their textures. Models are the essential building blocks of real-time 3D video games today.

➤ An *animator* creates the motion attached to objects or characters and gives them the ability of movement, fighting skills, or even facial expressions.

Some teams are fortunate to have a full-time concept artist and designer to create the look and design direction for the graphics, Valdez notes.

Where can a game artist draw inspiration?

People have different tastes and views on art, which makes it very unique and enriching to everyone. Art itself is an expression and can come in many forms. I personally look to music, cinematography in movies, architecture, car designs, and fashion trends. Some artists seek inspirations from the works of other artists, painters, photographers, and sculptors.

The hardest part about creating art and animation for games is developing a "look"—a goal that all art in the game must follow. It's crucial in dictating the theme and mood to the whole game and must be done very early in the process of developing a video game. That means that pre-production, the early research and development of an idea for a game, is the most important time to ensure the best art direction for the entire project.

Valdez explains what motion-capture animation (mo-cap) is, and how it's used in today's games.

Motion-capture is the technique of gathering realistic and accurate animation data by capturing movements of an actor using optical and magnetic technologies. Many games require realistic motion data to convey realism in their products. It also is a significant time saver for animators who must develop a bulk of animations in a short time. By far the most important reason why developers use mo-cap is to capture human motion and all the intricacies that even the most talented animator cannot replicate. With motion-capture in the *Ready 2 Rumble* series, we were able to show the intricacies in human motion that are apparent in our supporting animations, helping establish personality and character. Every boxer has a set of introduction, victory, taunting, and fighting animations that establish emotion and distinct personalities.

Get a taste of Valdez' work at `www.midway.com`.

Rick Stringfellow

Before leaving EA Sports in 2002, Rick Stringfellow was the senior art director on the *NHL Hockey* series—one of the company's best-selling and most-coveted sports franchises. In the past, he worked at Radical on *ESPN Sports Games*, *FOX Hockey/FOX Basketball 2000/2001*, and *Jackie Chan Stuntmaster*.

What are the most important things for an artist/animator to keep in mind when working on a game? Stringfellow replies:

How will consumers see or interact with a piece of game art? Will they understand it from a functional perspective? Will it make sense without any instructions? The art we make is for other people—often, junior artists forget that when you're making a game, it's for consumers.

Is this the best possible piece of art I can make within the time and technical constraints? It's not good enough to just get the work done—you have to do the best you possibly can.

Another point for junior artists to keep in mind is that during the course of making a game, the art they make will go through many iterations. Never assume that after it's completed, it's actually finished. I'm looking at a game we just finished, and I can't see any art that hasn't gone through several modifications since it was first conceived.

Good art is a result of a collaborative process between the artists and everybody else on the team— when making a piece of art, you must work with everybody from the conception of the idea through to the implementation of the art.

Many artists would be curious to know about the various art-related positions at EA Sports, so Stringfellow walks us through the five key areas:

> ➤ **2D texture artist**. Responsible for creating all art for team textures, player faces, arena textures, some front-end images.

> ➤ **Interface artist**. Builds the front-end interactive component to the game. Works on look and feel and interactive buttons and animations.

> ➤ **3D modeler**. Creates all the player and arena models; deals with animation weighting and mapping of 2D textures onto the 3D model.

> ➤ **3D animator**. Edits and creates all the motion within the game. Normally working on small clips of animation.

> ➤ **Art director/art lead**. Responsible for all aspects of all art within the game. Must be able to understand both the aesthetic needs and technical requirements of the art.

The *NHL* series is often under a microscope from diehard fans. Stringfellow was asked to recall any major challenges with this series.

As always with making a game, at some point you run out of memory. In this case, when all the final components came together, we blew way past the limits of the platform memory and basically crashed the game. Normally, when you exceed memory by a very small amount, with a bit of work you can get enough space to make it all fit. When you exceed memory by a huge amount, something big has to go!

The words of wisdom in this case are not to be afraid to start cutting or trimming. You normally have very little choice to do this—but the longer you delay the chopping, the more painful it gets. We managed to trim out a whole bunch of data that did reduce the quality of some art—however, not so much that it looked objectionable. When we made the cuts and began to fit back into memory, we went through a lengthy process of adding back some of the quality until we hit the limit but didn't exceed memory.

Making the art for *NHL* is incredibly challenging. There isn't any piece that can be singled out, and it's almost always teamwork that overcomes any hurdle that we encounter. The best advice on how to overcome challenging art is to plan so well up front that it seldom becomes a problem—and hire the most talented and self-motivated people you can.

Stringfellow believes that although learning how to use software programs is important for video game art and animation, it's *essential* that an artist be familiar with the basic principals of art and animation:

Understanding proportion, form, and movement is crucial to making good characters. Understanding architecture and the reasons behind the planning of urban spaces helps immensely when constructing lifelike environments. And knowing how to break away from reality is a must to create new and entertaining art.

As for the software tools, the most important piece of knowledge is the basic principles of how 2D and 3D art is technically constructed using software tools. I don't think learning a specific package really matters—the best advice would be to learn at least one of the major packages really well.

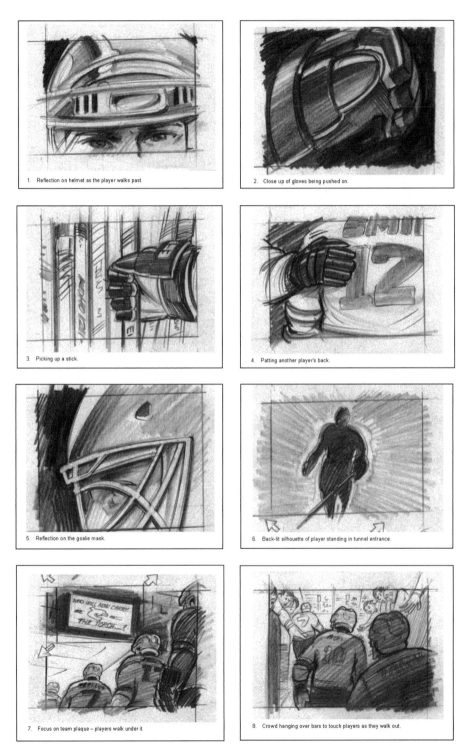

1. Reflection on helmet as the player walks past.

2. Close up of gloves being pushed on.

3. Picking up a stick.

4. Patting another player's back.

5. Reflection on the goalie mask.

6. Back-lit silhouette of player standing in tunnel entrance.

7. Focus on team plaque – players walk under it.

8. Crowd hanging over bars to touch players as they walk out.

As a very special treat for the millions of *NHL Hockey* fans out there, here's the storyboard artwork for the *NHL 2002* introductory sequence. A special thanks to Michael McCartie, the talented artist responsible for these conceptual drawings.
(Used with permission by Electronic Arts, Inc. and Michael McCartie.)

"Do we ever stop looking?" responds Rick Stringfellow, when asked where a video game artist looks for inspiration.

The best place is outside of your normal environment—external stimulation is the best motivator. And when you do get blocked, the best thing to do is stop trying so hard to be inspired—go off and do something different. Normally, the moment that you stop trying to force it is the moment that all the ideas flood out.

Stringfellow says he recommends that artists and animators go to school to sharpen their craft, but says to be careful when choosing the school and the course.

It's normally a huge investment for people with little cash. If you're not already a practicing artist, just learning a software tool will not guarantee work. If you're just starting out, consider schools that offer art and design along with learning a piece of software. Don't forget that a piece of software is just a tool—you have to figure out what to do with it creatively.

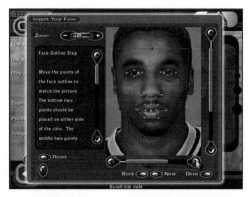

EA Sports was the first to bring "Face in the Game" technology to gamers. What is it? Stringfellow explains, "It allows us to take a player's photograph and wrap it onto the face model, and at the same time allow us to tie it into our Facial Animation system so players can celebrate a goal, or grimace from a hit!

(Used with permission by Electronic Arts, Inc.)

Dan Michelson, Electronic Arts

We touched on motion-capture (mo-cap) animation elsewhere in this chapter, but now we're in for a special treat. Sit back and enjoy this crash course on mo-cap with Dan Michelson, the senior motion-capture specialist at Electronic Arts Canada, home of North America's largest mo-cap facilities. And be sure to read Dan's very impressive bio in Appendix A, "Biographies!"

Motion-capture is a means of tracking the performance of a real actor in order to map that motion onto an animated character. This is done by attaching markers onto key locations on the actor's body. Highly sensitive cameras then are able to track the positions of these markers in 3D space. We take this positional data and then solve it onto the animated skeleton. By using several markers about a certain joint, we're able to derive rotational data as well.

The different types of technologies available are magnetic, biomechanical, passive optical, and active optical motion-capture. All of these technologies have their strengths and weaknesses. The right system depends on your project's needs. Motion-capture is used not only to save time, but to add realistic motion to a game. Electronic Arts uses optical motion-capture because it gives more accurate data.

Michelson highlights the different specialists needed to get the players in a game (such as a basketball or football title) to animate so realistically.

1. **Motion-capture operator**. This position is twofold. Some operators run the studio during production and are responsible for operating and maintaining the equipment. They also build sets and props as required for each project. Other operators deal with the data acquired from the motion-capture shoot. They must identify raw data and clean the missing or any bad data.

2. **Motion-capture specialist**. This person is responsible for communicating with the game team to ensure an efficient shoot. They're also responsible for solving the acquired data onto the game's skeleton and delivering the data to the team.

3. **Motion-capture actor**. The actor is the artist responsible for performing the needed motions for the game team during a shoot. This may be as simple as running through the capture space or as difficult as impersonating celebrities.

The hardest part about mo-cap work, says Michelson, is when you must deal with "occlusion." He explains:

As we use an optical system, it's dependent upon the camera's capability to see a marker. When we must capture wrap tackles for *Madden Football*, often markers can be occluded for long periods of time. Re-creating these markers requires a process known as virtual markers. This is extremely tedious and time-consuming work.

Tiger Woods, at an EA motion-capture session in Orlando, Florida.
(Used with permission by Scott Martin/AP and Electronic Arts, Inc.)

But hand-animating the players in a game can be even more painstaking, says Michelson:

> The alternative to using motion-capture is to hand-animate the characters' skeletons. This is done by a process called *keyframing*, in which an animator must move each bone on every frame to derive a realistic look. Because there are 30 frames every second in a typical game, this can be a very slow process, and it takes a very skilled animator to make it look natural. It can look realistic when done by a highly skilled artist who has lots of time to tinker with each move. This is not a luxury we can generally afford, given the speed and accuracy of our motion-capture animation.

There are a few key things when working with mo-cap technology, Michelson stresses:

- ➤ Begin with the end in mind.

- ➤ Decide where you want to spend the most time. Production schedules are tight, and you must often choose what you want to invest the most time and effort toward—for instance, gameplay gets far more attention than cut scenes, so make sure you get that working first.

- ➤ Remember that you're capturing personality along with motion, so be very picky when choosing talent. Working on *March Madness* [in 2001], we noticed after the capture session that the talent they chose for the bulk of their in-game moves leaned to his left. He leaned left when he was standing still, and it was even more noticeable when he was moving. Now, the problem arises when they must map his motions onto several players on the court at once. Suddenly, you run the risk of having all 10 players on the court, all leaning to their left. Not good. We were able to correct his curvature in our software, but only to a point.

Don Bluth, Don Bluth Films

As a special treat for this book, we have the distinct pleasure and honor to interview Don Bluth, a veteran animator and producer who has worked in Hollywood on such outstanding films as *Anastasia* (1997), *The Secret of NIMH* (1982), *An American Tail* (1986), *All Dogs Go to Heaven* (1989), *Thumbelina* (1994), *The Land Before Time* (1988), and (most recently) *Titan A.E.* (2000). In 1983, he also helped create the legendary *Dragon's Lair* laser disc arcade game. Bluth's last video game project was *Dragon's Lair 3D*, which debuted in the winter of 2002. Be sure to read his full bio in Appendix A, or visit www.donbluth.com.

Shortly after the Classic Gaming Expo 2002 held in Las Vegas (where Bluth spent a couple of days signing autographs and posters, and shaking hands with countless fans!), he took time out to chat about art and animation for video games.

What are the three most important considerations for an artist/animator to keep in mind when working on a game?

1. **Clarity**. It's almost the same as when animating for a feature film. The audience must see clearly what the character is doing. We deal with "silhouette" issues: When you find a good pose for your character, does the pose "read" well? If you painted it all black, could you still understand what the character is doing (in silhouette)?

2. **Believability**. Are your characters' actions believable? Can you show your character's personality; make him think and breathe? Bring him to life.

3. **Entertainment**. Find something in your character—a flaw in the design, a characteristic that makes him/her special and entertaining to your audience. Usually this is something in the character's personality; something maybe that you find entertaining in a friend or relative's personality.

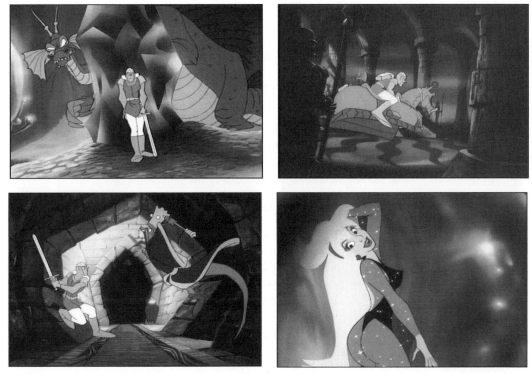

The success of *Dragon's Lair* is nothing to shrug at. The average arcade game has a life expectancy of about nine months, yet *Dragon's Lair* is on its 20th year. It has pulled in more than $131 million in revenue to date. Now that's a lot of quarters! Pictured here is Dirk the Daring from the original *Dragon's Lair* game, plus a shot of the damsel in distress, Daphne.
(Used with permission by Dragon's Lair LLC, © 2000 Don Bluth.)

What software tools should an artist and animator be familiar with?

We're not that technical and therefore really not that familiar with the various gaming software tools. However, we do use some artistic computer tools such as Softimage, Toonz, Maya, Photoshop, Matador, and so on.

Is it helpful to know classical art?

Knowing classical art is only background information, a platform to build on or take off from. The key to your art is learning the "language"—the pencil, the brush, the computer, and so on. Develop an ability to draw. The ability to draw or build in the computer is the "language" portion. This enables you to communicate through art.

The second major point is to get an education. We can learn the language of drawing, but we still have to have something intelligent to say. So a good education is extremely important.

Surprisingly, Bluth doesn't see a big difference between creating art for an interactive medium versus the film industry. "It's usually quite similar, especially if you're telling a story with your game. Construction is a little more demanding." He explains:

With *Dragon's Lair*, we had to design flowcharts to visualize the branching effect in the editorial process. You're also constantly thinking in terms of "threat-resolve"—not something that's there in standard film-making, although it's a great editing format to use when creating a threatening chase sequence.

The challenge is still to entertain and keep the attention of your audience. The game doesn't really afford you the privilege of developing thorough multiple personalities with details or small idiosyncrasies in your character, like you can in a film. Therefore, the personalities of your game characters must be simple and direct.

When and where does a video game artist look for inspiration? "When he's staring at the blank paper," teases Bluth. "Actually, we look everywhere: novels, TV shows, movies, magazines; or just observation of the entertaining events that happen in our lives with our coworkers, friends, and family. It's all around us. You never really know where the Muses dwell."

Explaining how Dirk the Daring from the *Dragon's Lair* series was created, Bluth says "Dirk is not really a complicated guy, but we did look for something about him that would give him mass appeal."

One [option] was to consider him "everyman," sort of like a Charlie Chaplin. Charlie Chaplin also didn't speak in his first films. He was not a hero, but a nice guy who always tried to do the right thing. He represented the masses, the everyday worker, just trying to get through life. So when we approached Dirk, we thought of him as not too smart and kind of muscular with a big weapon. He was to be uncomplicated, but not simple-minded. The fact that he didn't talk really helped in the international market. He ended up representing the same kind of personality in all countries, without having to dub him into those foreign languages and worrying about what he said.

There's no formula for creating a hit character. It's just as hard to find a hit character as it would be to come up with a hit song, hit movie, novel, or comic book. It's just the luck of the draw—no pun intended. I wish we had access to such a formula. Many times, it can be the vision of a single person, businessman or artist, engineer, technician, and so on. It may be the result of a brainstorming session. There are many ways to flush out good ideas. It's always good to test your ideas with your peers. If the idea works for the small group, it may work for the masses as well.

Finally, Bluth was asked to discuss the most challenging aspect of the animation in *Dragon's Lair* or *Dragon's Lair 3D* and how he overcome it. "Probably adjusting to the fact that we were dealing with gameplay and not story continuity," answers Bluth. He elaborates:

The art or animation is basically the same as in a feature film. The animators still have to show a good performance in drawing, acting, and entertainment. The challenge for me was dealing with the fact that we were not making a feature film with a message for the audience. It seemed, at the time, to be a frivolous use of a very expensive medium. I guess the way I got through it was to concentrate on the entertainment value of each scene, just as I would in a feature film. That approach must have worked, as it turns out; it's the one project that has brought us the most notoriety. This game has fans all over the world.

For more on creating hit characters such as Dirk the Daring, flip back to Chapter 6.

The first *Dragon's Lair* game had only 22 rooms—none of which could be explored—but in *Dragon's Lair 3D*, there was a whopping 230 rooms.
(Used with permission by Dragon's Lair LLC, © 2000 Don Bluth.)

Chapter 14

The All-Important User Interface (UI) and Game Control

Although it's likely that you'll find some conflicting advice in areas of this book on art techniques, level design suggestions, or the best way to animate a character, it's universally recognized that a bad *user interface (UI)* in a game can be its own demise, regardless of how good the content is.

While compiling this book, a number of designers were asked if there was any truth to the gaming industry adage that a user interface can make or break a game. For the most part, the designers agreed that it can indeed break a game. They were also clear that if the game itself isn't good, the UI certainly can't save it. Nonetheless, it's one of the most significant areas of game design that's often overlooked.

Keep in mind that there are two distinct areas of a game's interface. The first is the menu screen, or shell interface, used mainly to set up video or sound options, configure controls, launch a multi-player game, access saved games, exit to a desktop, and so on. The second is the in-game user interface—that is, what the player sees on the screen while playing.

THE EXPERTS

- Steve Rechtschaffner, Electronic Arts Canada
- Lorne Lanning, Oddworld Inhabitants
- Shigeru Miyamoto, Nintendo
- James Schmalz, Digital Extremes
- George Broussard, 3D Realms
- Pierre Rivest, Ubi Soft Entertainment
- Catherine Roy, Ubi Soft Entertainment
- Sid Meier, Firaxis Games
- Bruce Shelley, Ensemble Studios
- Don Hopkins, Freelance
- Mark Dickenson, The 3DO Company
- Steve Hunt
- Phil Saunders, Presto Studios
- Tim Cain, Troika Games
- Matt Householder, Blizzard Entertainment
- Richard "Lord British" Garriott, NCsoft
- Michael Waite, Electronic Arts
- David Wu, Pseudo Interactive
- Todd Howard, Bethesda Softworks

Control is another important aspect to game design, and many lump this area into user interface because they're closely related. Far too often, the player pays $50 for a game and can't control the character or machine (or "camera" angle of the action, in some games). In other cases, the control layout is fine, but the objects onscreen don't respond quickly or smoothly enough.

Many gamers would agree that the sports game genre seems to have the most difficulty when it comes to a good in-game UI. With team-based sports games such as football, soccer, basketball, or hockey, part of the reason is that the gamer must have all the players accessible at all times and must choose which player(s) to control. To complicate the issue even more, in some cases it's also necessary to give commands to other team members. I'll cover team-based sports games in a moment, but first let's look at sports games in which there's only one character to control—such as in golf, skiing, or boxing. These sports games have their own sets of UI challenges.

Steve Rechtschaffner, Electronic Arts Canada

Steve Rechtschaffner is the studio vice president and executive producer at Electronic Arts Canada. Earlier in this book, he shared some insight on game design with his games *SSX* and *SSX Tricky* as shining examples. His last game was *NBA Street Vol. 2*.

How do the development teams at EA Sports and EA Sports BIG handle the user interface so well when so many games fail to provide a good UI?

> Understanding the difference between primary controls and secondary controls is key. So many games ask you to do more complicated secondary controls way too early in the experience. I like a game that allows me to start with the basics in an intuitive way; then branch out and learn the more complicated, more controllable aspects of the game as I'm ready and no longer having to think about the basics. If I'm still trying to remember the basic controls and having to execute more advanced controls too early in the experience, I'm not going to stay interested. Feeling intuitive is also key. Your controller action should somehow emotionally equate to the onscreen maneuver. Done right, you feel the moment right back through the controller. Both *NBA Live* and *NBA Street* do this well on their jump shots.

On the *SSX* games, Rechtschaffner adds the following:

> We spent a considerable amount of time on designing and redesigning the interface on *SSX* and *SSX Tricky* to reflect this philosophy. I think its upfront simplicity and discoverable depth is what makes it a game that people aren't afraid to pick up and try. If a game is intimidating to control when you first pick it up, it's poorly designed.

The key to creating a successful user interface and control scheme, says EA's Rechtschaffner, is "understanding the difference between primary controls and secondary controls." Shown here are two shots from *SSX Tricky* for the Xbox platform.
(Used with permission by Electronic Arts, Inc.)

Lorne Lanning, Oddworld Inhabitants

The mind behind Abe and Munch speaks elsewhere in this book about creating successful game characters and designing action/adventure games. Here, Lanning shares some advice on creating a solid UI.

Lanning admits that creating a good UI and control has been a challenge for the team at Oddworld Inhabitants, and that their titles may have traditionally been "too complicated on the controls and with many of the puzzles." He notes, "This is a result of not doing focus testing." Lanning expands:

> This should be up to the publisher, but most publishers don't want to spend the money to focus test. When you build a game, it's very easy to get too close to it; something that feels good to the team that's building it may not feel good to a fresh gamer who just bought it. An awkward control that was used at the beginning of the games production, implemented just to keep the job rolling, might begin to feel okay to the designers after they've been living with it for several months. This is a dangerous trend.

But Lanning says they've likely licked this problem with their latest game:

> As we've felt that our controls have traditionally been difficult, we've put particular focus on getting them more intuitive for our latest game, *Munch's Oddysee*. This means laying out the buttons that are most commonly used in the most convenient places. You must also consider that the evolution of games has itself determined many patterns that gamers have grown accustomed to.

Years ago, Tommy Tallarico [see Chapter 15, "Sound Engineering," and Chapter 16, "Music and Games"] said, "People don't just play one game at a time; they typically play three or four games at a time. They might pop in a fighter for awhile; then pop in a racing game; then an adventure game later in the day." His point was that if you stepped off the well-beaten path of control configurations that most games use, you're walking the gamer through undiscovered and awkward territory. It's a dangerous move to do so. However, if you want to do more creative things than have been done before, you need to figure out how to synergize the way people are accustomed to with what you're now offering that's new and different.

An increase in the game's complexity, suggests Lanning, requires smarter, tighter controls:

For us, the majority of the game we felt needed to be played with only one button and the true analog joystick. More involved tasks, such as "gamespeak" [the ability to communicate with other characters in the game], would take advantage of the other buttons. This chemistry required the code to be smarter and the layout to be more tightly conceived. Then, because one button would operate most of the mechanics in the world, the mechanics couldn't be located too close to one another. A great deal of attention was put on this new control configuration—largely because we knew that awkward controls could kill a great game. With great and simple controls, we knew that more people would be able to play it and enjoy it.

Shigeru Miyamoto, Nintendo

Nintendo's superstar game designer, Shigeru Miyamoto, discusses how important game control and the user interface are in relation to action/arcade game design:

I am always conscious that I should make games as entertainment commodities rather than as artistic works. For players to enjoy themselves is taken for granted, so we look at the games from the players' point of view. The most understandable example of this consideration should be the *controllability*. When I'm making games, I make them with my utmost care so that my own thoughts can be reflected in the games through the controller. Perhaps this is something that evokes players' emotional sympathy.

Shigeru Miyamoto's *Pikmin* for the Nintendo GameCube is an action/strategy game like no other. In the game, the player assumes the role of an astronaut who crash-lands on a planet inhabited by "Pikmin." The goal is to rebuild your spaceship so you can go back home. This is accomplished by controlling these little beings and accomplishing tasks throughout many levels.
(Used with permission by Nintendo of America, Inc.)

James Schmalz, Digital Extremes

James Schmalz of Canada's Digital Extremes, the co-creators of the award-winning *Unreal*, *Unreal Tournament*, and *Unreal Championship*, gives us a good definition of what constitutes a non-gameplay user interface: "The graphical user interface for video games is the means by which the player interacts with the game startup, setup, and configuration—things such as selecting a game character, choosing music volume, selecting controller settings, and starting a new game or loading an old one."

What separates a poorly designed UI from a well-thought-out UI? "A good interface is nicely laid out and easy to manipulate and understand," says Schmalz. He continues:

> There should be an easy path through the menu system to get quickly into the game. It also should be easy for players to change whatever settings they want in the game. Overall, it needs to be obvious, easy to use, and as simple as the game developer can make it while still suiting the needs of the game.

How about some advice on creating a smooth UI for the player?

> The process of making a good UI involves thinking about the way the player will use it and then simply making that process as simple and intuitive as possible, while keeping the menus interesting-looking and professional. Usually, it requires several passes to get to the final layout. Once the rough draft is up and running and people can try it, there are usually many suggestions as to how it can be improved. Improvements go on for several iterations, until everyone is happy with the final layout.

Visit www.digitalextremes.com for more info on the company and its games.

George Broussard, 3D Realms

Let's move from *Unreal* to *Duke Nukem*. 3D Realms' George Broussard brings plenty of experience to creating a smooth control layout for the player.

> Game controls are intangible, binary, and critical. They're intangible because there are no hard rules to follow, and it's all about "feel." They're binary because they're either good or bad, with little middle ground. They're critical because if the controls are bad, people will lose interest in your game before they've even played much of it.

So what's Broussard's secret?

> You want a minimum of keys and interface pieces to deal with while you're playing, and you want controls that are responsive and that react to what the player wants to do. Players should never be frustrated with the controls. If they are, address it at once—there's something wrong. Never, ever blame the player; it's your fault. Look at popular games in your genre and see what they're doing right. See what fans of those games like or dislike about the controls. Don't try and reinvent the wheel because chances are that someone has already been down that road and put in the time to polish controls to perfection. Use that to your advantage.

Some games have done it right, says Broussard. If you're making a first-person shooter game, look at *Quake III: Arena*, *Unreal Tournament*, and *Half-Life*. For real-time strategy games, he lists *Command & Conquer: Red Alert 2* and *Starcraft*. His third-person game examples are *Max Payne* and *Heavy Metal: F.A.K.K. 2*.

Pierre Rivest, Ubi Soft Entertainment

Rivest, a designer for the *Batman: Vengeance* video game, agrees with the other designers in this chapter: UI and control method in a video game are extremely important. First, some words on the UI:

> It's the first thing the player sees when the game is booted. If the first look fails to excite the player, it's bad news. While playing, the UI informs and helps the player on the status of his current game, which is also quite important. *Batman* is a bit different in this sense. We let the player decide whether the UI will be displayed while playing; our goal is to give the player the impression that he's playing an episode of the animated series.

On control:

> This is also quite important. The player is going to be in constant interaction with the main character for the duration of his playing time. Thus, the controls must be easy to master and intuitive. The controls of the *Batman* game can be pretty complex; they adapt to the gameplay. For instance, if Batman is fighting, the game goes into the fight system mode, in which Batman can perform otherwise undoable actions. The controls slightly change to allow Batman to perform the fighting actions.

And next, more from Ubi Soft…

Catherine Roy, Ubi Soft Entertainment

The producer on Disney's *Tarzan Untamed* and *Jungle Book* games in Montreal speaks about the decision to limit Tarzan's movement to an invisible path when crawling along wide branches. In the following segment, Roy explains how this came to be and why it's better for the game's sake:

> When we started working on *Tarzan*, we wanted to do a pure 3D game. At first, we had gameplay ideas in which Tarzan could swing on a vine 360 degrees, and the player had to control Tarzan on the branches in 3D—without falling on the sides.

> But after a couple of focus groups, we found out that it was much too difficult to control Tarzan on the tight branches. The player would fall all the time, and Tarzan didn't look like a hero at all. We then tried a technique we called *smart control*. It's a kind of magnet that would help you stay on track if the controller was in a reasonable angle of tolerance compared to the right direction. It worked really well, but it was still too easy to fall off the branches. The level design had created a certain rhythm in the levels that was [enjoyed] at a fast pace, which could be reached only if the controls were made more straightforward. This is why we came up with the 2D control in the end. In fact, this was the only way we could have Tarzan do extreme things and be a hero while the player could enjoy the fast-paced gameplay.

As Roy's anecdote shows, level design and game control often work hand-in-hand!

Sid Meier, Firaxis Games

When creating *Alpha Centauri* a few years back, the UI was an important consideration to Sid Meier, and he tried to cater the UI design to newbies to the turn-based strategy genre, as well as to more seasoned game veterans. Says Meier:

> I wanted the game interface to be easy to use, with everything accessible with the mouse, but I also wanted keyboard shortcuts. In *Alpha Centauri*, we realized that people wanted to learn more about the information onscreen—units, terrain, buildings—so if you right-click a given area, it will tell you more information in depth.

Bruce Shelley, Ensemble Studios

As lead game designer and spokesman for Ensemble Studios and its incredibly popular "Age" series (*Age of Empires*, *Age of Kings*, *Age of Mythology*), Bruce Shelley has plenty of advice to share in this book, including advice on creating a real-time strategy game (Chapter 3, "General Game Design: Strategy Games"), breaking into the industry (Chapter 21, "Breaking Into the Industry"), writing design documents (Chapter 6, "Creating Characters, Storyboarding, and Design Documents"), and coding realistic AI (Chapter 12, "Artificial Intelligence [AI]"). Here, Shelley offers some advice on creating a successful user interface:

> Overall goals for the UI should be to allow information and commands to pass back and forth between the player and game quickly but with minimal effort.

He elaborates and adds to this advice:

> The UI should stay out of the player's way. A good UI is never noticed, but a bad one can spoil the experience or kill the game. The *Age* games can be played entirely with a mouse, and this is not an accident. A basic UI is good for the casual gamer. We provide hot keys for expert players so they can play more quickly and efficiently. We continually look for ways to give information to the player unobtrusively. For example, in *Age of Mythology*, a banner drops down from the menu bar to let you know that you have villagers not working. When everyone is working, there is not a banner in sight. Also, we provide rollover help for almost every object in the game.

Don Hopkins, Freelance

In Chapter 11, "Programming Theory," Don Hopkins shares his insights on programming a game like *The Sims*. Here, he shares why the UI in *The Sims* works so well. Hopkins says it took quite a bit of user testing and quality assurance and many iterations and changes: "We experimented with many different user interface styles and were not afraid to throw away the ones that didn't work...but I still miss the throbbing brain widget and hope to use it in another game some day!"

Hopkins discusses the importance of the UI:

> The user interface is deeply intertwined with the design of the game and its model of the world. So when one changes, the other might have to change. Some user interface problems can be worked around in the design of the game.

As an example of an executive UI-based decision with *The Sims*, Hopkins recalls the following experience:

> At first, time didn't stop while you built the house or bought new objects. But that caused many hard-to-fix bugs, such as when you moved things around when people were using them or built a wall in somebody's path. And undo/redo for the editing tools wasn't possible if the world was changing while the tools were being used. So the designers decided that build and buy mode would stop time, which solved a lot of problems.

One regret I have about *The Sims* user interface is that I wish it didn't use any modal dialogs that popped up and stopped time. Modal pop-up dialogs, such as the ones you get when you use the phone, display a message and freeze game time until you press a button. Although some will eventually continue after awhile if you don't answer them, modal dialogs interrupt the flow of the game, and it's a bad user interface technique that should be avoided in general. *The Sims* is the kind of game you want to leave running to see what happens over a long time, so the modal dialogs that pop up are a drag. But the pie menus don't pause the game when they pop up, and they're partially transparent so you can see the live action going on behind them.

More on this in a moment. Meanwhile, Hopkins reminds game designers that stopping time is possible in single-player games such as *The Sims* but not in real-time online multiplayer games such as *Ultima Online*. Therefore, *The Sims Online* won't be able to use time-stopping modal dialogs and must solve those user interface problems in other ways.

Some gameplay changes made in the creation of *The Sims* were spawned by an interface decision, says Don Hopkins:
"At first, time didn't stop while you built the house or bought new objects. But that caused many hard-to-fix bugs, such as when you moved things around when people were using them or built a wall in somebody's path."
(Used with permission by Electronic Arts, Inc.)

What are the "pie menus" that Hopkins mentioned earlier? Enjoy the following paragraphs, written by Hopkins to thoroughly explain what they are and why they were employed:

Pie menus are a naturally efficient user interface technique: directional selection of pie slice-shaped targets. The cursor starts out in the center of the pie, so all targets are large, nearby, and in different directions. Fitts' Law explains the advantages of pie menus, relating their fast selection speed and low error rate to their large target size and small distance. Pie menus are easy for novice users, who just follow the directions, and efficient for experienced users, who can quickly "mouse ahead" after they know the way.

When you click an object in *The Sims*, a pie menu pops up, and you can choose an action for the current person to perform with that object. In the center of the pie menu is the current person's head, looking around at the items you point at. The menu displays a list of actions that apply to the object under the cursor. You know what the object is because you pointed at it. But how do you know which person the pie menu applies to? Solution: Put the person's head in the center of the menu. Why just the dis-embodied head and not the whole body? Because the pie menu selection is meant to reflect a mental decision process, which the head suggests. (And the whole body couldn't fit in the menu and would have to be clipped somehow, which wouldn't look very nice.) The disembodied head is nice because it can turn around to face the selected menu item as feedback. It represents the "homunculus": the little person inside your head who decides how you're going to react to the environment.

The pie menu background is a transparent shadow, so it doesn't totally obscure your view of the world. The area behind the pie menu is desaturated to monochrome, its contrast is lowered, and the edges of the shadow effect are feathered (it gently fades out). This is so the colorful head stands out against the gray background, but you can still see what's going on behind the pie menu. The feathered shadow visu-ally separates the head into another layer, so it's obviously part of the user interface outside of the world, but without drawing any distinct borders or edges. Without the visual separation of layers, it would look like a giant head was floating around in the house, which would certainly violate the principle of least astonishment. The shadow desaturates and lowers the contrast of the background behind the menu, to soften the edges and reduce the visual clutter of the background. There are no sharp edges except for the head and the labels. Lines and edges attract your visual attention, and there is no reason to draw attention to the edge of the pie menu background—just the head and the labels.

And as a special treat to fans of *The Sims* (likely you're one of the millions of them worldwide!), Hopkins provides the following piece based on an early demo of *Dollhouse*, which was eventual-ly published as *The Sims*.

Designing User Interfaces to Simulation Games: A Summary of Will Wright's Talk, by Don Hopkins

Will Wright, the designer of *SimCity*, *SimEarth*, *SimAnt*, and other popular games from Maxis, gave a talk at Terry Winnograd's user interface class at Stanford. He reflected on the design of simulators and user interfaces in *SimCity*, *SimEarth*, and *SimAnt*. He demonstrated several of his games, including *Dollhouse* (known to consumers as *The Sims*).

Here are some important points he made at this and other talks. I've elaborated on some of his ideas with my own comments, based on my experiences playing lots of *SimCity*, talking with Will, studying the source code and porting it to Unix, reworking the user interface, and adding multiplayer support.

The anatomy of a simulation game

There are several tightly coupled parts of a simulation game that must be designed closely together: the simulation model, the gameplay, the user interface, and the user's model. In order for a game to be real-izable, all of those different parts must be tractable. There are games that might have a great user inter-face, be fun to play, and be easy to understand, but involve processes that are currently impossible to simulate on a computer. There are also games that are possible to simulate, fun to play, easy to under-stand, but that don't afford a usable interface. Will has designed a great game called *Sim Thunder Storm*, but he hasn't been able to think of a user interface that would make any sense.

On the user model

The digital models running on a computer are only compilers for the mental models users construct in their heads. The actual end product of *SimCity* is not the shallow model of the city running in the computer. More importantly, it's the deeper model of the real world, and the intuitive understanding of complex dynamic systems that people learn from playing it, in the context of everything else about a city that they already know. In that sense, *SimCity*, *SimEarth*, and *SimAnt* are quite educational because they implant useful models in their users' minds.

On the simulation model

Many geeks have spent their time trying to reverse-engineer the simulator by performing experiments to determine how it works, just for fun. This would be a great exercise for a programming class. When I first started playing *SimCity*, I constructed elaborate fantasies about how it was implemented, which turned out to be quite inaccurate. But the exercise of coming up with elaborate fantasies about how to simulate a city was very educational because it's a hard problem!

The actual simulation is a much less idealistically general purpose than I would have thought, epitomizing the Nike "Just do it" slogan. In *SimCity* classic, the representation of the city is low-level and distilled down compactly enough that a small home computer can push it around. The city is represented by tiles, indexed by numbers that are literally scattered throughout the code, which is hardly general-purpose or modular, but runs fast. It sacrifices expandability and modularity for speed and size, just the right trade-off for the wonderful game that it is.

Some educators have asked Maxis to make *SimCity* expose more about the actual simulation itself, instead of hiding its inner workings from the user. They want to see how it works and what it depends on, so it's less of a game and more educational. But what's really going on inside is not as realistic as they would want to believe: Because of its nature as a game and the constraint that it must run on low-end home computers, it tries to fool people into thinking it's doing more than it really is by taking advantage of the knowledge and expectations people already have about how a city is supposed to work. Implication is more efficient than simulation.

People naturally attribute cause-and-effect relationships to events in *SimCity* that Will, as the programmer, knows are not actually related. Perhaps it's more educational for *SimCity* players to integrate what they already know to fill in the gaps than letting them in on the secret of how simple and discrete it really is. As an educational game, *SimCity* stimulates students to learn more about the real world, without revealing the internals of its artificial simulation. The implementation details of *SimCity* are quite interesting for a programmer or game designer to study, but not your average high school Social Studies class.

Educators who want to expose the internals of *SimCity* to students may not realize how brittle and shallow it really is. I don't mean that as a criticism of Will, *SimCity*, or the educators who are seeking open, realistic, general-purpose simulators for use in teaching. *SimCity* does what it was designed to do and much more, but it's not that. Their goals are noble, but the software's not there yet. After kids master *SimCity*, they could learn Logo or some high-level visual programming language such as KidSim, and write their own simulations and games!

Other people wanted to use *SimCity* for the less-noble goal of teaching people *what* to think instead of just teaching them *to* think. Everyone notices the obvious built-in political bias, whatever that is. But everyone sees it from a different perspective, so nobody agrees what its real political agenda actually is. I don't think it's all that important because *SimCity's* political agenda pales in comparison to the political agenda in the eye of the beholder.

Some muckety-muck architecture magazine was interviewing Will Wright about *SimCity*, and they asked him a question that was something like "Which ontological urban paradigm most influenced your design of the simulator, the Exo-Hamiltonian Pattern Language Movement, or the Intra-Urban Deconstructionist Sub-Culture Hypothesis?" He replied, "I just kind of optimized for gameplay."

Then there was the oil company that wanted "Sim Refinery," so you could use it to lay out oil tanker ports and petroleum storage and piping systems because they thought that it would give their employees useful experience in toxic waste disaster management, in the same way that *SimCity* gives kids useful experience in being the mayor of a city. They didn't realize that the real lessons of *SimCity* are much more subtle than teaching people how to be good mayors. But the oil company hoped they could use it to teach any other lessons on their agenda just by plugging in a new set of graphics, a few rules, and a bunch of disasters.

And there was the X-Terminal vendor who wanted to adapt the simulator in *SimCity* into a game called "Sim MIS," that they would distribute for free to managers of information systems, whose job it is to decide what hardware to buy! The idea was that the poor overworked MIS would have fun playing this game in which they could build networks with PCs, X-Terminals, and servers (instead of roads with residential, commercial, and industrial buildings), which had disasters such as "viruses" infecting the network of PCs, "upgrades" forcing you to reinstall Windows on every PC, and business charts that would graphically highlight the high maintenance cost of PCs versus X-Terminals. Their idea was to use a fun game to subtly influence people into buying their product by making them lose if they didn't. Unlike the oil company, they certainly realized the potential to exploit the indirect ways in which a game like SimCity can influence the user's mind, but they had no grip on the concept of subtlety or game design.

On the gameplay

Usually, the game is separate from the simulation. Games can be based on conflicts and goals that are external to the simulation itself. The simulation goes on doing its thing, and the users can play different games with their own sets of goals. The simulation doesn't consider fires spreading between buildings to be an error condition or a source of conflict—that's just the way the simulator's supposed to behave. But users might, unless the game they're playing is pyromaniacal.

The design of the gameplay has a lot to do with the user's model of the system, and *SimCity* elegantly supports a number of different user models, games, and toys in one program. You can use the terraforming tools and natural features to play with it like a sandbox or landscaping toy, without even starting the city simulation phase of the game. You can even use it as a painting tool—drawing colorful designs and cartoons with land, water, roads, and buildings. *SimCity* comes with several scenarios with different conflicts and goals and also has a menu of disasters you can invoke to destroy your city or challenge yourself to recover. You can start your own city from scratch and develop it in any direction you want. A satisfying feature of *SimCity 2000* is the ability to put signs in your city, to name roads and buildings and parts of town. How else could you personalize a simulated city?

There was some interesting discussion about using *SimCity* as a medium for storytelling: encouraging people to imagine far beyond the bounds of what the computer is able to simulate. You can build cities to empathize with and tell stories about them, about their people, culture, buildings, and history. A class of students could label different parts of a city, and each person could tell a story about a different part that interacted with the stories going on in neighboring parts of the city. Then they could make a web site with the downloadable city and an image map of the whole city, linking to all the stories on web pages, with screen snapshots of their neighborhoods and lots of hypertext links between each story. This way, each student could collaborate with several others to write a web of interconnected stories, all about the same city!

On the user interface

Will demonstrated the close-up and overall views in *SimEarth* and showed how *SimCity 2000* integrated these with zooming in one window. He talked about information density and screen size.

Post Morta

After designing *SimCity* classic, then *SimEarth*, then *SimAnt*, then *SimCity 2000*, here's one way Will compares them: With *SimCity* classic as the standard against which to measure, *SimEarth* was too complex, *SimAnt* was too simple, and *SimCity 2000* was just right.

SimEarth

SimEarth and *SimAnt* didn't support the same level of creativity and personal imprinting that *SimCity* does. With *SimEarth*, anything you do is quickly wiped out by continental drift, erosion, and evolution; you can walk away from it for awhile, come back later, and it will have evolved life or shriveled up and died without you, looking pretty much the same as if you had slaved over it for hours. It was too complex a simulation for people to grasp or affect in a satisfying way.

The time scale slows down as the game progresses from geological time to when life appears, to when intelligence appears, to when technology is developed. There was some trouble conveying this to the users. One thing that supported the notion of time scale is how the view controls along the bottom of the global map were ordered in a temporal progression, in the order you'd need to use them, from the continental drift display to the technology display.

SimAnt

SimAnt had just the opposite problem—it was too simple—but that made it popular with younger kids. Like *SimEarth*, it didn't support creative personal imprinting as well as *SimCity* because one ant farm looks pretty much like any other, and ants are quite disposable and devoid of personality. The educational point of *SimAnt* is to teach about the emergent behavior of multicellular organisms such as ant colonies. I think *SimAnt* would make a fascinating large-scale multiplayer game.

Dollhouse

Imagine zooming into *SimCity 2000*, all the way down to the street level, and seeing little people walking around, waving at each other, asking for spare change, jumping up and down, gesturing, interacting with each other, living and playing in rooms with furniture and active objects, and you're one of them!

Will showed me *Dollhouse* several years ago, and it was amazing then and even more so now. To confirm, *Dollhouse* became *The Sims*—the best-selling computer game in history.

Dollhouse takes the third-person view (looking down on your character) instead of the first-person view (looking out of the eyes of your character). You view your character from above, with a 45-degree orthographic view like *SimCity 2000* uses to display buildings. Will has found that it works quite well because you can see yourself as others see you, as well as seeing other people around you. If there are a bunch of people gathering around some interesting person or place, it's easy to tell what's going on, and navigation is simple and direct. It doesn't suffer from the disorienting navigational problems that a first-person view like *DOOM* imposes. Being able to see yourself as others see you seems to make interpersonal interactions involving body gestures much easier.

Mark Dickenson, The 3DO Company

The *High Heat Baseball* games are one of the most critically acclaimed sports series on the planet, regardless of platform. 3DO designer Mark Dickerson says, "It cannot be overstated that a sports game is only as good as its interface." He expands on this comment:

Within a short period of time, the user must be able to forget about the mechanics of the interface. This is the only way users will truly believe they're playing the sport. Unfortunately, many aspects of sports are complicated. This is where a designer has to be creative and open to feedback. If you don't get the interface right, you won't have a successful sports game. This doesn't mean just implement something similar to your competitors. If your interface is too similar, your gameplay experience will be, too. If something works, sure, use it. If it doesn't cover what you're trying to achieve, explore the possibilities. But whatever you do, get it right.

Mark Dickenson believes that the user interface is critical in a sports game. "The user must be able to forget about the mechanics of the interface," he says. Shown here is a shot from High *Heat Baseball: Major League Baseball 2002.*
(Used with permission by 3DO, Inc.)

Steve Hunt

Steve Hunt of Rage Software fame agrees that, as with any game, a good graphical user interface (GUI) design is really important for the success of simulations, such as aerial combat games for the PC. "It's one of those things that if done well, no one will notice it; done badly, and it'll annoy the hell out of you," he jokes. How about some do's and don'ts?

> ➤ Use either a linear or tree-type menu structure. That is, you either go through a number of screens one after the other or you go down and up the tree but never across. The main thing to avoid is a web structure, in which multiple screens connect to other multiple screens.

> ➤ Consistent style and controls are also important—don't use a scrollbar in one window and an up-and-down button in the next.

Phil Saunders, Presto Studios

Are the interfaces for adventure games any different from those of other genres? Phil Saunders from Presto Studios offers this discussion, after completing *Myst III: Exile* for Ubi Soft Entertainment:

The best interface is the one that isn't there. The chief goal is to make players forget that they're using a computer as the portal to the world that they're experiencing. This is definitely an area where less is more.

Play testing and truly listening to the frustrations and irritations of the user are key. Requiring players to remember complex key commands or making them navigate a busy interface takes away from the immersiveness of the experience. Do you really need a database-like inventory management system, or can your gameplay be streamlined to make the use of objects contextually? Questions like these should always be asked, and the simplest answer is always the best. Remember that as the designer, you're ultimately responsible for each player's experience, and therefore you have the right to constrain it. If your game is properly designed, players won't miss the freedom that an infinite number of options would give them.

Tim Cain, Troika Games

Naturally, role-playing games require a good UI and control scheme. Designer Tim Cain, responsible for the coveted *Fallout* series (for Interplay) and more recently *Arcanum* (for Sierra Studios), agrees with Phil Saunders of Presto Studios (see the preceding section) that "the biggest trend for user interfaces appears to be no interface." He explains:

People want full-screen games. At most, they want a small translucent bar for health and maybe another for messages, but otherwise a wide-open field of view seems to be the optimal interface for many players. This means more hot keys (but not too many, or you have a "complicated" game) and pop-up windows to handle interfaces such as inventory or character maintenance. Also, assigning different functions to left- and right-clicking and to the mouse wheel is more popular and more accepted by most players (as opposed to even five years ago, when you couldn't even assume a right mouse button existed, much less convince people to use it).

Matt Householder, Blizzard Entertainment

On creating a successful user interface, Blizzard Entertainment's Matt Householder simply says the following:

> Don't frustrate the player's desire for perfect control within the game world. Any sense by the player of lack of control (however brief) can be fatal. The user interface must be intuitive and consistent. This makes it easy for new players to learn and encourages experienced players to become experts.

Richard "Lord British" Garriott, NCsoft

In Chapter 4, "General Game Design: Sports, Simulations, Adventure Games, and Puzzles," the godfather of graphical computer role-playing games offers some sage advice on creating single-player and massively multiplayer RPGs. Here, Garriott focuses on creating an effective user interface for the player.

"The more familiar the UI is to the player, the better," says Lord British. When elaborating on this "first hurdle," he says that this doesn't always mean it's the better interface, but the more familiar:

> Right now, the Windows interface is familiar to many gamers, with the left and right mouse-click functionality. I'm not necessarily endorsing it, but more people can relate to it. If the game has a UI that resembles or borrows from Windows, the gamer will be better off because of its familiarity.

Garriott's second principle stems from the familiarity factor and should be something every game designer strives for—making the UI so intuitive to the gamer that he or she becomes one with the onscreen avatar. Lord British calls this one "the backhoe operator syndrome." After familiarity, the key is to make the UI (from a dexterity standpoint) almost nonexistent, so the player no longer considers it an interface at all. Lord British elucidates:

> You know those backhoes on construction sites—those machines that dig dirt? After a period of time, the operator of the backhoe no longer thinks about how to tip the bucket and scoop up the dirt—he just does it.

"Lord British" says to keep the controls and interface as familiar to the gamer as possible to increase the immersion factor and decrease the learning curve. Pictured here is the massively multi-player role-playing game *Lineage: The Blood Pledge*.
(Used with permission by NCsoft US, Inc.)

A good UI should work the same way, says Lord British. The player should be the avatar onscreen, and not control it. To achieve this level of immersion, he insists that game designers should create as simple a UI as possible without forfeiting the player's options. He learned this the hard way through the evolution of the *Ultima* series, and recalls how the simplicity factor has come full circle:

> With *Ultima* on the Apple II, there were only a half-dozen commands, such as north, south, east, and west movement; and hot key letters that started with the first letter of that function, such as *s* for save and *l* for load. Then things got more complicated as the series matured. By *Ultima VI*, every letter meant some-thing—with no exception—so I had to stretch it. For instance, I had to use the *z* key to bring up stats because the s key was allocated for the save function. The problem was that I needed to add more com-mands, so I collapsed the keys into meta-commands, such as the word *use* to unlock a door or light a torch. Therefore, this noun/verb interface evolved, expanding into five graphical icons in *Ultima VII*, but it was still a two-step effort because you had to click "talk to" and then click a character, for example. Because the gamer had to do these two things, it was still difficult to get that "backhoe" effect. In *Ultima VIII* and *IX [Ascension]*, it's one direct command and all mouse-driven. The program now determines what the player wants to do. For example, if there's an NPC [non-player character] on the screen and you want to talk to him, all you have to do is talk to him. If your sword is drawn, he'll fight. The UI is now contextu-ally sensitive, with visual clues to confirm that this is indeed what the player wants to do before doing it.

In Lord British's opinion, the UI we use today could have been done 20 years ago, but we needed to go through this stage of reorganization.

Michael Waite, Electronic Arts

The producer and lead designer for *Motor City Online* shares some input on designing a graphical user interface (GUI) for a massively multiplayer online game or persistent state world (PSW) and the challenges that come with it:

> Designing a GUI for a PSW presents a huge range of challenges—it's a much more difficult proposition than creating a console game interface. In a console game, you can lead users down a single linear path (or let them choose between two or three linear paths). But in a PSW, you're dropping users into a massive world and saying, "Do whatever you want—good luck!" Players live in a PSW, so the GUI has to be built for long-term functionality—which means you'll want the user to be able to go anywhere and do anything as quickly as possible. This inherently means some loss of simplicity for the new user. (Power users and new users have an entirely different set of needs.) In *Motor City Online*, we have erred on the side of UI efficiency for the long-term resident. We've tried to ease the learning curve for new users with help aids like tutorials, screen help, and ToolTips. In the end, users get most of what they need from each other real-time, via *Motor City Online*'s persistent chat interface—the most powerful help tool in the game.

David Wu, Pseudo Interactive

How important is a good user interface in a game such as *Cel Damage*? David Wu, president, designer, and programmer at Pseudo Interactive, responds:

> A poor interface can kill a game. My advice is to keep it as simple as possible and to steal ideas from other successful titles. You want your players to know what to do as soon as they pick up the controller. Don't try to be innovative here; save your creativity for the game itself. A player should pay attention to the game, not the game pad. The best interface is one that's completely transparent to the player.

Todd Howard, Bethesda Softworks

And finally, a few words from Bethesda's Todd Howard, whose last project was *Morrowind*, the third chapter in the mega-popular *Elder Scrolls* computer game RPG series. As reiterated many times in this chapter, Howard says, "interface is everything."

> It's the player's way of using the game. From the controls to the aesthetics of the menus—it all plays a huge part. And never expect the player to read the manual. That's too much effort. They want to put the game in and just play.

> The other thing, especially when doing a console game, is to really pay attention to what buttons you use. Play your game for awhile, and see if your hand starts to cramp up. If so, try another combination. Spend time tweaking the turning speeds on your character and see how the stick feels. This can make a big difference in how much fun your game is.

Keep in mind that one way to check and modify a UI and control is to properly test the game. Flip to Chapter 17, "Proper Game Testing," to read how to test a game during and after the game's development.

Bethesda Softworks' Todd Howard says interface is everything, and you should never expect the player to read the manual. Pictured here is a shot from *Morrowind*. Visit `www.elderscrolls.com` for more info and images.

(Used with permission by Bethesda Softworks, Inc.)

Chapter 15

Sound Engineering

THE EXPERTS

- Matthew Lee Johnston, Microsoft

- Marty O'Donnell, TotalAudio/Bungie Studios/Microsoft

- Erik Kraber and Jack Grillo, Electronic Arts Los Angeles

- Tommy Tallarico, Tommy Tallarico Studios

- Clint Bajakian, The Sound Department

- George "The Fat Man" Sanger, Fat Man Music

Not too long ago, sound effects in arcade, console, and PC games meant the odd bleep or chirp from an internal speaker. Fast forward to 2003—during a heated game of *Battlefield 1942: The Road to Rome*, you can literally hear the breath of fellow soldiers and the shells from gunfire hitting the ground...

As audio software and hardware continue to evolve for consoles and the PC, sound is becoming an incredibly significant part of the gaming experience. And consider for a moment the rate at which this new technology is not only accessible, but affordable. During the past few years alone, we've witnessed the emergence of Digital Theater Surround (DTS), Dolby Surround Sound, Dolby Digital (AC-3), Dolby Surround Pro Logic, Microsoft DirectSound and DirectSound 3D, Creative Labs Environmental Audio, Aureal's A3D, surround sound speakers, multiple-channel surround sound speakers, DVD players, powerful subwoofers, USB 2.0, FireWire connections, Bluetooth and WI-Fi, and optical digital outlets for a cleaner channel and digital inputs for all kinds of supported musical gear.

Point made?

With this new technology comes a new breed of audio specialists, who are determined to breathe new life into the interactive entertainment industry. This chapter delivers advice from a number of well-known and respected sources in the gaming industry on getting into sound design as a profession, ways of achieving the effects heard in popular games, which archived sound packages are worth getting, and how sound design fits into the grand scheme of game design.

> **NOTE**
>
> Electronic Arts, the world's largest entertainment software company, announced in 2002 that they had the first interactive games to completely integrate DTS Interactive and SurroundSoundScape audio technologies into console games such as its NHL and SSX games for the PlayStation 2. For the uninitiated, DTS is a popular audio technology used in theaters and on DVD movies.

Matthew Lee Johnston, Microsoft

As the Audio Director at Microsoft, the extremely talented Matthew Lee Johnston has worked on many products for the PC and more recently for the Xbox console. Past products include Microsoft's *Train Simulator*, *Combat Flight Simulator*, and *Flight Simulator*, *Midtown Madness*, *Microsoft Golf*, and most recently, *Fable*, *BC* and *Voodoo*. Johnston works at "Studio X," Microsoft's internal publishing studio that handles the Rare and Lionhead relationships, as well as a few other smaller game companies. Be sure to read his impressive bio in Appendix A, "Biographies."

Asked for the three most important considerations for an audio lead working in the interactive entertainment industry, Johnston's response is simple: Earn. Listen. Originate. He explains thoroughly:

1. **Earn; then assert ownership over your discipline**. Because of its "black art" status, audio design tends to invite all kinds of pesky intervention by those who think of you as "the person who does all the sound work that I don't feel like doing myself." At some point in your career, the game designer will want to direct the voice acting, the marketing team will want to select the genre of music, and the 2D artist will want to make sound effects using an evaluation copy of "Amateur Sound Destructor Pro 2.0" that he downloaded yesterday. It's easy to get upset when this happens and feel like someone's stepping on your toes, but you can use the situation to your advantage.

   The often well-intentioned amateur audio annoyance is actually a confused exhibition of interest in what you do. Take the time and explain to the enthusiastic wannabe audio designer that you appreciate that he cares about the audio and that he took the initiative to mock up some demo material for you. Also, note that you would love to incorporate his opinions into your final design. Schedule a short meeting with him to "brainstorm," and start that discussion by explaining your role on the team and what you consider to be your scope of ownership over the audio portion of the project. Then mine him for ideas, use the good ones, discard the bad ones, and add him to the list of people you go to when you want some feedback. Not only will you have another fan among your team members, but it creates a vibe of collaboration, like having an "audio deputy." It also establishes you as the sheriff to be reckoned with in town, and that you will be making the final decisions 'round these here audio parts.

2. **Listen**. Direct questioning and listening is one process that, ironically, audio people don't do enough of in this business. As the "audio expert," you'll have a hard time finding someone on the team who will be able to truly "collaborate" with you on a discussion about audio design as it relates to the other aspects of the project. Not only will the majority of the people you're working with not have any experience with audio design, but most people have a difficult time discussing their aural experiences in general. Dialogue about aesthetic issues surrounding audio design with non-audiocentric folks often contain vague and random musings, such as "The guns should sound deadly," "I want the sound to make the gamer feel hungry," and "I can feel something like that music from that old movie in which John Denver played the cowboy working really well in this section." Ask for more specific information, and you'll likely find yourself facing more abstract references and wall-gazing than you can handle.

The key to overcoming this communication/perception barrier is to initially ask the right questions and then listen critically to the responses. It's your job as the "expert" to bleed the correct information from the various sources available to you. Get to know the people you're working with by asking them how they use their ears. Use questions as examples of how to think more actively about sound: "What do you think the top five most important ambient sounds are in relation to gameplay? How will the gamer use these sound cues while roaming the map to achieve more in the game?" This type of question establishes several important ideas:

➤ **Sound cues** can be important to gameplay and provide the gamer with critical information that's not appropriate for visual representation (objects coming from behind you, for example).

➤ **Sound events** can stand on their own and don't necessarily have to be associated with a visual object.

➤ **Sound interactivity** should be designed into the level, as opposed to simply dropping in sound effects to match visual objects when the level is complete.

By presenting your peers with higher-level audio design concepts in question form, you require them to consider the possibilities, which will make them better collaborators in the future. You'll also solidify your role as the person who thinks on a higher level about audio, and in turn will ensure that this person will come to you in the future when she needs some of your special brand of thinking.

Microsoft's Matthew Lee Johnston takes his job very seriously—
he is pictured here recording sounds for the computer game
Train Simulator on a train with associates Gordon Hempton and
Rod Fergusson; recording noises in Austria;
and random train users in Tokyo.
(Used with permission by Matthew Lee Johnston and Microsoft Corp.)

3. **Originate**. Many people find their way into audio design work through music, and in a way, a soundscape for a video game is a lot like a big interactive song in which half of the voices come from nontraditional instruments such as piston engines and arena crowds. Technically, however, music is only a portion of the audio environment for a game, and the sound effects are often undervalued by composer-heavy audio teams—the result is an extremely uneven

differential of originality between the music and the sound effects. What tends to happen is that a team will go to great efforts to create new and interesting instrument sounds and wonderfully unique original music and then break out the sound effects libraries for the "non-musical" sound design work. This is an incredible injustice to the gamer, in my opinion. All the games I've shipped in the last five years have contained sounds derived from entirely original sources. As a result, I've helped to build a high-quality and comprehensive internal sound effects library here at Microsoft.

Many designers cite budget and time restraints as reasons for leaning on libraries for source material. On a strictly practical level, expense should no longer be a barrier because recording equipment is so inexpensive these days. Any sound designer with a little research and a reasonable amount of trial-and-error can achieve amazing results with a very simple and inexpensive rig. You can also offset the expense of the more exotic recording excursions by involving the marketing department and allowing them to cover your recording adventures as "special-interest" stories in gaming magazines or "making-of" features in exchange for some extra budget dollars.

You'll also be building a library that will be incredibly valuable if there's a sequel, a similar game, a web site, and so on. An original sound effects library can be a huge asset to any game company or production facility, and if presented correctly to managers, it can be another great way to justify your field recording or Foley efforts.

If there's just no possible way to gather your own source, it can also pay to seek out someone with a private library. There are a number of really great field recordists out there who maintain their own libraries and license them for a reasonable fee. They also go out and get the recordings you need, and if you let them maintain ownership of the sound for their library, the expense can really be reasonable. I really think the best at this is Gordon Hempton, the SOUND-TRACKER. His work is amazing.

What are the differences in creating sound effects, voices, and music for a console game versus a PC game?

There are two ways to approach this question. On the hardware side, audio design for PCs is about delivering the same experience on a multitude of different hardware configurations. A lot of time is spent making sure that Dad, with his P200 machine, and 16-year-old son, with the lightspeed gaming system, get relatively similar experiences. A lot of tradeoffs need to be made in situations in which you anticipate selling a lot of product outside of the U.S. and Europe, in which the average system tends to be a bit slower and less predictable. A console game is much easier to dial in because of the known hardware entity, which allows the designers a greater ability to really exploit the box and deliver a fine-tuned experience.

Console games are often a bit different by design. The demographic for a console game is often younger, and the games are less complex. In the PC world, you have a lot of simulations and first-person shooters that require massive amounts of intricacy and complexity. Console games usually take the refined "arcade" approach and deliver a more focused, more accessible experience. When I design audio for console games, I'm usually spending less time on the vastness of the world and complexity of its mechanics and more time on the aesthetic issues, such as how well the sounds enhance gameplay and whether they motivate the gamer to keep playing.

Why is sound and music so often overlooked in the gaming industry?

I think it's because hearing is largely a subliminal sense that humans take for granted. People are not constantly pondering and evaluating what they're hearing like they do about what they see. Therefore, there isn't a cognitive storehouse of vocabulary relating to the act of listening in the average human mind.

Another reason is that development teams really haven't seen the payoff when throwing money at the game audio. A lot of audio professionals land in this gig because they use computers to make music. I think that this is mainly the fault of the hiring managers, as well as the pure lack of available talent, but a lot of composers get slapped into the audio designer role when they aren't qualified. If all you do is create audio "content," but there's no one designing the audio infrastructure or writing specs that outline how that content should be manipulated and triggered, you won't be considered as a driving force in the game development process. Therefore, I think that game designers and project managers have a low set of expectations for what the audio department can produce.

I think if more audio designers educated themselves about game design, programming, visual art creation, and project management, they would be able to infiltrate the various groups within the team as a true peer. Instead of waiting for the programmer or producer to hand them a list of sound files to create, audio designers should be actively seeking out that information and making their own lists. Audio designers should collaborate with the programmers on a technical spec that describes in detail what the engine that handles the audio will actually do to it. If the audio designers get more involved and educate themselves out of the "audio ghetto," they'll move themselves and their art into a better "neighborhood."

What software packages and hardware should a budding sound engineer have?

On the hardware side, a good digital audio workstation is mandatory, and a good sturdy I/O interface to get your work in and out of your computer is also key. The Mac and the PC both have strong and weak points, but the gap is shrinking very rapidly. Spending more is not necessarily the answer.

On the periphery, I would also invest in a field recording setup, such as a DAT machine or a MiniDisc recorder. This portable setup can also act as a moving Foley rig so you can set up a mini-recording studio in any room or location. It's also becoming more important to have the ability to create 5.1 surround mixes of your work. The next generation of consoles will be capable of delivering 5.1 audio, and you don't want to be passed over for a gig just because you can't deliver the desired target format.

The one thing I can't stress enough is how important it is to have a good set of monitors. It won't matter how cool any of your gear is if you can't accurately listen to what you produce with it. If there was one area in my studio where I spent the maximum percentage of my budget, it would be on the monitors.

If your desire is to create some cool original sounds, Johnston suggests again that you start with original source material. "After you get the source you need, the best thing to do is to experiment wildly and then refine until you get closer to what you're shooting for." He adds:

> One thing a few of the guys here have really perfected is the use of random generators to create original source material. I've heard a lot of great stuff come out of Jerry Schroeder and Peter Comley's studios that have been produced this way. Many of the sound modules commercially produced these days will generate random patch settings at the click of a button, which makes it pretty easy and fun to crank out a bunch of original, raw source material that can be masterfully tweaked into shape.

> Another magical combination of random processing occurred when I unleashed an aspiring young intern on our Kyma system and asked him to focus on the random features. The combination of the unadulterated experimentation, lack of knowledge about how to use this powerful system the "right" way, and the way that you can assign random values to pretty much any oscillator or filter produced a great variety of results that were truly original.

There's a complete chapter in this book on breaking into the industry for different game design disciplines (see Chapter 21, "Breaking into the Industry"), but Johnston throws in a few words here about the topic:

> The age-old Catch-22 about breaking in to any industry exists in the gaming world as well: It takes experience to get the experience. One angle that I really exploit on my projects is that innovations often come from the uninitiated people who are still exploring and aren't tied down to old habits and processes. I make sure that on every one of my projects, there's someone in the early stages of production—who is either an intern or a fresh hire—who can feed the more established sound designers with a new and interesting perspective. This person is often found by listening to demos or more commonly through various colleges that are known for encouraging creative use of technology as instrument rather than the trade-school approach of "Here's how to use it."

> For this reason, I would also avoid focusing on learning as many tools as possible. The truth is that any intelligent person can operate the tools that audio designers use, but it takes a truly talented person to produce an interesting listening experience. As long as you understand the underlying concepts surrounding the basic editing and sequencing packages—and just as importantly, the physical properties of acoustic sound and how it relates to the various audio technologies—you should be able to learn any tools very quickly. Chances are, you'll need to learn quickly because the tools are constantly changing.

> It would be easy to get discouraged by looking at job listings for sound design gigs; the HR departments who write those things are looking for the "best candidate" whom they automatically think is the "most qualified." I personally think that every team should constantly be developing talent within the team in order to maintain a strong and loyal crew. This can be done by giving people who exhibit independent thinking and creative flair, but perhaps lack the technical chops, a chance to get in and get dirty. If you represent yourself as this "fresh perspective" and market yourself to game companies regardless of open job postings, you'll have a better chance at getting in the door.

Marty O'Donnell, TotalAudio/Bungie Studios/Microsoft

Ten days after Marty O'Donnell accepted a full-time position with Bungie Software, focusing entirely on the audio production for *Oni* and *Halo*, Microsoft purchased the company and moved it to Redmond to develop games for the Xbox. Although still co-owner of TotalAudio with Mike Salvatori (who stayed in the Chicago studio), Marty is currently audio lead for Bungie Studios at Microsoft.

And if you've ever paid attention to the audio in *Halo*, you'll know why he was invited to chat in this book about his craft!

O'Donnell says that the following are the most important considerations for a sound engineer to remember when working on his/her first game:

➤ Nothing is more important than the final mix. You must know exactly how different game states will affect the differing types of audio you've created. In linear media, such as film, all the audio, sound effects, dialogue, and music are brought together and mixed and balanced precisely the way the designer wants the audience to experience it. In games, however, all these elements can be brought together in ways that might be impossible to anticipate—in effect, a real-time interactive final mix. An individual sound effect might be "cool" if it's played loud but be totally inappropriate if a character is supposed to be whispering at the same time.

➤ Get the best equipment and hire the best talent. Actors and musicians should be accomplished professionals. Equipment and software should be top-notch, but more importantly they should be tools that you're comfortable working with.

➤ Sounds make it real; music makes you feel. In commercial work, I've learned that one of the most important things to remember is that the actual sound of something is rarely exactly what people are expecting to hear. If you record the sound of a potato chip breaking, it might be accurate, but also quite boring. Most likely, adding the sound of a tree being felled in the forest will give the right dramatic impact to the slow-motion shot of a crispy chip. The same goes for game audio. The actual recording of a gunshot or an elevator is not enough to create the surreal mood of most game environments. Use the real sounds as starting points, and then add bigger and more exaggerated sounds to enhance and expand them. In one of the traps in *Riven*, we added a woman's twisted scream to the sound of scraping metal, just to give the player the sense that something really bad was happening. I beat on a bundle of dried grapevines with a metal pipe to create some of the bone-crunching hits in *Myth*.

The most important thing in effective sound effects is synchronization. A good mouth noise, if perfectly in sync with the visual, will be more convincing to the observer than the most realistic sound that's slightly out of sync.

"Carefully balancing the audio will give the game the best chance at creating a sense of reality and the right mood for the player," says Marty O'Donnell, who created the sound effects for *Halo* (pictured here). "This is not unlike balancing character strengths for gameplay." *(Used with permission by Microsoft Corp.)*

On the topic of game music—discussed in depth in Chapter 16, "Music and Games"—O'Donnell says his motto is "Less is more." He explains:

> Use music only where it will have an emotional impact, and not just as audio wallpaper. Remember that just as in film, in which music is subservient to the scene, game music needs to enhance and support gameplay, not overpower it. Also, I've been writing and producing music professionally for almost 20 years, and I've never been disappointed in the results of having other musicians perform on my compositions. Sometimes due to the budget or lack of time it's not possible, but I'm usually not as happy with the results. Game music needs to be malleable, and is often recorded or changed at the last possible minute. It's a good idea to produce placeholder tracks and then replace them with final recordings that include other musicians.

When asked if there's a difference in creating sound effects, voices, and music for a console game versus a PC game, O'Donnell says it's really just a technical difference:

> Consoles are a more stable platform, and therefore I don't have to worry about supporting different sound cards and sound systems. Other than that, the creation process is similar. The really nice thing now is that the consoles support great systems such as Dolby 5.1 surround sound.

O'Donnell comments on why music and sound design are often overlooked when creating a game (usually the smallest portion of the budget goes to the audio):

> The only place that music isn't taken for granted is in the music industry. That's because music is recorded for the sake of music and not to enhance another product. In all other media, music and sound are elements that are subservient to some larger work. Listening to a Beethoven symphony in a concert hall is quite different from listening to the same symphony underscoring a dramatic scene in a movie.

In the game industry of the past, music was used to set a single mood (per level) and played constantly because it was hard to get enough variety in the sound effects to react interactively with the gameplay. Now, we have the technology to have full-bandwidth music and audio, great actors, and some really great programming to get all this content to respond to the player's actions. But it will take some time for gamers and developers to desire that kind of content; their expectations are still based on the past. The good news is that new gamers are expecting the kind of quality they are used to seeing and hearing on radio, TV, and film; and the developer who doesn't realize that fact will be beaten in the marketplace by those who do. In Japan, game soundtracks sell quite well to the general public, and I'm hoping that the same thing will happen soon in the West. Interactive sound design is quite different from sound design for linear media; I think we're still working out some of the techniques that will help highlight the uniqueness of the art of interactive entertainment.

What's the best way to break into the sound industry, and what kind of equipment and software do you need?

At this point, I believe that a young sound designer or composer should probably find an established sound and music production company and try to get hired as an intern. It also helps to be a fan of games and be extremely computer-savvy. Be a student of the use of audio in film, TV, and games. Produce some sound and music tracks for QuickTime videos and have them available to show to your potential employer. Find friends your own age who are doing a game or independent film project and work with them. Look for every opportunity and go for it. Then be willing to do whatever is asked of you, and be open to learning any type of program that's thrown at you. It's also possible to get a position in a related industry, such as film, broadcast, or music. Having that valuable experience and track record can be attractive to game developers.

For the sound designer on the Mac, which is still my preference, [you should have] ProTools, Peak, Waves plug-ins, Barba Batch, QuickTime Pro, Media Cleaner Pro, a good portable DAT, and some good mics. If you work on the PC, ProTools and Sound Forge are essential. For a musician, sequencing software such as Digital Performer, Cakewalk, or Logic Audio are essential programs.

And don't forget to practice!

O'Donnell recommends the following (in)valuable sound design resources to sound engineers to better their craft:

Keyboard, *Electronic Musician*, *Mix*, *Surround Sound*, and *Game Developer* are all good magazines for game audio folks. There are many good listservs I like—the best for me are the Interactive Audio Special Interest Group (IASIG), Video Games Musicians list, Game Audio Pro list, and the DAW-Mac (Digital Audio Workstation—Mac) list. By the way, I think it's important for any audio engineer to be fluent on both PCs and Macs, but there's no doubt that Macs are essential for anyone who wants to produce music and audio.

Why should someone hire a sound company such as TotalAudio instead of doing it themselves? Is it financially feasible?

In the early days of game development, it was possible to get away with having one of the programmers who understood the sound code on the product to author the sounds. Maybe you could get someone who played an instrument to make some tunes for the game. Now we're at the stage where game audio rivals film audio. In the film industry, there are specialists in every area of audio production. Eventually, the same will happen in game audio. For a game to be competitive, the developer will need to hire specialists to create content. Some will be hired as staff, and some will be outside contractors who come in on an as-needed basis. Directing dialogue, creating sound effects, and composing music are three main areas that will continue to require specialization.

To learn more about Marty O'Donnell and the work produced by TotalAudio, drop into the official web site at www.TotalAudio.com.

Erik Kraber and Jack Grillo, Electronic Arts Los Angeles

If you've ever marveled at the sound in the coveted *Medal of Honor* series—you're certainly not alone—and you can thank Erik Kraber and Jack Grillo, EALA's Director of Audio and Lead Sound Designer, respectively. They were asked to provide some insightful advice for video game sound engineers.

"There are three key things that we are trying to be aware of in the sound design process: feedback, immersion, and emotion," begin Kraber and Grillo (who answered all questions together, by the way).

As we create and integrate the sounds needed for the product, we are always asking ourselves these questions:

Feedback

Is the sound clarifying the actions of the player? Without visual support, does this sound help the player understand what he is doing or what he needs to do? Is the sound tied appropriately with the event or action to form a cohesive energy? If the answer is "no" to any of these questions, we need to decide whether the sound itself is wrong, whether the sounds around it are wrong, or whether there even needs to be a sound at all. Often, clarity of feedback comes with the absence of sounds. Too many sounds sometimes just create chaos.

Immersion

Is this world fully realized—sonically immersive and dynamic? When you close your eyes, are you transported into the world, even without the visual support? Have all efforts been made to make the world organic: no gaps in loops; very low frequency of repeated recognizable sounds or short loops; constant subtle changes? If the answer is "no" to any of these questions, we need to look into a new approach to make sure this is achieved.

Emotion

Does this sound support the emotional energy of the moment? Does this sound support the emotional arc of the level or of the game? If the answer is "no" to any of these questions, we have to ask, "Is that okay?" Not all sounds can contribute to this equally. Obviously, this is an area that music generally dominates, but it is important to understand how sound effects, dialogue, and ambient sounds all contain emotional energy, too.

With *Medal of Honor: Frontline* as an example, Kraber and Grillo were asked to support their advice above. Their response is as follows:

Feedback

In *Frontline*, we experimented quite a bit with weapon distance sound modeling. We had a number of different sounds that would fade in and out, depending on how close the enemy was to the player. We came up with some amazing sounds that felt very real, but in the process we were obscuring the player's ability to identify weapon sounds. We found it was important for the player to know not just that they were being fired at, but exactly what weapon was being used against them. So, in order to promote better feedback for the player, we simplified our distance sound modeling and made sure that the unique characteristics of each weapon were preserved at most distances.

Immersion

D-Day in *Frontline* was a big focus for us. It is the first level of the game, and we had to immediately convince the player that he was about to hit the shores of hell. We spent a good deal of our time coming up with a long streamed Dolby surround file that would play in sync with the opening boat sequence. This allowed us to score the opening, just as we would for a film. This really helped the level of immersion because we could do almost anything we wanted with the main streamed file and then add many layers of individual sounds on top of it (artillery hitting water, plane flybys, bullet whizbys, exploding PT boats).

Emotion

We had fun experimenting with conflicting energies and emotions in the "Arnhem Nights" level. The battle is almost as intense as D-Day, but the music is very somber and tragic. We created this fine balance between the chaos of an intense firefight and the sadness of a boy's choir. Michael Giacchino and Scott Langteau's instincts were perfect with the music composition. Rather than have some action-packed music to fit over the battle scene, Michael created something deep and reflective, and the contrast worked very well.

So, what kinds of tools (that is, software and hardware) should a budding sound designer get hold of? Is this financially feasible?

"All you need to get going is a computer, digital multitrack editing software, an audio card with audio inputs, and some type of microphone," answer Kraber and Grillo. They continue:

These tools will give anyone exposure to the world of recording, editing, and processing sounds. If you can get a multitrack editor that allows you to edit in sync with a digital movie, that will allow you to experiment with sync sound and help you understand what sound is needed to support a visual. We use expensive software and hardware, but there are plenty of software-based, digital multitrack editors and sound cards on the market that are very affordable for both the PC and Mac.

Omaha Beach is the first level of EA's *Medal of Honor: Frontline*. "We had to immediately convince the player that he was about to hit the shores of hell," say Kraber and Grillo, EALA's Director of Audio and Lead Sound Designer, respectively.
(Used with permission by Electronic Arts, Inc.)

Next, a tough question: This duo was asked to provide a couple of specific tips or tricks for creating sounds in a game.

This is a very difficult question to answer because each type of sound has different tricks associated with it. For instance, weapon sounds tend to sound bigger if you can stagger the timing of a closely miked gunshot with a distantly miked gunshot. If you stagger the timing of the two separate sounds by a few milliseconds or more, gunshots tend to feel huge. For creature vocals [Kraber and Grillo also worked on EA's *Clive Barker's Undying*], we tend to play quite a bit with real-time pitch bending of animal sounds through a vocoder. Again, it all depends on what kind of sounds you are trying to design.

So, what's the biggest problem with sound in video games today?

"The single biggest problem in video game sound is the attitude that sound design ends at sound asset delivery," answer Kraber and Grillo. They explain:

The overall quality of the sound in any given game has very little to do with the individual sounds. Sound designers throughout the industry work very hard at creating unique and appropriate sounds, but they often sound out of balance after they are implemented. There is nothing more disappointing than a great sound asset integrated poorly. The way to make a game sound great is to give the sound designers access to mixing each sound in context. In the film industry, there are very talented and highly paid individuals tasked with nothing but mixing all the sounds of the picture together to make one cohesive whole. In the video game industry, this task is often left to junior programmers, or spread out among level designers, animators, producers, and so on. At EALA, the sound design team is very lucky to have complete control over the entire sound design process, including the final mix. We believe this to be the most important distinction of the *Medal of Honor* series, and it seems like it would be a simple standard to adopt. Creative ownership through the entire process is the most effective and efficient path to quality.

Finally, what are the three single best pieces of advice you can give a budding audio engineer who wants to break into the video gaming industry?

➤ **Make connections**. It is sometimes hard to break into this business if you don't know people in the industry who can support and market you. Usually, you can find a friend of a friend who knows somebody who works on games. Going through that person is probably going to be easier than trying to walk in the front door on your own.

➤ **Really know the industry and the products**. Be very informed about all the games that are currently on the market, and formulate opinions on what you like and what you don't. Listen to games and get a feel for how you could make them better. If you are applying for a position, make sure you know all about their products and think how you can help improve what they do.

➤ **When you apply for a position, be sure to send a demo that shows how you would like to be doing sound for a game**. Just sending a CD of music to a company that is looking for a sound designer may not be enough to get you in the door. I rarely have people sending me demo tapes with video game footage and sync sound, which I find very strange. Almost 90% of the time, I just get a CD. Seeing how your sound can enhance a game or a film is a huge selling point, and it can really help if you don't have much experience. If you prove to them that you can do it, and they can hear it with their ears and see it with their eyes, they will care less about your experience.

Tommy Tallarico, Tommy Tallarico Studios

Never heard of Tommy Tallarico? Impossible. Be sure to read his thoroughly impressive bio in Appendix A and his excellent advice on creating music for games in Chapter 16.

Tallarico shares some cool techniques when creating sounds for video games:

➤ **It's always best to combine existing sound libraries and going out and recording/editing your own sounds**. Too many sound designers use sound libraries too much. Sound libraries are great for certain things, but not for everything. Libraries also are great for layering in with sounds you've created.

With all the great audio software and tools available, it's easy to take a sound and manipulate it into something completely different. You can get some pretty amazing sounds just by pitching stuff down a few octaves! For some reason, it always seems like we need lots of wet mucky squishy sounds. For this, we use thick Jell-o mix about halfway before it gets hard. Makes a nice thick liquidy sauce.

➤ **Different types of microphones produce different outcomes**. My suggestion is to use a few different mics placed at different areas for the sound you're trying to record. After you get it back in your studio, you can decide which sounds (or layers of sounds) work best.

➤ **When in doubt, add a little low-end EQ to your sound**. It will always bring up the presence and make it sound a little bigger.

If doing a sports-related game, ask the publisher to get you into an event to record the sounds (crowds, chants, cheers, ambiance). A lot of times the publisher is paying lots of money in order to secure professional sports licenses, and it's very easy to get into special events if you just ask the publisher to ask the licensor.

Tommy Tallarico is one of the "rock stars" of the video game industry, shown here in his best James Bond outfit, and toying around in his recording studio to get new and exciting sounds for video games. "Work hard, play hard" is his motto.
(Used with permission by Tommy Tallarico.)

Clint Bajakian, The Sound Department

After working at LucasArts Entertainment Company from 1991 to 2000 as a composer and sound design supervisor, Clint Bajakian left to start his own company: C. B. Studios. In 2002, he cofounded The Sound Department (www.thesounddepartment.com) with Julian Kwasneski, offering state-of-the-art audio production services with an emphasis on computer and video games. Be sure to read his lengthy bio in Appendix A.

When asked about what The Sound Department is, Bajakian answers with a quote from his web site:

The Sound Department is an audio production company specializing in sound design, original music, and voiceover for games. With credits in over 50 leading titles and a combined 18 years of professional experience, its award-winning staff is a clear leader in the industry.

➤ Quality

➤ Reliability

➤ Collaborative Approach

These are what distinguish The Sound Department. The SF Bay Area company responds individually to each project's needs, often supervising custom teams assembled from an extensive network of game audio veterans.

Bajakian says that all game platforms are supported, including location-based entertainment and the emerging wireless and Internet markets. He explains a bit more about its services:

Julian Kwasneski and I are equal partners in managing The Sound Department and performing most all of the audio production, including sound design, music composition, and voiceover production. Occasionally, we subcontract out to other Bay Area audio professionals. We each have a lean and mean digital audio production studio, and we keep in touch daily. Often, we collaborate on various projects; just as often, we work on titles separately. Although we offer our services to all media industries, it is the game industry in which we have the most professional experience. We've scored a few independent films along with various smaller projects for industrial or communications clients, but by far and away, the vast majority of our business is the games industry.

Concerning audio in games, Bajakian was asked to give some insightful advice on creating sound for video games:

Play the game; know the game. Understand the dramatic pace and feel. Get concept art, get a design doc, post the art on your walls, get burns of the game to play, watch testers playing the game, and so on.

Manage the data and information with a high degree of organization. Set up specific pipelines for asset transfer to and from the project. Work out how revisions are to be handled, archives, and backups. Track information by using lists with search capabilities like databases. Effects and voice file databases are especially important. Place as much emphasis on this organizational, or administrative, aspect of the job as you do your creative art and craft.

It's very important to think of one's self as being a full-fledged member of the team as opposed to the audio provider off to the side. Talk to people; meet the artists, programmers, testers…shoot the breeze with them while learning more about the game and what input they may have for the audio. (One day, that tester will be a designer or producer, and may hire you!) Find out who to go to for what, and be lib-eral with your phone and email footprint with the team. Keep very close tabs with the producer as well as whomever has been designated your point person and/or audio programmer. Good implementation of the audio is as important as the relative quality or originality of the audio itself!

Bajakian was asked to support his advice with an example of a recent game he's worked on:

In *Jedi Knight II: Jedi Outcast*, Julian maintained a highly organized database for all the sound effects in the project. We got and played burns of the game and frequently went to LucasArts to observe the gameplay with Chuck McFadden, the lead tester, or Dan Pettit and Brett Tosti, the co-producers—

taking copious notes. We were in constant daily contact with Brett and Dan; members of the LucasArts sound department; and most importantly, the game designer, Kevin Schilder of Ravensoft. Not a single issue came up that we didn't iron out with the proper people, having fun the whole time. And the organizational procedures worked so well that we were able to focus on the creativity of the project and ship a critically acclaimed audio package, complete with an extraordinary interactive soundtrack.

And now a question asked a few times in this chapter: What are the most important audio software and hardware tools one needs to get going? And at what cost?

It used to be more expensive to amass the necessary gear to do this type of work. Now, with the advent of professional, computer-based, audio-production tools, one can put together a hot authoring environment for less than $10,000. What one needs is a computer, MIDI sequencing and multitrack audio editing software that can also play digital video in synchronization with the audio tracks, an effects processor or software effects plug-ins, an instrument sample set, sound effects libraries, DAT deck, mixing console, and speakers. Ideally, one would also have the ability to record his own sound effects or music tracks, either in the studio or remotely by using a portable recording rig. This, of course, necessitates a microphone and portable recoding device. The cost only really gets run up by the sample and sound effect libraries. The rest can easily be put together for less than $5,000.

On creating sound for *Jedi Knight II*, Bajakian says, "We got and played burns of the game, and
frequently went to LucasArts to observe the game play with Chuck McFadden, the lead tester,
or Dan Pettit and Brett Tosti, the co-producers—taking copious notes." Shown here: Bajakian at work.
(Used with permission by Clint Bajakian.)

Are there any beefs with sound in video games today?

According to Bajakian, the biggest problem is audio today is getting the attention and backing it deserves in order for it to rise to a level of quality and impact that the consumer demands. He explains:

My experience is that often the main reason audio in a game can be excellent and achieve new heights is the sound designer's and composer's own initiative to excel, often along with an enthusiastic audio programmer—despite a healthy budget and strong recognition commensurate with their hard work. The money is there in the games industry, but not enough of it is applied toward audio; the public relations and publicity entities are there, but give still only minor attention to audio; the leading game platforms have adequate resources such as RAM, disk space, and technical capabilities for audio to be totally awesome; the biggest problem is that the powers-that-be need to recognize the importance of the audio's contribution to dramatic entertainment and to back it accordingly. I always find it interesting that one of the first things consumers point out is the audio, although it remains one of the last pointed out by the press.

But Bajakian believes the trend is reversing: "More and more third-party developers are creating better and better tools and technology, the game platforms have given good attention to the audio element, and executives and producers are more and more realizing the importance of audio and the necessity for its strong backing."

"The use of live orchestras happening with more and more frequency in the industry is a testament to this, along with the advent of multichannel surround formats becoming commonplace," adds Bajakian.

Finally, Bajakian was asked to give some advice to those starting out:

Put the necessary software and hardware together to build and operate a simple but effective audio production studio. Practice in it, and take on as many interactive audio projects as you can—even for little or no money at first. Get credits in things as much as possible; build a résumé, including an internship if able.

Learn as much as possible about audio production, games, business models, and the Internet; be proficient with all the leading software applications such as MS Word, Excel, Outlook, database applications, PowerPoint, HTML (ideally), and of course, audio applications of as many kinds as possible.

And...

Keep a close eye on assistant- or associate-level job openings in the industry. Remember that personality is as important to a prospective employer as talent and skill base. And remember: Work hard and always have a positive attitude!

George "The Fat Man" Sanger, Fat Man Music

George Alistair Sanger, a.k.a. The Fat Man, has been composing music for games since 1983. Along with Team Fat, his legendary team of three other cowboy composers, he is internationally recognized for having created music for more than 200 games, including *Wing Commander*, *The 7th Guest*, *NASCAR Racing*, *Putt-Putt Saves the Zoo*, *Tanarus*, and *ATF*.

Sanger advises sound engineers to remember these pointers:

> ➤ **Get the gig**. You can't excel at the game if you're not on the playing field.

> ➤ **Be earnest**. This is not a gig in which you do whatever it takes to get money. This is a concert for potentially 10,000 people—in your time on the stage, I think it's good to try to make it a good time for them, even if it turns into a free show.

> ➤ **Be kind and patient**. This will solve untold numbers of unforeseen problems. In particular, sometimes it's very easy for the client to show himself in a way that makes him appear to be foolish or mean. Try to assume that he is *not* trying to make your life hard—he's probably just as new to this as you are and more scared of audio than you. Resist the urge to send angry email in reply to what appears to be a stupid evaluation of your audio. In the end, he probably wants what's best for the gamer, as do you.

Why should someone hire/outsource audio to Team Fat?

Hiring in-house and hiring what we in Texas call "out-house" take turns being in and out of fashion. If budding game builders can do all the audio themselves, there's a lot to be said for that. It's really fun, and you learn a lot. You could be like *me*! It might even be the best thing for your game. On the other hand, it might take you 20 years and 200 games before you're able to make the audio that your gamers deserve. See, that's where the experience thing pays off.

I think that efficiency is the biggest factor. Do you have the time, manpower, equipment to do it yourself; or the money to set up for that? If so, go for it! If not, look into the cost of independent audio houses. We may dress fancy, but we might not cost as much as you think—mainly because you're sharing the setup expenses with all our other clients. For a mid-sized company, I'd remind them to check into *all* the expense factors before hiring an in-house. We did a little cost comparison on our web site (`www.fatman.com/compose.htm#5`).

And there's a punchline. You'll *never* have exactly one man's worth of work, or two men's worth, and so on. It'll never be precisely a whole number. So you'll either have a half-man sitting around getting paid for nothing, or you'll need to hire another half-man. That's where the independents can be very handy.

Why are sound and music so overlooked in the gaming industry?

The game designer is like a rocket scientist. He's got *a lot* to do. He's up on the gantry, putting the finishing touches on his Saturn V, and you're down on the ground yelling, "I KNOW! PAINT IT UP TO LOOK LIKE A WATERMELON!" Even though you know and I know that nobody would ever forget a launch like that, it just isn't important to the game designer right now. He is likely concerned with more scientific details, such as wondering if the thing will fly and getting you off of the launch pad.

In truth, music is a hugely efficient area of game design, says Sanger. "You can do more good for your gamer, and it will cost less money than in any other area of the game."

What proportion of the game's entertainment value can potentially come from the music?

I did some research, and I've heard everything from 60% (um…uh…maybe) to 5%. Never lower. Now consider the fact that I've never heard of more than 1.5% of the game's development resources going toward music. Somebody's missing the boat (or rocket)….

Any key software packages and hardware that a sound engineer should have? Sanger replies, "I don't like to talk about hardware and software—it's overemphasized." That said, Sanger says he uses a couple of things that he feels strongly about, "because they work very well, are very helpful, and are inexpensive." Here are his picks:

➤ Anything by Sonic Foundry. Sound Forge is a must; Vegas Video is great.

➤ The RNC audio compressor by FMR (`www.fmraudio.com`). For $200, you get a $3,000 toy, and it's about as close to a "magic box" as you can get.

➤ I like the Sony Mini Disk Walkman. I got it for a hundred bucks with a mic, and it sounds 90% as good as the $100,000 digital two-track we used to use to master CDs in L. A.

➤ If you need a sampler, get a Gigasampler. Put it on a separate PC from any of your other software, run tape around the CPU three times, and never ever upgrade.

Howdy, ma'am. Here's a shot of "The Fat Man"—you can see a name isn't everything.
Sanger says Susan Penn, "tailor of the world's best suit," spent three years making it—
those snakes are all hand-embroidered.
(Used with permission by George Sanger.)

How about some cool tips on making great game sounds instead of using stock sounds?

It's fun to build sound effects from scratch and to use something unlikely to make your sound. I suppose there are altogether too many sounds in games that I've worked on that contain bits of my Rolls Royce or the sound of toilets flushing. There's a great deal to learn from the movie industry about beating up melons and breaking celery and cracking dowels wrapped in meat to simulate damage to the human body.

On the other hand, Sanger continues, "It's not that important to be clever—it's better to sound good. Often a branch makes a good branch sound, a fire makes a good fire sound. Sometimes, to get the best punching sound, I just hit myself!"

Kidding aside (or is he?!), Sanger says that to make the right sound effect, he tries to use his heart and his ear. "I think, 'What would I *really* like to hear right now?' and then, after imagining the sound, I think of the most efficient way to get a warm recording of that." The Fat Man tries to remember the sounds that he really loves and keep them handy. Here's a list of the sounds he enjoys using:

- ➤ Bubble paper
- ➤ Ping-pong balls
- ➤ Jell-o through a straw
- ➤ Big sheets of metal
- ➤ Our oven door
- ➤ A pan with a tiny bit of water in the bottom
- ➤ My computer being shut off
- ➤ Brake drums being dropped
- ➤ Fireworks
- ➤ Parades

Says Sanger:

I've recently allowed myself to collect sounds. I carry a Sony Mini Disk Walkman on most of my adventures—it has a great little mid-side microphone that comes with it. The mic goes in my hat. The very nice aspect of a mid-side mic for our business is that you get a stereo recording...*but* if you combine the right and left sides to make a mono recording, the recording is still perfect—there are no phase-shift or off-axis coloration anomalies introduced.

He adds that as he collects these sounds, he adds them to a big library on hard disk, sorted by sound type, which he backs up to CD from time to time.

There are a lot of ways to sort sounds, says Sanger, and they can be very personal. With that in mind, he does it something like this (see following list). He notes, "Some categories, such as light bulb taps, just occur because you have the sound; whereas other categories, such as ballistics, are there because you'd better have them in this business."

- Ambience
- Automotive
- Ballistics
- Boinks
- Buzz
- Cartoon
- Clops
- Combat Scenes
- Electronic
- Household Items (appliances, coins, cuts-snips, doors, ice, light bulb taps, Velcro, window, zippers)
- Human Body (burps, mouth, potty, footsteps)
- Machinery
- Monsters
- Musical Logos
- Nature (animals, dirt-gravel, environments, weather)
- Percussion
- Ring, Clang, Ping, Zing
- Rip
- Rumble
- Scrape
- Slide
- Snap, Crackle, Pop
- Spells
- Sports

- ➤ Squeaks

- ➤ Synth

- ➤ Thud

- ➤ Twang

- ➤ Voice Snippets

- ➤ Wet-Watery

- ➤ Whoop

- ➤ Whoosh

Sanger says what's very important is the implementation of sound effects in the game:

Don't associate a single sound effect with a single action. When something happens in the game, it shouldn't directly cause a .wav file to play. It should call something less direct, such as a routine that randomly picks a .wav from a pool of sounds. Perhaps that pool of sounds could grow, shrink, or change as the game progresses.

For some excellent examples of George "The Fat Man" Sanger's sound effects and music, visit `www.fatman.com/listen.htm`.

Chapter 16

Music and Games

THE EXPERTS

- Tommy Tallarico, Tommy Tallarico Studios

- George "The Fat Man" Sanger, Fat Man Music

- Chance Thomas, HUGESound Network

- Jeff Kliment, LucasArts

Few segments of the entertainment industry welcome as many different talents and specialties as the gaming industry. Where else can writers, programmers, artists, animators, sound engineers, and musicians all work together as a team for one single product? This is one of the key reasons why this young industry is so exciting. And the opportunities are virtually endless!

Fortunately, developers of console, PC, and portable gaming titles are slowly recognizing the importance of a good musical sound-track, and more effort and financial resources than ever before are being poured into music. Sure, it's still a tiny piece of the overall pie when compared with the money spent on graphics (and licensing, where applicable), but it's a growing field, and the top musicians in the gaming industry can make a good living. Sure beats playing seedy bars or giving it up for a day job.

Let's take a look at the top musicians in the business and listen to the advice they can give to those looking to break into the gaming industry.

> **NOTE**
>
> Total Audio/Bungie Studios/Microsoft's multitasking Marty O'Donnell, responsible for the audio for the groundbreaking game *Halo*, speaks quite a bit in Chapter 15, "Sound Engineering," about both sound and music design and implementation. Be sure to read his comments where both disciplines are discussed together.

Tommy Tallarico, Tommy Tallarico Studios

Arguably the most accomplished (and insanely busy!) video game composer in history is Tommy Tallarico, whose music for more than 200 games has been heard by hundreds of millions of people all over the world. Some of Tallarico's top titles include *Earthworm Jim*; Disney's *Aladdin*; *Cool Spot*; *The Terminator*; *Prince of Persia*;

the *Test Drive* series; *MDK*; *Tomorrow Never Dies*; *Tony Hawk Skateboarding*; *Spider-Man*; *Pac-Man World*; *Knockout Kings*; *Blitz, Unreal* and *Unreal 2*; *Time Crisis*; and *Metroid Prime*. Visit his web site at www.tallarico.com.

Tallarico chats in depth in this section about game music composition and implementation, and gives advice about how to best break into the industry as a musician.

"Some of the most important things to remember are creativity and integration," begins Tallarico. "Integration with the programmers and/or designers/producers is half of the work. After you've created a sound, it's important to make sure that the sound is being triggered properly and at the right volume, pitch, pan, and so on."

Making sure of the way the audio will be triggered is also a very important process that should be discussed very early on in the project, says Tallarico. "Keep in mind that every project you'll ever work on will be set up and handled entirely differently each time," he says.

On the creative side, you want your work to really stand out from anything anyone has ever heard:

> Using elements such as ambiance as opposed to music can sometimes create a more realistic and enjoyable atmosphere. Another secret is to try and do something that has never been done before. When I first took on *Tony Hawk's Pro Skater*, no one had any idea it was going to be as popular as it was. I liked it because there had never been a good-sounding skateboarding game, *ever*! I really like the challenge part of the job.

> It's important that the composer [avoids] being too repetitive. For example, if you're creating a two-minute song, the main motif shouldn't really repeat unless it changes a bit or other instruments are added, subtracted, changed, and so on. The thing to remember is that the player will be hearing your song over and over again, so you want to make sure that you deliver something unique each time before the loop happens.

> Not every score has to be completely interactive. It's okay to use full songs for certain sections. If the section or scene changes, you can go into another new song that reflects the current mood. Once again, I must stress that every project is going to be different and requires a different approach to audio. This is the challenge, and for me [it is] the "fun" part of doing what I do. Keeping an open mind to all of the technical possibilities is very important. Don't be afraid to speak up and try new ideas.

Where can musicians look for inspiration?

> Listening to and referencing movie soundtracks is a very good way to get a taste of the styles for certain games. Many times a producer or designer will come to me and say, "We want it to sound like *Conan the Barbarian*," or whatever movie best represents the feeling they're trying to convey. Keep in mind that a lot of movie music is incidental or "background"-type music. Whereas video game music, for the most part, is what I like to call "foreground" music—in your face, heart-pounding, adrenaline-kicking stuff.

> Referencing certain instruments in the music can also help convey a scene. For example, a didgeridoo will instantly put you in Australia. Big tubular bells or low male choir may give you a sense of spookiness. Wind trees and high female choir may give you an underwater or icy feel.

Discussing the possible differences in creating sound effects, voices, and music for a console game versus a PC game, Tallarico says there's a technical consideration, but it's changing very rapidly.

In most console games, you're a lot more worried about space constraints. For PCs, it's easy to download lots of sounds onto the hard drive or stream in various audio cues on-the-fly or from a memory chip. As the new platforms are becoming more capable of handling large files and streams, you'll eventually see this line disappear. Already, with Microsoft's Xbox, the console machine is more powerful (audio-wise) than 99% of all the PCs out there right now!

Is there a point when a game maker should hire a sound company?

A lot of times, a small developer is working on only one game and can't afford to build a digital audio studio. Compare [with] the movie industry. What would it be like if every producer or director had to use just one or two people to create all the music for every film they worked on? It would become stale very quickly. In fact, in the '40s and '50s, most composers were in-house working for the movie studios (as were the actors!). It really wasn't until the '60s and '70s that composers such as John Williams started making names for themselves as independents. Many times, smaller developers don't even employ a sound person because they don't need a full-time audio guy. Lots of publishers don't have sound people because they don't have an internal production staff at all. They deal mostly with marketing, PR, legal, and sales.

Over the long run, it makes a lot more sense to be able to choose the audio person and style that fits your current project. Over the last three or four years, there has been a major shift in audio—people leaving companies and starting their own businesses. There's also a lot more money to be made if you're on your own and make the right deals. But in-house is safer and more reliable.

This is all great advice, but why do so many gamers and industry professionals alike seem to overlook audio in game? "The answer is 'I HAVE NO FREAKIN' IDEA!'" jokes Tallarico.

A lot of times, sound in general is underrated by companies. I feel that there are three main elements to a video game that are all equally important to the whole experience: graphics, which is the art and animation; programming, which incorporates the visuals plus design, feel, and movement; and sound, which is everything you hear. So do most companies take the audio as seriously as the graphics and programming? I would say no for sure. We should have a bigger percentage of the budget (to do things such as have live orchestras, *talented* voice acting, intelligent script writing, and so on), but instead it's often [considered] post-production, similar to the film industry. But for video games, that's just not the case—the composer and sound designer need to be there from day one, figuring out technically how everything is going to be incorporated into each phase or level of the game.

But Tallarico says this has improved over the last five years. Why is that so? "Because all of us audio guys are complaining so much!" he laughs.

Every year, you see more live musicians and talented voice acting. Hopefully, we'll reach a point where almost every game is like that, as opposed to about 10%—15% of the stuff out there. If you look at the film industry, film composers are underrated when compared to movie stars and directors.

Okay, let's talk about key software and hardware. According to Tallarico, every musician needs a good sequencer for composing music. "Both Macs and PCs have great sequencing software—my advice would be to go online and download the different demos for each." Tallarico's personal favorites are Cakewalk (`www.cakewalk.com`) for the PC and Digital Performer (`www.motu.com`) for the Mac.

> Aside from the sequencer, you need a strong sampler with lots of different sounds. This will enable you to get very versatile. There really isn't any one style for video game music; therefore, you may be asked to incorporate lots of different sounds, styles, and techniques in your music writing. A good sampler will enable you to do this.

For the sound designer, he recommends Sound Forge (`www.sonicfoundry.com`) for the PC. "This is the most versatile, easy-to-use, and affordable audio software program on the market. There are even tons of plug-ins available to make it even more powerful," he notes. Another piece of equipment a sound designer will definitely need, adds Tallarico, is a portable DAT machine for grabbing all of those sound effects.

"When putting everything together for pre-rendered game cinematics (music, sound effects, dialogue, and so on), I use Digital Performer on a fast Mac with the Mark of the Unicorn 2408 digital interface," says Tallarico. "Once again, it's a very inexpensive way to get lots of tracks going without paying outrageous prices for hardware."

NOTE

Flip back to Chapter 15 to see Tallarico's cool tricks and techniques for creating sounds for video games.

Well-armed with examples to support his discerning advice, Tallarico offers the following thoughts on creating something that sounds different and is technically challenging.

> In the early days, I think mostly what I did was to give the players the kind of music they wanted to hear. I remember playing games and thinking, "This music sucks! It sounds like a merry-go-round tune or some childish bleeps and blips. Why weren't people doing rock, pop, blues, orchestral, dance, techno, and so on? No one had ever really heard a real guitar in a video game until the early '90s.

> Another thing I started doing was to introduce lots of musical samples right into the cartridge MIDI files. Back in the old days on the Sega Genesis, people would use the sample chip to play a scratchy voice sample ("FIGHT") or use it to intro the company name ("SEGA"). I decided, why not have that sample channel be playing as much as possible? I had convinced programmers that if they gave me enough space, I would make the Genesis sound like no one has ever heard. So I used kick drum and snare drum samples, guitar and horn hits, singing voices, and so on, right in the music. On top of that, I would use as many real sampled sound F/X as I could; by prioritizing every sound in the game, I was able to constantly have the sample chip playing without any recognizable dropout when other things took priority. If you go back and listen to a game such as *Earthworm Jim* or *Aladdin*, you'll hear samples going off all the time. No one ever really did that.

A lot of times, the game has to be the right kind of game in order for it to have great music. So sometimes the music or project finds you. I remember the first time I played *PaRappa the Rapper*, in which they used multiple streams going on at the same time to get the instruments to fall out or layer, depending on how well you were doing. I had just finished working on *Treasures of the Deep*, and we were kinda doing the same thing, but not to the same extent. I was really blown away that it worked as well as it did in *PaRappa!* Until you actually do something like that, you're never entirely sure how it's going to come off within the game.

Any advice to offer on breaking into the industry?

I think talent and determination are the two biggest assets you could have. With enough determination, you achieve/find/create luck. I would say to anyone who is serious about it to just go out and do it! Put together your best-written favorite couple of songs on CD and go to the E3 convention in Los Angeles and/or the Game Developers Conference in San José. Pass out CDs, make friends, learn, and network with people. Take your demo and send it out to all the game companies. It's all about being in the right place. It's hard to be discovered if you're sitting in your bedroom. I got in this industry by moving to California and starting as a games tester. That goes for getting into any part of the industry—it's all about working your way up and who you know! If you have a genuine love for games and want to be a producer or designer, start out in the testing department. You can't really just be a producer or designer; you have to work your way up to that. If you want to be a programmer, learn C++ and RISC or assembly language; same if you want to be an artist—learn 3D Studio Max. Usually, you have to know somebody in the industry and start out low, but one thing people don't realize is that this industry is starving for talented people right now—mostly artists and programmers.

Learn your art and then take a job for whatever it pays—do it for free if you have to, just to get your foot in the door. Then, when you get your chance, show them what you're made of…so much so that by the next project, you're writing your own ticket! Experience is everything when job hunting in this industry, so get it any way you can.

A great web site to find out all about the gaming industry is www.gamasutra.com [read Chapter 24, "Game Design Resources on the Internet"]. There, you find tons of interviews with gaming professionals. There are also lots of job postings every week.

While we're on the topic, Tallarico enlightens us on how he broke into the industry. It's an interesting story, so put your feet up and enjoy:

This is actually a pretty funny story! I'm originally from Springfield, Massachusetts. When I was a kid, I always wanted to move to southern California to be a musician. (Doesn't everybody!?) Anyway, when I turned 21, I left Mass. and drove across country to southern California. The only thing I really knew out here was Hollywood, so I drove to Hollywood. I didn't have a place to stay, didn't know anybody, didn't have a job, and—oh yeah—I didn't have any money!! So I showed up in Hollywood, took a look around, and said, "What the hell is this?!!!" Those of you who have been to Hollywood, you know what I'm talking about. Hollywood isn't exactly the way they portray it on TV—it's pretty much a dump! The only other thing I knew in California was Disneyland, so I stopped some bum on the street and asked him where Mickey Mouse lived. He pointed me about 45 minutes south to Orange County.

I was sleeping either in my car or on Huntington Beach at this point, so I was looking for anything I could find. So I picked up a newspaper and got a job the very next day selling keyboards at the Guitar Center. I knew about music and keyboards…what the hell. Believe it or not, the very first person I waited on happened to be a producer for a new software company starting up, called Virgin Mastertronic. I've loved music my whole life; I've been playing piano since I was three years old. My second love has always been video games. Never in my whole life did I ever think of putting my two loves together—until that day.

I became the first tester at Virgin the next day. (A tester is somebody they pay to play games and find things wrong with them.) The first game I worked on was David Perry's *Overlord—Supremacy* in the UK. He still says, "I can't believe you're the bastard who kept coming up with all those bug reports that kept me up at night." There were only about 15 people at Virgin at the time, so they didn't need a full-time musician. When the first opportunity arose for music (*Prince of Persia* on the Game Boy), I jumped on it. I would sit down with the programmers and technicians every chance I got, to learn about the machines. I know nothing about programming. I just know music and games.

It's definitely been a plus in my career. I mean, think about it—how do you program the blues or rock 'n' roll? That's just something you feel! Anyway, I worked on *Prince of Persia* for free on the weekends and after work. The VP of the company was so impressed, he made me the music guy! My next game was *Global Gladiators* on the Genesis, which won "Best Music of the Year," and I've been doing it ever since!

A few years ago, when Tommy Tallarico gave his keynote speech at the Game Developer's Conference (see Chapter 25, "Key Conventions, Organizations, and Awards"), he passed out copies of a standard audio agreement for folks to take a look at. Why? As Tallarico puts it, "Tons of musicians and sound designers have no idea what to ask for or what to expect contractually." Tallarico says he receives countless emails from people requesting his boilerplate agreement. As a special treat, Tallarico has provided it for use with this book.

> ### NOTE
> The audio contract is included in DOC format on the book page on the New Riders web site with the filename `Audio Contract.doc`. The DOC file is a Microsoft Word file, but many word processors can read and edit this format, including WordPad (one of the free Windows accessories). The document is designed with one-inch margins.
>
> We strongly advise that you have your own legal representative(s) look over the contract, to make sure that its provisions suit the needs of your business. You may need to make some changes to the form. In particular, section 12a notes that the contract is made in accordance with the laws of the state of California; be sure to specify the governing state or province in which your business operates.
>
> The last page of the form is a sample schedule of milestones for the contract; replace the text in italic with the appropriate date, amount, royalty/bonus terminology, and so on for the individual contract.

Tallarico urges anyone with questions regarding audio in the video game industry to contact him at `tallarico@aol.com`. Alternatively, budding sound engineers/musicians can send a demo tape to this address:

> Tommy Tallarico Studios, Inc.
> P.O. Box 1001
> San Juan Capistrano, CA 92675

> **NOTE**
>
> The next time you're online, check out Gamingforce Audio at `www.gamingforce.com`. As the name of the site suggests, it's completely dedicated to video game audio, namely music. Another stellar site is the Video Game Music Archive at `www.vgmusic.com`. You can listen to more than 10,000 video game music files at this site!

George "The Fat Man" Sanger, Fat Man Music

In Chapter 15, The Fat Man shares some insight on sound design and implementation. Here, he chats about creating music for games and how to best break into the biz:

"Repetition is by far your biggest enemy," says Sanger. "It's much more significant than the size of the listener's speakers, the resolution of your audio files, or even if you're licensing a hit tune from the radio."

Composition: Avoid Repetition

Your game will last 40 hours, your budget will cover one hour of music. So, game audio will repeat.

Therefore, emphasizing a musical theme is far less important in game audio than in conventional music. Variations play a much bigger role. Schoenberg has some clever things to say about contrasting familiarity with surprise—simply read it and ignore all the "familiarity" stuff because the computer will take care of that.

Essentially I think what the composer needs to keep in mind is this: At its core, all art boils down to a game of "peek-a-boo." Don't keep hiding in the same place unless you're setting us up for a BIG surprise.

Implementation: Avoid Repetition

Don't allow the same music to loop over and over and over and over. It's common for the game designer to think of one theme or tune per character, or worse, per level. This condemns the novice player to hours of repetition. If the same tune plays for five minutes, the sound system really should switch.

Communication: Repeat A Lot

See Chapter 15!

> **NOTE**
>
> The next time you're on the Net, click to GameSpot's "Top Ten Video Game Soundtracks." Think you can guess what a couple of them are? Here's the URL:
>
> www.videogames.com/features/universal/tenspot_soundtrack

Chance Thomas, HUGEsound Network

Before leaving to start his own production company in 2000 (www.hugesound.com), Chance Thomas was a senior music producer at Sierra's Yosemite Entertainment studio in Oakhurst, California, and chances are (er, sorry!) you've heard his melodic and memorable scores on dozens of games. Along with creating orchestral tracks, rock singles, and independently released game music CDs, he spearheaded the fight for game music to be considered at the Grammy Awards.

Believe it or not, Thomas is an Academy Award winner! He won an Oscar in 2003 for his work on *ChubbChubbs*, which won the Academy Award for "Best Animated Short Film."

But the ideal way to preface Thomas' advice is to read from the liner notes of Sierra's *Quest for Glory V* soundtrack. He writes:

> Music is mysterious, elusive, familiar, capricious…It's like a language we knew before our birth, its intimacy both surprising and obvious in turn. Writing music seems to be a tussled balance of discovery and ingenuity, of sheer will and catalyzed coincidence. The composer forages, struggles, demands, coaxes, curses, and finally relents. And often in the quiet humility of surrender, the Muse comes out of her hiding place, satisfied that our best efforts have sufficiently softened the soul. She speaks to us from the inside out, triggering emotions so subtle and profound, as her voice finds an inevitable path to the surface.

To start, Thomas lists his most important piece of advice for game musicians:

> Quality counts. Our ears are trained to expect sonic excellence through exposure to films, television shows, and popular music CDs. Game music will always lose impact if it loses credibility with the player. If a player ever has to make that dreaded mental downshift, "Oh well, this is just game music…" the composer has lost the game; the music has failed to capture the player's imagination and emotions as it should. Go for the highest-quality standard you possibly can. There's no technology sophisticated enough to make bad music sound good, nor to present amateurish efforts as polished gems. There's just no substitute for outstanding source material.

If time permits and it's financially feasible, Thomas recommends using real instruments rather than synthesized ones:

> No amount of technology can ever overcome poor source material. There's no "emotion fader" on a mixing console. That's why more and more of us are proponents of hiring real, living, feeling, passionate professional musicians to play as much music as we can possibly afford. There's nothing like capturing a brilliant performance of red-hot musicians pouring their feelings into fine acoustic instruments to give you emotionally stirring source material to work with.

Thomas' recorded works are filled with this approach. As an example, he used a 36-piece orchestra and then a 32-piece orchestra for various sections of the *Quest for Glory V* soundtrack:

> We recorded two passes on every track—recording multiple takes in each instance until we got the magic one—to create the sound of a 72- and 64-piece orchestra, respectively. I wish you could listen to the difference between the synthesized version and the live version of each. No comparison.

Okay, so most game musicians don't have a full orchestra accessible to them. Understood. "The point is, if you want to make a *big* emotional impact, you'd better pay big attention to your music," asserts Thomas. "George Lucas said, 'Sound is half the movie-going experience.' Please keep that in mind as you consider the role of music in your games."

So when exactly should a game musician get involved in the development cycle? As early as possible, says Thomas:

> There's an amazing synergy that's possible only with early and ongoing involvement. I've written pieces of music early in development that inspired entirely new sections of a game. Having music in place can assist voice actors in delivering a more powerful and dynamic performance. Not to mention the raw enthusiasm that a great tune or score can generate with the creative people on a team.

> Music is the language of emotion. It speaks to us in ways that words and images can never express. Ask yourself, "What do I want a player to feel in this game?" And if the composer is worth his salt, the score will induce that emotion.

Ironically, Thomas thinks music is often overlooked in the video game industry:

> The main reason is because most game audio is so bland. As the current chairman of the music and sound screening committees for the Academy of Interactive Arts and Sciences, I get to listen to lots of game audio. I hear exactly what developers are doing across a broad spectrum of the industry. In many cases, the audio is poorly (or at least unimaginatively) conceived and sloppily executed. It's obvious in those cases that the developer/publisher has paid very little attention to the audio. As a result, you can bet the audio will be only tolerated (or perhaps even shut off) by the audience.

> On the other hand, a steadily increasing number of game developers and publishers do pay attention to quality audio. Games brought to market by these savvy companies stand head and shoulders above the competition. It's an interesting sidebar to note that most often these are games whose developers have contracted with experienced independent specialists for their music, sound, and/or voices.

"One more thought about music in particular," adds Thomas. "Bland music has never been able to capture the imagination or passion of a human being. In any format. Games are no different."

Chance Thomas started composing and producing music more than 20 years ago. During his lengthy career, he has produced award-winning original scores for many formats: films, commercials, television, and computer games.

On breaking into the industry, something that's discussed in depth in Chapter 21, "Breaking into the Industry," Thomas contributes the following:

> As long as the industry remains in the transition period between a studio system and a specialty system, I think the best way for an audio beginner to learn the ropes is working as a full-time employee of a developer or publisher in-house and on-site. This will grow in them an instinctive feel for the development process—including what kinds of issues impact other aspects of the development—that's impossible to understand otherwise. HUGEsound only affiliates with such experience-enriched audio pros, most of whom began their game industry careers working in-house for a major developer or publisher.

Speaking of HUGEsound, why should a game developer or publisher hire them?

"In many ways, the evolution of the game industry has parallels to that of the film industry," begins Thomas. He explains:

> In the growing years of the film business, Hollywood functioned through the "studio system." Each major player owned its own distribution, production, and talent resources. For example, each company had its own in-house composers, sound guys, and so on. But as filmmaking evolved away from the old studio system in the late '60s and early '70s, independent contractors who had developed superior skills in certain specialties began to offer better value to films. Better than the studio system employees who were (by necessity) more generalized in their talents.

> Now we seem to be approaching a comparable turning point in the game industry. Today's competitive games need the advantage of specialized experts in all areas, but particularly in audio. Great audio can set classic games apart from wannabes. HUGEsound is one company that can now give developers such contract audio specialists. Each member of the HUGEsound Network is a proven performer with expertise in various styles of music composition, sound design, audio programming, voice casting, mixing, mastering, implementation, and so on.

> There's little room for error in today's tight marketplace. Game makers face fierce competition. As was pointed out in a *Game Developer* magazine editorial, the days of building a hit game in the garage are virtually gone. Specialty audio service providers such as HUGEsound can save developers money and headaches, give them dazzling results, and help bring in healthy profits.

How did Thomas break into the industry? "Unexpectedly at first; then relentlessly after I got a taste of it." He continues:

> Here's the unexpected part: I was pursuing a career as a fairly successful composer and music produc-er in the advertising industry (McDonald's, Nissan, Mall of America, and so on) when I was approached by a man developing an interactive educational game for the Orient. He hired me to create a ton of music for his game, but about halfway into the project, his funding ran out and we never got to finish.

> Here's the relentless part: After that, I developed a demo of my music targeted at game companies. I put together a résumé that highlighted the attributes I thought would be most enticing to a game company. Then I began to send out résumés and demos to the various software developers, as well as a head-hunting firm specializing in game industry employment. About this time, a friend happened to see a post-ing for a job opening at Sierra, so I sent to them, too. Sierra called back right away and said they were looking to hire a full-time composer. Things went extremely well during the interviews with Jay Usher (Project Manager), Jason Hayes (now at Blizzard), and Victor Crews (also at Blizzard); and they hired me to create the score for *Quest for Glory V*. I accepted the position on the terms that we would use a live orchestra for the project and release a soundtrack album. Sadly, the game did poorly, but the sound-track was a success. We moved about 50,000 units, and the press seemed to love it.

> I also worked on *J.R.R. Tolkien's Middle-Earth*, *SWAT 2*, *Navy SEALs*, and *The Realm* while employed there. When the company shut down the Oakhurst division and offered me a job in Seattle, I accepted at first. But later I decided I would try my hand at working for several game companies on a freelance basis. That's when I launched HUGEsound, and later launched the HUGEsound Network.

Want to increase your odds on breaking into the gaming industry? Chance Thomas says any budding sound engineer or musician should learn how to use the Pro Tools software package.

Read more about HUGEsound and Chance Thomas' work at www.hugesound.com.

Jeff Kliment, LucasArts

Jeff Kliment, the sound department manager at LucasArts, has been the lead sound designer on such games as *Star Wars*, *Rebellion*, *Grim Fandango* (including the soundtrack), *Star Wars: Episode I-Racer*, *Indiana Jones and the Emperor's Tomb*, and *Full Throttle II*.

On how he broke into the industry, Kliment says he's always enjoyed music and knew he wanted his career to be somehow music-related:

> But I really didn't have a specific plan. When I moved to San Francisco in 1978, I saw a listing in a cof-fee shop for a room for rent in a house full of jazz musicians, so of course I took it. One of the guys was a sax player who told me about a great recording program at San Francisco State University. It was the best tip I've ever received in my life. It's a long story, but the job at Russian Hill Recording was a direct result of my studies there.

Kliment says it's key for musicians to simply "learn their craft." If he was looking for someone at LucasArts, he would want "someone who had great chops, a sense of humor, and great people skills. Making music for interactive games also requires strong computer skills. An understanding of programming is a big plus. It helps if you're a gamer, too!" adds Kliment.

What are some of the personal or professional attributes you need to be a successful game musician? Why do so many games fail in this department? "Well, it takes more than simply being a good musician," answers Kliment. He continues:

> To be successful in our business, you have to have the right balance of all the things I mentioned above. Analytical skills are really useful. Flexibility, a good team spirit…the things that would apply to most professions also apply to ours. We are very fortunate here at LucasArts to have a team of people who bring a lot of depth to their work.

Jeff Kliment says designing game music for a console is very different than for a PC because of the varying hardware capabilities and shortcomings. "The composer must be aware of the specifics of each platform in order to find the best way of approaching the job."

Finally, on making it in this industry, Kliment reminds those reading this book, "I've always found that if you follow your heart and do what you love to do, the rest will happen as it should."

Part III

Post-Production

Chapter 17

Proper Game Testing

THE EXPERTS

- Bill Roper,
  Blizzard Entertainment

- Matt Householder,
  Blizzard North

- Chris Taylor,
  Gas Powered Games

- David Dienstbier

- David Jaffe,
  Sony Computer
  Entertainment America

- Steven Rechtschaffner,
  Electronic Arts Canada

- Bruce Williams,
  Microsoft

- Todd Howard,
  Bethesda Softworks

- Warren Spector,
  Ion Storm Austin

- Harvey Smith,
  Ion Storm Austin

- Randy Smith,
  Ion Storm Austin

- Brad McQuaid,
  Sigil Games Online

- Richard "Lord British"
  Garriott, NCsoft

- Sid Meier,
  Firaxis Games

- Eric Tremblay,
  Ubi Soft Entertainment

- Harry Gottlieb,
  Jellyvision

It has been mentioned innumerable times throughout this book that play testing a game is an extremely critical process that must be performed thoroughly before a product's release. So why are there so many bugs in computer games? Why does it seem there are multiple patches for each game these days? Are designers getting lazy in this department, or are they simply taking advantage of the Internet as an effective distribution method for patches?

There are a number of reasons for bugs and patches:

➤ Developing a computer game is not like developing a game for a console platform, in which the end user is playing the game on a fixed piece of hardware. That is, all the millions of PlayStation 2s, Nintendo GameCubes, and Microsoft Xbox units are built the same (although the software may vary for a geographic area, such as North America, Asia, or Europe). With computers, very rarely do you find two gamers with the same setup. If you think about it for a moment, there are literally thousands of combinations of software and hardware, making it extremely difficult for a game to work smoothly on all systems. Thus, designing a game for a PC is like trying to hit a moving target.

➤ Game companies are big business. If a product misses its shipment date, it loses money (especially during the profitable holiday season), and because many large game publishers are public, they must disclose quarterly fiscal results. One bad quarter may have an extremely adverse effect on the company's stock value. For this reason, on top of marketing commitments with various publications and distribution commitments with various retailers, many games are prematurely shipped out the door with the attitude of "We'll have a patch up on the Internet within a couple of weeks." Roughly one-third of console and PC games each year are sold during the month of December. The unfortunate reality is that many computer gaming publishers will prematurely ship their games to be on store shelves during this time. What game publishers are starting to understand, however, is that a gamer who is dissatisfied with a company's product may not purchase from that manufacturer again.

Keep in mind that companies must also test for gameplay issues, such as making sure puzzles aren't too difficult (for example, in adventure games), battle isn't too awkward (action games), a character's stats are accurate (RPGs), character control is responsive enough (sports games), and rival units are well-balanced (strategy games).

There are many ways for companies to test games for bugs as well as balancing and compatibility issues, as we'll see in this chapter, but generally speaking, there are two kinds of game testing:

➤ Although it varies from company to company, *beta testing* is an incremental procedure handled internally at the development studio or publishing house, and in some cases distributed to volunteer consumers in the gaming community in exchange for feedback. It usually begins semi-formally when the game is in late alpha/early beta stage—hence the name.

➤ *Quality assurance (QA) testing* is typically performed by outsiders in a proper testing environment, and is usually administered toward the end of the game's development cycle. Bug reports and any other queries, beefs, or comments are submitted for evaluation prior to the game's release. Then, after a game has shipped, technical support staff begin submitting user complaints (and developers read newsgroup postings and web site forums), and a list of fixes is collected and organized for the first patch. Keep in mind that in some cases, the patches are fully justified, such as when a new 3D video or audio card is introduced after the game has been released.

This chapter concentrates on how to properly test your game throughout its development, with suggestions from a number of reputable companies and spanning most genres.

Bill Roper, Blizzard Entertainment

Blizzard's computer game development studio is recognized internationally as one that takes its time releasing each game. Just look at how long it took to get *WarCraft III* and *Diablo II* out the door—but the stable games were well worth the wait! Proper game testing is absolutely crucial, agree Bill Roper and Matt Householder (see Matt's comments in the next section).

Roper says detailed, accurate bug reports are another area in which QA can really help the programmers track and eliminate
bugs in the code. In this segment, he explains how the process works at Blizzard Entertainment.
Shown here are a scene from *WarCraft III* and a publicity image.
(Used with permission by Blizzard Entertainment, Inc.)

Testing is an amazingly difficult process to do well, as is obvious from the number of bugs we see in big
games from big companies. Even the best teams and QA departments can't find everything, but the
important goal is to ship the game as bug-free as possible.

One area for which we could have done an even better job with this ourselves on *Diablo II* was to keep
making testing tools until the end of the project. Having the development team intimately interact with the
test department is essential to finding and fixing as many bugs as you can. Not only should the QA department request tools to make their tasks easier and their reports more informative, the development team
should always be thinking about what could go wrong with the game and make tools to test border cases.

Roper explains how the employees at Blizzard Entertainment take note of and manage the bug
reports:

We use an easily accessible, web-based database that everyone in the company can access to input,
track, and resolve bugs in the game. Management of this database is constant and comes from both
the developers and the testers to ensure that we're examining as many bugs as closely as possible. Also,
we have different elements assigned to test teams that directly interact with the programmers responsible for those areas. If a quest in the game is not working correctly, the QA team in charge of that part of
the game inputs the bug into the database and is a focused group that can work with the individual
programmers to resolve the issue.

Constant communication between everyone involved in the creation of the game is encouraged, especially at the lead level. Our leads in QA, programming, art, and production are always talking about what
the current goals are in the test process. What specific bugs are at the top of our priority list? What do
the programmers need tested? Is the glitch in the temple-level background a programming issue or an
art issue? Prioritizing and maintaining a clear focus on the tasks at hand, coupled with keeping everyone
in the loop, makes for smoother and more effective testing.

Finally, and most importantly, says Roper, there must be a true dedication to putting out less-buggy software:

> If you have a severe bug that locks up the game 10% of the time, you must be willing to not ship the game until it's fixed. There are many reasons why games miss their projected ship dates; and as developers and consumers, we should support the companies that do so to make the product better, not only in terms of balance or fun, but also in terms of stability.

Matt Householder, Blizzard North

Matt Householder adds to Bill Roper's remarks in the preceding section by saying that there are several kinds of testing that each game must pass through successfully. He partakes in the following:

> ➤ **Feature testing**. Here, you're looking to see that the game features are implemented, working as desired/designed, and ultimately tuned to be the most fun.

> ➤ **Compatibility testing**. Here, you determine how well (on a scale of "not at all" to "great") the game performs with different versions of hardware and software. Compatibility testing is a lot more work for computer systems than for consoles.

Householder adds that another way to look at testing is based on who's doing the testing:

> The programmers are the first testers, of course. They write and test the code as they go (with varying success). After that, the QA staff and other members of the production team test the game and report bugs they find in a database. After enough of the major bugs are fixed, computer games may undergo a beta test involving hundreds or even thousands of (hopefully) eager game players. A beta test can help expose compatibility problems, and opens the game up to a class of users who won't hold back criticism of any flaws or shortcomings.

Chris Taylor, Gas Powered Games

Sticking with the action/RPG genres for a moment, Chris Taylor from Gas Powered Games says that testing a game has gone from being some quick steps that a game was rushed through at the end of the development cycle to a very thorough and scientific process. Taylor's last game was the action/RPG *Dungeon Siege* for the PC.

> I don't want to oversimplify the testing process, but I can tell you that it involves planning, coordination, a database management system, strict protocol, and very competent personnel. A good tester can be trained on the job, and this is why it's a very popular entry-level position in the industry, but it's not to be confused with being an easy job or a fun job. It requires hard work, people who pay very close attention to detail, and people who know how to read game specification documents. That's not to say that there aren't the bright spots, but even people who are paid to play games all day long are glad to go home when it's quitting time!

David Dienstbier

On the importance of game testing, David Dienstbier (who left Acclaim in 2002) says that game testing is an absolutely critical part of game development. He likens game testing to medical testing on a number of levels:

> If a game were a patient, it would be pretty easy for someone to see what was wrong if it were covered in lumps, had four extra limbs, had no teeth, and so on. However, it's when you have a game that for all intents and purposes looks great that diagnosis becomes more difficult, and specialization is more valuable. Testers try everything they can to break a game. They record their steps, try different combinations of things to get a reaction, and in general pick the game apart piece by piece.
>
> When a problem is found, they report the problem—and more importantly how they found it—to the programmers or designers, who then determine how it can be repaired.
>
> Sometimes, the problem can be fixed easily by a designer looking for errors in the way a game was built (they can check scripts, links, and editor components), but most of the time it takes a programmer to dig into the game's code and repair the problem. What makes testing so crucial is the fact that they must make it their job to find problems that are not always obvious. Often, these bugs can be disastrous to a title if they're not eliminated prior to hitting the shelf. Testers are also great resources for input. It's often a good idea to get testers to give feedback into a game as it develops. As certain components of a project fall into place, input from gamers who are not on the core team can be quite enlightening.

David Jaffe, Sony Computer Entertainment America

The mastermind behind the coveted *Twisted Metal* series calls testers "the unsung heroes of the business." Jaffe continues:

> They get a bad rap sometimes (dunno why), but they are so important. A lot of people think all they do is try to find bugs. Well, this is a big important part of their job, but it's not all they do. They also are fresh but experienced eyes on a game that you may have spent so much time with, you can no longer make realistic judgment calls about it. So they always offer up lots of great ways to make the game better, and this adds so much to the process. (And they find bugs, too.) A buggy game is a terrible thing for a player to have to experience. A poorly balanced game is also a nightmare for players. Both things can be avoided, assuming that the team has the time and desire to listen to what the testers have to say.

Jaffe discusses the different kinds of testing in a game by using *Twisted Metal: Black* for the PlayStation 2 as his example:

1. **Collision testing**. This is where the testers try to get the 3D car/character to bust through the environments/3D worlds. There are several reasons why this may occur, and the tester needs to find every area of the game map where this happens. And it's frustrating because it doesn't always happen. Sometimes, it occurs only 50% of the time, and the tester needs to figure out the conditions under which the collision bug occurs. (Sometimes, it's because the vehicle has to be going a certain speed; sometimes, it's because a 3D artist has simply

forgotten to put proper collision in the area.) It's actually funny; on *Twisted Metal: Black*, I think the testers caught about 95% of these bugs, but every now and then I'll see a post or email about someone who busted out of the world—and while we think it's horrific on the development side, the emails are usually writing about how cool it is that they got to drive around this void outside of the main game! It's like peeking behind the sets of a movie and realizing that the house is just a facade and there's nothing inside! We hate it, but there are some bugs that players seem to get a kick out of.

2. **Shell testing**. Making sure that the game shell points you in the right direction. In *Twisted Metal: Black*, we had a bug where you won the game, and instead of showing you a win movie, it took you to the options screen—thank God a tester caught that!

3. **Weapon testing**. Making sure the weapons work as designed.

David Jaffe speaks on action game design in Chapter 2, "General Game Design: Action/Arcade Games."

Steven Rechtschaffner, Electronic Arts Canada

The *SSX* and *NBA Street* franchises are polished games, to say the least—in light of both gameplay balancing (between the competing _riders) and lack of bugs. On proper QA testing, Steven Rechtschaffner comments that it's "essential on one level and very helpful on another." He explains:

The essential aspect of quality assurance (QA) is finding and identifying everything that's broken and not working as it was designed to. They then work with us to make sure that all the various bugs get fixed. The helpful side of QA's participation is giving us feedback on the gameplay of a game. Lots of great ideas and creative solutions to problems have come from our testing teams. In short, QA plays a very important role in the making of any good game.

Bruce Williams, Microsoft

How do you go about testing a simulation such as the coveted *Flight Simulator* series? Does it differ from game testing? Interestingly, Microsoft's Bruce Williams says that most of the developers on the team are pilots, "So we have a lot of experience with flying in general." He explains why this is significant:

We know about air traffic control, navigation, cockpit controls, and so on. We also have aeronautical engineers on the team who work with data from aircraft manufacturers and other sources to ensure that the flight models are accurate. We fly many of the aircraft in *Flight Simulator* to validate our flight models, and we also spend time in full-motion, FAA-approved sims to make sure that we've accurately modeled the big airliners. And we talk to lots of experts. For example, when we included the Concorde in *Flight Simulator 2000*, we worked with the chief Concorde pilot at British Airways. For features such as air traffic control, we bring in working ATC specialists who help us make sure that everything's as realistic as possible.

Microsoft's Bruce Williams says the team tests its *Flight Simulator* products extensively, which includes flying real aircraft to compare the sim's authenticity; as well as talking with pilots, air traffic control specialists, and other experts.
(Used with permission by Microsoft Corp.)

Todd Howard, Bethesda Softworks

Bethesda is one of the largest independent game publishers, whose PC titles over the past few years including RPGs, action games, and simulations. Project leader and designer Todd Howard says the best way to test is the "perfect build" scenario:

> Whenever you get to a milestone or you've got a specific feature in, test it and write down everything it doesn't do correctly. You now have a choice—you can leave it in if you can live with what it's doing wrong, but the best choice is to take it out of the game and fix it completely right then. In this case, the current version of your game is a "perfect build." The game doesn't have everything in it, but what it does have works perfectly. It doesn't crash a lot or provide functionality that works incorrectly. [If ignored,] these things can really pile up in the end. Now, you'll be forced to leave some in, so you can go on and get other things working, and that's okay. Just make sure to keep very good track of what they are and what they need to do.

Howard also provides some advice on beta testing when your game is basically done and you need to find all the bugs:

> The other advice I'd give is not to send your game to beta testers too early. If your game isn't ready, or if you're not ready to deal with the feedback your testers give you, wait until you are. The worst thing for a tester is to send you feedback and then you say nothing back, or you don't fix the problems. They won't feel they're helping you, and will help you less when you really need to hear from them.

Warren Spector, Ion Storm Austin

The humble designer responsible for countless PC gaming classics (see Spector's bio section in Appendix A, "Biographies") says game testing is a very big topic and offers the following:

> ➤ You want constant team testing. Coders, artists, designers, and audio engineers who don't test their work and get feedback from their peers before they check it in don't last long in this business.

> ➤ As much as possible, you want development milestones that are testable as early as possible in your development cycle, and you want a small group of dedicated testers involved in the project as early as is practical to check milestone progress.

> ➤ After you hit alpha (the point at which the game is genuinely playable, with all game systems functioning, if not bug-free), you need a somewhat larger group of testers to provide information about bugs, but also to tell you whether the game is any fun. (Trust me, you're way too close to it by this point to have any degree of objectivity yourself!) This is also the point at which a lot of developers, myself included, turn to friends and colleagues and get some blind testing going. I usually look for people who have some understanding of the kind of games we make here; folks who've worked on similar games; folks I know well enough to know they won't sugarcoat their feelings about a game to spare *my* feelings.

> ➤ When you hit beta, you hope your "fun factor" problems are behind you, and you focus on fixing what's broken. Then there's the painful process (mostly for the QA folks!) of running through excruciatingly detailed checklists that outline every single thing a player can possibly do during the game. At the end, you hope your publisher has an adequate hardware lab to check compatibility with as many hardware configurations as possible.

And what the heck is "skippy testing?" Answers Spector:

> Throughout development, you do what we've always called "skippy testing" (not sure if that's a term coined at Origin or if it's a more widely used expression). Skippy testing is the process of doing everything you can think of to break the game—removing CDs at obviously dangerous times, banging your hands down on the keyboard to hit as many keys as you can simultaneously, and so on.

Harvey Smith, Ion Storm Austin

Ion Storm also boasts designers Harvey Smith and Randy Smith (no relation). The designers on *Deus Ex 2* and *Thief 3*, respectively, share their thoughts on proper game testing in this section and the next.

"Testers are like a troubleshooting focus group," begins Harvey Smith. "They help you figure out why the game is breaking, and they give you a read on how fun it is." On the importance of testing, Smith offers the following example from his recent experience on *Deus Ex*:

> Game environments are getting increasingly complex and flexible. Often, the game is capable of something that none of the developers could have dreamed due to the sheer number of elements or the depth of the simulation. For instance, we featured a unit in Deus Ex that exploded upon death. This unit encouraged the player to use range weapons instead of mêlé weapons—it caused some players to switch styles on the fly in order to avoid the death-explosion. We wanted each unit to be differentiated from the others in some way. The game also featured locked doors that could be opened with the player's (valuable) lockpick or explosive resources. After playing the game for weeks, we saw that the testers were luring the exploding units near locked doors before killing them; the resultant explosion would open the locked door (or cabinet) at no resource cost to the player.

> This sort of emergent strategy was not something we had foreseen, but the testers found it just because they were immersed in the game for so long. They often do some of their most inspired work after they play the game for so long that they get really bored—that's when they get clever, trying to entertain

themselves. After seeing this (and getting over our initial surprise, delight, and amusement), we made some decisions about whether we needed to reduce the death-explosion range in order to make this tactic less likely to occur by accident.

Randy Smith, Ion Storm Austin

Randy Smith, project director and lead designer on *Thief 3*, shares his thoughts on eliminating technical bugs and tweaking the quality of the gameplay through testing.

> While games are still in development, it's very common for them to crash, hang, or exhibit any of a number of unwanted behaviors while running. At a certain phase of the project, it's critical to lock down development, stop introducing new features, and focus exclusively on fixing those technical bugs. Bugs number in the thousands, and to make sure all the important ones get fixed, they're tracked with a giant database.

So how are all these bugs located, documented, and fixed?

> Finding them all requires a lot of play testing, so testers pretty much play the same game experiences over and over, try lots of new things, and do their best to break the game in inventive ways. Every time the game crashes or hangs, or when they observe something that doesn't belong, they make a new entry in the bug-tracking database.

Of course, another important thing to test for is overall game quality:

> Play testers provide critical feedback about which parts of the game are fun, not fun enough, too easy, too hard, and so on. These aren't technical bugs, usually, but they are legitimate bugs and are tracked with the same database. Play testers usually test for both types of bugs at the same time for as long as they're working on the project. In addition to formal play testing, there is also usually informal peer review, in which you mail early versions of your game to trusted fellow developers for their critical feedback. Initial reactions usually contain the best data, so it's smart to "save" a few people and wait to show them the game when it's close to finished and you've attempted to respond to earlier feedback.

Brad McQuaid, Sigil Games Online

Without a doubt, *EverQuest* is one of the most successful online role-playing games in the history of PC gaming, and many of the kudos can be attributed to Brad McQuaid's emphasis on proper game testing (see Chapter 5, "General Game Design: Role-Playing Games (RPGs) and Persistent Online Worlds") for a more lengthy discussion on MMORPG game design. In 2002, McQuaid left Sony Online Entertainment to start up Sigil Games Online.

On how to test a massively multiplayer online role-playing game, McQuaid offers the following:

> Testing is paramount to any game, massively multiplayer or otherwise. Nobody wants bugs or broken game mechanics that lead to an unstable or unbalanced game. The challenge with testing as it relates to MMORPGs is that the size and nature of these games require long periods of testing involving a lot of

people. Single-player games are typically tested internally with teams of perhaps 5–50 game testers for a period of time prior to the game's launch. MMORPGs, on the other hand, typically employ both internal teams of testers as well as large armies of external testers (beta testers). *EverQuest*, for example, was in beta testing for approximately nine months. We began with approximately 50 external testers and brought that number up to 25,000 the month before release. And there were still bugs and problems we had to address a year after release because 200,000 players will find problems that 25,000 didn't.

In game development, the terms alpha and beta are typically used to describe milestones prior to commercial launch. Alpha typically means "code and features complete," and beta means that the game is stable enough to begin serious testing. With MMORPGs, or at least with *EverQuest*, alpha meant the game was playable and ready for internal testing. Beta meant opening the game to people outside of Verant to help us debug, to offer suggestions, and to find problems with game mechanics. *Closed beta* typically means that the external people involved in the beta were handpicked on an invite-only basis, whereas open beta means that just about anybody from the public is welcome to participate.

Brad McQuaid, formerly of Sony Online Entertainment (and now with Sigil Games Online), says testing is paramount to any game, massively-multiplayer or otherwise, because no one wants a buggy or unbalanced game. In this segment, he discusses the extra challenges in a massively-multiplayer game like *EverQuest*.
(Used with permission by Sony Computer Entertainment America.)

Richard "Lord British" Garriott, NCsoft

The one and only Richard "Lord British" Garriott, conceiver of the legendary *Ultima* for Origin Systems and now at his new company, NCsoft (U.S.), says that a lot of effort is poured into game testing, especially for online games, as experienced with the popular *Ultima Online*.

A successful online game must have good engineering from the start; you have to have good code. And after you have good code, the QA testers can do their job well.

Unfortunately, there was no way to thoroughly test a breakthrough, massively multiplayer game such as *Ultima Online* early on in the process, as evidenced by a few unhappy players after the game's initial launch. But many more servers around the world have been added for less Internet congestion, whereas a handful of full-time engineers are handling the bandwidth issues back in Texas as well.

Garriott says that when they test their games internally, they attempt to play the game as a player would by going through a checklist procedure. This checklist includes all the game's features and combinations of features, and can become quite the tedious task. He elaborates:

> For example, if a magic system has 50 spells, a tester must test each of the spells and the spell combinations on all monster types, NPCs (non-player characters), and items on every map. This is a huge matrix—in fact, we have binders full of these [checklists]. And you have to do this with every version of the game [every "build" throughout the game development process].

On top of all this, Garriott reminds us that this all has to be done on all machine types and configurations. Sounds like fun, huh?

Sid Meier, Firaxis Games

Sid Meier's name has appeared many times throughout this book as he lends his thoughts on game design. When it comes to proper testing, he mirrors the sentiment offered by Richard Garriott.

> First is bug testing, which should be done by as many people [as possible] on many different machines. Also, it's important for the tester to use a method of reproducing and documenting the bug.

After all, finding a bug isn't worth its weight unless it can be captured and reported; therefore, Meier uses various techniques, such as an autosave feature in the game that bookmarks the game every 10 seconds or so. This way, a previous game can be loaded if a bug is found.

The second kind of testing done under Meier's supervision is to find out if the game is too hard or too easy:

> Designers have no way of telling because they're too close to the project to get an objective look at the game. The key is to give the game to people and watch what they're doing, and to see where they get stuck.

Meier believes that the first half-hour of gameplay is critical and is an important determinant of whether the gamer will keep playing the game.

Eric Tremblay, Ubi Soft Entertainment

Eric Tremblay started work as a tester at Ubi Soft in Montreal in 1997. The first title he worked on was *F1 Racing Simulation*, and after two months of testing the PC game, he was promoted to the position of lead tester on the same title. Tremblay has also worked as a lead on the sequel, *Monaco Grand Prix Racing Simulation 2*, while at the same time doing QA supervision on all the titles tested at the Ubi Soft Montreal QA department. After being upgraded to the rank of QA supervisor, he was named Worldwide QA supervisor. Quite simply, Tremblay's task is to oversee the work of all Ubi Soft's QA teams in the world: Montreal, Paris, Shanghai, and Bucharest. Finally, in February 2001, he was promoted to Worldwide Quality Assurance Manager. Not bad, huh?

Tremblay discusses the differences between QA testing and beta testing, and when both should begin and end.

> In a way, it's pretty much the same. QA testing is performed in-house, within our office, by our QA depart- ment, in a more organized way than beta testing. Each team has a lead tester. The lead person super- vises the work of all the testers on the team. He's responsible for the quality of the work, to ensure that the game is fully tested and that no aspect has been undertested. Before the game enters testing, it's his task to build a test plan to ensure that the game is well-tested. A test plan is a document in which all tests to be performed on the game are indicated: O/S, walkthrough, install, functionality, and so on.
>
> As for beta testing, it's generally used for massively multiplayer online games (MMOs) or even for single- player games when the developer doesn't have a QA department. It takes place before the release of the game, at the beta stage of the development. You want to have as many people as you can to play the game for a certain period of time so they can provide you with feedback [and] bugs through a data- base or emails. It's also used to test the stability of the game. The quality or stability of your game relies on the beta testers' work.

But Tremblay cautions that the difficulty with beta testing is that not all beta testers are thor- ough: "Some are beta testers just to get the game before it's released; others are very professional and will send you bugs."

Ubi Soft tests for collision bugs, graphical ones, and (as Tremblay says), "We also ask the tester if the game is well-balanced—if the difficulty level is progressive."

And, of course, because testers are gamers, Tremblay asks for their feedback on the game— suggestions on design modifications, gameplay, user interface, and so on. But he adds a caveat: "Testers must know that they're here to test the game, not to redesign it."

What are the differences in testing for a console games versus a PC game?

> For PC titles, games must be well-tested because we're the last step before the game is published. We're doing QA to avoid customers buying bad games, to sell quality titles. The name of the company often relies on us—we don't want to be responsible for killing the release of a game because we let it go too buggy.

As for console titles, says Tremblay, the game must be approved by the manufacturer (Sony, Nintendo, Sega, Microsoft):

> Console manufacturers have quality standards that our game must answer; our titles have to be clean and answer to all the quality criteria. They'll test the game; if it fails one of the standards, we can't release the game.

Tremblay reveals what's needed to run your operation smoothly and sends a message to prospective game designers and marketing reps:

> The key is to have a well-prepared test team. To have a lead building test plan to make sure that no aspect of the game is undertested. Listen to QA. Too often, marketing adheres to release dates—no matter what the condition of the game is, they'll release it. Yes, there is a time [at which] a game must go, but we're on the field, we test the game all day long, so please listen to us.

Ubi Soft has both part-time and permanent testers. To recruit testers, it places job openings on the Internet on its own official web site or it asks the testers to suggest friends who want to test. Says Tremblay: "At some times of the year, we double and even triple the number of testers in our QA department to be able to test all our games on time for their release."

So what's it like working there? How do you ensure good testing, a good working environment? Answers Tremblay:

> ➤ Be able to join new testers with experienced testers.
>
> ➤ Have a well-prepared team, good tools, people who like games and who are ready to spend nights and days testing games…and who like pizza and chicken (overtime meals!).
>
> ➤ One of my tasks is to always have up-to-date standards. In addition to good testing, our game must answer to certain Ubi Soft standards. Before being released, a game must pass all the requirements of our checklist or standards.

They also practice something known as *regression testing*. What the heck is that?

> We want to make sure that old bugs don't come back later to haunt us. For our new testers, I build a training program. New testers learn the tester job (the basis), how we test a game, the tools we use, and the proper terms to use when reporting bugs. There is also a practical training, where testers practice what they have learned in "class." Finally, they're introduced to a team, and experienced testers are assigned to support them and to supervise their work in the first week as testers.

Finally, Tremblay offers an example of a game that was tested well, and why.

> I remember a game tested here called *Solar* that proves how testers are great people and very experienced gamers. The testers were giving so many recommendations on how to improve the game that the producer told the developer to add in the game everything we were asking. Furthermore, they asked us to completely redo the design, the story, and the missions. So, for one title, the tester was tester-designer. [Tremblay says we shouldn't expect this to happen too often!]

> The quality of our games is in part the quality of our work, the work of the QA department. By creating standards and procedures, we're able to have our game approved by console manufacturers on the first submission, and fewer patches released on the Internet later on.

Harry Gottlieb, Jellyvision

Does the testing process differ for puzzle games, such as the renowned *You Don't Know Jack* series or MSN Zone's *Outsmart*? To answer this question, Jellyvision's lead designer Harry Gottlieb begins by stressing that game testing isn't just important; it's essential. He expands:

> Jellyvision doesn't release a program until we've confirmed that our audience thinks it's great and we as creators think it's great. I can't imagine releasing a program into the world that embarrassed me or that might flop creatively; a sip of hemlock is always preferable to a public stoning (and takes far less energy for all involved).

> We have a full-time Audience Information Services (AIS) group at Jellyvision (and have had it in place from [when Jellyvision numbered fewer than] 30 people). All sorts of testing are fully integrated into Jellyvision's design process. Someone comes up with an idea. A designer fleshes it out on paper, getting feedback from colleagues. We simulate the play of the game in a "paper-and-pencil" format: We use index cards, overhead transparencies, bells, whistles, and whatnot. The designer or one of Jellyvision's many improv actors (who double as writers, editors, audio producers, programmers, or artists by day) act as the host. First, we test with our own staff. If the core idea (what we call the interactive moment) is a complete flop, we drop the project. Otherwise, we shape it and bend it and keep testing it with our staff. This is surprisingly affordable.

Gottlieb explains the term *interactive moment*: "The interactive moment is a key activity that makes the entire program psychologically engaging (trying to figure out the answer to a question, deciding whether to force your opponent to answer, deciding what cards to play in your hand, figuring out what route to take to dodge the ghosts and eat all the blue dots, etc.). The interactive moment doesn't happen on the screen; it happens in the player's head."

> Once we think the program is brilliant, we then test it with outside folks—who often do us the favor of telling us otherwise. If the core idea is still engaging, we keep shaping. This is when things get exciting: Having your audience tell you that your "brilliant" ideas are merely "good" encourages a strong designer to come up with much better ideas—features to fix the problems are so creative that when the product is finished, you can't imagine it without them. When a good designer hears criticism, her imagination kicks into gear.

> Mediocre designers fix problems with obvious solutions (usually the ones that subjects suggest in focus groups). At Jellyvision, we're very clear about the role of the audience: its job is to tell us what's wrong. Our job is to come back with solutions that surprise the audience.

> We never "explain" a product to a focus group. We always create a simulation, demo, or prototype that's adequately close to the real thing (given where we are in the process) so that we can get real feedback. Our AIS staff helps us sort out the subject's biases created from the test instrument.

Before we start spending the big bucks to go into full production (adding teams of artists, writers, musicians, programmers, and so on), we do prototype confirmation testing. We create the full prototype with all the core gameplay features—including sample writing, music, performance, and well-honed timing—but without the pretty art. If that works, we paint on all the fancy colors. (The original prototype for *You Don't Know Jack* was done in black-and-white in HyperCard. Except for the artwork, it plays almost identically to the game today.)

A key thing that studios and production houses need to remember: Hire great designers (or creative folks with great design potential), give them the training and support they need, require them to listen to feedback—but let them make the decisions. Testing is sometimes used by well-intentioned marketing folks to backseat-design the program. That's why many creative development people hate focus groups instead of loving them. (Jellyvision designers love focus groups). A great program needs to be guided by someone with a clear singular vision who is smart enough to crave feedback and creative enough to respond to it in ways unexpected. But that someone needs the authority to run. A good designer in the right environment will know when to break out the hemlock on his own.

Be sure to hop back to Chapter 3, "General Game Design: Strategy Games," in which Harry Gottlieb covers a few of the game design "rules" that Jellyvision adheres to when developing award-winning pop culture trivia diversions.

Chapter 18

Technical Support and Customer Service

THE EXPERTS

- Robert Riley Jr., THQ

- Mark Linn, Interplay

- Ernest McCay

After a game is released via traditional retail channels or over the Internet, it's the manufacturer's responsibility to support the title for consumers. All this work done after the product ships is an essential part of the game's cycle. How the consumer's needs are met (or not met) becomes a critical determinant in whether he or she will deal with the company again in the future.

There are two main areas of support in the gaming industry: technical support and customer service.

➤ **Technical support** provides troubleshooting help for installing, setting up, and running software or hardware. Common issues for the PC gaming industry include driver conflicts, setup for 3D accelerator support, multiplayer gaming, joystick configurations, and more general DirectX problems.

➤ **Customer service**, on the other hand, focuses on help with orders (purchases or returns), warranty issues, billing inquiries, account information (if it's an online game or network), and other non-technical problems.

Both tech support and customer service provide consumers with avenues for satisfaction with their purchase.

Most gaming companies prefer to handle technical support and customer service internally, but in some cases, they hire outside agencies to control the traffic. And it's a common practice for publishers, rather than the development studio, to take care of the technical support and customer service issues. For example, LucasArts deals with any technical support calls, emails, and faxes relating to *Star Wars: Knights of the Old Republic*, rather than BioWare, the developers of the game.

This short chapter looks at the recommended ways of running a smooth technical support or customer service operation, whether you are supporting your own shareware or freeware title, or you want to get into this side of the gaming industry at a publishing company.

Robert Riley Jr., THQ

Rob Riley is the director of customer service and online at THQ, one of America's most successful video game developers and publishers.

Riley discusses the difference between customer support and technical support and the importance of support in general:

> In our environment, [customer support and technical support] are the same. It's a critical phase in a product cycle. From the customer's perspective, it may be their first direct interaction with the company. From the company's perspective, it's the most direct route to feedback from our end users. In both cases, we have an opportunity to strengthen our relationship with our customers.

What are the three most important things for a developer/publisher to keep in mind when it comes to proper consumer support?

> ➤ **Always be available**. When the customer service department is closed, make sure that there are alternative support routes available (online, user groups, automated voice systems, and so on).
>
> ➤ **Know your product**. A customer service engineer who can retain the confidence of the caller is far more effective in resolving a difficulty.
>
> ➤ **Be aware of your audience**. THQ develops products for different platforms and age groups. It's critical to deliver service appropriate to each group.

> There are no fixed rules in this aspect of our business. In general, it's always beneficial to capture and retain customer service history. This data can be used to improve the service process and can also be used to make better product. At THQ, we have seen a fairly dramatic shift in service contact method—from telephone a few years ago toward email and the web. We'll continue to provide support via phone, fax, and conventional mail as long as there's a demand.

This is great advice—but what if the publisher/developer has no money and it's a shareware/freeware game? Do the same principles apply?

> It's an issue of perception—a customer who is unable to find satisfaction is an unhappy customer. Providing comprehensive customer service is an expensive proposition, and many small companies choose to outsource this aspect of the business. It's not feasible to release a software package without a support infrastructure behind it.

What are the differences between customer support for a console game versus a PC game?

With a console game, tech support is limited to the replacement of the game software; console hardware is built to the same standard. With the PC, there are countless variables: software drivers, various video and sound cards, different CPU vendors, and different operating systems, to name a few. Further, a product that's 100% bug-free when shipped may not be compatible with newly developed hardware. Because the PC market is evolving so quickly, this challenge is substantial.

From a PC perspective, when should patches be released? Small, incremental patches? Or larger patches, but more spread out?

I think Microsoft has established an effective patch policy, in which critical issues are patched on an as-needed basis, but larger "point releases" are published less frequently. This allows the end user to enjoy a relatively consistent software environment, but also provides minor bug fixes to enhance stability and security.

Visit THQ's online home to customer service at `www.thq.com/support`.

THQ's Bob Riley says technical support is a "critical phase" in a game's development cycle. Pictured here are two snapshots from *WWF Smackdown! Just Bring It*, one of THQ's biggest franchises.
(Used with permission by THQ, Inc. © 2002 Worldwide Wrestling Federation, Inc.)

Mark Linn, Interplay

Mark Linn is the lead technician at Interplay's Irvine, California, headquarters, and has been part of the technical support team for close to seven years.

He explains that at Interplay, his technicians are trained to handle customer service calls, so they can resolve issues on the spot. "One-call resolution is best for the consumer and for us," explains Linn. He notes that phone calls are more effective than email or faxed queries, and it's also faster for both parties; therefore, it's less expensive for Interplay and more timely for consumers.

Because this book caters to budding game designers who may want to start their own company or who aim to get a job at an existing developer or publisher, we asked Linn for the best advice he can give on running a smooth technical support operation. The following sections provide his answers.

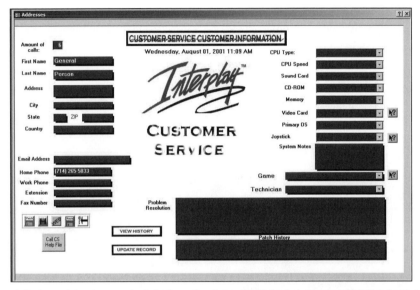

Ever wanted to know what customer service looks like on the other end? Well, thanks to Interplay's Mark Linn, here's a real data sheet that's filled out by the support rep when gamers call in with a question or comment about a given game.
(Used with permission by Interplay Productions, Inc.)

A Good Database

According to Linn, setting up a database and good call-tracking are the most important first steps. For larger companies, all technicians should be networked together, in case customers don't get the same person on the phone each time.

At Interplay, all calls are logged on a Microsoft Access database that records information about the user, his or her system, what happened during the last call, if the game in question has any known bugs (and how to get around them), and so forth. Linn notes that they tend to get calls from the same people repeatedly, so they call up the file by the customer's phone number. "Most of the people who call technical support are new computer users who are unfamiliar with the computer or older operating systems such as DOS," explains Linn. Because Interplay maintains a clean and organized database, it can often get to the root of the problem faster; therefore, it also reduces the hold time for customers calling in. "It's on their dime, so we try to make it quick and painless for them."

Proper Training

Linn emphasizes proper training because most of their applicants are familiar with computers, but they need to know the operating systems that are relevant to gaming and the games themselves.

> We won't even give them an interview before they pass a test to make sure they understand computers the way we need them to (for example, operating systems such as Windows 95/98 or higher, and DOS). Then, for the first few days of training, we sit them down and make them play the games. The more familiar they are with the games, the more they'll be able to assist the callers.

Be a Good Listener

Linn says it's crucial that his staff be good listeners and possess good customer service skills. Moreover, they must not take things personally. "Callers may be irate—and they don't think of it as 'something is wrong with *their* computer,' but more like 'something is wrong with *your* product.'"

"If these three rules are adhered to, any technical support operation should run smoothly and efficiently," says Linn.

For more on Interplay's customer support, visit `www.interplay.com` and click the Help tab on the left side of the screen.

Ernest McCay

Before leaving 3DO in late 2002 to pursue other interests, Ernest McCay was the customer service supervisor at 3DO. He has performed product support lead on a number of titles, such as the *Might and Magic* series, *Vegas Games*, and the *Family Game Pack Royale*.

McCay defines technical support and customer service and shares some sage advice on how to properly perform these tasks for a game company:

> Technical support is mostly a large subset of customer support:
>
> ➤ **Customer support**. Resolving technical issues (system tweaking); hearing suggestions and complaints; receiving and following up on bug reports and compatibility issues; product replacement; answering gameplay questions; providing feedback to the marketing and development teams.
>
> ➤ **Technical support**. Resolving technical issues and compatibility issues; following up on bug reports.

McCay discusses how they line up in the product cycle (this ties into proper game testing, as discussed in Chapter 17, "Proper Game Testing"):

> 1. During the design and alpha stages, the support team can bring up issues that occurred with similar products (this is particularly important with sequels) and the severity of customer reactions to them.

2. During the beta stage, the support team can review the bug database and prioritize efforts on those issues that will most impact customer satisfaction—this can save a fair amount of development time before and after release.

3. Prior to release, the support team can act as part of the signoff process, ensuring that the game is supportable. This is crucial because the motivation of the support team is to reduce its workload and act as customer advocate, whereas the development team is motivated to meet its milestones.

4. During the release, the support team should track issues as they come in, narrow them down to actual game issues, and prioritize them for the development team.

5. Post-release, the support team should track issues and provide customer feedback to the marketing and the development teams for future releases.

To support these endeavors, it's important for the support reps to develop good working relationships with the development team(s). It's also important for management to back them when they're right—otherwise, you're hamstringing them.

Customer support is (and should be) the first line of contact with customers. With the right tools, they can track a lot of information for the marketing and development teams, freeing up those teams for the tasks that only they can handle. In the process, this helps keep the support job interesting and lowers burnout/turnover.

According to McCay, these are the three most important rules for a support team:

> ➤ Keep your promises.

> ➤ Don't lie or make unreasonable promises.

> ➤ Know your products and their platforms.

He reiterates that it's important for management to support these rules with company policy.

McCay offers the following do's and don'ts:

Personalize your answers. Be warm but professional. Be thorough. Take the time to do any needed research. Keep your promises (can't emphasize this one enough). Stay focused. Project confidence in yourself and your products. Always remember that you are the most immediate representative of the company that the customer will experience.

(For management): Keep support in the loop. Give them correct and unambiguous information. Provide proper training. Provide paths of advancement. (You'll get much better performance this way.) Back them up.

Don't lose your cool. Don't lose focus—letting the customer ramble for an hour, for example. Don't give pat, generic answers. Don't give too much information at once; focus on the most likely problems, and accept the possibility of a callback. Don't give too little information, saying what to do but not how to do it. Don't lie; it will almost always come back and bite you, so it's not worth the risk—not to mention the moral and ethical issues. Don't pass the buck—very little frustrates a customer more in the long run—or allow the buck to be passed. (I can't count the times when consultants or computer manufacturers have blamed system issues on our games because they didn't want to deal with it, but you can't accept responsibility for things out of your control.) Don't let an unreasonable customer walk all over you—don't reinforce bad behavior.

(For management): Don't marginalize the support team. Don't shoot the messenger when support points out an embarrassing mistake on the part of the development team. Don't fail to utilize the resource.

What are the best ways to conduct support?

Email and phone support are the best venues for customer contact. Email is perhaps the most important because files can be transferred and long explanations to common questions can be scripted, saving time (although personalized editing of those scripts is still important). Phone support has the advantage of instant gratification (important for consumer happiness), quick resolution, and being able to redirect a confused customer onto the right path. Phone also has the advantage over email in that you can exert much greater control over how your comments are interpreted. Humor is dangerous via email, but often a saving grace over the phone. I strongly feel that both should be available, with the possible exception of a massively multiplayer game—it's a special case. There is usually a very small percentage of the total players with the odd psychological quirk of not being able to have fun unless annoying others; these few make phone access by players undesirable, given the disproportionate amount of resources they take up.

What if a game developer can't afford a professional customer support or tech support team like 3DO's?

The important thing for a shareware/freeware publisher to keep in mind is to not set support expectations any higher than can be reasonably managed by that publisher. If it's one person writing code during two hours a day off the job, promising to respond to all contacts within 24 hours is ill-advised at best.

The amount of support that should be provided by a shareware/freeware publisher really depends on the goals. If the product is meant as a fun exercise, support isn't as important. If it's intended as a means of breaking into the industry, support is potentially even more important than it is for an established company. Again, the important thing is to set a reasonable expectation and meet it without fail. Most people are accepting of reasonable conditions, but after the expectations are set, any failure of expectations becomes a breach of trust. Trust is the basis of successful sales.

On the differences in supporting a console versus a PC game, McCay maintains that "there is generally much less involved in supporting a console game—the hardware typically works or needs to be serviced (which is out of the purview of the game company's support team), and there aren't the large number of system tweaks that PCs need to have done."

3DO's *Army Men* games are one of the company's best-selling franchises.
(Used with permission by 3DO, Inc.)

Speaking of PC tech support, when should a patch be released?

Patches should generally be larger and more spread out. There are two big reasons for this. First, with every patch, there is the risk of breaking another part of the code. Second, the industry is so competitive now that keeping programmers on tap for a lot of incremental patches isn't practical—their talent is needed elsewhere. Test time isn't much different for a single big change or a single small one (or shouldn't be), so it's more economical to do a large fix. It also takes time to gather information, more of which can make the fix a better one. The big exception to this is where a bug slipped through that makes the game unable to be completed. These need to be patched ASAP.

For 3DO's customer service/technical support pages, visit www.3do.com/support.

Chapter 19

Public Relations and Marketing

The unfortunate reality is that no matter how good a game is, it just won't sell if nobody knows about it. In this day and age, hype, exposure, and distribution muscle are needed to sell games—or at least one of the three.

Public relations representatives (reps) and marketing reps have the same goal—to get the product known—but how they go about it varies greatly. Loosely speaking, *public relations* (PR) reps work with the press to get media exposure; whereas *marketing reps* tend to deal more directly with the consumer through advertising, packaging, and promotions. In some cases, they also deal with retailers regarding distribution channels and presentation issues.

Doug Lombardi, a savvy marketing representative at Valve Software, elaborates on the job requirements for each of these two important positions:

> Two key areas that every game publisher must address in garnering critical mind share for a product are marketing and public relations.
>
> Generally speaking, public relations representatives handle all communications with the press, who subsequently get the information to the end user via previews, features, news stories, and so on. Specifically, the PR duties include setting up press tours, promotional events, and editorial visits to the studio or development house. Additionally, the PR reps manage the creation of releases about the product, developer, and company—while also responding to all inquiries from the press for interviews, artwork, and so on.
>
> The marketing folks, on the other hand, manage the creation of more direct communications to the consumer, such as advertisements, packaging, and so on. In most cases, the marketing manager works

THE EXPERTS

- Tammy Schachter, Konami of America
- Jeffrey Castaneda, Rockstar Games
- Jeane Wong, Electronic Arts (EA)
- Tom Sarris, LucasArts
- Chris Olmstead, Golin/Harris International
- Mike Rubinelli, THQ
- Mary Bihr, LucasArts
- Peter Dille, VP, Marketing, THQ
- Mike Fischer, Sega
- Jason Enos, Konami
- Jay Miller, ZIOSoft

very closely with a creative agency to produce the product's visual identity as well as the aforementioned promotional materials. And in some cases, the marketing manager pursues third-party (or *co-op*) promotions and agreements, in which a software publishing house, for example, partners with a technology company to co-promote both companies' products.

Many gaming developers and publishers opt to hire an outside PR agency or marketing firm to handle their business. There are pros and cons for hiring an agency, as discussed in the next few pages.

The goal of this chapter is to shed some light on these two roles by delivering helpful advice from seasoned industry professionals. They'll cover the best ways to conduct successful public relations and savvy marketing for your game.

Public Relations

These folks are some of the best in the business, and they come through with excellent advice.

Tammy Schachter, Konami of America

With seven years of experience in public relations and publicity, Tammy Schachter, a Senior PR manager at Konami of America, has focused her expertise in games, entertainment, technology, and new media. Schachter has launched more than 80 titles on every major platform, including *Metal Gear Solid 2: Sons of Liberty* (Konami of America), *Rayman 2: The Great Escape* (Ubi Soft Entertainment), and *Crash Bandicoot: The Wrath of Cortex* (Universal Interactive).

Schachter defines PR in this context as "the art of evangelizing, promoting, and securing editorial coverage for a game company's new title in a strategic manner with a consistent, cohesive message." And she maintains that there are a few key considerations to keep in mind when promoting your own game:

> ➤ **Know the product**. Nothing is more important than being knowledgeable about the product. Understanding its strengths will arm you with the tools needed to promote it, while understanding its weaknesses will allow you to defend and protect it from harsh criticism.

> ➤ **Timing and planning**. It's critical that you make a plan. Working backward from the launch date, figure out when you will need to meet editorial deadlines in order to secure coverage in the appropriate magazine issues. A detailed PR plan and timeline allow you to identify the elements needed to execute the campaign (screenshots, box art, cover renders, beta samples, master code, and so on) and secure timely coverage. It also allows you to strategically organize the campaign and maximize your game's exposure.

As an example, Schachter says if you have a game that's scheduled to ship in October, you should plan to have reviews in the November issues of key enthusiast publications, which means submitting reviewable code in August.

> ➤ **Know the media and anticipate their needs**. As you begin to negotiate for coverage, you'll quickly realize that it isn't as easy as it looks to land the cover of *EGM* or a feature in *USA Today*. That is why it's critical that you understand the difference between enthusiast, trade, consumer, and broadcast outlets. Each one has its own personality, its own timetable, its own coverage focus, and its own audience demographic.

Understand, therefore, that each magazine needs its own reason to write about your game. Always be prepared with multiple customized pitch angles. It's important that you don't waste the time of a business journalist at the *New York Times* with a story about a game that would make more sense for the *Circuits* section.

If a budding game designer has no choice but to do his or her own PR, are there any do's and don'ts? Yep. Schachter provides the following Top 10 list of PR. Kick back and enjoy:

Tammy's Top 10 List

10. **Don't lie**. Lying might help you once, but never again. Lying is the best way to burn bridges and abuse trust. Lots of people think that PR folks are all liars because we put the best spin on things. However, putting a positive spin on something and lying are two very different things. Don't do it. Period.

9. **Do make a plan**. Think about the kind of game that you're promoting, and think about the kind of coverage that you want for it. Then make a plan that will reach your target audience. Think strategically about timing, messaging, and your demographic, and put it all down on paper. This will allow you to manage your campaign over time, focusing on your immediate needs while working toward your ultimate goal.

8. **Do get on the phone**. The phone is your most important tool. It's through the phone that you will build relationships. Although much of our business takes place in email, it's nevertheless a cold communications application. It can be used to enhance relationships but not build them. It's only on the phone (and in person, of course) that you will build personal relationships. So, do pick up the phone and call the press.

7. **Do follow up with all contacts**. I can't stress this enough. It's so important to follow up. When you tell a journalist that you will send a screenshot, send it. When you send a game, follow up to make sure that [the journalist] received it; and be available in case [he or she has] any technical issues, questions about the story, or other concerns.

6. **Don't be afraid to ask**. Journalists hold the key to the publication at hand, so don't be afraid to ask them about it. For instance, ask them what issue they're currently working on and what their deadlines are. They know their publication best. Work within their parameters.

5. **Do focus on previews to build momentum**. The more hype surrounding your game during its developmental stages, the better the chance of convincing the press that it's worth reviewing and convincing the buying public that it's worth buying.

4. **Do be creative**. Journalists receive hundreds of emails, phone calls, and pitch letters. Make yours stand out. Do the same for your press releases, events, and story ideas. Push yourself to your creative limits!

3. **Don't be rude. Ever**. This may seem obvious, but it shouldn't be taken for granted. You must always be respectful, courteous, and professional.

2. **Don't ignore any request**. Even when you can't fill a journalist's particular needs because product or other materials are unavailable at the time, always return their calls and reply to their emails.

1. **Do be proactive**. Always remember that you are the voice of your game and your company, and unless you scream from the rooftops, no one is going to hear you.

Wow, now that's good stuff!

Schachter says that even someone with a small budget—or no budget—can successfully get a product out there and get it reviewed by the press. "PR is all about saving money—not spending it. Looking at a marketing campaign (advertising, packaging, POP [point of purchase], and so on), one's PR budget should be only a fraction of the overall marketing costs." She continues:

> To successfully secure coverage (reviews) for your game, you need to build momentum and generate awareness. Your most important tool here will be your imagination. Think creatively about guerilla tactics that will build hype around your game. Use email to disseminate screens or product information. Go into chat rooms or bulletin boards to get people talking about the game. Give an exclusive to a key media outlet that will set the buzz going.

Schachter says that when you have momentum building, you need to get in touch with each journalist to discuss his or her coverage plans for your title:

> When you've agreed on the timing, the materials needed, and deadline due dates, send a complete package—including the game, the product info, screens, and all other relevant materials—and be sure to follow up.

Tammy Schachter, a seasoned public relations specialist at Konami, says securing highly visible coverage for a product is of critical importance. The cover of *Next Generation* magazine featured Solid Snake to promote *Metal Gear Solid 2: Sons of Liberty*. Schachter helped arrange this impressive cover story while at the Bender/Helper Impact PR agency.

(Used with permission by Tammy Schachter and Imagine Media, Inc.)

On securing a *Next Generation* magazine cover for *Metal Gear Solid 2*, Schachter says this was a real challenge because they had a very limited amount of information and assets to work with at the time:

> The details of this game were highly guarded by Konami. However, [because it was] one of the most anticipated games of 2001, we wanted to do something special with *Next Generation*. I worked closely with their editorial staff for over a month to make sure that they received everything they needed to write a top-notch story. Inch by inch it finally came together. *Next Generation* even went so far as to design their over-cover image because no high-res photorealistic image of Solid Snake had ever been released by Konami. In the end, they received exclusive screenshots, hands-on time with the game, and the all-important interview with Hideo Kojima.

Finally, Schachter was asked for a ballpark range to hire a PR agency. "This varies widely," she says. "But depending on the length, scope, and depth of the campaign, fees can range from under $5,000 to over $25,000 a month."

Often, the most cost-effective solution is to manage the PR internally, says Schachter. "However, when additional funds are available, it would be wise for a small developer/studio to hire an agency or freelance PR professional to consult with the internal team."

With big licenses comes extra responsibility: Schachter weaved her PR magic on *Crash Bandicoot 2: Cortex Strikes Back* and *Jurassic Park: Survival*

(2002, Used with permission by Universal Studios. Used with permission by Konami of America, Inc.)

Jeffrey Castaneda, Rockstar Games

The one and only Jeff Castaneda is the PR Director at Rockstar Games, and has been responsible for the launch of many successful console games, including the infamous *Grand Theft Auto III* (PS2 and PC) and *Grand Theft Auto: Vice City* (PS2 and PC). Other titles under Castaneda's belt include *Grand Theft Auto II* (PS2, Dreamcast, PC), *Max Payne* (PS2, Xbox, PC), *State Of Emergency* (PS2), *Smuggler's Run: Warzones* (GameCube), *Smuggler's Run 2* (PS2), *Smuggler's Run* (PS2), *Midnight Club: Street Racing* (PS2), *Oni* (PS2), *The Italian Job* (PSOne), *Surfing H30* (PS2), *Austin Powers: Oh Behave!* (GBA), *Austin Powers: WTMUL* (GBA), *Thrasher: Skate and Destroy* (PSone), *Monster Truck Madness* (N64), and *Wild Metal* (Dreamcast).

Future aspirations? "To continue to work with companies and people who possess a true vision and passion for the entertainment they create," answers Castaneda.

To start off our lengthy discussion about video game PR, Castaneda offers some sage advice to those who want to get into the PR biz. "If you can look yourself in the mirror and believe your own pitch, you've taken the first step," says Castaneda.

Next, he says to develop "relationships" with the media; treat the relationship with respect, and it will be reciprocated.

Finally, adds Castaneda, "In measuring the success of your PR efforts, don't always judge it by the quantity of coverage you get—make sure that it is also quality of coverage that is most important."

Castaneda was asked to support his advice with a recent PR effort at Rockstar Games:

> The *Official PlayStation Magazine* cover story (November 2001) for *Grand Theft Auto III* symbolizes my proudest moment ever in my seven plus years of doing PR in the video game industry. Prior to this point in my career, I had relatively successful stints doing PR at a couple of different companies within the video game industry, and attained high-profile press coverage in *Newsweek*, *The New York Times*, *Entertainment Weekly*, *Rolling Stone*, *Spin*, and so on. However, nothing could compare to what achieving that cover felt like.

Castaneda offers some background info:

> When I began working at Rockstar Games in July 1999, it was still in its infancy as a newcomer to the U.S. video game arena. It was a small operation filled with a crew of young, talented, and creative people who were passionate about work, passionate about the games they were making, and driven by the vision that company founders Sam Houser and Terry Donovan created. The vision for the company revolved around the fact that gamers were growing up, and therefore the content in their games had to grow to match their changing tastes and interests. The people out there buying the latest and hottest fashions, music, and so on were the same consumers that Rockstar wanted to attract because it became very clear that gaming had become an undeniable part of the young adult everyday lifestyle. However, more often than not, in the mindset of most gamers, games seemed to follow a set gaming formula of levels, missions, bosses combined with pretty graphics. Instead, Rockstar wanted to change that and give the players more freedom and provide more open-ended gameplay instead of confining them to traditional gaming standards. So, in this sense they were not just creating "games," but actual "experiences" for the player.

He continues:

> It was a lengthy and complex process trying to get the press to trust that Rockstar could actually accomplish these lofty goals. The press was skeptical because the company did not possess the sort of history or catalog of games that some of the other veteran publishers possessed. This caused some of the more jaded journalists in the industry to even harbor animosity or resentment toward the company because Rockstar did not operate under the "expected" or "traditional" norms of the industry.
>
> However, with each game that Rockstar published—games such as *Thrasher: Skate and Destroy* to *Midnight Club: Street Racing* and *Smuggler's Run*—one could get a taste of and introduction to what was about to come. The jewel in the Rockstar vision was to be found in its *Grand Theft Auto* franchise. *Grand Theft Auto*, *Grand Theft Auto: London*, and *Grand Theft Auto II* were absolutely brilliant games that on an international level had garnered critical acclaim and success for their addictive gameplay; edgy content; and wide-open, nonlinear gaming experience. However, they had only somewhat of a cult following in the U.S. There was a small and loyal fan base, but a majority of the U.S. press and public just couldn't look past the 2D graphics and top-down perspective in the game.

Castaneda says that when it came time to start PR on *Grand Theft Auto III*, it became very clear very quickly that it was going to be a daunting task—and a hard sell to the U.S. press. He recalls, "As time went by, we knew that it was going to be an all-out war if *Grand Theft Auto III* was even going to have any chance at succeeding."

Why? Three reasons:

➤ There weren't many fans in the U.S. press of the previous versions of *Grand Theft Auto*.

➤ According to some journalists, there were "So many great games coming out from bigger publishers, so good luck in trying to gain mindshare among consumers and in the pages of our magazines," or "Our readers just aren't into *Grand Theft Auto*, it's just not their style of game."

➤ At times, it truly felt like a battle of David and Goliath proportions. We faced an industry full of journalists who had practically already made up their minds as to what games were going to be the big hits of 2001. After a lot of determination and persistence, we began to win some of the mindshare that we so desperately sought after and put together some significant press coverage for the game. Momentum and buzz for *Grand Theft Auto III* was definitely growing. However, in our eyes, it still was average for a game that we at Rockstar knew was going to change the face of video games!

Castaneda says the one last puzzle piece missing in the equation was getting the cover of a major gaming publication—the "Holy Grail" for videogame PR professionals:

> Throughout the year, we had pitched every magazine in the industry for covers, and were turned down several times. Finally, we had one last chance with *Official PlayStation Magazine* for its November 2001 issue. That pitch was the most nerve-racking of my life, but in the end, the PR team proved triumphant. *OPM* believed in *Grand Theft Auto III* enough to give us the cover, and since that point, *GTAIII* went on to shock the industry and create history by becoming the biggest game to hit the video game industry in a very long time.

"It was a huge victory for me, both personally and professionally, as well as for Rockstar Games because that cover was a testament to all the hard work that everyone at Rockstar had put in," recalls Castaneda.

"It was a symbol that Rockstar had finally begun to attain the respect that it had been fighting for within the industry since its inception—it also marked the fact that Rockstar had truly 'arrived' as a force to be reckoned with, and that this was only the beginning."

Castaneda was asked whether it was easier or more difficult to do PR for games with so much hype, such as the *Grand Theft Auto* franchise. Admittedly, Castaneda says doing PR for the *GTA* franchise is "undoubtedly more difficult." He explains:

> In retrospect, it's easy to say that there was so much hype surrounding *GTAIII* because it eventually became the biggest-selling game of 2001 in the world, and has become a cultural phenomenon. But in all honesty, the huge hype on this game didn't actually truly take off until about two months or so before

the game's release in October 2001. Before that point, so many other games had gotten way more buzz and press coverage and attention then we did. In the eyes of the majority of the press and public, they had already picked and bet on who they thought the winners would be. They might have expected *GTAIII* to be a good solid game, but not the masterpiece that it would eventually become.

Castaneda continues:

I believe that this was due to the fact that I don't think a majority of the journalists and public could actually get their heads around what Rockstar and Rockstar North (formerly DMA Design) were actually trying to accomplish with *Grand Theft Auto III*. The free-roaming, nonlinear, open-ended, nontraditional gameplay experience that the *Grand Theft Auto* worlds provide was, in a sense, new and uncharted territory for most because it really hadn't been done yet (at least not in the magnitude that Rockstar created). They weren't ready or prepared to believe that Rockstar was creating a new paradigm in not just gaming, but in entertainment.

"Seeing the characters of *Grand Theft Auto III* on the cover of *OPM* surrounded in smaller print by almost every single game that many editors deemed 'more of what their readers wanted' was pure poetic justice," recalls Castaneda. Pictured here is the best-selling game of 2001 across all platforms: *Grand Theft Auto III*.
(Used with permission by Rockstar Games, Inc.)

Castaneda adds that changing people's perceptions and trying to get them to get over their skepticism for Rockstar and this game was a huge and extremely difficult PR undertaking:

"So many times, PR people tend to throw buzz words out like 'revolutionary' this and 'ground-breaking' that, but how often does that actually ring true?" asks Castaneda, rhetorically. "So, we had to figure out a way to convince jaded journalists that we actually had created a true revolutionary experience."

But don't forget—there was (and still is) a mainstream media backlash over *Grand Theft Auto III*. Needless to say, this can be a PR nightmare. Admits Castaneda:

> On a larger scale, managing the level of controversy the mass media created around *Grand Theft Auto III* made the PR effort extremely more difficult. Although the video game industry is not new by any means, it is still relatively young in the eyes of the public. Therefore, even if the industry has "grown up" and its players have grown up, society and the majority of mass media have failed to accept and acknowledge this fact. The video game industry doesn't have the history and level of acceptance that TV and movies have achieved in the eyes of the public. The result is a cable TV show like *The Sopranos* or a movie like *Goodfellas* being praised, whereas a video game like *GTAIII* becomes vilified—although the content of both pieces of entertainment are similar and deemed for mature audiences. There is an obvious double standard. This forged another level on the PR battleground we faced in trying to convince the mass media to try to cover *GTAIII* in a responsible journalistic fashion, as opposed to going with their first instinct to attack the game and sensationalize their stories because it would make a "better" story. We did not always win these battles, but at least the education process continued, and steps towards changing perceptions about the industry were moving forward. Video games are the coolest and most exciting forms of entertainment being created, and in time, the mass media will hopefully cover the industry in a fashion that won't undermine its true worth and brilliance.

So, was it all worth it?

"Doing PR for *Grand Theft Auto III* has undoubtedly been the most difficult and challenging experience of my PR career, but it has also been the most fulfilling and rewarding, as well" says Castaneda. "There were so many obstacles to overcome for this game in order to get the credit that *GTAIII* and Rockstar Games truly deserved." He continues:

> It's an honor to be part of a phenomenon and something as commercially successful as *Grand Theft Auto*. Rockstar provided a game that is not only technically brilliant and groundbreaking, but artistically amazing. The *Grand Theft Auto* franchise marks a new chapter in video game history that continues to capture the imaginations of new and old video game players alike, and will also drive the industry forward to reach even higher. Not many people get to be part of something that makes as big a cultural impact such as this, where it becomes part of society's fabric. It's definitely a blessing.

> However, the best part of it all is that Rockstar Games has raised the bar for itself and for the industry with *Grand Theft Auto III*, but last year was just the beginning. Rockstar is not one to rest on its laurels, and for all the achievements, this past year was just the stepping stone. Now, there is a whole new war to go on the offensive on.

"Everyone get ready," smiles Castaneda.

Jeane Wong, Electronic Arts (EA)

Jeane Wong is a PR manager of the EA Games department, has been with EA for six years, and has been involved in game publicity since 1994. Says Wong, "My original plan was to go into entertainment PR (music), but I happened to stumble upon the interactive gaming realm accidentally straight out of college, and have to say that it's been a great experience."

Wong was asked to define PR and discuss its importance and implementation. "PR is such a misunderstood concept," she begins. "I've got a journalism degree—with a concentration in PR—and have lived/breathed PR for more than eight (professional) years…but sadly to say, my family and the majority of my friends still have no idea what I do."

To Wong, PR is a service "in which professionals generate external and internal awareness for a product or company through media placements."

It's a field in which we, as publicists, develop solid media relationships to secure editorial coverage (TV, print, online, radio) on behalf of our products/companies. Unlike advertising or promotions, PR isn't bought through media buys (with dollar figures attached), but instead is secured by having publicists pitch and work with journalists on editorial opportunities.

How important is PR? Wong jokes, "Well, obviously, I'm quite biased with my answer. Honestly, even if I weren't in the PR field, I would still acknowledge that there is a high level of importance placed on quality PR coverage."

As I mentioned earlier, unlike advertising/promotions, PR placements are the result of publicists working with journalists to secure coverage that is from the press perspective. This editorial perspective can't be bought or altered by any publicist or company; therefore, it's often an invaluable tool for anyone or any company, given the credibility it provides the source. The mass audience—regardless of industry—relies on editorial to provide professional opinion on almost everything—game reviews, movie reviews, music reviews, trends, and so on. I would even be so bold as to state that the success of anything often results from a fantastic PR launch.

What are some important considerations for those who must do their own PR?

It's even more imperative that a new designer/company focus on the importance of PR. Assuming they have no choice but to do it themselves, they [probably] have a small budget and/or unknown product/individual. A major upside to PR is that the coverage secured often amounts to much more when compared to advertising—both financially and in volume. My current company/department decided to break down the amount of PR coverage we secured on a product by equating how much it would cost per spread/page/air time, and so on. One high-profile title had more than $1 million worth of PR coverage (when no more than $50,000 was spent). The payback was pretty impressive, considering how much it stretched itself out to be.

Wong describes the three most important considerations for a designer/company doing their own PR:

1. **Secure and develop solid media contacts**. These people are the ones writing articles, so you've got to know them.

2. **Prepare a healthy batch of assets and information**. A picture is worth a thousand words, so having an image accompany an article is a major coup!

3. **Develop a comprehensive PR plan and timeline**. Have a big-picture idea of how and what you want to achieve.

Wong maintains that a low-PR budget campaign doesn't necessarily mean low-quality coverage:

Money doesn't equate to success, at least not for PR. You have to be smart, strategic, and prepared in order to deliver a successful PR campaign. Persistence and follow-up are the two main components needed for PR. Press are bombarded by a million things, so it's up to a publicist to convince the journalist to cover their product/company. And it's definitely beneficial for a publicist to follow up because it's the end result that PR looks for—once filed, the journalist isn't necessarily too concerned about making sure that the publicist gets the article.

On creativity, Wong offers the following:

Being creative is definitely another aspect of PR that's a "lost art." A PR campaign can fall victim to cookie-cutter initiatives. Creative doesn't have to be expensive; being smart and strategic will have a much more positive end result. Taking the time to determine the unique aspects and elements of a product (or company) and applying those items when pitching press will be much more beneficial than a generic press release or product mailing.

As an example, Wong refers to working on *Black & White*, a computer game that had two very different sides (the player could engage as a good deity or an evil deity).

After brainstorming and thinking of cool ideas to reinforce the fact that there were two very different sides to the game, we came up with the idea of creating a press kit folder that reflected both sides—and we created documents that provided "good information" and "bad information." Needless to say, the press who received the two-sided press kits embraced the idea and appreciated the creativity behind the bipolar delivery of the game.

What are the advantages and disadvantages of working as a PR rep internally for a game company versus an independent PR firm?

If I had to mentor a fledgling publicist, I would advise that he or she start within a PR agency to get the full-on experience of what PR boot camp is like. My analogy to boot camp primarily revolves around the fact that if you can survive an agency, you can make it anywhere. It can be a grueling place, considering the volume of work and multitasking you have to be prepared for in order to succeed. At any moment, you can get calls from one client asking for a summary while you're involved in a project for another client. And you've got to be prepared to switch topics when appropriate, such as when a journalist is interested in one client/project, but it turns out that another is better suited for the editorial opportunity.

With a healthy dose of PR experience at an agency (Wong says a few years), the PR representative should become a much more marketable professional, at which time he or she can look into internal PR positions.

Tom Sarris, LucasArts

As director of public relations at the LucasArts Entertainment Company, Sarris has a number of very important video game franchises under his jurisdiction, including, of course, the famous *Star Wars* line of interactive entertainment products. Sarris has been in the industry for close to 11 years, nine of which have been at LucasArts.

"Strictly defined," begins Sarris, when asked to define PR in his words, "the practice of public relations is to gain third-party endorsement of a product or service through print, broadcast (television and radio), and Internet media."

Sarris says the overall goal is to gain positive editorial coverage that reaches consumers who may be predisposed to use your product or service. With that in mind, Sarris offers advice on securing positive editorial coverage:

> The best way is to inform as many game journalists as possible to ensure that they know that the product is actually in development. From there, a steady supply of art (screen shots, concept sketches, video, and so on) and editorial assets is absolutely invaluable to ensuring consistent coverage. When the game is at an appropriate stage of development to demo, in-person press appointments should be scheduled (either inviting the media to where you are or going to where they are) to give them a first-hand look at the game.

From his many years of experience, can Sarris suggest any do's or don'ts when it comes to game PR?

> Never complain about a bad review. It's akin to arguing with a baseball umpire. The call won't change, and all you'll end up doing is infuriating [the reviewer]. If a developer properly manages the expectations of an editor up front, the chances of a bad review are lessened. Although there's certainly no way to ever guarantee a positive review, properly managing expectations will go a long way to helping the media to feel positive about a game. Above all, *always* be open and honest with the media. If you lose their trust, it's very difficult to gain it back.

Is PR for an immensely popular franchise such as *Star Wars* more difficult because there are higher expectations or easier because everyone is familiar with the characters and universe (not to mention the existing marketing of the movies and related paraphernalia)?

> *Star Wars* is perhaps the most successful license in interactive gaming. It may sound surprising, but doing public relations for such a popular intellectual property is both a blessing and a curse. It's a blessing in that almost everyone in the world understands and likes *Star Wars*. But because of that, there are incredibly high expectations that are sometimes challenging to fulfill. Thankfully, the majority of the time LucasArts has gotten it right and produced *Star Wars* games that players have enjoyed.

For those who may be interested in taking a job as a PR rep for a game company, what are the different kinds of PR? According to Sarris, LucasArts has four positions in the public relations department:

➤ The *Director of Public Relations* sets and manages the overall strategic direction for all facets of worldwide product and corporate communications and ensures that those goals are met.

➤ The *Public Relations Manager* follows the overall strategy and manages the day-to-day contact with the press to ensure consistent coverage in the game and consumer media.

➤ The *Domestic Public Relations Coordinator* works under the direction of the PR director and PR manager to ensure timely dissemination of art assets and other materials.

➤ The *International Public Relations Coordinator* works with all of LucasArts' international partners and disseminates assets and materials so that they can appropriately promote LucasArts' games in their respective territories.

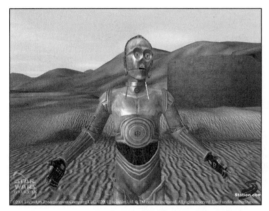

With the success of the Episode II *Star Wars* movie (Attack of the Clones), you bet the related video games are selling quite well. There are titles for all systems, including this one—the massively multiplayer *Star Wars Galaxies*. Read all about them at `www.lucasarts.com`.
(©2002 LucasArts Entertainment Company LLC and its Licensors. LucasArts and the LucasArts logo are registered trademarks of Lucasfilm Ltd. All rights reserved.)

Chris Olmstead, Golin/Harris International

For our chat with a successful and well-respected PR rep, let's go back to the agency side once again and talk with Chris Olmstead, Senior Media Executive at Golin/Harris International's Los Angeles office. Olmstead has worked primarily on the Nintendo account over the past nine years, and has helped launch the Nintendo 64, the Game Boy Color, the Game Boy Advance, and the GameCube.

His favorite Nintendo game? *1080 Snowboarding* for the Nintendo 64. Says Olmstead, "Not being a 'gamer,' I find this title to be very intuitive and easy for the non-gamer to learn."

As confirmed by the other PR specialists in this chapter, Olmstead explains that public relations is the art of positioning your client and its products and/or services in the news in a favorable light. He adds:

> By the same token, it's important to be up front with the media, letting them know the truth (as much as possible and at the appropriate time) about a company to avoid any "surprises" and creating mistrust with a journalist. Public relations is ultimately about relationships with the media—getting to know someone and providing them with information that will help foster their understanding about your client. As the relationship grows, the communication between media executive and journalist optimally becomes an open channel for information that's mutually beneficial.

> For the journalist, important information about a company can be divulged in confidence by the media executive that allows him or her to not only understand the company better, but also [gain] a better perspective of how the company works within its industry...

> For the media executive, the trust developed with the media in providing key information allows the opportunity to learn key details about industry competitors, and how the journalist and other key figures view your client as well as the competition and the state of the industry as a whole.

Olmstead talks about the most important things for a new game designer to keep in mind when doing their own public relations:

> The key in any PR campaign is "newsworthiness."

> > ➤ What is unique, different, new, or unusual about your game?

> > ➤ What developments does it play off of, expand, or divert from?

> This is where media relationships can pay off. By working with not only key game enthusiast print and online media, but also key consumer game reviewers, the developer can create a release or even "bullet point" the key facts/unique features of the game (even in a concise email).

> After sending media the game's key points, take a "road trip" to personally visit with key press— concentrating on New York, Los Angeles, Chicago, San Francisco, and Minneapolis/St. Paul. These are where most of the key game and consumer media are based. Plan on spending at least two to three days (even up to a week) in each city, personally giving each outlet a brief game "tour" so they can see the salient features.

But what if someone can't afford this?

> Then focus on two or three (say New York, San Francisco, and Los Angeles). If road money is completely out of the question, send beta copies of the game to the key reviewers at the game magazines, newspapers, and top consumer magazines (such as *Time*, *Newsweek*, *Wired*, *Rolling Stone*, *Playboy*, and so on). Ultimately, that's the most important part of your media outreach. You may want to include a brief intro and "tips" to help jump-start their entry into the game. Also, provide a "heads up" about key

features in certain levels to look for, as well as a "reader's digest" cheat sheet to help media move through the game more quickly (especially for those who are on tight deadlines—media really appreciate this).

Olmstead says that after you send the game, personally call each reviewer to make sure it arrived and to see whether he or she has any questions:

You should also follow up a week later to see how the journalist is progressing through the game, and offer tips/information to not only help the reviewer proceed through the game, but also illuminate its unique features. This will be appreciated by the reviewer and encourage him or her to contact you for additional questions/assistance (especially during the more challenging passages). It will also help develop your relationship with the reviewer. Again, this is ultimately the most important element of the campaign. Your ability to communicate the game's unique features to the media in an open and supportive manner can potentially mean the difference between a fair and a good review.

Olmstead describes the advantages and disadvantages of working as a PR rep internally for a game company versus a PR firm:

I work for a PR firm, but my only account is Nintendo. The potential disadvantages of working for a firm are being pulled in another direction by another client. But I've been told that an internal PR department can be pulled in other directions by internal pressures/management priorities that add to the work that needs to be completed. The key element (which often remains elusive) is balance. Allow yourself the opportunity to see the "big picture" on several levels. From a client perspective, [finding] the key elements that comprise the whole campaign and also the industry as a whole—keeping track of your competitors, and so on. On a personal level, giving yourself a breather now and then so you can provide positive energy to your client and not become "burned-out."

Chris Olmstead of Golin/Harris International discusses the ups and downs of
working in PR at an agency versus internally at a game company in this segment.
(Used with permission by Nintendo of America, Inc.)

Finally, how about an example that supports the aforementioned PR advice?

> Probably the most rewarding story I ever placed (both professionally and personally) was a *New York Times* profile on Mr. Miyamoto in April, 1999 (in conjunction with the Game Developer's Conference Lifetime Achievement Award he received several months earlier).

> Our goal going into the Game Developer's Conference was to secure a national print feature story on Miyamoto. This was very important because Nintendo was facing increased competitive pressure by Sega Dreamcast (already available) and a known PlayStation 2 demo that would be showcased during the conference. Miyamoto's presence allowed Nintendo to focus on the one thing it knew better than any other company: the importance of creating the most entertaining, challenging, and exciting games in the world. Miyamoto was (and continues to be) its best developer, and he is synonymous with some of video gaming's enduring icons: *Donkey Kong*, *Mario*, and *Link* from the *Zelda* series.

> We approached the *New York Times* and offered the business reporter, Sharon King, an exclusive story. Because she was heading to the conference and knew Miyamoto's award would be among the top news items from the show, Sharon was thrilled to be offered "behind-the-scenes" access to him during a pre-show dinner. She probably spent about three to four hours with Miyamoto, not only learning about his integral role in Nintendo's rise in the video game industry, but also the thinking behind his unique game perspective. *The Legend of Zelda: Ocarina of Time*, considered his masterpiece, had been released in November of 1998, and was the featured Nintendo title to illustrate his creative genius.

> Personally, this was my favorite article because an anecdote that emanated from the conference actually became the final paragraph of the article. I asked Miyamoto if he could give my son some game advice. His interpreter offered, "On how to beat *Zelda*?" I said, "No, he's already beaten *Zelda*." They both laughed. I then asked if he had any general advice on video gaming. Miyamoto pondered the question for a minute and then wrote the following message on my son's *Nintendo Power Magazine*: "To Jeremie, Play Outside on Sunny Days, Shigeru Miyamoto." I have this signed magazine framed, along with the *New York Times* Miyamoto story, in my living room.

Mike Rubinelli, THQ

This former Vice President of Product Development at THQ left the company in the fall of 2002 and is currently at Gotham Games, a subsidiary of Take-Two Interactive. We had the privilege to chat with the industry veretan prior to his departure, and he was asked whether he prefers working with an internal PR group or an external agency:

> Internally is much better—and I'm not saying that because I know they're going to read this before you get it!

He explains:

> I've worked in situations where marketing was not collocated and the PR firm was contracted, and it was far and away the worst situation you could possibly have for building market awareness for your game. There is a certain osmosis that takes places when marketing and PR interact in person on a daily basis. Often, you'll see the two groups play off each other in terms of the campaigns, as well as what the game should be.

But Rubinelli explains the differences in the kinds of video game PR:

> In our business, there are actually two types of PR: there is Corporate PR and Product PR. The differences are fairly obvious. The group I referred to earlier is Product PR. In most companies, Product PR is a group that operates under the Marketing umbrella. As you can imagine, most everything that they do is geared toward getting the title positive exposure, from the initial product announcement to the final product review campaign. If they are in-house, they are simply closer to the product. They become immersed in their individual project teams, working hand-in-hand with the game producers and the product marketing managers. A more seamless collaborative effort results. The marketing and PR people are always on message—effectively managing assets, communicating features, and so on. This is especially important in the video game world with the many variables that affect the product development process.

Marketing

We hear from some of the best in marketing in this section.

Mary Bihr, LucasArts

We heard earlier in this chapter from Tom Sarris, Director of Public Relations at LucasArts, about what it's like doing PR for *Star Wars* games. Now we've got Mary Bihr, Vice President of Worldwide Sales and Marketing, who describes the flip side. Bihr has been involved in sales/marketing for nearly every LucasArts launch since 1988, with the exception of a handful of the early PC and early console products. How would she describe video game marketing?

> Video game marketing is distilling the essence of the game—its attributes and its value to the customer—into a few succinct message points, and reaching out and evangelizing the customers. We want to convert them to our brand, provide them with a reason to believe in us, and build their loyalties over time.

> Marketing works hand-in-hand with public relations in raising the level of awareness of the product and providing customers with a compelling reason to take interest in the game. Both work together to stand out above the noise level and grab a little share of mind. There should be agreement about the common audiences to be reached in both the product marketing and public relations efforts, and there should be agreement about the key message points to the audience.

Bihr lists the most important things for someone in computer game marketing to keep in mind:

> ➤ Know your audience and how to reach them.

> ➤ Know your message and know that the game delivers on the message.

> ➤ Keep your marketing simple, clear, and on strategy.

With this in mind, is it easier or more difficult to market a game with worldwide familiarity and expectations, such as *Star Wars*?

> It's both. It's simple because you don't have to spend a lot of time explaining *Star Wars*. There are immediate associations with the name, and there are certain expectations as well. However, it's difficult because we're not providing the market with one *Star Wars* game, but many—whose messages must be balanced, whose audiences must be distinguished one from another, and whose points of commonality and points of uniqueness must be factored into management of the overall franchise. We don't want our customers saying, "Oh, LucasArts has just put out another one of those *Star Wars* games." Each game should be compelling in its own right, be different from other *Star Wars* games, and yet deliver a quality experience that's consistent with the overall brand and the expectations of the customers.

Aside from this inherent Catch-22 with *Star Wars* games, what are the other challenges in marketing a game?

> The most difficult challenge is trying to predict whether the game will actually deliver on the promise and timing this prediction so that by the time we make it, we still have time to calibrate the sales and marketing efforts correctly.

> Over the course of the last decade, we've had some games we thought would barely break even, which went on to become best sellers. And then there were those games we believed in with a passion, but which were never commercial successes. It's the challenge of the marketer to envision what the product will be from its early stages (sometimes with just a black-and-white document and a few concept sketches) to a finished product; to anticipate how the product will be received by the public; and to determine how well it will sell, given the marketplace dynamics at the time of launch. Then, believing the best for each product, we create the buzz that should make our customers want to pick up the game and play it.

Granted, LucasArts likely has a large marketing budget. But Bihr has some recommendations for game designers/developers who must do it on their own with limited resources:

> On a limited budget, focus the message keenly and use public relations as much as possible, creating unique opportunities to showcase the product. Employ the Internet to spotlight the product; and distribute information, demos, and product updates. Build your customer database so that you can communicate directly to them. Partner with your key retailers and key magazines to advertise the product in print and in-store. Get your demos in the hands of as many people as possible. It's the age-old technique of creating demand through sampler opportunities. If you've got a good game, let it speak for itself in the demo.

Peter Dille, VP, Marketing, THQ

As senior vice president of worldwide marketing, Peter Dille oversees all global corporate and product marketing functions, including advertising, publicity, promotions, and THQ's online presence. Prior to joining THQ, he served as senior director of product marketing for Sony Computer Entertainment America and was a key executive in the launch of the Sony PlayStation.

"Video game marketing is, in many ways, akin to movie marketing," begins Dille. "In both cases, the marketer is trying to establish a strong opening for the product. To do this, the marketing is actually geared toward building a 'buzz' around the product in the weeks and months leading up to the product's release." He continues:

In the gaming category, there are several different types of products, and the marketing can be very different for each. For example, for hardcore gaming products, the marketing often involves getting early adopters and opinion leaders excited about the product, talking it up, and establishing strong word-of-mouth. A recent example of this for THQ is *Red Faction* for PlayStation 2. On the other end of the spectrum, there is a very different kind of marketing for games geared toward younger children. These products often leverage an established licensed brand—whether a hit TV show like *Rugrats*, a movie property like *Jimmy Neutron*, or a toy product like Hot Wheels—and focus more on mass market retail.

For all the quirks and individuality of this business, video game marketing also involves all the "classical" marketing principles: pricing, promotion, place, and so on. Product marketing managers are assigned to a product at the inception of the project and are researching competitive products and making recommendations on features. They are responsible for managing the brand and developing a three- or five-year brand plan. Product managers work closely with sales to help forecast sales volumes. And, of course, marketing also prepares the strategy and execution of the more visible elements of the marketing campaign—the packaging and the advertising.

Does a well-known franchise such as *Rugrats*, *Power Rangers*, or *Scooby Doo* (seen here) make marketing easier, or are the consumer expectations challenging to live up to? "I wouldn't say it's more or less difficult, it's just a different process," says Peter Dille.
(Used with permission by THQ, Inc.)

So is it easier to market a game like *Rugrats* and *WWF*, with their built-in audience?

> Marketing a game with built-in brand awareness, like our *WWF* line of products, has many advantages. With any licensed product, the brand is already established, so the marketing challenge isn't to establish the brand; it's to deliver the brand. That brings with it a different set of challenges: Our WWF fans are so fanatical about the property that they have very high expectations for what the *WWF* video game experience should be. They want the WWF Superstars to behave exactly like they do each week on TV. They want the moves just right, and the storylines have to be accurate as well—which can be tough because the storylines are always evolving in the case of the WWF. So marketing works closely with product development to communicate the brand requirements and interfaces with the licensor. There are millions of WWF fans; to date, we've done a great job of delivering the experience based both on our sales results and the awards we've won for product quality.

Dille adds that on the marketing deliverable side, you need to deliver the brand in a way that's in keeping with how the WWF brand is portrayed. "Packaging and ads all have to go through a thorough approval process that doesn't exist for original products."

On the other side of the spectrum, he continues, "The marketing that we do for original products like *Red Faction* allows us to create our own worlds and our own campaigns."

> The marketing is all tied to the storyline of the game, which is about a mining colony on the planet Mars. As the miners realize they're being abused and killed off by an evil corporation, they form the "Red Faction" to unite the troops to fight back. Our campaign utilized the themes of the game's storyline to gradually leak information, screen shots, video and demo discs from the game, and so on. In other words, the marketing was created to feel like it was coming from the insiders in the Red Faction.

> To build a buzz around the launch of the game, we created a viral campaign that made heavy use of the Internet and email. Starting from ground zero with no *Red Faction* database (this is the launch of a new game, not a sequel—we're building this brand), we grew the database to more than 40,000 members of the Red Faction. Although this may sound modest when compared to millions of Napster users, it's actually crucial to our marketing to get the early adopter excited about our game and to fuel word-of-mouth. The PlayStation 2 installed base is still in its early stages, so to get the active participation of this many hardcore gamers is very important. After all, when they opt into our marketing, they're asking us for information—we're not trying to get their attention any more.

It sounds as if the responsibilities of marketing and PR are similar. How do these two disciplines work with each other? According to Dille, public relations in the video game world is actually a subset of marketing:

> In addition to packaging, advertising, promotions, and so on, the product manager is also responsible for setting the PR strategy for the product. Because PR is a specialized form of communication, most gaming companies either have dedicated PR staffs internally or they work with an outside agency. In both cases, the product manager is responsible for overseeing the efforts of PR, and works collaboratively with the PR manager to develop a compelling PR campaign. As discussed previously, the marketing of the product needs to be coordinated so that the PR for the product is hitting at the appropriate time and in conjunction with the other elements of the marketing effort.

What one key piece of advice can you offer for those who must market their own game?

I think the first recommendation I can provide to someone who is new to video game marketing is that you need to be flexible. Our business is a unique mix of entertainment, technology, and packaged goods. A lot of people come into this category from the packaged goods business, and they have a hard time understanding product slippage. They're used to a world in which someone can tell them when the product will be ready—or better yet, they're the ones that get to tell manufacturing when to have the product ready. Similarly, this business has a lot in common with the movie business. But movie marketers know when a movie is going to release months or years in advance of when the home video is going to ship. And when the home video is preparing to ship, they know how it performed in theatrical release. Which brings me to the third element of being flexible—as a marketer, you can plan for hit products, but it's not easy to know for certain when they'll show up. Software is software, and it's not finished 'til it's finished. And it may or may not be as good as you thought it would be when it was three months from completion, which is often well past when most of the marketing budget needs to be committed and spent.

Dille spoke earlier about specific challenges for different kinds of products, but are there always obstacles to overcome? He indicates that the biggest challenge in marketing a new game is to establish the anticipation and buildup for a product that can't be played or experienced yet.

PR becomes a big part of the equation. We try to focus on the early adopter who reads the gaming books and frequents the gaming web sites. When a product is far enough along, it's great to get a demo to gamers—either through a cover mount CD or a retail kiosk or traveling kiosk program. Finally, retailers pay a lot of attention to what the gaming "experts" say, so these game reviewers give our products the "thumbs up" or "thumbs down."

Finally, Dille warns that successfully marketing a product with a small budget may not be as easy as it once was:

The video game business today is more than $20 billion market worldwide, with over $9 billion in business done in the U.S. each year. That's about the same size as the domestic box office. Market share is really consolidating among a few larger players, with a growing gap between a few leading publishers and several more second-tier publishers. One of the primary reasons for that is the resources required to develop, market, and distribute a game title on a worldwide basis. So the days of making a game in the garage and getting it to market on a shoestring are long over. This is big business. That being said, there are techniques marketers can use that don't cost as much as a national TV campaign. Creative use of the Internet is one example, such as [we did with] *Red Faction*.

Mike Fischer, Sega

Gaming industry veteran Mike Fischer left Namco Hometek, the U.S. consumer software-publishing arm of Namco Ltd., to join Sega's team.

Fischer sees the primary role of marketing as a channel of communication between a company and the people who buy and play the products.

Through market research, consumer assistance, and the Internet, we listen to our consumers' opinions, trends, and tastes—and share this knowledge with the people creating our games. At the same time, we have to let the public know about our products. We do this through a variety of means—including advertising, PR, trade and public events, our web site, and so on.

Fischer agrees that PR is one component of a marketing plan and is crucial to spreading the word about products in ways that simple advertising can't accomplish—but he admits that PR is often viewed in a negative light:

Terms such as "PR flack" or "PR spin" are really unfair characterizations of this area. The fact of the matter is that the people who spend all day creating video games cannot be expected to divert attention away from their work to answer every press inquiry. Even if they somehow had this extra time, they may not necessarily be the most articulate spokespeople when it comes to providing the press with information on their projects.

A PR manager works closely with the game development team to gather any information and materials the press will need. Whenever possible, these materials should communicate not just a game's basic features, but also the creators' own vision and passion for their project. Every game has its own unique history, story, and features, which good PR should communicate in a compelling way.

Whenever possible, we do try to give the press direct access to the game development teams. When these teams are in Japan, scheduling pressures and language barriers can make the work especially difficult. But a good PR manager can judge when a publicity opportunity is worth taking some of the development team's time away from their project.

Fischer was asked to discuss the most important considerations for someone doing their own marketing of a game. "As far as I'm concerned, there are only two ironclad rules," begins Fischer. "Always be true to the product and your consumers, and share the passion that our customers have for their product." Here's why:

When one of our customers buys a game, he or she is investing up to $50 and many dozens (sometimes hundreds) of hours. It's the job of marketing to make sure that this is an informed investment of both time and money—one that leaves the customer not only satisfied, but eager to try our other games as well.

Let's say, for example, that I'm given the task of marketing a product with a relatively small sales potential. Maybe it's a quality game, but one with a niche appeal to a small market of hardcore enthusiasts—something like an old-school Japanese-style RPG or a complicated simulation game. It might (I said *might*) be possible to increase sales with a marketing campaign that misleadingly portrayed the game as a more fast-paced, action-oriented title for a more casual game player. What's the result? By trying to increase short-term sales for one product, I end up leaving consumers feeling misled and taken advantage of. Sequels for this title are guaranteed to fail, the company's brand image is hurt, and consumers will not trust anything the company says to them again. Word-of-mouth is the key to the success or failure of any game; and any marketing message that hurts the credibility of a game, brand, or publisher will ultimately cost a company more than the quick buck it might generate in the short term.

To drive his point home, Fischer says he started his career working at Sega's headquarters in Japan, and the hardcore gamers there "don't mess around." What does he mean by this? Recalls Fischer, "From time to time, customers who felt burned by a bad game experience would smash the cartridge and mail it back to us. They didn't want a refund, they just wanted to send us a message—that experience was a great lesson in remembering to respect my customers."

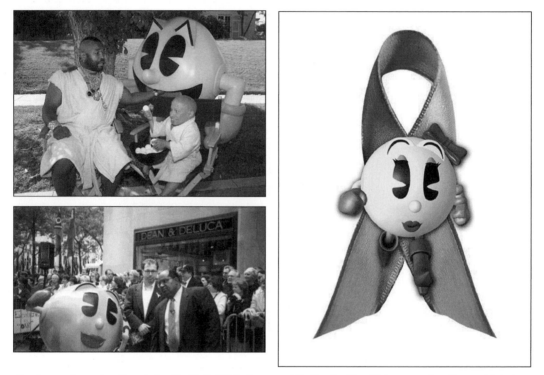

Seen here are images from Namco's *Pac-Man World: 20th Anniversary* and *Ms. Pac-Man Maze Madness* campaigns. Commercial shoot on location in "Beverly Hills," co-starring Verne Troyer ("Mini Me" from the last two *Austin Powers* movies) and the legendary Mr. T. Ms. Pac-Man on *The Today Show*. Marketing Ms. Pac-Man as part of the National Breast Cancer Awareness Month.
(Used with permission by Michael Tweed Photography. Used with permission by Namco, Ltd.)

Fischer adds that he has loved video games all his life and shares the passion that his customers feel for video games:

> I don't market discs in cases—I market an entertainment experience. It's impossible to effectively market the excitement and fun of a game without understanding that game firsthand myself. It's also critical to have insight into the perspective of the consumers whom we want to buy and play our games.

Fischer admits, however, that this may be no easy task:

> Of course, I'm not a teenager—or even a "young adult" any more—so staying in touch with our consumers requires constant work. Sometimes, I feel like an aging professional athlete trying to stay in competitive shape, but I do put a lot of effort into trying to understand the perspective of our audience. Watching focus groups and reading market research reports is not enough. You have to talk to and stay engaged with the consumer. One activity that I found helps a lot is to stay in a store for part of a day and observe how people buy our products. It's great to watch how people shop. Some of them shop alone, circling the product like a shark before picking it up. Many go with a friend, debating the relative merits of each title before making a decision. Here's one more piece of advice I can give for anyone who tries this: Identify yourself to the manager before loitering around too long. It can help avoid some *really* embarrassing situations!

Fischer was asked the question posed earlier in this chapter to other experts—is it easier or more difficult to market a game with worldwide familiarity and expectations (such as *Pac-Man*)? Fischer says it's undeniably easier:

> The "AIDA" model of consumer behavior describes four steps to a purchase decision: awareness, interest, desire, and action. A well-known franchise gets the awareness issue out of the way, so we're already to second base with a title like *Pac-Man*.

You can peruse Namco's 2002 lineup at www.namco.com.

Jason Enos, Konami

Jason Enos is product manager at Konami of America, whose past projects include *Zone of the Enders* (with the *Metal Gear Solid 2* demo), *Dance Dance Revolution*, *Silent Scope*, *Metal Gear Solid* (and all its iterations), *Silent Hill Greatest Hits*, and many more.

Enos says the term "game marketing" is a very specific subset of activities that stem from traditional consumer marketing or product marketing:

> Buzz words such as *game marketing* affect the mindset of the marketer, often limiting the imagination and creativity of the marketing efforts. It's very easy to fall prey to marketing myopia when the same "game marketing" activities are followed game after game. I constantly evaluate my marketing efforts in this industry to make sure that I'm approaching each game with a product-specific campaign that's tailored and tied to the game's premise and target audience.

What was it like being responsible for bringing an Asian phenomenon like *Dance Dance Revolution* (*DDR*) to America?

> The experience was very self-satisfying on many different levels. Before I was "product manager" on *Dance Dance Revolution*, it was necessary to convince my colleagues that this product could be successful in North America. I began working on this project (outside of company time) as soon as I joined the company in 1999. I spent the next 12 months building an archive of materials—such as music game sales data, consumer comments, press clippings, and industry trends—to help build my case.

When the key people were on board with bringing the product stateside, I spent the next 12 months building my relationships with the underground fan base, spreading the information online in bulletin boards, traveling across the country to meet the media, educating company staff about the game, and generally evangelizing the product wherever/whenever possible.

Even today, I give the same level of attention to *Dance Dance Revolution*, even though the game has released.

Is the marketing for *DDR* really different from that of any other Konami title?

The key advantage to marketing *Dance Dance Revolution* is that it's a completely innovative and unique concept. The concept of the game automatically differentiates *DDR* from every other game on the market. Moreover, the arcade version of the game drives the consumer awareness at high-traffic areas throughout the country, setting up demand for a home version. Unlike most video games, which appeal to one or two segments, *DDR* appeals to multiple segments (kids, families, dance music lovers, fitness-conscious, and so on), enabling the marketing efforts to target a larger group of the population.

From the arcade into the home—Konami's *Dance Dance Revolution* has become an
international hit, where players dance to the beat on special sensors.
(Used with permission by Konami of America, Inc.)

So what were the challenges in launching *DDR?*

The key challenge to marketing *DDR* is that it's a completely innovative and unique concept (exactly the same as the key advantage). Because *DDR* is an entirely new concept that involves the use of a special dance peripheral, it was difficult to accurately convey this message in traditional marketing methods, such as a one-page print advertisement. The other big obstacle was that the music game genre has not enjoyed commercial success in the U.S. market. This historical data was a negative stigma that was often attached to the sales potential of *DDR.*

With all of his experience in the console gaming arena, is there any marketing advice Enos can share with others? "To become an effective marketer in the video game business, it's extremely important to know the product and the target audience," he answers.

Consumers are bombarded with advertisements and messages every day, and the only way to ensure that your message sinks in with the right audience is to be an expert on what you're selling and who you're selling it to. The other big advantage, which is often missing from this industry, is marketing professionals who are actually hardcore gamers or at least know the history of video gaming.

And on becoming a successful marketing specialist, here's a short list of Enos' do's and don'ts:

Do:

1. Challenge the norm.

2. Know your consumer.

3. Know your products.

4. Know your competition.

5. Be creative.

6. Stick to your guns.

7. Build a strong relationship with R&D [Research and Development].

8. Ask gamers what they think.

9. Evaluate market conditions to identify new product ideas/consumer demands.

Don't:

1. Avoid outside input.

2. Think negatively about your products (even the bad ones).

3. Think you hold all of the answers.

4. Talk down to the consumer.

How could someone with little or no cash successfully market their game?

Enos says products with limited budgets are sometimes more fun than products with large budgets because it forces you to be more creative and resourceful.

> These products are perfect exercises for learning the marketing process, and can be very successful and personally rewarding if launched properly. It's very important to be realistic on the budgeting and spending. Always ask yourself if the money could be reallocated to an area that would be more beneficial for the success of the product. Rely heavily on targeted public relations efforts, grassroots marketing at the consumer level, and online tactics. Build a strong relationship with the fans of the product and the R&D [Research and Development] teams because these people will go the extra mile at very minimal cost to help your efforts. Save money by spending more of your own time to accomplish tasks that would normally require budget expense.

Jay Miller, ZIOSoft

As Director of Sales at ZIOSoft, Inc.—one of the most successful Palm and PocketPC game publishers on the planet—Jay Miller chats about the do's and don'ts of game marketing. Future ambitions? "I'd like to be the first to publish a million-unit seller for PDAs," smiles Miller. "Wouldn't we all!" he adds.

When it comes to dishing out marketing advice, Miller offers the following:

> The number one thing anyone from a heavily financed operation to a garage developer needs to do is to sit down and make a plan. In order for marketing to be effective, it has to be planned out and balanced against ROI. Write down a concrete set of goals, and do the research to try and achieve them. Follow the plan, but if it isn't working, don't be too afraid to make changes.

> Do your research. You are going to have to spend money on marketing, no matter what, so make sure that your budget includes an allowance for research. The better you know your market, the better you can position your product.

> If what you are doing is not working, try something else. It is not uncommon for people to do the same thing over and over, yet expect different results each time. If something didn't work the past three times you tried it, perhaps it's time to move on.

Miller was asked to give an example of a savvy marketing effort he's responsible for.

"Hmm…savvy marketing is a toughy because I'm actually a sales guy," Miller cautions, but "One thing I'm proud of, though, is a co-promotion that we worked out with a licensor."

Although Miller isn't permitted to give the name of the licensor, he continues as follows:

> We have a number of titles that are a part of franchises, and we were able to leverage the marketing efforts for a PC title in the franchise to our benefit. We put a special insert into the manual of our title to promote the PC product in return for enhanced online coverage of our product on the PC franchise web site. It has worked pretty well.

As far as setting up and inking the deal, it was fairly simple. I just worked with the marketing and production team to brainstorm the possibility and then figured out the details. From there on, it was fairly easy to agree to without needing a lot of legalese. We both knew what we were looking for, so it was just a matter of figuring out the best way to accomplish a cross-sell without committing a whole lot of additional resources to making it happen.

"Be creative and be flexible, and something will work," encourages Miller.

Is it easier or more difficult to market a PDA game than a console or computer game?

"That's a good question without a concrete answer," answers Miller. He explains:

Scale certainly plays an issue in marketing, and by that I mean that the size of the project has a definite impact on the budget for marketing. The amount of money and resources that have to be committed to a console or computer game suggest a larger marketing budget because more exposure may be necessary to sell enough units to meet your ROI. I would venture that working with a smaller budget to market a PDA title may be more challenging because you have to be creative to get the most out of your money, but the complexity of the program is likely to be much less than that of a premium console or PC game. To sum this up, I don't think that the platform dictates the difficulty, rather the scope of the project.

Finally, what are some of the cheap/grassroots ways to market/promote a PDA game for those running their own business?

"One of the best and least-expensive ways to get some word out is to supply reviewers with copies of your game," answers Miller. He adds:

Even better is to have a plan to distribute a very few prerelease samples to start building some excitement. You definitely want to build momentum up to the launch. It's important to try and establish a relationship with the people behind the [web] sites as well.

Part IV

How to Make It Happen

Chapter 20

Doing It Yourself and the Shareware Revolution

THE EXPERTS

- Howard Tomlinson, Astraware

- Chris Kantrowitz, 7ate9

- John Romero, Monkeystone Games

- Bill Bales, Friendly Software

- Ian Wall, Beermat Software

- Shawnee Sequeira, Small Rockets

- Steve Moraff, MoraffWare

- Thomas Warfield, GoodSol Development

Not all success stories in this book involve getting a job at a well-known development house or publishing company and climbing the ranks from within. Sure, it's probably beneficial to work around the likes of Shigeru Miyamoto or Will Wright, but (similar to what's happening in the music industry with the emergence of many popular independent bands releasing MP3 albums online) some designers have chosen to simply sell their own creations over the Internet, and work from home in many cases.

You can create your own company, corporation, or other legal entity to manufacture, market, and distribute your game, but this chapter focuses on those game producers who distribute and sell their games over the World Wide Web as shareware. For the uninitiated, shareware games are free to download, but a small payment from the user is requested or required to continue playing. This "try-before-you-buy" software may be limited in time (for example, two hours of play) or in features (perhaps three out of 10 levels are available), or the entire game can be given up front in good faith.

Is it really worth releasing your beloved game this way? What are the pros and cons for selling shareware, as opposed to working toward a packaged retail product? The following entries are from folks who made the decision to do it alone, and have succeeded. If this is the road you choose, take heed to this advice.

Howard Tomlinson, Astraware

Howard Tomlinson is the CEO and lead designer at Astraware Ltd (www.astraware.com), a celebrated game studio in the UK known mostly for its award-winning Palm and PocketPC-based titles. Tomlinson started with the PC game *Bzzz!* about 12 years ago, and has held the position of lead designer for the past 6 years. Its most successful products are *Zap!2000*, *Text Twist*, and *Bejeweled* for the PalmOS.

Tomlinson first offers the three most important pieces of advice he would give to a game designer who may want to sell his/her game online:

1. Get a solid group of beta testers to rip your game to shreds. Don't just trust your best friend and your mum, saying "Yup, it looks okay." The very best beta testers are those who give you a list of 50 bugs and complain about every little thing in the game. As much as it hurts you to read those bug lists (even though they only do it to help to improve the game), it's all worthwhile when you get to a version where they say, "Can't find any bugs"—and you know it's ready to meet the world.

Astarwave's Howard Tomlinson says another advantage of being your own boss is that "You can gain and keep a massive customer base, who (for the most part) will be happy to receive offers about your next game!" Check out this assortment of games for the Palm platform. *(Used with permission by Astraware, Ltd.)*

2. Successful games online are those that get the most downloads. And those that get the most downloads are the ones that then get downloaded most. (Everyone else liked it; it must be good, right?) So your real aim is to get those initial bursts of hits!

   Get your game on as many online sites as possible. About a month or two before release, get in touch with editors and reviewers at the sites you like, and let them know about the game. Send a review copy (and complimentary registration) way ahead of release, and ask if they'd like to feature it when it's released. Make sure you follow up with a reminder when it's time!

3. Choose your pricing carefully—too cheap and they won't buy it because "It can't be any good if it's only $10." But be realistic.

Advantages and disadvantages of selling games online? Tomlinson says there are more pros than cons. On the advantages, Tomlinson believes the following to be true:

➤ It's easy to start up—there are some great registration services out there for people who don't want to set up credit card handling themselves.

➤ You can release what you like when you like, and you don't have to go through lengthy box design, legal, marketing, shipping times.

➤ You get money back from your work much sooner—retail royalty checks may be six months behind the actual sales.

For disadvantages: "You're not going to hit the biggest audiences by sticking online. It's got to hit the shops sometime," says Tomlinson.

He offers a few pointers for attracting gamers to your site, aside from "having lots of really cool games on there!"

➤ Make your site attractive and fast, and people will spend longer browsing it.

➤ Make your downloads easy to get to, and make it obvious that the site has frequent updates. People will want to bookmark it then.

➤ Choose good keywords to help search engines find your site, and get other games sites to link to yours wherever possible.

It's one thing getting the players to visit your site (or other download sites where your games can be snagged), but once they download the game, how do you get people to pay for them?

In Tomlinson's opinion, true shareware ("If you like it, please send me some money") just doesn't pay. "I'm not saying that people aren't honest, but they need a good reason to get their wallets out and register software," he says.

> We use two methods to encourage registrations: level-limited demos and games that give a limited number of "free" plays; and after that number is up, put up a nag screen. (The length of this nag screen increases slightly each time.) We also use the ability to submit to our Internet high score tables as an enticement to buy. Some other people prefer to actually cripple their software until registered, but this doesn't seem to work so well for games.

Just how popular are Astraware's Palm and PocketPC games? Tomlinson estimates that in the first 18 months of the release of *Zap!2000*, they had about a half-million downloads. What percentage pay for the product? Tomlinson divulges:

> For most of our games, between 0.5% and 1% of those who download it [will] register. After a good "awareness" campaign or if we've been hyping it for a while, it can get higher than that. [Sometimes] we hit on a completely addictive and absorbing game—our license of the PopCap game *Bejeweled* got registration rates approaching 5% for the first few months. That's definitely not the norm, though!

How about making money as an independent shareware author? Tomlinson admits, "It took a few years of building up a portfolio of games being sold online for the revenue to be enough just to work at it full-time. I think making a reasonable living is attainable, but rich?! I'll still keep my fingers crossed!"

He shares some advice on being a success in this facet of the gaming industry:

> We did it by working full time at it in addition to having normal full-time jobs. Took a couple of years of hard work before it could start to support us enough to just work on the games! We didn't want to go down the route of trying to find external funding—and I don't know how seriously any venture capitalists would take anyone basing their millions on the Internet nowadays.

NOTE

Flip back to Chapter 19, "Public Relations and Marketing," to read advice from Jay Miller on PDA game marketing! Miller is with ZIOSoft (`www.ziosoft.com`), one of the most successful Palm and PocketPC publishers in the biz.

Chris Kantrowitz, 7ate9

Designer Kantrowitz recently left The Groove Alliance, a company best known for its fabulous Webby award-winning Flash games such as *Real Pool 3D*, to begin working with the creative 7ate9 in Atlanta (`www.7ate9.tv`). Here, Kantrowitz talks about the rewards and drawbacks of creating online games.

Kantrowitz talks a bit about what constitutes shareware game design, and in particular, the web games made at The Groove Alliance. "Online game development perspective involves creating games that are played for an average of 15 minutes per session," he begins. The goal is to create games that play in a browser and are accessible to as many players as possible." The online gaming space is like developing a sitcom—quick, entertainment, satisfaction." To achieve this objective, he adheres to a few fundamental design principles:

> ➤ **It's important for the controls to be simple**. Arrow keys and the spacebar are a good start. We start the process of development assuming that the user has no gaming experience at all.
>
> ➤ **Playability/re-playability**. Our games should be playable without reading the directions. The design should be good enough that all controls for the game are obvious, and the game should be fun enough that people are constantly coming back for more.
>
> ➤ **Use of resources**. The longer people have to wait for the game to download, the less likely they are to play it. Online game players are eight times more likely to be on narrow band than broadband. As a result, you have to be cognizant of how to use resources in a way that delivers your idea to the end user efficiently.

He adds, "Online games are today's equivalent of early consoles—the success is in the subtleties of the design. Graphics and audio are secondary to gameplay."

The best piece of advice for others?

> For someone who is just getting started in online, I will say that this is the best place to experiment. The barriers to entry on the distribution side are much lower. As a result, distribution partners are very willing to take risks on the types of content they'll bring to the consumer.

So how does The Groove Alliance make its money?

We are a platform, so most of our money is made through the licensing of our technology. These licensing deals take many forms. One scenario has us licensing games that were created by our developers. Our clients license our platform and the games that are created with the platform. The second scenario is when a developer has a project that requires a technology like ours. We would then license our technology straight to them for development.

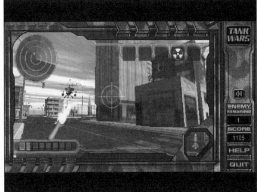

Kantrowitz says you should try to experiment in your game design and distribution methods whenever possible: "This opportunity is rare in the traditional game market; there's too much associated risk. Today, the game business takes risks only with successes, which creates a problem for those who have innovative ideas." Seen here are images from The Groove Alliance games *3D Pool*, *Tank Wars*, and *Dark Demon*.
(Used with permission by The Groove Alliance, Inc.)

The online gaming market has to be viewed in a very different way from the traditional game market. Online games are a media type similar to television and radio. The beauty of our distribution channel is that the traditional publisher becomes irrelevant. Our market works differently; we provide a platform to our developers, and they create content—we distribute it for them. We're concerned only about eyeballs. The more people play, the more valuable the real estate being sold.

Kantrowitz says they need worry only about creating the games—marketing of these titles is not their responsibility:

> Attracting people to our games is not an issue for us. The Groove Alliance's responsibility is creating good content. Our partner sites bear the responsibility of pointing their traffic to the games. This is why we consider our games more like traditional entertainment products. In television, the responsibility of bringing eyeballs to a show falls on the network. Creating good content is the responsibility of the producers. It works the same way for us.

And it seems to work quite well for them. Kantrowitz reports, "The Groove Alliance's games are being played millions of times per month—we've calculated that at any moment our games are being played by about 30,000 people."

The Groove Alliance is a relatively small team. Can someone become rich at doing it themselves without lots of commercial overhead?

> When the market grows the way we expect it to, there will be additional revenues that may double the size of the game industry. Online games have their own niche. The money generated by this growth will not necessarily flow into traditional channels. The most exciting part of the online gaming industry is the fact that it's not controlled by the major players. This leaves a very wide hole to be filled by smaller, more creative shops.

Kantrowitz believes there is potential for online games to produce more net profit than traditional games, and the developers who are involved in this market will do very well for themselves as a result.

Starting a new company is not a difficult task, says Kantrowitz. "File a few papers with the Secretary of State and off you go. But there are a few questions you have to ask yourself."

> ➤ What are we going to do? There's no point in starting the company unless you have a mandate.
>
> ➤ Why do I think I can succeed? Do you have an idea for a game/technology that's so unique that it distinguishes you from the rest of the market?
>
> ➤ Who is going to make up my team? No dopes allowed. If you're going to start a small shop, one bad egg can ruin the whole recipe. Take care during the hiring process to ensure that you check an applicant's background and that you truly understand his or her capabilities.

> From a business standpoint, remember that cash is king. There should be *no frivolous spending*. Buy used furniture (a lot of dot-coms have gone out of business). There's a simple mantra attached to this: Buy what you need, not what you want. There are a lot of useful items on eBay. It's amazing how fast $100 here and there can add up. There's always a temptation when starting a company to buy all of the "toys" before you recognize an actual need for them. We didn't have a proper phone system for three years.

He continues with the following thoughts:

> Publishers generally like to see companies make the most of their money. It's a sign of a well-run business. They'll garner a greater trust for you when they see smart money management.

The final thing to think about is what your end game is. Some people start companies, thinking that they'd like to run them for the rest of their lives. Others look to venture capital financing for a push to become much larger firms, and there are those who would love to be bought by a larger company at some point. Whatever your goal is, make sure that you structure your company in such a way that you can achieve that end game. This would require you getting a decent corporate attorney to advise you on the formation structure that would best accommodate your needs. If not done properly, it can sting you at a later date.

Where is the Net going in terms of game distribution? What about cell phone/PDA gaming? Kantrowitz believes that the Net will play a greater and more compelling role in gaming over time:

The Internet is a very broad concept. There are those who understand it to be the place you go when you're using a web browser. Some users don't associate email with the Internet. Everything that brings data over a distance is the Internet. Not just from the standpoint of bringing players together in multi-player environments, but changing how traditional publishers conduct their business.

The web game business is a separate issue. Thinking of traditional publishers, there are so many fantastic business opportunities that the Internet offers. The greatest example of this is the success of the persistent world games. EA sells *Ultima Online* at the stores for $50. It then charges $10 per month for the service that allows people to play together online. This additional $10 per month can make a company very profitable.

There's a much broader application for this concept. The broader application is to understand how subscriptions can add to the satisfaction of the player experience. Look at the sports business on the consoles. These games sell millions of units each year. Part of the development cycle for games requires that these games come out like clockwork each and every year so that player stats and the construction of the games mirrors (to the best of their ability) the current lineup of the teams. I believe that those who play these games would be more interested in paying a monthly fee to get stats updates, which would coincide with the current construct of the teams (during the season). Now that the console manufacturers have begun to add the hardware to make this idea feasible (modems/hard drives), I think there will be a shift in how these companies approach the timelines for their development process.

To wrap up, Kantrowitz says that on the device front, he doesn't think that games will play a huge role (in the near future) on PDAs and cell phones: "They don't have the ergonomic form factor to adequately play games on them. Trivia games, snake, puzzle games can work, and there's a market for them, but I don't think it's going to be the windfall that everyone is expecting."

To read about and play all of The Groove Alliance's titles, visit www.3dgroove.com.

John Romero, Monkeystone Games

Veteran game designer John Romero has been in the industry for more than 20 years, published more than 60 games, and founded three game development companies. His games—including the *DOOM* series, *Wolfenstein 3D*, *Quake*, *Heretic*, and *Hexen*—have sold millions of copies on a wide range of gaming systems.

Romero is currently running Monkeystone Games (www.monkeystone.com), a company that develops and publishes small games for several platforms, including cell phones and PDAs.

So, is this the end of PC game development?

On the contrary, answers Romero:

"We recently released our first in-house developed PC game, *Hyperspace Delivery Boy!* [The game] was originally developed on the PocketPC; then it was ported to the PC and enhanced with voice dialogue and crisper sounds and longer music," says Romero.

Romero was asked to chat about game design for those creating PDA games.

> ➤ Make sure you design your control interface to take advantage of the input offered by the device, which means no keyboard—but a really cool clickable screen.

> ➤ Design a game that people on PDAs will actually want to play, which is primarily a businessperson's gaming needs (quick in and out).

> ➤ Don't design too large a game; save space, reduce download times, and focus on your game being a replayable toy.

Monkeystone's John Romero (pictured here) says this about creating games for the PDA: "Don't expect huge sales numbers because they aren't there—this is still a really small market." Also pictured here are three screen grabs for the PocketPC game *Hyperspace Delivery Boy!*
(Used with permission by Monkeystone Games.)

Ironically, Romero admits that he broke all the rules:

> We did design the interface correctly, at least, but the game is too big for a PDA; it's not the kind of game that biz folks like because it's a long adventure, and it looks too cute for mainstream adults.

So, what are the key differences between creating a game for a PDA and one for a console or computer game?

"Well, you have to deal with a very small screen, so right there you have to make some very different choices," begins Romero. "Also, you can't make a game too fast because the PDA audience isn't dexterous enough for it—other than that, there are excellent sound, graphics, and input on the PocketPC."

But can someone really make a living by creating and selling PDA games? "You definitely need to have a stockpile of fun, cheap games that you're selling yourself to stay afloat with a small team," says Romero. "That's just staying afloat—to make more money, you really need to augment your income with other projects on platforms that have more users."

> **NOTE**
> Romero says it costs roughly $80,000 to create a PDA game in about six months. Considerably cheaper than a console, PC, or Game Boy Advance game!

Finally, from a career standpoint, Romero was asked to give some advice on breaking into the PDA game industry:

> ➤ Do it as a hobby first; don't dive into it without some experience.
>
> ➤ Don't expect huge sales numbers because they aren't there—this is still a really small market.
>
> ➤ If you develop a popular game on a PDA, make sure that your code is structured for portability, so you can move the game to other platforms and recoup your investment quickly.

Bill Bales, Friendly Software

Bill Bales is the CEO of Contus Corporation, which wholly owns Friendly Software, the developers of many golf games for Microsoft since 1988; and now, creators of AboutGolf.com's *World Tours Golf* titles for free on the Net (www.aboutgolf.com).

Bales offers some sobering words of wisdom on launching games solely on the Internet:

> ➤ Don't quit your day job.
>
> ➤ Research the market for which you want to build a game, and make sure that you're creating a viable product.
>
> ➤ Don't spend foolishly on the project, but instead use sweat equity and the sweat equity of others.
>
> ➤ Make sure that the product is outstanding.

If the game has already been made, Bales says much of his advice would be the same, with minor twists:

- ➤ Don't quit your day job.

- ➤ Pursue all means of exposing your game for free.

- ➤ If you have a truly viable game that people love, find a marketing partner that can get it exposed properly.

On various advantages and disadvantages to selling a game online (without a formal publisher or retail distribution partner), Bales says that these are the key advantages:

You don't have to follow the subjective design and product management desires of your publisher. When Friendly Software made golf games for Microsoft, the environment was oppressive.

If you can facilitate direct sales, you can net a lot more while selling for a lot less. Even with a marketing partner, this is true. We made $5 a unit with Microsoft on a $50 product, but if we were to sell with Real Networks as a marketing partner, we could make $10/unit on a $20 product.

The key disadvantages of doing it yourself, according to Bales: You don't get any guarantees; and you don't have the exposure, the distribution machine, or the publisher branding behind you. ("We got a lot of money from Microsoft—we still give our game away for free.") Seen here, two images from the free online game, *AboutGolf World Tours Golf*.

(Used with permission by Friendly Software Corporation.)

Bales adds the following:

Note that in the future, electronic distribution will become a real force. It might make it easier for little guys to distribute a product; I say *might* because the trend so far has been that the large web site brands are the ones that can attract the users and hence take the place of the traditional publishers. Nonetheless, this is better because there are fewer middlemen.

How do you attract gamers to the AboutGolf.com site?

> Admittedly, it's not easy without an ad budget, but we pursue all the free listings and exposure we can get. Plus, we run online events sponsored by sites that promote the game. We have a good product that download sites such as Cnet.com will expose for us (but only if the product is free). And, of course, the press helps expose the game.

After the game is downloaded, how are you paid for it?

> We really don't do that yet; our goal might be to have a superior product that people might pay for, but our preference would be for a new pay-for-play online facility to be compelling enough to drive revenues and allow us to continue to give the game away for free.

> We also will implement more and more tasteful strategies for putting promotional messages within the game for which we can get paid by advertisers. NCsoft's model for *Lineage* is our favorite "free game, pay for enhanced online play." We will still offer free online play also, at a lesser level.

Bales reminds gamers that Friendly's *World Tours* series of golf games are free to download, but they charge for some course add-ons and will soon launch a pay-to-play facility. "We've had about 300,000 downloads overall from c|Net, but were #1 for quite awhile at Softseek.com (now part of c|Net), and the #1 sports game at Go.com for a while."

Some game designers think they must reinvent the wheel—come up with a truly unique game. But Friendly Software proved it can be done building on an existing game that everyone knows (golf). What can game designers learn from this?

> It's great to reinvent the wheel. One out of a thousand will succeed. The most cost-effective and lowest-risk approach is to take a great idea and improve on it, or take a known product genre and do something better with it. Also, keep in mind that necessity is the mother of invention, and invention is *not* the mother of necessity. Translated: The market decides what they like—you don't. Hence, the best way to reinvent the wheel is to start out by not doing it—if the market steers you in a direction (necessity) that you figure out how to improve on things, you might find that you've reinvented the wheel without trying.

Without all that commercial overhead, can someone become rich at doing it themselves? "Yes, but it shouldn't be the goal, and it won't happen very often," says Bales. He expands:

> Rich should equal happy. If you're happy making games, very good at it, very good at getting it marketed, and very lucky, you just might make some money.

What's involved in starting your own development company?

> I asked this question in 1988 of some "experts" at that time. They told me not to go into the business—that was the sum total of their advice. But that made me want to do it more than ever.

> It takes a lot to put together a top-notch dev firm. But you've got to start somewhere. If you start by moonlighting or have other means of supporting yourself, it's a matter of being very smart and learning quickly and doing it. Know your market and know what it takes to be a dev operation. You've got to design the product and program it—everyone knows that. But you also have to do an outstanding job

of determining the optimum architecture so you can modify and upgrade the product—you need to control and document your source code, document and manage your dev process, and do lots and lots of testing. And more than anything, don't assume that there are zillions of dollars out there—maybe there are, but there are zillions of products chasing those dollars. A product that sells 50,000 units is a hit—so don't count on selling millions.

Bales is always up for some free personal advice and consultation, so be sure to drop him a line if you have any questions, comments, or suggestions: bill@friendlysoftware.com.

Ian Wall, Beermat Software

You may not have heard of Beermat Software, but chances are that you've played *Dope Wars*, one of the most popular (and controversial) free Windows games available. Focusing on the business side of selling and buying illegal substances, this game is not designed for players under 17 years of age.

For the past four years, Ian Wall has worked on products such as *EBBS/w* (*Backgammon* client for an Internet *Backgammon* server) and *Dope Wars*. Future products include a multiplayer version of *Dope Wars* and a trading game similar to *Dope Wars*.

Factoid: Beermat's *Dope Wars* is based on the concept of a 20-year-old DOS game, but all the code was written from scratch by Ian Wall. He says, "The look and feel is different from the original, and the feature set is greatly increased." Wall is honored to have received an email from the original author himself, who was "absolutely blown away that the concept is still alive and kicking today—he said he was impressed with where I had taken it. He even suggested some new features to add!"

In a lengthy interview, Wall first offers some helpful advice for game designers/developers looking to sell a game on the Internet.

- ➤ **Dedication**. It's *hard* to make a living off shareware software. A lot of shareware developers start off using their spare time to develop their products while holding down a regular job that actually pays the bills. That makes for long days and many lost weekends spent developing and testing your product, and supporting it as you try to grow a user base. It's easy to think, "Is this worth it?" when the hours are long, the money is short, and all your friends are in a bar having a good time! Dedicate yourself to your cause and give yourself a chance to succeed. It's better to have loved and lost than never to have loved at all…

- ➤ **Listen to and support customers**. They are your audience, your customers, and potential word-of-mouth marketers of your products. They probably use your product in ways you didn't envision and request features you didn't anticipate. You won't get a better focus group to advise you on your products, so take note of what they request—and if enough people request things, build 'em in, even if you can't see the need! If people have problems with your software, try to respond in a timely, polite, and helpful manner. You'll win a lot of friends and recommendations if you keep your customers happy, not to mention a bunch of willing beta testers!

➤ **Stay ahead of the competition**. A lot of early version shareware is generally easy for some-one to duplicate in terms of features. Compare someone trying to write a similar product to *Dope Wars* in their spare time to someone trying to write *Quake III: Arena* in their spare time. If you build it, and it's popular and relatively simple, expect a flood of knockoffs. I've experienced that myself. Try to keep improving your product on a regular basis (although not so often that you flood your customers with multiple versions).

With this advice in mind, what are the pros and cons for choosing this route?

Go to your local software retailer and count the number of products on their shelves. Then go to Download (www.download.com) and count what's available there (more than 20,000 products). At ZDNet.com, browse the products and read the thousands of user opinions about the products. Pick a box off the shelf at your retailer and ask, "What did *others* think of this?" and find the question unanswered. Take the box to the checkout and pay for it, and calculate how much goes to the retailer, how much goes to the distributor, how much goes to the publisher, how much goes to the developer, and how much of that load you as the customer are carrying—and as the developer, how little a percentage you would be getting!

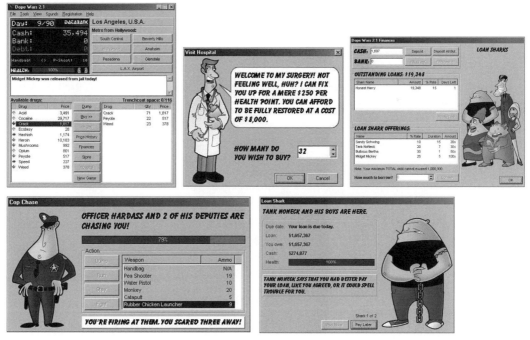

Images from the incredibly successful *Dope Wars*. The game's main window; a visit to the dodgy doctor to get fixed up; chased by Officer "Hardass"; manage your bank accounts, debts, and loans from sharks; and Pay now, or else…

(Used with permission by Beermat Software, Ltd.)

Compare that with buying it direct from the developer online. Think about updating your product and instantly making it available online, as opposed to out-of-date CDs sitting on shelves. Go to the same store two months later and see how many of the products you counted on the previous visit are still available, as opposed to being moved off to make way for newer products. Need I add more to the benefits of online distribution? Both the customer and the developer benefit.

From Beermat's perspective, we make cheap-and-cheerful low-technology software that's immensely popular (three million downloads and counting), but not substantial enough in itself to demand a sticker price that could cover the cost of manufacturing and distributing a physical product, as well as allowing the retailer and publisher to make a profit. We charge $5 to register the full version of *Dope Wars*. It's unlikely that a publisher would even pick up a product with such a low sticker price, and thus online distribution was our only option—a happy one at that, though.

How does Beermat attract gamers to `www.beermatsoftware.com`?

"Pictures of naked women work wonders for attracting the best male demographics," teases Wall. But seriously:

We've lived solely off word-of-mouth for *Dope Wars*. The game has now been in Download.com's top 50 downloaded games for 122 consecutive weeks, most of that in the top five, without a single penny being spent on advertising. We've tried to build a community around our web site—allowing people to create dealer accounts, post scores into the World Tables to see how they compare to other dealers around the world, form cartels (groups of dealers), have inter-cartel competitions for the best-performing cartels, message boards, and so on—in order to keep people interested in the software and keep them coming back to the site even after they've downloaded the game.

How do you get people to pay for these games?

I remember seeing statistics saying that fewer than one in 100 users will register shareware software, and if you can equal or beat that one percent conversion rate, you're doing well. The evidence we've seen with our shareware products bear that out. That can be quite disheartening for someone trying to break into the shareware industry! In terms of trying to generate revenue from shareware software itself, it's a tricky balancing act; you have to give customers enough features in the shareware version to get them hooked, but not so many that it isn't worth them paying to get the extra features of the registered version!

Other potential revenue streams exist:

➤ Advertising in the software is one way, although that market has recently taken a pounding.

➤ Distribution partnerships (piggybacking) is another—you distribute another company's software with yours, and if the user actually uses the piggybacked software, you'll receive a payment.

➤ Merchandising is another way (T-shirts, mugs, mouse pads, figurines, and so on), but you'd have to have a reasonably successful product out there in order to have a big enough target audience for the merchandise to make the initial outlay worth it.

The bottom line, says Wall, is that the best way to make money selling software is to develop something that people will buy. Fortunately, as touched on earlier, *Dope Wars* has been downloaded more than three million times—and registration payments have been received from more than 70 different countries! Wall adds, "Try to get *that* from retail distribution!"

Still on the topic of money, Wall was asked if selling games online could really pay off in the long run. Can you get rich at it?

> It's possible, but rare. For a while, I held out hope that *Dope Wars* would make me the next Bill Gates, but that "less than 1%" figure is holding me back somewhat! You have to be ready to embrace success if it arrives. If your garage-built product turns into a financial success, chase the market and try to expand the product in terms of quality and features, using the financial success gained to bring in some help with development and so on, and also to develop companion products. MS-DOS built Microsoft. *Wolfenstein* built id Software…

> Remember, though, that the vast majority of shareware developers are in it for the sheer pleasure of developing a product that someone else finds useful or fun. A lot of shareware starts out life as developers filling a need of their own and then wondering if others have the need. *Dope Wars* started that way; its original intended audience was 20 people in my office, and the thrill I got from my friends enjoying it was every bit as savory as the realization that millions of other people enjoy it, too!

Any tips on starting and running a shareware-based company? Wall says, "This is a little tough to answer because I've done my best to keep Beermat Software a one-man shop to keep overhead down." He continues:

> I contract out the necessary legal work and accounting work because that's beyond my skill set and knowledge, but have tried to do the rest myself. You have to be a bit of everything when you're starting out alone. I've been game designer, game developer, web site developer, principal test manager, deal broker, PR and media spokesman, support representative…

Where does Wall see the future of the Net and gaming?

> As broadband becomes more readily available, I see the Net taking over as the premier method of game distribution. More and more games are online-centric in their gameplay, and most of them have Internet-based patching mechanisms to download updates. When the day comes when you can download the big retail games in less time than it takes to visit the store, I expect to see the Net explode as a distribution mechanism. There is a significant lead time from "gold" code to the actual mechanics of retail distribution, such as pressing the CDs, printing and manufacturing the packaging, and distributing to the stores compared to making a download available digitally. As soon as developers figure out they can claw back (possibly) weeks of time from their shipping deadline and instead use that time to do the million last-minute fixes needed in their game, they'll embrace the Net, too.

What about PDA/cell phone gaming? As a gadget-orientated consumer, Wall is constantly disappointed by the quality of displays on cell phones, so he doesn't think this will take off too fast:

Sure, [cell phones] may be "Internet-ready" and SMS-capable, but with a four-line-by-nine-character display and just a numeric keypad, it's a chore to actually use those features. Throw in the low bandwidth of today's wireless Internet, and it will be awhile before it becomes fun for a consumer to play games on a cell phone. The potential is exciting, though, especially for a low-tech game such as *Dope Wars*. Imagine a central market data server issuing prices; and millions of people using their wireless phones on subways, trains, in meetings, and so on to buy and sell drugs in a real marketplace, possibly interacting with other wireless users in the locale, doing local deals, and so on; or having turf wars if they're in another user's proximity! Damn, that sounds like fun—where are my WAP manual and development tools?

Shawnee Sequeira, Small Rockets

"In terms of future aspirations, I want Small Rockets to continue to be the premier developer of wired/downloadable games on the planet!" says Shawnee Sequeira, co-founder and development director at Small Rockets (www.smallrockets.com), the UK-based developers of such popular shareware titles as *Tower of the Ancients* and *Art Is Dead*.

Sequeira offers three important pieces of advice for game designers selling their games online:

> ➤ **Be prepared**. Take the time to research the market for your game, ask yourself why you want to do your game, and make sure that your game will appeal to the right audience.

> ➤ **Be determined**. These things don't happen overnight, and anyone willing to get into this space and be successful will need to see the bigger picture and stick with it. It takes lots of stamina and hard work, but if you really want it, you'll make it happen.

> ➤ **Be smart**. The best company in the world can't live on code alone! You need to have capital to start up, you need money in case there are things outside of your control that affect your business, and you need to protect your rights and your IP. I've seen many small groups so desperate for cash that they give up any leveraging power they have and lose the one thing that's going to make them money—their game.

But Sequeira says following the preceding rules can pay off in the long run:

For Small Rockets, the advantages are numerous: We get to create games that we want to do and that people want to play. We get higher revenues because there aren't as many middlemen. And we get to tap into an audience that we may not have been able to reach in more traditional models. These are just a few of them.

As in any business, there are downsides to online distribution. Says Sequeira:

The disadvantages aren't as many, but I would say the big one is that it's not easy being the early adopter. With the changes in the web industry affecting games, too, the digital revolution is moving more slowly than expected. This means that there isn't necessarily a lot of upfront money for development, and you may have to wait longer for some of your investments to make their money back. But I guess even taking this into account, there's no denying the future, and that future is about digital distribution and the mass market. Surviving is what counts.

On getting gamers to the site to download the games, Sequeira says it's easy for Small Rockets because the games speak for themselves:

> They're small, easily downloadable, easy to pick up and play—and most importantly, they're fun. We've been lucky in that we haven't had to do a lot of marketing to generate interest. The games have done this in their own way. It's quite bizarre, really. I've never experienced anything like it. We've got a following without having to do much about it!

When the trial version is downloaded, how does Small Rockets get gamers to cough up the cash?

> It's really important to remember that your customers don't want to jump through a bunch of hoops to get something they want—when they want a game in a shop, they merely pick it up, take it to the register, and pay for it. That's it. With Small Rockets, we've tried to keep it that easy. Customers download the game demo (which is actually the whole game, compressed and locked). If they like it and want to purchase it, they go to our shop, buy a unique user key (which takes mere minutes), and then they're away and playing. There's no need to download more files; no need to buy a game that you've never played before; no more hassle.

> Look at it this way: In the time it would take me to get down to my local EB and back, I could have a new original game up and running on my PC for half the cost, and I didn't even have to leave the comfort of my own couch. That's pretty sweet if you ask me. And soon people will be able to download top-quality games for mobile phones, set top boxes, consoles—you name it.

Small Rockets has had success with remakes of classic games (such as *Tower of the Ancients*, which is based on *Tetris*), and Sequeira presents her opinion on why this is so:

> There's a reason why some game types are popular—it's because people are comfortable with certain game types and never get tired of playing them. Look at games like *Solitaire* and *Mahjongg*—people the world over play these games endlessly. Why? Because they're free? That can't be it entirely; there are a lot of free games on the Web and lots of free games that are bundled with PCs. It's got a lot to do with the fact that people know how to play them and they're simple. People don't want to feel stupid when they're playing a game; they want to be entertained. They don't want to read a manual for three hours or learn a complex set of button or key pushes; they just want to play and get some satisfaction.

> That's what gets me: Games keep getting bigger and more complicated and have more bells and whistles than people really want. When was the last time you finished a 40-hour, full-priced game? Who's got 40 hours these days to devote to something like that? What about people who've got a spare 30 minutes here or there while they're waiting for the kids to come home from school or while they're on their lunch hour? It seems so straightforward to me that I really don't understand what some developers are thinking.

> I don't think flooding the market with any old rubbish does developers any favors, either. The point is that you can take an established game and give it a twist or give it something different to make it unique. Instead of spending time trying to come up with the most original game ever, that time could be spent making a game that stands out among other games of that type or have that something quirky that your customer just can't resist.

How can a shareware designer cash in on this school of thought?

> I don't think it's realistic to say that someone can set up two inexperienced people in a room and get rich off making games. I know too much about what it has taken to set up Small Rockets. We have some of the most talented people in the UK games industry working in the company, and even with all their experience and know-how, it's still hard going and we're still learning.

> I could be putting my foot in my mouth and two 15-year-old hackers might create the next big game franchise from their garage, but the chances of that really happening are minute. The good thing about doing digitally distributed games is that anyone can do them—this is true. Are they going to get rich quick off it? No. At least, not right now. And besides, if you're only in it to make money, shouldn't you be a stockbroker, a doctor, a lawyer, or one of those professions your mom always tried to get you to do?

"If I knew then what I know now, would I still have helped start up Small Rockets?" asks Sequeira. "I think my parents ask me this a lot!"

> Starting up a business of any nature is about sacrifice and not having any free time. Don't expect to have a social calendar for the first two years. And do accept that some things are going to go fruity. It's also really important to do research to find out if you've really got what it takes to compete in your sector. Equally important is the discipline of having a good business plan and good cash-flow analysis. Be hard on yourself and your idea—is it going to work? What's realistic?

> After you think you've put yourself through a rigorous self-awareness program and have raised some cash, you need a great accountant, an honest lawyer, and a sympathetic bank manager. You'll count on these people heavily.

> The rest of it, like making the games, seems a cake walk after that. If you get through the initial setup of the company and you've been honest with yourself about what you expect to achieve, you should be in a pretty good position.

Is Small Rockets going in the direction of PDA or cell phone gaming, a current trend in the industry? Will portable PC gaming become huge?

> It's really hard to say. If I had looked in my crystal ball 12 months ago, I would've thought that the digital world would have progressed much farther than it has. Having said that, I do think there will be connected mass market devices that people will want to play games on, and that these devices will eventually be able to do all sorts of things that just can't be done right now. I think we're just now seeing the potential of devices such as mobile phones, PDAs, and so on.

> I think the biggest problems we face now as developers of games are a) the barrier to entry—that is, that a few powerful companies control the channels; and b) these companies aren't organized enough yet to standardize their technology.

How are we supposed to create compelling games with WAP and with no money? When is there going to be good technology and money for doing this stuff? "It'll happen eventually," Sequeira affirms. "And I can't wait for the day that I carry around one small portable device that I can talk to people on, play games on, go into a shop and buy something on—hell, even turn on my lights in my house!"

"The point about creating games is making ones that people want to play, that are fun, and that are of a high quality—it doesn't always have to be the most original game out there," says Shawnee Sequeira of Small Rockets. "Most of the time, those original titles crash and burn because people just can't get their heads around them." Shown here, a handful of Small Rockets titles: *Star Monkey*, *MAD: Global Thermonuclear Warfare*, *Kayak Extreme*, and *Art Is Dead*.
(© Small Rockets, used with permission by Small Software Ltd.)

Steve Moraff, MoraffWare

Steve Moraff was one of the first independent game developers to release shareware in the early 1980s, though he was not aware of the term *shareware* until a few years later. Some of his best-selling work includes *MoreJongg*, *SphereJongg*, and *RingJongg*—three variations of the classic Asian tile game *Mahjongg*, available from his Florida company, MoraffWare (www.moraff.com).

When asked why a game developer would prefer to go the shareware route as opposed to working at a development house, Moraff offers this straightforward guidance:

> The bottom line is that authors have to decide what kind of lifestyle they want. If they self-publish shareware, they have a real relationship with their users and they're their own boss, but they have to handle a lot of non-programming work to support their business. If they go with a publisher, they have to do what the publisher wants, and they're at the mercy of the random winds of the corrupt retail distribution system, but they don't have to deal with non-programming tasks as much.

Moraff and company's shareware offers full games, but with fewer background images, music, and tile sets to choose from. The following are Moraff's opinions on finding the right way to encourage gamers to pay money:

> Shareware reminders generally have to be somewhat obnoxious to work. Making games stop function-ing after a 30-day trial may be the most effective way, but it really annoys users and cuts down on dis-tribution. Annoying nag screens that have to be clicked off at the end of the game are what I use, and I find them to be the best balance between the need to get registrations and the need to maintain a desir-able shareware game.
>
> I do have a particularly annoying second nag screen that appears after about eight hours of use.

What are the most important pieces of advice Moraff can give a game designer who may want to sell his or her game online?

> This may seem trite, but my advice would be to make a real contribution to the world and forget the games. This is a world filled with problems and hope, and those of us who are skilled programmers can do a lot if we put our minds to it. Educational software, scientific software, and even business software can help make the world a better place.
>
> If you have to make games, make good games. There are plenty of mindless violence games out there, but games don't have to be that way. Try something unique, perhaps something that requires math or science to get through the game. My real advice for a new game designer who wants to make actual money as well as making games is to specialize and look for very small niches. Don't make a 3D shoot-em-up like everyone else, because only the top game or two in any niche makes any real money. That's why I suggest making unique games.

On the topic of selling your game online without a formal publisher versus a more traditional retail distribution partner, Moraff says he's in a good position to discuss this because his games are now available in stores:

> When you sell online, you can do anything you want. You are your own boss, and you make the rules. You also do all the work. There's no limit to how much money you can make because you're making your own rules. In retail, you can make only as much money as your publisher allows. They have to get the distribution for your product, and they have to spend money to promote it. When that works, it's nice because you have steady income with no overhead for production. Watch out, though—retail is a very cutthroat, nasty business. We have a very good publisher doing our retail work now, but previous com-panies that we negotiated with actually tried to wipe us out to prevent us from making deals with others. It's also not uncommon for publishers to simply not pay the royalties they owe. Several compa-nies we negotiated with are effectively bankrupt, and rumor has it they haven't paid royalties owed.

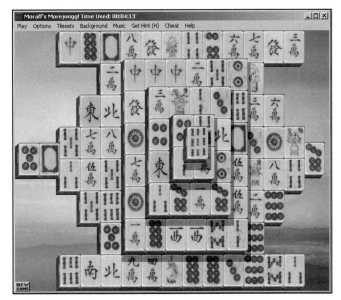

On promoting MoraffWare games, owner Steve Moraff says they have a webmaster on staff who has been in the online world since the early '80s: "He handles search engine placement, software distribution, and other marketing—single-person companies often find the programmer doing this work, but that slows new product development." Pictured here is Moraff's *MoreJongg*.
(Used with permission by Moraff Games.)

If someone gives in to the "nag screen" when playing a game like *MoreJongg* or *SphereJongg*, what does the gamer get in return after registering?

> We offer a lot when a customer buys from us. We support long hours on our 800 numbers, and we do whatever it takes to make every customer happy. We have always been dedicated to impeccable service. Game purchasing is very, very discretionary; and there are many, many free games, so you want to offer everything you can to paying customers.

And just how popular are Moraff's games? "All of our games together have 6–10 million copies distributed over the 16-year history of MoraffWare," says Moraff. And this doesn't count the many CD compilations that include his games.

Roughly, what percentage of users pay for the product? Moraff says their products enjoy a registration rate between 1 in 30 and 1 in 1,000.

Can someone look at the MoraffWare model and be as successful? Can someone make it rich selling their games online? Moraff says it certainly can be done. But with this caveat:

> If you focus on becoming rich, you will likely make no money at all. Except for a few cases, the money is made in this business by starting with the smallest of revenue amounts and then compounding small increases until the numbers are quite big. That has certainly been the MoraffWare way over our 16 years in business.

Thomas Warfield, GoodSol Development

If you've ever played *Pretty Good Solitaire*, you'll want to pull up a chair and read this interview with the president of GoodSol Development (www.goodsol.com), Thomas Warfield. This extremely popular *Solitaire* collection has been around since 1995.

> Selling via shareware is far more profitable for the developer than selling via retail with a publisher. If you sell retail through a publisher, you'll get at most 10%–20% of the wholesale price (which is maybe half of the retail price). This is assuming that you get paid by the publisher at all. Selling shareware, you typically get 80%—90% of the retail price, depending on e-commerce costs."

Like some products from the other shareware developers in this chapter, GoodSol's *Pretty Good Solitaire* is available at retail as well, so Warfield has a good grip on which distribution method brings in more dollars:

> There's a version of our program that has sold very well at retail (in the six figures of copies); nevertheless, the shareware sales have made far more money (more than 10 times) than retail sales because we get so much more from the sale. Retail publisher sales can be a nice add-on, but should never be relied on exclusively. In fact, the only way to do it is to not have that commercial overhead. Most retail games hardly make back their development cost. Most retail game companies lose money. Most shareware game companies make money.

Pretty Good Solitaire and *Free Solitaire* (GoodSol's freeware product) have (combined) been downloaded more than five million times, according to Warfield. "About three percent of the people who download our shareware products buy. The industry average for games is generally around one percent or lower," says Warfield.

So what's the secret to GoodSol's success? Warfield says to follow these rules:

1. Make a good game that's fun to play.

2. Either partner with someone who knows marketing or learn marketing yourself. No one will play your game, no matter how good it is, if no one has ever heard of it. For example, GoodSol enjoys various means of Internet marketing, such as search engines, download sites, links, Internet advertising, and so forth.

3. Unless you've found someone else to do it, expect to spend 80% or more of your time doing marketing and customer service rather than actual programming.

How does GoodSol ask gamers to pay for the product? "By asking them to pay for it," teases Warfield.

> Seriously, you start by asking for the sale in as many places as possible, on the web site and in the product. The best way to learn about the most effective ways to market shareware is to join the Association of Shareware Professionals at www.asp-shareware.org and learn from other members.

On the GoodSol web site (www.goodsol.com) is this warning: "*Pretty Good Solitaire* may be addictive. We are not responsible for lost productivity; neglected spouses, children, or pets. We are not responsible for lost sleep because you stay up to play 'just one more game.'"

But how does GoodSol ask people to pay for shareware, exactly? That is, are their games limited in time? Features? What are the ways shareware authors limit the play so people pay? What works best? Warfield answers with the following:

> Put links to the order page everywhere: in the menus, on nag screens, buttons in the game, and so on. Yes, the game is limited in time to 30 days trial. Actually, it keeps working after 30 days, but various features are taken away after a certain number of days. For example, some time after 30 days, the undo stops working and puts up a nag screen with an order link instead. Some authors have had success at completely stopping the game after 30 days, but I've found that a gradual decline in features works best for me.

Warfield suggests you avoid reinventing the wheel in game design:

> Inventing a totally new game—unless it's an absolutely groundbreaking classic, it's likely to be a good way *not* to make any money. The problem with inventing something totally new is that you have to create the market for it and explain what it is, which is very difficult. It's much easier to start with a game that everybody knows.

> Also, the gaming community seems obsessed with making games that only teenage boys are interested in. Ninety percent of all games are aimed at teenage boys, and teenage boys are only a small part of the population. Plus, they usually have a limited amount of money. On the other hand, there are lots of grandmothers, and they usually have a lot of money. If you want to make a game that makes money, don't make a game for a teenager—make a game that your grandmother would play.

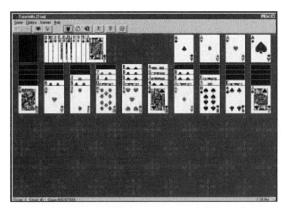

Why create a computer card game? GoodSol's Thomas Warfield says, "The market already exists and people already understand what the game is. Marketing is difficult enough as it is, without having to explain to everyone what your product is."

(Used with permission by GoodSol Development, Inc.)

A Final Word

Make some room on your hard drive because the following web sites contain thousands of PC and Mac shareware games, freeware, and commercial game demos. Every potential game designer/developer who is considering the shareware distribution option should be familiar with these sites:

➤ Shareware.com (www.shareware.com)

➤ Downloads.com (www.downloads.com)

➤ Games Domain (www.gamesdomain.com)

➤ Jumbo (www.jumbo.com)

➤ Tucows (www.tucows.com)

➤ Adrenaline Vault (www.avault.com)

➤ 3D Gamers (www.3dgamers.com)

➤ WinSite (www.winsite.com)

➤ 32bit.com/ServerFiles.com (www.32bit.com)

➤ Real Arcade (www.realarcade.com)

➤ GameSpot (www.gamespot.com)

Chapter 21

Breaking into the Industry

As evidenced by the interviews published in this book, there are many ways to break into the gaming industry. The two most common ways, however, are to get a job at an existing development studio or publishing company, or to create the game on your own terms and approach a publisher and/or distributor to pick up the title. Exactly what kind of company you launch on your own is another consideration altogether, and there many ways to do so.

Although the former is the more popular route, the gaming industry is full of success stories from people who have chosen either of these two avenues. Therefore, this chapter focuses on the best ways to present your idea for a game (or the game itself) to a publisher and on getting a job at a game company—and the best ways to get in the door. Keep in mind that other chapters, such as those on art, animation, programming, and music, offer specific advice for those fields.

Quite simply, consider this chapter the ultimate game developer round table of advice, going from sage to sage, asking how one should break into the biz today. How awesome is that?

THE EXPERTS

- Joel Jewett
- Paul Jaquays
- Bill Roper
- Tim Willits
- Erin Roberts
- Chris Taylor
- Chris Cross
- American McGee
- Cliff Bleszinski
- Denny Thorley
- Dave Davis
- Michael Rubinelli
- Brendan McNamara
- George Broussard
- Ed Martin
- Lorne Lanning
- David Dienstbier
- Mike McCoy
- Alex Garden
- David Jaffe
- Craig Alexander
- David Perry
- Scott Miller
- Peter Hirschmann
- Sid Meier
- Brian Reynolds
- Bruce Shelley
- Peter Molyneux
- Phil Steinmeyer
- Tim Schafer
- Phil Saunders
- Harry Gottlieb
- Matt Householder
- Warren Spector
- Ed Del Castillo
- Todd Howard
- Stevie Case
- Minh Le
- Kevin Bachus

Free Tools for Budding Game Designers

Fortunately for those looking to become full-time and famous game designers one day, many computer games offer free tools to help tweak your trade. Think about it—if you want to become a programmer, why not create a few MODs (modifications) for your favorite titles? Up-and-coming artists could start designing "skins" for these games, level designers can start work on maps, and so forth. And hundreds of computer games are released each year with these free tools, available on the CD or as a free download off the web. Examples include *Neverwinter Nights*, *Max Payne*, *Diablo II*, *Tony Hawk's Pro Skater* series, *Warcraft III*, the *Elder Scrolls: Morrowind*, and many more. And recently, Valve Software and Sierra Studios released the *Half-Life* Full SDK (Software Development Kit), which contains all the resources needed to build any type of game imaginable to run as an add-on for *Half-Life*.

So, instead of complaining about the quality of today's PC games, put your mouse where your mouth is and start creating your own!

At the end of the chapter is a special conversation with Kevin Bachus, Vice President of Publishing at Capital Entertainment Group and founding member of the Xbox project team at Microsoft Corporation.

Joel Jewett, Neversoft Entertainment

To ask how to best break into the video gaming industry, who better to turn to than the president of Neversoft Entertainment, Joel Jewett? In case you've been living under an Atari 2600 for the past few years, Neversoft is one of the hottest developers on the planet, responsible for *Tony Hawk's Pro Skater* and *Spider-Man* series on all platforms.

"So you want to become a game designer?" asks Jewett. "Well, first you need to know what a designer does." He expounds:

> A designer is that key person who's right in the middle of the development team. Your job is to create and maintain a vision of what's going to be fun for the player who ultimately buys your game; then use the tools and resources at hand to actually make that vision into something tangible. Your resources include not only software tools, but also other people on your team: artists, programmers, and other designers.

Is any formal training necessary?

> School is going to be critical to your success. Just because you have extensive knowledge of video games, that doesn't mean you can design one. A great game player doesn't necessarily make a great game designer.

Jewett says the following are some things to focus on during and after school:

> Make sure you get a solid, well-rounded education. Take as much math as you can. Math teaches you to solve problems analytically, and you'll be better prepared to communicate with the programming side of the development team. Develop your speaking, reading, and writing skills as much as you can. All of these things will help you communicate your ideas to your teammates, and enable you to get the most out of the rest of your team. In addition to the [preceding suggestions], if you can take programming classes, art classes, and classes in the use of various software art packages, you'll be even better prepared to communicate with the rest of the team because you'll have further insight into their respective disciplines.

Any secrets to share for game success?

> Great communication among team members is the secret to great video games. The smartest, most creative people in the world can't make a game if they can't work together as a team, and teamwork is built on good communication. You'll be one step up on other designers if you're the person who can make friends, talk freely, and earn the respect of people in all disciplines on your team. Meeting and talking to people may not be easy for you, but you can learn to get better at it. Challenge yourself, get out and do things that require you to hang out with other people. Try new things; meet new people.

> A good designer will often be called upon to draw from experiences in their lives, so the more you have under your belt, the better. Most video games incorporate some form of competition—either the player against himself or the player against other players. The competitive aspects of the game and how they're developed and presented to the player are what make a game fun. One of the best ways to help yourself to understand what makes a game fun is to get out there and compete, either with yourself or with others. Experiencing all forms of competition, from the debate team to golf, soccer, football, individual sports to team sports; all these things will help you to understand what's fun about learning to be good at something and then feel the thrill of the moment as you overcome a challenge. You need to experience these emotions so that you'll be able to create scenarios in your games that will draw these same emotions out of game players.

> And while you're out there playing golf, tennis, soccer, baseball—analyze those games while you're at it. Understand the rules. Figure out why those games have been around for so long and what makes them so fun. You can apply those fundamentals to video games.

To wrap up, Jewett says if inexperienced game designers focus a little more on all the things he mentioned previously, "You should be in pretty good shape by the time it comes to looking for a job because I'm thinking that you won't be reading this unless you've played about a million video games, too!"

> **NOTE**
> Veteran game designer Noah Falstein (check out his impressive bio in Appendix A, "Biographies") offers his two cents on breaking into the industry—go back to Chapter 6, "Creating Characters, Storyboarding, and Design Documents," to read his words of wisdom.

Enjoy these images from Activision's *Tony Hawk's Pro Skater 4*. Joel Jewett offers this tidbit of advice on breaking
into the industry: "Get out there and play; don't just hang out in front of the TV…you'll ultimately be a better designer for it."
(Used with permission by Activision, Inc.)

Paul Jaquays, Ensemble Studios

First a designer at id Software (developers of the *DOOM* and *Quake* series for the PC), and now
designer at Ensemble Studios (creators of the *Age of Empires* series), Jaquays offers a handful of
do's and don'ts on the topic of breaking into the industry:

➤ Experience is crucial. However, that job need not necessarily be actual employment in the
industry. Become involved in MOD work for the type of games you want to develop. More and
more, MOD teams are becoming the "farm clubs" for game development houses. Working on
a game MOD gives talented amateurs the chance to work in a team setting, develop the skills
that they hope to perform professionally, and potentially make industry contacts.

➤ What you can *do* and *create* is more important than where you go to school, or even what you
study. In the development side of the game industry, potential employers are usually not
impressed by your diploma.

➤ Create samples that showcase both your creativity and your technical skill.

➤ Don't represent the work of others as your own. Don't allow the work of others to be miscon-
strued as being your own. For example, if you're a level designer, your sample levels should

never include prefabs made by other designers. If you're a model maker but not a skin artist, make sure that your future employer can see samples of your meshes both with and without skins on them.

➤ If you choose to be active online, remember that the game development community is really very small. If you choose to be a jerk online, understand that the no-clue dweeb you flamed online or in a letter today may be the design department head offering the job you want tomorrow.

➤ Make an effort (and plan to budget the expense) to go to places in which game developers congregate, either professionally or socially. There's a lot to be said for putting a face to a name. All other things being equal (and sometimes even when they're unequal), developers are often more comfortable hiring services (or staff) from people they know and have met. If you can afford it, go to trade shows like E3 (Electronic Entertainment Expo), or professional gatherings like Game Developers Conference, or large sponsored LAN parties like QuakeCon.

➤ Be willing to relocate. Often.

➤ If you live outside the United States and have a goal of working for a company in the U.S., plan on getting some form of advanced educational degree (in addition to your outrageous development skills). U.S. immigration laws make it particularly challenging to "import" talent. The advanced degree is one of the yardsticks used to measure the worthiness of a potential immigrant to work in the U.S.

➤ Don't show up on the doorstep of a game developer unannounced and expect them to make time to review your portfolio and samples.

➤ Don't email samples to developers unless they're requested.

➤ Don't send unsolicited (un-asked for) game concepts to developers. It screams of non-professionalism.

➤ If you're coming out of a university program, make sure that your sample portfolio contains work other than your class projects. Student work—even good student work—still looks like student work.

➤ Whether you're an artist, a level designer, a writer, or a programmer, don't include samples in your portfolio unless they're things you would be willing to do again… and again… and again.

NOTE

Are you a video game artist? Or would you like to be? EA's John Miles, who is currently in charge of artwork for all Harry Potter video games, offers some exceptional advice on what to put in your portfolio and how to best break into the biz. Turn back to Chapter 13, "Game Art and Animation," to read his inspiring words of wisdom.

Bill Roper, Blizzard North

We heard from this industry veteran in Chapter 3, "General Game Design: Strategy Games" (on strategy game design), and in Chapter 5, "General Game Design: Role-Playing Games (RPGs) and Persistent Online Worlds" (on role-playing game design), for his work on the *WarCraft* and *Diablo* series, respectively.

Here, he offers some sage advice on breaking into the biz:

Take a Job—ANY Job

We are fortunate that as an industry, we have not lost the connection to our early roots, when two or three guys would get together in a basement or garage to create a game. The possibility for people to get into a game company at an entry-level position and then move into a career they really want is still here. We have people at Blizzard, for example, who started out in our Quality Assurance and Technical Support departments who now do everything from art to programming to level design to producing on projects throughout the company. I started out doing music for the PC version of *Blackthorn* and voice-over contract work for a *WarCraft: Orcs* and *Humans* demo based on a lead from an artist in the company. I sent in a cassette tape of me doing variations of the original *WarCraft* voices and some samples of my electronic compositions from college. Although I had never done music for a game before, they were tight on time, and I was offering to put in whatever hours were needed at the first price they offered. It was a lot of work because I had to keep my day job to pay my bills, but it got my little toe in the door. After finishing that music for *Blackthorn*, there were no other projects for me to work on, but I knew I had to get a full-time job at this company. I offered to do anything. I would be the customer service and technical support representative. I proposed running their BBS and using my desktop publishing knowledge to set up the manual for their upcoming game. I offered to wash the bosses' cars—and in fact, I even promised to hand over my Rock Hydra (an Alpha, nonetheless, for you *Magic: The Gathering* fans) if it would get me in the door. I am convinced they decided it was better to have me where they could keep an eye on me rather than to have to deal with me coming back every day with some new scheme; and I got not only my foot, but the rest of me, in the door. By the way, I did hand over that Rock Hydra…

Just Do It

First and foremost, find out what it is that drives your creative juices, and focus on becoming the best you can at it. Assuming you already have decided on something like programming or art or design, look at what else interests you and see how these elements of your life can intermingle. If you love sports and are also interested in AI programming, start working on creating the best football coach who has ever competed on the digital gridiron. If you love Westerns and horror and are an artist, start modeling or texturing a zombie gunslinger. If you have an idea for a game that you just haven't seen yet, make it out of cardboard and old Monopoly pieces. Whatever it is, give it a try. The single most impressive interview I ever took part in was with a programmer who simply loved designing games. His education and work history were standard and acceptable, but what stood out were the board game and card game he had not only designed, but also built himself and brought to the interview. His passion and ability were evident, and it showed that he truly wanted to be in this industry.

Location, Location, Location

The hours are long, you will be most likely be working on the same project for years, and you will find yourself emotionally attached to not only the game you are creating, but to the public perceptions of your game and your company. This is why it is vital to strive to get into a place where you really want to be, with people whom you want to be with. This may not be a possibility right off the bat, but it is something to keep as a goal. There are many people I have met in this industry that I know I will work with in some capacity because I have set that as a goal. If there is a company you admire, a designer or artist or programmer you want to work with, or a musician whose compositions move you, make sure you not only let them know (praise from peers is a wonderful thing, and we do not do it enough in this competitive industry), but keep tabs on where they are and what they are doing. Many of us at Blizzard grew up playing adventure games, and when we were looking for some help in punching up the puzzles on *WarCraft Adventures*, we leaped at the chance to bring in Steve Meretzky as a consultant. We spent three long days locked in a room going through the entire game, and although we never released the project, the chance to work with such a gifted designer was a real treat.

Tim Willits, id Software

Tim Willits is a senior designer, lead level designer, and project director on a handful of projects (including the upcoming *DOOM III*). You can imagine how many times they've been asked how to get a job at id, so Willits offers the following:

The best way to get into the business is to work on lots of material yourself on your own time. If you want to become a level designer, you should work on maps. If you want to become a programmer, you should write MODs or plug-ins. When interviewing for a job, the employer will always ask to look at something you've done, preferably something on the most current game released by that company. You'll need good, professional-looking material to demonstrate what you're capable of doing. Lots of applicants say they're creative and full of good ideas, and they might be, but if they can't demonstrate that before getting hired, the chances of getting a job are slim.

Erin Roberts, Digital Anvil

The producer on Microsoft's *Brute Force* for the Xbox, Erin Roberts (whose past credits include *Wing Commander*, *Privateer 2*, and *Starlancer*) offers the following tips on breaking into the biz:

1. **Be prepared to start at the bottom**. You may have the world's best design document, but it is incredibly rare that anyone will let you design your own game until you have a track record. If you're good and you put your time in, you'll get recognized pretty quickly.

2. **Create a demo and/or have plenty examples of your work**. Some of the easiest hires I've ever made have been from seeing a cool demo, finding out who created it, and getting them in. A demo shows you have the ability and skill to not only come up with your own concept, but to see it put into action. Same goes for other examples of your work, such as good paper

design abilities—well-thought-through design is always key. The type of person who loves doing this kind of thing in his/her spare time is the type of person every game developer wants.

3. **Be a jack-of-all-trades**. Designers, more than any other areas of game development, need to be incredibly diverse in their skill set. A designer has to be able not only to conceptually design; they then have to take that design and implement it. Your ability to implement that work will depend on how well you designed the original plan. For example, what tools do you need the programmers to create? If these tools are not specified properly, your job becomes a lot harder. The designer also is the conduit for the whole team. It is almost always left to the designer to deal with both programming and art and to bring together all the assets into a final product. So if you want to be a designer, not only do you need to have great ideas, but you need to be very organized, be communicative, have the ability to learn many varied tools (all which never work properly), have great troubleshooting skills, and have the ability to execute on the given plan... Good luck!

Read Roberts' advice on game design in Chapter 2, "General Game Design: Action/Arcade Games."

Chris Taylor, Gas Powered Games

As president, project leader, and chief designer at Gas Powered Games, the always-outspoken (and we all love him for that) Chris Taylor has quite a bit to say on breaking into the business, likely pooled from his experience while working on *Triple Play Baseball* for EA Sports, *Total Annihilation* for Cavedog, and *Dungeon Siege* while at Gas Powered Games.

"In order of importance," begins Taylor, "I would say you need to get your foot in the door at a company right away." He explains:

You'll learn 100 times more stuff, even if you're in the testing department, than if you're at home working on something in your spare time.

Then, pick something that you think you can do really well and focus on it. That could be programming, art, design, production, testing, management, scheduling—heck, it doesn't matter, but you really need to have something that you're going to be the best in the business at.

Finally, you need to have one hell of a great work ethic. Nothing is going to put you in first place like working your ass off. This is when you need to make a decision about whether you're going to be a superstar or it's just a 9 to 5 job. My advice is to go into it with the right attitude—to build the best games, no matter what it takes.

Taylor cites an example from his own professional experiences:

I started out in this business and did whatever I had to do to get a job. Personally, I'm not crazy about sports games, but I took the job to make *Hardball 2* anyhow. I worked almost every day for 15 months with only a few days off the whole time. I worked crazy hours and focused all my energy into making that first game. I wanted to impress management that I was the right guy for the job. Fourteen years later, I'm working harder than ever—12 to 14 hours a day, seven days a week. If you want to get ahead in this business, you have to be willing to put in the time.

What about formal training? How helpful is it in getting a job?

Art school is great for those who want to be an artist; an engineering degree doesn't hurt if you want to be an engineer. In other words, get some training in whatever area you want to specialize in, or be prepared to work your way up through an organization from the ground floor. Starting positions include the testing department, production, and administration. If you get some training, you can get a foot in the door and work your way up through the company much faster, but it's possible to do it with no prior experience if you have great people skills, can communicate effectively, and are a very hard worker.

Chris Cross, Electronic Arts Los Angeles (EALA)

As lead designer on the critically acclaimed *Medal of Honor: Frontline*, Chris Cross offers some savvy bits of game design advice in Chapter 2. Here, he discusses what it takes to break into the biz.

Essentially, it boils down to these three things, believes Cross:

Willpower

Keep driving, even when you think you can't take it any more. Some games are shipped by sheer willpower. If you can show that kind of drive getting in, people will have confidence in you and be willing to give you a chance. Walk the fine line between persistent and annoying. Always be polite, even when others turn you down or treat you badly.

Effort

Turn that willpower into results. Put up or shut up. This is really about integrity. Don't sell yourself just to get in the door. There's a long road and hopefully a career to be had. Pay off the faith that somebody had in you to hire you by working hard and turning out good—if not great—results.

Foresight and Opportunity

Keep your eyes open. Sometimes, what might seem like a step in the wrong direction may open up a chance at a later date to really shine. Don't be afraid to take a leap once in awhile. Just don't make a habit of it.

American McGee, Carbon6 Entertainment

A designer on *DOOM* and *Quake* and mastermind of *American McGee's Alice* (heck, it's got his name in the title—what did you think?) offers some helpful (and interesting) words here on breaking into the business:

> Unlike Hollywood, the game industry seems to be one of the last remaining creative industries in which you can break in on pure skill and motivation alone. In Hollywood, it seems to be all about who you know. Fortunately, for someone just getting into the game world, it's still mostly about what you can do. So in my opinion, just start *doing*. Write game treatments, create cool art, build interesting new levels, come up with awesome new music… Put it out there for people to see, and chances are that someone is going to recognize your talent and help you realize your dreams.

Cliff Bleszinski, Epic Games

Cliffy B, as he's known in the industry, has made a name for himself at a tender age as one of the "game gods" of the new millennium. And if you've ever marveled at the *Unreal* or *Unreal Tournament* series, you know why.

Here, he explains what budding artists or programmers should do to better their odds:

> **Artists**: Portfolio is everything. Résumé is secondary. I don't care if your résumé says you worked on *Jurassic Park*; for all I know, you may have painted the toe on a raptor. Send me a link to a web site that provides remarkable examples of digital as well as traditional art.

> **Programmers**: It's not quite that simple. The majority of programmers we've hired at Epic have produced something cool with our most recent game or in the MOD community. Steven Polge made the first "bot" AI for *Quake*. Jack Porter made a great Windows-style interface/server browser for *Unreal*. If you're a programmer, work toward making a cool programming demo. Make yourself heard online on message boards and keep in touch with industry folks at conferences such as GDC.

Does it matter where someone lives? Really?

> For 90% of the industry positions, it's crucial. Immigration is a total nightmare in the States. We seem to have little trouble bringing in relatively unskilled labor, but when it comes to any high-tech skilled workers, we seem to enjoy making it as hard as possible to bring these remarkable people into the nation— even though they're going to help bring millions in tax revenue in.

> The rare 10% of the industry that I've been able to work with on a contract basis includes a musician, sound effects guy, and some art pieces such as the occasional character models. Usually, there's so much that's programmer-dependent on any given project that having crucial people offsite is just not an option.

While wrapping up, Cliffy B chats about what budding game developers can do to be a success in the biz:

- ➤ DO have talent.

- ➤ DO play games.

- ➤ DO go to the Game Developer's Conference [www.gdconf.com, also see Chapter 25, "Key Conventions, Organizations, and Awards"] to meet various industry types.

- ➤ DO have a presence online: Have a web site, and send it to anyone and everyone.

- ➤ DO maintain high-quality samples of your work on this web site.

"Remember," concludes Bleszinski, "No one starts as a game designer—you have to pay your dues for years before you wind up in this position."

"Build levels, program, or make art. You must understand the development process and understand gaming as a cultural force to become a good game designer," says Bleszinski.

Denny Thorley, Day 1 Studios

The awesome *MechAssault* for the Xbox was Thorley's last baby—he served as the executive producer on the title at Day 1 Studios.

When asked to give some sage advice on getting a job in the biz, Thorley offers these following (and fantastic) pointers:

Initially, I would encourage individuals to specialize in an aspect of the game-creation process. Develop exceptional skills in a specific area that will get you noticed and open a door or two. Being average at modeling, texturing, animation, programming, or writing will not get you noticed. Being extraordinary at any one skill or even a subset of a skill will tell your prospective employer volumes about your potential to contribute.

When interviewing, obviously stress the quality of your work, but include the efficiency and speed of your work in your discussions. This indicates that you understand the need for speed and how your work can impact the development cycle.

Finally, do a little research on the company you are interviewing with. Who are you interviewing with? What was their last project? Go out and play the last game your potential boss created. Ask inquisitive, open-ended questions about the development cycle, the size of the team, and regrets on the project. The initiative you show here will stick in the minds of the interviewer long past your meeting.

Want to make a video game that has the whole world buzzing, like *Grand Theft Auto: Vice City*? Did you know it was the best-selling video game — across all platforms — in 2002? Read about what it's like to do marketing for the *Grand Theft Auto* franchise in Chapter 19, "Public Relations and Marketing."
(Used with permission by Rockstar Games, Inc.)

Dave Davis, Electronic Arts

As an 18+-year veteran in the video game industry (and five years at EA), Dave Davis has gathered some serious experience under his belt when it comes to picking the right team members for a project (such as his *Freekstyle from 2002*).

Here, he offers some tips to those just starting out:

First, make sure that you are passionate about making games. This industry went through a period in which it was flooded with new hires who didn't have a passion for games and simply thought that it would be a "fun job." The result was low-quality product, unhappy customers, and disillusioned employees who then left to seek other "fun jobs." The hours are long, the work can be tedious, and fame and successful product are elusive. However, seeing hundreds of thousands of gamers having a blast playing your game is an incredible rush. If you can't imagine yourself doing anything else but making the best video games possible, by all means step right up and apply.

"Second," says Davis, "decide what type of products you want to build, and target developers and publishers that specialize in that type of product."

He adds:

> If you absolutely love sports games, apply at a company such as EA. If you live for first-person shooters, contact the top companies in that genre. Companies will be most receptive if it is clear how they will benefit from your knowledge and skill set.

Finally, network as much as you can, advises Davis:

> Knowing someone in the industry is always the best way to get a job in a video game company. Do whatever you have to in order to attend industry events such as E3 or the Game Developers Conference [see Chapter 25], and make as many direct contacts as possible. Remember that we see thousands of résumés a month, so any advantage you can get definitely helps. Good luck!

Michael Rubinelli

As former Vice President of development at THQ, Inc., Michael Rubinelli managed the people who manage the game developers. Who better to ask about the best ways to approach a publishing company? We had the privilege to sit down with this industry veteran before he left THQ in late 2002. Rubinelli is currently working at Gotham Games, a subsidiary of Take-Two Interactive.

Rubinelli says there are three pieces to the puzzle, and although you don't need all three to spark interest with a publisher, the more you have, the better:

> ➤ First on the list is a compelling design document. To reiterate, this is a comprehensive outline of all the game's features and story, with information for all members of the design team [see Chapter 6]. Just like in Hollywood, in which every movie script is registered and logged with the writers' guild, most every company in the game business will require that developers sign a game-specific nondisclosure agreement (NDA) for that very reason. Ironically, publishers usually insist that an NDA be in place to protect all parties. There's no need for game designers to be nervous when they have a binding document in place.

> ➤ Second, a 2D colorized storyboard or character model collection is recommended. It's important to have an artist give the publisher an idea of the visual tone or flavor of the game by submitting sketches, rendered characters, or background drawings.

> ➤ Third on the list is some form of demo technology—that is, a working prototype of the game's engine.

It sure helps if you have a talented team already chosen to work on the game:

> I would say that in today's climate you're better off starting with an established group. Games and tools are getting so robust that building worlds gets removed from coders' and artists' hands more and more every day, and the people tasked with these jobs are game/level designers. When you get some experience under your belt and fully design well-known hit games, you could strike out on your own if you feel up to it!

Rubinelli also advises knowing the platform on which the game is going to be published. In other words, understand the strengths and limitations of the platform (for example, Sony PlayStation 2 or Nintendo GameCube), and make sure that the publishers know you're aware of the platform.

What kinds of games is THQ looking to scoop up? Rubinelli admits that his answer will sound trite, but couldn't be closer to the truth:

> I'm looking for a hit game. That is, I want to know what kind of game a designer has a real passion for. If the developers are working on something they really want to work on, it comes through in the game and everyone wins, regardless of the game genre.

> I think sports games are a little limited in scope, whereas action games have more flexibility to them, with more variations of gameplay.

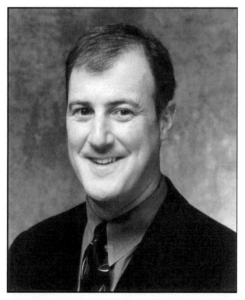

Industry veteran Mike Rubinelli says the cost of a console development kit has dropped over the past couple of years. He says it should now run about $5,000 to $10,000. This is something the publishers would likely purchase for the developers.
(Used with permission by THQ, Inc.)

NOTE
Hop back to Chapter 19 to read Rubinelli's opinions on what kind of PR to seek for your products and/or company.

Next, Rubinelli offers some advice on getting a job within an existing company:

> Instead of trying to get into a company as a game designer or producer, it's best to start at an entry-level position because these titles [game designer or producer] are usually given to those who have been in the industry for a while. The people who get those positions have a history, so if you're just starting out, it's best to start off in the testing department or perhaps customer service. The good news is that when a large company starts hiring, it often looks internally first; it looks to promote from within.

Good tip: Rubinelli says that many employers turn to the testing group when looking to promote an employee.

On the topic of looking for new games, he was asked to explain how the process works exactly. Does he fly to see developers around the world, or should they send in some code?

> There are three situations we typically come across. First, we will travel out to see developers to look at what they have been working on. Second, we get sent code with all the build notes. And third, we get developers who come in to present their ideas to us in person.

> Here are the three most important things I look for in a developer: Do they have a passion for what they are building? What is their track record (past games in the genre, existing technology, and so on)? And, oddly enough, what kind of people are they? At the end of the day, this is a business, and we are always "partnering up" with developers. You just like to know that your partners are good people.

Rubinelli was asked to discuss the pros and cons of working with a well-known franchise such as the *WWE*, *Scooby Doo*, or *Rugrats*:

> Working on a license can be a blessing and a curse. First, you have all the built-in expectations from people who are already acquainted with the property. If you do not translate what their idea of the interactive product should be, you run the risk of disappointing them. I think this tends to be more common with games based on books and comic licenses than cartoon, movies, or TV shows; but nonetheless, the risk still exists. On the plus side, you have all this built-in awareness and credibility for your game as soon as it is announced.

"It is much easier to get people to be interested in your game if it is based on a known entity as opposed to a completely original concept," admits Rubinelli. "Creating a successful original means much more work on the part of product development, marketing, and sales from interactive demos to quarterly press tours to the ongoing education of buyers."

Rubinelli was asked what he thinks the video gaming landscape will look like in five years, and how could the readers of this book benefit from it today?

> I think five years from now our industry will more closely resemble the record business. A few really big players and several small groups. I assume that there will be one to two strong upstart publishers that are not even in business today that will exist and have a good franchise or two. I think reading these books in general are very good if you can synthesize what the contributors are saying and apply it to whatever your goals are.

Finally, Rubinelli offers some final tips to those who want to break into the biz:

> Get your foot in the door any way possible (customer service, receptionist, mail clerk, and so on). It may be a small industry and seem somewhat closed, but after you are in, you can be in for life if you choose to.

> Play as many games as you can and figure out what they do well. Even the worst games probably do something well.

> Never give up.

Brendan McNamara, Sony Computer Entertainment Europe (SCEE)

In Chapter 2, the Director of Development at Sony's Soho studio in the UK talks about general game design and what it was like to develop *The Getaway*. Here, he chats about the do's and don'ts in trying to break into the industry.

"The one thing I always ask people in interviews is what game they would like to make if they were given the opportunity," begins McNamara.

He explains:

> It's really informative to find out what games somebody likes and how they see the future of games going forward. It also tells you whether someone has the ambition or vision to make their own game in the future. So I'd say it's important to know why you want to be in the business in the first place. What do you want to get out of a career in games? If you can answer that question clearly, you'll impress a lot of people at interviews. You would be surprised to see the amount of people who answer, "I thought it would be cool!" Maybe, but it's hard work, too, and it's good to know what you are working toward in your career.

Second, McNamara says to build a demo:

> If you're an aspiring game designer, and you come in with levels already built using a level editor for a popular game, it will give you a huge head start. We have all of our junior designers build us levels, and we play them to find out who can cut it. I give the same advice to artists and coders. Show people that you really want to make games, so much so that you spend your spare time writing code, creating art, or designing levels. It's much more concrete than coming in for an interview and listing your favorite games.

George Broussard, 3D Realms

Owner/Producer of 3D Realms, George Broussard is one of the geniuses behind *Duke Nukem*. Here, he offers a few tips for breaking into the industry:

> ➤ First, you should be a diehard gamer. If you don't live and breathe games, you should look for a job elsewhere. You'll work too hard for too little pay in this industry unless you really love what you do.

➤ Second, I think making MODs for current games is the best way to get noticed. Most people who create good models, animations, textures, and levels in the MOD scene are hired within a couple of years. It's primarily a matter of setting up a good web site; getting your stuff on there and seen.

➤ Third, you have to be able to finish what you start. It's important to show that you can take an idea from conception to finished product.

Ed Martin, Electronic Arts

This inspiring director of the *NASCAR Thunder* series at Electronic Arts dished out some great advice to newbie game designers in Chapter 4, "General Game Design: Sports, Simulations, Adventure Games, and Puzzles."

Here, he elaborates on what budding designers or developers can do to maximize their success in this multi-billion dollar industry:

Bring your dreams and aspirations to the table, but check your expectations of Fantasyland at the door. Working in the entertainment industry is fabulous; I wouldn't trade it for the world. But I have a job to do. Believe it or not, we don't play games all day, and I don't spend all my weekends at NASCAR races. Across the five different platforms that we're creating *NASCAR Thunder 2003* on, we have a team of more than 50 people, nearly 500 licenses, hundreds of thousands of lines of code, and less than a year to get it all done. Reality sets in quickly. It's not all fun and games. It is fun, and there are games, but there's a whole lot more to it.

Be prepared to start low and spend time working your way up. The computer and video game industry is now bigger than the motion picture box office; this is a big, mature industry. George Lucas and Steven Spielberg started low, and it took years to get to where they are. The top folks in this industry either started as flat-broke startups and fought for their lives, or they also came in low and worked their way up. You're not going to walk in the door with no experience and get handed the reins to a franchise that generates 50, 100, 200 million or more dollars. But someday, you just might get there. It takes time, though.

You don't know everything. This industry is filled with incredible people and phenomenal creativity. But it's spread all over the place. Spread out and get to know everyone in sight. It takes more than one person to make a hit game—at least today it does. Look around; work with lots of people. You'll be astounded by how much talent is around you if you open your eyes. And you'll have a lot of fun doing it!

Lorne Lanning, Oddworld Inhabitants

As the creator of *Oddworld: Munch's Oddysee* for the Microsoft Xbox, you can bet Lorne Lanning deals with many talented artists, animators, programmers, level designers, sound engineers, and musicians. How does he advise getting started in the industry?

> The best way to break into the industry is to start off as a game tester. Many game testers eventually get hired to do layout. Many layout artists eventually get the chance to design games. But of course, you need to keep on calling. People feel embarrassed about continually calling a company and continually getting turned back. However, the HR people know that those who keep calling are showing persistence and dedication. Persistence is a desirable trait to any employer.

Lanning was asked to give advice on applying for a job not as a game tester, but as a developer. What would impress the powers that be at Oddworld Inhabitants?

You would want to demonstrate to a game company that you...

> ➤ Are well organized.
>
> ➤ Play a lot of games and have a solid vocabulary of games as reference.
>
> ➤ Can illustrate your ideas solidly and consistently.
>
> ➤ Can communicate well with a team and are open to the ideas of others.
>
> ➤ Can solve problems even when faced with stifling technical limitations.
>
> ➤ Are fluent with basic 3D tools/layout tools (Max or Maya).
>
> ➤ Are willing to do whatever it takes to bring a project home and be there for your team members in the crunch.

Lanning continues:

> Today, game designers are operating almost entirely within virtual 3D worlds, which means they need to understand how to use 3D tools. If you can, show your ideas within a 3D representation. Create and use simple symbol-references to help illustrate your layouts and concepts. Use puppet shows (simple blocks acting out scenarios) to illustrate your ideas. Do anything you can to visualize how something will work and why you are able to communicate this to others. The more you show that you understand the tools and design concepts, as well as being able to effectively communicate them to others, the greater your chances of impressing upon someone that you can be a valuable asset on their team.

Lanning says the line between art and design is quickly growing more blurred as game machines get more powerful and the audience is demanding more realistic and convincing content. He explains:

> Today, the game designer has to exercise more sensibilities that would normally be the skills of a cinematographer, a set designer, a landscape architect, a writer/character developer, and programmers. We are at the point where these traits are all becoming more valuable to the individual game designer. So as games are taking on more and more film sensibilities, so the aspiring designers should also study film.

David Dienstbier

Before all else, "Educate yourself," recommends David Dienstbier, the man behind *Turok: Dinosaur Hunter*, among other successful console games. Dienstbier left Acclaim in 2002 to pursue other interests. He continues:

> The best way to get into game design is to be able to show work that you have actually produced yourself. There is a wealth of tools available today for little or no money that are invaluable to an aspiring game designer. Popular PC games often include level editors that allow a gamer to create their own game levels, or entire games. Talking about games is not enough. Playing games is not enough. There's a world of difference between being a food critic and being a chef. Entry-level positions are often the hardest to get in this industry for designers, and the best way to increase your chances is to be able to produce 3D work samples—along with any documents, critiques, drawings, or other samples you may have. This gives prospective employers a very well-rounded and comprehensive body of work by which to evaluate your skill set, and familiarizes an inexperienced game designer with the intricacies of the job.

> **NOTE**
>
> Chapter 24, "Game Design Resources on the Internet," houses a long list of killer web sites to check out if you're looking to get a job in the gaming industry. Some of these include `http://gamasutra.com`, `www.gamejobs.com`, `http://gignews.com`, `http://garagegames.com`, and many more.

Mike McCoy, Ubi Soft Entertainment

As lead designer on Tom Clancy's *Rainbow Six III: Raven Shield*, you bet he receives a number of applications from eager developers. The following is his advice to those just starting out:

Play Lots Of Games (and Not Just Video Games)

I play video games, board games, miniature games, card games, athletic games, and paintball/airsoft-type games. What I've found is that every game has something you can learn from it. I buy a lot of board games, learn how they work, but never actually play them. Something else usually distracts me before I find someone to try it with, but I learn from how they work. I recently created a miniature game that I played with my friends for about nine months. I couldn't believe how many of the lessons I learned while I created it translated into video gaming.

Work On Your Communication Skills

Game designers must have great communication skills. Not only do you need to be able to write coherent, logical design documents, but you also have to be able to back up and explain your ideas verbally. Game designers are also the team's cheerleaders and communicate through their emotions. When you have a bad day and go around upset, people notice it and react. During rough times, and they always happen at some time during every game's development, some people on the team will think that you are confirming their fears and doubts. Sometimes, you just need to walk around and talk to people to raise their morale. Get to know the team, offer to help if someone looks stressed, or just go have lunch with them. Finally, work on your public relation skills. As a designer, you will have to present the game to reporters, upper management, marketing and public relations staff in your own company; and even at trade shows and conventions such as E3. If you can't sell the game to them, how will they sell it to others?

Get In Any Way You Can

Most of the designers I've worked with came from some other job in the industry. Some came from tech support, others from testing, and still others from art and animation backgrounds. Don't be ashamed to take a starter level position. If you've got what it takes, show it, and you can work your way up and become a designer from within a company.

Read Mike McCoy's advice on creating games in Chapter 2.

Alex Garden, Relic Entertainment

The creator of *Homeworld* and *Impossible Creatures* says the best way to get a job in the industry is...any takers?...experience.

Garden has provided a couple of exclusive *Impossible Creatures* images from his upcoming game. A group of Chimpanzees (with a good range attack) crossed with Skunks (an area of effect unit); they're stationed on an ice cliff just above a battle in the distance. Another scene from the same mission shows hyenas crossed with komodo dragons. "The komodo have pack hunting abilities, frenzy, poison bite, and amphibious abilities," says Garden. "Off in the distance, you can see a flying unit patrolling."

(Used with permission by Microsoft Corp.)

Seriously, the single biggest thing we look for at Relic is experience. We judge you based on what you've done in the past. The work doesn't have to be professional because we're happy to look at contributions you've made to MOD groups, and so on. Identify what you're passionate about, get involved in MOD groups that will give you the chance to work on those things, and then *finish them*. This will speak volumes about your personality as a game designer.

Does it matter where you live if you want to be a famous game designer? Garden responds, "Absolutely not. Bruce Shelley lives in Delaware. That's in the U.S., right?"

David Jaffe, Sony Computer Entertainment America

"It's really not that tough right now," says David Jaffe, on breaking into the industry as a game designer/developer. The brains behind the *Twisted Metal* games provides two good ways:

1. **Start as a tester and show your work ethic**. Don't only be a good tester, but be available to give opinions, do game tuning, and run errands. I got hired out of testing because I did more than just test. I made it clear that I wanted more in the company and I worked hard to do other things (create design proposals, chat with producers, learn computer programs, and so on). And trust me, it works! I just hired our lead tester on *Twisted Metal: Black* out of testing to start work on our new game as a junior designer.

2. **Learn to make levels and tune gameplay on your own**. If you have a PC, you have no excuse. Most big games ship with level editors that let you make levels, tune AI, place pick-ups, etc. Basically, you can make your own game. If you want to design, don't worry about the fact that you don't have any new artwork (assuming that you can't draw) or new play mechanics (assuming that you can't code). Use what the editor gives you, and if you still make something fun, you know you're doing a good job. If someone came to me with 3–5 great levels made from Qradient (the *Quake* level editor) or WorldCraft (*Half-Life's* level editor), I'd totally consider hiring them, even if they'd never worked in the biz before.

So get the skills (they're easy to get on your own) and make sure you have a passionate work ethic.

What about the new video game systems that have debuted recently? Will this offer more opportunity for game designers/developers? Is it possible to get a development kit/license to make a game for any of these systems (including Sony's PS2)?

I don't think that picking up a PS2 dev kit will be an option for most budding game makers. And even if it is, you need more than one to make a PS2 game—you need a slew, with a whole team. And at that point, you're no longer a budding anything! You're in the games business at that point. And if you're not heavily funded, I'd say it's gonna be tough. Most games that sell a substantial amount these days are taking longer to make and costing a lot more. It's rare that you can make a game in 9–12 months any more and actually sell enough copies to make a dent. Honestly, I have my own plan for how a startup company should work in this day and age, and I ain't gonna share it until I try it and make tons of cash or go dead broke! Sorry!

Jaffe concludes by advising new game designers to simply make games with existing level editors or hook up with coders and artists and make a MOD.

Craig Alexander, Electronic Arts/Westwood Studios

Craig Alexander brings years of engineering and managerial experience to *Earth & Beyond*, most recently as the Vice President of Online and Executive Producer for Electronic Arts.

He was asked to reveal his thoughts on breaking into the industry in today's day and age.

"It really depends on the position the individual is pursuing, but if you want to be a producer, there are a few things to keep in mind," begins Alexander:

> As the complexity of games increases and the team size gets larger, a producer role demands a solid management education and training. In addition, producers should be well-trained in a specific game discipline. For example, it helps for producers of an MMORPG [massively multiplayer online role-playing game] to have an engineering background, due to the massive infrastructure these games require. RPG producers benefit from a strong game-design background.

"Aside from all that, a good liberal arts education is very important," adds Alexander:

> Producers need to draw on a broad base of knowledge because you never know what type of game you'll be working on. History, science, and literature all become important because producers need to manage people with many different skill sets. For example, although the producer may not be doing his own art, he'll be managing the art directors and need to be able to respond intelligently. I've always tried to staff my leadership team with people who have a diverse set of skills that complement my own strengths and weaknesses.

Finally, Alexander says producers need to love games: "It seems like a simple concept—playing games, loving games, and having a good instinct for games will take a producer far."

David Perry, Shiny Entertainment

One of the industry's veterans (and most recognizable personalities) is Shiny's David Perry, responsible for many games over the years, such as *Earthworm Jim*, *MDK*, *Sacrifice*, *Messiah*, and *The Matrix* games.

The best way to break into the industry, says Perry, is to find people like yourself and build a demo game on the PC. He expands:

> Take as long as it takes; upgrade your people until you have a really sweet playable demo. Then pitch it to companies that really *need* a game like that. Industry experience doesn't matter if you have a kickass playable *demo*. Financially, you'll get a much better deal if the game is far down the development road. Publishers hate risks, and the more you can remove the risk, the more their doors swing open.
>
> One thing I also suggest is to pick a designer you truly respect and then study their latest game down to every nut and bolt. Then, hand-write them a letter, and tell them technically *why* you like their work and cool things you're seeing in their competitors' games.

Perry pauses and inserts this caveat:

> Legally, developers can't read any game design ideas of yours—they're not being stuck up, it's just a legal thing—so be careful not to send them ideas that will have them folding up your letter and stuffing it back into the envelope! If you keep the conversation based on what's already public knowledge, you should be okay.

Regarding contacting designers, continues Perry, "The ones who have impressed me the most are the guys who show that they can really think and come up with solutions. I hate people who just say, 'It sucks'; I love people who say, 'It sucks, here's why, here's how other people fix it, and here's how I would fix it.'"

More on how to get in the door:

> If you catch their interest, just about any lead designer I know will keep your letter just in case they need a new assistant in the future. How do you contact someone? Simple: Just write a letter and send it to their company address with their name on it. Some will refuse to read it, some will just ignore you, and some will respond. (Many of the addresses are on my web site at `www.dperry.com`.) You can usually find the name of the lead designer of the game in the back of the game manual, in the game credits, or on the web being interviewed by gaming sites. Be sure to include your email address in your letter so it's easy to get back to you.

> Now, just a word of warning: Don't become a stalker. It's better to keep the letter interesting, not just a laundry list of niggles that don't really matter, and *not* your life story and every game you've played. (Just imagine that someone was writing to you; what would you like to see and how would you want it presented?) I sincerely wish you the best of luck.

Scott Miller, 3D Realms

Earlier in this chapter, we heard from 3D Realms' George Broussard, and now the other half of the terrible twosome shares his advice on the possibility of just selling an idea. According to Miller, "No—that's such a remote possibility it's not worth discussing." Here's why:

> Implementation and execution matter far more than ideas, which I consider a dime a dozen—even great ideas. Creative people simply never lack great game ideas. Also, with all the ideas that have been sent to me (hundreds), I've yet to see one that's worthy of turning into a game, mostly because amateurs—not unlike many publishers and developers, I guess—don't know how to create a game concept with franchise hooks.

Peter Hirschmann, LucasArts

Peter Hirschmann has been working in the entertainment industry for more than a decade. He joined DreamWorks Interactive in 1995 as a story editor and then went on to write and produce the award-winning *Medal of Honor* series for Electronic Arts. In 2002, Hirschmann left EA to work for LucasArts.

What's the first thing a level designer should do to get a job at a development studio? "These days, we'd never hire anyone for a junior designer position just off the street with no professional experience," confesses Hirschmann. He continues:

> The key word is "professional," meaning that you've actually worked in person with other live human beings, not just designing levels alone in your basement. The design department touches every element of a game's production, so being organized with your work, communicating ideas clearly, and having a

cheery personality (or at least one that allows you to get along with others) are all vital to your success. We tend to promote from within—that way, we already know how that person performs under pressure. Most of the stellar design team for the first *Medal of Honor* came up through the testing department.

How did Hirschmann break into the industry? "I was really lucky to get a production assistant job right out of college at Steven Spielberg's film company, Amblin," admits Hirschmann, "[though] I had been interning for their writers fellowship program while I was in school." The story continues:

> It was a wonderful education in how much effort needs to go into making a piece of popular entertainment—regardless of medium or subject matter—from its initial conception on through production, marketing, and distribution. This may sound blasphemous to some people, but I probably spent more time in the Amblin game room than in the screening room. I had been a big fan of LucasArts in the late '80s and early '90s, and I always thought that if Steven Spielberg started a game company, well, that'd just be it. I was just at the right place at the right time when he founded DreamWorks Interactive.

Is getting started in the game industry any easier now, or is it harder? "It probably works out to be the same," Hirschmann believes. He elaborates:

> The industry certainly has expanded a lot over the past eight years, so there's more opportunity, but projects have become bigger and team positions even more specialized, so it takes more time to ramp up into a full-fledged production job than it did before. This isn't necessarily a bad thing because the best way to learn about game production is from the bottom up, like from a testing job or a position as an asset wrangler. The Web is also a fantastic resource; almost every game studio has a career section, and even if they aren't hiring, you can often get a good idea of how they're organized by reading the job descriptions.

Any do's and don'ts when trying to break into the industry? What should you study in school?

➤ **Go to college**. Major in whatever interests you, whether it's molecular biology, European history, or (as in my case) creative writing. If major universities ever offer a "game production" major in the distant future, I imagine it would be a little of everything from almost every discipline.

➤ **Read a lot**. Have at least one hobby outside of gaming; embrace the notion of being a well-rounded individual. (I talk big—I'm one of the most boring people I know.) One of the most fun things about making games is that they can be about anything. You never know when you'll draw on some obscure fact you heard in a lecture or that you discovered during research for a paper.

➤ **Ask questions**. Developers usually toil away anonymously and always enjoy hearing from the people who actually play the game once the gold master goes out the door.

The best advice I ever heard as a kid was to try to do what you love for a living. If you love the thought of making games, make sure that you do everything you can to make it what you do.

Sid Meier, Firaxis Games

"Get involved as a play tester, and over time demonstrate your knowledge, be active, and offer suggestions," says Meier, outlining the best traditional way to climb the ladder. "Another way is to write manuals for a company. That is, do something related to game design; and if you have talent, it will be recognized."

But what about doing it yourself instead of this traditional way of getting in the industry? Meier responds:

> The second route is the quickest, but requires luck and a lot of talent. If this is what you want to do, and you're a programmer or are working with one, put together a playable demo of your game and shop it around. We all know of the story with *SimCity*. Will Wright took it to eight publishers who all turned it down, except Maxis. Now publishers are a lot more sensitive, but you must put together a good prototype. And it doesn't need full-motion video or polished graphics.

Brian Reynolds, Big Huge Games

Reynolds has worked alongside Sid Meier for many years and now is in charge at his own development studio, Big Huge Games. (Sounds big, doesn't it?)

Reynolds offers this advice:

> My first piece of advice to young people considering the game industry as a career is this: Don't do it unless you know it's something you really, really want to do. This is an extremely competitive industry—partially because it's perceived as fun, glamorous, and so on; so it's filled with people who do really truly love making games and are willing to work appallingly hard in order to realize that dream. If you're only so-so on the concept, this industry's probably not for you—you'll be competing with people who live and breathe computer games.

Big Huge Games' web site (`www.bighugegames.com`) provides quite a list of job perks. What do Reynolds and company look for in a potential employee? "Someone who not only has the commitment described previously, but also a top-notch skill set in a particular area—for entry and mid-level people, that usually means programming or art," says Reynolds. He continues:

> For anything but entry level, we look for industry experience (meaning specifically the computer game industry). Larger companies also hire full-time testers at the entry level, and this can be a way to break into the industry for those who don't meet the specific skill set requirements in one of the development areas.

Bruce Shelley, Ensemble Studios

Shelley's tenure at Microprose alongside Sid Meier and at Ensemble Studios is worth its weight in gold. He starts off by saying that it's easy to break into the business if you're a brilliant programmer or highly talented computer animator. "But for us normal people, it's more difficult," teases Shelley. "Designers I've known got their start most often by beginning as play-testers." He expands:

> To start here, you must be a good analytical player and be able to communicate where the game you're testing is working or not. Real play-testing is hard work. Most games in development are not fun because they're incomplete. If you can hold the vision of the game in your head, test according to the design team's needs, provide great feedback, and offer design solutions in those areas where a game is not working, you'll be recognized as being valuable as a designer.

> Testers I worked with at Microprose are now in the industry as programmers, designers, producers, and test managers. Ensemble Studios has hired several highly ranked *Age of Empires* players as testers. Some of these people are already getting opportunities on the design team because their ability to analyze and discover new tactics and strategies is valuable. We've also hired designers with no professional experience because they could demonstrate basic design skills by creating excellent scenarios using our in-game scenario editors. I started my game career by play-testing paper war games for free. I later got a job at the company for which I tested. Now the paper industry is quite small, but the same type of opportunity is available in the much larger computer/video game industry. The jobs are there. Every major developer/publisher uses testers, even if just part-time. Take a part-time job at night if you have to, but get inside. Once inside, if you work hard and well, get along with your team, and can communicate, you're on your way."

Peter Molyneux, Lionhead Studios

Does breaking into the industry differ overseas? Legendary "god game" designer Peter Molyneux describes what he looks for when hiring at Lionhead Studios:

> It's not getting any easier to break into the game industry…so obviously a degree or Masters helps get your foot in the door. Also, if you're prepared to start at the bottom, game companies will take you on as a tester or junior programmer. If you choose this route, the best advice I can give is don't sit back, but be prepared to work harder and longer and come up with as many observations and solutions as possible to get yourself noticed. The only other way is to put together a demo, although these days to do this on your own is becoming very difficult, indeed.

Phil Steinmeyer, PopTop Software

The designer behind *Railroad Tycoon* and *Tropico* series says it's helpful to be in the U.S. if you want to make a good living in game design: "The U.S. seems to be the center of gravity for much of the game-related press (especially on the PC side; for video games, Japan is probably king)." He continues:

The UK isn't bad either. Developers in other places will struggle a bit to get their message and PR out there, with both a language and a geography gap. This can be overcome, though it might be helpful to partner with a U.S.-based company or publisher. Remedy, the Finland-based developer of *Max Payne*, is a good example of this. It's partnered with 3D Realms, the well-known Texas-based game-maker. 3D Realms has helped Remedy refine its gameplay, get great marketing and PR, and so on. Once released on the PC and then multiple console platforms, *Max Payne* proved to be a big hit.

Tim Schafer, Double Fine Productions

The genius behind many of the most memorable adventure games and characters spoke earlier in this book on creating great games and clever puzzles, but here he chats about breaking into the industry.

I think it's hard to break in as a designer. Usually, people get in as something else. I came in as a programmer who could write dialogue. People like me just start designing when nobody's looking, and before you can stop us, we have the job! The industry is not mature enough at this point to recognize design as an art unto itself, unfortunately, so your best bet is to sneak in as something else: a programmer, an artist, or a tester. More and more, I've seen the testing department being used as a source for fresh talent. Which is strange, because usually testing departments don't smell all that fresh.

Schafer couldn't just leave us like this, so he offers the three most important skills you should have to "make it" in this crazy business: "Enthusiasm, creativity, and skill." He expands:

Enthusiasm—because you're going to need it. You have to love games because the games industry is hard. I'm not just feeling sorry for myself there: It's long hours of working with frustrating technical problems, and the pay is not so great that it makes up for all the pain you're going to go through. The only way it's worth it is if you love it. If you feel like you can't do anything else. Then, and only then, would I recommend a career in games to you. And if that describes you well, then you probably will love this industry because for those people it is a dream come true.

Creativity is an indispensable trait; not just in artists, but in programmers, producers, everybody. The medium that we work in changes completely every few years, and every generation of games comes with a new batch of problems that demand creative solutions. People can't just learn a basic skill and then milk it for the rest of their game career. They have to be able to face a problem they've never seen before and come up with a fresh approach.

And you have to have skill in something that will help bring your ideas to light. If you're an artist and you have an idea, you can use your skills to draw it out well enough so that other people will see what you mean. Or if you can program, you can wire up a demo of your idea. It almost doesn't matter what your skill is, as long as it helps you communicate your creative ideas to others. Actually, it does matter, because if your only skill is Riverdancing, everybody's going to get annoyed before you're done with your pitch!

If someone is new to the industry, should he start a development studio, or should a developer join an existing one?

If you're new to the biz, there's no way you can start your own development studio, unless you're sitting on an enormous pile of money or you're so famous that you can get a pile of money with one phone call.

And even then, why would you want to do that? You'd be better off getting some experience first working at a good game studio—you'll always make mistakes in the beginning, and it's important that you make those mistakes with SOMEBODY ELSE'S money!

Good point! Thanks, Tim.

Phil Saunders, Presto Studios

Phil Saunders, creative director at Presto Studios, the developers responsible for *Myst III: Exile* and other adventure games, offers his thoughts on the matter:

The first thing an aspiring game creator must do is decide on an area of the game design process that they're passionate about, and focus on developing those skills. Are you interested in programming or animation, 3D modeling or writing? It's great to have a varied skill set, to be able to "do everything." But in starting out, an employer is going to be looking for focused talent in one particular area.

One of the best things to do is to find the name of someone working in the field that you admire, and contact him or her. Often, professionals are just as passionate as you are about their job, and will remember what it was like to be in your position. If you don't harass them, they'll be happy to lend you what advice they can.

Harry Gottlieb, Jellyvision

Asked to discuss some do's and don'ts on breaking into the business, Jellyvision founder and chief designer Harry Gottlieb teases, "Don't." No, that's not his answer. Here's the more serious one:

Go get a job at a decent company to learn the production process. But if you want to be a designer, design. Experiment. I'm not saying a book like this can't be helpful [ahem!], but really, you've just got to get into the sandbox yourself and start playing. Use your intuition, mock things up, test it out on others, shut up and let them criticize your "brilliant" ideas, take it in, refine your intuition, and do another rev. If you've got talent, you'll end up making something great.

Matt Householder, Blizzard North

The producer on the coveted *Diablo* series takes a systematic approach to guiding those looking to make games for a living. His instructions are divided into the varied ways it can be done successfully. "There are really three major routes. Which is best depends on your skills and abilities," says Householder:

1. Get a job in QA—as a game tester—at a major publisher. Often, you work through a temporary employment agency for these kinds of positions.

2. Study computer programming at a top engineering/computer science school and get excellent grades while spending time on popular entertainment such as music, computer/video games, science fiction novels, comics, movies, and TV.

3. Learn 3D modeling, texturing, and animation while (again) spending too much time on popular entertainment such as computer/video games, science fiction, comics, movies, and TV.

"For all these routes" continues Householder, "you vastly improve your odds by attending major trade shows such as E3, ECTS, The Game Developers' Conference, or SIGGRAPH; by being persistent (yet not annoying) in applying for jobs; and in general by finding ways of meeting others already working in the game field."

Warren Spector, Ion Storm Austin

Not everyone can create such groundbreaking PC titles as *Ultima Underworld*, *System Shock*, and *Deus Ex*, so let's listen to the sage advice given by the one and only Warren Spector:

There are as many ways to get into the game business as there are people who want to do so. If I had to pick what seem to be the "easiest" routes, I'd say this:

➤ Whether self-taught or classroom-trained, become the best programmer on the planet. Spend your spare time generating demo games so you have a portfolio to show off. Someone will find a place for you.

➤ Become an ace artist, probably one with a specialty (low-poly modeling, animation, texturing, and so on). Put together a demo reel that shows you understand not only how to generate pretty pictures but what sort of artwork is useful in games.

➤ Get involved with a MODs group, and put together a 3D map or mission portfolio that shows you know what good gameplay is and how to achieve it.

➤ Become a tester for a developer or publisher. Many of the best and best-known designers and project directors in this business got their start in QA. This is a great way to get your foot in the door.

➤ Regardless of what your area of expertise is, try to find employment with a studio that makes the kind of games you like to play. Making games can be grueling work, and the idea of slaving away on something you don't really love sounds like hell on earth to me!

Ed Del Castillo, Liquid Entertainment

Ed Del Castillo, president and co-founder of Liquid Entertainment, juggles his management responsibilities with active participation in all aspects of product development, especially design and art direction. Before Liquid, Castillo oversaw the development of the *Command & Conquer* franchise at Westwood Studios.

Castillo offers his top five pieces of advice on breaking in, and making it in the industry:

1. Do your research.

2. Find a place you really believe in. You believe in their philosophy or their leaders.

3. Find people who are willing to believe in you. They're out there. They're just not easy to find.

4. Commit yourself fully. Half-assed commitment leads to half-assed output.

5. *Do not* get an ego. We make games, not nuclear weapons. The first time you catch yourself saying something s----y about the gaming public, slap yourself until you realize you've become an arrogant ass, and then thank God and the world for letting you have a job where you get to make video games.

Todd Howard, Bethesda Softworks

The project leader on *Morrowind* at Rockville, Maryland's Bethesda Softworks says, "First, find a place that makes games you like." Hmm, that seems pretty easy, no? He continues:

Whether you want to be a programmer, artist, or designer, a great demo is a must. If you have a great demo, you're in. Be prepared to start at the bottom, but don't be afraid to really push yourself on a company. Say that you'll do the crap and work your way up. Programmers should do some 3D code or special effects. Artists should have a demo tape or portfolio that shows off their skills. Show off your 3D models. Show the wireframe and modeling, show the base texture, and show the final result. Designers should try to build a level for *Unreal* or *Quake* and send them in. For *Elder Scrolls*, we also require writing samples from those who will be doing those kinds of things. But ultimately, if you can prove you're smart and willing to work really hard, you'll get a job.

Stevie Case, Monkeystone Games

Starting in the computer or console gaming industry? Be prepared to work for free, says Stevie Case, level designer on *Daikatana* and *Anachranox*:

The best way to get into the industry—the way I got in, as well as many of my friends—is to first learn your craft as a hobby. Pick a discipline—whether 2D art, modeling, level design, coding, sound, or whatever you choose—and begin to create.

Suck up any and all information you can find, and live your hobby. If you don't love it enough to spend copious evenings and weekends with your computer, you probably aren't going to enjoy doing it on a deadline. Become an active member of the online community that surrounds the gaming industry. Get to know both pro and amateur designers, share your knowledge, and seek their guidance. Join a MOD team, or just make your own.

The most important thing is to grow a portfolio of work that can be shown to a potential employer. Many MOD authors start out as amateurs and are quickly snapped up by eager design houses based on a promising product. Create a web site to showcase your work, but make sure it looks professional. Many companies hire without even announcing positions publicly, so don't be afraid to send out your résumé and a thoughtful email to potential employers. Include a link in your mail to the web site where some of your screenshots can be seen. Don't ever send unsolicited files of any sort, including maps and screenshots. If a company is hiring, a tasteful résumé and cover letter will be enough to draw them to your web site showcase. Most importantly, have a great attitude, display some modicum of social skills, and be patient! If you stick with your art and continue to improve, it won't be long before someone is willing to take a chance on you.

Minh Le, Valve Software

The creator of *Counter-Strike* is a perfect person to ask how to break into the industry because he created this MOD for *Half-Life* and was eventually snagged by the developers of the game. Says Le:

> You can use the tools to produce new content, and you can release that new content on the Internet, and from there you're bound to get a lot of feedback. Being a part of the MOD community is probably the best way to get yourself noticed by a professional development company.

Be sure to read how Minh Le got started in Chapter 2.

Kevin Bachus, Capital Entertainment Group

Kevin Bachus has been in the computer and video game industry for more than 20 years, when he began writing a series of successful arcade games for early personal computers. Bachus was a founding member of the Xbox project team at Microsoft Corporation, where he was instrumental in conceiving of the console and securing funding for the project. Currently, Bachus is Vice President of Publishing at Capital Entertainment Group (CEG).

So, what is the CEG, and why would a game developer be interested in the organization? Bachus explains:

> Pretty much everything about CEG is new to the game industry, but many of the parts of our business model are "borrowed" from other sectors of entertainment. For example, think about an independent production company in the film industry, such as Imagine Entertainment. They select the projects they think have the most potential, fund them, manage the production, and then work with a large studio to market and distribute their films. Along the same lines, you have record labels that find artists, pay for and manage the process of producing an album, and then deliver them to one of the larger music groups to distribute to retailers.
>
> Similarly, we go out and meet with development companies around the world who have fresh, exciting ideas that they're passionate about. We select the ones that we think have the potential to break new ground and to strike a chord with gamers. We work closely with the developer to help them achieve that full potential—both creatively (making the most of art, technology, gameplay, and so on) and logistically (tracking day-to-day progress relative to schedules, budgets, and bug reports). Unlike many publishers,

we don't have many of the financial pressures that lead sometimes to rush a game to market. But we do have an obligation to be mature and professional in our approach to development because we're spending our own money.

Bachus says when a game is about halfway done—when you can play a level or two, focus-test it with a real audience, track the team's ability to hit milestones, maybe read a few previews in leading gaming magazines—the CEG meets with potential publishing partners to find a home for it.

But Bachus says they're "not looking to *sell* it to the publisher." He explains:

We're just looking for them to commit to distributing the game and setting aside a proper budget to market it. We still pay for all the costs of development out of our own pockets, and we never pass those costs on to the publisher. As a result, the publisher's risk is about half of what it would be if they were producing the game themselves. And similarly, when the product is released, we share equally in the revenue from the game.

Bachus emphasizes this important point: They also pay developers more than they would receive if they were funded by a publisher (and sooner!)

Because we're sharing the risk and are entitled to more of the revenue, we have a larger pie to divide between ourselves and the developer than in a traditional publishing relationship, in which the publisher is on the hook for all costs.

The conversation turned to the way the CEG works and then what the alternative is for unsigned developers looking for help:

My partners (Gene Mauro, Mark Hood, and Seamus Blackley) and I set up CEG because we saw a growing disconnect between developers and publishers when it comes to getting original content produced. Today, given the enormous costs of developing and marketing top-notch games, publishers are more risk-averse than ever. This isn't a criticism of the publishers; they want to do innovative games as much as anyone, but they also need to be responsible when it comes to spending the huge amount of money required to get a game off the ground. We see an enormous opportunity for CEG to step in and fund and manage the production of those innovative (and hence riskier) games for the publishers so they can concentrate on what they do best.

Beyond working with CEG, developers can—as always—look to a publisher to fund development of their game. But, again, publishers are more conservative and cautious than ever when it comes to funding new, original game ideas.

Third, you can also try to fund development yourself:

Assuming that you don't have enough cash in the bank, you can always try to get a loan. With interest rates as low as they are today, if you can get it and then you can pay it back, it's a nice way to go. Of course, if you can't pay it back, you're done—bankrupt. In addition, there are private investors and venture capitalists who may be more interested in long-term potential, but they will take a significant portion of your company in exchange for the investment.

Finally, Bachus says that recently a number of "prototype" funds have emerged that are designed to help developers create a prototype that will ultimately be sold to a publisher. He explains:

> The publisher pays a premium and then assumes management of the game to completion. It may seem like a good way to demonstrate why a "risky" game has potential. After all, if you can show a publisher the game, they can understand your vision and it certainly helps *your* game stand apart from the other proposal documents on a publisher's desk. However, there's a big difference between building a prototype in order to make a sale and building a game. The order of tasks, the amount of work that goes into bells and whistles versus basic gameplay and mechanics, the investigation of production risks—all of these things are handled differently in the two cases, and it's not always easy to make the transition from one development style to another after the sale is made.

Having been in this industry for a long time, Bachus was asked to offer his best pieces of advice for someone who wants to break in the industry. He breaks it down into the following pointers:

1. **Get experience any way you can**. The most important element when trying to break into the industry is experience—not your training or your degree, not your intelligence or charming personality, and certainly not your high score on *Tony Hawk 3* or your vast collection of classic games for 8-bit and 16-bit systems (although that last one certainly gives you something to talk about!). The great thing about game development is that anyone can put together a reasonably good portfolio on their own—simple demos, character designs, game designs—anything that demonstrates your aptitude. After you have a few showpieces, hit the pavement and try to find whatever opportunities you can. The odds of being made lead designer on a multimillion dollar project are… slim. But if you can get onto a team in some capacity and excel in that role, you'll find that you're given more and more opportunities. Very few development teams have such rigid job structures and formality that you won't get more and more chances—if you're up to the task. But first, you have to put yourself into the position, however you can, to get those chances.

2. **Specialize**. Think of the most successful companies or individuals; what most of them have in common is that they do one thing really, really well. First-person shooters. Character animation. 3D engines. Level design. Racing games. Ultimately, you want to be known as the BEST character designer for platform games, or the BEST physics programmer for racing games, or the BEST level designer for real-time strategy games—so that when a team is looking for someone to fill a position, they think of you first. Remember: jack-of-all-trades, master of none.

3. **Be patient**. It takes time to build a career in any profession. Doctor, lawyer, rocket scientist; game development is no different. But with time and hard work, the opportunities will be there for you to seize.

Bachus was asked to discuss how to get development kits and what the process is like.

> The easiest and best way to get a development kit is to sell a concept to a publisher and have the publisher deal with the console manufacturers to arrange for your development kits.

> If you're not in a position to secure a publishing deal, but really need the development kits, you can try contacting the console manufacturers directly. Most of them have some sort of program for independent developers that can give you access to the technology you need. Of course, development kits aren't cheap: Don't expect the console manufacturers to cut you a special deal because you're just starting out.

However, most developers who think they need development kits probably don't. Bachus adds:

> If you're just looking to prove your team's skills to a publisher or put together a prototype of a game concept, you can do it more easily and more effectively on a PC. If you've set up your development environment properly, when you get your publishing deal you should be able to migrate your code to any of the consoles quickly and efficiently. I would approach a console manufacturer for hardware only if I had reached the limits of what I could do on a PC or if a publisher insisted on seeing experience on the specific console.

How can someone protect their idea?

"The best and only way I know to protect an idea is to reveal it only to people or companies they trust," answers Bachus. He explains:

> As any lawyer will quickly point out, ideas cannot be protected under copyright law—only the specific implementation of those ideas. It doesn't matter whether the idea is notarized or kept in a mason jar in the basement of the Wishy-Washy Washing Machine Co. If you have a great concept for a game about a time-traveling ninja/high school student, and someone else makes a game about a time-traveling ninja/high school student, you're out of luck. If they copy specific levels or puzzles or interface elements, you might have more of a shot at making a case. Of course, even then you're talking about months of court time and thousands of dollars in legal bills with no guarantee that you might win your case.

However, Bachus says that this sidesteps "the fundamental concern that's at the core of your question: How likely is it that someone will rip off your idea?" He explains that in his experience, the answer is not very likely at all:

> First of all, most publishers aren't just looking for good ideas. They're looking for teams that can successfully execute on the vision of the product. The success of most games isn't based on the "hook." It's based on the gameplay, the art, the audio, the technology: a million different things that all come together in the hands of a skilled team. Most publishers also know that very few successful games resemble their original concept because most successful games find their "voice" during the development process.

> It's way easier for a publisher to pay a designer a fee to purchase their idea or to walk away from an idea than to steal the idea and try to get someone else to make use of it.

On the other hand, many publishers are understandably concerned about novice game designers accusing them unfairly of stealing ideas. At CEG—as at many publishing companies—we won't accept an unsolicited game idea unless the designer signs a form acknowledging that we may already have other similar games in development. This isn't because we're looking for a license to steal. Quite the contrary. It's because many game designers have similar influences; and although they believe their idea is the most original, most unique idea ever, it's not only possible that two or three other people who have also come up with that same "most original, most unique idea ever"—it's probable. I've actually been in meetings at E3 where I will hear nearly the same idea two or three times in a day. It can be very surprising and very worrisome if you want to choose one of the various similar ideas, knowing that the other designers might accuse us of taking their idea and feeding it to the other team.

Bachus asks, "Would you hand your car keys, or house keys, or wallet to someone you barely know?"

If you have any fears that someone might want to rip off your idea, get to know them first. See if they seem ethical and honorable. Figure out what criteria they will use to decide whether to fund your game or not. Ask them how they've dealt with situations where they see similar concepts from different developers. Only then should you submit your concept.

"And if they tell you they already have a similar game in development... believe them," concludes Bachus.

So, what about video game agents and headhunters? Are they worth pursuing? Flip the page to read the pros and cons of working with 'em...

Chapter 22

Game Agents and Headhunters

THE EXPERTS

- Melanie Cambron
- Jeff Brunner, Representing Entertainers & Developers (R.E.D.)
- Marc Mencher, Virtual Search
- Pat Bigley, Prime Candidate

Let's face it—not all game designers have the *savoir faire* or courage to successfully sell themselves or their games to a reputable publisher. And in many cases, game designers *prefer* to concentrate only on the game itself and leave the number-crunching (and schmoozing!) to others.

As in other entertainment industries, such as film and music, game agents and headhunters represent designers and publishers, respectively. Although they work differently, their goal is the same—to unite talented game designers and their products with publishers and/or distributors.

This chapter is dedicated to both of these third parties by covering how they work—and more importantly, how you as a game designer can take advantage of the services they offer.

Melanie Cambron

Melanie Cambron, a.k.a. the "game recruiting goddess," is a recruiter for game industry leaders such as EA, THQ, Infogrames, and Sony. Her words of wisdom have been published in various books, plus she speaks each semester at the University of Texas at Austin and the University of North Texas on the game development industry. Visit www.melaniecambron.com for more information.

Cambron was first asked to explain what a "game recruiting goddess" does.

"I do it all," she begins.

> ➤ I locate top talent for my clients.

> ➤ I interview candidates.

> ➤ I review art and sound demo reels as well as code samples.

➤ I proofread and correct résumés.

➤ I take references for potential employees.

➤ I negotiate salary and benefit packages.

➤ I play tour guide and realtor for candidates.

➤ I dole out advice to those wanting to break into the game industry.

➤ I guest lecture at universities on the same subject.

➤ I assist candidates and their families with the often-cumbersome task of relocation.

➤ I provide spouses with information for their job searches.

➤ I am a liaison with immigration attorneys.

➤ I schedule travel for interviews.

➤ I then spend the afternoon lounging by the pool having cabaña boys bring me drinks with little umbrellas.

Okay, so we asked for it!

So, why would someone want a recruiter? Is a recruiter the same as a headhunter?

She responds:

A reputable recruiter is able to professionally market your qualifications to potential employers. That same well-established recruiter has developed strong relationships with key industry players and can get the résumé under the nose of the right person. Not only does the recruiter understand the intricacies of the hiring process, but he/she can be a wealth of information and support in dealing with salary negotiations, work visas, and relocation issues. Furthermore, because only 20% of available jobs are advertised, the recruiter has access to many "hidden" jobs through well-cultivated relationships and industry knowledge. "Headhunter" is simply cannibalistic slang for "recruiter."

Cambron was asked what she looks for in a candidate.

"Credit on current shipped games," she answers. And then clarifies:

I really look for folks who are able to stick with a project through ship. This is a volatile industry, and I sympathize that there are things that affect the project that are beyond your control. Publishers cancel projects; management misuses funds. But I am paid to find the best talent out there—the type of talent able to get the product out the door, even against all odds.

Do game designers/developers seek her services or does Cambron find them? The answer is "a bit of both."

She explains:

> When a client, the hiring game development company, asks me to conduct a search for talent, I actively seek out experienced individuals with the specific qualifications for that particular position. Thankfully, I also receive a great number of referrals from friends, clients, and candidates.

Is Cambron concerned only with established developers?

"I would love to assist every one in his/her job search," she begins. "However, I feel at the early stages of one's career, using recruiting services is not the best approach."

Why is that?

> Without a couple of years of professional game development experience, recruiting firms can hinder breaking into or furthering one's career. Companies pay fees to recruiters to find them specific talent that they cannot otherwise locate themselves. Most recruiting contracts with game companies specify a 12-month representation period. What this means is that after a recruiting firm submits your résumé, that studio cannot hire you for one year without that price on your head: the recruiter's fee. I would advise not utilizing any recruiting services during your first foray into the game industry. You will be much more effective in approaching companies by submitting your résumé directly.

Cambron offers a few web sites that provide game company names and links:

- ➤ `www.gignews.com`: Development tips, open jobs, job hunting advice

- ➤ `www.gamasutra.com`: Development tips, open jobs, job hunting advice

- ➤ `www.gamejobs.com`: Open jobs, job hunting advice

- ➤ `www.neoseeker.com`: Game product reviews, identifying companies by genre/platform

- ➤ `www.vgyellowpages.com`: Video game Yellow Pages

Cambron also offers a few suggestions for job hunting and interviewing:

- ➤ `www.gignews.com/perfectresume.htm`: Creating a perfect resume

- ➤ `www.gignews.com/jobcampaign_part1.htm`: Your personalized job hunt campaign

- ➤ `www.gignews.com/interview_questions.htm`: Interviewing tips

- ➤ `www.gignews.com/gamereferences.htm`: Your references

When asked what's the best advice to give an up-and-coming game developer, recruiter Melanie Cambron says, "Have samples," "Will travel" and "Manners matter." Read here for the elaboration.
(Used with permission by Melanie Cambron)

Next, Cambron was asked to provide an inspiring game developer success story that she was part of.

"Ah, my favorite Cinderella story," begins Cambron:

A studio head, who also happens to be a very dear friend of mine, was desperate to hire a top-notch lead PS2 programmer. This was back when they were as scarce as a full set of teeth at a square dance contest. I did some research and found a very talented lad working for a studio in Scotland. Luckily, he had a very unusual name, so I called information for the town in which the studio was based—and behold! He was listed. He returned my call and told me that he was not interested in moving to the United States at this time. I left him with some points to ponder; he called me the following day and informed me that indeed he was ready to move across the pond. Ultimately, he was hired by my client, tripled his income, gained all new furnishings, bought a new sports car, and paid off his student loans in just a couple of months. To his former colleagues back in Scotland, he emailed a photo of himself in front of his new car with the caption "God bless America!"

Melanie Cambron recommended a few good web sites and online articles previously, so she was asked to further explain her relationship with GIGnews.com:

GIGnews recruited me to utilize some of my connections with big names in the game industry to provide valuable insight into what they do and how they do it. Through the column, we hope to inspire as well as inform. I also get some great restaurant recommendations. I absolutely love doing the monthly interview with game industry celebrities, and have received wonderful feedback on the column. One recent interviewee said that it was the only article that her mother had ever appreciated.

Finally, what are the three single best pieces of advice Cambron can give to a budding game developer/designer who wants to break into the video gaming industry?

> **Have samples**. Samples—or better yet, a game demo relevant to your discipline—are an absolute must. Code samples for the budding programmer; 3D art samples for the budding artist; and writing and design samples for the designer. These samples not only illustrate your skills to potential employers; they also show that you are dedicated, professional, and prepared.

> **Will travel**. Be willing to move to land that first job. Flexibility in your geographic requirements will provide many more opportunities than if you limit yourself to jobs within 20 minutes of your current address.

> **Manners matter**. When approaching a company, be respectful of their time, be appreciative for any response, be appropriate in your correspondence. Correct grammar and spelling is becoming as rare as the Northern Spotted Owl. Take the time to properly compose your emails, and proofread your résumé. This is not casual banter with a friend via instant messaging. Follow each interview with a "thank you" email.

Jeff Brunner, Representing Entertainers & Developers (R.E.D.)

Jeff Brunner is the founder and a partner in Representing Entertainers & Developers—otherwise known as R.E.D (www.red-la.com). The primary mission of R.E.D. is to help independent game development companies to secure game development contracts and to work with game publishers and other entertainment companies to locate the right teams to develop their properties.

Brunner is also the president and cofounder of Interact, the interactive game industry's leading talent-recruitment company. Interact was founded in 1993 as the first recruiting company dedicated to the video game space. The individuals whom Interact has placed over the years are now senior decision makers at leading game publishers and studios. Interact recruits for these organizations, including Electronic Arts, Activision, THQ, Sega, and Acclaim.

Interact and R.E.D. are sister companies with distinct missions, but they share information and resources in order to provide broader opportunities for their respective clients.

Brunner explains why a budding artist, programmer, or game designer should consider using the services of a recruiting agency:

Probably the biggest benefit of using a reputable recruiting agency is gaining access to its extensive industry contacts. Interact has been in business for more than nine years, and we've built a pretty massive network of contacts, which enables us to match our candidates with job opportunities they would never have found on their own. The developers we've placed during those years have risen to positions in which they are hiring authorities at their companies, which helps our candidates get in the door.

Brunner adds that time is an important factor in the job search:

> Developers can find jobs on their own—they do it all the time. However, it's very time-consuming, espe-
> cially while in crunch mode during the home stretch of the development cycle—which is precisely when
> a developer needs to be looking ahead to the next assignment. It's hard to mount a methodical job
> search in your scarce spare time. Opportunities come and go quickly in our fluid industry. Recruiters
> spend all day on the phone finding out where the jobs are, so they're likely to find the kind of job you
> want much more quickly than you could on your own.

> Good recruiters not only uncover job opportunities; they help prepare their candidates for a successful
> interview. They've helped dozens of developers through the interview process and have a good idea
> what works and what doesn't. We also tap into our near-decade of experience to counsel candidates
> on advancing their careers. For example, we always advise against changing jobs in mid-project because
> it makes them look unreliable to potential employers.

R.E.D.'s and Interact's services are free to the developer. How does this work?

> Our revenues are contingent on us finding our clients work. In the case of R.E.D., our fees are normally
> a function of the development budget. We typically receive 10%, but that can vary depending on the
> project. In the case of Interact, a recruiter's commission is paid by the employer, based on (not taken
> from) the candidate's compensation package—and only if the candidate stays at the job for a guaran-
> teed minimum time (usually three months). This is added inducement for recruiters to negotiate the best
> possible deal for their candidates—and an incentive to match candidates with professionally satisfying
> positions.

How exactly does the recruitment process work? In the following sections, Brunner provides
a detailed step-by-step description of what happens after someone signs on.

Interact

I'll start with Interact because it follows a more defined, consistent process. Candidates come to us in a
variety of ways. Interact recruiters seek them out proactively; for example, by attending industry events
such as the Game Developers Conference and E3, reading game credits, following industry media, and
calling developers directly. Candidates also send us their résumés through our web sites or through listings in online outlets such as Gamasutra.com or the Videogame Yellow Pages. Relationship building is
a big part of finding developers to represent; candidates are referred to us by friends and colleagues
whom we've helped in the past.

After a candidate gives us his or her résumé, we do an intake to determine objectives, skills, and preferences (location, genre/platform, salary). We want to find out what kind of games the candidate wants
to develop.

We then distribute the résumé internally and examine it as a team in order to determine the candidate's
strengths and weaknesses and to discuss the candidate's objectives.

Following our evaluation, we contact employers to find available jobs that best match the candidate's objectives, skills, and preferences, which we then discuss in detail with the candidate. If the candidate is interested in a position, we get his or her approval to send a résumé and work samples. Only then do we send the résumé and samples, and only to companies that the candidate has specifically approved.

The next step is selling our candidate to the hiring authority and convincing him or her that this is the right person for the job. A lot depends on us having the hiring manager's ear—and our positive reputation and track record lend weight and credibility to our recommendations.

If the hiring person agrees to interview our candidate, we set it up and prepare the candidate—counseling on successful presentation and interview techniques, going over likely questions, and helping the candidate polish his or her answers.

After the interview, we get feedback from the hiring manager, mollify any concerns or objections, and set up a second interview. (It's our experience that the hiring process almost always involves at least two interviews.)

We also talk to our candidate to see whether he or she is still interested in the job. If so, we set up the second interview. When it gets to the offer stage, we negotiate a compensation package and present it to the candidate. If it isn't acceptable, we renegotiate until we come up with a mutually agreeable package and then set a start date.

The relationship doesn't end there. Only a shortsighted recruiter just goes for the commission and then it's "goodbye and good luck." A good recruiter stays in touch with the candidate, providing advice and making sure that things are going well. Our goal is to ensure that candidates have a positive experience working with a recruiter, so they'll call on us again in the future and refer friends and co-workers.

R.E.D.

There's really no "typical" process when we sign a client—it depends entirely on the client's situation. Some are established studios looking to augment their own business development efforts. Some are startup teams that need a publisher for their original game idea or a nearly completed game. Other times, it's a new studio that just needs a project to get the business going. We also work with publishers, looking for the best talent to develop their projects, and we help venture capitalists find investment opportunities in game development.

The level of preparation with a startup is more involved. Startup studios are generally intact development teams that have broken off from a publisher or larger development studio. Some have an original game idea for which they're seeking a publisher, and others are more interested in securing deals to develop games in a particular genre.

Some studios sign exclusive representation agreements, but more often they simply authorize us to represent them to publishers. Although we're called "game agents," we're more accurately characterized as a business development arm for our clients, negotiating deals and bringing them projects.

I'll illustrate our trade with a familiar example: an independent studio looking for the next project. After the studio signs with us, we consult with them about what sort of projects they're looking to do—platform, genre, and so on.

If it's a new studio, we evaluate its demo because producing an impressive demo is the single most important factor in grabbing a publisher's interest—especially if the studio lacks a track record in the genre of the project in question. Although the climate is shifting away from awarding development projects based on name and pedigree alone, publishers are assuming larger financial risks as game budgets increase. That's why they need to see an outstanding playable demo as proof that a new studio can deliver.

At this point, we begin contacting publishers that we think would be a good match for our client, and set up meetings with the client. (Between R.E.D.'s ongoing work with publishers and information shared by our sister company Interact, we have a fairly complete idea of what projects are available.)

Prior to these meetings, we sit down with the client and prepare them to answer the questions that publishers would ask. We review any design documents they have and make constructive recommendations where possible.

There are generally several meetings along the road to signing a contract, and many phone calls from us to the publisher to help them realize that our team is the right match for their project. If the publisher decides to go with our client, R.E.D. then negotiates the best terms possible. A Letter of Intent (LOI) is signed, and our client is paid an advance on the budget while details of the formal contract are being ironed out. After the deal is finalized, we monitor progress, involving ourselves as needed so we can focus on bringing the client additional projects. Via our sister company Interact, we assist the studio in staffing their development team.

There really aren't any other game talent firms that negotiate all the aspects of a deal (subscription fees, royalties, development budget, interactive and non-interactive rights), function as the client's business development arm, and provide the recruiting resources to staff development teams.

Interested game designers/developers can visit Interact at `www.interactjobs.com`.

Marc Mencher, Virtual Search

Former software engineer Marc Mencher worked for game companies such as Spectrum Holobyte and 3DO before founding Virtual Search (`www.vsearch.com`), a game industry recruiting firm. Virtual Search has a worldwide clientele servicing a variety of game development companies. In addition to traditional recruiting services, Virtual Search is unique in that the company is focused on career development, ensuring that the talent it represents achieve their short-term and long-term career goals.

Marc Mencher provides the following comprehensive (and lengthy) summary—created for this book—on what recruiters are, how they work, and why using a recruiter may be a good idea.

Along with lawyers and used car salesmen, recruiters are often the people that other people just love to hate. Admittedly, there are unprofessional recruiters in almost every industry, including the game industry, just as there are certainly unprofessional programmers, artists, producers, developers, and so on. But an experienced, ethical, and competent recruiter can mean the difference between your dream job and no job at all.

What is a recruiter?

Generally speaking, a recruiter matches job candidates with open job positions. For example, if Hot Smokin' Games, Inc. is looking for a producer, a recruiter will help find the right person to fill that position. Hot Smokin' Games, Inc. then pays the recruiter a fee if it hires that producer. If a recruiter asks you (not the company) to pay a fee for placing you, don't use that recruiter.

Why use a recruiter?

What if you're in a high demand/low supply position? For example, if you're a PSX programmer, why should you use a recruiter? Why should anyone use a recruiter? If you went to the hypothetical Hot Smokin' Games web site, you might find a link for "Employment Opportunities" and a series of job openings listed, as well as contact information where you can send your résumé. If you can send your résumé directly to the company, why even bother with a recruiter?

> ➤ **Avoid wasting time**. By using a recruiter, you don't spend your time searching for job postings, company contact information, and application requirements. There are thousands of computer game companies just in the United States. A simple web search will turn up dozens of game companies in the San Francisco Bay Area, and that's just the tip of the iceberg. And most of the companies have different application requirements. Recruiters have immediate knowledge of hundreds of job openings and they know exactly how each company wants your résumé to look.

> ➤ **Leap over the HR pile**. When you send your résumé to a company, you rely on Human Resources (HR) to route it. HR departments receive hundreds, if not thousands, of résumés for every position, from secretary to CFO. Your résumé will land somewhere in that pile and hang there until the busy HR staff has the time to sort and distribute the résumés to the appropriate hiring managers. Good recruiters, on the other hand, have long-term relationships with hiring managers and can market you directly to the appropriate manager within the company. For example, a recruiter who has a longstanding relationship with the Hot Smokin' Games hiring manager could give her a call and speak directly with her about you and your qualifications. On the other hand, if you cold-called the hiring manager, chances are she would be "away from her desk," or would just ask you to send your résumé. And, to be honest, you couldn't blame her. These folks get tons of calls and inquiries, and there is just so much time in a day. In short, recruiters help hiring managers cut to the chase.

> ➤ **Benefit from honest feedback and savvy spin control**. Recruiters get frank feedback from the company on how you performed in an interview. Generally speaking, hiring managers are reluctant to give honest feedback directly to a job candidate. However, they usually feel

completely free to let loose and give the recruiter the real lowdown on what transpired. Armed with this candid information, an effective recruiter can clean up any "mess" made by the candidate during the interview. For example, one recruiter represented a technically qualified candidate, but despite preinterview prep with his recruiter, the guy exhibited a bad attitude due to past work experiences. Not impressed with Mr. Bad Attitude, the hiring manager didn't extend a job offer, despite dead-on technical qualifications. Immediately after learning that the candidate was rejected, the recruiter contacted the hiring manager to discuss exactly what went wrong in the interview. Armed with the hiring manager's candid information, the recruiter was able to perform some savvy spin control, clean up the candidate's mess, and convince the hiring manager to give the guy a second interview. The second interview went much better. The candidate understood what went wrong, the hiring manager understood why it went wrong, and Mr. New Attitude was hired.

➤ **Reap the rewards of inside information**. Recruiters—at least the ones you should work with—are paid by the hiring company, not the candidate. As a general rule, if a company can pay a recruiter's fee, it's not in it for the short run. That is, companies who work with recruiters are typically more financially stable, so you won't find that you've relocated to Austin from San Francisco just to be out of a job two weeks later. Recruiters will focus you on the stable paying jobs and keep you informed of unadvertised and unique opportunities.

➤ **Enjoy a higher salary and better employment package**. A recruiter who is focused in the game industry market will know what your salary level should be, compared with others who have similar skills. If you haven't done the best job in the past negotiating your base salary and benefits program, a good recruiter can help you in this area. A recruiter knows the hiring company and what can and can't be accomplished for the specific position for which you're interviewing. A recruiter knows how much stock, vacation time, and bonus percentages are typically awarded for your employment level. A good recruiter also knows how far to push the salary negotiations, and so on. If you wonder why you're more qualified than your office mate, but she has a much better compensation package, odds are it's because she had a strong recruiter negotiate her employment package.

➤ **Benefit from long-term career management**. Career growth doesn't simply happen on a wish and a prayer. After you've found a recruiter you can relate to, let him help you formulate your short-term and long-term career goals. When you've outlined a plan of action, you and your recruiter can execute it over the next several years. Keep in mind that it's no coincidence that most managers, directors, or VP-level people within your company have longstanding relationships with a recruiter and obtained their senior level position through this recruiter.

So, why the bad rep?

If all of the preceding is true, and if recruiters are so darn helpful for company and candidate, why the bad reputation? Well, professional, ethical, and well-established recruiters play out the previous scenarios. The bad rep comes from recruiters who do things such as scan job ads, match buzzwords off your résumé, and blast-fax your information—often without asking your permission—and risking your confidentiality.

How do you find a good recruiter?

The best way to find a good recruiter is by word-of-mouth. A good recruiting firm should have established a reputation in the game industry. If you're thinking of looking for a new job, ask your friends and colleagues in the industry. Certainly, looking for a new job can be a very confidential matter, and if you don't feel comfortable asking anyone, do a little game industry reading. Well-established recruiters frequently appear as contributors in game industry publications such as GIGNews.com, GameWEEK, Gamasutra, and so on. You can also do a web search for recruiters. A Yahoo! Search for game jobs or game recruiters should be a good start. Then visit the recruiter's web site. Is it professional? Does it give you information about the firm? Check out their job listings. Are they current?

How do you work with a recruiter?

Establishing and maintaining a long-term relationship with a recruiter is one of the best-kept secrets in personal career advancement and management. And working with a recruiter is simple. If a recruiter contacts you, there are three easy steps to take:

1. **Be flattered**. Rest assured; no one headhunts a loser.

2. **Be helpful**. The first call is usually a polite request for information about you and your job status. The recruiter is not going to—nor has any incentive to—leak information. So take a moment and answer a couple of questions. If you're uncomfortable talking at work, simply get the recruiter's number and call back from home or give the recruiter your home number.

3. **Be nice**. As the saying goes, it costs nothing to be polite. Remember that nothing in life is certain but death and taxes, and although you may not be looking for a job the day a recruiter calls, you may be a jobseeker in the future. Don't burn any bridges.

Get in touch

If a recruiter contacts you and you're interested, or if you've found a recruiter on your own or by recommendation, your next step is simple: Give that recruiter a call or send an email. To use an overly clichéd phrase, a recruiter is usually a "people person" and will probably be more than happy to speak with you. At that point, the recruiter will want details about what you're looking for as well as your past experience. Assuming that you're the kind of person that recruiting firm works with, you'll need to send in your résumé. Although it's in your best interest to have your résumé in good shape before you send it to the recruiter, another benefit of working with a recruiter is the résumé assistance you'll receive. Recruiters know what companies are looking for and they know how to make a résumé shine.

Even if the recruiter doesn't have any job openings that fit your particular profile at that time, things always change; the next time he needs to fill a position for an art director in Minneapolis, you'll be on the "call" list.

Stay in touch

When you're working with a recruiter, it's important to keep an ongoing dialogue. If you have concerns about a certain position, talk it through with your recruiter. And be sure to always contact your recruiter following interviews that he has set up for you. Give your recruiter a complete rundown of your take on the interview—what questions were asked and how you responded. After he speaks with you, your recruiter will talk to the company. As indicated in the example mentioned previously, if anything went slightly awry, your recruiter may be able to administer some job-saving spin doctoring.

Above all else, be open and honest with your recruiter. To paraphrase Tom Cruise in Jerry Maguire, "Help your recruiter help you." Recruiters succeed only when you succeed. Make sure that you're on the same page in terms of what you want to do, as well as how and where you want to do it.

What should you expect from your recruiter?

➤ **Creation of a professional and effective presentation package**. A good recruiter will not just take your existing résumé and blast-fax it—you can do that yourself. Rather, a good recruiter will help you work on your presentation package. A presentation package includes a résumé, but one that's laid out to correctly highlight your experience as it relates to the specific job you want. Blasting out a generic résumé results in a high rejection rate. In addition to a tailored résumé, a presentation package also includes a minibiography on who you are, along with complete references. This is an important first step. Your résumé and presentation need to open doors. If a recruiter is interested only in getting his hands on your résumé and doesn't spend any time working on your presentation, you have a weak and ineffective recruiter working for you. Your résumé will probably be blasted out to every game company on the planet, risking your confidentiality and getting you rejected from consideration for a job that you're totally qualified to handle.

➤ **Creation of a job search strategy**. When your presentation package is in order, a good recruiter will co-create with you a job search strategy that considers your location desires, salary requirements, and career objectives. This search strategy is particularly important because you don't want your recruiter submitting your résumé to companies in which you have strong personal contacts. The search strategy will include a list of companies that you will approach yourself and a list of companies the recruiter will approach on your behalf. The search strategy keeps both parties on the same page. You never have to ask yourself, "What's the recruiter doing for me?" It's outlined in a mutually agreed-upon search strategy!

➤ **Complete job description and company education**. After the search strategy is established and you indicate interest in some of the jobs the recruiter has highlighted for you, expect to see written, detailed job descriptions from the recruiter. If these aren't provided, your recruiter probably doesn't have a good relationship with the hiring companies. The recruiter should also be able to educate you about the company: the company's financial strength; how well the management team works together within the company; short-term and long-term company plans; how well the bonus program has worked for other employees. In other words, all the upfront information you need to make the decision about whether you're really interested in the job. Only after you've established interest will a good recruiter release your résumé.

➤ **Feedback and constant communication**. A good recruiter will constantly update you on the status of your search. During an active job search phase, you can expect to hear from your recruiter on a weekly basis or more often. If you're passively looking around (just want to hear about new things when they pop up), you can expect to hear from the recruiter every other month or so.

➤ **Preparation for an interview**. A good recruiter, having a strong relationship with the hiring client, will prepare you for interviews—whether face-to-face or via telephone. The recruiter knows the hiring manager and what the company seeks technically, as well as interpersonally. Because you'll enter the interview process with much more information and insight into the company than someone who hasn't used a recruiter, your chances of getting the job are much better!

➤ **Support and negotiation**. Job hunting can be emotional and stressful. Your recruiter is your support system—scheduling all interviews as well as managing the process and flow of your communication with the hiring company. Your recruiter not only helps you and the hiring company establish a mutually beneficial employment relationship, she helps ensure—when choosing between several job offers—that you stay in line with the search strategy you set in motion for your short-term and long-term career goals.

➤ **Relocation and continued communication**. Finally, you can expect your recruiter to help you with the resignation process from your current job, help you and your family move (if needed), locate housing, address any visa issues, and so on. You can also expect to hear from your recruiter from time to time, ensuring that you've adjusted properly to your new work situation and troubleshooting problems if any exist.

Visit Virtual Search at www.vsearch.com.

Pat Bigley, Prime Candidate

Pat Bigley is the vice president of Prime Candidate, Inc. (www.primecandidateinc.com). Prime Candidate is an executive recruiting company specializing in the computer game industry. It recruits at all levels, including executives, sales, marketing, and all areas of development.

Why would a designer/developer or executive in the gaming industry use a recruiter such as Prime Candidate?

The market is flooded with every Tom, Dick, and Harry today looking to either get a job or to get into this industry. It's a very exciting and fast-paced industry, and it has a lot of interest for young people—but most wouldn't know how to get started in the industry and would certainly benefit by using a recruiter to get them introduced properly.

Also, many people don't want to be one of the many candidates thrown into the stack of résumés on an HR person's desk. If recruiters do their job properly, they market individuals so their credentials stand out and draw attention. Also, a good recruiter is usually very connected and can take a good résumé directly into one of the hiring authorities rather than through HR. It's a much quicker route and a more polished one.

As with the other recruitment agencies, individuals who sign with Prime Candidate don't pay for the service—rather, the hiring company pays. How does this service work? Bigley breaks it down into a dozen steps:

1. We ask for a résumé. If it reads correctly and is polished, we accept it. If it needs to be rewritten, we help the candidate with the rewrite.

2. We ask a lot of questions regarding salary range, geographical parameters, type of position the candidate is most interested in, skill set, and other general information to help us figure out which position we might be working on that best fits the candidate's needs and skills.

3. We send a list of the companies that we suggest might have interest in the candidate. Sometimes, we can supply the candidate with a job description; sometimes, we don't have a specific job, so we merely include the name of the company and the city.

4. We ask the candidate to let us know which companies should get a response—we always get permission to send a résumé.

5. Based on our communication, we send the résumé. This is usually done via email.

6. Some companies are good about communicating. They either ask to set up a phone interview with the candidate or they pass.

7. If the company wants to speak with the candidate, the company representative usually calls the recruiter and schedules a time to talk. This process can last for a few minutes to an hour.

8. After the initial phone screen, if the company representatives seem interested in the candidate, they usually then schedule an onsite meeting. If the company is local to the candidate, they merely agree on a time and set the meeting. If the company is in another city, state, or country, the company schedules a flight, hotel accommodations, and car as necessary. These interviews are usually a one-day or two-day process, and the actual interviews could go all day because the candidate will be meeting with many different people.

9. Sometimes, there are second and third interviews. If the company needs to meet with the candidate again, the next set of meetings is scheduled.

10. Decisions are made. Does the company want the candidate, and does the candidate want to work at the company? Remember that the interview process is for both parties—not just the company.

11. Either the company and/or candidate passes at this time, or both parties agree that they want to have an offer made. If everyone agrees on an offer, it's presented to the candidate at this time. He or she should work with the recruiter to decide whether the offer is good and viable. If the candidate wants to accept the offer, he or she can either accept via the recruiter or can speak directly with the company representative. If the offer has to be negotiated, it's decided whether the recruiter or the candidate will discuss the changes with the company.

12. The offer is accepted and the recruiter steps back—a start date is set and the process is complete.

Bigley says that many of the candidates they've placed have had successful tenures in the industry. "We've given many people the chance to fulfill their dreams and thus open up their own development company," she adds.

Is a recruitment company for everyone?

In some cases, that's the only way they'll get hired. But then again, some companies won't use recruiters because of the cost of the service, and some companies prefer to do it themselves.

On why a prospective employee should use Prime Candidate versus other similar agencies, Bigley maintains that it's a highly respected company, and people want to use its service because of its reputation. "We actually agent our talent to the respective company and find the specific talent that the company wants. We're very selective with the companies we have our agreements with, and extremely selective with the talent we represent. We respect the interests of our candidates and our companies."

For more on Prime Candidate, Inc., visit www.primecandidateinc.com.

Chapter 23

Design Schools and Courses

KEY TOPICS

- DigiPen Institute of Technology

- Full Sail

- Other Schools and Courses to Consider

As evident by their entries in this book, dozens of successful game designers, programmers, and artists believe that some level of advanced schooling is an important asset and serves as a solid foundation on which to build a career in the interactive entertainment industry. In fact, many project leaders and producers won't employ someone unless he or she has a degree related to that specialty (such as a university or college computer science diploma for programmers). There are hundreds of such courses for programmers, artists, animators, musicians, and sound engineers; but there are very few that focus specifically on how these disciplines relate to computer or console gaming. And it comes as no surprise that even fewer focus strictly on game design.

This chapter looks at a few schools and courses that cater to individuals who want to make a living as a developer in the computer or console gaming industry.

DigiPen Institute of Technology

Jason Chu, registrar of DigiPen Institute of Technology (www.digipen.edu), chats with us about what this unique school has to offer.

First, a bit of history. DigiPen Corporation was founded by Claude Comair in Vancouver, British Columbia, Canada in 1988. Its beginnings were as a company that provided services in 3D computer animation and special effects to the entertainment industry. Comair and company recognized that there was a tremendous shortage of 3D computer animators and decided to do something about it. DigiPen started to offer educational programs for artists to become 3D animators.

In 1991, they had a meeting with Nintendo of America (NOA) and discussed the possibility for DigiPen to offer educational programs in video game programming. This idea became reality in September of 1994, when they started the computer game programming program, supported by NOA. According to Chu, they realized that this program was the only one of its kind in Canada or the U.S. It was a two-year program; however, games were becoming more complex to program when the trend shifted to 3D. Therefore, DigiPen expanded the course to a four-year Bachelor's degree program. In February 1998, DigiPen opened a larger campus in Redmond, Washington.

Chu explains that video games are essentially interactive simulation programs in real time, hence the name they chose for the discipline: Bachelor of Science Degree in Real-Time Interactive Simulation.

Attending DigiPen U isn't all fun and games, says Max Szlagor, a recent grad who received a Bachelor's degree in Real-Time Interactive Simulation. "A typical DigiPen work week might stretch 12 plus hours a day, including weekends, in order to finish a project," says Szlagor. Here's a shot of the school grounds.
(Used with permission by Digipen Institute of Technology.)

This curriculum currently consists of nine levels of mathematics, two levels of physics, four levels of computer animation, 23 levels of computer science, and four complete projects in game implementation. The degree, in total, consists of 154 credits. DigiPen also offers a two-year associate degree program and a high school summer course, and there is talk of offering Master's and Ph.D. degrees in the near future.

Asked why someone who wants to learn about game programming or 3D animation would want to attend DigiPen, Chu answers in light of the current curriculum on programming:

> This is a highly specialized educational program in the area of game programming. As far as we're aware, we were the first and are currently the only degree-granting institution in the world dedicated to video game programming. If one is committed to becoming a game programmer as a career, this is the right school for the training.

Want to know what it's like to attend DigiPen? What about after you graduate? Max Szlagor, a recent grad, received a Bachelor's degree in Real-Time Interactive Simulation and graduated in April of 2001. He talks about life at DigiPen U and beyond.

Was Digipen all fun and games?

> Well, it was fun in the sense that we got to work with great classmates and excellent teachers while finishing several high-quality games. Although we played games for fun and research, most of our time was focused on making killer games. A typical DigiPen work week might stretch 12 plus hours a day, including weekends, in order to finish class work and polish any projects that were being worked on.

Sixty hours a week is a lot of work—creating games or otherwise! How much money can a grad start to make once finished at DigiPen U?

> Like any job, salaries vary widely. It all depends on the company you work for, the region you work in, the degree you get, and the skill level of the graduate. A four-year graduate can expect to make $40,000–$60,000, though the upper end would be pretty uncommon in most areas.

Are you working now?

> I am currently working at Nintendo Software Technology Corporation (NST). Some of the games produced by NST include Ridge Racer 64 and Pokémon Puzzle League for the N64, as well as Bionic Commando and Crystalis for the Game Boy Color. So far, work has been amazing, and my DigiPen education is serving me well.

Full Sail

Another high-tech college with a program dedicated to game design is Full Sail in Winterpark, Florida (for details see www.fullsail.com or www.fullsail.com/fs1/gd). Its motto is "real-world education," and game design is but one of the digital media programs offered. Full Sail's Game Design Associate of Science degree program was established to teach students the skills necessary to design and create single-player and multiplayer computer games for networks, PCs, and dedicated gaming consoles.

The course starts at an introductory level, beginning with basic mathematical and programming techniques and a sweeping chronological perspective of the computer gaming industry, in order to study and identify market trends that determine successful gaming hardware and software. This preface provides the foundation needed for the heart of the course: math and physics, programming in C++/DirectX/OpenGL, artificial intelligence techniques in modeling opponent behavior, coding multiplayer games, and ultimately a game project and significant clock hours on the PC.

Full Sail has a placement assistance department to arrange postgraduate internships in game development companies.

> **NOTE**
>
> Although the end of this chapter lists a number of schools and courses in North America for game design, programming, or animation, be sure to use your favorite search engine (such as Google) to type in the name of a desired city and then "video game school" to see what else you can come up with. Happy hunting!

Other Schools and Courses to Consider

Following is a list of additional schools and courses to consider for game designers, programmers, and animators:

- ➤ Academy of Art College (www.academyart.edu)
- ➤ The Art Institute of California—San Francisco (www.aisf.aii.edu)
- ➤ The Art Institutes (www.artinstitutes.edu or www.aii.edu)
- ➤ California Institute of the Arts (www.calarts.edu)
- ➤ Carnegie Mellon University (www.cmu.edu)
- ➤ Center for Advanced Digital Applications at New York University (www.sce.nyu.edu/cada)
- ➤ Center for Digital Imaging and Sound (CDIS) (www.gameschool.com or www.artschool.com)
- ➤ The Centre for Creative Communications at Centennial College (www.bccc.com)
- ➤ Centre National d'animation et de Design (www.nad.qc.ca)
- ➤ Cogswell Polytechnical College (www.cogswell.edu)
- ➤ DePaul University (www.depaul.edu)
- ➤ DeVry Institutes (www.devry.edu)

- DH Institute of Media Arts (www.dhima.com)
- Eastern Business Computer Institute College of Applied Art and Technology (www.ebci.ca)
- Game Institute (www.gameinstitute.com)
- Georgia Institute of Technology (www.gatech.edu)
- Herzing College (www.herzing.edu)
- Indiana University (www.indiana.edu)
- Marycrest International University (www.mcrest.edu)
- Massachusetts Institute of Technology (MIT) (www.mit.edu)
- Mesmer Animation Labs (www.mesmer.com)
- Middlesex University School of Computing Science (www.cs.mdx.ac.uk)
- MIT Artificial Intelligence Laboratory (www.ai.mit.edu)
- National Centre for Computer Animation at Bournemouth University (http://ncca.bournemouth.ac.uk)
- (NBCC) Miramichi (www.miramichi.nbcc.nb.ca)
- New York University (www.nyu.edu)
- Parsons School of Design (www.parsons.edu)
- Pratt Institute (www.pratt.edu)
- Rochester Institute of Technology (www.rit.edu)
- San Francisco State University (www.cel.sfsu.edu)
- San José State University (www.sjsu.edu)
- Savannah College of Art and Design (www.scad.edu)
- School of Communication Arts (www.ncsca.com or www.sca3d.com)
- Seneca College—Digital Media Centre (www.dmc3d.com)
- Stanford University (www.stanford.edu)
- University of Abertay Dundee (www.abertay.ac.uk)
- University of Advancing Computer Technology (www.uact.edu)
- University of Birmingham School of Computer Science (www.cs.bham.ac.uk)
- University of California, Irvine (www.uci.edu)

➤ University of California, Los Angeles (`www.ucla.edu`)

➤ University of Central Florida (`www.ucf.edu`)

➤ University of Maryland, Baltimore County (`www.umbc.edu`)

➤ University of Michigan AI Lab, Electrical Engineering and Computer Science Department (`http://ai.eecs.umich.edu`)

➤ University of North Texas Department of Computer Science (`www.cs.unt.edu`)

➤ University of Southern California Computer Science Department (`www.usc.edu/dept/cs`)

➤ Vancouver Film School (`www.vfs.com`)

Chapter 24

Game Design Resources on the Internet

KEY TOPICS

- Gamasutra
- Key Sites
- Essential Gaming E-Zines and Other Game Development Sites

This book may cover a lot of ground in a number of areas, but by no means is it the final word on game design and how to break into this bustling industry. The Internet is an outstanding medium for both novice and seasoned designers and other game developers to learn, interact, and contribute as members of the thriving gaming community. The purpose of this chapter is to present a number of enlightening stopovers while surfing the information highway.

Throughout this book, dozens of URLs and handy Usenet newsgroups have been offered for further and future reference, but this chapter is dedicated to more general game design.

> **NOTE**
> Like most things on the Net, site names, URLs, and such for the gaming industry are subject to change. If you don't find a site listed here, keep looking! Try Google.com. It's one of the best search engines on the Net.

The following web sites and Usenet newsgroups are generally listed alphabetically. But first, one web site that is arguably the most important for any budding game designer/developer to bookmark: Gamasutra.

Gamasutra

Gamasutra (`www.gamasutra.com`) is the premier game design web site, covering a wealth of topics from programming to graphic design; sound engineering to music; even areas dedicated to the production, legal, and business angles of the gaming industry. Each section provides regularly updated news, editorials, interviews, columns from experts in the industry, job classifieds, free utilities and source code, and much more. In short, make this your startup page on the web.

Alex Dunne, executive producer at Gamasutra, joins us here for a discussion of what Gamasutra is, what the site offers, and how it relates to its sister paper publication (*Game Developer*). Plus, Dunne has some tips for game designers looking to break into the biz. Incidentally, Dunne is also the chairman and founder of the Independent Games Festival (`www.igf.com`), an annual event, first launched in 1998, which recognizes innovation in independently developed video games (see Chapter 25, "Key Conventions, Organizations, and Awards"). Let's start right off with Dunne's description of Gamasutra.

> Gamasutra is the largest independent game development site, and it is part of the Gama Network (`www.gamanetwork.com`). It serves up daily news and technical articles, and as the sister site to Game Developer and the Game Developers Conference, many magazine articles and conference papers are published on Gamasutra. Besides news and articles, Gamasutra provides a range of services that help game developers connect with one another: résumé hosting (which is free, of course) and résumé searching; industry job listings; contract work listings (great for finding freelancers for your game); and a directory of contractors in the industry (freelance programmers, animators, composers, sound effects engineers, and so on). Gamasutra also features a comprehensive buyer's guide of game development products and services. The site currently has more than 100,000+ registered members, and it's free to join.

How is Gamasutra related to *Game Developer*?

> I handle issues related to the magazine's web site, which is dedicated primarily to customer service issues related to the magazine's circulation, and to generating subscriptions as well—magazine articles are found on Gamasutra.

What are the three most important things that budding game developers—that is, programmers, artists, level designers, game designers and so forth—should keep in mind when trying to break into the business?

I have just one: "Show, don't tell." By that, I mean that a demonstration of your abilities is far more important to a potential employer than practically anything you could write about yourself in your résumé. If you aspire to become a game programmer, show demos of what you've done in the past as they relate to the job you'd like to land at the company. If you're an animator, have a solid demo reel. If you're a level designer, show levels you've worked on. In this industry, talk is cheap, so examples of your work are critical to prove to employers what you're capable of.

What would you say are some of the best resources on the Net or in print?

Because I've worked on them for years and I'm extremely attached to them, I have to start out by mentioning our own site, Gamasutra.com, and our magazine, *Game Developer*. Both of them feature information that will help people looking to get into the industry. Our postmortems in particular should be of interest to budding developers—you read about what working on a game is really like, especially the things that can go wrong during development. But, of course, there are plenty of other great sources of information out there. I'd recommend flipCode (`www.flipcode.com`) and GameDev.net (`www.gamedev.net`) for development information, Fatbabies (`www.fatbabies.com`) for the ugly underbelly of the industry, and Blue's News (`www.bluesnews.com`) for excellent news about new games and projects in the pipeline.

You're involved in the Game Developers Conference, held each March in San José, California. What are some of the side projects you or your company are involved in?

Over the past three years, we assumed management of the International Game Developers Association. The IGDA is a nonprofit industry association that helps build communication among professionals in the game development industry. There are local chapters in various cities around the world that meet on a regular basis and help introduce game developers to one another. The IGDA also has a number of committees that address particular issues related to public policy and other areas of general concern to the community of game developers—such as education, online games, software patents, violence, and women in game development. The Gama Network also produces the Independent Games Festival (www.igf.com), an annual event held at the Game Developers Conference, which recognizes the most innovative independent games of the year. The IGF is to the game industry a bit like what the Sundance film festival is to the movie industry: a place in which small innovative projects are held up for the industry to see. Now in its fourth year, the IGF has helped a number of independent games find publishers, and has given out tens of thousands of dollars to independent game developers.

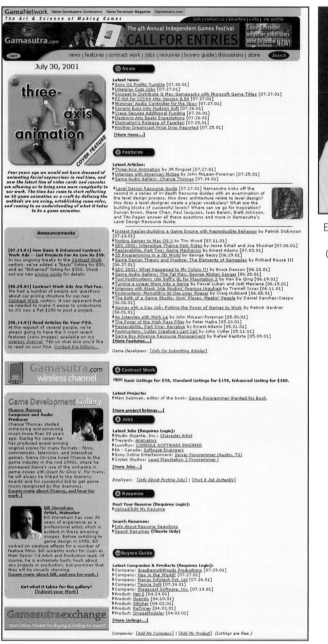

Easily the most celebrated webzine dedicated to the game design and development community is Gamasutra. This chapter features an interview with Alex Dunne, executive producer at the site.

(Used with permission by Alex Dunne.)

Dunne discusses some of the key media events, trade shows, and conventions to attend if you want to make connections and learn more about the industry:

The Game Developers Conference (`www.gdconf.com`) is the biggest event exclusively for game developers. There are hundreds of classes on various game development topics, lots of opportunities to meet people in the industry, and an expo floor full of companies involved in the game development industry. The Electronic Entertainment Expo, or E3 (`www.e3expo.com`), is another great event that showcases most of the games coming out in the upcoming year. SIGGRAPH (`www.siggraph.org`) is an excellent conference targeting the computer graphics industry. Although not strictly a game development event, many of the technologies are applicable in our arena.

Chapter 23, "Design Schools and Courses," discusses game programming schools—but does Dunne feel that education in this area is even necessary? He replies, "My general recommendation would be to attend any college that will offer you a firm grounding in math and computer science (to help your technical skills), and a good dose of humanities and liberal arts (to help develop your game design skills). Education is always a necessity in my book."

Let's switch gears for a moment. Is it easier to start a development company or get a job at an existing development company? What are the pros and cons of each? "If you're weighing these two options, it comes down to your goals," begins Dunne. He continues:

> Do you need a steady source of income? If so, I'd go with getting a job because there are a lot of talented independent game development companies just barely getting by. As an independent developer, you'll be going up against big publishers—companies that throw a lot of money into marketing budgets every year. Do you think your independent game can compete with word-of-mouth? Or will it be good enough to be picked up by a publisher? If it is good enough, would you be willing to relinquish some amount of creative control to satisfy your publisher? Another aspect to consider, which many people forget when they go the independent route, is that as a company leader much of your time will be spent on issues unrelated to game development—you're a business manager. As such, you'll have to get involved with public relations, marketing, sales and/or raising capital, and paying creditors. If you plan to have employees, you'll also have to manage payroll and benefits and be an office manager. There are a lot of details that company ownership entails. That said, the upside is that you have the ability to be your own boss, and you can fulfill your vision for your game—not someone else's vision of their game. It's a tough route, but if you're successful, it's probably more rewarding, both personally and professionally.

> The safer route for newcomers is to find a job. Being a "worker bee" at a large company doesn't sound nearly as romantic as being the founder of a startup, but it's the safer route to go, in my opinion. You'll spend more time working on games and developing your technical skills, and if things don't pan out, it's a lot easier to leave a job than ditch the company you're in charge of and legally bound to. After working at another company, you'll presumably have experience under your belt, and you'll have formed industry connections. At that stage, you'll be better prepared to make the leap to game industry entrepreneur.

Finally, what are some of the do's and don'ts for someone trying to get a job in the industry?

Play every game you can get your hands on, and try to understand what makes them tick from both a technical and a design point of view. Have demos of your work ready to show to prospective employers. Understand that there are numerous back doors into the industry. The often-cited example of this is starting in the QA department and moving over to development at some point. Meet and talk to as many people in the industry as possible. Like practically everything else in life, finding work in this industry is often about who you know. Consider using a recruiter to find a job. However, if you do go down this path, make sure that you research the recruiter first. Some recruiters out there are pretty shady, and if you have someone representing you who has a bad reputation within the industry, they're hurting you, not helping. Be prepared to sacrifice salary expectations for the chance to work on a good project that will teach you important skills.

Key Sites

The following are some other key sites to check out, listed in alphabetical order.

flipCode

`www.flipcode.com`

flipCode is an outstanding game design/programming community web site that houses countless feature articles, the latest news headlines, regular columns, discussion topics, key files, contests, and links. It's a must-see.

Game Design Newsgroup

`rec.games.design`

To keep abreast of all the latest happenings, to exchange ideas or ask questions, the Usenet `rec.games.design` newsgroup is a must for game designers to visit at least a few times a week. Common posts include "An idea for a new multiplayer game," "Any game musicians out there?" and "Need help in creating rules for..."

The `rec.games.design` FAQ is available at the following address:

`www.qucis.queensu.ca/home/dalamb/Games/design/design.html`

Game Developer Magazine

www.gdmag.com

Game Developer magazine is undisputedly the ultimate monthly bible devoted to game designers and developers, and its online counterpart offers a comprehensive look at the entire game development spectrum. At the web site, users can subscribe to the magazine (it's strongly recommended!), search for back issues, or link to sister site Gamasutra (www.gamasutra.com) for exclusive content.

> **NOTE**
> In Chapter 22, "Game Agents and Headhunters," game recruiter extraordinaire Melanie Cambron offers a handful of extraordinary web sites and online articles to help those just starting out. These include essays such as "Creating a Perfect Résumé," "Your Personalized Job Hunt Campaign," and "Interviewing Tips." Flip back to take note of 'em.

Game Development Search Engine

www.game-developer.com

The one and only Game Development Search Engine is a definitive search engine and directory to many of the game developer sites on the Internet. It's a must-visit site for those in the industry.

GameDev.Net

www.gamedev.net

GameDev.Net is an excellent webzine devoted to the development of computer games with news, feature articles, community info, editorials, Q&A, helpful books, and other resources.

GameJobs

www.gamejobs.com

GameJobs serves as a comprehensive listing of companies involved with the video games industry, with a direct link to the appropriate human resources page for each company.

GameSlice

www.gameslice.com

Simply one of the best behind-the-scenes web sites for those who want to know what's happening in the computer gaming industry. Editor Geoff Keighley has his finger on the pulse of the biz and delivers news, reviews, hard-hitting editorials, feature interviews, and company profiles to his many readers.

GarageGames

www.GarageGames.com

GarageGames is the first web-based publishing label for independent games and game makers. It provides everything needed to make and sell high-quality games.

GIGnews

www.gignews.com

"Get In the Game" News allows visitors to peruse a hearty collection of news stories, tutorials, features, job opportunities, and interviews—all about the thriving computer game industry.

Loony Games

www.loonygames.com

Currently on hiatus, Loony Games is nonetheless an excellent bookmark for game designers/developers. This comprehensive site houses many feature stories and columns written by some of the industry's finest game designers, programmers, and artists.

Makegames.com

www.makegames.com

Diana Gruber's well-written and wonderfully laid-out step-by-step guide to breaking into the business, "So You Want to Be a Computer Game Developer?" covers everything from self-promotion to working with other people to the nature of the industry. A large area is devoted to writing your first and second games, plus a list of helpful books to ease the programming pain. The site also includes links, reviews, articles, tutorials, and resources.

Sloperama

www.sloperama.com

Okay, so the name isn't the best. But this site is quite helpful for those who want to learn about breaking into the video gaming biz. New (and free) lessons are provided every month, including "How to Sell a Game Idea," "Basic Outline for a Game Design Document," and "Preparing for a Career in Game Design."

Ultimate Gaming Resource

`www.ugr.net`

In addition to this site's feature articles and game reviews, UGR's directories of software and hardware companies and gaming services offer hundreds of resources (`www.ugr.net/listings/listings.htm`). All entries contain the link to their official home page, plus many of them include their phone, mailing address, and email contact information for those looking to send in a résumé or work sample. This is definitely a page to bookmark.

Video Game Yellow Pages

`www.vgyellowpages.com`

The Video Game Yellow Pages is the only comprehensive online directory servicing every market segment of the electronic gaming industry, from ad agencies and PR firms to developers, retailers, and distributors. The site is a simple database designed to supply relevant information about companies involved with and related to the interactive entertainment industry.

Essential Gaming E-Zines and Other Game Development Sites

The following is an alphabetical list of some of the top PC and console gaming e-zines, job sites, game development destinations, and other key bookmarks on the Net:

- Adrenaline Vault (`www.avault.com`)
- AllCube (`www.allcube.com`)
- Blue's News (`www.bluesnews.com`)
- Classic Gamer Magazine (`www.classicgamer.com`)
- Computer and Video Games (CVG) (`www.computerandvideogames.com`)
- Computer Games Online (`www.cgonline.com`)
- Computer Gaming World (`www.gamers.com/cgw`)
- Console Domain (`www.consoledomain.com`)
- CoolGameJobs (`www.coolgamejobs.com`)
- Cprogramming.com (C/C++ resources) (`www.cprogramming.com`)
- E3 Awards (`www.e3awards.com`)
- Electric Playground (`www.elecplay.com`)
- Electronic Gaming Monthly (`www.gamers.com/egm`)

➤ Fatbabies (www.fatbabies.com)

➤ Fun Xbox (www.funxbox.com)

➤ GameDaily (www.gamedaily.com)

➤ Game Depot (www.edepot.com/game.html)

➤ GameFAQs (www.gamefaqs.com)

➤ GameInformer (www.gameinformer.com)

➤ GamePen (http://gamepen.ugo.com)

➤ GamePro (www.gamepro.com)

➤ Game Rankings (www.gamerankings.com)

➤ Game Revolution (www.game-revolution.com)

➤ GameCube Network (www.gamecubenetwork.com)

➤ GameCube XL (www.gamecubexl.com)

➤ Gamers.com (www.gamers.com)

➤ GamersEmpire (www.gamers-empire.com)

➤ GamersNews (www.gamersnews.com)

➤ GamerWeb Network (www.gamerweb.com)

➤ Games Domain (www.gamesdomain.com)

➤ Gamespot (www.gamespot.com)

➤ Games Radar (www.gamesradar.com)

➤ GameSpy (www.gamespy.com)

➤ GameZone (www.gamezone.com)

➤ Gaming Force (www.gamingforce.com)

➤ Happy Puppy (www.happypuppy.com)

➤ ieMagazine (www.iemag.com)

➤ IGN/Snowball network (www.ign.com, http://cube.ign.com, http://dreamcast.ign.com, http://n64.ign.com, http://pc.ign.com, http://pocket.ign.com, http://ps2.ign.com, http://psx.ign.com, http://xbox.ign.com)

➤ Imagine (www.imaginemedia.com)

➤ Independent Game Network/MadMonkey (www.madmonkey.net)

➤ Just Adventure (www.justadventure.com)

➤ Nintendojo (www.nintendojo.com)

➤ Nintendo Power (www.nintendopower.com)

➤ Old Man Murray (www.oldmanmurray.com)

➤ PC Gamer (www.pcgamer.com)

➤ Planet GameCube (www.planetgamecube.com)

➤ PSM Online (www.psmonline.com)

➤ Sharky Extreme (www.sharkyextreme.com)

➤ Team Xbox (www.teamxbox.com)

➤ Templar Studios (www.templar.com)

➤ UnderGroundOnline (UGO) (www.ugo.com)

➤ VgNation (www.vgnation.com)

➤ Virtual Search Job Listings (www.vsearch.com/jobs.html)

➤ Xbox 2K (www.xbox2k.com)

➤ Xbox Addict (www.xboxaddict.com)

➤ Xbox City (www.xboxcity.com)

➤ Xbox Gamers (www.xboxgamers.com)

➤ Xbox Now (www.xboxnow.com)

➤ Xbox Users Group (www.xboxusersgroup.com)

Chapter 25

Key Conventions, Organizations, and Awards

In the information age, it's possible for members of the gaming industry to work virtually anywhere in the world. With electronic file transfer via the Internet and relatively cheap overnight deliveries from courier services, there's no reason why game programmers, artists, and musicians need to work together in the same room, although there are obvious advantages in doing so.

However, if you're trying to get a job at a development company or attempting to get your game picked up by a publisher, or you want to keep an eye on what your competitors are up to, it's highly recommended that you get out there to meet and greet the gaming community in the flesh. In fact, in this book, many game designers recommend getting out there to talk face-to-face because this makes a much better impression than dealing with someone via email or over the telephone. Therefore, the first half of this chapter deals with all the gaming industry's top conventions, trade shows, and conferences around the world. Each listing explains what the show is all about and who it is best suited for, and lists the official URL for that show. The second part of this chapter lists a number of essential organizations in the industry, including various academies and associations that cater to different facets of the gaming industry.

Conventions and Trade Shows

Gaming conventions and trade shows run the gamut from huge and general to intimate and focused.

Electronic Entertainment Expo (E3)

The Electronic Entertainment Expo (E3) is the largest and most extravagant event in the gaming industry. Period. More than 60,000 members of the international computer gaming, video gaming, and "edutainment" industry flock to see—or display—the hottest products of the year. E3 is not only a gathering for exhibitors to showcase their upcoming gaming software and hardware to the media and retailers, but also a place for enlightening conferences and workshops hosted by the top names in the business. E3 is strictly a trade event; therefore, only professionals from the industry are allowed to attend.

And what a party it is! Techno music blasts through the booths; multiplayer games take place over 40-foot video screens; celebrities are present to rub elbows; larger-than-life mechanical creations of favorite video and computer game characters appear; and concerts at night feature famous bands sponsored by the likes of Sony, Nintendo, and Microsoft. The event usually takes place during mid-May each year.

For more information, visit www.e3expo.com.

Game Developers Conference (GDC)

Another extremely important conference for game designers to attend is the Game Developers Conference (GDC). This annual show takes place in the late winter/early spring (usually March) and has something to offer for all roles of the industry: programming, visual arts, sound and music, production, general game design, and even the business and legal sides of the gaming industry.

The multiple-day event is loaded with keynote speakers, tutorials/workshops, seminars, contests in each field, awards, and exhibitors. Be sure to check out past and future keynote topics and speakers at the official web site: www.gdconf.com.

Also check out GDC Europe at www.gdc-europe.com.

The Game Developers Conference includes a special sideshow and festival, described in the following section.

Independent Games Festival

This event is intended to promote interactive entertainment as an art form and to provide a forum for independent game developers from around the globe to show their work, receive recognition, and meet with potential publishers and/or distributors. Categories are based on platform: PC, Macintosh, Sony PlayStation, Nintendo, or online games. Awards are also presented for technical excellence, art, audio, game design, and audience choice.

For festival info, rules, and application procedures, interested developers should go to www.indiegames.com, www.igf.com, or www.gamanetwork.com.

Is this the gaming industry's answer to the Sundance Film Festival?

D.I.C.E. Summit

In 2002, the Academy of Interactive Arts and Sciences (www.interactive.org) held the first annual D.I.C.E. Summit in Las Vegas. (D.I.C.E. stands for Design, Innovate, Create, Entertain.) This summit was created to bring together some of interactive entertainment's most celebrated and prolific minds in order to foster discussion and evolution within the gaming world. Also at this event is the Academy's annual Interactive Achievement Awards ceremony, honoring the best in computer, console, and online entertainment—as determined by the Academy's voting membership. Click to www.interactive.org/awards to read the winners from the fifth annual awards from 2002. To read more on the D.I.C.E. Summit, visit www.interactive.org/dice.

Electronic Consumer Trade Show (ECTS)

Electronic Consumer Trade Show (ECTS), Europe's premier gaming conference, is held every fall in London, England. Game developers and publishers from Europe and around the world display their top interactive products (software and hardware) for the fourth quarter and the following year. Like E3, ECTS is a glitzy trade show, but for members of the industry only. And it's on a much smaller scale, too—fewer than 2,000 attendees. Every year ECTS also hosts an awards ceremony for the top interactive entertainment products of the year. For more information, punch in www.ects.com while surfing the web.

Milia

Cannes, France hosts a spectacular annual event: Milia, the International Content Market for Interactive Media, which includes a separate entity exclusively reserved for the gaming industry, dubbed the Game Developer Village. New game showcases, title announcements, keynote speeches and conferences, and the Milia awards ceremony are but a few of the festivities here. There's also a developer's day, with hundreds of freelance programmers, graphic and sound designers, and scriptwriters invited from around the world. In short, this event caters to the entire gaming industry, including designers, publishers, and distributors. Access more information on this event at www.milia.com.

SIGGRAPH

For computer graphic artists and animators, SIGGRAPH is one of the most important conventions of the year. Its main purpose is to promote "theory, design, implementation, and application of computer-generated graphics and interactive techniques to facilitate communication and understanding." The three-day event includes dozens of conferences and workshops, exhibits by software and hardware companies, and a career resource center for aspiring computer graphics specialists. To learn more about SIGGRAPH as an organization and/or the annual conference, visit www.siggraph.org.

Gen Con

Gen Con is one of the oldest—and certainly the largest—"unplugged" gaming conventions for role-playing game (RPG) enthusiasts. The event is sponsored by Wizards of the Coast, producers of such popular RPGs as *Magic: The Gathering*. For details, see www.gencon.com.

Comdex, International CES, MacWorld Expo, Toy Fairs

While wrapping up this half of the chapter, it should be noted that Comdex (www.comdex.com), the International Consumer Electronics Show (www.cesweb.org), MacWorld Expo (www. macworldexpo.com), and the various international toy fairs may also be good places for a game designer to attend throughout the year. They're not nearly as crucial as E3, GDC, or ECTS, but you may find inspiration or make good contacts with other members of the gaming industry.

Organizations

Without a doubt, the most important organization for the purposes of this book is the International Game Developers Association (www.igda.org). As a special treat, program director Jason Della Rocca (jason@igda.org) has taken the time and effort to chat about the IGDA and its purpose for this chapter.

According to Della Rocca, the IGDA is an independent, nonprofit professional organization for developers of entertainment software, which helps the game development community achieve its common goals. The IGDA focuses on providing value to its members in the following areas:

➤ Building community among members to facilitate communication, support, and an understanding of common goals

➤ Providing a voice for the community, including representing game developers on issues of public debate

➤ Promoting relevant education and training for the next generation of game developers as well as professionals in the industry today

➤ Promoting the art form of games, including increasing artistic and financial recognition for developers

➤ Providing business services, including financial, legal, and strategic planning resources for individual developers and development companies

"That's the somewhat more verbose version," says Della Rocca. "The shorter interpretation is that the IGDA does good stuff for the game development industry and community!" Asked to discuss some of the programs, events, and awards with which the IGDA is involved, Della Rocca fills in the gaps:

> Chapters connect members in specific geographic areas and help promote regional game development communities. Chapter members network, learn from each other, identify upcoming challenges and issues in their work, and help define the characteristics of the professional community where they live and work.
>
> Committees are occasionally formed by the IGDA to address particular issues, whether related to public policy or another area of general concern to the community of game developers. Committees are usually formed for a specific time period and with a specific end result, such as a white paper or a resolution. Committees are responsible for reporting their findings and proposals for future action to the membership through the IGDA; results may be published in the IGDA newsletter, on the web site, and/or in other vehicles.
>
> Special interest groups (SIGs) connect members who are interested in a specific topic or discipline relevant to the art or business of making games. SIG members learn from each other, promote their specialties, identify upcoming challenges and issues in their work, and advance the state of the art and the industry. SIGs communicate primarily through ongoing online discussion groups, facilitated by a moderator, and are given the opportunity to meet annually at the Game Developers Conference (GDC).
>
> Furthermore, one of the goals of the IGDA is to promote games as an art form, which includes increasing the artistic and financial recognition for developers. In our efforts to recognize the amazing talents of those in our industry and the games they make, the IGDA presents the Game Developers Choice Awards—a chance for developers to honor and recognize the individuals and teams who have transcended the current state of the art, with all nominees and winners awarded solely by professional game developers. The IGDA presents the Game Developers Choice Awards annually at the GDC.

The IGDA goes above and beyond all of the preceding programs with the GDC Student Scholarship program, newbie outreach efforts, industry research, and more.

How and why does/should a game designer or developer get involved with the IGDA?

> There are two aspects to this question: what I refer to as the tangible and intangible benefits of being an IGDA member. On the tangible front, it means you get stuff such as a free subscription to *Game Developer* magazine (an invaluable developer resource), discounts on books and events, special offers on products, and so on. On the intangible—and more important—side, being an IGDA member connects you with the rest of the community, both locally and worldwide, whether this is via discussion with pros in the online forums, during a live encounter during a chapter gathering, or by volunteering on a committee with other developers. Not only does this allow budding game developers to be part of and closer with the development community, but they're supporting the industry, making a difference, and doing the right thing.

Regular annual membership is $100 a year, or $35 for students.

Della Rocca lists some other key organizations to consider:

> In North America, there are really only two organizations: the IGDA and the IDSA (Interactive Digital Software Association) [see the discussion on this organization later in the chapter]. Although the IGDA is 100% focused on developers, the IDSA concerns itself much more with the publishing and retail aspects of the industry.

> Outside North America, many countries have an equivalent to the IDSA to handle ratings and other such standards. However, there is nothing quite like the IGDA anywhere else. The IGDA is, of course, a global entity with chapters and members around the world.

Along with the IGDA logo, pictured here are a few members of the board of directors of the IGDA: program director Jason Della Rocca; chairman of the IGDA and president of Outrage Entertainment Matt Toschlog (shown here with IGDA executive director Jennifer Pahlka at the IGDA suite during the SuiteNight parties at GDC), and Warren Spector, ION Storm Austin studio director and IGDA board member, shown here opening the Game Developers Choice Awards.
(Used with permission by Jason Della Rocca.)

And a word on key trade shows:

> For developers, the Game Developers Conference is a must. Period. GDC is an invaluable resource for building your skills, gaining new knowledge, making connections, and simply staying in touch with the dev community. Attending E3 is great, too, and helps give you an idea of what games are in production—perhaps providing some inspiration. There are many other conferences and shows to attend (SIGGRAPH, ECTS, Meltdown, Game Technology Seminars, Extreme GDC, Milia, Comdex, and so on), but GDC and E3 are the two biggies.

Finally, Della Rocca offers some helpful advice on breaking into the industry:

> ➤ **You need skill, knowledge, and talent**. It doesn't really matter where you get it from, but you need it. Without skill, knowledge, and talent, you won't get far in the game development industry. Some are born with a certain amount of talent; others must work on it every day—this is true for all aspects of game development (coding, design, art, and so on). In terms of knowledge, you need to be prepared to be a "sponge" for pretty much your entire game dev career.

> ➤ **You need passion**. Without the love for games and a passion to help create, you can pretty much forget about it. Those who do have the fire will sense the lack of passion and desire.

> ➤ **You need to communicate**. Communication and the ability to work in a team setting are critical for today's increasingly complex projects. Leaving your ego at home and being able to take constructive criticism play a big part in this.

Other Organizations

And now, other important organizations, listed in alphabetical order.

Academy of Interactive Arts & Sciences (AIAS)

The Academy of Interactive Arts & Sciences (AIAS) is a nonprofit organization dedicated to the advancement and recognition of the interactive arts and sciences. As stated in its bylaws and published on the web site, this is the formal mission of the academy:

> ➤ Promote and advance common interests in the worldwide interactive community.

> ➤ Recognize outstanding achievement in interactive content and the interactive community.

> ➤ Conduct an annual awards show, and enhance the image and awareness of the interactive arts and sciences.

The annual awards show mentioned previously takes place during the annual Electronic Entertainment Expo (E3). For membership information, news, events, and award winners, visit the AIAS at www.interactive.org.

American Association for Artificial Intelligence (AAAI)

The American Association for Artificial Intelligence (AAAI) is a nonprofit society devoted to advancing the scientific understanding of the mechanisms underlying thought and intelligent behavior and their embodiment in machines. Its aims include increasing public understanding of artificial intelligence (AI), improving the teaching and training of AI practitioners, and seeking funding for important developments. As outlined at its official web site (www.aaai.org), there are many benefits for members, including conferences, symposia and workshops, magazines, and more.

Computer Game Artists (CGA)

This membership association, headed by a "benevolent dictator," exists to form a community of computer game artists who interact with (share, learn, teach, and influence) each other and their industry. Find out more about what they are and how they work at www.vectorg.com/cga/CGA.htm.

Entertainment Software Rating Board (ESRB)

You may have seen a sticker in the corner of most computer game boxes that says *ESRB*, accompanied by an age rating. The Entertainment Software Rating Board is an independent group that with the support of the industry has developed a standardized rating system for interactive entertainment software products and web sites. The ESRB ratings are designed to give consumers information about the content of an interactive video or computer entertainment title and the ages for which it's appropriate. For more info and the various age ratings, visit www.esrb.com.

European Leisure Software Publishers Association (ELSPA)

This organization was founded in 1989 to establish a collective identity for the European computer and video games industry. ELSPA is concerned with the publishing and distribution of interactive leisure and entertainment software, working to promote the interests of all its members, and addressing issues that affect the industry as a whole. Point your browser to www.elspa.com to learn more.

Interactive Digital Software Association (IDSA)

The Interactive Digital Software Association (IDSA) is a U.S. association exclusively dedicated to serving the business and public affairs interests of companies that publish console and computer games for video game consoles, PCs, and the Internet. Today, its members account for more than 90% of the $6 billion interactive entertainment software sold in the United States. In short, the IDSA offers services to game publishers, such as a robust anti-piracy program, government relations, business and consumer research, and First Amendment and intellectual property protection efforts. The official IDSA web site can be accessed at www.idsa.com.

Interactive Entertainment Merchants Association (IEMA)

CyberActive Media Group, Inc. founded and manages this leading retail trade association representing interactive entertainment product retailers (see `www.iemag.com/cyberactive/about.asp`). Its official publication, *ieMAGAZINE* (the former *GameWEEK*), is the only trade magazine for the interactive entertainment industry.

Project Bar-B-Q

Hosted by George "The Fat Man" Sanger and sponsored by Cirrus Logic, this annual conference is meant to serve as a think tank for computer musicians and sound engineers to solidify their opinions and put those opinions to work for the good of the manufacturers, developers, and primarily the consumers of computer/audio products. The web address is `www.projectbarbq.com`.

Software & Information Industry Association (SIIA)

The mission statement of this trade association expresses its purpose:

> First, we seek to show the world that the software and digital information industry is the fastest-growing industry sector and a major contributor to the global marketplace. Second, we protect the intellectual property of members, and advocate a legal and regulatory environment that benefits the entire industry. Finally, SIIA empowers our member companies with knowledge by serving as a resource to them on a wide range of traditional and emerging subjects that affect their businesses.

Some of the SIIA's efforts go toward anti-piracy, government affairs, and many other programs, publications, conferences/symposiums, and awards. SIIA's Codie Awards is one of the oldest annual awards ceremonies held for the software industry, and includes game categories. In 2001, SIIA incorporated its Immy Awards (recognizing creative and effective marketing efforts) with the Codie Awards as new special categories. Tap into `www.siia.net` for more information.

Appendix

Biographies

Alas, we've come to the end of the book. It's time now to learn a little more about the fine folks who have offered their discerning words of wisdom.

Although a few of our sages in the gaming industry were unable to supply a bio, most are listed here in alphabetical order for easy reference. Perhaps you, too, will be listed in a book like this some day.

Alexander, Craig—Electronic Arts

Craig Alexander brings 16 years of engineering and general management experience to Earth & Beyond, most recently as the Vice President and Executive Producer for Westwood Studios and Electronic Arts. Prior to that, he held the position of General Manager for Sierra Online's original development studio from 1996-2000. When Sierra Online consolidated operations, Craig sold the Yosemite-based studio to another publisher.

Craig has extensive entertainment software and online experience overseeing Sierra's entry into the massively multiplayer Internet gaming segment. In addition, Craig is also an experienced engineer, having worked at TRW Space and Technology on microprocessor designs. Prior to his engineering work, Craig began his career at TRW in the project control office, scheduling large NASA spacecraft programs.

Craig holds a computer engineering degree from the University of Southern California and an MBA from the Anderson Graduate School of Management at UCLA. Game credits include *Phantasmagoria, Lighthouse, Space Quest 6, Gabriel Knight 2, Quest for Glory V Dragon Fire, SWAT 1* and *2*, and the pioneering massively multiplayer title, *The Realm*.

Bachus, Kevin—Capital Entertainment Group

Kevin Bachus, vice president of publishing at Capital Entertainment Group, began his career in the computer and video game industry more than 20 years ago when he began writing a series of successful arcade games for early personal computers. During that time, he has worked as a developer, marketer, production executive, and platform manufacturer.

Most recently, Bachus was a founding member of the Xbox project team at Microsoft Corporation, where he was instrumental in conceiving of the cutting-edge video game console and securing funding for the project. He continued as the company's first director of third-party relations for Xbox; he was successful at signing more than 200 of the world's leading developers and publishers to bring their hottest new properties to Xbox. In that capacity, he was also responsible for managing the portfolio of third-party titles in development for Xbox; and developing the processes, business models, and strategies behind that portfolio.

Before starting the Xbox project, he was the group product manager for DirectX: responsible for promoting Windows as an entertainment vehicle and ensuring that the DirectX suite of tools became the primary choice for games and multimedia developers. During his time in this group, he listened closely to what the developers wanted, and oversaw the launches of versions 5–7 of DirectX. As part of that work, he was instrumental in developing the concept that eventually became Xbox.

Prior to joining Microsoft, he served in a number of product development, business development, and marketing functions at Mindscape, Inc., including entertainment product acquisition and the management of U.S. operations for the company's European development studios. He also worked as an editor and writer at Ziff-Davis Publishing Co.

Bachus is a graduate of the University of Southern California School of Film and Television and held a number of creative positions in the film and television industry prior to his career in interactive entertainment.

Bajakian, Clint—The Sound Department

Clint Bajakian worked at LucasArts Entertainment Company from 1991 to 2000 as a composer and sound design supervisor before leaving to create his own company: C. B. Studios. In 2002, he co-founded The Sound Department with Julian Kwasneski, offering state-of-the-art audio production services with an emphasis on computer and video games.

Clint Bajakian received a Musical Achievement Award from *Computer Gaming World* magazine in 1998 for his soundtrack to *Outlaws*. This soundtrack and his score for *Escape from Monkey Island* were finalists in the Interactive Academy for Arts and Sciences original music category in 1998 and 2001, respectively. Fluent in many musical genres—including jazz, rock, world, and electronica—Bajakian's specialty is dramatic orchestral composition, as heard in *Outlaws*, *Indiana Jones and The Fate of Atlantis*, *Indiana Jones and The Infernal Machine*, and *Star Wars: TIE Fighter*. In 1991, Bajakian was the national recipient of the Academy of Arts and Sciences film music internship. He last composed an orchestral score to be recorded by a live orchestra for *Indiana Jones and The Emperor's Tomb*.

Currently, Clint Bajakian is acting as vice-president of G.A.N.G. (Game Audio Network Guild), a new organization that serves the interactive audio community, and serves on the board of the IA-SIG (Interactive Audio Special Interest Group). Bajakian is a member of AIAS (Academy of Interactive Arts and Sciences), Project Bar-B-Q, NARAS (National Academy of Recording Arts and Sciences), IGDA (International Game Developers Association), FMN (Film Music Network), AFI (American Film Institute), and AFTRA (American Federation of Television and Radio Artists). Clint was also a faculty speaker at the 2002 Game Developers Conference on the topic of audio production for games. He holds a double Bachelor of Arts degree with high honors in guitar performance and music theory from The New England Conservatory and a Master of Music degree in music composition from the University of Michigan.

Bigley, Pat—Prime Candidate, Inc.

Pat Bigley began her career as a booking agent for musical talent and variety artists. Her agent skills were developed where she ran the "one niter" division of a large Midwest booking agency. After the agency closed due to ill health of the principals, she operated a large CPA firm in Columbus, Ohio. When the firm was sold, she relocated with her family to California and opened up The Bigley Talent Agency in 1991. The agency primarily placed actors in film and television and was also very active in the literary arena. The agency was very adept at "packaging" entire projects for the film and television industries. For personal reasons, Pat later closed the agency and found her way to Search Associates, Inc., in which she was an executive recruiter for the electronic media/entertainment group.

Bleszinski, Cliff—Epic Games

If the gaming world were to name an "It List," Cliff Bleszinski would be at the top. Named one of the "Next Gaming Gods" by *PC Gamer* at the ripe age of 25 and featured on the cover of the magazine, CliffyB is an internationally synonymous title for his unique vision of gaming. Bleszinski is also a newsworthy subject because he served as producer for *Unreal Tournament 2002*, which was recently released (October 22, 2002) and sold nearly 400,000 copies in the first two weeks.

Despite his young age, Bleszinski has been designing and building best-selling games for more than 10 years. Few developers under the age of 30 can claim to be 10-year veterans of the gaming industry, but CliffyB's record speaks for itself. CliffyB has always seen gaming as the true next generation of consumer level entertainment. He believes that gaming provides a much more compelling experience than film or television due to its interactive nature.

Bleszinski has been a leader in the development of the following best-selling products:

➤ *Unreal* (PC)

➤ *Unreal Expansion 1* (PC)

➤ *Unreal Tournament* (PC, Dreamcast, Playstation 2)

➤ *Unreal Tournament 2002* (PC)

➤ *Unreal Championship* (Xbox)

➤ *Unreal 2* (PC, Q1 2003)

➤ *Jazz Jackrabbit 1* and *2* (PC)

➤ *Jazz Jackrabbit* (Gameboy Advance)

CliffyB operates as lead designer for Epic Games internal products and as executive producer for all externally developed products. CliffyB acts as Epic's creative filter for current and upcoming titles as well as assisting with any extensions of Epic's franchises—from action figures to feature film negotiations.

Known for his outspoken attitude and flamboyant style, CliffyB is well-known among gamers. When Hollywood was looking to model a character in an upcoming unannounced Revolution Studios project, Zak Penn (prolific screenwriter) contacted CliffyB and consulted him on the characterization and script. Ultimately, the character would come to be based on CliffyB.

Every *Unreal* franchise product has gone on to win numerous game of the year awards from both hardcore and mainstream press. The *Unreal* franchise has sold more than four million units since its debut in 1998 and remains one of the top brands in the controversial "first-person shooter" genre.

Epic Games was founded by Tim Sweeney in 1992 and is in its 11th year of operation. In a business increasingly dominated by large-scale industry, Epic remains one of a handful of independent and profitable studios.

Bluth, Don—Don Bluth Films

Producer/director Don Bluth is one of the most prestigious animators in the industry—admired by peers all over the world for his creative talent and his versatility in bringing memorable characters to life. While working on his films, Bluth wears many hats. He designs all the characters, serves as key storyboard artist, and (when the mood strikes) has been known to write some clever songs to accompany his lively and amusing characters. As if these duties don't keep him busy enough, he also writes and/or collaborates on most of the scripts for his projects.

Bluth was born into a family of seven children in El Paso, Texas. He grew up on a farm in Payson, Utah, in a highly creative environment. After watching *Snow White and the Seven Dwarfs*, he found his calling. From the age of six on, Don was always drawing. It soon became his dream to work for Walt Disney Studios and to bring his drawings to life as he had seen accomplished in films. Upon graduation from high school, Don took a portfolio of his drawings to the Disney Studio in Burbank. He landed a position in the animation department as an "in-betweener." This job required him to create the drawings in between the animator's key drawings to complete a movement. Bluth worked with Disney from 1955 through 1956 on the classic motion picture *Sleeping Beauty*. He left after one year.

Don spent the next two and a half years as a Mormon missionary in Argentina. Upon his return, he made the decision to continue his formal education; he enrolled at Brigham Young University, studying English literature. During this time, he continued to work during the summers for Disney.

After completing his education, Bluth and his brother, Toby, started a live theater in Santa Monica, California, in which they produced and directed popular musical comedies. Although this venture proved to be exciting, Bluth decided to commit to a career in animation after three years.

His first job upon re-entering the animation field was as a layout artist for Filmation Studios, a television production company. In this capacity, he was required to draw and design the backgrounds and create the character poses for the animators. Bluth was extremely adept at this and was soon promoted to the head of the department, a post he held for three years.

In 1971, Bluth returned to Walt Disney Productions as an animator, beginning what would be considered a skyrocket ride to the top of the animation field. He started as an animator on the feature film *Robin Hood* (1973) and was promoted within two years to directing animator on *Winnie the Pooh and Tigger Too* (1974) and *The Rescuers* (1976). Don was director of animation on *Pete's Dragon* (1977) and was producer/director on *The Small One* (1978).

Inspired by many of Disney's classics and filled with the desire to restore that quality to animated films, Bluth began a short project in his garage with two fellow Disney animators: Gary Goldman and John Pomeroy. This short project, known as *Banjo, the Woodpile Cat*, began production in March 1975. For the next 41/2 years, the trio worked nights and weekends in all areas of production to accomplish the finished project. During this time, they still kept their day jobs at Disney. In early 1979, Bluth, Goldman, and Pomeroy were approached by film industry businessmen who offered to fund them on a feature film. Banjo served as an excellent portfolio and showed that they could create the "classical" look. In September 1979, the trio resigned from Walt Disney Productions to start their own independent production company. For their first feature film, they selected Robert C. O'Brien's award-winning novel *Mrs. Frisby and the Rats of N.I.M.H.* In July 1982, they released their first non-Disney animated feature with the altered title *The Secret of NIMH*.

With the introduction of new laser disc technology in 1983, Bluth and partners created the first interactive laser disc game: *Dragon's Lair*. In December 1984, they began work on the acclaimed family feature about a young mouse's struggle to survive in a new land, entitled *An American Tail* (a collaboration with Steven Spielberg).

At the invitation of the Irish government, they moved their studio and its employees to Dublin, Ireland in November 1986, and their studio grew to be the largest in Europe. Their third feature film, *The Land Before Time*, was their first production created entirely in Ireland. Released by Universal Pictures during the Thanksgiving 1988 holiday, it achieved a record-breaking opening weekend gross for an animated film. Their subsequent efforts include *All Dogs Go to Heaven* (1989), *Rock-a-doodle* (1990), *Thumbelina* (1993), and *A Troll in Central Park* (1994).

In September 1994, Bluth returned from Ireland to head the Fox Animation Studio in Phoenix, Arizona, in which he shared the creative leadership with his partner producer/director Gary Goldman through June of 2000.

During those years, the duo produced and directed the hit animated musical *Anastasia* (1997), which received two Oscar nominations; the direct-to-video musical *Bartok the Magnificent* (1999); and the animated space opera *Titan A.E.* (2000), now on video and DVD.

Don and Gary have returned to independent filmmaking with the establishment of their new company, Don Bluth Films, Inc. Based in Phoenix, Arizona, they have begun pre-production work on a film version of *Dragon's Lair*. Their web site, www.donbluth.com, will enable them to communicate directly with their audience. There are plans to expand the web site to include animation education and the sale of animation artwork. Don Bluth's *ToonTalk* magazine was launched in June of 2000 at the San Diego Comicon. This magazine discusses the "behind-the-scenes" world of animation. It will be used to entertain and educate the audience in the principles of classical animation.

Don Bluth has been an active member of the Academy of Motion Picture Arts and Sciences since 1976.

Brunner, Jeff—Interact/R.E.D

If you're looking for Interact president and founder Jeff Brunner, don't look in the corner office—he'll be in a cubicle with the recruiters, on the phone, or in a meeting. He tried an office for a while, but felt that it kept him out of the action—and that's exactly where he wants to be. He will eagerly confess that the part of his job he loves the most is "the hunt," as he calls it—continuously networking until he finds the right candidate for a position.

Jeff has more than a decade of experience in identifying individual interactive talent and working with candidates and development studios to develop high-quality games. He is actively engaged in all facets of the company operations: formulating corporate strategy, building and training the recruiting team, and maintaining positive relationships with both clients and candidates.

Jeff maintains a special focus on the industry's individual talent because he believes it's the bedrock upon which the success of all Interact ventures is built. He relentlessly works the phones to contact talent and find out what they want to do, where they want to work, and how much they want to be paid. During more than a decade of recruiting in the video game space and high-tech industry, Jeff has garnered tremendous knowledge of the industry and its talent base.

Jeff subscribes to the adage, "It's amazing what you can accomplish if you don't care who gets the credit." Although his name may not be attached to every candidate placement, his efforts are instrumental in making them happen.

Jeff earned his Bachelor of Arts from the University of California at Irvine, in which he studied pre-law, psychology, and sociology. His favorite video games are *Spyro the Dragon*, *Spyro II: Ripto's Rage*, and *Spyro: Year of the Dragon*.

Bushnell, Nolan—uWink

Nolan Bushnell, CEO and founder of uWink, Inc., is best known for bringing *Pong*, Atari Corporation, and Chuck E. Cheese's Pizza Time Theater to the masses. He is justifiably revered as the "father of the video game industry."

Over the past 20+ years, Bushnell has built upon his flair for business and innovation by creating more than 20 companies, including Catalyst Technologies, Etak, Androbot, Axlon, Irata, AAPPS, and ByVideo. Additionally, he has provided consulting services to numerous corporations, including Commodore International, IBM, Cisco Systems, and US Digital Communications. He sits on the board of directors of several leading companies, including WAVE Systems, TradeWorld, and Webquest. He is a regular content contributor to the "Webby"-nominated MetaMarkets.com online "Think Tank" web site.

With his current venture, uWink, Inc., Bushnell and his team intend to make significant inroads into changing the face of Internet entertainment by streaming it into public portals and establishing mass multiplayer gaming tournaments worldwide.

Bushnell received his Bachelor of Science degree in electrical engineering from the University of Utah, where he is a Distinguished Fellow, and attended Stanford University Graduate School. With a passion for enhancing and improving the educational process and a desire to motivate others, Bushnell frequently lectures at major universities and corporations throughout the United States, inspiring others with his views on entrepreneurship and innovation.

Bushnell holds several patents on some of the basic technologies for many early video games and is also the inventor or co-inventor of many worldwide patents in various other fields and industries.

Over the years, Bushnell has received numerous awards of distinction, including being named ASI's "Man of the Year" in 1997, as well as being inducted into the Video Game Hall of Fame. In January 2000, Bushnell became one of the first 50 inductees into the Consumer Electronics Association's Hall of Fame, which gave public recognition to his significant contributions to 20th century technology. Bushnell is also highlighted as one of Silicon Valley's entrepreneurial icons in "The Revolutionaries," an historical view of Silicon Valley (part of the renowned Tech Museum of Innovation in San Jose, California).

He and his wife Nancy live with their eight children in the Los Angeles area.

Cain, Timothy—Troika Games

Timothy Cain started working in the game industry in 1982, programming a bridge card game for Electronic Arts while he was in high school. After completing a Master's degree in computer science at the University of California at Irvine, Tim returned to the industry in 1992. He made several games at Interplay, including the award-winning RPG *Fallout*; and juggled the roles of programmer, designer, and producer. In 1998, Tim co-founded his own company, Troika Games, whose first computer game was the stellar RPG *Arcanum*. Tim has also taught undergraduate courses in computer game design at UCI.

Cambron, Melanie—Virtual Search

Melanie Cambron is a recruiter for game industry leaders such as EA, THQ, Infogrames, and Sony. Melanie wrote the foreword to the successful book *Game Programming with Direct X 7.0* and its follow-up. She will also be contributing to a forthcoming book on the business of the game industry, due for publication in 2003. She speaks each semester at the University of Texas at Austin and the University of North Texas on the game development industry. Melanie is frequently interviewed by major media such as the *Dallas Morning News* for her industry expertise, and serves as a consultant to the City of Austin's Interactive Industry Development Committee.

Case, Stevie—Monkeystone Games

Stevie "KillCreek" Case is best known for beating John Romero, co-creator of *DOOM* and *Quake*, among other legendary titles, in a one-on-one *Quake* deathmatch. Stevie is a lifelong gamer with a specific interest in first-person shooters. She left the political science program at the University of Kansas in 1997 to pursue a career in gaming. In July of that year, Stevie signed on as the first full-time professional gamer with the Cyberathletic Organization, later to become the Cyberathlete Professional League (CPL). After designing several user levels for *Quake II* and writing two strategy guides for Prima Publishing, she signed on as a quality assurance tester at Ion Storm. Several months later, she was promoted to the position of level designer on John Romero's creative team. In 1999, Case rejoined the CPL as a member of the board of directors. In her free time, Stevie enjoys modeling and writing, and has appeared in such publications as *Yahoo! Internet Life*, *PC Accelerator*, *Details*, Playboy.com, and *Rolling Stone*. *Forbes* magazine recently named Case one of its "Top 100 Celebrities" for the year 2000. She travels extensively, representing the CPL at gaming tournaments in locales from Brazil to Berlin. Stevie currently serves as vice president and production coordinator at the newly formed Monkeystone Games, an interactive entertainment studio focusing on handheld platforms and emerging technologies.

Castle, Louis—Electronic Arts

Louis Castle's 13-year career has included positions as a designer, executive producer, programmer, and art director on such titles as *Blade Runner, Lands of Lore Guardians of Destiny,* the *Monopoly* CD-ROM, and *The Lion King*. More recently, he worked at Westwood Studios on titles including *Command & Conquer Renegade* and *Pirates: The Legend of Black Kat.* His background in fine arts and computer science has helped him maintain the artistic and creative vision crucial in the interactive entertainment industry.

"In art school, you find out pretty quickly that no matter what you come up with, some guy who died hundreds of years ago already did it," he says. "Creating fine art on computers, however, was this vast uncharted territory."

But even artists have to pay the bills. Castle did so working at a computer store and consulting and programming on the side. It wasn't long before he was freelancing full-time, along with new partner Brett Sperry. Castle considered himself a starving artist type; Sperry was a starving programmer. Odd couple though they were, they were both hungry for better paychecks. So Sperry tossed out the idea of striking out on their own. "Brett had big ideas about growing and prospering and becoming industry giants," Castle says, "while all that mattered to me was doing what I loved and having a great time at it."

In 1985, they started their own company, then called Westwood Associates, in the modest environs of Castle's converted garage (which also housed his bed and his beloved pinball machine). Since then, Castle's versatility has led to juggling several crucial roles within the company, from design guru to finance whiz to operations honcho. He is now drawing on all of his experience in the gaming industry in his role of general manager of Westwood, in which he oversees all the company's operations. Recently, Electronic Arts brought the Westwood team internally.

"What drives me today is seeing other team members succeed and thrive as they continue to make great computer gaming products," he says.

Church, Doug—Freelance

Doug Church has been doing game design and programming for more than 11 years, mostly working on PC games. His initial projects, such as *Ultima Underworld* (*UW*), used small teams of four to eight people to do all the programming, designing, level building, and so on. Since *Ultima Underworld*, he has worked on *UW2*, *System Shock*, *Flight Unlimited*, and *Thief*. Church also did lots of firefighting and bug fixing on various other projects. For the last two years, he has been doing design and programming consulting, helping out on some PC games as well as working on a PS2 music game.

Davis, Dave—EA Sports

Dave Davis, executive producer of EA Sports BIG's Freekstyle, has been with EA for the last six years. In addition to being the visionary behind Freekstyle, Dave is the executive producer for *Knockout Kings* and was the instigator of the massive reworking of the franchise in 2002. In the past, Dave produced the highly successful *MotoRacer* series as well as the EA Sports *Supercross* series.

At age 38, Dave has been working in the video game industry for 18+ years and has produced games for more than 14 years. An original founder of Radical Entertainment, he has also worked for SEGA, Distinctive Software, and Broderbund Software.

Del Castillo, Ed—Liquid Entertainment

Ed Del Castillo, president and co-founder of Liquid Entertainment, juggles his management responsibilities with active participation in all aspects of product development, especially design and art direction.

A graduate of the University of California in San Diego, Ed majored in economics and minored in psychology and visual arts. He began his career in the interactive industry at Mindcraft in 1991, in which he worked on *Siege*, *Ambush at Sorinor*, *Bloodstone*, and *Magic Candle*. In 1994,

Ed moved to Westwood Studios and became the sole producer in charge of the entire *Command & Conquer* franchise, including *Red Alert* and its expansions, ports, and foreign language versions. During 1997 and 1998, Ed was at Origin, in which he served as the producer responsible for Sid Meier's new startup, Firaxis. He eventually transferred to Austin, in which he worked with Richard "Lord British" Garriott, founder of Origin, on *Ultima: Ascension*.

In late 1998, Ed finally struck out on his own with the goal of bringing the highest-quality people together to create the highest-quality games. In early 1999, he created Liquid Entertainment with his partner, Mike Grayford.

Dille, Peter—THQ

As senior vice president of worldwide marketing for THQ, Peter Dille oversees all global corporate and product marketing functions (including advertising, publicity and promotions) and THQ's online presence. Prior to joining THQ, Dille served as senior director of product marketing for Sony Computer Entertainment America and was a key executive in the launch of the Sony PlayStation. In this role, he oversaw all PlayStation advertising and directed all hardware, software, and peripheral product marketing. Dille's eight-year tenure at Sony also included executive marketing and communications roles throughout Sony's interactive electronic divisions. Before working at Sony, he managed advertising, promotion, and corporate identity for the New York Stock Exchange. Dille graduated from Rutgers University with a Bachelor's degree in English and communications.

Dunne, Alex—Gamasutra

Alex Dunne is the executive producer of Gamasutra.com, a game development web site that publishes technical articles and offers services to professional game developers. He is also the chairman and founder of the Independent Games Festival (www.igf.com), an annual event, launched in 1998, which recognizes innovation in independently developed video games. Dunne was formerly the editorial director of the CMP Game Media Group, overseeing content in *Game Developer* magazine and Gamasutra.com, and was the editor-in-chief of *Game Developer* magazine. He sits on the advisory board of the Game Developers Conference and co-authored the book *The Game Developer's Marketplace*, published by Coriolis.

Falstein, Noah—The Inspiracy

Noah Falstein's love of games began with board games at an early age. At age 15, he first played *Computer Space*, the first commercial video game that Nolan Bushnell made a few years before *Pong*, and was hooked. His senior project in college was "Koronis Strike: A Simulation of Mining and Combat in the Asteroid Belt." Upon graduation, he began work at Milton Bradley's Advanced Research division, programming speech synthesis software and motor control for a personal robot that was never released. Five unreleased projects later (including some cool VCS games and a game for the [surprise!] unreleased MB home computer), he left to work for Williams Electronics. There, he became the project leader for the arcade game *Sinistar*, the first commercial video game to use speech. "Beware, I Live!" "I Hunger!"

After the arcade implosion in 1983, Falstein moved to California to become the seventh employee of the Lucasfilm Games Group—later to become LucasArts Entertainment. He worked on many games there, leading projects such as *Koronis Rift*, *PHM Pegasus*, and *Strike Fleet*; and co-leading *Indiana Jones and the Last Crusade*. He also co-designed *Indiana Jones and the Fate of Atlantis*, and served as producer for *Battlehawks 1942* and very early versions of *The Dig* and *Day of the Tentacle*. As the first (of four) project leaders on *The Dig*, he had the enviable task of leading brainstorming sessions that included George Lucas and Steven Spielberg. He also conceived of the "Insult Swordfighting" subgame in the first *Monkey Island* game, and was renowned (or was that disowned? reviled?) for contributing puns to that game and its first sequel. He also did some work for the short-lived Rebel Arts and Technologies group, designing location-based simulator rides.

After LucasArts, Falstein became one of the first employees at the 3DO Company, and produced the initial demos and early internal games for that new game platform.

After a brief stint in consulting, he once again was bitten by the startup bug—he became the third employee at DreamWorks Interactive, and worked on its first titles. But corporate politics and the lure of being his own boss led him quickly back to freelance work, and he founded The Inspiracy, doing game design and production consulting.

Through The Inspiracy, Falstein has worked on a myriad of projects, ranging from interactive comic books through PC and console titles to location-based simulators. Some highlights include lead design for DreamWorks' *Chaos Island* and Health Media Lab's *Hungry Red Planet*; writing for *Total Annihilation: Kingdoms* and its expansion set; and design consultation for many projects, including Microforte's MMOPRG *Big World* and I-Imagine's new Xbox driving title: *Chase*.

Falstein is also a well-known industry speaker, having given talks at most of the GDCs since 1990, as well as many at E3, Milia, SPA, Intermedia, Digital Hollywood, and myriad other conferences. He was the first elected chairman of the CGDA (now the International Game Developers' Association), and also has served as a judge for the Independent Game Developer's Festival and the European Multimedia Awards (EMMAs).

More information, as well as numerous articles on game design and production, can be found at The Inspiracy web site: www.theinspiracy.com.

Foster, Chris—Raven Software

Chris Foster has a background in art, writing, and the classics. He started work at Raven Software in the spring of 1995, and has worked on nearly all the titles begun by the company since that time, including *Heretic II*. In addition to his work at Raven, Chris is creating his own role-playing game; he is also a published poet and prose writer, as well as being the assistant editor for a small, independently run local magazine: *The Writer's Block*. Chris was lead designer on *Star Trek Voyager: Elite Force* and *Jedi Knight II: Jedi Outcast*.

Garden, Alex—Relic Entertainment

Johnny Wilson, former editor-in-chief of *Computer Gaming World Magazine*, called Alex Garden "the game industry's next Sid Meier." Alex began his career in the video game industry at age 15, working as a game tester for Vancouver B.C.-based Distinctive Software Inc. Over the years, Alex has worked with some of the world's leading developers at Electronic Arts Canada, Radical Entertainment, and Sierra On-Line.

Alex's most recent venture, Relic Entertainment, is one of North America's premiere game development studios. Relic's first title, *Homeworld*, has won more than 50 awards, including the prestigious "Game of the Year" award from CNN.com, MSNBC, and the world's largest computer game magazine, *PC Gamer*.

Alex's recent nomination for "Canadian Young Entrepreneur of the Year" and other business accomplishments have received feature coverage from *The Globe and Mail*, *The Financial Post*, *The CBC National Magazine*, CNN Online, Vicki Gabereau, *Forbes*, and *BC Business Magazine*.

Garriott, Richard—NCSoft

Richard "Lord British" Garriott published his first game in 1980, making him—the author of the best-selling *Ultima* series, including *Ultima Online*, the first major commercial success in the online games market—a true veteran of the computer gaming industry. Throughout his career, Lord British has received extensive praise and many awards, including *Computer Gaming World's* "15 Most Influential Industry Players," *Next Generation's* "America's Elite," *PC Gamer's* "Game Gods," and *PC Games'* "Designer of the Year" and "Entrepreneur of the Year." In an industry that now rivals the movie industry in popularity, Richard Garriott is one of the few well-known "stars."

Richard began developing games for his Apple computer as a teenager. While in high school and while working at a Texas computer retail store, he developed a small game called *Akalabeth* in his spare time. A copy of the game found its way to a software publisher, who bought publishing rights to it on the spot. *Ultima* soon followed, and by the time *Ultima II* was released in 1982, publishers were vying to get him to sign the dotted line.

In 1983, the Garriotts—including Richard and his brother, Robert—established Origin Systems, Inc. Based in Austin, Texas, the company is recognized as one of the innovation leaders in the ever-changing world of entertainment software. In 1992, Origin merged with Electronic Arts, a global leader in the entertainment software industry.

"Lord British," a trademark of Richard's, is the pseudonym under which Richard created the *Ultima* series. Lord British also appeared as a principal character in the storyline. The *Ultima* saga transpires in the realm of Britannia, and he was the benevolent ruler of this oft-beleaguered land. Spanning two decades, the *Ultima* series is one of the longest-running and most successful series in the history of entertainment software—selling millions of copies and winning innumerable awards throughout the world. In 1997, the *Ultima* series ventured into the realm of the Internet with the release of the technologically groundbreaking title *Ultima Online*. Winning many awards and accolades, *Ultima Online's* continued success is measured by the hundreds of thousands of people who enjoy playing the game from all over the world, with more people joining every day.

Richard "retired" from Origin/EA in April 2001 and formed Destination Games with his brother. Richard has a large fan base that follows his work closely and is eager to hear about his next game. The computer gaming press is always eager to interview him and quote him on his view of the industry and plans for the future. In an industry plagued with short-term employees who change jobs for promotions, Richard has inspired a loyal development team and business group to eagerly join him on his new endeavors.

A year later, Richard formed NCsoft Austin, located in Austin, Texas. It is a subsidiary of NCsoft (Korea). Its first title was a North American version of the popular Asian online RPG, *Lineage: The Blood Pledge*.

Gibbons, Mark—SCEE, Cambridge

Mark Gibbons last worked on *Primal*, the debut title on the PlayStation 2 computer entertainment system for this developer. The Cambridge Studio has been responsible for the *Medievil* series and *C-12* for the PSOne and PlayStation game consoles. The studio existed previously as Millennium Interactive, creating such titles as The *James Pond* series, *Starray*, *Kid Gloves*, *Defcon5*, *Frogger*, and *BeastWars*.

Gibbons was hired by Sony Computer Entertainment Europe in 1999 as a concept artist. A year later, he became lead artist on *Primal*. His background is in illustration, largely sci-fi- and fantasy-themed. He worked for several years as an artist for Games Workshop.

The birth of the PlayStation opened his eyes to the potential of working in an industry that had always fascinated him. He thinks that as technology developed and game graphics became more sophisticated, studios began recruiting artists with traditional skills to generate concept designs and bring fresh perspectives to game development.

The days of programmers pushing pixels around to create sprite graphics are long gone.

Gilbert, Ron—Hulabee Entertainment

Ron Gilbert has been professionally designing and building games for more than 16 years. He spent eight years at Lucasfilm, for which he created such groundbreaking adventure games as *Maniac Mansion* and the *Monkey Island* series, which are considered two of the most influential games in the industry. Gilbert is proficient in creating products and technology for the PC/Mac market, as well as the Palm. He co-founded Humongous Entertainment in 1992, in which he was responsible for the creative and technical direction of the company. He was the creator and designer of Freddi Fish and Pajama Sam, two of Humongous Entertainment's most popular characters. Gilbert has been credited by *Computer Gaming World* as one of the game industry's "15 Most Influential People" and was recently featured in *PC Gamer* as one of the industry's best game designers. He is a member of the advisory board of the Game Developers Conference.

Gottlieb, Harry—Jellyvision

As founder and chief designer at Jellyvision, Gottlieb worked on the many *You Don't Know Jack* games, plus Disney's *Who Wants to Be a Millionaire?* CD-ROMs, and many more online trivia games. His future aspirations include pioneering a new form of communication: the Interactive Conversation Interface (ICI), pronounced "icky," which supercedes the graphical user interface (GUI) for interactive mass communication—and using it to create positive, engaging, and meaningful interactive programs.

Gray, Richard—Ritual Software

Richard Gray is known more familiarly in the industry as the Levelord. He designs levels for first-person and third-person action games, and began his career by designing amateur levels for *DOOM*. These four levels were noticed by Nick Newhard, then of Q Studios, and the Levelord began making contract levels for the game *Blood*. These levels, in turn, were noticed by Scott Miller and George Broussard of Apogee/3D Realms. When you ask how someone gets into the industry, remember this progression.

Gray's first professional work was in *Duke Nukem 3D* while he was at 3D Realms. He did half of the levels for Duke, and being part of this killer game really launched his career. He then started his own company with Robert Atkins and Tom Mustaine, called Ritual Entertainment. They produced the first add-on pack for *Quake*, followed by two AAA titles, *SiN* and *Heavy Metal*. After doing *Blair Witch III*, Gray helped Rogue Entertainment with its game *Alice*.

The two levels that Levelord is most famous for are HIPDM1 for the first add-on pack for *Quake* and Spry for *SiN*. HIPDM1 was the first platform (fighting areas suspended in empty space) deathmatch level, a paradigm that's often appropriated today in many deathmatch levels. Spry was the first professional deathmatch level in which the players were the size of mice, battling each other in a huge room.

Before entering the industry, Richard Gray was an aerospace engineer. He wrote the code that tests and certifies fuel controls for commercial and military aircraft. He received his Bachelor of Science degree in engineering from UCLA in 1990. Before that, he was a business applications programmer, and before that, "a devoted sailor in the United States Navy, listening for Soviet submarines with the SOSUS system."

Greenberg, Daniel—Freelance

Daniel Greenberg is an award-winning game designer with almost two decades of experience making high-selling, critically acclaimed games. He has created designs and interactive scripts for titles as varied as *Lord of the Rings, Star Trek: Starfleet Academy, Vampire: The Masquerade— Redemption, Star Control III, Tenchu II: Birth of the Stealth Assassins, Independence War II: The Edge of Chaos, Sea Dogs, Advanced Dungeons and Dragons: Al Qadim/The Genie's Curse*, and *X- Men: The Mutant Wars*. He has consulted for Activision, Interplay, Infogrames, Sierra, Accolade, SSI/Mindscape, Bethesda Softworks, Walt Disney, Virgin, Universal, Time/Warner, and even Apple Computer.

In addition to computer games, Greenberg has a nearly 20-year history of creating dice and paper RPGs, trading card games, and game books. He started in the early days of *Advanced Dungeons and Dragons* and has designed dozens of games for TSR, White Wolf, West End Games, Holistic Design, Last Unicorn, and more. These games include the critically acclaimed *Who Watches the Watchmen* RPG for DC Heroes, the seminal *Who's Who Among Vampires: Children of the Inquisition*, the AD&D adaptation of the Ian McKellen movie *The Keep*, the fan favorite *Giovanni Chronicles: The Last Supper*, the cult hit *Malkavian Clanbook*, the top-selling *Star Wars* role-playing game adventure *Tatooine Manhunt*, and many more.

His games have won the Excellence in Software Award (SPA), the RPGA award, the GAMA/Academy of Gaming Arts, and numerous magazine and fan awards. He has lectured many times at the Computer Game Developers Conference, and has been a featured speaker for other industry groups. He has written more than 100 articles on computer and entertainment technology for *The Washington Post* and has written for *USA Today* and *DV Magazine*.

Daniel Greenberg has always worked freelance, completing all his designs without ever accept- ing a position within a company. This flexibility allows him to launch projects quickly, thus saving his clients time, money, and sanity. His next goal is to create The Sopranos of gaming; the mature, literate crowd-pleaser capable of thrilling a mass-market audience.

Greenblat, Rodney—Freelance

Rodney Alan Greenblat is a creator of intriguing and whimsical art. His paintings and sculpture have been exhibited in galleries and museums around the world. He is an author and illustrator of children's books and is director of the Center for Advanced Whimsy, an independent creative company that makes artwork, design, and music for children and adults.

Rodney's sculpture was featured in the 1985 Whitney Biennial, and his work was a major com- ponent of the East Village art scene. His first touring museum show, entitled "Reality and Imagination: Two Taste Treats in One," premiered at Penn State University in 1987. A touring museum show called "Land Ho," commissioned by the Chrysler Museum of Norfolk, Virginia, opened in February 1992. The show, which is a walk through a storybook consisting of paint- ings, drawings, sculpture, and computer graphics, reopened in February of 1993 at The World

Financial Center in New York City and began a tour of Japan starting with Osaka in 2001. Rodney's painting and sculpture is represented by Gracie Mansion Fine Arts in New York City.

Four children's books—*Uncle Wizzmo's New Used Car*, *Aunt Ippy's Museum of Junk*, *Slombo the Gross*, and *Thunder Bunny*—have been published by Harper Collins. Rodney's latest books, *Rodneyfun Comic Collection 1*, *Thunder Bunny and Wonder Mew*, and *Thunder Bunny Pops Up*— have all been published in Japan during 2000.

The Center for Advanced Whimsy has created a series of commercially available software products. *Rodney's Funscreen* (1991) is an entertaining learning game for children, published by Activision. *Rodney's Wonder Window* (1992) is a collection of interactive animation. *Dazzeloids* (1994) is a comic storybook. Both are published by The Voyager Company.

PaRappa the Rapper (1997) and *Um Jammer Lammy* (1999) are musical action games for Sony PlayStation and are collaborative projects published by Sony Computer Entertainment. These games have sold more than three million copies worldwide.

RodneyFun is a line of consumer products based on original characters. Sony Creative Products, a licensing division of the Sony Corporation, creates and distributes the products to more than eight hundred stores in Japan.

Cafe Rodney is a cafe and restaurant designed and owned by Rodney Greenblat and Tak Iwayoshi. Located in a prime shopping district in central Tokyo, it opened to the public May 2000.

PaRappa the Rapper is a weekly animated television series that aired in Japan in April 2001. It is based on characters designed by Rodney Greenblat, and is produced by Sony Visual Works and Fuji TV in Japan.

Rodney Greenblat also worked on *PaRappa the Rapper 2*, published for the PS2 by Sony Computer Entertainment America in 2002.

Hirschmann, Peter—LucasArts

Peter Hirschmann has been working in the entertainment industry for more than a decade, beginning at Steven Spielberg's production company, Amblin Entertainment. While there, he spent four years working up the ladder from unpaid college intern to production supervisor on the live-action portion of "Steven Spielberg's Director's Chair." Joining DreamWorks Interactive at the company's inception in 1995 as its story editor, Hirschmann went on to write and produce the award-winning *Medal of Honor* for the PlayStation platform. In 2002, Hirschmann left EA to work for LucasArts.

Hopkins, Don—Freelance

Don Hopkins enjoys researching, designing, and programming interactive graphical user interfaces, visual languages, games, and interactive artwork. Since 1988, he has been developing "pie menus," a reliable and efficient gestural user interface technique. He's implementing pie menus for many different platforms and applications, including *The Sims* and Internet Explorer. Don worked with Will Wright at Maxis to develop the character animation system, user interface, programming, and content-creation tools for *The Sims*. He has also developed a free JavaScript implementation of pie menus, available at www.piemenu.com.

His favorite programming languages include Python, Lisp, PowerPC AltiVec instructions, NeWS PostScript, ScriptX, MaxScript, Bounce (also know as Body Electric), Forth, various obscure special-purpose extension languages, and his own XML-based Lisp-like programming language. But just because something sucks doesn't mean it's not useful, so he also tolerates Windows, Mac OS, Unix, C++, X11, and DirectX. But he steadfastly refuses to stoop to Perl and has never had a good reason to use Java. His interests include visual programming, real-time graphics, image processing, cellular automata, artificial intelligence, reading and writing good code, and applying the works of Philip K. Dick and Stanislaw Lem to software design.

Don has worked as a migrant research programmer for the University of Maryland Parallel Processing Lab, Heterogeneous Systems Lab, and Human Computer Interaction Lab; as well as The Turing Institute in Glasgow, Carnegie Mellon University, Kaleida Labs, and the Interval Research Corporation.

He's also worked in the real world as a software developer, programming an Open Look NeWS toolkit in PostScript for Sun Microsystems, porting *SimCity* to Unix, and adding multiplayer collaboration for DUX Software, developing a real-time visual dataflow programming language for Levity and Interval, creating a visual NeWS programming environment for HCIL and Grasshopper Group, hacking Gosling Emacs for UniPress Software, and developing *The Sims* at Maxis. As an independent contractor, he developed The Sims Transmogrifier, a tool that allows players to create the own objects for *The Sims*. He also ported *The Sims* to Linux and optimized it to function as *The Sims Online* server.

Householder, Matthew—Blizzard Entertainment

Rather than include a formal bio, Matt Householder provides us with his "career credits" in chronological order. Heck, it's impressive nonetheless.

➤ *Krull*—coin-op original published by Gottlieb in 1983, programmer/designer.

➤ *Moon Patrol*—ColecoVision conversion not published by Atari in 1984, programmer/artist/sound effects.

➤ *Atari ST* operating system—GEM API line and polygon graphics primitives converted from 80×86 to 68000 assembly.

➤ *Winter Games*—C64, Apple II, DOS, Mac, Amiga, Atari ST, NES, and so on, published by Epyx and Milton Bradley in 1985, producer.

➤ *Rogue*—*Mac/DOS conversions published by Epyx in 1986, producer.*

➤ *World Games*—C64, Apple II, DOS, Amiga, Atari ST, NES, and so on, published by Epyx in 1986, producer/designer.

➤ *Championship Wrestling*—C64, Apple II published by Epyx in 1986, producer.

➤ *Sub Battle Simulator*—C64, DOS, Amiga published by Epyx in 1986–87, producer.

➤ *California Games*—C64, Apple II, DOS, Amiga, Atari ST, NES, Genesis, Lynx, etc. published by Epyx, Acclaim, Sega, and Atari in 1987–89, producer/designer/creator.

➤ *Rad Gravity*—NES published by Activision in 1990, producer.

➤ *Todd's Adventures in Slime World*—Genesis conversion published by Renovation in 1990, producer.

➤ *Chip's Challenge*—*DOS conversion published by Epyx in 1990, producer.*

➤ *Laptop Getaway*—DOS, Win 3.1 published by Epyx in 1991, producer/designer.

➤ *California Games II*—DOS, SNES published by Epyx and DTMC in 1990–91, producer.

➤ *Lester the Unlikely*—SNES original published by DTMC in 1992, producer/designer.

➤ *Ranma 1/2: Hard Battle*—SNES import published by DTMC in 1992, producer.

➤ *The Adventures of Dr. Franken*—SNES import published by DTMC in 1993, producer.

➤ *3DO Games: Decathlon*—Win95 published by The 3DO Company in 1996, producer/designer.

➤ *Hellfire*—Win95 Diablo expansion published by Sierra Online in 1997, *Diablo's* advocate/producer.

➤ *Diablo*—Sony PlayStation conversion published by Electronic Arts in 1998, Diablo's advocate/producer.

➤ *Diablo II*—Win9X/2K/NT/Mac published by Blizzard Entertainment in 2000, producer.

➤ *Diablo II: Lord of Destruction*—Win9X/2K/NT/Mac original published by Blizzard Entertainment in 2001, producer.

Howard, Todd—Bethesda

Todd Howard spawned from Earth's waters several years ago and quickly learned to breathe air in fear of dying. He has been a designer and producer for Bethesda Softworks since 1994. Howard was the project leader for *Morrowind*, the third chapter in the *Elder Scrolls* series. His major credits include design on *Daggerfall* (1996 Role Playing Game of the Year: *Computer Gaming World* and *PC Gamer*), producer and designer of *The Terminator: Future Shock* and *SkyNET* (1996 *PC Gamer* Editor's Choice, 5 Stars Next Generation), and project leader and designer of *Redguard* (1998 Adventure Game of the Year Finalist: *Computer Gaming World* and *PC Gamer*). Before that, Todd was playing such games as "doctor" and "I'll show you mine" while telling everyone that games would one day actually lead to the creation of a robot army to do his bidding.

Jaquays, Paul—Ensemble Studios

Paul Jaquays currently hangs his professional hat at Microsoft/Ensemble Studios in Dallas, Texas, where he works as a content designer. He began his career in the mid-1970s as a pioneering artist and designer in the area of pre-created game adventures for the *Dungeons & Dragons* pencil and paper role-playing game; he moved on to designing and directing the design of video games for Coleco in the early '80s. He then went on to freelance as an artist and game designer until the early '90s, when he joined TSR, Inc., the publisher of *Dungeons & Dragons*, as a cover illustrator. In 1997, he took up level designing for id Software before moving on to Ensemble Studios in early 2002. Paul Jaquays' early career is best defined by RPG adventures such as *Dark Tower* for Judges Guild and *Griffin Mountain* for Chaosium. As eventual director of game design at Coleco, he had a hand in nearly every video game coming out for ColecoVision and the ADAM computer. He designed the encounters for Interplay's version of *FellowShip of the Ring*. As a TSR illustrator, he is best known for a distinctive bright red dragon that was used on the cover of *Dragon Mountain* and on the *Dragonlance* story collection, *Dragons of Krynn*. While at id, he created levels that appeared in *Quake II*, *Quake III: Arena*, and *Quake III: Team Arena*. His current project with Ensemble Studios is yet to be announced.

Johnston, Matthew Lee—Microsoft

Matthew Johnston is Audio Director at Microsoft Game Studios. His past products include *Quantum Redshift Racing*; *Microsoft Train Simulator*; *Combat Flight Simulator* (1 and 2); *Microsoft Flight Simulator '95*, *'98*, and *2000*; Microsoft Phone; Windows 95; Windows 98; Windows 2000; Auto PC; *Midtown Madness*; *Microsoft Golf 3.0* and *'99*; *Microsoft Full Court Press*; *Microsoft Inside Drive 2000*; *Microsoft Monster Truck Madness* (1 and 2); *Playernet 1.0*; various MSN properties; *CART Precision Racing*; *Flight Sim 95*; *Cinemania 2.0*; *Ancient Lands*; and *Home Repair*; along with user interface sounds for PocketPC, Playernet 1.0, Kid's Interactive TV programming, 3D Movie Maker, and Dangerous Creatures.

Kojima, Hideo—Konami

Born on August 24, 1963, in Setagaya, Tokyo, Hideo Kojima moved to Kobe at the age of 3. It was there that he began shooting 8mm movies and writing short stories. In 1986, Kojima joined Konami as a game planner and made a powerful debut as the director of *Metal Gear* (*MSX*) in 1987. The title earned international praise for its innovative concept, dramatic script, and detailed real-world setting—all of which was totally new to action games. At Konami, Kojima spearheaded the development of *Snatcher* (1988), *Metal Gear 2: Solid Snake* (1990), *Policenauts* (1994), *Tokimeki Memorial Drama Series #1* (1998), *Metal Gear Solid* (1998), *Metal Gear Solid Integral* (1999), *Metal Gear Ghost Babel* (2000), *Zone of the Enders* (2001) and *Metal Gear Solid 2* (2001). At last check, Kojima was working on *Metal Gear Solid 3: Snake Eater*, slated for a 2004 release.

When not working on games, Kojima enjoys Luc Besson, David Lynch, and John Carpenter movies; reading Michael Crichton and Teru Miyamoto books; and listening to Joy Division, New Order, and Sisters of Mercy, among others.

Kriegler, Richard—Electronic Arts Pacific

Richard is an art director, conceptual artist, and digital matte painter. He began his career in advertising—creating concept and finished art for many Fortune 500 companies and Hollywood studios, including Paramount, DreamWorks, Universal, and Microsoft. He graduated with an M.F.A. from Cranbrook Academy of Art, and taught design for 12 years at Pasadena Art Center. He then moved on to spend three years as the art director at Santa Barbara Studios. His film credits include such blockbusters as *Spiderman*, *Contact*, and *What Dreams May Come*. Currently, he serves as the art director for EA Pacific, and last worked on conceptual and finished art for the real-time strategy game *Command & Conquer: Generals*.

Lane, Jeff—Valve Software

Jeff Lane started his career doing graphic design for the print industry. In a series of leaps and bounds over more than 13 years, he moved into doing graphics for video projects, then graphics for commercial multimedia, and finally graphics for games. He hasn't looked back since. After creating 3D art at Hyperbole Studios on their Quantum Gate interactive movie projects, he spent five years at Sierra Studios, at which he worked as an art director on *Phantasmagoria 2* and as a level designer for *SWAT3: CQB* before coming to Valve. At Valve, Jeff has worked on *Team Fortress Classic* and *Team Fortress 2*.

Lanning, Lorne—Oddworld Inhabitants

Lorne Lanning is the president and creative director of Oddworld Inhabitants. Prior to forming Oddworld with CEO Sherry McKenna in 1994, Lorne was the creative director of special projects and visual EFX supervisor at Rhythm & Hues Studios in Hollywood, CA. At Rhythm & Hues since 1989, Lorne worked on numerous award-winning commercials, films, and theme park simulation attractions. Prior to Special Effects production, Lorne was a technical director for aerospace visualization at TRW. He began his career as a freelance illustrator in New York City.

Lloyd, Ian—Electronic Arts

Ian Lloyd was the character and animation lead on *SSX Tricky* at the Electronic Arts Canada studio in Vancouver, B.C. In this capacity, he was responsible for character design and development, supervising a team of 11 exceptionally talented modelers and animators. Ian has been with Electronic Arts Canada since 1997 and worked previously for Gray Matter, Inc. in Toronto, Ontario.

While working at EAC, Ian has contributed animation to three iterations of *Triple Play* for the original PlayStation, as well as leading the animation and eventually the art teams on the wildly successful *SSX* for the PlayStation2.

Ian is a graduate of Sheridan College's three-year classical animation program in Oakville, Ontario, in which he was taught by gifted instructors such as Wayne Gilbert, Charlie Bonafacio, Maury Whyte, John Wheeler, Susana Wald, and Brian Lemay.

Magnin, Ed—Magnin & Associates

How do you go from teaching deaf students to designing and programming video games? Ed Magnin bought an Apple II computer in 1978 and taught himself to program. By 1979, he realized that he knew as much about programming the Apple as anyone else, quit his day job, and never turned back. Later, he had the opportunity to work at MicroProse with Sid Meier, and then at Cinemaware, doing Apple II and Apple IIgs games. At Virgin Games, he switched to cartridge platforms: Game Boy, NES, and SNES.

In 1993, he started his own company to develop Game Boy Color and (more recently) Game Boy Advance projects. It has established a reputation for being on time and has a 100% first-approval record with Nintendo. And if Magnin's life weren't busy enough, he also has been teaching game programming part-time at a local community college. As a service to aspiring game programmers, he maintains a large career info section on his web site (http://EdMagnin.com) and personally answers dozens of career-related emails each week.

McCoy, Mike—Ubi Soft

Mike McCoy's formal education is in meteorology, and has nothing to do with gaming. After graduating, he got a job as an environmental scientist and started programming human exposure models in FORTRAN. Before long, he was also managing projects and contracts.

After three and a half years, he decided that environmental consulting wasn't the career for him, and he started looking for interesting career opportunities everywhere: friends, Internet, and newspapers. Lo and behold, he came across a newspaper job posting for someone to "make military-based computer games without knowing how to program." He figured that because he knew how to program and was a self-taught military historian, he should call them up.

After a brief telephone interview and two in-person interviews, he got a job at Interactive Magic (I-Magic). He started as the lead designer on a military flight simulator game called *iF-22 Raptor*. He took to it instantly by using his military knowledge, programming logic, and project/team management skills. McCoy says he looks back on it and can't believe his luck.

While at I-Magic, he was the lead designer on *iF-22 Raptor*, the lead designer and producer on *iF-22 Persian Gulf*, and a designer on *iF/A-18 Hornet*. When I-Magic hit rough times, McCoy, a lead artist, and two lead programmers decided to try to start their own company. They started a short-lived company named Top Floor Games. Don't worry if you never heard of it because they merged with Sinister Games after only four months.

Sinister Games was a new company less than a year old. It had only eight employees at the time; with the addition of the four of them from Top Floor Games, they were able to complete *Shadow Company*, *Soldier* (completed but never published), *Dukes of Hazzard*, *Dukes of Hazzard II*, and *Batman: Gotham City Racer*.

Ubi Soft Entertainment purchased Sinister Games shortly before they completed Shadow Company, and thus began McCoy's relationship with Ubi Soft Montreal. He worked with third-party producers and designers in Montreal and Paris over the next year and a half, at which point they asked McCoy to move to Montreal to be the lead designer on *Rainbow Six III: Raven Shield*, published by Ubi Soft in March 2003. He has to say this is a match made in heaven because he previously worked as a police officer for three years.

With lots more planned for the franchise in the future, McCoy says he should be a very busy and happy man.

McGee, American—Carbon6 Entertainment

American James McGee is the creative director (CCO) of Carbon6 Entertainment, based in Los Angeles (www.carbon6.com). Past projects include *DOOM*, *DOOM II*, *Quake*, *Quake II*, multiple *DOOM* and *Quake* spin-offs, *American McGee's Alice*, and a number of other projects while at Electronic Arts. With his new company, he's hoping to bridge the gap between Hollywood and the games industry (wipe that look off your face, he says). McGee recently signed a writing/

producing/directing deal with Dimension films that has him working on a number of film and television projects as a writer, director, and producer. He is attached as a producer to the film version of *Alice*, now in development.

McQuaid, Brad—Sigil Games Online

Before forming Sigil Games Online in January 2002, Brad McQuaid served as the vice president of product development at Sony Online Entertainment and was co-founder of Verant Interactive, Inc. prior to the Sony takeover. He is the executive producer of *EverQuest*, one of the greatest graphical online role-playing games of all time, and has more than 10 years of experience in the gaming industry. Prior to forming Verant, McQuaid was with 989 Studios, in which he was a lead programmer and the producer of *EverQuest*. In addition, he was the senior partner at MicroGenesis, in which he was the lead programmer and producer of *WarWizard*.

Meier, Sid—Firaxis Games

Sid Meier is the chairman and director of creative development at Firaxis Games. Recognized as the "father of computer gaming," Sid Meier has been honored with virtually every major award in the gaming industry and was the second person ever to be inducted into the Academy of Interactive Arts and Science's Hall of Fame in 1999.

Just a glance at his career reveals a series of "firsts." In 1982, Sid co-founded MicroProse Software and created one of the very first combat flight simulators, *F-15 Strike Eagle*—a title that sold well over one million units worldwide. After *F-15*, he continued to create thought-provoking, innovative titles such as *Silent Service*, a submarine simulation; and the breakthrough *Pirates*, a unique blend of historical simulation, arcade action, strategy and role playing. By introducing strategy into flight simulation with *F-19 Stealth Fighter*, he created one of the most popular flight sims ever. And with addictive strategy games such as *Sid Meier's Railroad Tycoon* and *Sid Meier's Civilization*, he ushered a new genre of "god games" into computer gaming. *Civilization*, one of the best-known games in the industry, with worldwide sales of more than one million units, was recently honored as the best game of all time by *Computer Gaming World* magazine.

As co-founder and director of creative development at Firaxis Games, Sid continues to lead the industry into new territories. In 1997, the company's first release, the award-winning *Sid Meier's Gettysburg!*, was a groundbreaking real-time tactical-level war game, the first ever to provide virtually inexhaustible depth of play, detailed tactical decision-making, and superb AI in a real-time environment. In early 1999, Firaxis released *Sid Meier's Alpha Centauri*, which won "Turn-Based Strategy Game of the Year" from both *PC Gamer* and *Gamecenter*; and enhanced it later in the year with *Sid Meier's Alien Crossfire*, voted 1999's "Best Expansion Pack of the Year" by several industry magazines. *Sid Meier's Antietam!*, the stellar follow-up to *Sid Meier's Gettysburg!*, was also released in 1999 and received "War Game of the Year" from *Computer Gaming World* magazine. Firaxis is currently developing the highly anticipated *Sid Meier's Civilization III* and *Sid Meier's SimGolf*. Sid continues to lead the creative process at Firaxis Games, creating innovative games for players around the world.

Mencher, Marc—Virtual Search

Marc Mencher, a software engineer, has worked for game companies such as Spectrum Holobyte and 3DO before founding Virtual Search, a game industry-recruiting firm.

Marc's game-oriented career articles have been featured in GiGnews.com, *GameWEEK*, Gamasutra, *Game Developer*, and other industry publications. Marc does volunteer outplacement counseling for graduating students from colleges such as Full Sail, which specializes in training game development professionals. He is on the advisory board for the International Game Developers Association.

Prior to working in the game industry, Marc was a project lead for the advanced research facility of robotics manufacturer Cincinnati Milacron. In this role, he led the design and development of an advanced artificial intelligence project in collaboration with the U.S. Air Force, Carnegie Mellon Universities Robotics Research, and Pratt Whitney Aircraft Engine Group.

Michelson, Dan—Electronic Arts

Dan Michelson has been involved in film, television, and stage productions in the Los Angeles area for more than a decade. He graduated Summa Cum Laude in 1995 from the Chapman University Film School in Orange, California. While there, Dan directed and produced a variety of productions, including "The Ladies' Room," which received rave reviews from both faculty and students. Since graduating, Dan has directed more than 20 stage productions, including Ted Tally's "Hooters" and David Mamet's "Sexual Perversity in Chicago." He also directed the soap opera spoof *The Young, Dumb, and the Restless* for cable television. Dan's producing credits include the independent feature *The Last Drive-In* and eight episodes of the irreverent comedy *Blood, Sweat & Beers*, to name just a few. Dan took a position with Santa Monica Studios in 1997 and quickly become the resident expert on FutureLight's active optical motion-capture technology. While there, he earned a film credit on Sony's mega-blockbuster *Godzilla* and worked with such high-profile celebrities as Tim Burton and Jackie Chan on FutureLight's state-of-the-art motion-capture stage.

Dan also worked on a variety of sports titles for Radical Entertainment. Other credits include project coordinator on both *Interstate '82* for Blur Studios in Venice and a "Hollywood Gum" commercial for Ring of Fire Advanced Media in Hollywood. Dan also worked with Sony Pictures, capturing motion for its *Starship Troopers: Roughneck Chronicles* animated series. Since taking the position of senior motion-capture specialist with Electronic Arts, Dan has worked on many sports titles, including *Tiger Woods Golf*, *FIFA World Cup Soccer*, *Triple Play Baseball*, *NBA Live*, and *March Madness*.

Mikami, Shinji—Capcom Entertainment

Shinji Mikami is the general manager of Capcom Entertainment. His current project is *Devil May Cry*. He has been with Capcom for 11 years, working on projects such as *Goof Troop* (SNES), *Aladdin* (SNES), the *Bio Hazard* series (known in the U.S. as *Resident Evil*), and the *Dino Crisis* series.

What inspired him to join the video game industry? "I was lured to the free buffet lunch Capcom had for their recruiting party."

His favorite games are *The Legend of Zelda* and *Derby Stallion* (horse racing game). Hobbies include collecting watches and watching movies—with such favorites as *Jaws*, *Alien*, *Leon* (*The Professional* in the U.S.), *The Empire Strikes Back*, and *North by Northwest*.

Miller, Scott—3D Realms

Scott Miller began writing computer games in 1975 on a Wang 2000 and wrote more than 100 games, large and small, until 1990. More than 20 of the games he wrote were commercially released in disk magazines such as *I.B.Magazette* and *Softdisk*. During the mid-1980s, he wrote professionally for several national gaming magazines, including *COMPUTE!*, as well as writing two weekly syndicated columns for *The Dallas Morning News*, "Video Vision" and "Computer Fun," for more than four years. Miller also co-authored (with George Broussard) a book on beating arcade games.

In 1990, Miller quit his day job to focus on Apogee full time (Apogee had been a part-time business since late 1987). He recruited several developers, such as id Software (before they were id) and Todd Replogle (author of the first three *Duke Nukem* games) to work with Apogee and use its shareware marketing approach.

Scott says he spent far too much time and money playing arcade, video, and computer games throughout the 1980s, and managed an arcade location for several years early in that decade.

At Apogee/3D Realms, Scott manages the company and oversees most of the marketing tasks. He wrote games such as *Beyond the Titanic*, *Supernova*, *Trek Trivia*, and all seven *Kroz* games. He also designed levels for many of the later-released games, including the entire first episode of the first *Duke Nukem*.

Miyamoto, Shigeru—Nintendo

Considered by his peers to be the greatest video game designer in the world and called "The Spielberg of Video Games" by *Time Magazine* (May 1996), Shigeru Miyamoto is General Manager of the Entertainment Analysis and Development Division as well as a Director for Nintendo Co., Ltd. in Kyoto, Japan. In this capacity, Miyamoto serves as the creative force behind the world's most popular and enduring video games for the Nintendo GameCube, Game Boy Advance, Nintendo 64, Super Nintendo Entertainment System (Super NES), Game Boy, and Nintendo Entertainment System (NES).

Miyamoto joined Nintendo in 1977 as a staff artist. As the creator of the hugely popular *Mario* and *Zelda* games, he is one of the most revered figures in the video game world. In 1981, Nintendo released Miyamoto's first masterpiece, the arcade game *Donkey Kong*. In 1985, Nintendo released the NES with Miyamoto's *Super Mario Bros*. The classic side-scrolling action game set the standard for all future home console video games. Eventually, more than 50 million units were sold worldwide, and a series of mega-hit titles was born, including the 1996 N64 best-seller, *Super Mario 64*.

To date, Miyamoto has worked on more than 70 different Nintendo video game titles. More than 140 million video games in the *Super Mario* series have been sold worldwide.

In the mid-to-late 1990s, Miyamoto's video game projects included *The Legend of Zelda: Majora's Mask, Star Fox 64, Mario Kart 64*, and *The Legend of Zelda: Ocarina of Time* (which has been called the greatest video game of all time). More recently, Miyamoto brought to market a handful of critically acclaimed GameCube titles: *Pikmin, Metroid Prime,* and *The Legend of Zelda: The Wind Waker*, to name a few.

In 1998, Miyamoto was honored as the first inductee into the Academy of Interactive Arts and Sciences Hall of Fame.

Miyamoto holds a degree from the Kanazawa Municipal College of Industrial Arts and Crafts in Kyoto, Japan.

Molyneux, Peter—Lionhead Studios

Peter Molyneux is one of the best-known names in the international world of computer games. In 1987, he formed Bullfrog Productions Ltd. to develop an idea he had for a new type of strategy game. His unique approach, in which the player is a sort of deity ruling over his minions, was (inevitably) copied by other designers and became known generically as a *god-sim*. *Populous* was an instant success and has since sold more than four million copies, placing it among the top 10 most successful computer games of all time.

Populous was followed by *Powermonger, Magic Carpet, Syndicate, Magic Carpet 2*, and *Theme Park*. Each sold more than 400,000 copies, and Peter's reputation as one of the leading computer game designers in the world was firmly established.

In 1995, Bullfrog was purchased by California leisure software giant Electronic Arts. The deal made Peter a wealthy man while maintaining his position as managing director of Bullfrog. However, he discovered that working within a large corporation involved spending more of his time in managerial meetings and less on game design and development, so Peter decided to resign his position. His new plan was to put together a team of like-minded enthusiasts to develop games and leave the distribution and marketing business to the corporate experts. The result was Lionhead.

Before leaving Bullfrog, Peter completed his most ambitious design project yet. *Dungeon Keeper*, released in July 1997, is a masterpiece of design. Packed with original features, the game received "highest ever" scores from several magazines and won awards even before it was released. It became Electronic Arts' most successful release, selling more than 500,000 units in its first month.

An articulate and eloquent speaker, Peter has given talks at the British Film Institute, the American Museum of the Moving Image, the Institute of Contemporary Arts, and the Dortmund Museum of History and Culture. At one business symposium in Japan, Peter was the lead speaker, billed above another of the PC industry's gurus, a certain Bill Gates of Microsoft.

At 41, Peter is, as one newspaper put it, "an eccentric character," and is still obsessed with games. In addition to its secret passages, his home has pinball, table football, and pool machines. He spent several thousand pounds on a specially designed boardgame table with pop-up screens and drawers for the players. He also has a reputation as a party animal who loves arranging events. His lavish bash to celebrate the completion of *Dungeon Keeper* has taken on legendary status within the industry.

Muzyka, Ray—BioWare

Dr. Ray Muzyka is a joint CEO and co-executive producer at BioWare Corp. He co-founded BioWare in 1995 with Dr. Greg Zeschuk. Ray was the producer on *Baldur's Gate* and was/is the co-executive producer on *Shattered Steel*, *MDK2*, *Tales of the Sword Coast*, *Baldur's Gate II*, *Baldur's Gate II: Throne of Bhaal*, *Neverwinter Nights* and *Star Wars: Knights of the Old Republic*.

In addition to his development role, Ray also co-manages (with Greg) the financial and legal/business side of BioWare, and has just completed an executive M.B.A program at the Ivey School of Business, UWO.

Newell, Gabe—Valve Software

Before becoming founder/managing director of Valve Software, Gabe Newell held a number of positions in the systems, applications, and advanced technology divisions during his 13 years at Microsoft. His responsibilities included running program management for the first two releases of Windows, starting the company's multimedia division, and, most recently, leading the company's efforts on the Information Highway PC. His most significant contribution to *Half-Life* was his statement "C'mon, people, you can't show the player a really big bomb and not let them blow it up." *Half-Life 2*, published by Vivendi Universal Games, should be out by the time you read this.

Nomura, Tetsuya—Square

Tetsuya Nomura is the director and character designer for *Kingdom Hearts*. Past credits include character designer for *Final Fantasy VII* and *VIII*, *Parasite Eve*, and *The Bouncer*. Nomura's ability to create a wide range of characters will be key in creating a world that is a blend of Disney's and Square's classic styles. Deeply involved in all aspects of the title, Nomura's touch will be apparent throughout *Kingdom Hearts*.

O'Donnell, Marty—TotalAudio/Bungie Studios/Microsoft

Ten days after Marty O'Donnell accepted a full-time position with Bungie Software, focusing entirely on the audio production for *Oni* and *Halo*, Microsoft purchased the company and moved them to Redmond to develop games for the Xbox. Although still co-owner of TotalAudio with Mike Salvatori, who stayed in the Chicago studio, Marty is currently audio lead for Bungie Studios at Microsoft. *Halo* has been reworked from the ground up in order to take full advantage of the Xbox's amazing graphic and audio capabilities.

Pajitnov, Alexey—Microsoft Games Group

Alexey Pajitnov, the well-known creator of the legendary puzzle game *Tetris*, joined Microsoft as a game designer in September 1996 to lead the development of a series of mind teasers and puzzle games. Currently, Pajitnov is the lead designer on *Pandora's Box*, a new game featuring some of the most visually stimulating puzzles ever created.

Pajitnov was born in Moscow, Russia, in which his love for strategy gaming started at the early age of 14, when he became fascinated with math, puzzles, and tasks. Pajitnov's interest in gaming intensified over the years, culminating with the creation of his first puzzle game in 1984: the highly entertaining and addicting *Tetris*. It took Pajitnov a mere three weeks to program the code that became the main prototype for *Tetris*, the legendary game that has sold more than 50 million copies worldwide, hooked millions, and set the standard by which all video puzzle games have since been judged.

In 1989, Pajitnov and Vladimir Pokhilko founded AnimaTek, a 3D software technology company, in Moscow. After immigrating to the U.S. in 1991 and establishing a domestic AnimaTek office in San Francisco, Pajitnov and Pokhilko created such popular games titles as *El-Fish* and *Ice and Fire*. Pajitnov also has produced games with Bullet-Proof Software for Nintendo and Spectrum Holobyte, which include *Faces*, *Welltris*, *Knight Moves*, and *Hatris*.

Pajitnov holds a Master of Science degree in applied mathematics from the Moscow Institute of Aviation and undertook postgraduate work at the USSR Academy of Science Computer Center. In addition to his studies in the USSR, Pajitnov worked on automatic speech recognition and problems in artificial intelligence.

Perry, David—Shiny Entertainment

After authoring numerous books, David Perry moved from his homeland of Northern Ireland to England in 1981 to develop professional games for Mikro-Gen, Elite Systems, and Probe Software. After hits such as *Teenage Mutant Ninja Turtles* and *The Terminator* for Orion Pictures, in 1991 he moved to the United States to work for Richard Branson's Virgin games company. There, he headed up the team responsible for award-winning games such as Disney's *Aladdin*, 7-Up's *Cool Spot*, and Sega's Game of the Year: McDonald's *Global Gladiators*.

In 1993, Perry formed Shiny Entertainment, based in Laguna Beach, retaining around 40 staff. He has won many "Game of the Year" awards, including the prestigious European Golden Joystick Award for Best Console Programmer. Shiny's *Earthworm Jim* game became a Universal Cartoon Studios/Warner Kids Network television hit, a toy line, comic book, and other licenses. Perry is also an active advisory board member of The Game Developers Conference and has a web site at www.dperry.com, which is dedicated to helping new gamers into the industry.

Romero, John—Monkeystone Games

John Romero brought to Monkeystone a long history of successful gaming businesses and experience in all major areas of game development. John has invested more than 20 years in the game industry, published more than 60 games, and founded three game-development companies. His games have sold millions of copies on a wide range of gaming systems.

John's extensive list of accomplishments has established him as one of the most successful, influential, and well-known creative forces in the business. Legendary among his endeavors are the *DOOM* series, *Wolfenstein 3D*, *Quake*, *Heretic*, and *Hexen*.

As a result of his financial and creative successes, John has been instrumental in the formation of several leading game companies, including Raven Software, Human Head Studios, Parallax Software, Ritual Entertainment, Dwango, Rogue Entertainment, and Valve Software. John's corporate endeavors have spun off several additional companies, including CrackDotCom, Fused, Third Law Interactive, 10K Wizard, and Gathering of Developers.

In 1998, John took on the role of Chairman of the Advisory Board of the Cyberathlete Professional League, the leading professional computer gamer's league in the world, in an effort to realize the concept of computer gaming as a professional sport. The field of competitive computer gaming is based on John's concept of multiplayer deathmatch and has garnered such international attention from large corporate sponsors that yearly prizes in this field now near the $1,000,000 mark.

In July 2001, John co-founded Monkeystone Games, Inc. with a radical new focus on wireless and mobile gaming devices. Funded by his own investments, Monkeystone now employs a staff of eight full-time employees for the creation of games on several diverse platforms, from cell phones to the Game Boy Advance.

Game Design

John has designed games from the simple one-person, two-month project to the tremendously complex multiyear development cycle that requires a staff of more than 20. In addition to fully conceptualizing entire products, John also has considerable experience with creating well-designed playable environments—the actual areas in which the games take place.

Always on the forefront of game design, John was instrumental in pioneering the field of level design. He has participated in numerous discussion panels on the subject and contributed to books on level design, game design, and gaming history. His work has inspired legions of amateur designers to follow in his footsteps.

While developing the concept of linking computers together for network play, John coined the word "deathmatch" for this new mode of play, in which multiple players fight in a battle to the death. *DOOM* was the first game to immerse the player in a realistic three-dimensional world in which players compete head-to-head. Currently, tens of thousands of people all over the world participate in deathmatches on a daily basis. Even MTV has named a popular show after the concept: *Celebrity Deathmatch*.

Programming

John has been programming computers for 20 years on a variety of systems, beginning with an HP mainframe in 1979. Over the years, John has programmed on the Apple II, Commodore 64, Cromemco minicomputer, NeXT computer, Super Nintendo, Atari Jaguar, and finally the PC. He has extensive experience coding in a variety of languages such as BASIC, 6502 Assembler, Pascal, 8086 Assembler, Objective-C, and ANSI C.

His programming experience is broad—encompassing subjects as diverse as applications, graphics, game logic, and tools coding. Each of these areas is essential to game development. The ability to cross over between the programming and design fields has enabled John to create highly effective development tools.

John's game code has been published in several computer magazines, with the intent of teaching fledgling programmers how to code games. Due to the positive response, his games have garnered several magazine covers and feature articles.

Awards

John has twice been recognized by *TIME Digital* as one of the Fifty Cyber Elite (in the October 1997 issue and again in 1998). *Texas Monthly* honored John in September of 1998 as one of the Texas Twenty, described as the "most impressive, intriguing, and influential Texans." In 1998, *Entertainment Weekly* listed him among the Top 100 Most Powerful People in Entertainment, and MIT honored him as one of its Technology Top 100. Numerous times, John has been recognized by the gaming industry's magazines in their yearly listings of influential industry icons.

Over the span of his career, John's games have won all the industry's highest awards, including three Game of the Year awards. In total, John's games have accrued approximately 50 awards.

Roper, Bill—Blizzard Entertainment

As vice president of Blizzard North in San Mateo, Bill Roper oversees and manages all external projects, coordinates internal development teams, and heads Blizzard's project oversight teams. Most recently, he participated on the oversight team for *WarCraft III: Reign of Chaos*, in which he was instrumental in shaping the direction of the game.

Regarding his work on *WarCraft III*, Roper says: "This game is one of our greatest accomplishments to date. We started out hoping to create a fitting sequel to *WarCraft II*, and we ended up crafting a world of epic proportions. *WarCraft III* offers players an incredibly fun and dynamic experience."

Roper worked directly on all of Blizzard's top-selling products, including *WarCraft II: Tides of Darkness* (producer), *Diablo* (producer), *Starcraft* (producer), *Diablo II* (senior producer), and *Starcraft: Brood War* (executive producer). He also played a key role in the world design and managed the manual design for *WarCraft*, *WarCraft II*, *StarCraft*, *Diablo*, and *Diablo II*.

Furthermore, Roper served as a producer on several Macintosh versions of these games and worked as a member of the project oversight teams for the console versions of *WarCraft II: The Dark Saga*, *Diablo*, and *StarCraft 64*. He also managed the authorized add-ons for *WarCraft*, *Diablo*, and *StarCraft*. Currently, he's helping to manage the development of many new Blizzard projects.

In addition to his managerial responsibilities, Roper, who studied commercial music with a vocal emphasis at California State University, Long Beach, was also involved with providing Blizzard's voice content, having both acted in and assisted with the direction of the voice recording for the *WarCraft*, *Diablo*, and *StarCraft* franchises.

Roy, Catherine—Ubi Soft Entertainment

Catherine Roy is a producer at Ubi Soft Entertainment in Montreal. She started with the company in 1997 and has worked on four projects: *Laura's Happy Adventures*, *Alex Builds His Farm*, Walt Disney's *The Jungle Book Rhythm 'n Groove*, Disney's *Tarzan Untamed and Jungle Book*. She was an associate producer on her first two projects and producer on the last three.

Rubinelli, Mike—Gotham Games

When at THQ, Mike Rubinelli served as vice president of product development. He left in 2002 and currently works for Gotham Games, a subsidiary of Take-Two Interactive. Rubinelli oversaw the day-to-day management of THQ's external development. His responsibilities included ensuring overall product quality and increasing product management predictability. Before joining THQ, Rubinelli was vice president of product acquisition at Midway Home Entertainment, where he was responsible for the coordination of third-party game production and development. He also served as a producer at Electronic Arts, where he was responsible for *John Madden Football* and various other EA Sports titles.

Sakaguchi, Hironobu—Square

Hironobu Sakaguchi has led the development division since joining Square Co. Ltd. in 1986. He has produced more than 42 million units of computer game software worldwide, with his smash-hit *Final Fantasy* series selling more than 35 million units.

At Square, Sakaguchi was promoted to executive vice president in 1991. He recently entered into an exclusive production arrangement with Square, in which he plans to oversee the development of Square's future games as well as producing feature film projects.

Sanger, George—Fatman Music

The Fat Man, or George Alistair Sanger, has been composing music for games since 1983. Along with Team Fat, his legendary team of three other cowboy composers, he is internationally recognized for having created music for more than 130 games, including such sound-barrier-breaking greats as *Loom*, *Wing Commander I* and *II*, *The 7th Guest I* and *II*, *NASCAR Racing*, *Putt-Putt Saves the Zoo*, and *ATF*. He wrote the first general MIDI soundtrack for a game, the first direct-to-MIDI live recording of musicians, the first Redbook soundtrack included with the game as a separate disk, the first music for a game that was considered a "work of art," and the first soundtrack that was considered a selling point for the game.

Team Fat is the original out-of-house source for music for games. More than once, it has set trends and raised the bar for what is expected musically from games, significantly increasing sales of hardware and software. On a 380-acre ranch on the Guadalupe River, The Fat Man hosts the annual Texas Interactive Music Conference and BBQ (Project BBQ), the computer/music industry's most prestigious and influential conference.

Saunders, Phil—Presto Studios

Phil Saunders is the creative director at Presto Studios, Inc. He has worked on all of Presto's titles to date, which include *The Journeyman Projects 1, 2* and *3*, *Pegasus Prime*, *Gundam 0079: The War for Earth*, *Star Trek: Hidden Evil*, *Stephen King's F13*, and the recently released *Myst III: Exile*. Phil, a native of Toronto, Canada, graduated with honors in industrial design from The Ontario College of Art and Design in Toronto. He started out during college doing freelance product design, some special-effects work, and eventually some theme-park design work for Japan. After college, Phil got a job designing cars for Nissan Design International in San Diego, which brought him together with Presto and the Journeyman Project games—he left Nissan after four and a half years and joined Presto full-time as creative director in 1995.

Sawyer, Chris—Freelance

As a game developer, designer, and programmer, Chris Sawyer is responsible for such amazing works as *Transport Tycoon*, *Transport Tycoon Deluxe*, *RollerCoaster Tycoon* (the number-one PC game overall in the U.S. in 1999) and its add-on packs *Corkscrew Follies* and *Loopy Landscapes*, as well as many PC conversions of Amiga games including *Frontier Elite 2*, *Xenomorph*, *Conqueror*, *Campaign*, *Virus*, *Goal*, and *Birds of Prey*.

Schachter, Tammy—Konami

With nearly seven years of experience in public relations and publicity, Tammy Schachter has focused her expertise in games, entertainment, technology, and new media. Schachter has developed and executed PR campaigns for large international companies and small startups, thus allowing her to reach all aspects of public relations including consumer, trade, and enthusiast media relations, special events planning, development of PR collateral (digital press kits and b-roll packages), and international media tours.

Holding her greatest expertise within the video game space, Schachter has launched more than 70 titles on every major platform, in every genre. She has led the campaigns for some of the industry's most prominent and successful titles, including *Rayman 2: The Great Escape* (Ubi Soft Entertainment), *Metal Gear Solid 2: Sons of Liberty* (Konami of America), and *Crash Bandicoot: The Wrath of Cortex* (Universal Interactive).

Prior to joining Konami in 2002, Schachter work at Bender/Helper Impact in Los Angeles. Before that, she enjoyed a two-year tenure in a management position at Ubi Soft Entertainment. Schachter also worked at Matrox Graphics Inc. in Montreal. Schachter holds a Master of Arts in communications from McGill University.

Schafer, Tim—Double Fine Productions

Tim Schafer has spent the last 10 years at LucasArts. He was a programmer and assistant designer on the first two *Secret of Monkey Island* games, co-designer and co-project leader on *Day of the Tentacle*, and designer/project leader on *Full Throttle* and *Grim Fandango*.

Last year, Tim founded Double Fine Productions, a San Francisco-based design studio dedicated to inventing new characters and worlds and creating games with them that push the boundaries of interactive storytelling. His first game with Double Fine will be *Psychonauts*, scheduled for a late 2003 release.

Schmalz, James—Digital Extremes

James Schmalz, founder and creative director of Digital Extremes and his latest venture, Brainbox Games, is one of the foremost visionaries in the interactive entertainment industry. At the early age of seven, he was captivated by the gaming world when he was introduced to the now classic video game, *Pong*. And by age 12, he started programming his first creation, an Ultima clone called *Sorcery*, on an Apple IIe computer.

This passion for games continued to grow over the years; in 1993, James founded Digital Extremes on the revenue he built making games during the shareware craze of the early '90s. *Epic Pinball* was one of the most successful shareware games ever made, trailing behind only such industry greats as *Duke3D*, *DOOM*, and *Wolfenstein 3D*. A sequel soon followed (*Extreme Pinball*), and together they helped fund what would soon be one of the industry's blockbuster franchises and James' brainchild: *Unreal*.

Both *Unreal* and *Unreal Tournament* received numerous industry awards for their excellence in gameplay, graphics, and technology—including the prestigious Game of the Year award from the IDSA in 1999 for *Unreal Tournament*. To date, the scope of games in the award-winning *Unreal* franchise has sold more than 3.5 million units worldwide across the PC, PlayStation 2, and Dreamcast platforms.

Through the power of technology, imagination, and innovation, James' vision has helped create a new interactive world; and his passion will continue to push games to the forefront of the entertainment industry.

Digital Extremes last worked on the long-awaited sequel to *Unreal Tournament: Unreal Tournament 2003* for the Xbox.

With the industry's next-generation platform transition in 2001, James saw an opportunity to expand on Digital Extremes' success, and started up a second studio to focus solely on games for the next-generation systems. Brainbox Games opened its doors in November 2001, and is currently in production on its first title.

A graduate of the University of Waterloo, James received a degree in mechanical engineering. Luckily for the games industry, he didn't pursue a career in engineering.

Game History Timeline

➤ 1982: *Sorcery*—first game, an *Ultima* clone for the Apple IIe

➤ 1988: *Legends of Murder*—published by Big Blue Disc

➤ 1990: *Legends of Murder II*—published by Big Blue Disc

➤ 1992: *Solar Winds*—shareware published by Epic MegaGames

➤ 1993: *Epic Pinball*—shareware published by Epic MegaGames

➤ 1993: Digital Extremes founded

➤ 1994: *Silverball*—published by MicroLeague

➤ 1994: *Unreal* development begins

➤ 1995: *Extreme Pinball*—published by Electronic Arts

➤ 1998: *Unreal*—published by GT Interactive

➤ 1999: *Unreal Tournament*—published by GT Interactive

➤ 2000: *Unreal Tournament PS2*—published by Infogrames

➤ 2001: *Adventure Pinball*—published by Electronic Arts

➤ 2002: *Unreal Tournament 2003*—published by Infogrames

➤ 2002: *Unreal Championship Xbox*—published by Infogrames

Sequeira, Shawnee—Small Rockets

Shawnee Sequeira is the development director for Small Rockets, responsible for the company's games production, online partner development, and joint planning of company strategic policy.

She has already acquired a vast portfolio of games under her management at Small Rockets, including *Hot Chix 'n' Gear Stix*, *Jetboat Superchamps*, *Tower of the Ancients*, *The Red Ace*, *Super Chix '76*, *Jetboat Superchamps 2*, *Backgammon*, *Mah-Jongg*, and *Poker*; as well as *MAD*, *Art Is Dead*, *Kayak Extreme*, and *Star Monkey*, launching in 2001.

Sequeira previously served as a game producer for Fiendish Games and Criterion Software, Ltd., both wholly owned subsidiaries of the Canon Group. While working at Criterion, she produced titles for Dreamcast, including *Redline Racer* and *Suzuki Alstare Extreme Racing*. She also managed the Studios Technology team, a development group responsible for the creation of 3D applications and tools.

Sequeira started her online games career as an online producer and team leader at Online Magic, Ltd., in 1996, working for BMG Interactive's and then Take 2 Interactive's online development: www.take2games.com. She left when Online Magic was bought out by Agency.com, the world's largest web agency, in 1998.

Shelley, Bruce—Ensemble Studios

Bruce C. Shelley has been a professional game designer and developer since 1980. He began working with paper and board games, and switched to computer games in 1987. He has helped start or worked for five game companies. Prior to the start of Ensemble Studios in 1995, Bruce was best known for assisting Sid Meier on the design of the original editions of *Railroad Tycoon* and *Civilization* when they were colleagues at Microprose. He is a designer at Ensemble Studios, where he helped organize the company and evolve its development methodology. He now serves mainly as a spokesman for the company and its games. He contributed to the design of *Age of Empires*, *Age of Empires II: The Age of Kings*, and *Age of Mythology*. In 2002, he was elected to the Board of Directors of the Academy of Interactive Arts and Science for a third term.

Smith, Harvey—Ion Storm Austin

Harvey Smith is the project director of *Deus Ex 2* and lead designer of the original *Deus Ex*. Prior to joining Ion Storm Austin, he was lead designer of *FireTeam* (an Internet squad game that allowed players to cooperate using real-time speech). He worked at Origin before that, in which he started work as a tester in QA and eventually ended up working in Warren Spector's development group. His favorite role at Origin was lead tester for *System Shock*, when he got to work with a few key people from Looking Glass for almost a year. He comments that the experience was "super useful and influential in helping me understand what type of game design I wanted to explore."

Smith, Randy—Ion Storm Austin

Randy Smith (no relation to Harvey Smith) is project director and lead designer of *Thief 3* at (what is currently known as) Ion Storm Austin. Before joining Ion Storm, Randy worked at Looking Glass Studios as a designer on *Thief*, *Thief 2*, and *Thief 3* (the latter of which moved to Ion Storm after Looking Glass went out of business).

Spector, Warren—Ion Storm Austin

Warren Spector received his B.S. in speech from Northwestern University and earned an M.A. in radio-TV-film from the University of Texas, Austin. In 1983, while working on his as-yet uncompleted Ph.D., Warren joined Steve Jackson Games as an associate editor. He rose to editor-in-chief and worked on several games, including, *TOON: The Cartoon Roleplaying Game* before accepting a position with TSR, Inc. in 1987. There he collaborated on *Top Secret/S.I.* and the *Bullwinkle & Rocky Game*, wrote a novel (*The Hollow Earth Affair*), and worked on several board games and role-playing adventures.

Warren left pen-and-paper gaming in 1989, joining Origin Systems, Inc. where he co-produced *Ultima VI* and *Wing Commander*, and produced *Ultima Underworld*, *Ultima VII: Serpent Isle*, *System Shock*, *Wings of Glory*, and others. In 1997, after a one-year stint with Looking Glass Technologies, Warren founded the Austin office of Dallas-based game developer Ion Storm. Two years later, he accepted a partnership position and seat on Ion's board of directors. He is also on the board of the International Game Developers Association.

Warren and his team released the award-winning action/role-playing game *Deus Ex* in June 2000. *Deus Ex 2* and *Thief 3* are currently in the works, to be published by Eidos Interactive.

Street, Greg—Ensemble Studios

Greg Street is a game designer with Ensemble Studios, a part of Microsoft Corporation. A former college professor with a Ph.D. in marine science, he joined Ensemble in 1998. Greg was lead designer on the *Conquerors* expansion pack and was responsible for the campaigns and random maps in *Age of Kings*. In 2000, he won the Academy of Interactive Arts and Sciences award for Outstanding Achievement in Character or Story Development. His last project was *Age of Mythology*.

Suzuki, Yu—Sega of Japan

Yu Suzuki, one of Sega's leading video game producers, is recognized worldwide as one of the forefathers of console gaming for his contributions to the electronic entertainment industry in computer animation and 3D graphics. Suzuki joined Sega Enterprises in 1983. Early in his career at Sega, Suzuki served as a programmer and game producer. He quickly commanded much larger projects, and in his second year he created the world's first simulation arcade game, *Hang On*.

Suzuki vitalized the video game industry both technologically and culturally. In 1993, he created the internationally renowned arcade hit *Virtua Fighter*, the first 3D-animated computer fighting game. For the first time in the history of the Japanese gaming industry, *Virtua Fighter* was added to the Smithsonian Institution's Permanent Research Collection on Information Technology Innovation and is currently kept at the Smithsonian's National Museum of American History in Washington, D.C. The *Virtua Fighter* series is highly recognized by both the computer graphics development community and the Smithsonian Institution as an application that made a tremendous contribution to society in the fields of art and entertainment.

Suzuki is best known for industry firsts and genre-breaking games such as *Space Harrier*, *Outrun*, and recent arcade racing simulator *F355 Challenge*, which gained instant recognition from the gaming industry as well as the automotive community. Suzuki's latest creation is *Shenmue*, a highly anticipated epic for the Sega Dreamcast that far surpasses all previous games in content, quality, and graphics. The game, including an unparalleled interactive experience, has coined a new game genre, FREE (Full Reactive Eyes Entertainment). *Shenmue* was launched in Japan in December 1999, achieving an unprecedented number of sales. With fully interactive 3D environments and cinematic visuals that overwhelm the player's senses, *Shenmue* is the next step in the evolution of video games and the next masterpiece from Yu Suzuki.

Sweeney, Tim—Epic Games

Tim Sweeney is the founder and lead programmer at Epic Games, and has worked on many games over the years: *ZZT* (1991), *Jill of the Jungle* (1992), *Unreal* (1998), *Unreal Tournament* (1999), and *Unreal 2* (2003). He has some ambitious long-term future aspirations:

➤ Render photorealistic outdoor scenes such as forests with all their wind and fluid dynamics, shadowing, and illumination in real time.

➤ Build a large-scale multiplayer game supporting hundreds of thousands or millions of players in a distributed, open sense—the web model, not the CompuServe model.

➤ Write a scripting language combining the power of C++ with the simplicity and ease of use of Java, with the goal of making gameplay programming significantly easier than it is now.

➤ Factor RSA-2048.

Tim comments, "To the extent that these goals are unrealistic or infeasible... hell, I say aim high!"

Tallarico, Tommy—Freelance

Tommy Tallarico is the most successful and accomplished video game composer in history. He has helped revolutionize the video game industry and has shown time and again his ability to create unique soundtracks that truly enhance the overall gaming experience. His music has been heard by hundreds of millions of people all over the world on media such as video games, television, motion pictures, radio, soundtracks, and even on floats in the New Year's Day Rose Bowl parade in Pasadena, California.

Some of Tallarico's top titles include *Earthworm Jim*, *Disney's Aladdin*, *Cool Spot*, *The Terminator*, *Madden Football*, *Prince of Persia*, the *Test Drive* series, *MDK*, *Tomorrow Never Dies*, *Tony Hawk Skateboarding*, *Spiderman*, *Pac-Man World*, *Knockout Kings and the Blitz*, *Unreal*, and the *Time Crisis* series. Upcoming titles include the highly anticipated *Unreal 2*, *Metroid Prime*, *Maximo*, and *Casper*.

Tommy has been writing music for video games for more than 10 years. Founded in 1994, Tommy Tallarico Studios, Inc. is the industry's largest multimedia post-production audio house on the planet, having produced more than 30 titles in 2000 alone. Tallarico and his team have won more than 20 industry awards for best video game soundtracks and have worked on more than 175 games—totaling more than 50 million units sold and grossing more than 2 billion dollars in revenue! Tallarico was the first musician to release a video game soundtrack worldwide (*Tommy Tallarico's Greatest Hits Vol. 1*—Capitol Records). He has released five soundtrack albums since then, including the highly acclaimed James Bond *Tomorrow Never Dies* soundtrack, available in record stores around the globe.

Tommy was also the first to use 3D audio in a game (Q-Sound) and is currently working on one of the first interactive 5.1 (six-channel) games. Tommy has written, recorded, and produced for a wide range of talented musicians, including the Hungarian National Symphony Orchestra, Budapest Chamber Choir, and the Fear Factory band. He has worked in the industry as a games tester, product manager, producer, writer, designer, and head of music and video departments.

In 1999, Tommy co-designed (with Electronic Arts) the award-winning boxing game *Knockout Kings* for the N64, which went on to win the Best Console Sports Product of 1999 by the Academy of Interactive Arts & Sciences. He is a consultant for DTS (5.1 audio), Intel, and Apple and has given lectures all over the world about audio and video games (including the 1999 Keynote Address at the Game Developers Conference and Milia 2000 in Cannes, France). He also teaches courses and has been the guest speaker at many schools, organizations, and universities—including UCLA. Tommy has been featured on numerous nationwide and worldwide television networks, such as CNN and MTV. He has appeared on the covers of national and international magazines and newspapers, including the *Los Angeles Times* and the *Chicago Tribune*.

Tommy is the host, writer, and co-producer of the worldwide weekly video game television show, *The Electric Playground* (www.elecplay.com). The television show airs in prime time six times a week on the Discovery network and is syndicated internationally.

Taylor, Chris—Gas Powered Games

Chris Taylor began his career in the video games business at Distinctive Software in Canada. His first title, *Hardball II*, was a sequel to the popular *Hardball* and won the SPA (Software Publishers Association) award for best sports game of the year. Next, Chris created *4D Boxing*, which won many accolades for its innovation as a 3D title. Chris later served as designer and project lead for the original *Triple Play Baseball* at Electronic Arts.

Chris went on to create the highly acclaimed RTS *Total Annihilation* at Cavedog Entertainment. After completing the expansion pack, *The Core Contingency*, he decided to start his own company.

Chris founded Gas Powered Games in May of 1998 in Kirkland, Washington. GPG released its first title, *Dungeon Siege*, for the PC in April 2002. Gas Powered Games has established itself as an innovator in both technology and gameplay, and is now working on its next round of games to be released in the near future. *Dungeon Siege II* was announced in May of 2003, slated for a 2004 release.

Thomas, Chance—The HUGEsound Network

Chance Thomas is a composer and audio producer, as well as president of the HUGEsound Network of audio specialists.

Thomas creates heroic music scores of superb quality. His proven approach balances the range, richness, and drama of a live film orchestra with rare acoustic instruments and human voices. Electronic elements add supporting layers of intensity and distinctiveness to his sound.

He started composing and producing music more than 20 years ago. During his career, he has produced award-winning original scores for many formats: films, commercials, television, and interactive games.

Chance discovered the expressive capacity of a symphony orchestra while writing for films. Working in this field brought him valuable experience in emotive scoring (harmonic movement, rhythmic pacing, melodic exposition), orchestration, music preparation, and conducting. His skill with the orchestra is now widely admired.

As a commercial composer, he developed a reputation for quick turnaround times and excellent service. For example, he once received a frantic phone call from a media producer at Bonneville Communications. The agency needed original music scored to 12 radio commercials, and the client wanted them overnight. No problem. The 12 commercials were individually scored, the music recorded, and the masters delivered by 10:00 a.m. the next day.

Television experience taught Chance how to extract the best possible sound from small TV speakers. Choices of instruments, particular voicing of arrangements, equalization tricks, and custom digital effects were all honed for maximum impact. This combination of techniques and technology now form the nucleus of Thomas' proprietary HUGEsound audio-enhancing process.

Sierra On-Line lured Chance to the game industry in the mid-1990s. He pioneered Sierra's use of a live orchestra with the award-winning score to *Quest for Glory V*. He introduced ancient and unusual acoustic instruments such as the Hurdy-Gurdy, Rebec, and Viola di Gamba into the score for *J.R.R. Tolkien's Middle-earth*. For the sequel to *S.W.A.T.*, he produced a radio-friendly theme song that resulted in thousands of downloads from the game's web site.

His most obvious contribution was to the company's bottom line. For instance, when the music from *Quest for Glory V* was released as a soundtrack CD, fans snatched up the entire 50,000-unit production run. The cash return was phenomenal. The last figures disclosed in writing show more than $620,000 in additional revenue associated with the soundtrack. It was like having a briefcase full of free money handed to the team.

In July 1999, Chance resigned his position at Sierra to announce the launch of HUGEsound, a savvy group of pros dedicated to providing superior quality audio and fast service. In addition to his personal expertise, HUGEsound offers a reliable network of audio programmers, sound designers, audio technology consultants, composers, and voice-casting professionals. Specialists such as Tim Larkin (*Real Myst, Riven*), Phil Morris (*Tomb Raider, Silver*), Alexander Brandon (*Deus Ex, Unreal*), Thor Call (*Monster Trucks, Fox Sports*), and Michael McDonough (*Star Trek Insurrection, Demolition Man*) are easy to work with and guarantee the right results every time.

HUGEsound is based in the wooded foothills surrounding Yosemite National Park (located between Los Angeles and San Francisco). The glass walls of HUGEsound studio offer a spectacular outdoor setting, and Chance draws inspiration for his music from Yosemite's granite peaks and rich forest groves.

Today, Chance is a proud contributor to the professional audio community. He serves as chairman of the Music and Sound screening committees for the Academy of Interactive Arts and Sciences. He has been a featured speaker at the Game Developers Conference, a voting member of NARAS, and a presenter at the Interactive Academy Awards. For many, he will always be linked to the Grammy Awards and his winning game music Grammy campaign in the late 1990s.

He has been honored by the Emmy Awards, Telly Awards, Addy Awards, Aurora Awards, Vault Network Awards, and others. His music is widely recognized, having been broadcast to every television market in the United States and across five continents. A national marketing survey found that individuals from every ZIP code in America have a copy of Chance's music in their home.

Chance's work and professional opinions have been featured in the *New York Times, Los Angeles Times, USA Today, Hollywood Reporter, Entertainment Weekly, Wired News, PC Gamer, Grammy Magazine, EQ Magazine, CNN, c|Net*, and many other prominent media outlets.

His credits include original music for such successful enterprises as Electronic Arts, CBS Television Affiliates, McDonald's, Infogrames, Sierra On-Line, Feature Films for Families, the Mall of America, the Church of Jesus Christ of Latter-Day Saints, Amoco Oil Company,

Explorati, Family Services Adoption Agencies, Legend Entertainment, Rexall Drugs, Tupperware Corp., Salvation Army, Children's Miracle Network, In-Focus Systems, American Stores, Vivendi-Universal, and many more.

His gifts for creating intense orchestral scores, producing to audiophile standards, and pampering his clients continue to win loyalty among developers and earn high praise from the press. His current game projects (as of this writing) include *Unreal 2*, *Robota*, and Sierra games based on *J.R.R. Tolkien's The Hobbit* and *Lord of the Rings*.

Last, but certainly not least, Thomas won an Academy Award in 2003 for his work on *ChubbChubbs* for Best Animated Short Film.

For newly updated information, see www.hugesound.com.

Tørnquist, Ragnar—Funcom

Ragnar Tørnquist is the lead designer on Funcom's next big online game: *Midgard*. He's also the creative director at Funcom, which means that he has to think about the Big Issues: where games are heading, how the industry is evolving, and what designers can do to make better games. His prior convictions include the hit console title *Casper* (for the PlayStation and Sega Saturn), *The Longest Journey*, and most recently the background story for *Anarchy Online*, a massively multiplayer online role-playing game.

Ragnar has a degree in writing and directing for film and television from New York University's Tisch School of the Arts, and he's naturally intrigued by the possibilities of interactive storytelling, characterization, and immersion. Games are the next step in communication and entertainment, and he feels we haven't even begun to scratch the surface of what this medium can do.

Future aspirations include telling stories in a variety of media, although he's particularly intrigued by the possibilities in immersive, persistent online worlds, in which, he says, "players have the freedom to do anything, interact with anyone at any time, experience personal stories, and live interesting virtual lives." He predicts, "That's where the future of gaming is, and that's where I'll be!"

White, Stephen—Naughty Dog

Stephen White is the programming director of Naughty Dog, Inc. He was instrumental in the development of Naughty Dog's extremely successful *Crash Bandicoot* games (more than 22 million copies sold) as well as Naughty Dog's recent hit release *Jak & Daxter: The Precursor Legacy* for the PlayStation 2. Stephen is an industry veteran, with more than 16 years of published programming experience on a wide variety of platforms, and has programmed multi-award-winning projects, such as *Deluxe Paint ST* and *Brilliance*. Stephen was honored with a nomination for "Excellence in Programming" at the Game Developer Choice Awards at GDC 2002 for his work on *Jak & Daxter*. He has been a speaker at GDC and E3 as well as other industry events, and has written a couple of technical articles for *Game Developer Magazine* and *Programming Gems 3*. Stephen is currently working on Naughty Dog's next epic title, which is being developed for the PlayStation 2.

Highlights of Past Products

➤ *Jak & Daxter: The Precursor Legacy*—PlayStation 2

➤ *Crash Bandicoot 3: Warped*—PlayStation

➤ *Crash Bandicoot 2: Cortex Strikes Back*—PlayStation

➤ *Solar Eclipse*—SEGA Saturn

➤ *PGA Tour Golf 486*—PC

➤ *Brilliance*—Amiga

➤ *Deluxe Paint ST*—ATARI ST

➤ *Day of the Viper*—ATARI ST and Amiga

➤ *Bar Games*—ATARI ST

Recent Lectures

➤ "Navigation Meshes," Nordic Interactive Media Expo 2002

➤ "The Making of *Jak & Daxter*," Nordic Interactive Media Expo 2002

➤ "Global Game Trends 101," Electronic Entertainment Expo 2002

➤ "Teaching an Old Dog New Bits," Game Developer Conference 1999

Published Articles

➤ "A Fast Approach to Navigation Meshes," *Programming Gems 3*, published by Charles River Media; co-authored with Chris Christensen

➤ "Postmortem: Naughty Dog's *Jak & Daxter: The Precursor Legacy*," *Game Developer Magazine*, April 2002

Williams, Bruce—Microsoft

Bruce Williams is the product planner for flight simulations at Microsoft. He has worked on the *Flight Simulator* team since *Flight Simulator* was released for Windows 95. Bruce has been a pilot since the early 1970s. He holds a commercial pilot certificate with single-engine, multi-engine, and instrument ratings. He is also a certified flight instructor and he teaches part-time at a flight school in Seattle. Before joining Microsoft in the late 1980s, Bruce was a reporter and editor at several publications; in the mid-1980s, he was the editor for the newspaper *The Flyer*.

Willits, Tim—id Software

Tim Willits holds degrees in computer science and business from the University of Minnesota. His current position is as game director at id Software, in which he has been intimately involved with the familiar game series *DOOM*, *Ultimate DOOM*, and *Quake*. Prior to joining id, he worked for Rogue Entertainment on Strife. His hobbies are spending time with his family and stealing ideas from movies.

Wong, Jeane—Electronic Arts

Jeane Wong is PR manager of the EA Games department. She has been with EA for approximately five years and involved in game publicity since 1994. Her original plan was to go into entertainment PR (music), but she happened to stumble upon the interactive gaming realm accidentally, straight out of college. Previous gigs included working on the E3 1996 show at Neale-May & Partners, a PR firm based in Palo Alto. Prior to that, she was at Bender, Goldman & Helper (now Bender, Helper Impact), a PR firm in Los Angeles in which she worked with numerous interactive clients including Spectrum Holobyte (now MicroProse), 7th Level, New World Computing, Creative Wonders (EA Kids), Compton's New Media, and so on.

Jeane's future aspirations include growing with the interactive industry and seeing exactly how large (and successful) it can become.

Wright, Will—Maxis Software

Will Wright, Maxis' chief designer, co-founded Maxis with Jeff Braun in 1987. Wright began working on what would become *SimCity: The City Simulator* in 1985. Using a complex technique, he found a way to bring realistic simulations to desktop PCs. Previously, simulations of this sort were available only to the military, scientists, and academicians. But now, with an easy-to-use graphic interface, the world of simulations has opened up to consumers.

Wright has had a lifelong fascination with simulations. His interest in plastic models of ships and airplanes during his childhood in Georgia eventually led to designing computer models of cities, ecosystems, and ant colonies.

SimCity was released in 1989 and became a hit within a few months. The game has since won 24 domestic and international awards. With Fred Haslem, Wright co-designed *SimEarth: The Living Planet* in 1990, a simulation of a planet based on the Gaia theory of James Lovelock. In 1991, Wright and Justin McCormick designed *SimAnt: The Electronic Ant Colony*, a scientifically accurate simulation of an ant colony. *SimCity 2000* and *SimCopter*, a helicopter flight game, are also part of Wright's recent repertoire. The latest incarnation of *SimCity*—*SimCity 3000 Unlimited*, the definitive version of 1999's best-selling game *SimCity 3000*—has continued the tradition.

Taking computer entertainment to its most personal level, Wright's ground-breaking game *The Sims* puts players in charge of the lives of a neighborhood of simulated people. Released in February of 2000, this wildly popular title has become a cultural phenomenon, sold more than four million copies worldwide, and has received numerous "Game of the Year" accolades. To date, *The Sims* has inspired three expansion packs: *Livin' Large*, which allows players to put their simulated families from *The Sims* into new extreme situations and settings; *House Party*, which gives players the chance to host outrageous parties for their Sims; and, due out this November, *Hot Date*, which represents an entirely new experience for *The Sims*—dating!

Wright's latest achievement is the much anticipated *The Sims Online*. *The Sims Online* enables you to take your Sims to an online world in which you get to be yourself or whoever you want to be. In this world, you have your own piece of land to do with as you please. In this open-ended online world, you choose your role, your attitude, and your destiny.

Wright has become one of the most successful designers of interactive entertainment in the world. In 1999, he was included in *Entertainment Weekly*'s "It List" of the 100 most creative people in entertainment, as well as *Time Digital*'s "Digital 50," a listing of the most important people shaping technology today. However, his interests are not limited to computer games. Each year, Wright (along with his daughter) takes part in the annual Battlebot competition, which is broadcast nationally on Comedy Central. His past robots, which do battle with robots designed by other contestants, have taken top honors. Interestingly, it was Wright's interest in robots that eventually led him into computer programming.

Zeschuk, Greg—BioWare

Dr. Greg Zeschuk is a joint CEO, one of the founding partners of BioWare Corp., and a co-producer of *Baldur's Gate*, *Tales of the Sword Coast*, *Baldur's Gate II: Shadows of Amn*, *Baldur's Gate II: Throne of Bhaal*, *MDK2*, *MDK2: Armageddon*, and *Shattered Steel*. As co-executive producers, Zeschuk and his partner Ray Muzyka oversee and manage BioWare's games, including *Neverwinter Nights* and *Star Wars: Knights of the Old Republic*.

In addition to his development role, Greg also co-manages (with Ray) the human resources side of BioWare, and he is sleeping when not playing games.

Index

Symbols

E

M

VOICES THAT MATTER

HOW TO CONTACT US

VISIT OUR WEB SITE

W W W . N E W R I D E R S . C O M

On our web site, you'll find information about our other books, authors, tables of contents, and book errata. You will also find information about book registration and how to purchase our books, both domestically and internationally.

EMAIL US

Contact us at: **nrfeedback@newriders.com**

- If you have comments or questions about this book
- To report errors that you have found in this book
- If you have a book proposal to submit or are interested in writing for New Riders
- If you are an expert in a computer topic or technology and are interested in being a technical editor who reviews manuscripts for technical accuracy

Contact us at: **nreducation@newriders.com**

- If you are an instructor from an educational institution who wants to preview New Riders books for classroom use. Email should include your name, title, school, department, address, phone number, office days/hours, text in use, and enrollment, along with your request for desk/examination copies and/or additional information.

Contact us at: **nrmedia@newriders.com**

- If you are a member of the media who is interested in reviewing copies of New Riders books. Send your name, mailing address, and email address, along with the name of the publication or web site you work for.

BULK PURCHASES/CORPORATE SALES

The publisher offers discounts on this book when ordered in quantity for bulk purchases and special sales. For sales within the U.S., please contact: Corporate and Government Sales (800) 382-3419 or **corpsales@pearsontechgroup.com**. Outside of the U.S., please contact: International Sales (317) 581-3793 or **international@pearsontechgroup.com**.

WRITE TO US

New Riders Publishing
201 W. 103rd St.
Indianapolis, IN 46290-1097

CALL/FAX US

Toll-free (800) 571-5840
If outside U.S. (317) 581-3500
Ask for New Riders
FAX: (317) 581-4663

New Riders

VIEW CART 🛒　　　　　　　　［　　　　　　　　　　　　］　search ▷

▸ Registration　already a member? Log in.　▸ Book Registration

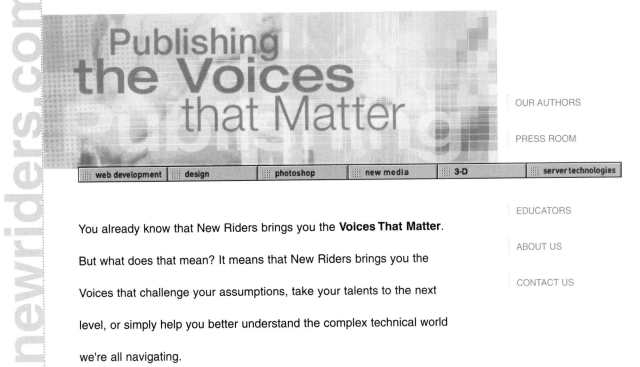

OUR AUTHORS

PRESS ROOM

| web development | design | photoshop | new media | 3-D | server technologies |

EDUCATORS

ABOUT US

CONTACT US

You already know that New Riders brings you the **Voices That Matter**.

But what does that mean? It means that New Riders brings you the

Voices that challenge your assumptions, take your talents to the next

level, or simply help you better understand the complex technical world

we're all navigating.

Visit **www.newriders.com** to find:

- ▸ **10% discount** and **free shipping** on all book purchases
- ▸ Never before published chapters
- ▸ Sample chapters and excerpts
- ▸ Author bios and interviews
- ▸ Contests and enter-to-wins
- ▸ Up-to-date industry event information
- ▸ Book reviews
- ▸ Special offers from our friends and partners
- ▸ Info on how to join our User Group program
- ▸ Ways to have your Voice heard

New
Riders

WWW.NEWRIDERS.COM

www.informit.com

YOUR GUIDE TO IT REFERENCE

New Riders has partnered with **InformIT.com** to bring technical information to your desktop. Drawing from New Riders authors and reviewers to provide additional information on topics of interest to you, **InformIT.com** provides free, in-depth information you won't find anywhere else.

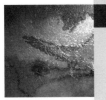

Articles

Keep your edge with thousands of free articles, in-depth features, interviews, and IT reference recommendations— all written by experts you know and trust.

Online Books

Answers in an instant from **InformIT Online Books'** 600+ fully searchable online books.

POWERED BY

Catalog

Review online sample chapters, author biographies, and customer rankings and choose exactly the right book from a selection of over 5,000 titles.

Maximize
Your Impact

0735700443
George Maestri
US$50.00

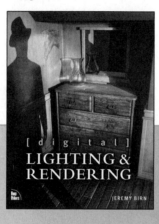

1562059548
Jeremy Birn
US$50.00

0735709181
Owen Demers
US$55.00

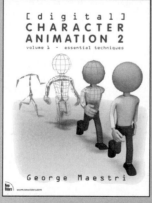

0735712581
Dan Ablan
US$45.00

1562059300
George Maestri
US$50.00

New Riders